MARKETING RESEARCH

MARKETING RESEARCH

DONALD R. LEHMANN
Columbia Graduate School of Business
Columbia University

SUNIL GUPTA
Columbia Graduate School of Business
Columbia University

JOEL H. STECKEL
Stern School of Business
New York University

 ADDISON-WESLEY

An imprint of Addison Wesley Longman, Inc.

Reading, Massachusetts • Menlo Park, California • New York • Harlow, England
Don Mills, Ontario • Sydney • Mexico City • Madrid • Amsterdam

Acquisitions Editor: Michael Roche
Assistant Editor: Ruth Berry
Project Coordination: Electronic Publishing Services Inc., NYC
Design Manager: Regina Hagen
Cover Designer: Linda Wade
Project Supervisor: Louis C. Bruno, Jr.
Manufacturing Manager: Hugh Crawford
Printer and Binder: R. R. Donnelley and Sons
Cover Printer: Lehigh Press
Marketing Manager: Jodi Fazio
Marketing Coordinator: Joyce Cosentino

For permission to use copyrighted material, grateful acknowledgment is made to the copyright holders throughout the text, which are hereby made part of this copyright page.

Library of Congress Cataloging-in-Publication Data
Lehmann, Donald R.
    Marketing research / Donald R. Lehmann, Sunil Gupta, Joel H. Steckel.
        p.   cm.
    Includes bibliographical references and index.
    ISBN 0-321-01416-2 (hardcover)
    1. Marketing research.   I. Gupta, Sunil, 1958–   . II. Steckel,
Joel H.   III. Title
HF5415.2.L3883 1997
658.8'3—DC21   97–34741
                                       CIP

ISBN 0-321-01416-2

12345678910—DOC—0100999897

Brief Contents

Contents

Chapter 3

The Research Process 58

Chapter 4

Sources of Information 78

PART II ▬▬▬▬▬▬▬

DATA COLLECTION 130

Chapter 5

Qualitative Research 130

Chapter 6

Experiments 143

Chapter 7

Survey Design   170

Chapter 8
Measurement and Scaling 234

Chapter 9

Sampling In Marketing Research 284

Chapter 10

Data Coding and Editing 335

PART III ▬▬▬▬▬
ANALYTICAL METHODS 362

Chapter 11
Basic Analysis 362

Chapter 12
Comparing Differences in Key Variables 420

Chapter 13
Regression Analysis 464

Chapter 16

Factor Analysis 600

Chapter 17

Geometric Representation of Objects 629

Chapter 18
Discriminant Analysis 656

Chapter 19
Logit Models 691

Chapter 20
Additional Data Analytic Techniques 716

Preface

Marketing research is at something of a crossroads. As we point out, much of the focus (at least in the developed economies) has shifted from collecting data to interpreting the deluge of information available. At the same time, companies are pressing for justification for expenditures on advertising, new products, etc. The consequence of this is a strong emphasis on "proving" the impact of decisions.

As a parallel development, battles over mature markets and rapidly-evolving technologies (e.g., the Internet) have taxed the ability of standard methods (e.g., surveys) to assess customer reaction in a thorough and detailed manner. The result of this has been renewed interest in qualitative methods such as focus groups which provide richer explanations (if not necessarily projectable ones) and ideas for segmentation and communication.

Put together, these trends mean marketing research (as opposed to research done by the marketing department) has the potential to emerge as a central basis for strategy and subsequent profitability. Further, a focus on customers has emerged as an important aspect of non-marketing functions such as operations. Thus it becomes critical for managers to understand research and to be able to specify what needs to be studied, how to study it, and how to interpret the results from studying it. This book focuses on those issues. In doing so, it takes primarily a method approach. That is, while problems and discussions related to pricing, advertising, etc. occur throughout the book, the book is organized around sources of data (chapters 1–9) and interpretation of data (chapters 10–20).

Users of this book interested in a basic understanding can obtain it by focusing on chapters 3 through 13 (regression analysis, which is the most useful and widely used of the analytical techniques). The next most useful chapters are chapters 14 (conjoint analysis, a way to assess customers' preferences), 15, (cluster analysis, a means for generating segments), and 16 (factor analysis). Chapters 17–20 provide discussions of specialized procedures such as discriminant analysis, logit, multidimensional scaling, and CHAID which are increasingly being used in commercial settings.

This marks the "rebirth" of a book used for many years in marketing research courses taught by, among others, Lehmann and more recently, Gupta and Steckel. The book is based on the premises that (a) research is useful, (b) research skills can be learned, and (c) not everyone reading this book does so voluntarily. Consequently there are attempts to convey some of the fun as well as the agony involved in doing and using marketing research, while still providing a fairly complete coverage of technical issues. Some basic features of the book are:

1. While there are descriptive sections, the basic writing style is instructive rather than encyclo-pedic, under the assumption that most people need to follow a learning process in understanding marketing research which is more than just memorization of facts.

2. The authors feel that the best way to learn the nuances of research is by doing some. They have found that a simple project (define a problem, make up a questionnaire, go get 150 respondents, analyze the data, and write a report) is the best learning experience in the course. Next to that, analysis of results seems to be the best way to increase understanding. For that reason, the analysis chapters contain studies already analyzed so the reader can see how inferences can be drawn from actual results.

3. A common data base involving 940 female heads of households' responses to a survey about usage of and attitudes toward foods is used throughout much of the book as an ongoing case example. This provides readers with the opportunity to view a large survey as it is analyzed by several methods and to compare the methods in a concrete situation.

4. The "fancy" analytical techniques are discussed mainly in words in the chapters. Mathematics are generally banished to appendixes. (How's that for market segmentation?)

5. Sample computer output from the SPSS and SAS programs is reproduced in the appendixes to the analysis chapters. This allows practice in interpreting essential results from actual output.

6. The target reader is a user rather than a producer of marketing research. Still, in order to be a good user, one must know enough about the subject to ask good questions. Therefore, the book will try to explain how or at least why many of the basic procedures are used.

7. The writing style will be, at times, light. This is based on the assumptions that (a) some readers may not be passionately interested in the subject and need to be kept awake, (b) it is dangerous for an author to take himself too seriously, and (c) this book should help introduce the subject but cannot possibly say everything relevant about it.

The authors would like to thank many people for their assistance and encouragement on the revision including Mike Roche, Anne Smith, Ruth Berry, and Christine Moore. Unfortunately, the blame for any shortcomings is not as easily conveyed.

Special thanks are due Kris Lehmann, without whose efforts at editing, typing, drawing figures, etc., this book would not have been completed.

Donald R. Lehmann

Sunil Gupta

Joel H. Steckel

PART I
Basic Concepts

CHAPTER 1
The Role of Marketing Research

The term *marketing research* means different things to different people. For this book, the following definition is used:

> Marketing research is the collection, processing, and analysis of information on topics relevant to marketing. It begins with problem definition and ends with a report and action recommendations.

This is purposely a broad definition and is intended to include the large variety of things done under the name of marketing research. The definition excludes, however, maketing/sales gimmicks that masquerade as marketing research (e.g., the old opening gambits of many encyclopedia or real estate salespersons, see McDaniel, Verille, and Madden, 1985).

An expanded version of this definition was adopted by the American Marketing Association in 1987:

> Marketing Research is the function which links the consumer, customer, and public to the marketer through information—information used to identify and define marketing opportunities and problems; generate, refine, and evaluate marketing actions; monitor marketing performance; and improve understanding of marketing as a process.
>
> Marketing Research specifies the information required to address these issues; designs the method for collection information; manages and implements the data collection process; analyzes the results; and communicates the findings and their implications.

To understand what marketing research is about, it is useful to understand where it comes from. Set in a business environment, marketing research is practically oriented. Aligned as it is with marketing, producing results that "sell" (are accepted) is very important. Yet in juxtaposition with this pragmatic framework is the connotation of research—scientific, scholarly, logical pursuit of truth. As will be seen, this juxtaposition leads to perpetual conflict between the demands of expediency and truth seeking.

As an applied field, marketing research has been a large importer of methodologies and concepts from other fields. These "benefactors" have included the following:

Psychology and *sociology*, from which most of the theories about how consumers think and process information have been drawn. Particularly relevant is the field of social psychology.

Microeconomics, from which utility theory and related concepts have been appropriated.

Statistics, from which most of the analytical procedures have been borrowed.

Experimental design, from which the fundamental concepts of testing and research design have largely been drawn.

As would be expected in such a hybrid field, the terminology also is drawn from separate areas, and learning the jargon can be a nontrivial barrier to understanding the subject (as the reader may already be aware).

The term *research* encompasses widely disparate approaches to gaining and analyzing information. Some of the major contrasts are as follows:

Orientation. This can range from tightly focused research (e.g., what the effect on sales would be of a 10 percent price cut) to very general, scholarly styled investigations (e.g., finding out what our customers think about when they use our product).

Formality. While most people associate research with studies that are structured with budgets, time schedules, and computerized analysis, both introspection and informal contacts with customers or salespersons are excellent ways to gain information.

Amount of data collection. Again, a common stereotype of marketing research is that it involves extensive data collection, usually in the form of either an experiment or a survey. Not only are there many other kinds of data collection, but a large and increasing amount of marketing research involves analysis of data that are already available.

Complexity of analysis. Research can include nothing more complicated than counts of the responses to a single question (i.e., how many people bought blue shirts) or "fancy" multivariate statistical procedures that simultaneously examine several variables in a variety of ways.

Marketing research and analysis is thus something of a hodgepodge of different approaches and heritages.

WHO DOES MARKETING RESEARCH?

The people who do marketing research are a widely disparate group. There are no marketing research schools, no certification exams, and few schools where a marketing research major exists. Hence, the academic backgrounds of those in research are varied, with psychology and statistics the two most common courses of study of those in research. Many people enter research on rotational assignments from line marketing positions, so it may be somewhat surprising that there is considerable collegiality among members of the research business. Job movement between suppliers (companies that provide research services to other companies for a fee), advertising agencies and consulting companies, and manufacturing and service companies is common.

The research function is traditionally a staff function, often aligned with the planning function. In the past, this has been synonymous with dead-end jobs and a certain lack of respect. Recently, this has begun to change as job mobility and integration have increased. Still, in many organizations, research is something of a stepchild, and it is especially vulnerable during recessions and "reengineering." Even firms with a half billion dollars or more in revenue tend to have fewer than 10 full-time market researchers. The result is that most research is actually done by outside suppliers.

WHAT IS MARKETING RESEARCH?

A list of market research activities closely parallels the information needs for developing a marketing plan:

1. *Monitoring Performance* (sales, margin, share, turnover, returns, satisfaction)
2. *Idea Generation* (advertising copy, new product concepts)
3. *Industry Evaluation* (growth rate, technological change, regulatory environment, likely entrants and exits)
4. *Customer Analysis* (who they are; why, where, and how they buy; what they like and buy and intend to buy; segmentation; brand equity and satisfaction measurement)
5. *Competitor Analysis* (who they are, what they are doing, strengths and weaknesses, what they are likely to do)
6. *Potential Estimation and Sales Forecasting* (territory potential)
7. *Marketing Mix Evaluation*
    Product (concept tests, test markets)
    Distribution (sales by channel, level of support)
    Price (elasticity estimation, impact of promotions, determining appropriate price)
    Advertising (what to say—copy; who to say it to—targeting; when to say it—timing; where to say it—media selection)
    Service (level of satisfaction, voicing of complaints, adequacy of response to complaints)

It is interesting to realize how the research business differs in various situations. Consumer packaged goods research often involves large-sample surveys or experiments as well as frequently employing multivariate statistical procedures. Industrial marketing research is much more likely to use existing data or small samples of key accounts along with relatively simple analytical procedures. Research in the developing nations is most likely to be a struggle to collect reliable data, although recently the ability to get research done in remote (from the U.S. point of view) areas of the world has improved markedly. The "moral" of this discussion, then, is that marketing research is many things to many people.

THE ROLE OF MARKETING RESEARCH IN A BUSINESS

Understanding the role of marketing research requires some conception of how a business operates. One useful way of portraying a business is as a collection of three principal activities: intelligence, operations, and strategy development. Intelligence consists of any activity devoted to collecting or portraying information for use in operating or strategic decisions. Accounting, which is primarily internally focused (e.g., reporting profits, inventory), and marketing research, which is externally oriented (primarily to customers and competitors), are two major intelligence functions. Operations consists of the current focus of a business, including manufacturing, marketing programs (e.g., sales, service, delivery), finance, etc. The strategic element of a business is concerned with the long run and includes such activities as long-range planning and research and development.

Marketing research thus exists to serve the information needs of both operations and strategy development. At its most basic level, monitoring sales and market shares provides data for evaluating operations. More imaginative research might focus on alternative program evaluation (e.g., advertising testing). Finally, the most ambitious types of marketing research attempt to assess future markets in terms of customer preferences and competitive actions.

Marketing research has often been confined, especially in earlier conceptions, to providing information related to operational needs by both the narrow perspective of its producers and an unenlightened view on the part of its users. As an extreme example, "marketing research" in one major airline in the 1980s referred to a single task: periodic surveys of passengers of the airline. Pricing decisions were studied in a separate organization, and volume forecasting in still another unit. Our position is that all these activities are correctly considered as part of the task of marketing research. Moreover, it also is appropriate for marketing research to be involved in longer run and hence, in some sense, more important decisions (e.g., providing input to R&D). Table 1.1 indicates analyzing industry trends and pricing studies are the most widely practiced research activities.

THE ROLE OF THE MARKETING RESEARCHER VIS-À-VIS THE MANAGER

The role of the company marketing researcher is that of an internal consultant. In a research project the role is essentially threefold. First, the researcher serves as a technical consultant who provides expertise in such areas as sampling and implementation (generally by knowing available suppliers, selecting an appropriate one, and working with the supplier during execution of data collection). Second, he or she is generally responsible for analyzing data and providing an initial interpretation of the results. Third, the researcher should act as a consultant to the manager in both the problem definition and action recommendation stages of the project.

In contrast, the manager is primarily responsible for defining the problem and the final recommendations. To be comfortable with the results, a manager must have at least a logical, nontechnical understanding of the research project, especially the logic behind its basic design.

The manager must also maintain a reasonable perspective on what research can and can't do. Research cannot make a bad product sell, nor can it exactly forecast sales in the year 2010. A manager who asks for a single estimate of, for example, sales, ignores the uncertainty associated with such predictions. Knowing whether forecast sales of 1.2 million are reliable within 10,000 or 200,000 is critical to proper contingency planning. Also, the manager who sets unrealistic time schedules (e.g., two weeks for a study where data collection should take three) or budgets will end up with less reliable research. Finally, managers should recognize that some apparently simple questions (e.g., What is the effect of advertising on sales?) are actually very complex. In addition to a variety of measurement issues (Do we measure sales in terms of units, dollars, or market share; advertising in terms of dollars, exposures, share versus competition, or media used?), the basic nature of the cause and effect relationship among variables is often unclear (e.g., Does advertising cause sales, or is the advertising budget set as a percentage of sales?). In short, a manager must accept research projects as a useful but imperfect aid to decision making rather than a panacea.

Conflicts occur between managers and researchers. Managers often think of research as an unnecessary optional expense, the benefits of which are difficult to measure. They view it as slow to arrive, dull, overly qualified, and overly technical. In contrast, researchers criticize managers for poor and changing problem definition, and as technically semiliterate, unsupportive, and superficial with a predetermined right answer. Firms that minimize such conflicts, generally through direct contact leading to mutual understanding and respect, are likely to find their research function more beneficial.

The typical goal of an MBA is to be a manager, not a researcher. Managers do not generally like to be bothered with technical details. Consequently, this book tries to be understandable to technically competent managers. Basically, the manager needs to do three things:

1. Manage/interpret available information.
2. Recognize when additional information is needed and contract for it.
3. Communicate clearly with both researchers and others in the organization (e.g., bosses). In particular, to listen and distill information regarding strategies and problems (i.e., from bosses) and define specific research issues for researchers. (While not particularly glamorous, listening is essential to good communication.)

These tasks suggest a basic distinction in competence and responsibilities between researcher and manager. The manager should have an in-depth knowledge of the business and be primarily responsible for problem detection. The researcher, in contrast, should be technically knowledgeable (about sampling, data collection, and methods of analysis) and focus on project specifications and analysis. Interpretation of results is a joint task that blends the researcher's technical skills and fresh perspective with the manager's knowledge of the subtleties of the particular situation.

Some (i.e., many students and managers) question whether it is important for managers to know what analysts do. There are at least four reasons why basic understanding (i.e., at the level of this book) is beneficial:

1. By understanding the process better, a manager can interpret results better and be less at the mercy of an "expert," whose opinion/interpretation a naive manager must either accept or reject in toto. Also, while top-line (short summary)

TABLE 1.1 Research Activities of 435 Companies

	Developed by Mkt. Res. Dept.	Developed by Another Dept.	Developed by Outside Firm	% Doing
A. Business/Economic and Corporate Research				
1. Industry/market characteristics and trends	56%	12%	30%	92%
2. Acquisition/diversification studies	28	20	11	50
3. Market share analyses	49	13	27	85
4. Internal employee studies (morale, communication, etc.)	38	24	18	72
B. Pricing				
1. Cost analysis	20	37	6	57
2. Profit analysis	15	39	5	55
3. Price elasticity	30	23	10	56
4. Demand analysis:				
a) market potential	55	20	13	78
b) sales potential	48	26	11	75
c) sales forecasts	34	18	9	71
5. Competitive pricing analysis	40	28	10	71
C. Product				
1. Concept development and testing	51	6	23	78
2. Brand name generation and testing	32	4	21	55
3. Test market	33	9	18	55
4. Product testing of existing products	40	8	17	63
5. Packaging design studies	31	6	17	48
6. Competitive product studies	30	12	14	54

reports are useful, important insights often come from more detailed, subtler analyses.

2. By understanding what an analyst typically does as well as what can and cannot be done, a manager can better specify research tasks—i.e., ask the right questions.

3. Because the ability to perform analysis is being decentralized through advances in information technology (i.e., a computer on every desk), the ability to analyze and interpret data as well as the responsibility for doing so is moving from a secluded analyst to the operating manager. Those managers who adapt to this are more likely to succeed.

4. Technically competent managers tend to be better leaders. Managers who both understand and have empathy for research are more likely to have researchers put in the effort required to do a quality job. In contrast, an uninformed manager who looks down at the research function is likely to be given less than the highest quality effort by research suppliers.

TABLE 1.1 *(Continued)*

	Developed by Mkt. Res. Dept.	Developed by Another Dept.	Developed by Outside Firm	% Doing
D. Distribution				
1. Plant/warehouse location studies	13	15	3	25
2. Channel performance studies	22	17	7	39
3. Channel coverage studies	18	13	7	31
4. Export and international studies	13	15	7	32
E. Promotion				
1. Motivation research	33	4	21	56
2. Media research	36	7	28	70
3. Copy research	35	6	29	68
4. Advertising effectiveness testing				
a) prior to marketplace airing	35	6	28	67
b) during marketplace airing	26	6	19	66
5. Competitive advertising studies	24	5	18	43
6. Public image studies	37	6	26	65
7. Sales force compensation studies	15	21	6	34
8. Sales force quota studies	13	15	3	28
9. Sales force territory structure	15	21	2	32
10. Studies of premiums, coupons, deals, etc.	32	10	13	47
F. Buying Behavior				
1. Brand preference	47	4	30	78
2. Brand attitudes	46	4	30	76
3. Product satisfaction	54	5	31	87
4. Purchase behavior	48	5	30	80
5. Purchase intentions	47	4	30	79
6. Brand awareness	42	3	34	80
7. Segmentation studies	50	6	33	84

*Note that "% Doing" does not equal sum of "Developed by" responses due to multiple responses in "Developed by" categories
Source: Thomas C. Kinnear and Ann R. Root, *1994 Survey of Marketing Research* (Chicago: American Marketing Association, 1994), page 49. Copyright © 1994 by the American Marketing Association. Reprinted with the permission of the publishers.

As a consequence of the belief that a technically competent manager is a better manager, this book devotes much of its effort to describing the tools available to a researcher. Put differently, in addition to describing what the manager does (i.e., problem definition) and must know (i.e., in general, what methods are available), this book discusses what the manager benefits from knowing (i.e., what the analyst/researcher is doing).

STATISTICS AND MARKETING RESEARCH

As mentioned earlier, marketing research is a heavy user of several fields including psychology. Perhaps its strongest association, however, is with statistics. Indeed, research includes a heavy dose of applied statistics.

There are at least three views of statistics:

1. As an insufferable bore and irritating annoyance (to some extent due to the way math in general, and statistics in particular, are often taught)
2. As a high form of logic, pure and absolute
3. As a way to get a better handle on the way the world operates

This book rejects the nihilistic first view as the equivalent of throwing out the proverbial baby with the bath water. While not every aspect of statistics provides immediate gratification, it provides a series of signals and insights that benefit its users. Also, not surprisingly, this book rejects the second view and holds that statistics is a means and not an end in itself.

HOW COMPANIES GET RESEARCH DONE

Where research is done is also interesting and occasionally surprising to the uninitiated. Few companies have the staff to actually collect data. Rather, most companies contract data collection to a host of supplier companies ranging from large, well-known firms with offices in many major cities to small job shops with fewer than 10 people. While advertising agencies often serve as a vehicle for getting research done, typically they serve as conduits to the same suppliers. The suppliers in turn may subcontract data collection work to a network of field supervisors. Similarly, computer analysis is often handled by outside firms. Hence, data collection and analysis involve a whole series of subcontractors who work on various parts of a job.

The size of the research business in terms of revenue is relatively small. Typically, marketing research budgets run about 1 to 2 percent of sales at consumer packaged goods companies and less than 1 percent at financial services and health service companies (Kinnear and Root, 1994).

The internal organization of firms is quite variable. Still, in the current economic climate "lean and mean" means small. The research supplier business is also relatively small (Honomichl, 1996a). The total revenue of the 165 members of CASRO (Council of American Survey Research Organizations) is about $5 billion, with 61 percent of their revenue coming from the United States (Table 1.2). In 1995, D&B Marketing Information Services, which included Nielsen, had revenues of $2.4 billion, whereas second-ranked IRI had only $400 million and third-ranked Arbitron $137 million. As of 1997, D&B had spun off its research operations into a separate organization. Most firms are quite small, both in relation to other services (e.g., advertising agencies, accounting firms) and to the sales of the firms they serve.

WHAT RESEARCH DOES NOT DO

Research can possibly be best understood in terms of what it can't do. The following are two major things research cannot do:

> *Make decisions.* Research's role is not to make decisions. Rather, research takes data on a confusing/uncertain market and rearranges them into a different

form that hopefully makes the market more understandable and, consequently, good decisions easier. However, researchers often do make recommendations that become the decision after the appropriate approval is gained.

Guarantee success. Research at best can improve the odds of making a correct decision. Anyone who expects to eliminate the possibility of failure by doing research is both unrealistic and likely to be disappointed. The real value of research can be seen over the long run, where increasing the percentage of good decisions should be manifested in improved bottom-line performance and in the occasional revelation that arises from research.

FORCES SHAPING RESEARCH

A number of factors influence the nature of marketing research:

1. Limited Budgets

Interestingly, the money spent on physically developing a particular part or system is considered an investment, whereas the money spent on understanding customers and providing input to design and development is typically treated as an expense. Intense competition and slow economic growth has led to cost cutting and restructuring (a.k.a. downsizing, reengineering, etc.) designed to trim expenses. Since marketing research's payback is typically longer term, the marketing research budget is often among the first to be trimmed (in spite of the obvious inconsistency of spending less on research while talking about a fast changing world, marketing orientation, learning organizations, the information superhighway, etc.).

Research has gained importance in some firms. Goodyear's turnaround was based heavily on Aquatred, the tire that had 150,000 ordered before ads even appeared and sold 1 million in its first year. The product was based on research that showed that wet traction was second in importance to durability in tires. Similarly, when Goodyear began selling through Sears, it first conducted research with consumers which indicated, contrary to popular opinion, that this would not cannibalize Goodyear dealers (which apparently it did not).

2. The "De-Siloing" of Business

As has been widely proclaimed, the traditional functional view of business persists more in some MBA curricula than in successful organizations. The distinction between quality programs (which are often run by the operations function) and satisfaction measurement (typically a marketing research task) is largely semantic. Cross-functional teams such as those in the new product area require research to be relevant to and decipherable by not just its traditional client, marketing management, but by operations and R&D as well. Perhaps most interesting, some firms now see a distinction between investment activities (which include R&D, capital investment, marketing research, and advertising), and expenses such as promotions. For companies with such an orientation, research competes for funds with capital investments as much as with other marketing tasks.

TABLE 1.2 Top 50 U.S. Research Organizations

Rank 1995	Rank 1994	Organization	Headquarters	Phone	Total Research Revenues* (millions)	Percent Change from 1994**	Percent and Revenues from Outside U.S. ($ in millions)
1	1	D&B Marketing Information Services	Wilton, CT	(203) 834-4200	$2,388.1	9.0%	63.9% $1,525.8
2	2	Information Resources Inc.	Chicago, IL	(312) 726-1221	399.9	11.0	11.0 66.3
3	3	The Arbitron Co.	New York, NY	(212) 887-1300	137.2	11.5	
4	4	Westat Inc.	Rockville, MD	(301) 251-1500	124.0	4.2	
5	5	Maritz Marketing Research Inc.	St. Louis, MO	(314) 827-1610	122.4	12.0	21.4 26.2
6	6	Walsh International/PMSI	Phoenix, AZ	(602) 381-9500	111.6	6.5	28.1 25.1
7	—	The Kantar Group	London, UK	(44-171) 656-5599	91.9	6.5	6.5 6.0
8	7	The NPD Group	Port Washington, NY	(516) 625-0700	85.8	24.6	15.0 12.9
9	8	NFO Research Inc.	Greenwich, CT	(203) 629-8888	73.1	17.4	2.7 2.0
10	9	Market Facts Inc.	Arlington Heights, IL	(847) 590-7000	64.6	13	9.9 6.4
11	13	Audits & Surveys Worldwide Inc.	New York, NY	(212) 627-9700	54.6	24.4	24.0 13.1
12	10	The M/A/R/C Group	Irving, TX	(214) 506-3400	52.1	3.2	
13	14	Opinion Research Corp.	Princeton, NJ	(908) 281-5100	44.1	.9	23.1 10.2
14	12	Abt Associates Inc.	Cambridge, MA	(617) 492-7100	42.9	-8.1	2.3 1.0
15	19	The BASES Group	Covington, KY	(606) 655-6000	41.6	11.0	20.0 8.3
16	17	Intersearch Corp.	Horsham, PA	(215) 442-9000	41.1	12.3	
17	18	MAI Information Group	Livingston, NJ	(201) 717-0500	38.0	12.0	
18	20	Macro International Inc.	Calverton, MD	(301) 572-0200	37.8	7.1	40.7 15.4
19	15	Walker Information	Indianapolis, IN	(317) 843-3939	37.7	-10.9	15.3 5.8
20	11	Elrick & Lavidge	Tucker, GA	(770) 938-3233	34.6	21.7	1.5 .5
21	25	Roper Starch Worldwide Inc.	Mamaroneck, NY	(914) 698-0800	31.5	18.0	5.7 1.8
22	24	J.D. Power and Associates	Agoura Hills, CA	(818) 889-6330	30.3	6.3	
23	23	Burke Inc.	Cincinnati, OH	(513) 241-5663	29.0	10.3	5.0 1.6
24	27	Creative & Response Research	Chicago, IL	(312) 828-9200	27.1	8.0	
25	32	Lieberman Research Worldwide	Los Angeles, CA	(310) 553-0550	23.4	20.0	11.9 2.8

		Organization	Headquarters	Phone				
26	29	Chilton Research Services	Radnor, PA	(610) 964-4602	23.3	5.7		
27	30	Yankelovich Partners Inc.	Norwalk, CT	(203) 846-0100	23.2	12.6	6.0	1.4
28	33	M.O.R.-PACE Inc.	Farmington, MI	(810) 737-5300	22.5	22.2	13.1	3.0
29	34	Wirthlin Worldwide	McLean, VA	(703) 556-0001	22.3	21.2	3.8	.9
30	31	ASI Market Research Inc.	Stamford, CT	(203) 328-7000	21.1	14.4		
31	39	Total Research Corp.	Princeton, NJ	(609) 520-9100	20.9	16.4	26.3	5.5
32	35	Market Strategies	Southfield, MI	(810) 350-3020	19.3	6.6		
33	37	Data Development Corp.	New York, NY	(212) 633-1100	18.6	11.1		
34	36	Custom Research Inc.	Minneapolis, MN	(612) 542-0800	18.5	9.5		
35	38	ICR Survey Research Group	Media, PA	(610) 565-9280	17.9	7.1		
36	40	Response Analysis Corp.	Princeton, NJ	(609) 921-3333	17.2	11.3		
37	—	IntelliQuest Inc.	Austin, TX	(512) 329-0808	17.0	30.7	29.2	5.0
38	43	Market Decision	Cincinnati, OH	(513) 721-8100	15.1	8.0		
39	41	Research Data Analysis Inc.	Bloomfield Hills, MI	(810) 332-5000	14.4	10.9	20.0	2.9
40	45	Martrixx Marketing Research	Cincinnati, OH	(513) 841-1199	14.1	28.7	52.9	7.5
41	44	Conway/Milliken & Assocs.	Chicago, IL	(312) 787-4060	12.4	6.9		
42	42	National Analysts Inc.	Philadelphia, PA	(215) 496-6800	12.0	-6.8		
43	48	Guideline Research Corp.	New York, NY	(212) 947-5140	11.7	20.1		
44	46	Gordon S. Black Corp.	Rochester, NY	(716) 272-8400	11.5	13.5		
45	—	Ross-Cooper-Lund Inc.	Teaneck, NJ	(201) 836-0040	10.3	35.7	1.0	.1
46	47	BAI (Behavioral Analysis Inc.)	Tarrytown, NY	(914) 332-5300	10.0	2.9	10.8	1.0
47	49	Newman-Stein Inc.	New York, NY	(212) 777-2700	8.6	-3.3	5.0	.4
48	—	TVG Inc.	Fort Washington, PA	(215) 646-7200	8.6	4.9		
49	—	Marketing Research Services Inc.	Cincinnati, OH	(513) 772-7580	8.5	23.8		
50	—	FRC Research Corp.	New York, NY	(212) 696-1000	8.4	3.8	3.0	.3
		Subtotal, Top 50			$4,552.2	9.4%	$1,760.1	38.7%
		All other (115 CASRO member companies not included in Top 50)**			413.0	6.7		
		Total (165 organizations)			$4,965.2	9.2%		

*Total revenues that include nonresearch activities for some companies are significantly higher. This information is given in the individual company profiles in the main article.

**Rate of growth from year to year has been so as not to include revenue gains or losses from acquisitions. See company profiles for explanation.

***Total revenues of 115 survey research firms—beyond those listed in Top 50—that provide financial information, on a confidential basis, to the Council of American Survey Research Organizations (CASRO).

Source: Jack J. Honomichl "1996 Business Report on the Marketing Research Industry" from Marketing News (June 3, 1996): H4. Copyright © 1996 by the American Marketing Association. Reprinted with the permission of the publishers.

3. Information Technology

The existence of networked computers and employees accustomed to using computers has made access to data more widespread. As a consequence, the old view of marketing research as something that someone else does is giving way to the view that it is part of a manager's job. Moreover, information technology has contributed to a deluge of information, which changes the question from what data to collect to how to summarize and interpret the data already available.

THE ETHICAL AND LEGAL ENVIRONMENT

The public is not enamored of marketing research, and often groups it with direct marketing as an invasion of privacy (or at least an interruption to dinner). A 1992 Harris-Equivax "Consumer Privacy Survey" as well as many others evidence widespread concern about the use of customer record data by companies. Similar irritation exists because of sales pitches under the guise of marketing research. And the credibility of research is further damaged by the call-in polls (often to 900 numbers), which represent only highly involved individuals. As a consequence, the Research Industry Coalition, a group of the major organizations such as the American Association for Public Opinion Research (AAPOR) and the Market Research Council (MRC), drafted statements with respect to these dubious practices (Table 1.3). Not surprisingly, enforcement remains elusive.

Similarly, the American Marketing Association has developed a code of ethics for the conduct of research (Table 1.4). While limited in scope, this at least provides some general guidelines for research conducted in the United States. For study participants, assurances of anonymity, safety (physical and mental), privacy, honesty, and voluntary participation are basic rights. While subjects can be deceived temporarily (i.e., as to the purpose of the experiment to prevent them from trying to please the experimenter), debriefing that reveals the nature of the study and corrects any false information is required. Put most bluntly, treat subjects as humans, as you would want to be treated.

The legal environment of research has also expanded. In the United States, research is used to assess misleading advertising and trademark infringement as well as to assess damages of an unfair or illegal practice (cf. Morgan, 1990). Legal action was also recently taken by a manufacturer (Beecham) against a research supplier on the grounds that the supplier's forecast for Declare (a competitor for Woolite) was too high (about 50 percent share), causing the company to enter the market but only obtaining a 20 percent share. Beecham claimed the error was due to use of an incorrect estimate of the percent of households using the product category (30 percent vs. 75 percent), whereas Yankelovich, Clancy, and Shulman argued that weak marketing support explained the result. Though this suit was settled out of court, it raises important issues for the conduct of research. It also points out the risks in simply accepting research reports without careful scrutiny and questioning of assumptions.

Some research is explicitly designed to provide support for positions in legal proceedings involving allegations of deceptive advertising, unfair practices, or trademark infringement. Given the scrutiny imposed by the adversarial nature of proceedings in U.S. courts, research that has information value but is open to multiple interpretations is often discounted. Put differently, the standards are more exacting for research in the legal arena.

THE CHANGING NATURE OF MARKETING RESEARCH

The traditional view of marketing research focuses on conducting studies to address a particular problem or issue. A major emphasis of such studies is data collection, usually in the form of a survey that may or may not include an experimental stimulus (e.g., an ad, a new product concept). The results of such studies are used to make a discrete decision (e.g., which ad to run, whether to further develop or introduce the new product).

While problem-focused research continues to be important, much research involves more continuous learning about customers and markets. Similarly, while surveys are still in widespread use (for example, in the measurement of satisfaction), both more qualitative procedures (focus groups, interpretive methods) and analysis of routinely collected data (customer records, scanner data) have grown in importance.

Since marketing research is in the business of "producing" information, it is useful to consider which production (now called operations) process best describes it. While many are possible, two particularly salient alternatives emerge:

1. A job shop where all (or at least most) of the jobs are customized, special orders
2. A production line that focuses on generating consistent product efficiency

When problems are defined unsystematically in response to mini-crises, a research department tends to resemble a job shop. As a consequence, the operation tends to be flexible with low fixed costs but also not to "learn" much from past work unless a strong effort is made to facilitate comparability across studies. This is not easy, as one company's strenuous but abortive efforts to require a single standardized question to measure intention to buy across studies demonstrated.

When problems are consistent (i.e., monitoring quality and customer satisfaction, tracking share using panel data, tracking sales by customer or region), it is possible to design a system using consistent data collection, analysis, and reporting methods. Often called a *Marketing Information System* (MIS), periodic reporting enhances comparability and efficiency. However, like any standardized system, it also tends to be inflexible and to discourage innovation.

Partly as a reaction to the inflexibility of many marketing information systems, attention has recently turned to *Decision Support Systems* (DSSs). Essentially, these systems combine the systematic/standardized data with both special-purpose data, sometimes including subjective judgment, and analytical methods to address particular problems (i.e., planning sales territories). In some sense, DSSs provide the "right" way to think about marketing research: as a tool that provides information relevant to decisions and even actual decisions (as in so-called expert systems). Moreover, as standard data becomes more prevalent (which seems likely to be the case), designing "systems" will become increasingly crucial. However, this book will still provide extensive coverage of the traditional research project, for several reasons:

1. Information and decision support systems are changing rapidly as developments occur in the area of artificial intelligence, and hence anything said here is likely to be very general (i.e., make the systems user-friendly) or out of date. Put differently, the study of such systems is a topic in its own right.

TABLE 1.3 Acceptable Research Practice Statements

Statement about Certain Unacceptable Practices When Performed under the Guise of Research	Research Industry Privacy Statement: Safeguarding Respondents and Data

In recent years, certain misleading practices, performed in the name of research, have become increasingly evident. **The Research Industry Coalition wishes to state that in no case are the following practices deemed legitimate or acceptable as elements of professionally conducted research:**

requiring a monetary payment or soliciting monetary contributions from members of the public as part of a research process

This set of practices amounts to fund raising under the guise of research. It takes unfair advantage of the cooperative attitude that a majority of the public manifests when asked to take part in a legitimate information gathering process. In some cases, unwary members of the public are enticed to contribute money as a condition of gaining some future "benefit" from their participation.

offering products or services for sale, or using participant contacts as a means of generating sales leads

A common practice is to gain entry or acceptance in order to make a sales pitch by initially defining the contact as being made for "research" purposes. This trades on the prestige of science, and it exploits the willingness of people to reveal information about themselves in the public interest. In some cases, questions establish respondents' susceptibility to sales pressure or their interest in some product or service. Follow-up contacts are then made to those so identified, all in the name of "research."

revealing the identity of individual respondents to a survey or of participants in a research process without their permission

It is a normal research practice to pledge anonymity and confidentiality to the public in order to secure their cooperation and frankness in responding to questions. Revealing the identity of individuals, for whatever purpose, is a violation of that pledge unless a respondent's prior informed consent has been obtained.

Concern has mounted among the general public about the intrusions of business and government into their private lives. The Research Industry Coalition wishes to emphasize our deep and long-standing commitment to protecting the privacy of research participants and the confidentiality of the data we gather.

Communicating these concerns is important both for the public and for the research industry

It is important for the public because the information we gather is used to understand the public's reaction to government policies and social and political events. It is also used to understand the public's preferences for products and services and the rationale for those choices. Such understanding facilitates at the marketplace for ideas and products. Existing policies, products, and services are improved; new and better ones are created.

It is important for the research industry because we rely on public cooperation to gather information. We feel that we will get better cooperation when the public understands our interest in protecting both their identities and the information they contribute

For many years marketing and opinion research practitioners of our member organizations have subscribed to the codes of standards and professional ethics that emphasize the need to protect the privacy of respondents and the confidentiality of the data collected for research purposes. **Our codes of professional ethics and practices stress honesty, respectful treatment, and professionalism in our contacts with the public.**

In fact, RIC issued a statement in 1990 that "revealing the identity of individual respondents to a survey or of participants in a research process without their permission" was not acceptable in professionally conducted research.

Our objective is to reassure the public that the information they provide for marketing and opinion research purposes will be handled in accordance with professional standards that safeguard their privacy.

| RIC members endorsing this statement: AAPOR, AMA, APA, ARF, ASA, CASRO, MRA, MRC, NAA, NCPP, QRCA, TTRA | RIC members endorsing this statement: AAPOR, ACR, AMA, APA, ASA, CASRO, MRA, MRC, NAA, NCPP, QRCA, TTRA |

TABLE 1.3 *(Continued)*

Statement about the Unacceptable Usage of Call-In "Polls"

In recent years, the misuse of 900-number and other types of call-in "polls" has become increasingly evident.

These "polls" report the opinions of only those people who called in, and not those of the general public. Nevertheless, many people believe such polls are scientific, believable, accurate, and representative of the entire population. The Research Industry Coalition believes that any publicizing or promotion of such "polls" not only damages legitimate marketing and survey research practice, but can be very misleading or damaging when used to influence public policy or simply to disseminate information on perceptions of the general public.

The results of so-called 900-number call-in "polls," and other types of self-selection "polls," are based solely upon the responses of those people who were exposed to a written or broadcast stimulus, were strongly motivated to register an opinion, and were willing to pay to do so. Hence, such "polls" do not measure the opinions of a projectable cross-section of the general public or of some other predefined group (no matter how many responses are received) because they fail to use scientific sampling methods in which everyone in the given population has a known chance of being selected for survey participation.

Research surveys based upon scientific sampling yield findings that are often sharply at variance with the results of call-in "polls," which merely tally the opinions of a self-selected set of respondents. Further, such "polls" generally frame issues in highly simplified terms and thus do not measure the often complex opinions that exist on a given issue.

Self-selection "polls" are not legitimate research, and when publicized or promoted in any way to any part of the general public, ought to be accompanied by an appropriate disclaimer statement.

The Research Industry Coalition recommends the following disclaimer statement for use with call-in "polls":

> "These 'polls' represent the opinions of only those people who have called or written in, and not the general public."

RIC members endorsing this statement: AAPOR, ACR, AMA, APA, ASA, CASRO, MRA, MRC, NAA, NCPP, QRCA, TTRA
Source: Reprinted with the permission of The Research Industry Coalition.

2. A lot of marketing research is still ad hoc, particularly in some parts of the world.

3. The same issues and methods that arise in designing and analyzing ad hoc studies apply to designing and maintaining systems as well. Issues such as missing data, unclear wording, and even analytical method become "invisible" as user-friendly decision support systems emerge. Unless you understand what data exist, can evaluate their quality, and comprehend what various analytical methods do, an information and decision support system becomes an incomprehensible black box to be supported/worshiped or attacked blindly.

As a consequence, for pedagogical reasons this book focuses on designing (rather than maintaining) data collection methods. Similarly, the analysis section describes methods that are applicable to any data set. Examples of systematic data (i.e., scanner panel data, sales records) are presented where appropriate.

Still, the view of research promoted here (we're all in marketing, aren't we?) is more general than a series of independent projects. While the research project remains a basic building block of the researcher-manager interface, a more interactive view is appropriate. At least in developed economies, data has moved from being a scarce commodity to a burdensome surplus. For example, packaged goods manufacturers are inundated with special surveys, scanner-based purchase and store records, and detailed sales

TABLE 1.4 Process of Marketing Research

Code of Marketing Research Ethics for the American Marketing Association

A. For Research Users, Practitioners and Interviewers

1. No individual or organization will undertake any activity which is directly or indirectly represented to be marketing research, but which has as its real purpose the attempted sale of merchandise or services to some or all of the respondents interviewed in the course of the research.

2. If a respondent has been led to believe, directly or indirectly, that he is participating in a marketing research survey and that his anonymity will be protected, his name shall not be made known to anyone outside the research organization or research department, or used for other than research purposes.

A. For Research Practitioners

1. There will be no intentional or deliberate misrepresentation of research methods or results. An adequate description of methods employed will be made available upon request to the sponsor of the research. Evidence that field work has been completed according to specifications will, upon request, be made available to buyers of research.

2. The identity of the survey sponsor and/or the ultimate client for whom a survey is being done will be held in confidence at all times, unless this identity is to be revealed as part of the research design. Research information shall be held in confidence by the research organization or department and not used for personal gain or made available to any outside party unless the client specifically authorizes such release.

3. A research organization shall not undertake marketing studies for competitive clients when such studies would jeopardize the confidential nature of client-agency relationships.

C. For Users of Marketing Research

1. A user of research shall not knowingly disseminate conclusions from a given research project or service that are inconsistent with or not warranted by the data.

2. To the extent that there is involved in a research project a unique design involving techniques, approaches or concepts not commonly available to research practitioners, the prospective user of research shall not solicit such a design from one practitioner and deliver it to another for execution without the approval of the design originator.

D. For Field Interviewers

1. Research assignments and materials received, as well as information obtained from respondents, shall be held in confidence by the interviewer and revealed to no one except the research organization conducting the marketing study.

2. No information gained through a marketing research activity shall be used directly or indirectly for the personal gain or advantage of the interviewer.

3. Interviews shall be conducted in strict accordance with specifications and instructions received.

4. An interviewer shall not carry out two or more interviewing assignments simultaneously unless authorized by all contractors or employers concerned.

   Members of the American Marketing Association will be expected to conduct themselves in accordance with the provisions of this Code in all of their marketing research activities.

Source: Reprinted with the permission of the American Marketing Association.

records. These billions of bits of information indeed make it difficult to see the information in the data (or to quote T. S. Eliot, "Where is the information we have lost in the data?"). Thus while special studies remain important, so is a system for dealing with available data and establishing baseline norms against which to compare new results. The development of decision support systems (i.e., computer-based procedures for integrating data, analytical methods, and managerial judgment) is, in fact, an appropriate goal of marketing research.

THE INTERNATIONAL PERSPECTIVE

When one broadens the view of research beyond U.S. organizations, it appears that currently most of the revenue and activity occurs in the developed world. Several major firms are not based in the United States: The Kantar Group (UK, second with revenue of $433 million), GFK (Germany), SOFRES (France), Infratest Burke AG (Germany), and Video Research (Japan). While it seems inevitable that the importance of currently less-developed companies will increase in the research business as in all businesses, for the present most of the activity is in the United States and Europe, each with about 40 percent of the total business (Honomichl, 1996b).

This book thus has as its focus the types of research most commonly used in the United States. There are at least three reasons for this, in addition to the current preponderance of work in the United States and Europe and by U.S. firms. First, the basic principles of design and analysis transfer across cultural boundaries, although many details of data collection procedures may not. Second, for better or worse, there seems to be a trend toward reproducing many of the developed world's procedures in the rest of the world. Of the top 25 research organizations in 1996, 18 were based in the United States and another (the UK-based Kantar Group) does 60 percent of its business there (Table 1.5). Third, the authors don't know much about much of the world, and so it would be presumptuous (not to mention very difficult) for them to write about it. For those who don't buy the first two arguments (or condone the third), the book by Douglas and Craig (1983) might be worth pursuing.

THE APPROACH OF THIS BOOK

Many people argue that marketing research is more of an art than a science. Actually, it probably most resembles a craft in that it requires both adherence to some basic principles and some skill gained from experience. This book will approach the topic by attempting to explain the methods most commonly used—what they are, how they work, and what their weaknesses are. As much as possible, the book will be user oriented and will stress practicality over purity.

Stylistically, this means the book is both informal and informative. In terms of content, the book begins by discussing the need for and types of studies (Chapters 2 and 3) and the design of studies (Chapters 4–8). Sampling is covered in Chapter 9. Coding and basic analysis are covered in Chapters 10 and 11. More advanced analytical material appears in Chapters 12–20. Finally, some general comments on the future of research are provided in Chapter 21.

TABLE 1.5 Top 25 Global Research Organizations

Rank 1995	Organization	Headquarters	Country	No. of Countries with Subsidiaries/ Branch Offices (1)	Full-time Employees	Total Research Revenues (2) (Millions)	Percent Change From 1994 (3)	Revenues from Outside Home Country US$ (Millions)	Percent of Total
1	D&B Marketing Information Serv.	Wilton, CT	USA	1	25,000	$2,388.1	9.0%	$1,525.8	63.9%
	A.C. Nielsen	Stamford, CT	USA	61	17,000	1,286.1	6.0	977.4	76.0
	IMS International Inc.	New York, NY	USA	57	6,000	818.5	11.0	507.7	6.20
	Nielsen Media Research	New York, NY	USA	1	2,000	283.5	13.5		
2	The Kantar Group Ltd.	London	UK	1	2,758	432.9	15.7	263.6	60.8
	Research International	London	UK	16	1,250	233.3	18.1	161.7	69.3
	Millward Brown International	Warwick	UK	10	959	137.4	22.0	73.2	53.3
	MRB Group Ltd.	London	UK	6	549	63.3	-2.9	28.4	45.6
3	Information Resources Inc.	Chicago, IL	USA	13	4,000	399.9	11.0	66.3	11.0
4	GFK Holding AG	Nuremberg	Germany	32	2,000	311.2	16.6	123.2	39.6
5	SOFRES Group S.A.	Paris	France	19	2,584	251.7	5.5	177.5	70.5
6	Infratest Burke AG	Munich	Germany	13	750	152.1	9.3	69.5	31.9
7	Video Research Ltd.	Tokyo	Japan	316	145.3*	2.3*			
8	IPSOS Group S.A.	Paris	France	10	1,000	142.8	6.4	93.0	65.0
9	PMSI/Source Informatics	Phoenix, AZ	USA	1	850	139.7	7.8	48.1	34.4
	Pharmaceutical Marketing Serv.	Phoenix, AZ	USA	7	450	91.3	11.8	48.1	52.7

10	The Arbitron Company	New York, NY	USA	1	527	137.2	11.5		
11	Westat Inc.	Rockville, MD	USA	1	810	124.0	4.2		
12	The Maritz Marketing Research Inc.	St. Louis, MO	USA	3	842	122.4	12.0	26.2	21.4
13	NOP Information Group	London	UK	5	750	120.3	12.7	41.5	34.5
14	Taylor Nelson AGB Plc.	London	UK	7	1,053	108.6	14.5	23.0	21.2
15	Marketing Intelligence Copr.	Tokyo	Japan	1	359	104.7	9.2	.3	.3
16	The NPD Group	Port Washington	USA	11	650	85.8	24.6	12.9	15.0
17	NFO Research Inc.	Greenwich, CT	USA	4	614	73.1	17.4	2.0	2.6
18	Market Facts Inc.	Arlington Heights, IL	USA	2	450	64.6	13.0	6.4	9.9
19	Dentsu Research	Tokyo	Japan	1	98	57.3*	6.4*	2.7*	4.7*
20	Audits & Surveys Worldwide Inc.	New York, NY	USA	4	287	54.6	24.4	13.7	25.1
21	The M/A/R/C Group, Inc.	Irving, TX	USA	1	250	52.1	3.2		
22	Sample Institut GmbH & Co. KG	Molln	Germany	7	283	45.7	7.4	21.9	47.9
23	Nikkei Research Inc.	Tokyo	Japan	4	187	45.2	11.2	1.5	3.5
24	Goldfarb Consultants	Toronto, ON	Canada	6	155	44.6	29.8	19.0	26.1
25	Opinion Research Corp.	Princeton, NJ	USA	3	256	44.1	.9	10.2	23.1
	Total				47,629	$5,648.0	10.3%	$2,550.0	45.2%

(1) Includes countries which have subsidiaries with an equity interest or branch offices, or both.
(2) Total revenues that include non-research activities for some companies are significantly higher. This information is given in the individual company profiles in the main article.
(3) Rate or growth from year to year has been adjusted so as not to include revenue gains or losses from acquisitions. See company profiles for explanation. Rate of growth is based on home country currency.
* For fiscal year ending March 31, 1996.
Source: Jack J. Honomichl "1996 Buisness Report on the Marketing Research Industry" from Marketing News (June 3, 1996): H4. Copyright © 1996 by the American Marketing Association. Reprinted with the permission of the publishers.

REFERENCES

Cox, William E. (1979) *Industrial Marketing Research*, New York: John Wiley and Sons.

Douglas, Susan P., and C. Samuel Craig (1983) *International Marketing Research*, Englewood Cliffs, N.J.: Prentice-Hall.

Ferber, Robert, ed. (1974) *Handbook of Marketing Research*, New York: McGraw-Hill.

Honomichl, Jack J. (1996a) "1996 Business Report on the Marketing Research Industry," *Marketing News*, June 3, H1–H39.

—— (1996b) "Honomichl Global 25," *Marketing News*, September, H1–H19.

Kerlinger, Fred N. (1973) *Foundations of Behavioral Research*, 2nd ed., New York: Holt, Rinehart and Winston.

Kinnear, Thomas C., and Ann R. Root (1994), *1994 Survey of Marketing Research*, Chicago: American Marketing Association.

McDaniel, Stephen W., Perry Verille, and Charles S. Madden (1985) "The Threats to Marketing Research: An Empirical Reappraisal," *Journal of Marketing Research*, 22, February, 74–80.

Morgan, Fred W. (1990) "Judicial Standards for Survey Research: An Update and Guidelines," *Journal of Marketing*, 54, January, 58–70.

Perreault, William D., Jr. (1992) "The Shifting Paradigm in Marketing Research," *Journal of the Academy of Marketing Science*, 20, Fall, 367–75.

Twedt, Dik W. (1983) *Survey of Marketing Research*, Chicago: American Marketing Association.

CHAPTER 2

The Value of Information

Information plays a central role in many of the key concepts in marketing such as market and customer orientation, quality, and satisfaction assessment. Day (1991) and Glazer (1991) describe knowledge and the ability to learn about markets as a key competency and source of competitive advantage. In this chapter, we explore three aspects of information: (1) what it is used for; (2) what influences its use; and (3) how it can be valued.

INTRODUCTION

One reason information is valuable is that, in general, we don't know as much as we think we do and what we think we know is often wrong. One clear example of not knowing as much as we think we do is overconfidence (cf. Mahajan, 1992). Typically when we forecast, we place too small a range around a forecast. For example, if you ask a number of people for a forecast of, say, sales of a new product (e.g., HDTV) and a range in which they are 90 percent sure the actual result will fall, you will find only something like 10–20 percent of the forecasts will fall in the 90 percent range of an individual. This tendency is actually stronger for experts than for novices. While overconfidence can be reduced by highlighting extreme possible results and encouraging people to think of what could cause a result to be different, its prevalence suggests we may need more information than we think we do. Similarly, in a study by Armstrong (1991), a sample of experts was asked to rate the likelihood that 20 hypotheses about consumer behavior "proved" to be true as in articles in the *Journal of Consumer Research*. The percent of correct responses was remarkably similar and close to 50 percent (range 51–58%) for three groups: practitioners, academics, and high school students. The conclusion is pretty clear: we don't do much better than chance in predicting many aspects of behavior based on experience and intuition.

Information needs exist for both new and existing brands. While the impetus for Kodak's Disc Camera was the peaking of Instamatic sales in 1978, the design was the result of research indicating that "trouble-free" photography in a broader range of situations than was possible with Instamatics had appeal to the market. Design of specific features followed extensive customer testing. The introduction of the Disc Camera and subsequent products such as the Falcon, a single-use camera first introduced in Japan in 1994, represent blends of marketing, marketing research, and research and development (which doesn't always guarantee great success).

Research is often less dramatic but at least as prevalent among existing brands. Consider Gillette and its mature products: razors and razor blades. Their research includes annual national surveys of men and women, an annual interview of an existing panel, a national telephone brand awareness study, numerous consumer use tests, and their own as well as syndicated retail audits. Thus, the collection of information plays a crucial role in many companies.

The basic thrust of this chapter is that the value of information is related to the improvement to which it leads in actual decisions. When considering the value of information, it is important to recognize that many uses of information are only indirectly related to decisions, profit and loss calculations, or both. In addition to aiding decision making, information also is collected for the following reasons:

> *Tradition.* As is the case with any organization, patterns of behavior become established. A budget allocated to research is a budget that will be spent. While marketing research typically is a very weak competitor in the bureaucratic battles for funds, it does have a certain permanence: Those involved in information collection and analysis tend to recommend further research.

> *To gain agreement.* Often, research is used not to influence the person who orders the research (who has already made a decision) but as a document to gain support for the decision within the organization. Here, research serves both a legitimization and a quality control function.

> *To prepare a defense in case of failure.* Research serves as a defense in case a decision goes awry. While there is a fairly low limit to the number of blunders a person can be associated with and still be employed, it is a lot easier to explain a decision if you can produce a report that said it was the right one.

> *To stall.* One of the best ways to delay a decision is to postpone it by suggesting that it can be studied further.

> *Legal.* An increasing amount of research is related to legal issues, such as claim substantiation and trademark infringement. Also, deceptive advertising complaints to the Federal Trade Commission create a demand for marketing research studies.

> *PR/advertising.* Research often serves as the basis for advertising claims (e.g., "7 of 10 doctors . . ."). Here its role is to convince consumers either of the truth of a particular claim or of the trustworthiness and high-mindedness of the company in general.

> *Consciousness raising.* In some cases, conducting a study is designed to focus attention of either respondents or interviewers on a topic. For example, a manager at a major computer manufacturer used a customer survey as a way of increasing the sensitivity of the sales force to particular nontechnical benefits and problems from the customer's perspective.

TABLE 2.1 Different Uses of Information

1. To help make a decision
   a) Accurate use (use that accepts the results as relevant)
   b) Inaccurate/biased use (selective use to support a position)

2. To gain knowledge
   a) Content (specific knowledge from the study)
   b) Process (general knowledge about procedures, customers, etc.)

3. For political purposes
   a) Include others in the process
   b) Tradition/policy
   c) Signal importance
   d) Delay a decision
   e) Impress others

4. To increase comfort
   a) Reduce uncertainty about a decision
   b) Feel did a thorough job

One typology of information use, based on Menon and Varadarajan (1992), stresses the intended use (Table 2.1). They draw a distinction between use for decision making versus use for the decision makers (e.g., for knowledge/learning, comfort/uncertainty reduction, or political purposes). Menon and Wilcox (1994) have developed a scale to measure the use of market research. Based on their analysis, they break use into six categories:

1. Congruous (consistent with the results)
2. Incongruous (inconsistent with the results)
3. Cynical (for appearance or political reasons)
4. Positive (to draw attention to the area)
5. Process (learning because of participating)
6. Product (specific learning)

WHAT IS WORTH RESEARCHING

One perspective on what is worth researching comes from the Marketing Science Institute (MSI). A foundation with over 60 corporate member firms, MSI is dedicated to encouraging research by academics on topics that are relevant to practice. Every two years, it prepares a statement of research priorities based primarily on practitioners' views. The 1996–98 (Table 2.2) priorities indicate interest in fairly broad strategic issues (e.g., really new products, long-term customer relations, the impact of information technology). While the standard topics of advertising and pricing are relevant, it is clear that the practitioners (of whom the largest subgroup is in the market research function) view the potential of marketing research to be greater than simply testing elements of the marketing mix.

TABLE 2.2 1996–98 MSI Research Priorities

1. Customers and Consumers
2. Innovation and Really New Products and Markets
3. Information Technology and New Media
4 Marketing Management Organization and Processes
5. Global Marketing
6. Management Use of Information and Market Research
7. Brand Equity and Product and Brand Management
8. Marketing Measurement, Engineering, and Empirical Generalization
9. Pricing and Promotions
10. Service
11. Channels and Sales/Value Chain
12. Understanding Competition
13. Market Orientation
14. Marketing Communications
15. Public Issues

Another perspective comes from recognizing the imperfect understanding of even experts. For example, Hock (1988) found that marketing experts were no better than ordinary consumers in predicting general consumer opinions—and neither was very good. Consequently, one might assume we know less than we think we do and hence more is worth researching than we think.

INFLUENCES ON INFORMATION USE

The likelihood that managers pay attention to research findings depends on several factors. One study (Deshpandé and Zaltman, 1982) found that research that had impact tended to:

Be confirmatory rather than exploratory in nature
Not produce surprising results (see also Lee, Acito, and Day, 1987)
Occur in a decentralized organization
Have a high level of interactions between researchers and managers
Be of high technical quality

In a follow-up study focusing on industrial firms, Deshpandé and Zaltman (1987) again confirmed that surprising findings are less utilized (confirming the obvious but often overlooked fact that new ideas are rarely welcomed). They also found greater utilization in more formal organizations when the objective was more exploratory.

Perkins and Rao (1990) studied the use of information in a controlled setting and found that more experienced managers relied more on "soft" information, particularly when the decision was less structured or routine. Maltz and Kohli (1995) studied the dissemination of information from marketing to other functions. They found that information use is influenced by research quality (measured by its accuracy, relevance, clarity, and timeliness), which in turn is influenced by confidence in the researchers (their trustworthiness and competence).

The role of trust has received considerable attention. Studying interactions between 779 providers and users of market research including intra- and intercompany relationships, Moorman, Zaltman, and Deshpandé (1992) found that personal trust and perceived quality of interaction were the main determinants of information use. Further, the impact of trust tended to be indirect, influencing the perceived quality of interactions between research users and providers, which in turn influenced information use. Interaction quality was measured in terms of (a) handling of disagreements, (b) insight production, (c) strategic understanding, (d) customer orientation, and (e) productive interaction. Trust is enhanced most by the (a) integrity and also by the (b) confidentiality, (c) sincerity, (d) tactfulness, and (e) timeliness (including honesty in making promises) of the researcher. Interestingly, congeniality actually led to decreased trust. In addition, the researcher's expertise (training and experience) and willingness to reduce uncertainty (interpret inconclusive data) contribute to trust (Moorman, Deshpandé, and Zaltman, 1993a,b).

The continual flow of information makes it likely that firms will frequently deviate from or change plans. Moorman and Miner (1995) suggest that the availability of real-time information increases both organizational improvisation and its effectiveness when knowledge of past information (i.e., organizational memory) is high.

Specific issues of information use also arise. The massive amounts of scanner data available motivated a conference on "Building an Information Strategy for Scanner Data" (Weinberg, 1989). Goldstein (1993) studied the use of scanner data by product managers. He concluded that managers organize their knowledge as a series of stories, which they update in the light of unexpected results. Also interestingly, analysis tended to be simple and based on limited data rather than extensive statistical analysis of available data.

In a more qualitative vein, Zaltman (1989) focused on the relationships between advertising agencies and their clients. He found a tendency to focus on evaluative rather than developmental research and to use only convenient measures of effect (e.g., awareness rather than the interaction effect of advertising on price elasticity). One conclusion reached was that a market research group should be attached to each major marketing unit and its charter should be broad.

THE VALUE OF INFORMATION FOR DECISION MAKING

In valuing research this way, we take a basically "transactional" view. That is, we view information in the context of a single decision. Clearly, this understates the value if any general knowledge is generated that is then applied in future situations. Further, as discussed earlier, there are many uses of information that don't relate to decision making per se (e.g., political uses). Here, we narrow the focus and present a framework for assessing the value of information in terms of making a single decision.

There are many decisions where the situation is sufficiently clear that no additional information is likely to change the decision, and hence the value of information is very small. (For example, if the boss asks if you could work late, the answer is, "Yes.") On the other hand, some decisions cry out for information that may not be available at any price. (For example, secret information about the price of Polaroid stock six months in the future would be crucial to the decision whether to buy or sell the stock, except for certain legal issues.) More likely, however, is a situation where information will improve the odds of making a good decision (such as getting a better measure of the market potential for a new product).

The concept of the odds of making a good decision is crucial to the concept of the value of information. For example, assume that a decision maker is faced with a tough decision—one where there are two choices and each one seems about equally likely to be correct. By relying on experience, the decision maker might be able to increase the odds of choosing the correct action from 50:50 to 60:40. By collecting the best available information, the odds might be increased from 60:40 to 80:20 in favor of making the correct decision. Hence, the value of information in this case comes from increasing the chance of the correct decision from three out of five to four out of five. Information is not perfect (there is still a one in five chance of making a wrong decision), and in fact it is possible that we will make the wrong decision after collecting information, whereas we would have made the correct decision without the information. Still, over the long run, one is clearly better off with information than without it whenever there is uncertainty about the consequences of alternative decisions.

Another point worth making is that unless a decision changes as the result of information, the information has no value in this context. This truism has two separate levels of meaning. First, unless the manager is willing to change his or her mind based on data, the data collection is an unnecessary expense. Second, if all the decisions after information collection are to go ahead and the prior decision was also to go ahead, the information has no value. For example, it could be relatively obvious that we wish to enter a market. If we collected further information, we might better pinpoint the size of the market. However, we would be unlikely to find a market that would alter the enter/not enter decision, so the information would not be worth anything. This leads to two other key points. In general, information is most useful in cases (*a*) where we are most unsure what to do and (*b*) where there are extreme values (either huge losses or profits), which would be extremely important if they came to pass. What collecting information really does is lower the odds that you will go ahead with a flop or, conversely, fail to proceed with a success. Exactly how much information is worth depends on the following three things:

1. The amount the odds of making the correct decision increase when the information is collected and used
2. The relative benefit (profitability) of the alternative decisions
3. The cost of the information

This chapter presents a formal framework for decision making and for evaluating the worth of information. While this framework is rarely used formally, both the logical structure itself and concepts concerning the value of information underlie the decision to collect information. The chapter closes by reemphasizing some real-world considerations in assessing the value of information. The reader is warned that the treatment that follows is at least semiformal. If such treatment leads to intimidation or frustration, the reader should concentrate on understanding the concept of the value of information, as this is by far the most important concept in the chapter.

DECISION ANALYSIS AND INFORMATION VALUE: CONCEPT

Before discussing decision analysis and the value of information in detail, it is useful to highlight the concepts by considering the case of whether to introduce a new product. New product introduction is a risky undertaking, with the risk varying by, among other things, the level of study prior to entering the market, the relative benefits and costs of the new product versus the products it competes with, and the general level of competitive activity.

In structuring the decision, one first needs to identify the possible alternatives. Here, we will assume the possible decisions are to go ahead and introduce the product, to not introduce the product, or to conduct a test of the product and then either go ahead or not. Next, we need to specify the possible results. While clearly there are an infinite number of results (e.g., sales = 0 units, 1 unit, 2 units, . . .), we can (over)simplify this by considering only two levels of sales: low and high.

The consequences of the various combinations of decisions and market results are pretty obvious. Introducing the product to a low sales level leads to a loss, while introducing it to a high level leads to a profit. Not proceeding has no cost or profit associated with it. Performing the test adds to the cost.

Notice that we are ignoring the very real possibility that the study would uncover information that would allow us to improve a product and thus improve the chances of a high sales level. This simplification is made solely to prevent the discussion from becoming any more complicated than it already is.

We now need to assess how likely each of the possible results is. In this case, we begin by assuming that the likelihood of a successful new product is so low that, if we directly introduce the product, sales are more likely to be low than high (i.e., the likelihood of low sales is high and high sales is low). Next, we consider how likely a test is to produce a positive result. Since, at least for most new products that are similar to existing ones, test results are likely to be better than eventual market results, we assume the likelihoods of negative or positive results are both about 50 percent. Assuming we get a negative result, we know from experience that the chances of a low sales level are very high and those of a high sales level very low. On the other hand, if we get a positive result we have learned that there is a moderate chance of then achieving either a low or high level of sales.

This information is summarized in the tree in Figure 2.1. The viable decisions are thus pretty clear: don't introduce, introduce without testing, or test and proceed to introduce if the test result is positive (it generally makes no sense to test and ignore the results, which going ahead after a negative test would imply). The impact of these decisions can be summarized as follows:

Do not introduce. You are certain that there will be no impact (loss or profit).

Introduce without test. The likelihood is high you will incur a loss and low you will produce a profit.

Test. There is about a 50 percent chance you will introduce the product with a moderate chance of a loss and a moderate chance of a gain, and a 50 percent chance you will decide, based on the negative test result, not to introduce the product. You are certain you have to pay for the test.

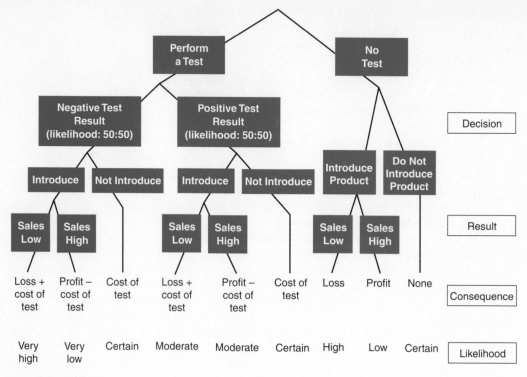

FIGURE 2.1
Conceptual Example: Product Introduction and Testing

What this informal decision analysis does is structure the discussion about decisions around possible events, consequences, and likelihoods, rather than preferences. For example, faced with this decision most people would, if they did not test, prefer not to introduce the product. The decision to test would then be based on whether the decision maker(s) preferred a certain result of no net income or to pay for the test and have a 50 percent chance of no net income and a 50 percent chance of either a loss or a profit (which is basically a 50 percent chance of no income, a 25 percent chance of a loss, and a 25 percent chance of a gain). The difference in the value of the result if the test was run and the value without the test is then the value of the test (soon to be called *the value of information*).

DECISION ANALYSIS

In this section, we discuss decision analysis as a way to structure decision making. The term *decision analysis* refers to a logical framework for choosing among alternative courses of action. Much has been written on the subject (Assmus, 1977; MaGee, 1964; Raiffa, 1968; Schlaiffer, 1959) including a fairly readable book by Jones (1977). The framework is typically visualized in terms of a tree diagram (Figure 2.1). The typical method of constructing such a tree is as follows:

1. Delineate the possible courses of action.
2. List the possible results ("states of nature") of each course of action.
3. Estimate the payoff (usually in monetary terms) of each possible combination of courses of action and results.
4. Assign likelihoods of occurrence (probabilities) to the different possible results for each given course of action.
5. Select the course of action that seems to lead to the most desirable results.

Example

To see how decision analysis is used more formally, consider the following problem: The XYZ Transportation Company, which specializes in freight deliveries, is considering a new rate on its New York to Paris route. In the past, there has been a two-tier pricing system for one-pound packages: $20 for "first class," which guarantees next-day delivery, and $10 for "regular," which typically takes two to three days. We are now considering instituting a same-day delivery service at the price of $30 or $40 (we have a thing about prices in $10 increments and will consider no other prices—boss's orders). After some preliminary analysis, we decide that one of three possible results is likely to occur if we price at $30: getting 100, 60, or 20 new packages per day. Similarly, if we price at $40, we can get either 50, 30, or 5 new packages per day.

Also, at the new prices we expect some of our present customers to trade up to the new service. At the $30 price, we think either 20 or 30 packages per day will be sent same-day instead of first class, whereas at $40, either 10 or 20 will move to same-day.

The daily cost of setting up and running the new service will be $700. The variable costs to send a package by the three classes of service are $18 for same-day, $12 for first class, and $8 for regular. What should we do?

Even though this is a fairly simple situation, the data are sufficiently extensive to make analyzing the decision in one's head fairly complicated. Hence, to provide a structure to the decision-making process, one could quite logically begin by drawing a tree to represent it (Figure 2.2).

Having delineated the situation faced by identifying (a) the courses of action and (b) the possible results (outcomes), one would now proceed to estimate (c) the monetary consequences of each of the possible results. Consider the value of a single new piece of business at the $30 price. Since XYZ gets $30 and it costs them $18, they gain $12 for each new piece of business. Similarly, for everyone who trades up, they make $12 instead of $20 − $12 = $8, for a net gain of $4. Hence, for the result of 20 new packages plus 20 trade-ups, they would make incrementally 20 × $12 + 20 × $4 = $320 per day. When the fixed cost of $700 per day is figured in, the incremental profit becomes $320 − $700 = −$380. (Note here that we are using the incremental profit compared with doing nothing. We could also have calculated actual profit; we chose incremental because, quite frankly, the numbers are smaller.) One can get the profit results for each of the profit combinations in a similar manner (Table 2.3).

Having identified the profit implications of the various results, the next step is to estimate the relative likelihoods of the different possible results. This is typically done

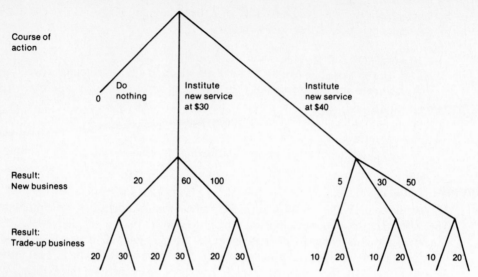

FIGURE 2.2
Package Pricing Decision Tree

TABLE 2.3 Profit Results Given Different Market Results

Course of Action; New Service Price	Result: New Business	Result: Trade-Up Business	Incremental Daily Profit[a]
None	—	—	0
$30	20	20	320 − 700 = − 380
		30	360 − 700 = − 340
	60	20	800 − 700 = 100
		30	840 − 700 = 140
	100	20	1,280 − 700 = 580
		30	1,320 − 700 = 620
40	5	10	250 − 700 = − 450
		20	390 − 700 = − 310
	30	10	800 − 700 = 100
		20	940 − 700 = 240
	50	10	1,240 − 700 = 540
		20	1,380 − 700 = 680

[a]For the $30 price, incremental profit is $12 × New business + $4 × Trade-up business − $700; whereas for $40, incremental profit is $22 × New business + $14 × Trade-up business − $700.

by assigning probabilities to each of the possible branches of the tree. These probabilities may be based on survey results, experience in analogous situations, or expert judgment. In the present situation, assume that the probabilities of the different possible levels of new business for the $30 price are 20 units, .2; 60 units, .5; and 100 units, .3. Also assume the trade-up business probabilities are 20 units, .6; and 30 units, .4. For the $40 price, the probabilities of new business are 5 units, .2; 30 units, .6; and 50 units, .2. The trade-up business probabilities are 10 units, .5; and 20 units, .5. The decision tree can then be redrawn with the appropriate probabilities and profits (Figure 2.3).

To estimate the probability of a particular profit for a given course of action, simply multiply the probabilities of the results that must occur to produce the profit result. For example, 20 new packages and 20 trade-ups produce an incremental profit of −$380. The probability of the result of 20 new and 20 trade-up packages for a $30 price is .2 × .6 = .12.

Thus, each course of action produces a distribution of possible profits with probabilities attached to them (Table 2.4). Hence, the decision about which course of action

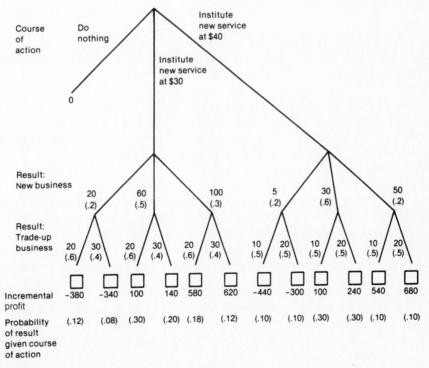

FIGURE 2.3
Package Pricing Decision Tree with Probablities and Profits

TABLE 2.4 Profit Distributions for Three Possible Courses of Action

Course of Action	Incremental Profit	Probability of Profit
Do nothing	0	1.00
Institute new service at $30	− 380	.12
	− 340	.08
	100	.30
	140	.20
	580	.18
	520	.12
Institute new service at $40	− 450	.10
	− 310	.10
	100	.30
	240	.30
	540	.10
	580	.10

to take has been converted to a decision about which distribution of results is more appealing. Several selection procedures are possible. Three of the most common are:

1. Choose the decision that guarantees the best result if everything goes wrong. This criterion (known as *minimax*) is the most conservative procedure and leads to very conservative decisions—in this case, doing nothing since both the other decisions could lose money and doing nothing would not.

2. Choose the decision that gives the chance for the best possible result. This is the gamble strategy (called *maximax*), which explains why people are willing to buy lottery tickets—they are willing to expect to lose a little money on the chance they will earn a lot. Since the $40 price offers the greatest potential gain ($680 if 50 packages and 20 trade-ups are generated), the new service would be instituted at a $40 price under this criterion.

3. Choose the course of action that provides the largest expected monetary reward. This is the criterion most often associated with decision trees (although not necessarily the best one). It requires calculating the expected monetary consequences of each of the possible courses of action by "weighting" the possible monetary results by their probabilities of occurrence. In the present example, this involves the following:

a. Do nothing and make $0 incremental profit.
b. Institute the new service at $30 and expect to make $164 per day incremental profit (Table 2.5).
c. Institute the new service at $40 and expect to make $148 per day incremental profit (Table 2.6).

Since the $164 per day net incremental profit from instituting the service at the $30 price is the maximum of the three possibilities, we would institute the new service at $30.

TABLE 2.5 Expected Incremental Profit of $30 Price

Result		(A)	(B)	
New Business	Trade-Up Business	Increment in Daily Profit: IP| R	Probability of Result: P(R)	(A) × (B)
20	20	− 380	.12	$ − 45.60
	30	− 340	.08	− 27.20
60	20	100	.30	+ 30.00
	30	140	.20	+ 28.00
100	20	580	.18	+ 104.40
	30	620	.12	+ 74.40
				$ 164.00

Problems with Using Decision Trees

Decision analysis has been around for a long time, and its pros and cons are fairly well known (MaGee, 1964; Villani and Morrison, 1976). There are a number of problems inherent in using decision trees, which are discussed in this section.

Specifying the Alternative Courses of Action and Their Consequences In many situations, the alternatives are fairly clear-cut. For example, the vending machine companies' options in pricing are pretty much limited to 5-cent increments, given the equipment already in place. Similarly, a product manager at some stage may be faced with a choice between launching a new product nationally or regionally, test marketing it, doing further tests or refinements, or dropping it. What makes things complicated is the possible responses of competition or, as is becoming more important, regulatory bodies or lobbying groups. Since these responses can affect both the results (i.e., if a rate case finds against a utility, they can't raise rates) and their profitability (beating back consumer or competitive challenges is expensive), these potential responses can greatly complicate the tree. Even in the example used in this chapter, we would expect some probability that the rate would not be approved by some relevant regulatory agency and a good likelihood that competition would react to the new service in some way. These would in turn

TABLE 2.6 Expected Incremental Profit of $40 Price

Result		(A)	(B)	
New Business	Trade-Up Business	Increment in Daily Profit: IP| R	Probability of Result: P(R)	(A) × (B)
5	10	− 450	.10	$ − 45.00
	20	− 310	.10	− 31.00
30	10	100	.30	+ 30.00
	20	240	.30	+ 72.00
50	10	540	.10	+ 54.00
	20	680	.10	+ 68.00
				$ 148.00

lead to further actions by XYZ Co. In short, a series of courses of action and results are needed to realistically represent most decisions.

Finally, it is important to recognize that for a "real" problem, no single tree is drawn. Rather, a first-cut tree is constructed to select those alternatives that seem most promising. Then, the other branches of the tree are dropped and those that are retained are refined, sometimes by collecting data, until the "best" decision emerges.

Estimating Possible Results and Their Probabilities   There are three basic sources of the possible results of a decision and their probabilities: logic/deduction, past experience/empirical evidence, and subjective estimates.

   1. *Logic/deduction.* In certain very simple situations, it is possible to deduce the probabilities of the results from the situation. For example, the probability of a head on the flip of a coin, a 7 on the roll of two dice, or a full house in a game of poker can be deduced from the situation and a few basic rules of probability and statistics (although students have a disarming tendency to do so incorrectly on tests). Unfortunately, in most marketing research situations this method is not applicable.

   2. *Past experience/empirical evidence.* Past experience is one source of estimates of the possible results and their probabilities. When Procter and Gamble introduces a new soap, it has a pretty sound idea of possible sales levels because it has introduced so many similar products in the past. Similarly, data analysis is often performed and sales levels forecast based on models using such variables as GDP, market growth rate, and so forth. The models in turn can be used to formally generate the probabilities of different results. Unfortunately, the past data and analyses rarely seem perfectly compatible with the situation under consideration. Hence the analysis of past data typically only serves as a basis for subjective estimates of the possible results and their probabilities.

   3. *Subjective estimates.* In the absence of hard data, a manager must make guesses about what the results will be. While these guesses should be based on as much analysis and experience as possible, they still involve some subjectivity. It is this subjectivity that, for many people, causes the greatest consternation over the use of decision analysis.

   The first major issue in obtaining subjective estimates of the possible results and their probabilities is to decide from whom to collect the estimates. Aside from the obvious—finding someone who is knowledgeable, honest, and willing to provide estimates—knowing exactly who to talk to is something of an art. One obvious source is salespersons who are in direct contact with buyers and hopefully (but not always actually) in tune with the market. Another source is so-called experts, both inside and outside the organization. Since the responsibility for the decision under consideration will ultimately fall on someone, however, it is appropriate to involve the person or persons (i.e., the product manager) whose evaluation depends on the decision in estimating possible results and their probabilities. (A side benefit of this is that those people who give estimates will be involved in the analysis and, therefore, more committed to the results. This benefit can, of course, turn into a cost if individuals involved give false probabilities to affect the outcome of the analysis.)

   The second major issue in assessing the possible results and their probabilities is how to obtain them. This turns out to be a very tricky task since most people don't understand probability concepts (Tversky and Kahneman, 1974). The most obvious approach is to directly ask an individual to list the possible results and their probabilities of occurring. Unfortunately, many people (and especially nonquantitatively oriented managers) don't respond well to such direct assessments of probabilities; and when they do respond, they are often inaccurate (Russo and Schoemaker, 1990; Bazerman, 1994). Hence, a variety of devices are employed to get the probabilities less directly.

The most commonly used gambit to elicit probabilities involves asking an individual to indicate various levels that sales will exceed with a certain likelihood. For example, the individual might be asked to indicate:

1. What level will sales exceed 90 percent of the time? (e.g., 5,000 units)
2. What level will sales exceed 50 percent of the time? (e.g., 10,000 units)
3. What level will sales exceed only 10 percent of the time? (e.g., 20,000 units)

By using the answers to these questions, a researcher can develop an entire distribution of possible results (Figure 2.4).

Alternatively, a researcher may ask a key individual to first list some possible results. Then, the researcher can ask the individual to indicate the relative likelihood of occurrence (from which probabilities of the results can be deduced). Detailed discussion of methods for eliciting results and their probabilities is beyond the scope of this book. For further reading, see Hogarth, 1975; Jones, 1977; Sarin, 1978; Savage, 1971; Winkler, 1967a,b.

Considerable opposition exists to using subjective probabilities. This comes from two basic schools of thought. The first position of opposition is that anything based on subjective probabilities is essentially worthless. Assuming the person making the estimates has experience, the subjective estimates will in fact be based on data (experience in analogous situations, etc.). The difference between subjective and data-based estimates (which should be and typically are subjectively adjusted) is thus not as great as it first appears. The other major opposition to using subjective probabilities is that since they are not perfectly accurate or easy to obtain, they are not worthwhile. Development of the probabilities of results is a nontrivial task. It is, however, doable.

FIGURE 2.4
Derived Distribution of Possible Sales Levels

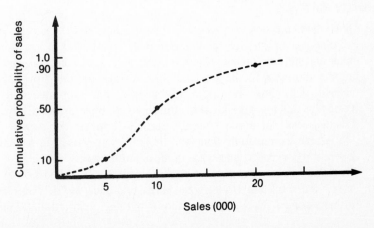

Assessing the Monetary Consequences of Different Results While this is possibly the easiest of the problems to deal with, it is by no means trivial. For example, estimating future costs of production given changes in energy costs, raw material prices, and so forth, is very difficult. Hence, the monetary consequences are really estimates; their effect on the decisions should usually be checked at least by sensitivity analysis if not by incorporating multiple monetary results and attendant probabilities into the decision tree.

Choosing an Appropriate Criterion The most obvious criterion to apply is expected monetary value. This, though, is a good criterion to use only in the case of repetitive decisions that are independent of each other and when the outcomes are not so large as to greatly affect the organization. The independence notion is rarely true, since the condition of the general economy alone dictates that either most things go well or many go sour together. Also, in many cases the decision will have a sufficiently large impact that it will affect the organization, or at least the part with which the decision maker is associated. For example, certain possible results may seriously damage the financial position of the company, and decisions leading to these will typically be avoided in going concerns.

Another barrier to the expected value criterion is individual behavior. Since turning a profitable product into an unprofitable one may lead to being fired, whereas doubling profits may only lead to a 10 percent raise, the personal consequences of the results may be asymmetric and, hence, the expected value criterion inappropriate. In short, individuals may be understandably more cautious (risk averse) than is implied by the expected value criterion.

It is possible to develop a formula that translates the different monetary results into utilities and then to compute expected utilities. A more pragmatic approach, however, is to calculate the expected value and the range of possible results and then check to see if any of the likely results of the indicated decision are sufficiently bad to cause reconsideration and possibly a change to a less risky decision. It is also sometimes appropriate to check other decisions that result in lower expected values to see if there is a possible result under these decisions that is so desirable it is worth going against averages.

Sensitivity Analysis

Given that any decision tree is typically at best a facsimile of the world, it is useful to examine the sensitivity of a decision to small changes in the tree. For example, would changing the new business demand estimates in Figure 2.3 change the decision? If changing the estimates in the tree does not change the decision, then the decision is relatively insensitive to those estimates, giving one more confidence that the decision is optimal. If, on the other hand, the decision changes as a result of small changes in the tree, then it is less easy to argue strongly that the optimal decision is known.

Whenever sensitivity analysis reveals something on which a decision does seem to depend, it suggests that this type of information is relatively crucial and is possibly worth further investigation. Put more simply, if a decision is portrayed as a tree, then those pieces of information that seem to affect the decision are the ones that should be further studied. While this sounds obvious, many dollars have been spent fine-tuning advertising copy when the major uncertainty was the possible entrance of a new competitor or a ban by the FDA. Hence, one should generally study those elements of a decision that (*a*) matter (no sense studying irrelevant material, as any student knows), (*b*) are uncertain (no sense studying something that is already known), and (*c*) can be learned about (if you can't reasonably expect to reduce uncertainty, it is not very intelligent to spend much money trying to do so).

Summary

Having spent considerable time pointing out the weaknesses of decision trees, it is important to indicate that they still are useful devices. Their major advantage is that they provide structure in what appear to be largely unstructured situations. It seems far more constructive to have people debating the likely results in sales of a decision, rather than arguing whether they like the decision or not. (Such discussions are also more likely to be based on facts than on political clout or debating skills.) There is also some evidence that suggests that breaking a decision into small parts leads to better decisions. Decision trees also provide an indication of what key uncertainties exist. If the expected value criterion is used, it provides a very useful starting point for deciding what to do. In short, given an uncertain world, decision trees are a useful device for structuring a problem and getting an indication (relatively quickly and inexpensively) of what is the best decision to make. Since managers are ultimately judged more by results than by method, however, it is the managers' prerogative to make choices any way they choose.

VALUE OF INFORMATION: QUANTITATIVE ASSESSMENT

Before investing time and money in collecting information about a decision, most people make a judgment (at least implicitly) on whether the information will be worth the trouble. Consider, for example, an individual choosing a new dishwasher. That person may already have a choice in mind (e.g., I have a GE now that I bought from store A and it worked well, so I will buy a GE there next time). In deciding whether to gather more information (e.g., read *Consumer Reports*, comparison shop), several major considerations exist:

1. Under what kind of time pressure is the individual? (Is the present dishwasher flooding the kitchen or just getting old? How much "free" time does the individual have?)
2. How easy is it to collect more information? (Does the individual subscribe to *Consumer Reports*, live in an area where shopping is easy, etc.?)
3. What is the cost of a bad decision? (What is the cost of buying another new machine, cost of a service contract, etc.?)
4. How different are the available alternatives? (Does which brand is bought make much difference in either length of life or quality of service?)
5. How likely is it that more information will change the decision? (If the individual is fairly certain that he or she will buy a GE at store A, then more information is probably irrelevant.)

Of these considerations, 1 and 2 are related to the cost of information, 3 and 4 to the relative results of the alternative decisions, and 5 to the relative odds of making a good decision with and without more information. If a sample of people were asked whether they would collect information in a set of situations/scenarios, we would expect more of them to collect information when (*a*) the cost of information was low, (*b*) there was a noticeable difference among alternatives, and (*c*) they felt a relatively high degree of uncertainty about which decision alternative to select.

While the preceding seems sensible, it does not directly produce a quantitative assessment of the value of additional information. To get a quantitative assessment, one procedure uses decision trees. The procedure has three basic steps:

1. Build a decision tree for the situation assuming current information. Then calculate the optimal decision and its expected value (EV|CI).
2. Build a decision tree for the situation assuming that additional information were available. Then calculate the optimal decision given the additional information and its expected value (EV|AI).
3. Estimate the expected value of additional information (EVAI) as EVAI = EV|AI − EV|CI. Hence, the value of information is the expected improvement in profit that would result if the information were obtained.

Example

A more complete discussion of the methodology appears in the appendix to this chapter. However, for illustrative purposes a simpler example will be used here. Assume a product manager is trying to decide whether to continue selling the old formulation of a product and end up with essentially certain profits of $50 or switch to a new one, which will end up with profits of either $10 or $80 (e.g., the decision on New Coke). It seems equally likely it will produce $10 or $80 given current information. Hence, we get the picture in Figure 2.5. The expected values of the two decisions are as follows:

$$\text{Continue selling old formulation:} \quad \$50(1.0) = \$50$$

$$\text{Sell the new formula:} \quad \$10(.5) + \$80(.5) = \$45$$

Therefore, given current information, we would keep the old formulation and EV|CI = $50.

Now assume we could get a research report on market acceptance of the new formulation, which would be either unfavorable (in which case the probability that the prof-

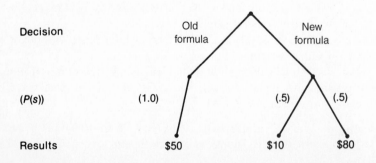

| Decision | | |
| Old formula | | New formula |

FIGURE 2.5
Decision Tree with Current Information

(P(s))   (1.0)   (.5)   (.5)

Results $50 $10 $80

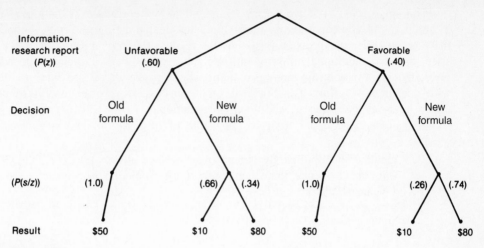

FIGURE 2.6
Decision Tree with Additional Information

it would be $10 increases to .66) or favorable (in which case the probability that the profit would be $10 decreases to .26). Also assume that we expect the probability of an unfavorable report to be .60. We can represent the choices given this additional information by Figure 2.6.

The results of the two decisions under the two possible research reports are determined as follows:

Unfavorable report:

Old formula: $50(1.0) = $50

New formula: $10(.66) + $80(.34) = $33.80

Favorable report:

Old formula: $50(1.0) = $50

New formula: $10(.26) + $80(.74) = $61.80

Hence, given an unfavorable report, we would, not surprisingly, keep the old formula and make $50; while given a favorable report we would use the new formula and expect to make $61.80. Since 60 percent of the time we expect an unfavorable report, the expected value given additional information is

$$EV|AI = $50(.60) + $61.80(.40)$$
$$= $54.72$$

Thus, the expected value of the additional information (in this case, the research report) is

$$EVAI = EV|AI - EV|CI$$
$$= $54.72 - $50.00$$
$$= $4.72$$

This approach is relatively easy to extend to more complex situations. The problem in applying the approach comes in obtaining reasonable estimates for the monetary results that are possible, the probabilities of these results, the probabilities of the various possible results of additional information, and the probabilities of each of the actual results given the information. In many situations, these probabilities are hard to deduce even with considerable effort. For this and other reasons, it is often useful to calculate an upper limit on the value of additional information.

To calculate the upper limit on the value of information, two steps are employed:

1. Calculate the optimal decisions given perfect information (i.e., the decision you would make if you knew what the result would be in advance) and its expected value (EV|PI).
2. Calculate the expected value of perfect information (EVPI) as EVPI = EV|PI − EV|CI.

Returning to the example in Figure 2.5, we see that, if profits for the new formula would be $10, we would want to stick with the old formula (and make $50); whereas if profits for the new formula would be $80, then we would want to use the new formula. Since half the time the profit from the new formula will be $10 and half the time $80,

$$EV|PI = \$50(.5) + \$80(.5)$$
$$= \$65$$

Hence,

$$EVPI = EV|PI - EV|CI$$
$$= \$65 - \$50$$
$$= \$15$$

The most we would be willing to pay for information would be $15. If someone offered to sell us research for $20, we would politely decline the offer no matter how good the person's forecasting record was.

Problems in Assessing the Value of Information

The methodology just described for quantitatively assessing the value of information, once learned, is relatively simple to apply. Its conceptual use is widespread. Yet its application in a formal sense is limited. There are several reasons for this limited use. They are as follows:

Difficulty in Application It is possible to argue that the technique is not used because it is perceived to be hard to apply. This argument is, however, both largely incorrect and self-serving. The cost of using such procedures is fairly low; and their level of use is even lower, indicating other explanations are needed.

The Expected Value Criterion Does Not Apply This limitation is an important one. For a small firm, operating on an expected value basis ignores the very real problem of bankruptcy. Similarly, the job security of an individual may require avoidance of bad results more than attainment of spectacular ones.

Prima Facie Decisions Many apparent decisions may in fact be preordained. This can be because the situation dictates the decision (i.e., if I'm a small firm producing a commodity, I may have to match price cuts). Alternatively, it may be that political realities dictate a decision. (We may all know that the idea is dumb; but if it is the boss's pet idea, we may prefer to have the market test tell the boss so.)

Company Policy In many cases, it is company policy to proceed in a certain manner. For example, it may be policy to test commercials on samples of 100 in Albany, New York. Therefore, the value of information is not the issue—the only feasible course of action is to proceed. (It is, of course, possible to argue that the company policy is in need of revision. While this may make you a star, it is more likely to make you unpopular, unemployed, or both.)

SUMMARY

As discussed earlier, the value of information is related to several factors:

> *The accuracy of information.* Obviously the more accurate the information, the greater its value.
>
> *The cost (both dollar and time) of information.* Data already on hand or contracted for are relatively costless, whereas collecting new data is both costly and time consuming.
>
> *The ability and willingness to accept information and act accordingly.* The more receptive management is to information, the greater the value of the information.
>
> *The lack of clarity over what the right answer is.* The more obvious the decision, the less the need for information.
>
> *The extreme results and their consequences.* The more serious the extreme results are, the greater the need for information.
>
> *The degree of risk aversion on both a company and a personal level.* The greater the risk aversion, the greater the information need. On a personal level, getting the right information may protect one to some extent in case the decision is bad. (At least we can blame luck or some other factor rather than lack of diligence.)
>
> *Competitive reaction to information gathering in terms of "jamming" the information and being given more time to plan a counterattack.* Competitors will often do their best to destroy the information value of data collection, especially test markets where tripling advertising, cutting price, and offering large trade deals to fill the channels of distribution are only a few of the common gambits. The motivation for this is to feed you bad information and make it harder for you to make the right decision. Also, the more time you

spend gathering data, the more obvious it becomes to competitors what you are planning to do and the more time they have to react to it.

Company policy. Company policy often dictates the "need" for information collection.

The need to gain agreement. Information collection is perhaps most important in that it facilitates the establishment of reasonable agreement among the many parties to a decision about the advisability of the decision and the way to proceed.

The need to stall or build momentum. Often, a decision is sufficiently controversial that people look for a way to postpone it. Opponents of a position who feel open opposition is unwise can and do line up in favor of gathering more data, a much less risky position. By the same logic, supporters of a proposal who believe they do not have sufficient support to push the proposal through at the present may suggest getting data (a "pilot" study) to determine feasibility as a means of getting a toe in the door.

Managers use information for a variety of reasons: to make decisions, for political ammunition, and to make themselves more comfortable with a course of action. All of these make information valuable. For example, being comfortable with a decision lends to pursuing it with great vigor, which in and of itself improves the odds of success. Focusing on information as a decision-making tool/aid, it is important to recognize that managers, like other humans, show evidence of a number of biases in judgment. Often referred to as context effects, or more generally behavioral decision theory, response to information is influenced by its presentation/context (cf. Bazerman, 1994; Russo and Schoemaker, 1990). For example, in addition to being overconfident in forecasts as mentioned in the introduction, managers tend to

1. "Anchor." In other words, once they have an opinion, they tend to hold on to it. One way they do this is to look for "confirming" information, that is, information that is consistent with their opinion.

2. Rely on "available" information. That is, they pay attention to information that is easily recalled. This is a variant on the "a picture is worth a thousand words" cliché, which suggests that vivid information is weighted more (too) heavily. Hence, a single comment in a focus group or a single experience with a product or customer may have a disproportionate effect on opinions/decisions.

3. Ignore "base rate." In many circumstances, the general population produces information that makes an event extremely likely (or unlikely), as well as some specific data that suggest a different outcome. People often rely too much on the specific/"case" information in forming a judgment. Consider, for example, a father evaluating the possibility that his son will be a professional football lineman, of whom there are perhaps 350. The base information (350 out of thousands who play high school football) suggests the odds are low/essentially nil. On the other hand, the son is 6 feet 3 inches tall, 250 pounds, runs a 5.0 second 40-yard dash, and was all-county. The father is convinced the son will be an all-pro. While the son's statistics are indeed encouraging and similar to those of many pro linemen, they are similar to those of many more couch potatoes. The father has ignored

the base rate, partly because he wants to believe the case information. Similarly, the conviction that a new product concept is a winner based on initial results often ignores the fact that even among new products that are introduced, most fail.

4. Misuse of information/feedback. In one study, the presence of accurate information actually decreased the performance of managers in a simulated market (Glazer, Steckel, and Winer, 1992).

The point here is not to discuss "behavioral decision making" in detail—indeed, there are many articles and books on the subject (cf. Bazerman, 1994). Rather, the point is simply to indicate that information may be used in nonoptimal ways by human beings, hence altering its value as well as its impact. Moreover, experienced managers may use different information from that used by inexperienced managers in new product promotion decisions. Perkins and Rao (1990) found experienced managers relied on more information in general and more "soft" information in particular. Hence, the same biases are unlikely to be evidenced by all decision makers or in all situations. In the extreme, data may be as much like an inkblot test ("What do you see in it?") as a "fact" to be analyzed clinically and statistically.

The formal determination of the value of information can be a fairly tricky task. Nonetheless, the concept of comparing the value of information with its cost is a useful step. In doing so, it is essential to define both benefits and costs broadly enough to take into account the positions and proclivities of the various parties to the decision. Based on the assumption that at least occasionally one will find information of positive value (a hoped-for result if those individuals in market research positions are to continue to eat), the rest of this book is devoted to alternative means of collecting, analyzing, and utilizing information.

PROBLEMS

1. Assume you were considering changing the formulation of a food product by substituting one ingredient for an existing one.
   a. List the concerns you would have.
   b. Draw a decision tree to represent the problem.

2. What do you think would be the value of additional information in each of the following situations:
   a. A decision by P&G about whether to market Tide next year.
   b. A decision about which style dial to put on GE dishwashers this year.
   c. A decision whether or not to drill an oil well.
   d. A decision to launch a new packaged goods product.
   e. A decision to change the format of a ballet company's performances.

3. Bernie C. owns an ice truck. He sells ice cream on his lunch hour. When the weather is good, hot, and humid, he can net about $120 per day at the beach or about $60 per day if he sells ice cream around his home. When the weather is poor, cold, and rainy, his net at the beach is about $15 per day, and at home about $25 per day.

In this area, there is a 20 percent chance of fair weather (and therefore an 80 percent chance of poor weather).

a. What should Bernie do?

b. How much should Bernie pay for a perfect forecast?

c. How much should Bernie pay for an 80 percent reliable weather forecasting service? (i.e., the probability of forecast matching weather is .8).

4. Draw a decision tree that would help the phone company assess the effect of raising the price of pay-phone calls 10 cents.

5. In considering three different positioning strategies for Slurp, a new soft drink, I assume one of three possible market conditions can occur. These will influence the profits as follows:

Market Condition			
I	II	III	Position
12	14	18	Conservative
16	12	12	Moderate
4	8	30	Flaky

My subjective estimates of the probabilities of the three market conditions are .5, .3, and .2, respectively.

a. With no other information, what should I do?

b. What is the most I would pay for information about which market condition will occur?

c. A firm proposes to test what market condition will exist. It traditionally is right 80 percent of the time. When it is wrong, it is equally likely that anything else can happen. How much is this firm's research worth to me?

6. Assume demand for a machine I rent/lease is as follows:

Demand (units)	Probability
200	.05
220	.05
240	.10
260	.15
280	.20
300	.25
320	.15
340	.05

The item costs me $80, and I can rent it for $120.

a. How many should I stock?

b. What is EVPI?

c. If you were legally committed to stock 300, what would EVPI be?

7. Assume that I had a brilliant concept for a new product. It is company policy to test products sequentially. I estimate the probabilities of this idea passing each screen, given that it passes the previous screens, are as follows:

Stage	P (pass)	Cost
Initial screen	.5	1,000
Concept test	.8	10,000
Product test	.5	30,000
Economic analysis	.4	10,000
Test market	.5	400,000

If I pass the test-market stage, I will roll out nationally (fixed cost = $4 million) with three possible results: failure (gross margin of $1 million), so-so (gross margin $5 million), and success (gross margin of $14 million). The probabilities of these three results are .4, .4, and .2, respectively.

a. What is my expected profit if I begin the process and proceed until screened out?

b. What is the expected value of perfect information?

c. Assuming you had passed the concept test, what is the expected profit in proceeding?

8. I am considering changing my package design for Munch, my best-selling dog food. I suspect one of three market conditions will exist. The expected profits associated with each of the possible results are as follows:

	Market Condition		
Packaging	A	B	C
Old	10	10	4
New	12	7	5

The probabilities of occurrence of the three market conditions are .5 for A, .3 for B, and .2 for C.

a. With no other information, what should I do?

b. What is the most I would pay for information about the future market condition?

c. My market research department has proposed a test to determine which market condition will hold. Its characteristics can be described as follows:

Market Condition	Probability of Test Result Given Market Condition		
	X	Y	Z
A	.8	.1	.1
B	.2	.7	.1
C	.2	.1	.7

What is the value of this test?

REFERENCES

ARMSTRONG, J. SCOTT (1991) "Prediction of Consumer Behavior by Experts and Novices," *Journal of Consumer Research*, 18, September, 251–56.

ASSMUS, GERT (1977) "Bayesian Analysis for the Evaluation of Marketing Research Expenditures: A Reassessment," *Journal of Marketing Research*, 14, November, 562–68.

BAZERMAN, MAX H. (1994) *Judgment in Manager and Decision Making*, 3rd ed., New York: John Wiley and Sons.

BLOOM, PAUL N., GEORGE R. MILNE, AND ROBERT ADLER (1994) "Avoiding Misuse of New Information Technologies: Legal and Societal Considerations," *Journal of Marketing*, 58, January, 96–110.

DAY, GEORGE (1991) "Learning about Markets," MSI Report 91-117.

DESHPANDÉ, ROHIT, AND GERALD ZALTMAN (1982) "Factors Affecting the Use of Market Research Information: A Path Analysis," *Journal of Marketing Research*, 19, February, 14–24.

—— (1987) "A Comparison of Factors Affecting Use of Marketing Information in Consumer and Industrial Firms," *Journal of Marketing Research*, 24, February, 114–17.

GLAZER, RASHI (1991) "Marketing in an Information Intensive Environment: Strategic Implications of Knowledge as an Asset," *Journal of Marketing*, 55, October, 1–19.

GLAZER, RASHI, JOEL E. STECKEL, AND RUSSELL S. WINER (1992) "Locally Rational Decision Making: The Distracting Relationship Between Information and Managerial Performance," *Management Science*, 38, February, 212–26.

GOLDSTEIN, DAVID K. (1993) "Product Managers' Use of Scanner Data: A Story of Organizational Learning," MSI Report 93–109. Cambridge, Mass.

GUPTA, SACHIN, PRADEEP CHINTAGUNTA, ANIL KAUL, AND DICK R. WITTINK (1996) "Do Household Scanner Panels Provide Representative Inferences from Brand Choices: A Comparison with Store Data," *Journal of Marketing Research*, 33, November, 383–98.

HOCK, STEPHEN J. (1988) "Who Do We Know: Predicting the Interests and Opinions of the American Consumer," *Journal of Consumer Research*, 15, December, 315–24.

HOGARTH, ROBIN M. (1975) "Cognitive Processes and the Assessment of Subjective Probability Distributions," *Journal of the American Statistical Association*, 70, June, 271–89.

JONES, J. MORGAN (1977) *Introduction to Decision Theory*, Homewood, Ill.: Richard D. Irwin.

LEE, HANJOON, FRANK ACITO, AND RALPH L. DAY (1987) "Evaluation and Use of Marketing Research by Decision Makers: A Behavioral Simulation," *Journal of Marketing Research*, 24, May, 187–96.

MAGEE, JOHN F. (1964) "Decision Trees for Decision Making," *Harvard Business Review*, 42, July–August, 126–38.

MAHAJAN, JAYASHREE (1992) "The Overconfidence Effect in Marketing Management Predictions," *Journal of Marketing Research*, 29, August, 329–42.

MALTZ, ELLIOT, AND AJAY KOHLI (1995) "Market Intelligence Dissemination Across Functional Boundaries," Cambridge, Mass.: MSI Report 95–115.

MENON, ANIL, AND P. RAJAN VARADARAJAN (1992) "A Model of Marketing Knowledge Use Within Firms," *Journal of Marketing*, 56, October, 53–71.

MENON, ANIL, AND JAMES B. WILCOX (1994) "USER: A Scale to Measure Use of Market Research," Cambridge, Mass.: MSI Report 94–108.

MOORMAN, CHRISTINE, ROHIT DESHPANDÉ, AND GERALD ZALTMAN (1993a) "Factors Affecting Trust in Market Research Relationships," *Journal of Marketing*, 57, January, 81–101.

—— (1993b) "Relationships Between Providers and Users of Market Research: The Role of Personal Trust," Cambridge, Mass.: MSI Report 93-111.

MOORMAN, CHRISTINE, AND ANNE MINER (1995) "Walking the Tightrope: Improvisation in New Product Development and Introduction," Cambridge, Mass.: MSI Report 95–101.

MOORMAN, CHRISTINE, GERALD ZALTMAN, AND ROHIT DESHPANDÉ (1992) "Relationships Between Providers and Users of Market Research: The Dynamics of Trust Within and Between Organizations," *Journal of Marketing Research*, 29, August, 314–28.

PERKINS, W. STEVEN, AND RAM C. RAO (1990) "The Role of Experience in Information Use and Decision Making by Marketing Managers," *Journal of Marketing Research*, 27, February, 1–10.

RAIFFA, HOWARD (1968) *Decision Analysis: Introductory Lectures on Choices under Uncertainty*. Reading, Mass.: Addison-Wesley.

RUSSO, J. EDWARD, AND PAUL J. H. SCHOEMAKER (1990) *Decision Traps*, New York: Fireside.

SARIN, RAKESH KUMAR (1978) "Elicitation of Subjective Probabilities in the Context of Decision Making," *Decision Sciences*, 9, January, 37–48.

SAVAGE, L. J. (1971) "Elicitation of Personal Probabilities and Expectations," *Journal of the American Statistical Association*, 66, December, 783–801.

SCHLAIFFER, ROBERT (1959) *Probability and Statistics for Business Decisions*, New York: McGraw-Hill.

TVERSKY, AMOS, AND DANIEL KAHNEMAN (1974) "Judgment under Uncertainty: Heuristics and Biases," *Science*, 185, September, 1124–31.

VILLANI, KATHRYN E. A., AND DONALD G. MORRISON (1976) "A Method for Analyzing New Formulation Decisions," *Journal of Marketing Research*, 13, August, 284–88.

WEINBERG, BRUCE (1989) "Building an Information Strategy for Scanner Data," MSI Conference Summary 89-121. Cambridge, Mass.

WINKLER, R. L. (1967a) "The Quantification of Judgment: Some Methodological Suggestions," *Journal of the American Statistical Association*, 62, December, 1105–20.

—— (1967b) "The Assessment of Prior Distributions in Bayesian Analysis," *Journal of the American Statistical Association*, 62, September, 776–800.

ZALTMAN, GERALD (1989) "The Use of Developmental and Evaluative Research," MSI Paper 89-107. Cambridge, Mass.

APPENDIX 2-A

AN EXAMPLE OF EXPECTED INFORMATION VALUE CALCULATIONS

Assume a supplier of parts to automotive manufacturers just developed a new van accessory. Tooling and other fixed costs would be $3 million. Sales would be through an established distribution channel, and the price to the distributors would be $110. The variable costs per unit are $70. Analysis indicates four possible levels of sales:

Sales (s)	Probability of Market Result: P(s)
5,000	.4
50,000	.2
100,000	.2
200,000	.2

TABLE 2A.1 Probability of Test Result Given Actual Sales

$P(z|s)$

Sales (s)	Test Result (z) Winner	Test Result (z) Also-Ran	Test Result (z) Loser
5,000	.2	.2	.6
50,000	.3	.6	.1
100,000	.6	.2	.2
200,000	.7	.2	.1

QUESTIONS

1. With no other information, should the company market the accessory?
2. What is the most the company should pay for information about likely sales?
3. A firm specializing in projecting sales for products based on a scale that characterizes products as winners, also-rans, or losers offers to do research for the company. Based on their claims and discussions with former clients, their accuracy is estimated to be expressed as in Table 2A.1. How much is this survey worth?

DECISION WITH NO FURTHER INFORMATION

The decision of what to do with no further information can be addressed by means of the decision tree approach of the previous section. First, convert sales to profit figures:

$$\text{Profit} = \text{Sales}(110 - 70) - 3,000,$$

Hence, we have the following:

Sales(s)	Monetary Profit Given Sales: M(s)	Probability of Result: P(s)
5,000	− 2,800,000	.4
50,000	− 1,000,000	.2
100,000	+ 1,000,000	.2
200,000	+ 5,000,000	.2

Next, compute an expected value given current information (EVCI) by multiplying the profit given result times the probability of that result for each of the four results and summing the results:

$$\text{EV}|\text{CI} = \sum_{\text{all results}} (\text{profit result}) \cdot P(\text{result})$$

$$= \sum M(s)P(s)$$

$$= (-2,800,000)(.4) + (-1,000,000)(.2)$$

$$+ (1,000,000)(.2) + (5,000,000)(.2)$$

$$= -1,120,000 - 200,000 + 200,000 + 1,000,000$$

$$= -120,000$$

Since −120,000 is less than zero (which I could achieve by not marketing the accessory), my decision on an expected value basis would be not to go ahead at the present time. Still, the possibility of making $5 million is sufficiently intriguing that I may not want to completely drop the idea.

EXPECTED VALUE OF PERFECT INFORMATION (EVPI)

The key to deciding whether to drop the concept or not is to find out *in advance* what market result I am facing. Obviously, it is impossible for nonmystics or those who are not friends of the Delphic Oracle to know the results in the future. Still, it is a useful step to calculate the value of such perfect information.

The concept of getting perfect information is that one would know what sales were going to be in advance but could not alter them. (In other words, you would be omniscient but not omnipotent.) Therefore, a decision maker would proceed whenever the profit were positive and not proceed (and hence have a zero rather than a negative profit) whenever the profit would be negative. This is equivalent in poker to knowing what cards the opponents hold: You drop if they will beat you and stay if you will beat them (assuming no successful bluffing can be done). The expected profit given perfect information (EV|PI) would then be

$$\text{EV}|\text{PI} = \sum_{\substack{\text{all results} \\ \text{where profit} \\ \text{is negative}}} P(s)(0) + \sum_{\substack{\text{all results} \\ \text{where profit} \\ \text{is positive}}} P(s)M(s)$$

In this case, that becomes

$$\text{EV}|\text{PI} = (.4)(0) + (.2)(0) + (.2)(1{,}000{,}000) + (.2)(5{,}000{,}000)$$
$$= 1{,}200{,}000$$

The expected value of perfect information then is the *net* difference between the expected profit given perfect information and the expected profit under the optimal decision given current information:

$$\text{EVPI} = \text{EV}|\text{PI} - \text{EV}|\text{CI}$$

In the present case, this becomes

$$\text{EVPI} = 1{,}200{,}000 - 0$$
$$= 1{,}200{,}000$$

(Notice that we subtract 0, rather than a −120,000, since, under current information, the optimal policy is not to proceed.)

Thus, EVPI is an upper bound on the amount we would be willing to pay for additional information. If a firm offers to do a $2 million study for us, we can reject it out of hand since in expected value terms even perfect information is only worth $1.2 million. We also would be very leery of proposals close in cost to the EVPI, since most information is far from perfect.

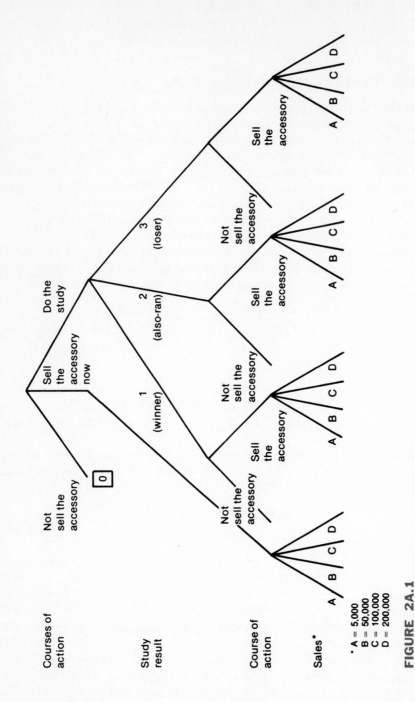

FIGURE 2A.1
Decision Tree Including Additional Information

Courses of action

Study result

Course of action

Sales*

* A = 5,000
  B = 50,000
  C = 100,000
  D = 200,000

Not sell the accessory

Sell the accessory now

Do the study

0

1 (winner)

2 (also-ran)

3 (loser)

Sell the accessory

Not sell the accessory

Sell the accessory

Not sell the accessory

Sell the accessory

A B C D

EXPECTED VALUE OF ADDITIONAL INFORMATION (EVAI)

The concept of the expected value of additional information is, like EVPI, a net value concept. EVAI is the difference between the expected profit given the additional information and the expected profit given current information. Calculating EVAI requires estimating the expected value given additional information, which in turn requires quantifying how accurate the information is likely to be.

To see this problem more clearly, it is useful to construct a decision tree to represent the situation (Figure 2A.1). To make a decision, we must attach monetary values to each of the results and probabilities to each of the branches of the trees. We see that we should either do the study or not sell the accessory. Unfortunately, to analyze the results of doing the study, we need two sets of probabilities: the probabilities of the study results ($P(z)$) and the probabilities of sales given the study results ($P(s|z)$). There are two basic approaches to getting these:

Directly estimate them. It may in some cases be possible to directly estimate $P(z)$ and $P(s|z)$ based on experience. This is the exception rather than the rule, however.

Indirectly estimate them. In many cases, it is not very easy to estimate the $P(s_i|z_j)$ and especially the $P(z_j)$ (as in the given example). However, $P(z_j|s_i)$ values may be more easily estimated. The method for transposing the $P(z_j|s_i)$ values into $P(z_j)$ and $P(s_i|z_j)$ values is based on something called *Bayes theorem.*

Bayes theorem is the result of the penchant of an English vicar for playing with probability theory. Its use has become synonymous to many with incorporating subjective probabilities in analysis (as well as so many four-letter words on the part of students that the good vicar would wonder what he had wrought). Nonetheless, the concept is simple enough that it can be applied fairly easily (if somewhat cumbersomely).

The basic notion is that the probability of a sales level given a test result is the probability of a sales level *and* the test result divided by the probability of the test result:

$$P\left(s_i|z_j\right) = \frac{P\left(z_j \cap s_i\right)}{P\left(z_j\right)} = \frac{P(\text{sales level and test results})}{P(\text{test result})}$$

By clever manipulation, this converts to

$$P\left(s_i|z_j\right) = \frac{P\left(s_i\right)P\left(z_j|s_i\right)}{P\left(z_j\right)}$$

The secret then is to calculate $P(z)$, since the $P(z|s)$'s are already known. The procedure followed has three basic steps. First, we construct a table as follows: Since we know that $P(z_j \cap s_i) = P(s_i)(P(z_j|s_i))$, we can use the information originally given to calculate a table of the joint probability of a particular test result and a particular market result. Returning to the numerical example, $P(\text{test result 1 and sales of 5,000})$ is calculated as $P(\text{sales of 5,000}) \times P(\text{test result 1}|\text{sales of 5,000}) = (.4)(.2) = .08$. Similarly, we compute all the numbers in the table down through $P(\text{sales of 200,000 and test result 3}) = (.2)(.1) = .02$. We now have Table 2A.2, which represents all possible combinations of test results and sales levels.

TABLE 2A.2 Joint Probability of Test Result and Sales Level: $P(z_j|s_i)$

Sales (s)	Test Result (z)		
	Winner	Also-Ran	Loser
5,000	.08	.08	.24
50,000	.06	.12	.02
100,000	.12	.04	.04
200,000	.14	.04	.02

The next step is to calculate the probability of the different test results—$P(z)$. Since a test-market result must occur in conjunction with one of the four sales levels, we can get $P(z)$ by simply summing numbers down the column of the previous table:

$$P(z_j) = \sum_{\text{all } i} P(z_j \cap s_i)$$

Hence, we get Table 2A.3.

The final step is to calculate the probabilities of the market given the test results. This is done by using

$$P(s_i|z_i) = \frac{P(s_i \cap z_j)}{P(z_j)}$$

For example, the probability of a sales level of 5,000, given test result 1, is

$$\frac{P(\text{sales of 5,000 and test result 1})}{P(\text{test result 1})} = \frac{.08}{.40} = .20$$

Similarly, I can calculate all elements $P(s_i|z_j)$ by dividing each element in the $P(z_j \cap s_i)$ table by its column sum (Table 2A.4). We can now attach all the necessary probabilities to the decision tree as in Figure 2A.2.

TABLE 2A.3 $P(z_j)$

Sales (s)	Test Result (z)		
	Winner	Also-Ran	Loser
5,000	.08	.08	.24
50,000	.06	.12	.02
100,000	.12	.04	.04
200,000	.14	.04	.02
$P(z_j)$	.40	.28	.32

TABLE 2A.4 $P(s_i|z_j)$

Sales (s)	Test Result (z)		
	Winner	Also-Ran	Loser
5,000	.20	.29	.75
50,000	.15	.43	.06
100,000	.30	.14	.13
200,000	.35	.14	.06
	1.00	1.00	1.00

The next step is to calculate the expected values of the decisions given the test results, so that we can determine the optimal decision based on the test information.

Test result: Winner

Expected profit given do not sell the accessory = 0

$$\text{Expected profit given sell} = .20(-2,800,000) + .15(-1,000,000)$$
$$+ .30(+1,000,000) + .35(+5,000,000)$$
$$= -560,000 - 150,000$$
$$+ 300,000 + 1,750,000$$
$$= +1,340,000$$

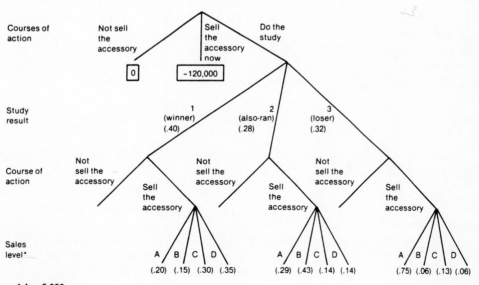

* A = 5,000
  B = 50,000
  C = 100,000
  D = 200,000

FIGURE 2A.2
Decision Tree with Computed Probabilities

Hence, given that the test result indicated a winner, we would go ahead.

Test result: Also-ran

Expected profit given do not sell the accessory = 0

$$
\begin{aligned}
\text{Expected profit given sell} &= .29(-2,800,000) + .43(-1,000,000) \\
&\quad + .14(1,000,000) + .14(5,000,000) \\
&= -812,000 - 430,000 \\
&\quad + 140,000 + 700,000 \\
&= -402,000
\end{aligned}
$$

Given this test result, we will not market the accessory.

Test result: Loser

Expected profit given do not sell the accessory = 0

$$
\begin{aligned}
\text{Expected profit given sell} &= .75(-2,800,000) + .06(-1,000,000) \\
&\quad + .13(1,000,000) + .06(5,000,000) \\
&= -2,100,000 - 60,000 \\
&\quad + 130,000 + 300,000 \\
&= -1,730,000
\end{aligned}
$$

Here, we also do not market the accessory. (Actually since result 2 indicated not to market and result 3 suggests a lower chance of success than 2, we could have saved ourselves the calculation time.)

We are now (finally) ready to calculate the expected value given additional information. Returning to the tree, we have Figure 2A.3. The expected value given additional information is the weighted sum of the expected profit of the *optimal* decision given each of the test results:

$$
\text{EV}|\text{AI} = .40(1,340,000) + .28(0) + .32(0) = \$536,000
$$

We now calculate the value of additional information as the net increase in expected profit given the information:

$$
\begin{aligned}
\text{EVAI} &= \text{EV}|\text{AI} - \text{EV}|\text{CI} \\
&= \$536,000
\end{aligned}
$$

This result means that, if the cost of this particular study is less than \$536,000, we should go ahead with the study. If the study's costs are greater, however, we should not do the study. While this process may seem tedious, it is actually quite straightforward (Figure 2A.4). It is also possible to convert these steps to a series of matrix operations. (See D. H. Mann, 1972, "A Matrix Technique for Finite Bayesian Decision Problems," *Decision Sciences*, 3, October, 129–36.)

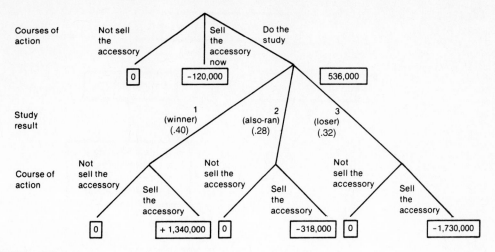

FIGURE 2A.3
Expected Profit Given Additional Information

SOME COMMENTS ON THE METHODOLOGY

In reviewing the methodology just presented, two points seem worth emphasizing. First, the conclusions are only as good as the input data. Since suppliers will tend to be overly optimistic in their presentation of the accuracy of their service in predicting results, it is often necessary to tone down these predictions. Put differently, it is desirable to do sensitivity analysis by varying the input values—$P(z)$, $M(s)$, and $P(z|s)$—to see if the decision would change. If the decision is sensitive to small changes in these input values, then it is often worth reconsidering the input values. A final point can be made concerning the relationship between information value and the accuracy of additional information. Since the accuracy of additional information is measured by $P(z|s)$, we can see how information value could be related to the $P(z|s)$ values for a hypothetical three-equally-likely-states-of-nature, three-test-result case. Perfect information would look like the following:

(Pz|s)	Test Result *(z)*		
Sales Level *(s)*	*1*	*2*	*3*
A	1	0	0
B	0	1	0
C	0	0	1

FIGURE 2A.4
Steps to Calculate *EVAI*

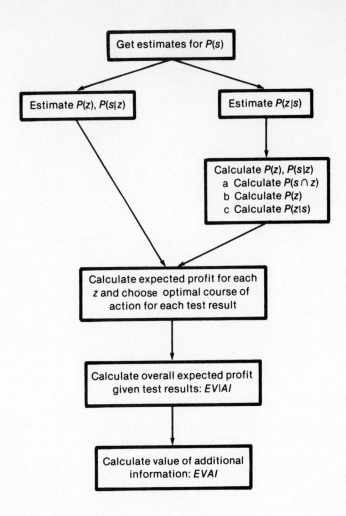

In other words, the test results will be a perfect match with the sales level. Information of no value, on the other hand, would appear as follows:

($Pz\|s$)			
	Test Result (z)		
Sales Level (s)	**1**	**2**	**3**
A	.33	.33	.33
B	.33	.33	.33
C	.33	.33	.33

Put differently, if the test result is independent of the sales level, then the test results will have no information value. Clearly, the closer the situation is to the perfect information case (especially for extreme/serious market results), the greater will be the value of the information.

The concept of when information has value can be demonstrated further by considering the example in Table 2A.5. First, notice that variation alone does not mean information has value. In case I, the variation of the results under decisions 2 and 3 is much greater than it is in case II. Yet decision 1 dominates decisions 2 and 3 in case I: the worst result under decision 1 (18) is better than the best result under either decision 2 or 3 (17). Consequently, decision 1 is optimal in case I, and information about which market condition will occur has no bearing on the optimal decision. Second, notice that the same market result may not produce the best results for all decisions (e.g., in case II, decision 1 works best in market condition A, whereas decision 3 works best in condition C). What gives information value in case II is the dependence of the optimal decision on the market condition [i.e., decision 1 produces under one market condition the best possible result (30), and under another the worst possible result (−15)].

TABLE 2A.5

I. Information Has No Value

Decision	Market Result	Consequences (profit)
1	A	20
	B	19
	C	18
2	A	14
	B	12
	C	− 200
3	A	17
	B	9
	C	− 300

II. Information Has Value

Decision	Market Result	Consequences (profit)
1	A	30
	B	10
	C	− 15
2	A	8
	B	6
	C	4
3	A	− 4
	B	2
	C	12

CHAPTER 3

The Research Process

Discussions of research design often appear to be a series of platitudes and caveats that, if taken together, would void almost all research actually done. Nowhere is the conflict between "scientific" and real-world considerations more apparent than in the selection of a research design. To be purely scientific is so costly that research becomes more of a cost than a benefit; to ignore sound research design may cut costs drastically, but this also cuts the value of the research to zero (or even negative if the results are sufficiently misleading). The key to research design, then, is to make an intelligent compromise between scientific correctness and easy execution.

There are two basic kinds of research processes. One involves "first-time," one-shot research, which is treated as an "open" design problem. The discussion in this chapter implicitly focuses on this type of design problem.

The other type of research process involves the repeated use of an approach. To some extent, even first-time research uses elements of this type. For example, a particular product may require a sampling frame of 7- to 10-year-olds and a survey that includes certain questions in order to be comparable with past research. However, there is some research where the information to be collected, method of collection, and basic reporting format are repeated over time. Basic analysis of and reports on scanner data, customer records/activity data, and periodic satisfaction surveys tend to be pretty standardized, as are the data. Managing such information systems is an increasingly important task for marketing research in particular and the firm in general.

Designing "permanent" (notice how when someone gets a hair permanent, it lasts about two months?) systems involves a research process more complicated than but not unlike that involved in first-time projects. One major complication is that the system needs to be designed not for a currently identified problem but to answer questions and address issues that may not yet have been articulated. This requires effort at defining future scenarios, a perilous task at best. Second, because one can anticipate lots of problems that may arise and many people should be involved in a permanent research project, the possible information needs soon dwarf any reasonable reporting system. As a consequence, information has to be prioritized into (*a*) that which will be provided in some basic form, (*b*) that which will be easily accessible for analyses and presentation, and (*c*) that which will be either archived and/or aggregated or destroyed. This also requires limiting information collection to a level that will not swamp current and rapidly expanding future information handling systems (i.e., computers and data storage devices).

Designing a permanent information system, then, follows an initial design process that roughly matches that of a first-time study. Subsequent use then becomes a constrained version of a first-time study where most of the elements are fixed. Failure to consider the design issues that went into the system, however, can lead to problems in interpretation. For example, in 1994 scanner data for consumer packaged goods products such as food and toothpaste came primarily from supermarkets. Given the rise in importance of "mega" retailers (e.g., Wal-Mart, Price Club), this leaves out a substantial fraction of some categories and, hence, requires careful interpretation of sales and share information. For that reason, we focus this chapter on first-time research design issues.

This chapter gives an overview of the research process. The process can be viewed as a series of 10 steps (Figure 3.1):

1. Problem definition
2. Determining information needs
3. Setting research objectives
4. Selection of type of research
5. Design of data collection
6. Development of a plan of analysis
7. Data collection
8. Analysis
9. Drawing conclusions
10. Reporting

The first six steps encompass what is known as research design, and the last four represent execution.

FIGURE 3.1
The Research Process

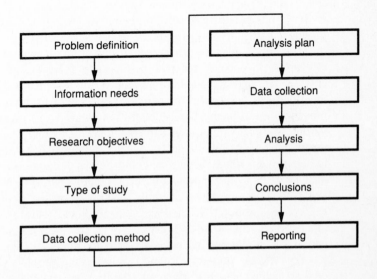

In a company, multiple research processes are in progress at any time, in various stages of development. For a particular process, the stages of problem definition, determining information needs, and setting research objectives require cooperation between manager and researcher. Typically, selection of a type of research through analysis is primarily the task of the market researcher. Drawing conclusions and reporting also require cooperation between researcher and manager.

This chapter proceeds by briefly discussing each of these 10 steps. More detailed discussions appear in ensuing chapters.

PROBLEM DEFINITION

The most important phase of any research is the definition of the problem to be addressed. In spite of this, there is a tendency to spend very little time on this issue. Partially due to the pressure of busy schedules, partially because people assume that the stated problem is the real one, and partially from a reluctance to appear foolish by asking such a naive question as "What is the real problem?" a large percentage of research turns out to be of little or no value.

It is very easy to assume that the stated problem is the real one if it is worded as a research problem. If someone asks if a particular analysis can be performed (e.g., a regression analysis of price on sales), it is much easier to answer this technical question rather than inquire why you want to do the analysis (e.g., to set the price on a new product, choose a promotion plan for an existing product, or evaluate the decisions of a product manager). Put differently, the stated problem is often the tip of the real problem iceberg (a mixed metaphor, but hopefully an informative one); its relation to the real issue is often quite small.

While it is often the case that the stated problem is the tip of the iceberg, the opposite problem also exists: the managerial problem may be sufficiently broad so as to be nondirective (e.g., "Why are sales sluggish?"; "What do we need to do to double share?"). Such managerial problems frequently arise when a gap is anticipated between actual and planned or budgeted performance. The job of the manager and the researcher is then to translate the broad problem into a set of specific information needs and then to select some of these needs as research objectives.

The moral of this discussion is that both managers and researchers should continually probe to uncover the real problem. In a large percentage of cases where practitioners feel that researchers have produced useless results, the source of this feeling is the unwillingness or inability of the practitioner and the researcher to jointly define and comprehend the problem. The problem can range from making a particular decision to providing political ammunition for convincing someone that a particular course of action is useful (and if it fails, at least logical), giving a learning experience or sense of prestige to the person whose budget is being tapped, or simply using up a budget so it isn't cut next year. It is not unusual for the problem definition to change in the mind of the person paying for the research while a study is in the field. Hence, it is strongly advisable to ask the question, "What is the real problem?" several different times and ways (including by observing what the person paying for the research is both personally interested in and rewarded for by the organization), and then put the agreed-upon problem in writing.

It is clearly preferable to ask "What is the problem?" in a probing, supportive, cooperative manner. Overtly blunt questioning can provoke hostility and defensiveness on the part of a manager. Hence, it is best to begin asking about general concerns and specific decisions that are important to the manager. In essence, then, the market researcher plays the role of consultant at this stage. However, it is important to continue one's questions about the nature of the problem, rather than suggesting solutions at this stage.

A key element in defining a problem is distinguishing a problem symptom from a problem situation. Put differently, it is easy to spend one's effort stopping a runny nose rather than treating the flu that is causing it. This occurs because the person asking for research often states the symptom rather than the underlying problem. Consider, for example, the following situations that have occurred:

1. *Stated problem*: To improve the motivation of the sales force.
    Real problem: Sales were falling below quotas. As it turned out, the cause was a combination of a quality control problem in the company's product and aggressive competitive activities. Motivation was a symptom of the situation, not a cause.

2. *Stated problem*: To use regression analysis to forecast sales.
    Real problem: A textile manufacturer was interested in developing a forecasting system for its many lines of fabrics and patterns. As it turned out, business was so volatile that regression analysis (or any other mechanical forecasting system) proved to be of limited value.

3. *Stated problem*: To study the relationship between price and sales for an ethical drug market.
    Real problem: A pharmaceutical manufacturer was considering introducing a drug in the market. A key concern was what price it could charge for it, which was the result of someone's suggestion that a very high price could be set since prescriptions were insensitive to price. Investigation of the relation between the price of existing drugs and sales indicated that the higher-priced goods were in fact the major sellers, hence suggesting a high price was appropriate. Further study, however, indicated that the high-price/high-sales brands were the first to enter the product category as well as the most highly rated by doctors. Hence, studying historical data relating price to sales was at best of little value and at worst misleading. The use of old data in this area has become even more perilous with the growth of managed health care in the United States.

4. *Stated problem*: To evaluate methods of forecasting sales of a major new durable.
    Real problem: A major manufacturer was in the process of developing a new durable for a potentially large but undeveloped market. The manufacturer needed to decide (*a*) whether to continue with development, (*b*) what particular features of the product would be most appealing and, hence, should be developed further by the R&D/engineering department, and (*c*) what level of sales to plan for. While describing different forecasting methodologies is interesting, it does not solve the basic problems facing the manufacturer.

5. *Stated problem*: To find out what consumers think of a company's advertising.
    Real problem: A company faced a possible cease and desist order from the FTC concerning their advertising. The problem was to collect evidence (*a*) that showed

whether the ads were in fact having a measurable and inappropriate effect on consumer perceptions of the product (obviously, the "right" answer was no) and (b) that would be admissible and persuasive in legal proceedings. The outcome was a national probability sample done by Gallup, which surveyed consumers and became a key element in the company's defense. Knowing that the real problem was legal, rather than informational, led to a different approach to data collection, analysis, and result presentation.

6. *Stated problem*: To determine whether a new formulation of a product was perceived to be better than the old one.

Real problem: The major competitor was gaining share. In blind tests, the competitor's product was considered better by a majority of customers. Therefore, the question was whether a new formulation closer to the competitor's would be better.

The astute reader (in this case, anyone who contributed to our retirement fund by purchasing this book) will notice this last problem is the situation faced by Coke versus Pepsi prior to the introduction of New Coke. This managerial problem was translated into the research problem: which formulation tasted better? Since the New Coke formula was preferred in blind taste tests, the decision was made to replace the old (now, "Classic") formula with New Coke. The market results, however, did not match the test results. What apparently happened (I am also good at criticizing Sunday sports on Monday) was that, as a product, Coke involved image and association as much as taste. Hence, the publicized change in formula also had the effect of reducing the brand's goodwill, and hence, sales were disappointing. The moral of this story is that a product offering is much broader than the physical product, so blind product tests alone may not indicate how well a particular formulation will do.

There is another key issue to be addressed along with problem definition: When must the results be available? This is a question to which the first answer is typically unrealistic (i.e., yesterday), and some thought must be given to deciding what the real deadline is.

It is possible to spend so much time defining the problem that nothing is accomplished. It also may be uncomfortable for someone in a staff position or consultancy role to probe a "superior." Also, there is a limit to how long the "What is the problem?" game can be played. (Some people cover up inability or unwillingness to proceed by stalling with general questions.) Nonetheless, problem definition should receive more attention than it typically does.

INFORMATION NEEDS

Having satisfactorily defined a problem, the next step is to determine what types of information are most useful for resolving the problem. It is generally desirable to search for both broad descriptions and a relatively extensive list of information needs at this stage. The list becomes a starting point from which the specific research objectives are selected. Generally, information needs can be uncovered as an extension of the process of defining the problem.

Consider the problem of explaining why sales are falling short of expectations. A number of information needs are apparent, including:

1. Industry sales and key drivers of them
2. Sales of competitors
3. Competitive activity (pricing, advertising)
4. Attributes of products gaining and losing sales (e.g., are sales moving from lower- to higher-quality products?)
5. Behavior of past customers (satisfaction, brand switching, amount purchased)
6. Sales by distribution channel

Clearly, a single study cannot hope to answer all these questions. Thus a decision must be made about which are (*a*) most important and (*b*) most researchable (i.e., can be addressed in a reasonable time for a reasonable cost). The need(s) that are the highest on both importance and researchability then become research objectives.

RESEARCH OBJECTIVES

In contrast to information needs, research objectives should be both specific and limited. One of the greatest causes of dissatisfaction with research is vaguely worded or overly optimistic objectives, which are rarely achieved. For example, a research objective might be "to determine the effect on the market share of brand B of a 5-percent-off promotion run for two months." While the research is likely to provide other information, requiring it to serve too many masters will often result in a study being (*a*) expensive, (*b*) late, and (*c*) inconclusive. Put differently, if the goal is to develop segments of the market based on lifestyle measures, this should be agreed to in advance. Obviously, any additional insights the research uncovers will only add value to the study.

TYPE OF STUDY

Deciding on research objectives first requires understanding of the type of research being done. The most common categorization ranges from exploratory (which assumes no preconceived notions) to causal (which assumes a very specific preconception of how one or more variables influence one or more other variables). A useful categorization is exploratory, descriptive, and causal.

Exploratory   This is a study designed to find out basic information and potentially to formulate hypotheses. It stems from general problem descriptions, such as finding out how consumers make decisions about life insurance. Typically, such studies have few if any formal hypotheses and use "soft" methods, such as in-depth interviews, focus groups, or employee testing.

Descriptive   Descriptive studies are part way along the continuum from exploratory to causal. These studies assume that the identity of the relevant variables is known (e.g., for life insurance purchase, income, age, family status, and risk aversion). Hypotheses are of the general type: x and y are related (e.g., life insurance purchase is related to age). Results tend to be profiles, such as of purchasers versus nonpurchasers.

Causal   This is the most demanding type of study. Such studies assume that not only do we know the relevant variables but we also know (hypothesize) how they affect each other. Hence, we are concerned with two basic problems:

1. Confirming or disproving the hypothesized relationships
2. If the hypotheses are so specific that the mathematical form of the relationship between variables is known (e.g., $Y = a + bx$), estimating the parameters and strength of the relationship

Exploratory research tends to be qualitative and is very important in that it prevents preconceived notions from excluding potentially useful results. It is easy for a researcher or brand manager to forget that they are not typical consumers. Pure exploratory research, however, is rarely done. By selecting who to get data from and the general form of that information, a researcher betrays his or her preconceptions about the problem. Also, though exploratory research is useful for generating ideas (hypotheses), it typically fails to be a good basis for decision making. The results of exploratory research also often defy statistical analysis. Because of this, there is substantial pressure to make research less exploratory and more causal. Nonetheless, qualitative methods are very useful and will be discussed at some length.

Selection of a type of study depends heavily on the research objectives. It also depends on available data, budgets, time pressures, and the experience of the potential users. Actually, in many cases, a research objective will require multiple research approaches, often in sequence. For example, Frank (1983) describes an extensive approach for repositioning an existing brand of a consumer packaged good, which has five stages:

1. Qualitative (focus groups, depth interviews)
2. Positioning study of the market
3. Study of the potential for alternative positionings
4. In-home use tests
5. Advertising testing

The discussion in this chapter focuses on the approach to designing each stage in such an effort.

Stating Hypotheses

Partly because of its psychological and statistical heritage, marketing research often refines its research objectives into formal hypotheses. In stating hypotheses, we are really explicitly stating our preconceptions about the way the market we are concerned with works. While the hypotheses can be simply prejudices or hunches, they are more appropriately based on prior research or existing theories. It is possible and often useful to state hypotheses quite explicitly. For example, H_0: A 10 percent increase in advertising will generate an 8 percent increase in brand mentions. Such explicitness is not necessary, however, and often is a symptom of pseudoscientification. If the strongest reasonable guess you have is that increasing advertising will increase brand mentions, then your hypotheses should state just that.

For descriptive or causal studies, stating hypotheses has two major benefits. First, it translates a problem statement into a series of assertions (questions) that can be addressed with data, and thus largely determines the research design by specifying the data needed. Second, being forced to make implicit notions explicit is a healthy exercise, which often leads to modifications of opinions even without data collection. It is possible to overly bureaucratize the hypothesis-generating process by demanding such things as a formal hypothesis for every question asked and a significance test and cutoff level in advance of data collection. Unfortunately, then the form of the hypotheses may become more important than the substance, to the detriment of the research. Still, with the caveat of avoiding foolish rigor, explicit (as opposed to formal) statements of expected results (a.k.a. hypotheses) are very beneficial.

Existing versus New Data

Before spending the time, money, and effort to collect data, it is useful to see if usable data are already available. Existing data are more widespread and useful than most people realize and should be considered first. Sources of secondary data are described in Chapter 4.

DATA COLLECTION METHODS

Assuming new data are required (and can be justified in terms of a cost/benefit analysis), the following basic alternatives are available: observation, questioning, and simulation.

Observation

One of the most obvious ways to collect data is to simply observe behavior. This can be done in a natural setting (where people are allowed to go about their "normal" business) or a controlled (laboratory) situation. This can also be done either unobtrusively, so people are unaware they are being observed (i.e., with hidden cameras), or obtrusively, with either personal or mechanical observation.

One advantage of observing behavior is that one can directly obtain information that is "bottom line"—did they buy our brand, use the coupon, read the point-of-purchase ad? Another, which requires a skilled observer, is that the observer can notice subtleties and nuances of behavior that purely objective observation may not reveal. The disadvantages are, first, direct observation can be costly (try following an individual around a store with a videotape camera to observe a shopping trip, or a salesperson to see which accounts he or she calls on). Second, the fact that a person is being observed may affect the behavior that is directly exhibited. (In public, most people do the right thing and always support socially desirable causes.) There is also a very important indirect effect on behavior of any obtrusive measurement method. By focusing an individual's attention on a particular aspect of behavior, the individual may think about it more consciously, which may in turn cause a behavior change. Hence, care should be taken to be sure that the behavior being obtrusively monitored is typical and not an artifact of the data collection process.

Questioning

By far the most widely recognized method of collecting data is questioning. (Who hasn't been asked to fill out some survey at one time or another?) Market research is equivalent in many people's minds to survey research. Even when observation studies are done, it is common to supplement them with a questionnaire.

One advantage of surveys is that they are generally less expensive than observation. They also can systematically cover information that is not subject to direct observation, such as awareness, attitudes, and intentions. The major disadvantage of surveys is that the responses may not be accurate. This can be true because of either a simple memory error (what brand of gas did I buy last?) or a conscious attempt to distort the facts (most people won't admit to being "against" ecology, good nutrition, etc.). In fact, the tendency to present socially desirable responses is a major problem with survey research. There are also some common results, such as the overstatement of intentions (of those who say they definitely will buy something in the next six months, typically less than half do so), that make interpreting survey responses difficult.

Simulation

One type of study that is very different falls under the broad title "simulation." Simulation studies are not directed toward collecting data but rather at using existing (past) data and models to project the answer to "what if" questions. Based on a model of a situation (e.g., Sales = 2.73 + 4.12 × advertising + log(percent distribution) + . . .), the results are projected for different hypothetical situations, simulating actual results. While simple models can be solved analytically, many models are sufficiently complex to defy easy analytical solution. In these situations, results are simulated over many trials, usually by means of a computer program. It is these large-scale computer models that are typically associated with the term *simulation*.

The advantage of these models is that they can be directed toward answering managerial questions without collecting new data. The disadvantage is that, if the model is incorrectly constructed or the past data that were used to calibrate the model are no longer relevant, the results will be misleading. Unfortunately, there is no mechanism built into simulation (or into any other projection method, for that matter) that would enable the user to know a priori when the results are bad. In general, simulation models are not used to generate marketing research data.

The term *test instrument* is used here to signify the method by which data are actually secured. Hence, for a lab experiment involving placement of chips into piles to indicate the relative importance of attributes, the chips serve as the test instrument. In the case where the test instrument is a survey, one issue that arises is that of direct versus indirect questions. Indirect questions may sometimes "trick" respondents into giving a more truthful answer about touchy subjects (i.e., the projective technique of asking what does your neighbor think about . . .). On the other hand, indirect questions may provide false information (my neighbor is a mechanic who likes working on cars, while I prefer Nautilus workouts). Another issue is whether to use aided/structured versus unaided/open-ended questions. Structured response questions get results that are easier to analyze, whereas unaided responses have less measurement effect built in but tend to be dominated by the verbal respondents and those with strong positions on the issues involved. The overall format of the questionnaire, the order of questions, and length are among numerous other issues that must be considered in designing such an instrument.

One potential hazard of designing a test instrument is that it can become a catchall for many different individuals' research needs. Nice-to-know questions are interesting but they usually are not worth their cost. Questionnaires designed by committee are usually long and disjointed. While it is obviously desirable to piggyback questions on a study if the cost is low, the point is often reached where the costs are substantial and some brave soul must say "Enough," lest the instrument become so cumbersome that it no longer serves its original purpose.

Who Will Be Sampled

A key question in any study is, Who will be studied? If an industrial company has four major clients, then a sample of all four clients (a census) is often in order. For a consumer packaged good, however, there are obviously too many customers to include all in a study, and thus we must choose a sample to represent them. The question of who will be sampled really breaks down into the following four separate but related issues:

1. Who is the target population? This question requires specification of who the subjects are from whom you desire information (e.g., the largest accounts, female heads of households between 21 and 39, . . .).
2. How many will be sampled? This question deals with trading off accuracy, which requires making the sample large, against cost constraints, which lead to making the sample smaller.
3. How will the subjects be contacted? While various means exist for contacting target subjects, the vast majority of studies use either personal contact, phone contact, or mail. Recent practice has shown a tendency toward telephone interviewing, with phone interviewing accounting for almost half of the data collection revenues of 94 research suppliers in the United States (Table 3.1).
4. How will sample points be selected from the target population? Another budget-constrained decision, the choice of sample points ranges from pure random selection (which is often expensive and almost never employed) through methods designed to ensure representation of key groups (e.g., stratified or quota samples) to convenience sampling procedures.

Sampling can be considered as a separate step in the research process, but here it is considered jointly with the data collection method, since the two are related. For example, it doesn't make sense to design a detailed written questionnaire for the illiterate—which, incidentally, represents up to 30 percent of the U.S. population, depending on the definition used.

Who Will Do the Work

One of the first questions addressed is, Who will do the work? The answer is overwhelmingly a supplier/outside contractor. Next, the question of who will work on it both from the company and the supplier (a critical factor that is often overlooked) must be addressed.

TABLE 3.1 1992 Revenue from Data Collection		
	Dollar volume (in millions)	Percent of total
Telephone interviewing	$350	44.6%
Central location	150	19.1%
Mail questionnaires	90	11.5%
Personal face-to-face interviews	85	10.8%
Focus groups, one-to-one in-depth interviews	60	7.6%
Mail diaries	20	2.5%
All other	30	3.9%
	$785	100%

CASRO report based on 94 firms
Source: Honomichl, 1993, p. 8.

How Much Will Be Spent

The amount of money to be spent has a (the) critical effect on the type of study chosen (e.g., budgets of $10,000 exclude complex field experiments). While in theory the amount of money budgeted should be the result of an analysis of the likely value of information, in practice it is more likely to be a predetermined figure. Also, most budgets have ranges, such as $20,000 ± 15%. (Guess whether the plus or minus occurs more often.)

ANALYSIS PLAN

Before data are actually collected, an analysis plan should be developed. Since most commercial research is done on a tight timetable, all relevant analyses should be prespecified. A side benefit of this prespecification is that it allows one to check to see if the data being collected are adequate for the form of analysis planned. This cuts down considerably on the after-the-fact "why didn't we get data on . . ." questions.

It is often also important to specify in advance what results lead to what actions. Prespecifying these "action standards" prevents a lot of agonizing over what the results mean as people with different desires interpret the results to suit their positions. For example, at this stage it is usually possible to agree on a target share for a new brand of, say, 10 percent. Specifying this as the cutoff prior to data collection makes the decision making, once the results are in, less subject to political persuasion. While it is important not to overlook unexpected events that affect the results of a study, it is also useful to have predetermined decision cutoffs.

An example of a situation requiring predetermined action standards is a test market for a new food product. The key decision is whether to introduce the product nationally, and the key piece of information needed is what level of sales the product will attain nationally. Because the first months of sales will largely be pipeline (wholesale and retail trade stocking up), factory shipments are a poor indicator of sales. Hence, an indicator of retail sales is needed.

To develop action standards, the national share needed to achieve a satisfactory rate of return must be calculated (assume it is 8 percent). Next, characteristics of the test market must be considered. These include advertising levels (likely to be higher than normal), prices (likely to be lower than normal), and other factors that might be thought to affect market share. Assume an inflation of 1 percent. Thus, since 9 percent share in the test market is needed to indicate profitability, the resulting action standards might be

Test-Market Share	Decision
12% or more	Expand aggressively
10–12%	Limited expansion
8–10%	Continue to test
Under 7%	Reevaluate the product

A final point concerning analysis is that the availability and requirements of analytical routines (mainly computer programs) must be considered. If the planned analyses require certain forms of data, then those data must be included in the test instrument. Similarly, the availability of analytical procedures and the ability to interpret them will influence which analyses are planned; only rarely is it worth developing a new procedure for a single application.

DATA COLLECTION

The data collection phase is typically a period of waiting for the researcher. Having specified what is to be done, a manager can sit back and let the supplier work. This can be a mistake. Keeping in touch with the supplier helps ensure quality control. Observing data collection gives insights that often are unavailable from the summarized results, which is why companies often encourage managers to observe research in the field. Also, the data collection phase is an opportunity to try out and debug the analytical procedures needed when the data become available.

It is crucial to pretest a procedure before going to a big sample. At the very least, researchers should force themselves and a few convenient subjects to go through the process. It is amazing how many bad design decisions (e.g., poor questions) can be screened out this way. It is also desirable to run a pilot of 50 to 100 typical subjects. This tests whether the procedure works on subjects in the target population and whether the data have any variability. (If everyone answers a question the same way, it is probably not worth asking.) While a pilot test has both time and monetary costs associated with it, its benefits usually far exceed its costs.

ANALYSIS AND INTERPRETATION

Analysis is, in one sense, the least interesting part of most research. The analyses prespecified by the analysis plan are simply (assuming computer gremlins are absent) carried out and the results reported. In contrast, the interesting and creative part of the work involves interpretation. Interpretation may suggest further work. However, conducting extensive further work usually indicates inadequate planning as well as the lack of budget and time constraints—a rare combination indeed (except, of course, for academic researchers).

Interpretation of results is rarely literal. For example, 40 percent of a sample may say they remembered a given ad. While this sounds good in absolute terms, it is not clear what it would translate into in dollar sales. The key to interpretation is to gather information on a previously used scale. For example, assume in the past I ran 34 similar studies in which an ad was actually used and sales as well as ad recall were measured. These results could be portrayed graphically as in Figure 3.2. Given this background, a 40 percent favorable rating seems likely to produce between a 6 and 11 percent increase in sales. Hence, we might interpret the 40 percent recall as an indication that the ad, if run, would produce an 8 percent increase in sales.

So important is the calibration issue that design of the basic elements of the test instrument should almost always be restricted to previously used methods. Even such seemingly innocuous changes as going from five- to six-point intention scales make interpretation of the results difficult (are 20 percent "top box" responses on a five-point scale the same as 17 percent "top box" responses on a six-point scale?). Similarly, to know 70 percent of respondents are satisfied with our brand is not very informative unless I know what percent are satisfied with our major competitors. In short, measured values often are misleading. It is only by examining measured values relative to either historical data or concurrently gathered measures of competitive products that useful interpretations can be made.

Reconciling results with prior conceptions is often difficult. Whenever analysis of data conflicts with strongly held preconceptions, the natural inclination is to question the data, the analysis, or both. This is a healthy reaction, since innumerable biases may creep into a study and errors in analysis, both conceptual and computational/ programming, are far from uncommon. Still, at some point, a manager must be willing to give up preconceptions or information collection loses its real value and becomes a ceremonial exercise. The art of using marketing research is to know when that point has been reached.

FIGURE 3.2
Historical Relation of Question Answers and Actual Sales Results

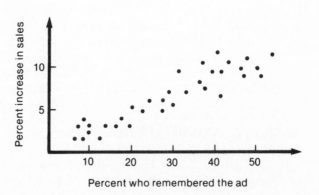

DRAWING CONCLUSIONS

The final step of a well-ordered research process is drawing conclusions. The ex post value of the conclusions depends on how well they assist in resolving the problem. Unfortunately, much research ends up by concluding (a) that the problem needs to be modified, (b) that the data don't address the problem, or (c) that more research is needed. (This is the favorite conclusion of both academic research and reports from consultants, for obvious reasons.)

THE RESEARCH REPORT

The reporting of research results is a marketing task, and hence, it requires understanding the talents and preferences of the readers. Nonetheless, for most situations "the" research report should be a series of reports in various stages of detail and technical language.

The basic report should be a one- to two-page memorandum with the following basic information:

1. Problem
2. Method of study (e.g., a survey of 139 railroad workers)
3. Basic results (findings)
4. Conclusions

The basic report should be written in nontechnical language and be readable by any reasonably intelligent person.

The next level of detail would be a 10- to 20-page version, which expands on the basic report by including more detail on study methods (e.g., a questionnaire, sampling plan, and response rate). It can also contain key analytical results (e.g., cross-tabs or a crucial regression analysis) as well as a brief discussion of the limitations of the study.

The third level of detail is a complete record of what was done and of the results, including tabs on every question (if the study is a survey). This is supported by a fourth level, which includes the raw data and computer output and is typically stored in a basement until it rots due to age.

The purposes of the most general level are (a) to be widely circulated, (b) to summarize *the* key result, and (c) to make it possible to decide intelligently whether to read the longer (10- to 20-page) version. The second level of detail is written to be available to interested readers who are competent but not necessarily technical specialists. Put differently, this report should also be in the native tongue and not statistical jargon. The third level is for the few experts who both exist and care to examine the results in detail. The fourth level is designed to (a) make reanalysis possible and (b) give archaeologists a challenge in the future. The four levels can be summarized as follows:

Level of Detail	Target Audience	Length
1	Broad, managers	1–2 pages
2	Limited	10–20 pages
3	Research-oriented readers	"Longish" (e.g., 100 pages)
4	Future researchers, rats and roaches, professors	Excessive

In producing these reports, a useful approach is to complete level 4 first, then 3, 2, 1, so that each report is essentially an abstract or synopsis of the previous one.

For better or worse, many people rely on an oral presentation of research findings to learn what happened in a study. The oral presentation, like the research report, should be available in several levels of detail. For maximum impact, nontechnical language and proper use of visual aids are invaluable. Put differently, it is best to (a) overprepare, (b) start out simply, and (c) be willing to accelerate or amplify the presentation, depending on audience reaction. The last point is crucial. Intelligent people are offended by slow, inflexible presentations. On the other hand, no one likes to feel they aren't smart enough to follow a presentation. Therefore, the pacing of a report is often as important as its content.

Increasingly, reports are circulated in electronic form through a computer network. Design of this form of report has not been extensively studied, but the usual suggestions of brevity, clarity, and nontechnical description seem to apply as well.

A TYPICAL APPROACH

The research process was described as a sequence of logical steps. In practice, this approach is more goal than reality. In the first place, the sequence is typically attacked iteratively with problem definition, statement of hypothesis, selection of type of study, sample definition, and analysis plan all considered almost simultaneously. While not pure in an academic sense, this approach has much to recommend it when there are time and money constraints as well as established company procedures for certain types of research.

What is often disastrous, however, is when the sequence is used out of order. For example, assume that using a particular analytic procedure is the goal of the study (i.e., "I want to do a market segmentation study using multidimensional scaling"). This is appropriate for basic research but certainly not for applied research. The effect of such bad priorities, where the analytical procedure dictates problem definition, is generally the production of research that is skimmed and then appropriately filed but does nothing to aid management. Put differently, it is perfectly reasonable to build a data collection method or analytical technique into a study to assess its value for this and future problems, but it is generally wasteful to build a major study around a technique. This is especially true of fancy multivariate techniques, which make good add-ons but should rarely be used in the absence of more standard techniques that serve as the "fail-safe" in case the fancy techniques fail to uncover anything interesting.

The typical approach, then, is to see what approaches are feasible, given multiple constraints, such as:

1. Time (a two-month deadline eliminates many approaches)
2. Budget ($10,000 does not lend itself to large probability samples and personal interviewing)
3. Standard practice (standard procedures have big edges: they are easier to interpret because of comparability with past results, and easier to justify and communicate because of familiarity)

The culmination of any good research design is a time line summarizing when different stages will be completed. This time line is often constructed with the ending date given (i.e., "We expect a report on March 1"). While it is possible to use elaborate CPM or PERT procedures, the example in Figure 3.3 of the process for a survey is more typical. Notice that it is common to do several activities simultaneously. Also notice that the entire process was scheduled for five months, indicating the need to plan well in advance. While this can be cut, the tendency to save six weeks by eliminating the pilot test stage is probably the worst bargain imaginable. It is also worth pointing out that large projects usually have built-in evaluation/exit points. These points provide the option to discontinue the research once the results become sufficiently clear without spending the entire budget.

Completion Date	Duration (weeks)	Task
February 1 needs	4	Finalization of problem and information
March 1	4	1. Development of questionnaire (test instrument) 2. Selection of sampling plan 3. Analysis plan
April 1	4	Pilot test and tabs
April 15	2	1. Revision of questionnaire 2. Final analysis plan 3. Payment of federal taxes
June 1	6	Field work
June 15	2	Data coding, punching, and initial tabs
July 1	2	1. Complete analysis 2. Initial ("top-line") results produced
July 15	2	Final report presented

FIGURE 3.3
A Research Time Line

EXAMPLES

Example 1: Nutritional Knowledge

This section describes a project that serves as a point of reference for the book (but not as a model of how to do research) and will be discussed in more detail later. The subject of the project was the nutritional knowledge, attitudes, and practices of U.S. households (Lehmann, 1976). The project was undertaken for two basic reasons: (a) the issue was interesting and important and (b) a budget was available to spend on it. It now provides an interesting snapshot of views approximately one generation ago.

Obviously, a variety of approaches are available for studying this problem. A variety of constraints, however, largely dictated the following design:

1. A budget ceiling of $10,000
2. A single principal researcher with no staff
3. A five-month time frame in which to complete the research
4. The principal researcher's familiarity with survey methodology and fondness for large data sets and multivariate procedures

Given these constraints, the resulting design should have been no surprise. A series of notions about how nutritional knowledge would affect behavior were considered. Changes in behavior and perceptions were also deemed important pieces of data. To gather data, a survey of 1,200 female heads of households was undertaken. These respondents were chosen from an existing mail panel (thus guaranteeing both demographic information and a high response rate as well as removing the sample selection, mailing, and data punching jobs from the principal researcher). The analysis plan was to establish a simple question-by-question tabulation as the basic report for wide dissemination and to play with "fancy" techniques both to understand the determinants of weekly food expenditures and to see how various foods, nutrients, and parts of the body were perceived to relate to each other. A pilot test of 100 was also included, and it resulted in one major change in the questionnaire. While the results came in late (so much for the timeline), the study provided some interesting findings, some of which will be discussed later.

Example 2: The Impact of Price Promotions on Coffee Purchases

Understanding the impact of price promotion is a major concern for manufacturers of frequently purchased products. It has been suggested that promotions may either cannibalize existing sales (basically because current customers stock up at reduced prices) or induce brand switching (by encouraging customers of other brands to switch to the promoted brand). There is also concern over the long-run impact of promotion on perceived value of a brand (i.e., if it's on sale all the time, it probably isn't very good). In the present case, the focus was on the effect of price promotion on purchase timing, quantity, and brand choice. This problem is both a real one and one that has sparked considerable academic interest (e.g., Gupta, 1988).

In choosing a study, it is clear that causal information is needed. Data could be collected by means of a survey, but at additional expense and with the caveat that people don't always do what they say they do. Fortunately, an existing database, a scanner panel

---

TABLE 3.2 Research Criteria

Sample Selection Criteria

1. The sampling frame should reflect the population of interest, and the conclusions drawn and generalizations made should be limited to this sampling frame.
2. The sample should be representative of the population from which it is drawn.
3. The sample size should be large enough to provide reasonably precise estimates for all subgroups being studied.
4. Nonresponse rates should be reported, and the effects of nonresponse should be estimated.

Measurement Criteria

5. Individuals gathering and coding the data should not know the purpose, hypotheses, or sponsor of the research study.
6. The data collection instrument or questionnaire should be pretested.
7. The measures, procedures, and questions should not suggest a response.
8. Wording and topics in the data collection instrument or questionnaire should be unambiguous and easily understood by the target population.
9. Whenever possible, several methods and measures should be used to assess beliefs, attitudes, or behavior.

Additional Criteria for Associative and Causal Research

10. Whenever possible, associative and causal studies should use different methods and scales to measure the constructs under investigation.
11. Associative and causal studies should report the test statistics used and their level of significance.

Additional Criteria for Causal Research

12. Research designed to establish causality should rule out reverse spurious associations caused by unobserved variables.
13. Research designed to establish causality should rule out reverse causality.
14. Research designed to establish causality should rule out simultaneous causality.
15. Research designed to examine constructs, such as behavior, that are distant in time from the communication should give strong emphasis to controlling additional factors.
16. Designs using a control group should ensure that the control and treatment are not different prior to the treatment.
17. When different groups cannot be controlled for *a priori,* the study should control for differences statistically.

Criteria for Conduct of Researcher

18. The researcher should publicly acknowledge all research sponsors and affiliations that might have had input into the research.
19. The researcher should make available at no charge or at a nominal charge the research instruments, the sampling plan, and the analysis plan to any interested party.
20. When generalizing the finding to broader contexts, the researcher should temper the conclusions to reflect the study's limitations.

Source: Paul N. Bloom, Julie Edell, and Richard Staelin, "Criteria for Assessing Research on the Effects of Marketing Communication" (Cambridge, Mass.: Marketing Science Institute, 1994) Report #94-123, pp. 15–17. Reprinted with the permission of the Marketing Science Institute, Cambridge, Mass.

in a particular city, was available. While generalizability (since only a single city was available) is in question and there are questions of coverage (not all purchases are necessarily included) and completeness (we can only tell if a coupon was or wasn't redeemed, not if a household had one and didn't redeem it), the ability to track households over time made this the database of choice.

In terms of analysis, the basic results consist of reporting sales on and off deal. However, given the turbulent competitive environment (i.e., other brands were also on and off deal) and the possible carryover effects (due to stockpiling when an item is on deal), a more sophisticated analysis is needed. Basically, this analysis adjusts for "baseline" sales (that is, what sales would have been in the absence of promotion). Practically, this meant building a model of the choice process and estimating it with regression-type analysis.

SUMMARY

Research design is the crucial stage of research. As will be seen later in this book, many of the issues raised here have been well delineated and the alternative solutions examined. The six keys to a good research design are common sense, logic, knowledge of the problem, attention to detail, effort, and luck. No matter how good the first five elements, nature can provide surprises or changes (i.e., earthquakes) that invalidate well-designed research.

Research design takes on even greater scrutiny in the public policy arena. In hearings and judicial proceedings, fairly reasonable procedures are often criticized as part of the advocacy process. In this domain, especially strict standards must be maintained. A set of criteria designed to relate to assessing the effects of marketing communications developed by Bloom, Edell, and Staelin (1994) provides a useful set of considerations for most studies (Table 3.2).

This book proceeds as follows. The next chapter provides a basic overview of the types of studies that are available. Chapters 5 to 8 address in more detail issues related to specific kinds of studies. Chapter 9 focuses on sampling. Chapter 10 deals with coding and editing responses, and the following chapters focus on methods of analysis.

PROBLEMS

1. Assume you had eight packages of a certain product and knew one had been short-weighted. Design the most efficient scheme for using a balancing scale (assume each use of the scale is expensive) to find the short-weighted package. (This is a classic logic problem.)

2. Mr. Smart has just been assigned the task of recommending a way to test the effect of shelf facings (2 vs. 3 vs. 4) and promotions (5-cent, 10-cent, and 20-cent discounts) on Slop-out, a new toilet bowl cleaner and sterling silver wash. Suggest three alternative approaches, list their pros and cons, and make a recommendation.

3. Estimating the effect of advertising on sales is a key problem in marketing.

   a. Suggest some alternative research designs for addressing this problem.

   b. Indicate why this problem is so elusive.

4. Assume you wanted to monitor food consumption patterns of 20- to 25-year-olds in the United States. What could be done?

5. A certain school points proudly to the average salaries of its graduates (highest in the country) and claims this proves it has the best program. What counterarguments might be made?

6. Assume you wanted to know whether attitude change preceded or followed behavior change for a new food product. What would you do?

7. Is it possible to prove causality? To disprove it?

8. A certain chemical manufacturer noted that its sales of a given compound were flat. It knew that its sales were distributed across several industries: utilities (60 percent), paper manufacturers (20 percent), chemical producers (15 percent), and miscellaneous others (5 percent). It wanted to know its market share, the share of its three major competitors, and how clients perceived its product versus those of its major competitors. What study would you design, given a $10,000 budget?

REFERENCES

BLOOM, PAUL N., JULIE EDELL, AND RICHARD STAELIN (1994) "Criteria for Assessing Research on the Effects of Marketing Communication," Cambridge, Mass.: MSI Report 94–123.

CAMPBELL, DONALD T., AND JULIAN C. STANLEY (1966) *Experimental Designs for Research*, Skokie, Ill.: Rand-McNally.

FRANK, NEWTON (1983) "An Approach to Repositioning Currently Marketed Brands," *Marketing Review*, 38, April–May, 21–25.

GUPTA, SUNIL (1988) "Impact of Sales Promotions on When, What, and How Much to Buy," *Journal of Marketing Research*, 25, November, 342–55.

HONOMICHL, JACK (1993) "Revenue Picture Brighter for Some Firms," *Marketing News*, November 8, 8.

LEHMANN, DONALD R. (1976) "Nutritional Knowledge, Attitudes, and Food Consumption Patterns of U.S. Female Heads of Households," Columbia University Graduate School of Business, Research Paper no. 121.

CHAPTER 4

Sources of Information

The purpose of this chapter is to delineate the various sources of information available for marketing research. As will be seen, there are enough sources that keeping up with them is a full-time job. The extent of the job is such that most larger firms establish research libraries. A user of research used to need to support a good library (a.k.a. information resource center) and librarian. Beyond reading in your spare time, making friends with the librarian is one of the best ways to keep informed about available information.

Recently, increasing amounts of information are becoming available through the information highway via the Internet. Services such as Prodigy, CompuServe, and America Online provide entrée to an ever increasing mass of data. While it is not possible for matter that is printed every four to five years (e.g., this book) to keep up with the evolving world of the information highway, it is possible to recommend that one try to do so.

The chapter begins with a brief discussion of secondary sources (i.e., those that already exist). The rest of this chapter describes some of the most important types of information (summarized in Table 4.1).

INTERNAL SECONDARY SOURCES

Sales/Accounting Data

A major source of data is company sales records. Sales records by territories, factory shipments, and marketing programs are all typically available. The problem comes in getting them into a form that is relevant for marketing. A discussion of some of the major problems follows.

1. Data Are Not Comparable Much of the data available are gathered for accounting purposes. This implies that many of the profit figures, for example, will be based on fully allocated costs and may not be directly usable for abandonment decisions. It is also not unlikely to find production, sales, and profit figures all measured in slightly dif-

TABLE 4.1 Types of Data

Secondary
    Internal:
        Sales/accounting data
        Customer records
    External:
        Public domain
        Private
Primary
    Syndicated
    Special purpose

ferent time frames (as well as in some conflict with each other). In short, since much of the data are not gathered for marketing research purposes, they are often in a form that requires adjustment before they are useful. They also tend to be at variance with external measures, such as those obtained from sales audits by firms such as Nielsen.

2. More Data Are Available than You Know Exist Few companies have accurate filing systems on the information and research that has already been completed. Decentralized management and product or category management systems may be excellent for increasing incentives but are inefficient for conveying information. It is not uncommon for essentially the same study to be done in two or more regions as well as at the corporate staff level. Therefore, it is advisable to have a central information clearinghouse in a large company. Failing that, it is usually a good investment to have occasional lunches with people outside your immediate group to find out what's going on elsewhere in the company.

3. The Data Are Overly Aggregated To investigate a variety of issues (i.e., advertising's effect on sales), it is desirable to have data as disaggregated as possible (i.e., sales by regions, districts, or even individual consumers on a daily or weekly basis). Yet much data are available only in summary form (i.e., national sales and advertising figures on a monthly or annual basis), and analyses that could be performed if the original data were accessible are often precluded by the retention of only aggregate information.

4. Report Formats Are Rigid Most of the data are available in the form of periodic reports. These reports are typically imposing collections of tables in the form of computer output. These reports might, for example, break down sales by region and income category. If someone wanted sales broken down by educational background, this would entail a special report, a time delay, and a budget outlay. If the data were available via a computer network, this means some additional programming/analysis is needed. Because of this, many of the reports serve more to fill up empty shelves (or space in computer memory) than to help make decisions. In spite of these problems, however, sales and accounting data are very useful forms of information.

Customer Records

For many firms, the most useful source of information is their own customer records. This is especially true for industrial firms, services, direct marketers, utilities, and durable goods manufacturers. Put differently, any business that has direct contact with customers has the opportunity to "capture" information about its own customers. Companies are increasingly recognizing the value of customer records as a source of both information and a basis for establishing a more profitable relationship with the customer. In many ways, research and marketing are merging as in the checkout service offered by Catalina Marketing, which customizes coupon distribution based on a customer's purchases (another bonus for holders of shopper's cards).

Customer records data come from several sources:

1. *Billing records.* The simplest source of customer records is billings/sales data. These data are both extensive and quickly available. The disadvantage of such data is that you don't know what other (competitive) products and services the customer also bought. However, for monopoly businesses and those where customers tend to deal with a single supplier (e.g., public utilities, phone companies), the data are quite complete. An attempt was made by Citibank to create a syndicated database based on use of their credit card, but the venture was eventually canceled.

2. *Warranty and registration forms.* Consumer durable manufacturers and many industrial firms typically sell most of their products through retail outlets or representatives and therefore do not have direct contact with their final customers. However, many include warranty and registration forms with the product, which are then sent directly to the manufacturer. While not all customers return such forms, enough do so that they provide a useful information service.

3. *Rebates and coupons.* Any rebate or coupon program provides a data source. For consumer products, ZIP codes provide a basis for relating response to a variety of demographic and marketing mix variables.

4. *Salesforce call reports.* Salesforce customer call records (reports) are another potentially useful source of data. Given the increased level of salesforce automation, it is much easier to capture this information, frequently via fax or modem.

5. *Service/information centers.* The proliferation of toll free numbers coupled with computerized databases has made this an extremely important source of information. Companies such USAA (an insurance company with a base of military families) have extensive operations that do everything from answering questions to sending birthday and graduation cards to targeting products to families based on their characteristics. Ford's customer service center has been made a center of the operation with information on problems transmitted both to manufacturing and engineering departments and to dealers.

6. *Satisfaction surveys.* Often collected in conjunction with quality improvement programs, satisfaction surveys provide a rich database for assessing customer loyalty and likelihood of retention as well as detecting problems in need of attention. Such surveys are now standard in many companies. While they don't provide data on competitors' customers, examination of trends and comparison with other products such as those monitored by the University of Michigan and the American Society for Quality Control are possible.

EXTERNAL SECONDARY SOURCES

Probably the two most underutilized sources of information are the library (both the company's, if a good one exists, and the public library) and the Internet. There seem to be two principal reasons for this. First, knowing something is in a library does not make retrieving it in an up-to-date form easy. Second, some managers feel that each problem is sufficiently different to require special research (i.e., "that may be true for toothpaste, but we're talking about mouthwash"). The second point is true, but only to a certain extent—surely, something about toothpaste purchase behavior is relevant to mouthwash purchase behavior, at least to the extent that it suggests the kind of research that might be useful. This section, therefore, will proceed to mention some of the most useful secondary sources. For a more complete discussion, see Stewart (1984).

Trade Associations

Trade associations often maintain extensive information on sales and profits. In addition, they often keep a file on reported research dealing with their industry. Finally, a few actually collect data from consumers, such as the Textile Manufacturers Association, which maintains a panel who report their clothing purchases. Another useful source of basic information is The Conference Board.

General Business Publications

In addition to specific industry-oriented publications (e.g., *Progressive Grocer*, *Steel*, *Chemical and Engineering News*), a variety of general publications often carry useful information. Among the most useful are *Advertising Age*, *Business Week*, *Forbes*, *Fortune*, *Industrial Marketing*, *Brand Week*, and *Sales and Marketing Management*. Also, the *Wall Street Journal* and *New York Times* provide additional sources of general information. In addition to these publications, two sets of handbooks contain useful information. The Dartnell Corporation series of handbooks includes *Advertising Manager's Handbook*, *Direct Mail and Mail Order Handbook*, *Marketing Manager's Handbook*, and *Sales Promotion Handbook*. The McGraw-Hill Handbook Series includes *Handbook of Advertising Management*, *Handbook of Marketing Research*, and *Handbook of Modern Marketing*.

Academic Publications

A variety of professional journals exist that contain articles of value for marketing research. These journals provide a means of communication both between academics (usually the theoretically/quantitatively oriented ones) and other academics, and between academics and practitioners. Those most directed toward practitioners include *Harvard Business Review*, *Journal of Marketing*, *Journal of Advertising Research*, *Journal of Advertising*, and *Journal of Retailing*. The most practically oriented is *Marketing Research*. The more theoretically/methodologically oriented include *Journal of Consumer Research*, *Journal of Marketing Research*, and *Marketing Science*.

Annual Reports

Annual reports provide substantial companywide information. Each company is also required to provide information about its various lines of business annually in a form known as a 10-K report. These reports are filed with the Securities and Exchange Commission and are available on request from the company. Since this type of reporting, in addition to being expensive, provides some useful competitive information, it is not surprising that companies are not eager to comply with this requirement.

Financial Analysts

A major source of distilled information is the reports of financial analysts. While rarely based on primary data, these reports provide considerable information about companies and industries.

Government

Perhaps the most common source of information is the U.S. government. Since your taxes already have paid for it, it is strongly advisable to gather any possible benefit from the various government offices. Most of the data are aggregate in nature (product, rather than brand; region, rather than individual oriented). Its major value is often in assessing market potential.

Department of Commerce/Bureau of Census   The single most useful publication is the *Statistical Abstract of the United States*. This book contains tables of statistical data on income, sales by product categories, and so on. It also provides references to other sources and, hence, serves as an excellent starting point in any data collection process. For a comprehensive reference guide, see the *American Statistics Index*, published by the Congressional Information Service. Another useful reference guide is *Measuring Markets: A Guide to the Use of Federal and State Statistical Data*. Also see *Current Survey Statistics Available from the Bureau of Census*.

Much of the useful data available come from the Commerce Department/Bureau of Census, so making contact with someone there is a wise move. Some of the most useful sources you are likely to be guided to include the following:

Survey of Current Business   More than 2,500 indicators are reviewed, including commodity prices, real estate, labor force, employment, earnings, foreign trade, and various raw material industries. In addition, a verbal review of the current situation and other articles are included. The data reported here are summarized every two years in *Business Statistics*.

Census of Business (Economic Censuses)   For purposes of reporting, similar companies are grouped together by means of a Standard Industrial Classification (SIC) coding system. This system is described in detail by the *Standard Industrial Classification Manual*. The grouping method is based on the principal product or service the company produces. Consequently, companies with multiple product lines and those companies that are vertically integrated are difficult to classify, as are the many companies that operate in miscellaneous categories. Classification is done first by major groups (two-digit SIC code), then by subgroups, which are broadly defined industries (three-digit SIC code), and then by specific industry (four-digit SIC code). For example, Major Group 34 is Fabricated Metal Products, Group 344 is Fabricated Structural Metal Products, and Industry 3442 is metal doors, sash frames, molding, and trim.

While sensible in principle and useful for small, focused companies, classifying large companies with multiple product lines (and allocated costs) is difficult. Ignoring the issue of whether the basis should be sales, profits, or assets committed (and if so, plant and equipment, working capital, or human capital), large companies often are engaged in a number of alliances and partnerships as well as partial ownership through stock of other companies. Hence, SIC codes and their equivalent (e.g., JANs in Japan) or any other classification scheme are imperfect indicators of actual activity.

Censuses of the following areas are prepared: Agriculture, Retail Trade, Wholesale Trade, Selected Service Industries, Construction Industries, Manufacturers, Mineral Industries, Transportation, and Government. For example, the census of manufacturers is a production-oriented report geared to measuring number of establishments, output, costs, value added, and wages. Reports are also available both on a product basis in the industry series (e.g., Fabricated Structural Metal Products SIC Group 344) and on a regional basis in the Area Series (e.g., New Jersey). Data are collected by mail canvass on employment, payrolls, labor-hours, inventories, capital expenditures, and costs of materials, resales, fuels, electricity, and contract work. In addition, the *Annual Survey of Manufacturers* surveys 65,000 firms to update these data and also collects information on type of fuel consumed, supplemental labor costs, quantity of electricity, gross value of fixed assets, and rental payments.

Current Industrial Reports These are the periodically updated production statistics for the various product classifications (SIC codes), often based on a sample of firms (e.g., 600–1000).

Current Business Reports These reports summarize business in different areas. Monthly retail trade by product category is a widely used form of this report.

County and City Data Book These documents report data on employment and payroll for type of business (two- and four-digit SIC codes) and by geographic area (states, counties, and MSAs—Metropolitan Statistical Areas) as well as for the total United States.

Census of Population and Housing The census of individual households done every 10 years provides a wealth of consumer data on a regional basis. The following are key points:

1. In addition to the questions everyone answered in 1980, one long form (which included extensive demographic and other information) went to 19 percent of the total population (with the sample selected to overrepresent rural areas).
2. Governmental areas include the following:
   a. The United States, Puerto Rico, and other areas under U.S. jurisdiction.
   b. States, counties, and county equivalents.
   c. Incorporated places (cities, villages) and minor civil divisions (MCDs), such as townships.
   d. Congressional districts and election precincts.
   e. American Indian reservations and Alaska native villages.
3. Statistical areas include the following:
   a. Census regions (Northeast, South, Midwest, and West) and divisions.

    b. Metropolitan Statistical Areas (MSAs), Primary MSAs (PMSAs), and Consolidated MSAs (CMSAs). These replaced the SMSAs and SCSAs used until 1983.
    c. County census divisions (CCDs).
    d. Census designated places (these used to be unincorporated places).
    e. Urbanized areas.
    f. Census tracts and block numbering areas (BNAs) averaging 4,000 people.
    g. Census blocks (usually city blocks).
    h. Block groups averaging 900 people.
    i. Enumeration districts (EDs) averaging 700. EDs are used when census blocks are not available.
    j. Neighborhoods.
    k. ZIP codes.
  4. The pattern of data collection crosses governmental and statistical areas and is fairly complex, as Figure 4.1 indicates.
  5. Data are available in several forms, including printed reports, microfiche, and computer tapes, and are also accessible via an online service.

The census data are very useful for assessing potential by area. Firms such as CACI, Claritas (Prizm), and Donnelley provide census data matched to ZIP codes. In spite of the massive effort entailed, however, it is not a true census in the sense of being completely accurate. Interviewing cheating is a factor, and so is the desire of some people to provide false data. For example, since welfare depends on the presence of a male head of household, there is an obvious incentive to falsify those responses. Hence, it is unfair to deify the census results or castigate too harshly other results that are at slight variance with them.

Inquiries about Bureau of the Census programs should be directed to Data User Services Division, Customer Services, Bureau of the Census, Washington, DC 20233; (301) 763-4100.

Other Government Sources

Department of Labor. The *Monthly Labor Review* provides data on employment, wages, and consumer price indexes. The department also publishes *Employment and Earnings Statistics* annually.

Department of Agriculture. The Agriculture Department has monthly and special publications as well as such annual reports as *Agricultural Statistics*, *Crop Production*, and *Crop Values*.

Department of Health and Human Services. HHS provides data on population in the monthly *Vital Statistics Report* and the annual *Vital Statistics of the United States*.

Federal Reserve System. The monthly *Federal Reserve Bulletin* reports on financial indicators, such as interest rates, fund flows, and national income data. Each of the 12 Regional Federal Reserve banks also puts out periodic reports.

Council of Economic Advisors. Publishes the monthly *Economic Indicators*.

Congressional Information Services. Provides a variety of information.

These figures illustrate the principal hierarchical or "nesting" relationships among census geographic areas. Note that the hierarchies overlap; for example, counties are subdivided into MCDs or CCDs (part A), into urban and rural components (part C), and, inside MSAs, also into census tracts (part B).

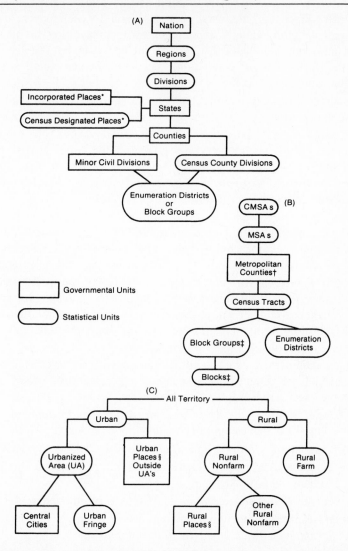

*Places are not shown in the county, MCD, and CCD hierarchy, since places may cross the boundaries of these areas. ED and BG summaries do, however, respect place boundaries.
†In New England, metropolitan towns (MCDs) and cities replace counties as the components of MSAs.
‡In MSAs, blocks and block groups generally cover only the urbanized area and places of 10,000 or more.
§Includes both incorporated places (governmental units) and census designated places (statistical units).

FIGURE 4.1

Principal Hierarchical Relationships among Geographic Units
Source: 1980 Census of Population and Housing, modified.

Other Sources

Thomas Register of American Manufacturers contains information on products manufactured and services rendered by company, including brand names.

Standard Rate and Data Service publishes advertising rates and data for periodicals, direct mail, network, spot radio and TV, newspaper, and transit. Also, newspaper circulation is audited annually. In addition to rates, the newspaper and spot radio and TV reports include data by state, city, county, and metropolitan area on population, spendable income, retail sales, farm population, and farm income.

Other sources on media include *Ayer Directory of Publication* and *Standard Periodical Directory*.

Morton Reports gives more than 500 industry reports. These reports cost a few hundred dollars per industry and go into some detail in describing an industry. Other companies that provide industry reports include *Frost and Sullivan*, *Predicasts*, *Information Source*, and *Find/SVP*. Predicasts has an online database that combines several sources of data.

Sales and Marketing Management Survey of Buying Power gives data for cities, counties, metropolitan areas, states, and the total United States on population, number of households, per capita income, retail sales in total and nine categories, along with indexes of buying power and sales activities.

Editor and Publisher Market Guide profiles 1,500 newspaper markets in terms of a variety of standard measures (population, housing, transportation facilities, salaries, number employed) as well as such other measures as principal industries, utility meters, temperature, shopping days, and retail outlets.

A Guide to Consumer Markets contains census information plus population, prices, employment, and so forth, on statewide or larger regional unit bases. Ownership of durables and spending by categories, often cross-tabbed by income, age, and so forth, are given.

Rand-McNally Commercial Atlas and Marketing Guide contains population figures plus 40 statistics on each county in the United States.

Dun and Bradstreet's Market Identifiers provides data on various businesses.

Leading National Advertisers (LNA) reports information on media expenditures by company and product.

United Nations Statistical Yearbook is a source of international statistical data.

The *United Nations* publications include *World Economic Survey* and *Handbook of International Trade and Development Statistics*.

International Monetary Fund provides mostly financial data.

World Bank produces data such as its Annual Atlas.

Department of Commerce publishes *Foreign Trade Reports*.

Guides and Indexes

Obviously, there are a variety of sources of information that may be useful for specific problems. The key is to know which are relevant. Guides to data sources are available. Two useful ones are the *Business Periodicals Index*, a cross-indexed source of major business periodicals and the *Encyclopedia of Business Information Sources* (Gale Research Company). Other guides include:

> *Directories in Print*, Detroit: Gale Research.
>
> *Encyclopedia of Associations*, Detroit: Gale Research, published annually.
>
> *F & S Index:* Predicasts

Computerized literature surveys are now also widely available.

In the 1980s, many firms began providing computerized information search services. An example was Lockheed's DIALOG, which, for an hourly fee, searched databases, such as *Chemical Industry Notes* and *Standard and Poor's News*, for information of interest (Fries, 1982). Given the amount of information extant, a computer-generated bibliography is often a good investment. Other guides to information include those of Findex and the online Nexis and ABI/Inform services. There are several guides to computerized information, such as the *Encyclopedia of Information Systems and Services* (Detroit: Gale Research).

Finding the data is not the only problem, however. The accuracy of the data is often questionable, government sources included. Most of the data sources are good for relative comparisons (comparing current sales with last year's). On the other hand, almost no source (the census included) is perfectly accurate in an absolute sense. Accurately measuring, for example, the unemployment rate requires assumptions about how to compute the total labor force, what to do about so-called underemployment (e.g., a Ph.D. working as a waiter), and so forth. Also, apparently accurate statistics are frequently gross approximations. For example, the number of umbrellas bought in the United States could be estimated based on a sample of 1,000 in Buffalo, New York, and then projected to the United States as a whole. When the data are reported, however, the numbers take on a permanence and aura of truth that their estimation rarely justifies. Hence, care must be taken not to interpret reported data as perfectly accurate.

The Internet

Currently the biggest growth area in information acquisition is online services. Both services such as CompuServe, America Online, and Prodigy and various Web browsers make the search for information desk-based rather than library-based. This area is undergoing rapid evolution, so it makes little sense to catalog it in hard copy. Still it will soon be the case, if it isn't already, that the most efficient way to begin gathering secondary data is via the nearest online keyboard.

PRIMARY DATA SOURCES

Primary data here refers to data that are collected for the purpose (information needs) at hand. Normally, this refers to data collected directly by the company. There is also a hybrid category of data, that of syndicated services. Basically, these sources arise when a number of companies need similar data and some enterprising soul decides to provide it at a fee to multiple companies. Examples include audience measurement services, media and product use surveys, and scanner-based sales records. Basically, firms choose to buy into syndicated services to benefit from the reduced hassle and cost of pooled efforts at some cost in terms of the ability to customize information. That is, they use syndicated data rather than collect their own (primary) data. A large amount of data comes from syndicated sources, some of which we proceed to describe during our discussion of the different types of primary data (Table 4.2).

INFORMAL

It may seem strange to begin a discussion of sources of information for research by considering informal sources. Yet much useful information can be gained from introspection, discussions with acquaintances, and listening to consumer comments and complaints. For example, while usually overlooked or downplayed by marketing research, some introspection about the problem at hand is very useful. While no one can logically argue that brand managers, marketing researchers, or their associates and spouses are typical consumers, they are both consumers and (at least hopefully) fairly knowledgeable about the product or service in question. They also are observers of how others behave. Hence, "insiders" should have a fairly good notion about the product or service under investigation and may be able to list such things as alternative product uses, attributes important to the selection process, and so forth. While such "results" may not be perfectly projectable, they are an extremely useful starting point for further research. Introspection also has the potential to generate a genuinely new idea, something that rarely results from standard surveys. These ideas can either be applied directly or submitted to more formal research for substantiation or rejection. Given the minor cost of informal research, any good idea that emerges is a bargain.

TABLE 4.2 Primary Data Source

Informal
Qualitative:
      Participant-observer
      Depth interviews
      Focus groups
Observations
Surveys:
      Personal
      Phone
      Mail
Panels:
      Continuous reporting
      Special purpose
      Standby
      Scanner
Experiments:
      Laboratory
      Field
Models/Simulations

A side benefit of conducting informal research is that it forces researchers and managers to address problems directly, rather than simply considering the information that is filtered through various reports. One often feels that many of the bad management and research decisions that are made could have been avoided if someone had taken the simple step of directly talking to customers and/or looking at the problem from the customer's point of view.

QUALITATIVE

The research discussed in this book is largely directed toward generating quantitative measures of constructs for the purpose of aiding understanding of the market and, consequently, decision making. Since structured questions presuppose that the relevant responses are known and the only issue is their relative frequency, they are not amenable to first-cut analysis of a problem. Qualitative methods, on the other hand, provide such a starting point and are largely useful prior to the use of structured surveys. Interestingly, the use of "soft" methods seems more prevalent in Japan than in the United States (Johansson and Nonaka, 1987).

At one time, the author as well as many other researchers treated qualitative research as an interesting anachronism but as somehow less pure and useful than quantitative studies of large samples. Recently, due to cost considerations, a realization that big samples don't necessarily produce truth, and a feeling that one- and two-page summaries of large studies are relatively sterile in providing insights, qualitative research has reemerged as an important part of marketing research. In fact, one article suggested that the success of Japanese companies may be partly attributable to their use of more qualitative research techniques in general and of focus groups in particular (Trachtenberg, 1987). For that reason, we devote a subsequent chapter to the topic.

Qualitative research is widely recognized as useful for structuring problems and helping design quantitative studies. Quantitative studies, on the other hand, are generally preferable when numerical counts or forecasts are needed. Hence, an obvious "do qualitative work first, then a quantitative study" suggestion emerges. Less obvious is the role both play in providing insight, the real goal of research. Quantitative studies often produce results (e.g., uncover a customer segment, find an unexpected correlation with behavior) that require further understanding, often by means of qualitative research. Thus, quantitative and qualitative methods are complementary tools. Moreover, since qualitative methods are essentially ways to engage customers in conversation on their terms, they are quite consistent with the normative dictum of "getting close to the customer." (Certainly, at least in form, qualitative methods seem more user-oriented than surveys, which appear closer to tests than friendly conversations to many respondents.)

The value of qualitative procedures depends almost totally on the insight and intuition of the researcher. Moreover, a portion of qualitative research is driven by the presumption that humans are driven by emotions (Zajonc and Markus, 1982; Hirschman and Holbrook, 1982; Havlena and Holbrook, 1986) and by values and social systems (Rook, 1985; Mick, 1986) as much as "rational" economic factors. The combination makes many people uncomfortable, since the research seems "unscientific." However, since the goal of research is to provide information and insight (Langer, 1987), blanket rejection of any method is inappropriate, especially one that can provide different perspectives.

Several qualitative methods are available; three will be discussed here: participant-observer, depth interviews, and focus group studies.

Participant-Observer

The use of a participant as the primary data source is common in such fields as anthropology. In this method, the observer (researcher) actually becomes a participant (e.g., a member of a buying committee) and after some time passes makes observations about how the group behaved. While such methods are subject to bias, skilled participant-observers do produce meaningful insights. In fact, because they are involved in greater depth and over time in compiling information, they may be able to explain behavior that, based on a single survey, seems incomprehensible. It is the importance of "social context" that led Bonoma (1985) to call for the expanded use of case research in marketing. Still, the use of the classic participant-observer, who might live with the other subjects for from six months to several years, is rarely utilized in marketing research.

Depth Interviews

Depth interviews consist of probing questions being directed at a single subject by a single interviewer. These interviews often last over one hour and require a highly trained (and highly paid) interviewer. The purpose of a depth interview is to continually probe so superficial responses (e.g., "I use brand X because it is pretty") are translated into more specific responses (e.g., "I have a thing about pink, and brand X's wrappers are pink").

Depth interviews were borrowed from psychology and during the 1950s enjoyed considerable popularity. People like Ernest Dichter specialized in probing respondents to uncover basic motives (which, incidentally, often proved to be Freudian/sexual in nature). Now the trend is to use questioning methods such as laddering and repertory grids to gain in-depth understanding of attitudes.

Focus Groups

Focus groups are basically open discussions between 6 to 12 people, with the focus provided by a trained moderator. These sessions typically cost about $1,500 each (for normal consumers) and run for one to one and a half hours. The moderator's role is to gently direct the group to discuss items of interest to the buyer of such research, probing what appear to be superficial answers and moving on when a topic seems to be exhausted.

Focus groups, including some of the best, are often conducted by single entrepreneurs operating out of their living rooms, although major firms have considerable experience in conducting focus group sessions. Focus groups can be used for a variety of purposes (Calder, 1977):

To generate hypotheses about the way consumers think or behave.

To structure questionnaires by uncovering relevant questions and appropriate response categories.

To overcome reticence on the part of subjects to respond. The group setting often encourages participants to say things they would not say in a one-to-one setting. This can occur because of a "safety in numbers" effect or the snow-balling/egging-on that takes place in group situations.

To generate or evaluate new ideas for products or product uses.

To find explanations for results of other studies.

Focus group sessions are handled in many different ways. However, a common approach when the focus is brand preference and use is to have members of the group progress through three stages. First, group members discuss products they use for a particular situation/need with very little intervention by the moderator. Second, the members are guided to discuss how they rate alternative products. Finally, the moderator probes their feelings in order to uncover why they favor one product over others.

Focus groups are flexible tools. They allow much greater probing than even relatively detailed questionnaires. Because they are flexible, they can take advantage of unexpected responses and probe areas previously thought unimportant. Also, people in the group may egg each other on so they will say things they never would say individually. Sensitive subjects, such as birth control, are often probed in focus group sessions. Moreover, a variety of interesting questions that are not suited to structured question format may be asked. In fact, the session is basically one big open-ended question. Finally, since the entire session is usually recorded, analysts can review the results several times before drawing any conclusions.

OBSERVATIONS

Direct observation of behavior is a very important tool. In many circumstances, it is the most accurate way to measure overt behavior. In some cases, observation is the only way to measure behavior due to either unwillingness (anorexics and steroid users are unlikely to recount their actions very accurately) or inability on the part of a consumer to report past behavior (ever asked a two-year-old something?). Its major disadvantages are (*a*) it cannot be used to measure thoughts, preferences, and so forth, and (*b*) it can be fairly costly. Actually, several types of observation methods exist. Some of the major choices to be made include scope of observation, degree of control over the setting, direct versus indirect measurement, observer (human versus mechanical), and obtrusiveness of observer (known versus hidden observer).

Scope of Observation

An observation can be highly structured if the key behavior is well established in advance. For example, in observing soap purchased at a given store, one might observe only the brand purchased. Alternatively, an observation could include all aspects of behavior, including number of packages examined, length of time to make the choice, number of people talked to, and so forth. The scope of the observation has a great deal to do with the problem definition. A vague problem definition and exploratory research (e.g., "let's see how people buy soup") calls for all-inclusive observation, while a tight problem definition (e.g., "measure the relation between brand bought and time spent shopping") leads to much more structured and less extensive observations.

Degree of Control over the Setting

In observing behavior, there is a choice between observing behavior in a natural setting (where observation is fairly difficult) and a more controlled situation (where observation and control of extraneous and desired influences is easier but behavior may be more artificial). Not surprisingly, controlled observation is usually less expensive, easier to interpret, and less projectable.

Direct versus Indirect Measurement

Most observational methods involve directly measuring behavior. A variety of indirect methods have been employed. One example involved newspaper readership in New York City. Surveys consistently showed that the *New York Times* was the paper of choice even though the *Daily News* was clearly a large seller. Given the large social pressure to give the "right" answer (the *Times*), one enterprising researcher decided to check the garbage cans of a number of residents. In addition to some fairly unpleasant items, the researcher found a preponderance of *Daily News*es.

A related and interesting approach for measuring food consumption was based on a "census" of items found in household refuse (Rathje and Ritenbaugh, 1984). By examining items in a family's garbage, some conclusions concerning differences in consumption across national identity, ethnicity, region, income, and minority status were derived (Reilly and Wallendorf, 1987).

A more common indirect method for measuring food purchase behavior is a pantry audit. By literally going through a kitchen and recording what is on the shelves, an estimate of food shopping and consumption patterns can be made. It is only an estimate, however, since the items will be on the shelf or in the refrigerator because they were bought but not consumed (including some food received as gifts such as a fruitcake). These audits can uncover rarely used and bad tasting foods as often as popular/commonly used ones.

A final example of indirect observation research is TV ratings. By attaching a recording device to TV sets or using remote sensing devices, the programs that are on can be monitored. Whether they are being watched or slept through, however, is unknown. In fact, any audit is a form of indirect observation. Hence, almost all accounting data (sales records, inventories, and so on) involve observations and, except in the case of physical audits, usually indirect observations.

Observer (Human versus Mechanical)

The choice between human and mechanical observations usually depends on which is easier to utilize in a given situation. When choosing between human and mechanical observation, the accuracy of mechanical observation must be contrasted with the less accurate but often more insightful human observations. One form of human observation is to have a person under observation also serve as an observer. This *participant-observer* then records both his or her own behavior as well as that of other participants.

One of the most widely used types of mechanical observation is *optical scanning*. Here customer purchases are automatically recorded and keyed to the customer's account via a credit card. Products are coded in terms of the Universal Product Code (UPC), and information on price, quantity, etc., is gathered for each transaction. This allows extensive data to be collected by store, product type, brand, or customer. These data are now extensively used by packaged goods manufacturers.

Another basic type of mechanical response observation is *physiological measures*. An eye camera can be used to monitor what an individual is looking at. These have been used in studies of both shopping behavior and advertising response. A *pupilometer* is a device that attaches to a person's head and measures interest/attention by the amount of dilation in the pupil of the subject's eye. A *galvanometer* measures excitement by means of the electrical activity level in a subject's skin. For example, one toy company exposed 400 children to a collection of new toys and, based on galvanometer readings and other physical measures, selected a single toy to emphasize in a particular selling season. Obviously, the subject is acutely aware of such observation because of the equipment involved. Still, these "unnatural" measurement devices have in some cases accurately measured the level of response to an ad.

Two less obtrusive measures are response latency and voice pitch analysis. *Response latency* measures how long a person takes to respond to a question. The length of time is often thought to be related to the difficulty of the decision. *Voice pitch analysis* measures interest by monitoring the voice of a respondent.

Obtrusiveness of Observer (Known versus Hidden Observer)

The choice between hidden and revealed observers depends on how differently the researcher believes the subject will behave if the subject knows that he or she is being observed. One can imagine all kinds of modified behavior in which the subject attempts to appear more logical, and so forth, than he/she/it really is (Webb et al., 1966). In many cases, however, this source of bias is likely to be fairly small.

The question of obtrusiveness also raises myriad legal and ethical questions concerning protection of subjects. Many situations require that formal consent forms be signed by the subjects in advance. Moreover, whenever subjects are exposed to a manipulation (e.g., a mock-up ad), it is important to debrief the subjects at the end of the observation by explaining the purpose of the manipulation to them. The debriefing is especially crucial when one or more of the manipulations involve false information. The principles of consent and debriefing apply both to observational and experimental settings.

In summary, then, observation is really a broad category involving a variety of techniques. Examples are found in Table 4.3. It is important to remember that observations can be used as complements to surveys or other methods. In fact, most experiments involve both observations and surveys to assess the results.

SURVEYS

Surveys are one way of collecting data, and unfortunately for marketing research are sometimes thought of as the only way. Several companies prepare massive (syndicated) surveys, usually annually, that collect data on a variety of topics, such as background (age, income, and so on), media exposure (magazines read, TV shows viewed), and

TABLE 4.3 Some Examples of Observational Methods

Method	Characteristics				
	Scope (Structured versus Extensive)	Degree of Control (Natural versus Controlled)	Directness (Direct versus Indirect)	Observer (Human versus Mechanical)	Obtrusiveness (Known versus Hidden Observation)
Hidden camera	Extensive	Either	Direct	Mechanical	Hidden
Store clerk with checklist	Structured	Natural	Direct	Human	Known
Physiological measurement (galvanometer, etc.)	Structured	Controlled	Direct	Mechanical	Known
Pantry audit	Structured	Natural	Indirect	Human	Known
Nielsen TV ratings	Structured	Natural	Indirect	Mechanical	Known
Participant observer	Extensive (usually)	Either	Direct	Human	Either

products used/ownership. For a fee, a company can buy into such a survey. In addition, a company can add a few special questions of its own. The advantage is that by cooperating with others, the costs are shared and thus lower for each of the participants. The disadvantages are

1. The timetable for the survey is rigid and may not match the decision-making process.
2. The number and types of questions a company may add are very limited.

Custom-designed surveys are much more flexible than syndicated surveys. Among their disadvantages are the requirements (both time and monetary) of sample selection and questionnaire design. Actually, these surveys can be conducted in a variety of ways including personal, mail, or phone interviews. Interestingly, the popularity of data collection method varies by country, with central location interviews most common in France, telephone in Sweden, and at-home or work surveys in Switzerland and the United Kingdom (Demby, 1990). Surveys are discussed in detail in Chapter 7.

PANELS

Continuous Reporting Panels

Many companies maintain panels of individuals who agree to report (explicitly when they keep a record of purchases, implicitly when they use a preferred shopper card) all their purchases of a certain category of products, such as groceries and clothing. These panels allow tracking of brand, size, and quantity purchased over time. This allows both the continuous monitoring of shares by brand, size, and so forth, and the identification of which brands compete most closely as well as the reaction to marketing mix variables such as promotion. The problems with continuous reporting panels are unfortunately fairly severe (Boyd and Westfall, 1960; Sudman, 1964). Yet in spite of these problems, panels are widely used and useful.

Panel Membership Bias   The panel recruitment process produces a high level of non-participation. A 10 percent or smaller recruitment rate for diary panels is typical. Reporting every bottle of catsup purchased by brand, size, store, price, whether it was on special, whether a coupon was used, and so forth, is an activity in which most people refuse to participate. While the people who are eventually included in the panel are typically matched to the general population in terms of obvious characteristics, such as age and income, there is a nagging worry that the same motivation that led someone to join the panel would cause him or her to behave differently from those "normal" people who refused (similar to people who want to be jurors on long trials).

False Reporting   Reporting forms are often sufficiently complex that a variety of short-cuts may appeal to the respondents. One obvious way to shorten the task is to simply fail to report some purchases. Alternatively, it is convenient to report multiple purchases of a single brand and size or to report more purchases of the brand previously reported. Finally, there is the real problem of forgetting and either failing to report a purchase or reporting it incorrectly. Thus, reporting rates and accuracy vary (McKenzie, 1983).

Panel Aging and Dropouts   A problem all panels struggle with is aging. A panel with the right average age in 1990 will be on average about 10 years too old in 2000 if no one drops out. Hence, it is important to continually update the panel by adding members, both to keep the average age down and to replace respondents who for one reason or another (moving, loss of interest, death) depart from the panel.

Panel Conditioning   The mere fact that an individual is reporting purchases of a product is likely to make the person think more carefully about the product. Consequently, being on the panel may create an expert consumer whose behavior no longer is representative of consumers in general.

Getting the Data in Shape for Analysis   The problems involved in transforming returned forms into computer-ready data are legion. As such, the chance for error is great.

Special-Purpose Panels

To avoid the aging, conditioning, and other problems with existing panels, as well as to collect data on subjects not covered by existing panels, it is possible to set up a special-purpose panel to gather data. The two main problems with this approach are:

> *Recruitment of panel members* is expensive both in terms of effort and money.
> *The dropout rate* may be a problem (Sobol, 1959). For example, in one study a special phone panel was established to monitor sales of a new car over an 18-month period in five measurement waves. In spite of the strong "guarantee" of the supplier that dropouts would be 5 percent or at most 10 percent per wave, the actual dropout rate was nearly 20 percent per wave. By wave 5, less than half the original panel members remained (Farley, Katz, and Lehmann, 1978). Since dropouts were, as expected, less interested in new cars, this dropout problem led to a biased sample in later waves, which required some gyrations to overcome (or at least reduce).

Standby Panels

To ensure a large response rate, it is possible to utilize panels of people who have previously agreed to provide information on any subject. Background information, such as age and income, is maintained on these panel members. The most common form of the standby panel is the mail panel. These panels are often maintained in units of 1,000, each of which is intended to be representative of the total United States in terms of age, region of the country, and so on. For example, NFO (National Family Opinion) maintains a panel of 450,000 households in the United States. Similar panels are maintained by Market Facts and NPD. Two problems with this approach are the low recruitment rate and the underrepresentation of minority groups.

Low Recruitment Rate   Typically, fewer than 1 in 10 people will agree to serve on a standby panel. Those who do obviously are more interested in filling out questionnaires and, hence, are at least in one aspect atypical of the general population. They are also relatively literate. (Illiterates have problems with six-page mail questionnaires.)

Underrepresentation of Minorities   Mail panels typically underrepresent minority groups, such as African Americans and Hispanic Americans. The minority members included tend to be older. Therefore, for some purposes, these panels are seriously (no pun intended) biased.

Scanner Panels

A relatively recent development is so-called scanner panels. These panels collect data by means of optical scanners, which record items purchased and prices paid at a checkout counter. These data are often augmented by advertising data (e.g., newspaper ads) and promotions (e.g., if a coupon was used). Panel members are identified by means of a special shopper card.

Scanner data contain a wealth of information. For example, they make it possible to track the effect of ads or promotions at the store level. Such tracking, however, is far from trivial. The basic unit of data is the individual transaction (e.g., a tube of toothpaste purchased by J. Doe on March 15 for 87 cents). This information is then typically stored in separate files relating to the store and the family. The resulting data files for even a single store or family are amazingly long. Moreover, data on advertising or family characteristics (age, income, and so forth) are typically stored in separate files. Hence, even attempting to study the impact of advertising on sales involves a tedious task of file manipulation.

Aside from the problem of handling the essentially infinite quantity of scanner data, other problems have been noted. First, the data are at the family rather than the individual level. Second, many influences on sales, such as TV advertising, point-of-purchase displays, and number of shelf facings, may not be included in the data set. Third, behavior of nonbuyers must be inferred (e.g., did they not buy the toothpaste at 87 cents because they failed to receive a coupon, were on vacation, . . . ?). Fourth, store coverage by scanners is not complete and many purchases are not included in the database (e.g., purchases made for cash at a local deli or on trips when the customer forgets the special card). Fifth, certain customers refuse to join such a panel, leading to possible nonresponse bias. Finally, scanning accuracy is less than 100 percent. Goodstein (1994) found that scanners both over- and undercharge and therefore misreport the price paid on 5–10 percent of the items.

In spite of these and other problems, however, scanner data provide a welcome addition to the market research arsenal. They are particularly useful for tracking the effects of price and promotions on sales. Still, care is needed in selecting a sample of scanner households to analyze; selection weighted by purchase frequency seems to produce more accurate estimates of the impact of price (Gupta et al., 1996). Moreover, as more of the current limitations are overcome, scanner data seem destined to be the primary source on frequently purchased goods. (Obviously, it is not likely to be a major data source for studying the process by which $10 billion construction projects are awarded.) Partly for that reason, the competition between the two principal suppliers (Nielsen, IRI) is particularly intense. (For example, in summer 1996, IRI sued Nielsen, claiming Nielsen used exclusive contracts with retailers to keep IRI from gaining access.)

EXPERIMENTS

An important source of information is experiments. These come in two basic types: laboratory and field.

Laboratory

Laboratory experiments are the epitome of tightly controlled experiments. Here, essentially all the stimuli the respondent is exposed to can be controlled. Therefore, the effect of a single variable (e.g., a particular ad) can be assessed. The disadvantage of a lab setting is its lack of realism and the resulting likelihood that lab results will differ from field results, usually in the form of being more dramatic. For this reason, absolute results are generally recalibrated according to the past correspondence between lab results and subsequent field results.

Field

The opposite of a lab experiment, a field experiment is the ultimate in realism but the worst in terms of control. To be effective, one must ensure (*a*) that the controlled variable did, in fact, vary according to the design and (*b*) that other things that influence the results did not change concurrently (i.e., when the ads shown were changed, the prices did not also change). Field experiments form the basis of much of direct marketing as various catalogs, offers, etc., can be tested and responses compared with customer sales records.

In constructing these polar extreme types of experiments, it is important to realize that intermediate services are available. One of the best known is a controlled store test, where "real" shoppers in a real store are exposed to an experiment (e.g., changes in shelf facings or prices). Such tests are designed to achieve most of the control of a lab experiment plus most of the realism of a field setting. Another important distinction is between *controlled* and *natural* experiments. In a controlled experiment, the subjects are assigned to a "treatment" by the researcher. If you were testing three prices, you could assign every third person to a particular price setting. In contrast, in a natural experiment, respondents are allowed to select (naturally) their own treatment. For example, if I were interested in assessing the effect of education on job choice, I could try to control the situation by assigning subjects to educational levels. This, however, would be both gross-ly expensive and morally questionable. Hence, an alternative is to simply observe how job choice and education correlate in a sample of individuals. The problem with this (nat-ural) approach is that the education level is likely to be related to a set of variables, such as parents' education and income, attitude toward school, and IQ, that also influ-ence job choice. Consequently, a natural experiment is cheap in terms of data collection but expensive in terms of the analysis required to deduce correctly the effect of the treat-ment variable on the criterion. (Survey data, a mainstay of marketing research, are basi-cally treated as a series of natural experiments when they are analyzed.)

MODELS/SIMULATIONS

At the polar extreme from focus groups is the collection of models that are formal/math-ematical descriptions of a situation. These models are typically the result of analysis of some form of data plus a theory and are calibrated to answer "what if?" questions (e.g., "What if I increase price 10 percent?"). What is available to a potential user is typi-cally a general description of the model plus the model's answer to a series of ques-tions.

Actually, models are at least as much users of data as sources of data. They typi-cally require one of the other forms of input data (panel, special survey, or the like) for calibration. Only after these data are available and analyzed do the models become sources of information. For that reason, they are not discussed extensively here.

SUMMARY

This chapter has described several sources of information. Often, unless both secondary sources have been examined and some qualitative research has been performed, pro-ceeding to collect more primary data is premature. The following chapters provide more extensive discussion of three methods of primary data collection: qualitative, experiments, and surveys. It is important to recognize that these methods, while they compete for budget dollars, are complementary in terms of the information they provide and are often used in conjunction with each other.

PROBLEMS

1. Discuss the appropriateness of a continuous panel versus a revolving panel (new respon-dents each wave) for monitoring:

   a. Advertising awareness.

   b. Brand-switching patterns.

   c. Attitude toward a brand.

2. What were U.S. dishwasher sales in 1987? Compare several sources and explain the disparity.

3. Where would you go to find out information about the PVC business?

4. What would you do to estimate the growth rate of sales of microcomputers and microwave ovens in the United States?

5. Assume you were employed by L. L. Bean. How could you use data on customer response to catalog mailings to understand preferences and hence more efficiently use resources?

REFERENCES

Agricultural Statistics, Washington, D.C.: Department of Agriculture, published annually.

Annual Survey of Manufacturers, Washington, D.C.: Department of Commerce, Bureau of the Census, published annually.

Ayer Directory of Publications, Philadelphia: Ayer Press, published annually.

BELLENGER, DANNY N., KENNETH L. BERNHARDT, AND JAC L. GOLDSTUCKER (1976) *Qualitative Methods in Marketing*, Chicago: American Marketing Association.

BONOMA, THOMAS V. (1985) "Case Research in Marketing: Opportunities, Problems, and a Process," *Journal of Marketing Research*, 22, May, 199–208.

BOYD, HARPER W., JR., AND RALPH L. WESTFALL (1960) *An Evaluation of Continuous Consumer Panels as a Source of Marketing Information*, Chicago: American Marketing Association.

BRITT, STEUART H. (1973) *Marketing Manager's Handbook*, Chicago: Dartnell.

CALDER, BOBBY J. (1977) "Focus Groups and the Nature of Qualitative Marketing Research," *Journal of Marketing Research*, 14, August, 353–64.

Census Catalog and Guide, Washington, D.C.: U.S. Government Printing Office, published annually.

Census of Business, Washington, D.C.: Department of Commerce, Bureau of the Census, published annually.

Crop Production, Washington, D.C.: Department of Agriculture, published annually.

Crop Values, Washington, D.C.: Department of Agriculture, published annually.

DEMBY, EMANUEL H. (1990) "ESOMAR Urges Changes in Reporting Demographics, Issues Worldwide Report," *Marketing News*, January 8, 24.

Digest of Educational Statistics, Washington, D.C.: Department of Health and Human Services, published annually.

Editor and Publisher Market Guide, New York: The Editor and Publisher Co., published annually.

Encyclopedia of Information Systems and Services, Detroit: Gale Research.

FARLEY, JOHN U., JERROLD P. KATZ, AND DONALD R. LEHMANN (1978) "Impact of Different Comparison Sets on Evaluation of a New Subcompact Car Brand," *Journal of Consumer Research*, 5, September, 138–42.

Federal Reserve Bulletin, Washington, D.C.: Federal Reserve, published monthly.

FERBER, ROBERT, ED. (1974) *Handbook of Marketing Research*, New York: McGraw-Hill.

FRIES, JAMES R. (1982) "Library Support for Industrial Marketing Research," *Industrial Marketing Management*, 11, 47–51.

GOODSTEIN, RONALD C. (1994) "UPC Scanner Pricing Systems: Are They Accurate?" *Journal of Marketing*, 58, April, 20–30.

A Guide to Consumer Markets, New York: The Conference Board, published annually.

GUPTA, SACHIN, PRADEEP CHINTAGUNTA, ANIL KAUL, AND DICK R. WITTINK (1996) "Do Household Scanner Panels Provide Representative Inferences from Brand Choices: A Comparison with Store Data," *Journal of Marketing Research*, 33, November, 383–98.

Harvey, Joan, ed. *Statistics—Europe: Sources for Social, Economic, and Market Research*, Beckenham, Kent, England: CBD Research Ltd., published monthly.

HAVLENA, WILLIAM J., AND MORRIS B. HOLBROOK (1986) "The Varieties of Consumption Experience: Comparing Two Typologies of Emotion in Consumer Behavior," *Journal of Consumer Research*, 13, December, 394–404.

HIRSCHMAN, ELIZABETH C., AND MORRIS B. HOLBROOK (1982) "Hedonic Consumption: Emerging Concepts, Methods, and Propositions," *Journal of Marketing*, 46, Summer, 92–101.

HODGSON, RICHARD S. (1976) *Direct Mail and Mail Order Handbook*, 3rd ed., Chicago: Dartnell.

JOHANSSON, JOHNY K., AND IKUJIRO NONAKA (1987) "Market Research the Japanese Way," *Harvard Business Review*, 65, May–June, 16–22.

LANGER, JUDITH (1987) "The Process of Insight: How Researchers Turn Qualitative Research into Marketing Insight," *Marketing Review*, 43, November, 11–15.

MCKENZIE, JOHN (1983) "The Accuracy of Telephone Call Data Collected by Diary Methods," *Journal of Marketing Research*, 20, November, 417–27.

MICK, DAVID GLEN (1986) "Consumer Research and Semiotics: Exploring the Mythology of Signs, Symbols, and Significance," *Journal of Consumer Research*, 13, September, 196–213.

Monthly Labor Review, Washington, D.C.: Department of Labor, published monthly.

Morton Reports, Merrick, N.Y.: Morton Research, published annually.

Rand-McNally Commercial Atlas and Marketing Guide, Skokie, Ill.: Rand-McNally, published annually.

RATHJE, WILLIAM, AND C. K. RITENBAUGH (1984) "The Household Refuse Analysis," *American Behavioral Scientist*, 28, September–October, 115–28.

REILLY, MICHAEL D., AND MELANIE WALLENDORF (1987) "A Comparison of Group Differences in Food Consumption Using Household Refuse," *Journal of Consumer Research*, 14, September, 289–94.

RISO, OVID, ED. (1973) *Sales Promotion Handbook*, 6th ed., Chicago: Dartnell.

ROOK, DENNIS W. (1985) "The Ritual Dimension of Consumer Behavior," *Journal of Consumer Research*, 12, December, 251–64.

Sales Management Survey of Buying Power, New York: Bill Brothers, published bimonthly.

SOBOL, M. (1959) "Panel Mortality and Panel Bias," *Journal of the American Statistical Association*, 54, 52–68.

Standard Industrial Classification Manual, Washington, D.C.: Office of Statistical Standards.

Statistical Abstract of the United States, Washington, D.C.: U.S. Department of Commerce, Bureau of the Census, published annually.

STEWART, DAVID W. (1984) *Secondary Research*, Beverly Hills, Calif.: Sage.

SUDMAN, SEYMOUR (1964) "On the Accuracy of Recording of Consumer Panels," *Journal of Marketing Research*, 2, May, 14–20, and August, 69–88.

Survey of Current Business, Washington, D.C.: Department of Commerce, Bureau of Economic Analysis, published monthly.

Thomas Register of American Manufacturers, New York: Thomas, published annually.

TRACHTENBERG, JEFFREY A. (1987) "Listening, the Old-Fashioned Way," *Forbes*, 140, October 5, 202–04.

United Nations Statistical Yearbook, New York: United Nations, published annually.

The U.S. Market for On-Line Databases, New York: Frost and Sullivan.

Vital Statistics of the United States, Washington, D.C.: Department of Health and Human Services, published annually.

Vital Statistics Report, Washington, D.C.: Department of Health and Human Services, published monthly.

WEBB, EUGENE J., DONALD T. CAMPBELL, RICHARD D. SCHWARTZ, AND LEE SECHREST (1966) *Unobtrusive Measures*, Skokie, Ill.: Rand-McNally.

ZAJONC, ROBERT B., AND HAZEL MARKUS (1982) "Affective and Cognitive Factors in Preferences," *Journal of Consumer Research*, 9, September, 123–31.

APPENDIX 4-A ▬▬▬▬▬▬▬▬▬
RESEARCH SUPPLIERS

Even in the largest companies, data collection is rarely carried out by company personnel. Rather, the company subcontracts the work to suppliers. Hence, most marketing research work involves dealing with suppliers. It is important to remember, however, that the responsibility for problem definition and a good part of the burden of design and interpretation should rest with the company, not the supplier.

This section is designed to acquaint readers with some of the major issues in supplier selection and monitoring. It has been described (probably accurately) as both boring and useful. This chapter begins by briefly discussing supplier selection and quality control. Then, some of the services offered by the larger research firms are highlighted. The chapter then concludes with a brief summary.

THE SUPPLIER BUSINESS

For many years, the supplier business was pretty much a cottage industry. A large number of small firms existed with particular product or regional specialties. Recently, however, consolidation into full-service companies has increased, as has the merging, acquiring, and diversifying common to much of U.S. business. For example, in 1986, Control Data sold 40 percent of Burke to Time, Inc., which combined it with SAMI (Selling Area Markets, Inc.), a warehouse withdrawal auditing firm. SAMI/Burke then formed a joint venture with Arbitron (a TV ratings supplier owned by Control Data) called ScanAmerica to combine TV viewing measurements with product purchase data. Then, in late 1987, Time, Inc., announced plans to sell SAMI/Burke back to Control Data. SAMI folded in 1989, selling its assets to IRI. Control Data's decision was reportedly influenced by Dun and Bradstreet's proposed acquisition of IRI. Since Dun and Bradstreet already owned Nielsen, which in turn was involved in a joint venture with NPD, Dun and Bradstreet would have controlled most of the consumer household purchase tracking business. As it turned out, the Dun and Bradstreet–IRI merger plans were dropped because of objections by the FTC on antitrust grounds. The point of this discussion is that the research business has emerged as an industry where consolidation and economies of scale seem to be increasing, the recent employee buyout of NFO notwithstanding.

SELECTING A SUPPLIER

Probably the key decision a researcher makes is which suppliers to employ. A variety of considerations are relevant for this decision.

Reputation of the Supplier

The supplier's reputation is important for lending credibility to the results. Even if firm XYZ, Inc., can do a better job, a study by Gallup or Nielsen will have more clout with the average person. This is important when the study is designed to have impact on someone who is not knowledgeable about marketing research suppliers and practices (e.g., in a legal trial).

Technical Competence of the Supplier

The technical competence of a supplier should always be assessed. Many suppliers who are good at basic studies do not possess the personnel or computer capability to do complex analyses. Those who profess to possess such capabilities may have one technician who is supposed to oversee all "fancy" analysis, or even an outside consultant who serves as a hired gun on technical matters.

Experience of the Supplier

General experience is very important in doing good marketing research. Often overlooked, however, is experience in a particular type of research. It is generally advisable to avoid paying a supplier's development costs to learn about a new type of analysis if an experienced alternative supplier is available.

Costs

The instinct to cut costs is essentially sound. A little price shopping is desirable. After a point, however, cost cutting may be false economy. Suppliers are in business to make a profit and can only be squeezed so far before they lower the quality of the results by hidden methods, such as cutting the number of callbacks or time spent on the project, or obvious methods, such as cutting sample size or pretests.

Reliable Delivery

Most suppliers require approximately the same amount of time for a given project. Still, checking to make sure the supplier consistently delivers on time is advisable.

Project Director

The person who will be project director is the key to the success of a project. An experienced director with sufficient time, interest, and knowledge is a quantum improvement over an inexperienced, harassed, or uninterested one.

Since no one supplier is always dominant on all these criteria, a reasonable approach is to compare a few (e.g., three) viable alternative suppliers in terms of their abilities à la Table 4A.1. While all of the elements in the table are important, two often are especially so: the skill of the person handling your account (job), and the likely effort level expended on your behalf. Consider both their competence and how badly they want your business.

The previous discussion has focused on the selection of a supplier on a one-shot basis. Given the increased use of standard/syndicated data and the emphasis on comparing results across time, regions, or brands/companies, another important concern is consistency. Firms

---

TABLE 4A.1 **Some Criteria for Evaluating Suppliers**

Design
    Product knowledge
    Experience with type of study
    Skill of the account person
    Technical backup staff

Sampling
    Basic design
    Nonresponse follow-up procedures
    Procedure for checking responses

Supervision of Data Collection
    Level of personal involvement
    Procedures

Data Processing/Analysis
    Procedures for coding
    Editing and cleaning of responses
    Basic reports
    More complex analyses

Interpretation and Follow-Up
    Interpretation skills
    Follow-up work

Overall Quality
    Competence
    Likely effort level

Specific Factors
    Delivery time
    Cost

---

attempting to be customer-focused, market-oriented, learning organizations (important goals as well as overused buzzwords) need data that is comparable. Hence, like much of business, working with research suppliers takes on a relationship management/partnering character.

The Research Proposal and Job Specifications

Before going to outside suppliers, it is important to carefully specify what the task of the supplier is. In general, the more detail the better. Specifically, all of the following should be addressed:

1. Sampling requirements, including screening criteria and callback procedures, as well as size.
2. Data collection method. If it is a questionnaire, this includes content by type (e.g., demographics) and a rough idea of the number of each type of question.
3. Pilot testing: size, method, and number required.
4. Data coding and editing procedures.

5. Analysis to be performed, including basic tabs and multivariate procedures.

6. Ownership of results and their "final resting place"—that is, who gets to keep the data and analysis.

7. Reports required in terms of content.

8. Time/work schedule.

9. Price (preferably broken down by component) and contingencies (e.g., ±15 percent).

10. Payment schedule.

Also, you may wish to obtain a confidentiality agreement so that the supplier agrees not to work with your major competitor for X months.

QUALITY CONTROL

There are two basic methods of employing suppliers. One is to request bids on a project. This requires either (a) well-defined specs, which might be prematurely drawn, or (b) loosely defined specs, which can lead to widely disparate proposals and, hence, comparisons of very different approaches to a problem. The other approach is to deal over time with a small number of suppliers (e.g., two to four). This strategy has the advantage of economies of scale, in the sense that the time spent by the supplier in understanding the company's business is greatly reduced, especially if the supplier assigns a permanent account representative to the client. Also, dealing consistently with a given supplier makes comparability of results across studies somewhat easier. The disadvantage of this approach is that new ideas/approaches may be overlooked and that research may become routine. This approach also may raise costs by making the supplier take the business for granted. In any event, a price quote should be obtained before work begins so that neither party (company or supplier) faces an unpleasant surprise later on.

Checking up on suppliers is advisable. Without being a complete stickler, it is advisable to monitor what is going on by such activities as spending a day in the field and keeping in contact with the supplier during the course of the study. This both helps ensure attention to the project and tends to give insights into what happened that are unavailable from the summary report.

At this point, a few words can be said about academic suppliers. With the exception of those who have genuine businesses established, academics are typically understaffed. Consequently, they are relatively poor at meeting deadlines and giving polished presentations. On the other hand, they are witty, have low overhead, and occasionally have novel ideas. If one can put up with their occasional lapses into academic jargon, they are often useful in helping specify research design or analytical procedures. Basically, they are complementary to, rather than replacements for, "real" suppliers. (This commercial was brought to you by your local chapter of the Hire/Employ Local Professors Association.)

The rest of this chapter exposes readers to the real data sources—suppliers. The number of suppliers is enormous. What this chapter does, therefore, is to concentrate on the major data sources, especially those that apply to consumer packaged goods (Figure 4A.1). The reasons for this focus are (a) research suppliers have concentrated on packaged goods, and their services are extensively developed, and (b) the information on them is widely available. Also, by examining the services offered by these suppliers, an understanding can be reached of the kinds of services that are perceived as valuable.

Company	Principal Focus	Principal Services
1. Dun & Bradstreet A.C. Nielsen	Consumer Packaged Goods (grocery, health and beauty aids)	Scanner Data
Cognizant IMS International	Pharmaceuticals	Pharmacy Sales Physician Treatment Records
Nielsen Media Research	Television Viewing	People Meters
2. Information Resources	Consumer Packaged Goods	Scanner Data Decision Support Software
3. Arbitron	Media/Audience Measurement	Diaries
4. Westat Crossley	Government Commercial Firms	Surveys Surveys
5. Maritz	Consumer, Business-to-Business	Surveys; Custom Work
6. Walsh/PMSI	Pharmaceuticals	Pharmacy Sales
7. Kantar Group (WPP)		Surveys
Millward Brown		Copy Testing
Research International		Copy Testing; Custom Work

MRB Group
   Simmons Market Research
   Winona
	Media; Product Usage	Syndicated Surveys
		Custom Surveys

8. NPD	Consumer Packaged Goods	Syndicated Industry Data Custom Surveys
9. NFO	Consumer Packaged Goods Yellow Pages	Mail Panels; Surveys Syndicated Surveys
10. Market Facts	Consumer Packaged Goods	Mail Panels; Surveys
11. Audits and Surveys		Store Audits Surveys
12. M/A/R/C	Consumer Packaged Goods	Surveys Consulting
13. Opinion Research		Surveys
14. Abt	Government	Surveys
15. BASES	New Products	

FIGURE 4A.1
1995 Largest U.S. Research Organizaitons
Source: Drawn from Jack J. Honomichl, "1996 Business Report on the Marketing Research Industry" from *Marketing News* (June 3, 1996): H4. Copyright © 1996 by the American Marketing Association. Reprinted with the permission of the publishers.

It is important to understand that this chapter is not an endorsement or advertisement. Many excellent suppliers are not discussed here. Moreover, the information is presented largely as it is given to prospective clients by the suppliers themselves. Therefore, editorializing is minimized. Suffice it to say that there are enough war stories around so that, before using one of these services, it makes sense to talk to some past users.

Research suppliers provide two basic types of service: standard/syndicated and custom. An excellent extensive summary of standard services for consumer packaged goods is provided by Curry (1993). Here, we highlight some of these as well as some custom and business-to-business services offered by the largest research suppliers.

DATA SOURCES
Retail Scanner Data

Two companies dominate the scanner business: IRI (which first introduced the service) and Nielsen. Ironically, in 1979, IRI founders John Malec and Gerry Eskin (a professor, no less) were told by Nielsen that their concept for a new product was not viable (Kreisman, 1985). These firms battle for both clients and employees, which both switch between the two suppliers.

Scanner data are collected in two separate forms (household level and store level) and for two distinct sets of clients (manufacturers and retailers). In addition, three other sets of data are also maintained:

1. Prices, features, and displays at the retail level
2. Coupons and other promotions
3. Advertising (TV, print, radio)

Most of the data come from in-store scanners and households who use "special shopper" cards at the checkout. At the store level, both Nielsen (Scantrack) and IRI (InfoScan) utilize samples of several thousand supermarkets spread over 50-plus markets. Within each market, scanned stores generally have sales over $2 million and account for over 80 percent of all commodity volume (ACV) in the market. IRI has a larger number of households (60,000+) per market in total. In addition, IRI and Nielsen also get scanned data from drugstores. They also collect data using in-home scanners. Panel members use these to scan products once they are home. This allows collection of data based on purchases at nonscanned stores. On the other hand, it requires more effort on the part of panel members, and hence the possibility of mis- or nonscanned purchases increases. Household-level scanning represents another major data source. IRI had more than 600,000 households in the panel in 1995.

In addition to the major scanning services, IRI's Behavior Scan collects data in six smaller, more self-contained markets (e.g., Eau Claire, Wis.). Using a panel of 3,000 per market, this service allows for testing alternative marketing programs (e.g., in-store promotions and, through special TV devices, advertising at the household level).

Both Nielsen and IRI offer a number of special reports and modeling services based on these data. For example, IRI's Promotion Scan focuses on trade and consumer promotion, while Nielsen's SCAN*PRO concentrates on in-store prices and displays as well as newspaper advertising.

Retail Audits

In the 1970s and 1980s, the biggest part of the Nielsen portfolio was its auditing service, covering food, drug, mass merchandise, and alcoholic beverage outlets. Scanner panel data have now largely replaced audit data in food and drug outlets. Still, audit data continue to be used in some areas (e.g., to measure snack items in gas stations and mom-and-pop stores, as well as alcoholic beverage sales in liquor stores). Moreover, since the auditing service was responsible for Nielsen's position as the largest research supplier, and the method is still applicable to areas where scanner data are inadequate, a discussion of the auditing system is presented here.

The heart of the system was in-store audits. Every two months, an auditor (there were more than 500 of them) arrived at each store in the sample and recorded

Beginning inventory

Ending inventory

Purchases

Price at date of audit plus special prices (if any)

Distribution (if stocked and levels)

Deals (factory packs)

Local advertising

Displays

Total sales (all products)

In addition, major media advertising (newspaper, magazines, network TV, and spot TV) was also monitored. For each brand, sales were estimated, as shown in Figure 4A.2

	For June–July	
	Packages	Value
Inventory:		
May 30	114	
July 30	93	
Change	21	
Purchases:		
From manufacturer (1 order)	12	$ 3.72
From wholesalers (4 orders)	48	15.00
Total	60	$18.72
Consumer sales:		
Packages	81	
Price, per package		$ 0.39
Dollars, total		31.59
Adv. 1 2 3 4 5		
6 7 8 9		
Display X		Selling price, 39¢
		Special price, 35¢

FIGURE 4A.2
Principles of Nielsen Retail Index Auditing ("Alpha" Brand of Spot Remover–3 Ounces in Super X Market)
Source: *Nielsen Retail Index Services* (A. C. Nielsen Company, 1975). Reprinted with the permission of the ACNielsen Corporation.

The audit period actually ran over several weeks. Auditing began about two weeks before the end of the bimonthly period and continued two weeks after the next one started. Hence, the auditing cycle looked like the following:

February–March Period							
	First (Prior) Audit				*Second (Post) Audit*		
	Jan. 10,	*Jan. 11,*	*... ,*	*Feb. 12*	*Mar. 10,*	*Mar. 11,*	*... ,*	*Apr. 12*
Store group 1	x				x			
Store group 2		x				x		
Store group 3			. .				. .	
		:						
Store group n				x				x

Sales in the February–March bimonthly period were thus a "smoothed" average of sales January 10–March 10, January 11–March 11, and so forth, through February 12–April 12. This average was an annoying problem in certain modeling endeavors, especially in estimating the effectiveness of advertising and promotion (Shoemaker and Pringle, 1980).

The sample used for the audit was a set panel of stores. Stores were recruited and induced to participate based on (*a*) an appeal for cooperation in the spirit of learning, (*b*) information provided to the stores about trends in business, and (*c*) monetary compensation (an above-the-table payment).

Until 1976, 1,600 stores were included in the grocery index. These stores were grouped into five categories and selected disproportionately to reflect the sales volume accounted for by five store types, rather than just their number—see Figure 4A.3. In early 1976, the sample of stores was changed (*a*) to reflect changes in the market and (*b*) to cut cost. The new

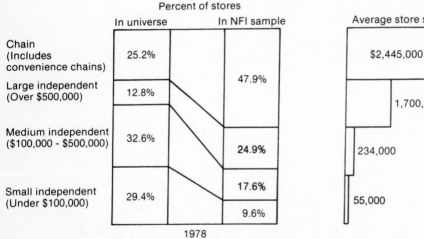
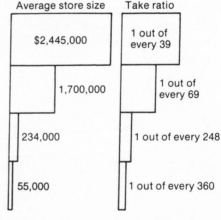

FIGURE 4A.3

Disproportionate Sampling Concept

Source: "Management with the Nielsen Retail Index System" (A. C. Nielsen Company, 1980): 11. Reprinted with the permission of the AC Nielsen Corporation.

sample of 1,300 stores (fewer stores means less cost) differed mainly in that A & P stores were now included, and many mom-and-pop stores were eliminated. For a single two-month period, both the old and new stores were monitored. This was supposed to provide a means of assurance that the sample change did not affect the results. For most brands, the national results were in fact stable (i.e., the share in the old sample was 29.1 versus 28.9 in the new sample). For some brands, however, national shares changed by three or four points. Since a difference of this size means a lot in terms of profits (and jobs retained or lost), a big question arose about which share was correct.

Special-purpose audits are still often used for specific market tests, especially when a test occurs in a limited market area. Audits and Surveys, Burgoyne, Ehrhart-Babic, and Westat all provide such services. For example, Elrick and Lavidge developed a computerized audit panel of 1,000 stores that sell consumer electronics to track that industry.

Warehouse Audits

Warehouse (as opposed to retail) audits used to be another staple of packaged goods research in the United States. These audits focus on an intermediary in the value/distribution chain (e.g., wholesalers) and have value in areas of the world (e.g., Eastern Europe) where accurate retail-level data are unavailable. The best-known syndicated service of this type was maintained by SAMI (Selling Area Markets, Inc.). Audits of withdrawals from central warehouses were conducted every four weeks. While there was a lag between warehouse and actual customer sales (and sometimes a disconnect if the product didn't sell at all), the system provided a low-cost way to estimate sales and gauge distribution by retail stores.

Two major factors doomed warehouse audits for packaged goods. First, scanner-based retail data provided faster and more accurate measures of consumer response to market conditions. Second, ECR (efficient customer response) initiatives made the role of the wholesaler less pivotal as inventory moved directly from manufacturers such as P&G to retailers such as Wal-Mart. In the end, SAMI's main asset, its client list and historical data, was sold to IRI for $7 million, and the service terminated in 1989.

Diary Purchase Panels

Diary panels are an older and, in the absence of accurate scanner data, the most obvious way to assess household purchasing behavior. Given the effort involved, it is more difficult to recruit members for such panels (would you rather join a panel where you get a discount or bonus for presenting a card to the cashier or had to record by hand all your purchases?). The chances for misreporting are also greater than for a scanner panel. Still, diary panels exist. For example, NPD maintains a panel of 16,000 households that record purchases in 20 categories. A sample format appears in Figure 4A.4.

Most diary panels now are created for special purposes. Often, members are recruited by mail. Dropout rates can be 40–50 percent, an obvious potential source of bias. These can be one-shot panels, as in the NFO example in Figure 4A.5.

MRCA specializes in diary panel data. The Menu Census is MRCA's best-known service. Two thousand households are queried about what they typically eat and drink. The households report for a period of 14 days by filling in a daily menu diary, 500 doing so each quarter. The information includes the following:

1. Every food dish served at home plus time of day served

2. Food eaten away from home

PAGE 1

TOYS & GAMES/HOBBY & CRAFT PURCHASES - For Children & Adults

Include ALL ELECTRONIC TOYS, VIDEO GAMES, TRADING CARDS & BICYCLES.
Report ALL JUVENILE and CHILDREN'S BOOKS on Page 2.

STORE CODES

01	Book Store	50	Electronics Store
10	Department Store	60	Restaurant
20	Mail Order	65	5 & 10/Variety
21	Hobby Store	70	Grocery/Supermarket
22	Gift/Card/Stationary	80	Drug
24	Sporting Goods	85	Catalog Showroom
26	Gas Station	90	Door to Door
28	Hardware	95	Warehouse Club
30	Discount	97	Home Shopping via TV
40	Video Store	99	Other
45	Toy Store		

SPECIAL OFFER CODES

1 Manufacturer Coupon
2 Store Coupon
3 Store Sale
4 Manufacturer Rebate
5 Other Special Offer

CATEGORY CODE GUIDE

10 Infant Toys: Activity Centers, Crib Toys, Mobiles, Rattles, Etc.
14 Role Playing/Home Making: Appliances, Dress Up Sets, Kitchen Sets, Hairdresser Sets, Mowers, Play Make-Up &, Jewelry, Play Phones, Play Tools, Toy Guns/Weapons, Etc.
16 Audio/Visual Toys: Microphones, Radios, Slide Viewers/Reels, Etc.
18 Musical Toys: Instrument Replicas, Musical Instruments, Etc.
22 Dolls & Accessories: Baby, Collectible, Fashion, Mini Dolls, Doll Accessories, Doll Clothes, Doll Houses, Etc.
26 Stuffed Toys/Puppets: All Plush Including Animated, Musical, Talking, Plush, Etc.
30 Action Figures/Accessories: Action Hero, Military, Robot, Space, Warrior Figures, Etc.
38 Building & Construction Toys
42 Remote Controlled Vehicles: Aircraft, Boats, Cars, Trucks, Etc. (Connected By Wire)
46 Radio Controlled Vehicles: Aircraft, Boats, Cars, Trucks, Etc. (No Wire Connection)
54 Wind Up / Friction Vehicles: Aircraft, Boats, Cars, Trucks, Etc. Powered By Friction, Rubber Bands, Wind Up Mechanism, Etc.
58 Other Vehicles: All Other Aircraft, Boats, Cars, Trucks, Etc.
60 Vehicle Playsets & Accessories
62 Electric Cars/Trains & Accessories
64 Video Games & Accessories: Learning Aids, Flash Cards, Globe, Letters, Magnetic Letters, Telescopes, Etc.
65 Games: All Games For Children
66 Puzzles: Cardboard, Foam, Plastic, Wood, Etc.
67 Children's VCR Videos
74 Educational Toys: Electronic Learning Aids, Flash Cards, Globe, Letters, Magnetic Letters, Telescopes, Etc.
78 Arts & Crafts: Crayons, Design Toys, Markers, Paint, Sculpture Kits, Sewing Kits, Etc.
80 Model & Accessories: Aircraft, Boat, Car, Truck, Etc. Model Kits & Supplies.
86 Junior Sports Equipment: Non-Professional Equipment: Fishing, Frisbees, Jump Ropes, Scooters, Skates, Sleds, Etc.
90 Bicycles/Ride Ons: Battery & Pedal Powered, Riding Vehicles, Push Toys for Children, Metal/Plastic Tricycle, Rocking Horses and Accessories, Etc.
99 All Other Toys: Suckles, Childrens Furniture, Exercise/Playground Equipment/Swing Sets, Pools, Trading Cards, Water Toys, Themed Sleeping Bags & All TOYS NOT MENTIONED ABOVE

SPECIAL QUESTIONS: Enter correct codes in far right columns above

Answer A – D for Both Toys & Games/Hobby & Craft and Juvenile Books

A. How is the receiver(s) of this Toy/Book related to the buyer? (Write in all numbers that apply)

CODE
01 Self
02 Daughter
03 Grandson
04 Granddaughter
05 Cousin
06 Niece
07 Nephew
16 Brother
13 Wife
14 Friend (No Relation)
15 Don't Know Recipient Yet
16 Son(s) and/or Daughter(s)
17 Grandson(s) and/or Granddaughter(s)
99 Other
10 Bought for Entire Family

B. Did you plan to buy this specific item in advance?

CODE
1 Yes
2 No

C. What was the occasion?

CODE
1 Christmas/ Chanukah
2 Easter
3 Birth of Baby
4 Birthday
5 Other Special Occasion
6 No Special Occasion

D. Did recipient influence purchase?

CODE
1 Asked for this Toy/Book by name
2 Asked for this Toy/Book
3 Had no direct influence

Answer E & F for Toys & Games/Hobby & Craft Only

E. How was the purchaser made aware of this item? (Enter one code)

CODE
1 Magazine Advertisement
2 Newspaper Advertisement
3 Newspaper Insert/Flyer
4 Recommendation
5 Recipient Asked for Item
6 Store Display
7 TV Advertisement
8 World Wide Web/Internet

F. What MOST influenced the final purchase decision? (Enter up to 2 codes in order of importance)

CODE
01 It's an Accessory/Refill
02 Adding to Collection
03 It's Educational/Developmental
04 Manufacturer Reputation
05 Price/Special Offer
06 Quality/Durability
07 Recipient Asked for Specific Item
08 Recipient Likes this Type of Toy
09 Specific Character
98 Other Influence
99 No Direct Influence

Answer G & H for Juvenile Books Only

G. Is the book...

CODE
1 Hard Covered with Paper Pages
2 Hard Covered with Board Pages inside?
3 Soft Covered?

H. Is the item...

CODE
1 A Book?
2 A Book and Record Set?
3 A Book and Cassette Set?
4 A Book with Sound Pad?

FIGURE 4A.4
Diary Panel Format

Source: Reprinted with permission of American Shoppers Panel, 1979.

3. Items added to a dish
4. How item was served (main dish, dessert, etc.)
5. Who prepared the meal
6. Who ate the meal
7. Leftovers
8. Cooking fats and oils used as frying agents; flour used for dusting
9. Brand name of packaged products used and type (ready-to-eat, canned, etc.)
10. How the dish was cooked
11. Recipes used

In addition to actual food usage and preparation, other data collected include the following:

1. Diet status of household members
2. Attitudes, interests, and opinions about homemaking, nutrition, etc.
3. Demographic data

Standby Panels

A number of firms maintain panels of respondents who agree in advance to participate in surveys, typically by mail or phone. Response rates within the panels tend to be high (70–80 percent) and a variety of demographic and lifestyle information is already available on members. Further, the panels are matched to the general population in terms of age, income, etc. On the other hand, the recruitment rate is less than 50 percent (10–15 percent is closer), leading to concerns about selection bias (people who like answering surveys may not be typical) and maturation/conditioning (if overused, the respondents become professional survey takers). Four firms maintain large panels of this type: NFO, NPD, MARC, and Market Facts. For example, NFO has 450,000 members (one of every 224 U.S. households), and Market Facts more than 400,000.

Special-Purpose Panels

Syndicated specialty panels are also widespread. For example, NFO has diary-based panels on beverage consumption, pleasure travel, and carpet and rug purchases. Other panels focus on specific groups (e.g., Hispanic Americans).

Omnibus Surveys

The Simmons Study of Media and Markets is a massive study of 23,000 adults. Data collection includes two home interviews, a booklet about the use of more than 800 products and services, and diaries. Media studied include magazines (where participants are taken through the magazine to assess aided recall), newspapers (based on reported "yesterday reading"), television (based on two-week diaries), radio (based on "yesterday listening"), outdoor advertising, and Yellow Pages usage. Information on respondents' demographics and psychographic and lifestyle indicators (VALS) are also collected. Segmentation is available via Prizm (Claritas) and Acorn (CACI) demographic clusters and VALS lifestyle segments. Data are available in the form of printed reports and direct online access. Special surveys of 2,000 children (ages 6–14), 2,500 teenagers (12–19), and 10,000 Hispanic Americans are also conducted. A similar and competing service is offered by MRI (part of NDP Information Group).

SAMPLE CONCEPT TEST

Automated e-mail Responder (AeR)

The electronic age brings new headaches for the busy executives—junk e-mails. Now a group of acclaimed computer scientists have used the latest technology to develop a software which saves time of busy executives by automatically responding to e-mails.

What is AeR and How does it work?

AeR is an expert system based on pattern recognition technology. After you install this software, it works in three phases: learning, testing, and actual operation. In the learning phase, you respond to e-mails as usual and AeR "learns" from your way of responding. In the testing phase, AeR responds to e-mails and asks you to approve or disapprove the way it responded. AeR then adjusts its response style. Once you are satisfied, AeR is ready for actual operation where it automatically responds to most of your e-mails. If unsure about an e-mail, the software leaves it for you to respond.

Based on this description, please answer the following questions.

1. How attractive do you find the idea behind this software?

   ❏ Very Attractive
   ❏ Somewhat attractive
   ❏ Slightly attractive
   ❏ Not attractive at all

2. In your opinion, how unique is this software?

   ❏ Very unique
   ❏ Somewhat unique
   ❏ Slightly unique
   ❏ Not at all unique

FIGURE 4A.5

3. If this software were available for a reasonable price, how likely are you to buy it?

❑ I will definitely buy

❑ I will probably buy

❑ I might or might not buy

❑ I will probably not buy

❑ I will definitely not buy

4. Which software package (e-mail) would this need to work with for you to consider purchasing AeR

❑ GroupWise

❑ cc Mail

❑ Eudora

❑ Lotus Notes

❑ other _____

5. Would an automatic response function to your pager or cell phone for emergency e-mails be an attractive feature?

❑ Very attractive

❑ Somewhat attractive

❑ Slightly attractive

❑ Not attractive at all

6. Were you to receive an AeR response to one of your requests, would you be:

❑ offended

❑ insulted

❑ pleased

❑ neutral

FIGURE 4A.5 *(continued)*

The survey booklets used contain about 100 pages of questions about media and product use, travel, and eating outside the home.

Special-Purpose Surveys

A large number of firms offer capabilities to execute surveys. While mail surveys are common, most work is now done via telephone. Phone surveys are collected via central location phone centers, many with 100 or more calling stations. Central locations allow for control over interviewers. Control is also maintained by computer-generated interviewing (Computer Assisted Telephone Interviewing, or CATI). Some of the larger firms offering such services include Westat/Crossley Surveys, Maritz, NPD, NFO, Elrick and Lavidge, Market Facts, M/A/R/C, Walker, Abt, MRB/Winona, Bruskin (part of NOP Information Group), Intersearch, Millward Brown (part of WPP), Opinion Research, Burke, Roper-Starch, and Research International. Many of these firms (e.g., Walker and Maritz), offer specialized services in the important area of satisfaction measurement. They also maintain samples of special groups of respondents ranging from doctors and dog owners to those who eat away from home (e.g., NPD CREST). For example, besides a Hispanic panel, NFO maintains special panels on households that have *recently moved*, households with *new babies and expectant mothers*, households with members *over 50*, and a panel of 150,000 households with members with 60 different *chronic ailments* (allergies, Alzheimer's disease, angina, . . .). Market Facts weekly surveys 500 mall shoppers.

Multiclient (Cooperative) Surveys

Many firms produce surveys that allow a client at a low cost to add one or two questions to a periodic survey. For example, Market Facts offered TELENATION, a weekly survey of 1,000 American consumers at a 1994 cost of $750 for a closed-end question, $1,200 for an open-end question with a precoded response list, and $1,400 for a general open-end question. Standard demographic questions (Figure 4A.6) are also asked. Turnaround is rapid, with results available Wednesday for questions turned in the previous Friday.

Media Measurement

In addition to the general media information available from the surveys by Simmons and MRI, specific audience measurement services are available. The best-known media rating service is Nielsen's TV ratings, which has withstood competitive offerings, including one by AGB in the early 1990s, and remains the standard for measuring television audiences.

Arbitron is well known for its diary panel-based measures of radio audiences (Figure 4A.7). Arbitron specializes in measuring media (radio and TV) audiences on a local basis. It dominates radio audience measurement as Nielsen does TV; its main competitor, Birch, ceased operations in 1991. Data are collected on a regional basis and grouped, among other ways, according to a measure called ADI (area of dominant influence). The basis for this breakdown is areas where media (radio and TV stations) reach from the "center" of the area. Hence, a county is included in the area from which the majority of its radio or television programs are broadcast.

Data were once collected exclusively by diaries. The steps used in the radio diary panel are:

1. Preplacement letter (to listed numbers).
2. Placement phone call.
3. Diary mailed for each person in household, along with token ($1 per person) premium. (More is sent in minority households.)
4. Reminder call.
5. Letter containing additional dollar per household premium.

Telenation's interviews are conducted Friday through Sunday through Market Facts' proprietary research facilities.

Each interview consists of client-specific questions and standard demographic questions.

Standard Demographic Questions

All TELENATION respondents are first screened to ensure that they are 18 years or older, that no one in the household works in marketing research or marketing, and that they have not participated in a research survey in the past three months.

1. Are you the male/female head of household?

   Yes   No

2. Do you consider yourself to be the primary grocery shopper in your household?

   Yes   No   Don't know

3. May I please have your age as of your last birthday? (Do not read list unless respondent hesitates)

Under 25	45 to 49	65 to 74
25 to 34	50 to 54	75 to 84
35 to 44	55 to 64	85 or older

4. What was the last grade of school you completed? (Do not read.)

Completed grade school or less	Some high school, not completed
Completed high school	Some college, not completed
Completed college	Post graduate work started or completed

5. Are you...(Read list)

   Employed full-time   Employed part-time   Retired   Not employed

6. Are you married?

   Yes   No

7. How may people live in your household at the present time? Please include yourself and any babies.

   1, 2, 3, 4, 5, 6, 7, 8 (or more)

8. How many in your household are...

   Under six years old   6 through 12 years old   13 through 17 years old

9. Do you or does someone else in your household own your place of residence?

   Yes   No

10. Now I would like to read a series of income groups. Please stop me when I read the group that describes your total household income, from all sources, over the past year.

Under $15,000	$30,000 to less than $40,000
$15,000 to less than $20,000	$40,000 to less than $50,000
$20,000 to less than $25,000	$50,000 to less than $75,000
$25,000 to less than $30,000	$75,000 or more

11. Are you...

    White   Black   Asian   Member of another race

FIGURE 4A.6
Telenation's Approach to Research
Source: Reprinted with the permission of Market Facts, Inc.

Initial contact is made by phone to homes with up to four callbacks (five attempts) to each listed number in the sample and nine callbacks to unlisted numbers. Premiums are not mentioned in gaining cooperation. Names of sample members are drawn from the list maintained by Metro-Mail of households with listed telephone numbers. This is then augmented with numbers that are not listed and that appear to be residential phone numbers.

The sample size varies, depending on the size of the market. Standard market samples vary from 550 to 4,000, while condensed market samples range from 250 to 400 (Arbitron, 1987b).

For radio, every person age 12 or older is sent a diary. The diary covers one week, with a page for each day of the week (Figure 4A.7).

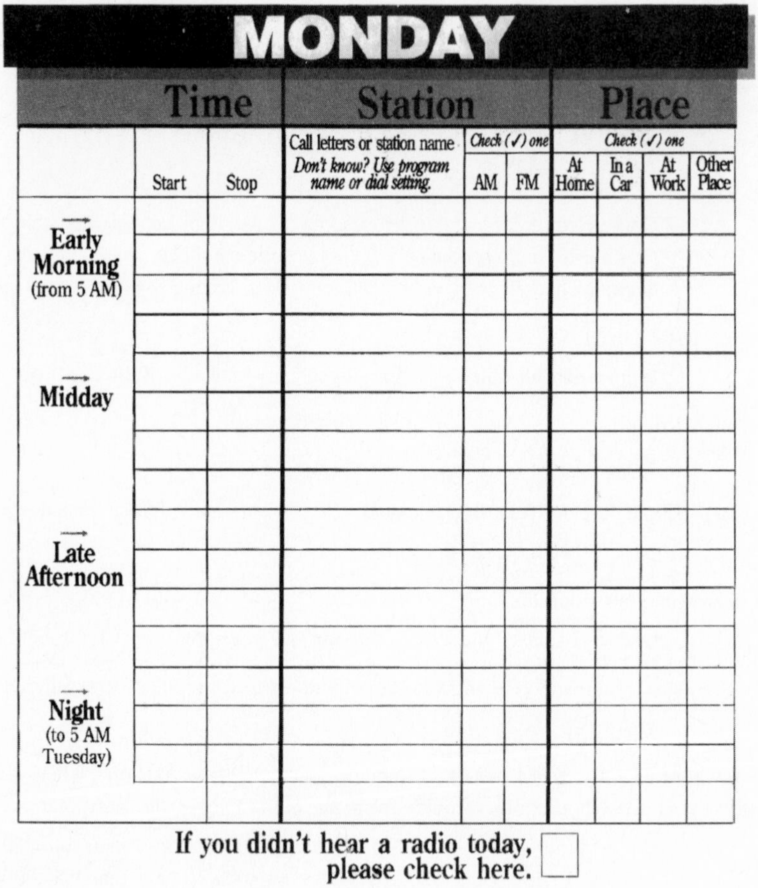

MONDAY

	Time		Station			Place			
			Call letters or station name *Don't know? Use program name or dial setting.*	*Check (✓) one*		*Check (✓) one*			
	Start	Stop		AM	FM	At Home	In a Car	At Work	Other Place
Early Morning (from 5 AM)									
Midday									
Late Afternoon									
Night (to 5 AM Tuesday)									

If you didn't hear a radio today, please check here. ☐

FIGURE 4A.7

Arbitron Ratings Radio Diary

Source: Arbitron Ratings/Radio, 1997. Copyright © 1997 by The Arbitron Company. Reprinted with the permission of Arbitron. No further reproduction permitted without the permission of Arbitron.

A major use of these data is in evaluating advertising alternatives. In each area, audience by station is estimated in hourly blocks of time as well as in larger aggregations (e.g., 6 A.M. to noon). For each period, the following are calculated:

1. Average *number* of persons listening
2. Average *rating* (average number/population of area)
3. Metro *share* (shares of listening audience)
4. *Cume persons* (number of persons who listen during at least some part of the time period, often called *Reach*)
5. *Cume ratings* (Cume persons/Population)

These numbers are used to derive several key figures:

1. *Gross impressions* (Average number of persons × Number of spots of a given ad aired during the time period)
2. *Cost per thousand* (CPM = Cost/1,000 gross impressions)
3. *Gross rating points* (GRP = Average rating × Number of spots)
4. *Frequency* (Gross impressions/Cume persons)

The data are also used to rank stations and programs based on audiences. The makeup of station audiences is available in terms of basic demographics.

The television diary data are essentially the same as the radio data. Its diary is a bit more structured; other than that, though, the two services are basically twins. Television ratings based on diaries of one week in length are produced.

Another well-known media service comes from Worldwide Roper Starch. Starch is best known for its Starch Message Report. This report attempts to measure the impact of ads in magazines and newspapers. Between 100 and 150 men and 100 and 150 women over age 18 are interviewed. Only individuals who have read at least some part of the magazine issue being studied are used as respondents. For each ad studied, respondents are classified in terms of:

1. Nonreader (does not remember reading the ad)
2. Noted reader (remembers reading the ad)
3. Associated reader (remembers the brand or advertiser)
4. Read most (read more than half the ad)

The data are summarized for each individual ad, and also each ad is compared with other ads in the same issue in terms of both raw readership scores and readership/cost ratios.

Other well-known media measurement services are Burke's day-after TV ad recall scores, McCollum-Spielman's commercial tests, and ASI's commercial tests.

Focus Groups

Any firm that does custom research is almost certain to do focus group work. Some (e.g., M/A/R/C) even maintain a standby panel of respondents who, in addition to being available for personal and phone interviewing, will come to central locations (malls) for product testing or participation in focus groups.

Concept and Product Tests

IRI's ASSESSOR, BASES, and NPD's ESP are well-known new-product testing services. Screening of commercial or product concepts can be done through mailed videos. NFO in conjunction with ASI has such a service for copy testing where participants are interviewed by telephone 24 hours later, with the feature that once the material has been viewed, the tape self-destructs. Allowing people to view ads in a natural setting increases the realism but loses the control present in a controlled setting (e.g., ringing phones, barking dogs, and screaming kids).

Mercer offers an "information acceleration" service based on the work of Glen Urban at MIT. Essentially, this is designed to test significantly new products (e.g., electric cars) for which simple concept tests are not reliable. It provides (via computer/multimedia presentation) the respondent with information about the future environment, the opportunity to view the product in 3-D, actually seeing different parts of it (e.g., the engine, trunk, dashboard), and the option to get word-of-mouth reactions from various people. Currently such a study might cost $300,000—about double what the straightforward (no information acceleration) concept test would cost.

Probably the best-known product testing service is BASES. BASES specializes in simulated test markets. This service evaluates new product concepts and products (including mail-in surveys in partnership with NFO and markets in partnerships with IRI) in a controlled but realistic environment. It compares four basic measures (purchase intent, value, uniqueness, and intensity of liking) of reaction to a concept with its historical database of 5,000 cases in the United States and 3,000 in other countries to get a relative reaction to the product. Subjects expressing interest are given the product for testing and then contacted by phone for their reactions.

Medical

In order not to leave the impression that all services deal with consumer goods, we describe briefly the two major research suppliers to the medical industry: IMS, which is part of Nielsen and on its own would be the second (after Nielsen) largest research supplier in the world, and Walsh/PMSI.

IMS is the major supplier of research to the pharmaceutical industry, and it does a large portion of its business in countries other than the United States. Its services include the following:

> *Pharmaceutical market studies.* The purchases of a sample of 840 pharmacies, proprietary stores, and discount houses are audited and reported monthly. (This sample also provides data on toiletries and beauty aids.) Similarly, the purchases of 350 hospitals are audited. In addition, pharmaceutical warehouse withdrawal data are also collected.
>
> *Prescription Audit (NPA).* Based on a computerized panel of pharmacies, data on prescription volume, price, dosage information, and so forth, are collected weekly and reported biweekly, monthly, or quarterly.
>
> *National Disease and Therapeutic Index (NDTI).* Based on 2,100 physicians who report case histories over a 48-hour period four times a year, reports on drug use, diagnosis, etc., are prepared.

The New Product Digest. A monthly report on use during the first three months of introduction of new drugs, based on surveys of 360 office-based physicians.

National Mail Audit. A panel-based report of pharmaceutical mail received by the 300 panel members.

National Journal Audit. A monthly audit of advertising in 350 medical journals.

National Detailing Audit. Monthly reports of 2,800 office-based physicians on the personal selling activities of pharmaceutical sales representatives.

Audatrex. A sample of 1,000 physicians who provide copies of each prescription they write. A subpanel of 300 physicians (called Medilink) also furnishes qualitative information on heart-related disorders and musculoskeletal ailments (who said only researchers used big words?).

PMSI (Pharmaceutical Marketing Services, Inc.) similarly provides a number of services, including:

- A prescription report based on 3,000 retail pharmacies
- A nonretail sales database, based on deliveries to institutions such as hospitals, nursing homes, clinics, surgery centers, and HMOs
- A survey of physicians that focuses on prescribing behavior by therapy class and attitudes toward new products
- Basic data on medical professionals, pharmaceutical products, and managed care providers (HMOs, PPOs)

Other Services

The number of other services offered is huge. Some examples include

Market Facts' "Conversion Model". Basically, users and potential users are divided along a continuum: users are described as (1) entrenched, (2) average, (3) shallow, and (4) convertible (a.k.a. at risk) based on their brand loyalty/commitment. Nonusers range from (1) available to (2) ambivalent, (3) weakly unavailable, and (4) strongly unavailable (a.k.a. loyal to someone else).

J. D. Power car buyer and dealership surveys.

Survey Sampling specializing in (surprise) sample design.

Geodemographic descriptions of areas such as Cluster Plus, Acorn (CACI), Prizm (Claritas), and Vision (National Decision Systems).

The annual *MONITOR* study by Yankelovich Partners. This survey concentrates on basic values and social trends.

Dun and Bradstreet Business Marketing Services provides a variety of services to industrial markets. The most widely used is the Dun's Market Identifiers (DMI). This service is based on a data bank of more than 4 million businesses in the United States and Canada. The companies are grouped according to four-digit SIC codes. For example, at one time there were 7,130 truck rental and leasing firms (SIC code 7513), 2,919 metal door, sash, and trim firms (SIC code 3442); and 27 firms mining bauxite and aluminum ore (SIC code 1051).

The main use of this service has been for industrial marketers to estimate market potentials. The data are also used to help define sales territories and to pinpoint particularly good prospects as well as to provide a mailing list of potential customers. For each firm, 27 variables are available (Figure 4A.8). A customer selects the type of business he or she is interested in (typically described by geographic area or SIC code, or both, but sometimes by a variety of measures, such as sales volume or employment size). The customer then receives anything from the name of the businesses that pass the screen to a complete profile of each of the companies based on the 27 available variables, depending on how much they are willing to pay. The majority choose the "Sales Prospecting Service," which provides information as in Figure 4A.9.

While this list is by no means complete, we hope that it will give the reader a sense of the type of research available as well as the large number of suppliers. Besides, more complete coverage would have an unduly soporific effect on the author (and, no doubt, the few readers who have struggled to arrive at this point).

SUMMARY

This appendix has attempted to outline some of the major types of services available from suppliers. In using suppliers, it is important to note that performance should be carefully evaluated (Mayer, 1967). Numerous others exist, and many are quite specialized. For example, if you sell athletic shoes, you might use SMART—an audit service focused on 1,500 sporting good chains and athletic footwear specialty retailers offered by NPD.

While most of the major suppliers are honest, they are under time and profit pressures, which suggest continued involvement (but not harassment) on the part of the client is generally advisable from a quality control as well as an information perspective. Also, in using suppliers, be careful to check out exactly what is going on—this chapter is not gospel and did not attempt to list the many criticisms each of the services has encountered.

One final point concerns the use of "other brands." A variety of small research shops exist. Some are very competent (e.g., Sawtooth Software, which specializes in computer-designed interviewing and conjoint analysis). The disadvantages of using a small operator are (a) they will have to do more subcontracting, (b) they usually do not have the same experience base as larger operators, and (c) the results are less impressive to the average reader of the report if he or she has never heard of the company. On the other hand, small companies often have novel approaches to problems that may be particularly useful.

In the future, the research business seems destined to move toward increased concentration as well as the use of higher tech methods of data collection (e.g., scanners). Also, the use of sophisticated analytical methods seems to be increasing. (Marketing brochures of suppliers now casually mention sophisticated statistical procedures.) Finally, the next move for suppliers will be to provide hands-on decision-support programs in response to the information deluge facing managers. NPD has a brochure headlined by a quote from T. S. Eliot: "Where is the knowledge we have lost in the information?" The successful suppliers of the future will not only collect and analyze data, they will also convert it to a form that adds to knowledge rather than overwhelms it.

PROBLEMS

1. Why do you think companies, including big ones like General Foods, hire suppliers rather than gathering and analyzing data themselves?

Identification:
1. Name of establishment.
2. D-U-N-S number.
3. D-U-N-S number of headquarters.
4. D-U-N-S number of parent.

Classification:
5. Headquarters.
6. Branch.
7. Subsidiary.
8. Manufacturing or nonmanufacturing location.
9. Single or multiple location.

Location:
10. Street address.
11. Mailing address (if different).
12. Zip code.*
13. City.
14. Country code.
15. SMSA code.†
16. State (or province).
17. Telephone number.
18. Area code.

Products or services:
19. Primary line of business (SIC).
20. Up to five secondary SICs.

Size:
21. Sales volume.
22. Employees at this location.
23. Total employees.

Financial strength:
24. Net worth.‡
25. Credit rating.‡

Other:
26. Year the business started.
27. Chief executive (and title).

* First three digits of zip code denote sectional center.
† Standard metropolitan statistical area.
‡ Credit and net worth data available only to subscribers to the D & B Credit Service at an additional charge.

FIGURE 4A.8
Dun & Bradstreet Basic Marketing Facts
Source: Dun & Bradstreet, Inc., *Dun's Market Identifiers*, 1976. Copyright © 1976 by Dun & Bradstreet, Inc. Reprinted with the permission of Dun & Bradstreet, Information Services.

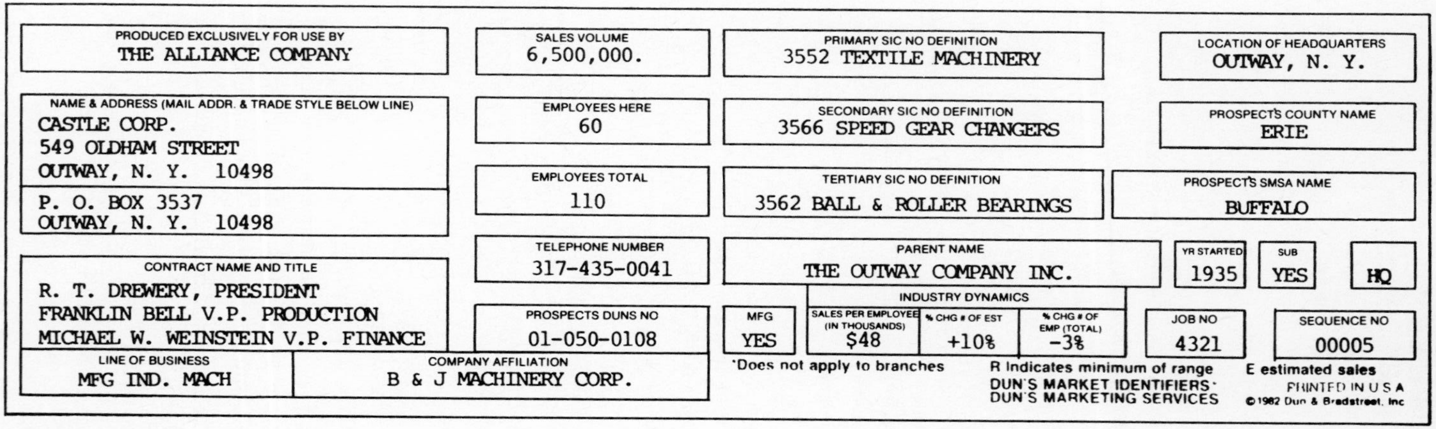
PRODUCED EXCLUSIVELY FOR USE BY
THE ALLIANCE COMPANY

SALES VOLUME
6,500,000.

PRIMARY SIC NO DEFINITION
3552 TEXTILE MACHINERY

LOCATION OF HEADQUARTERS
OUTWAY, N. Y.

NAME & ADDRESS (MAIL ADDR. & TRADE STYLE BELOW LINE)
CASTLE CORP.
549 OLDHAM STREET
OUTWAY, N. Y. 10498
P. O. BOX 3537
OUTWAY, N. Y. 10498

EMPLOYEES HERE
60

SECONDARY SIC NO DEFINITION
3566 SPEED GEAR CHANGERS

PROSPECT'S COUNTY NAME
ERIE

EMPLOYEES TOTAL
110

TERTIARY SIC NO DEFINITION
3562 BALL & ROLLER BEARINGS

PROSPECT'S SMSA NAME
BUFFALO

CONTRACT NAME AND TITLE
R. T. DREWERY, PRESIDENT
FRANKLIN BELL V.P. PRODUCTION
MICHAEL W. WEINSTEIN V.P. FINANCE

TELEPHONE NUMBER
317-435-0041

PARENT NAME
THE OUTWAY COMPANY INC.

YR STARTED
1935

SUB
YES

HQ

PROSPECTS DUNS NO
01-050-0108

MFG
YES

INDUSTRY DYNAMICS
SALES PER EMPLOYEE (IN THOUSANDS)
$48
% CHG # OF EST
+10%
% CHG # OF EMP (TOTAL)
-3%

JOB NO
4321

SEQUENCE NO
00005

LINE OF BUSINESS
MFG IND. MACH

COMPANY AFFILIATION
B & J MACHINERY CORP.

*Does not apply to branches
R Indicates minimum of range
E estimated sales
DUN'S MARKET IDENTIFIERS*
DUN'S MARKETING SERVICES
PRINTED IN U S A
©1982 Dun & Bradstreet, Inc

FIGURE 4A.9
Sample Business Profile
Source: Dun's Marketing Services. "Sales Prospecting Services," 1982. Copyright © 1982 by Dun & Bradstreet, Inc. Reprinted with the permission of Dun & Bradstreet, Information Services.

2. For each of the following problems, suggest the likely research approach(es) and at least two potential suppliers:

   a. Estimating the effect of a proposed TV advertising copy for shampoo
   b. Estimating eventual sales of a new food product now in test market
   c. Evaluating the appeal of various hypothetical product designs for a dishwasher
   d. Understanding how consumers approach the decision to purchase a house
   e. Studying the use of a new drug by physicians
   f. Measuring the closeness of competition between two food products

3. Interpret the following audit share data, assuming you were brand manager for Znarts:

Total U.S.	Brand	Brand Share by Store				
		A & P	Finast	Grand Union	Other Chains	Others
18%	Znarts	12%	18%	17%	21%	16%
25	A	19	28	32	25	28
18	B	21	18	15	20	16
28	C	31	30	26	24	28
4	Other	3	3	5	4	10
5	Private label	15	3	5	6	2
100%						

4. Assume you were monitoring sales in a region and found the following results concerning market share:

	Jan.– Feb. 1978	Mar.– Apr. 1978	May– June 1978	July– Aug. 1978	Sept.– Oct. 1978	Nov.– Dec. 1978	Jan.– Feb. 1979
Audit data	29%	29%	28%	30%	32%	31%	30%
Panel data	29	28	27	28	31	29	33

   a. Is anything happening?
   b. If so, what might be the explanation for the data?

5. Assume you switched suppliers for audit data and overlapped suppliers for one period. The estimated shares were as follows:

	Jan.– Feb. 1978	Mar.– Apr. 1978	May– June 1978	July– Aug. 1978	Sept.– Oct. 1978	Nov.– Dec. 1978	Jan.– Feb. 1979	Mar.– Apr. 1979	May– June 1979
Old Supplier	29.2	28.7	26.9	27.3	28.3	27.9	28.1	27.0	—
New supplier	—	—	—	—	—	—	—	29.2	30.0

a. Are we better or worse off than we were one year ago in May–June (and by how much)?

b. What do you expect to happen to share next period (July–August)?

c. Suggest how you might estimate what sales in July–August 1978 would have been under the new supplier.

6. Which brand is doing better?

Brand	Percent of Distribution ACV	Sales Units
A	70%	18,000
B	90	23,000

7. Assume I wanted to know how much a new brand would cannibalize sales of an existing brand. What research methods might be employed?

8. Explain the calculations of reach, frequency, and gross rating points. How accurate do you think the calculations are and what does this accuracy depend on? Under what circumstances would each be the appropriate objective to maximize in setting a media advertising schedule?

9. Given the breakdown on sterling silver flatware purchase by magazine readership (shown on p. 125), how would you go about constructing a magazine advertising schedule?

10. Assess the effect of the 80-cents-off coupon run by Wisk in the second four-week period of the following data compiled by AdTel from their panel:

	Period							
	1	2	3	4	5	6	7	8
Total share	4.7	6.4	16.5	10.6	5.4	4.6	4.5	5.8
Deal share	0.7	3.3	11.7	7.9	1.8	0.6	1.2	1.9
Nondeal share	4.0	3.1	4.8	2.7	3.6	4.0	3.3	3.9

Source: reprinted with permission from AdTel, Inc., New York.

11. Interpret the following data based on a two-year AdTel study (July 1969-1971). The data show percent of Brand Buyers' Total Furniture Polish Volume accounted for by their favorite brand.

Favorite Brand	Favorite Brand Share of Total Purchases
Lemon Pledge	41.5%
Regular Pledge	34.4
Favor	34.1
Behold	32.7
Pride	31.1
Jubilee	30.2
Old English	28.8
Endust	22.9

Average Issue Audience

Flatware—Place Settings Personally Purchased, Amount Spent, and Purpose of Purchase in Last Year
Total Adults (in thousands)

	U.S. Total	American Baby	American Home	Barron's	Better Homes & Gardens	Business Week	Car & Driver	Cosmopolitan	Esquire	Family Circle	Family Week-	Field & Stream	Forbes	Fortune	Girl Talk	Glamour
Total	14,9056	1,871	4,446	1,054	24,743	3,837	3,180	9,498	4,634	20,908	18,451	10,061	1,773	1661	1,320	7,256
Rating	100.0	1.3	3.0	.7	16.6	2.6	2.1	6.4	3.1	14.0	12.4	6.7	1.2	1.1	.9	4.9

Bought flatware
(Sterling, Silver Plate, Stainless)

	U.S. Total	American Baby	American Home	Barron's	Better Homes & Gardens	Business Week	Car & Driver	Cosmopolitan	Esquire	Family Circle	Family Week-	Field & Stream	Forbes	Fortune	Girl Talk	Glamour
in last year	11,233	**102	591	**39	2590	383	*261	956	544	2,242	1,648	682	174	154	**107	847
PCT. comp.	7.5	5.5	13.3	3.7	10.5	10.0	8.2	10.1	11.7	10.7	8.9	6.8	9.8	9.3	8.1	11.7
Index	100	73	177	49	140	133	109	135	156	143	119	91	131	124	108	156
Rating	100.0	.9	5.3	.3	23.1	3.4	2.3	8.5	4.8	20.0	14.7	6.1	1.5	1.4	1.0	7.5

Place settings
Bought less

	U.S. Total	American Baby	American Home	Barron's	Better Homes & Gardens	Business Week	Car & Driver	Cosmopolitan	Esquire	Family Circle	Family Week-	Field & Stream	Forbes	Fortune	Girl Talk	Glamour
than 8	4,088	**50	*260	**9	1,001	*95	*109	319	*219	765	654	*226	**54	*104	**39	324
PCT comp	2.7	2.7	5.8	.9	4.0	2.5	3.4	3.4	4.7	3.7	3.5	2.2	3.0	6.3	3.0	4.5
Index	100	100	215	33	148	93	126	126	174	137	130	81	111	233	111	167
Rating	100.0	1.2	6.4	.2	24.5	2.3	2.7	7.8	5.4	18.7	16.0	5.5	1.3	2.5	1.0	7.9
Bought 8	5,173	**33	*244	**17	1,031	*204	**118	454	*227	926	644	345	**65	**36	**50	396
PCT comp	3.5	1.8	5.5	1.6	4.2	5.3	3.7	4.8	4.9	4.4	3.5	3.4	3.7	2.2	3.8	5.5
Index	100	51	157	46	120	151	106	137	140	126	100	97	106	63	109	157
Rating	100.0	.6	4.7	.3	19.9	3.9	2.3	8.8	4.4	17.9	12.4	6.7	1.3	.7	1.0	7.7
Bought 9 or more	1,972	**18	**87	**13	557	**84	**33	*182	**98	551	*350	**112	**55	**15	**19	**127
PCT comp	1.3	1.0	2.0	1.2	2.3	2.2	1.0	1.9	2.1	2.6	1.9	1.1	3.1	.9	1.4	1.8
Index	100	77	154	92	177	169	77	146	162	200	146	85	238	69	108	138
Rating	100.0	.9	4.4	.7	28.2	4.3	1.7	9.2	5.0	27.9	17.7	5.7	2.8	.8	1.0	6.4

Amount spent

	U.S. Total	American Baby	American Home	Barron's	Better Homes & Gardens	Business Week	Car & Driver	Cosmopolitan	Esquire	Family Circle	Family Week-	Field & Stream	Forbes	Fortune	Girl Talk	Glamour
Less than $40	6,889	**66	*288	**8	1,427	*189	**191	560	349	1,247	901	352	*106	*112	**48	469
PCT comp	4.6	3.5	6.5	.8	5.8	4.9	6.0	5.9	7.5	6.0	4.9	3.5	6.0	6.7	3.6	6.5
Index	100	76	141	17	126	107	130	128	163	130	107	76	130	146	78	141
Rating	100.0	1.0	4.2	.1	20.7	2.7	2.8	8.1	5.1	18.1	13.1	5.1	1.5	1.6	.7	6.8
$40 or more	4,343	**36	*303	**31	1,163	195	**69	396	*196	995	748	330	*69	*42	**59	378
PCT comp	2.9	1.9	6.8	2.9	4.7	5.1	2.2	4.2	4.2	4.8	4.1	3.3	3.9	2.5	4.5	5.2
Index	100	66	234	100	162	176	76	145	145	166	141	114	134	86	155	179
Rating	100.0	.8	7.0	.7	26.8	4.5	1.6	9.1	4.5	22.9	17.2	7.6	1.6	1.0	1.4	8.7

Source: W.R. Simmons and Associates Research, 1976/77, *The Study of Selective Markets and the Media Reaching Them*, New York ©1977.

12. Interpret Figure 4A.10 and the following table, both taken from AdTel results. What other data sources could be used to collect such data?

Deal Loyalty			
	Ajax	*Comet*	*Total Scouring Cleanser*
Brand buyers puchasing 50 percent or more of brand volume on deal	27.1%	17.1%	15.9%
Volume accounted for by buyers purchasing 50 percent or more of brand volume on deal	20.1	9.9	11.5
Brand buyers puchasing 80 percent or more of brand volume on deal	17.7	9.1	5.1
Volume accounted for by buyers purchasing 80 percent or more of brand volume on deal	10.6	3.4	2.9

Source: reprinted with permission from AdTel, Inc., New York.

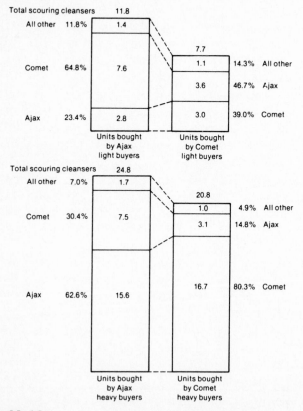

FIGURE 4A.10

Combination Buying Patterns Among Heavy/Light Buyers of Scouring Cleanser (equivalent units bought during two-year period)

Source: Reprinted with permission from AdTel, Inc., New York.

13. Using scanner data in Kansas City, a company found its share was 14 percent and increasing. Audit data put share at 10 percent and constant. A diary panel indicated share was 9 percent and dropping. Company sales records indicated sales were 150 percent of the level reported by the diary panel. SAMI warehouse withdrawal showed a 12 percent share.

a. Explain why these measures can differ.

b. Suggest a logical (as opposed to methodological) explanation for the results.

14. What does this purchase record suggest this consumer is doing?

Actual Purchase Record—Margarine

N.CP. Family: #46141–Product Class: 34–Size: 00100

	Day of Purchase	Type	Units	Deal	Price	Outlet	Weight
Mazola	7–7	02	1	X	$.36	13	1.00
Mazola	8–4	02	1		.43	12	1.00
Imperial	8–8	00	1	X	.36	60	1.00
Gold O'Corn	8–9	02	1		.35	12	1.00
Gold O'Corn	9–19	02	1	X	.35	12	1.00
Nucoa	9–21	00	1		.30	12	1.00
Gold O'Corn	9–22	02	1	X	.35	01	1.00
Miracle	9–26	00	1		.35	12	1.00
Fleischmann's	9–28	02	1	X	.33	12	1.00
Fleischmann's	10–6	02	1	X	.35	12	1.00
Gold O'Corn	10–12	02	1		.35	60	1.00
Gold O'Corn	10–13	02	1		.35	12	1.00
Gold O'Corn	11–2	02	1		.35	12	1.00
Golden Glow	11–15	03	1	X	.35	12	1.00
Gold O'Corn	11–24	02	1		.35	60	1.00
Golden Glow	11–27	03	1	X	.35	12	1.00
Fleischmann's	12–7	02	1	X	.34	12	1.00
Gold O'Corn	12–15	02	1	X	.35	12	1.00
Fyne Spread	12–20	00	2		.35	12	2.00

Source: Market Research Corporation of America, *National Consumer Panel Diary*, p.1.

REFERENCES

AdTel (1973) "How to Test and Measure the Sales Effectiveness of Television Advertising and Consumer Promotion," New York.

Arbitron Ratings Company (1987a) "A Guide to Understanding and Using Radio Audience Estimates," New York.

—— (1987b) "Radio Description of Methodology," New York.

—— (1987c) "Television Description of Methodology," New York.

Arbitron Television Research (1976) "Diary of Television Viewing," New York, November 3.

ASSESSOR (1994) "Sales Forecasts Marketing Insight ... and More," M/A/R/C Group, Irving, Tex.

Audits and Surveys (1987) "What Can We Do for You?" New York.

BASES Group (1994a) "BASES by Mail," Covington, Ky.

—— (1994b) promotional material, Covington, Ky.

BASES Group/NFO (1994) "Turning Ideas into Winners," Covington, Ky.

Burke Marketing Research (1994a) "Burke Marketing Research," Cincinnati.

—— (1994b) "Burke Qualitative Services," Cincinnati.

—— (1994c) "Customer Satisfaction—Are Your Customers Secure?" Cincinnati.

Curry, David J. (1993) *The New Marketing Research Systems*, New York: John Wiley and Sons.

Data User News, Washington, D.C.: U.S. Department of Commerce, Bureau of the Census, published monthly.

Dun & Bradstreet Corporation (1976) "Dun's Market Identifiers," New York.

—— (1986) "1986 Annual Report," New York.

Elrick and Lavidge, Inc. (1994) promotional material, Tucker, Ga.

Eskin, Gerald J. (1973) "Dynamic Forecasts of New Product Demand Using a Depth of Repeat Model," *Journal of Marketing Research*, 10, May, 115–29.

"Factfinder for the Nation" (1982) Washington, D.C.: U.S. Department of Commerce, Bureau of the Census, No. 18, December.

Green Book. New York: American Marketing Association, New York Chapter, published annually.

Honomichl, Jack J. (1986) "Ranking Top Players in Growing Global Arena," *Advertising Age*, 57, November 24, S-1–S-2.

—— (1996) "1996 Business Report on the Marketing Research Industry," *Marketing News*, June 3, H1–H39.

Information Resources, Inc. (1994a) 1993 Annual Report, Chicago.

—— (1994b) "The Difference in Decision Making," Chicago.

Kreisman, Richard (1985) "Buy the Numbers," *INC. Magazine*, 7, March, 718–21.

M/A/R/C, Inc. (1994a) "The M/A/R/C Group, 1994 second quarter report," Irving, Tex.

—— (1994b) "M/A/R/C Power," Irving, Tex.

Maritz Marketing Research, Inc. (1994) "The Fine Art of Marketing Research," Fenton, Mo.

Market Facts, Inc. (1994a) "The Conversion Model," Arlington Heights, Ill.

—— (1994b) "MarkeTest 2000," Chicago.

—— (1994c) "Market Facts—The Right Combination," Arlington Heights, Ill.

—— (1994d) "TeleNation National Telephone Research," Chicago.

—— (1994e) "TeleNation Overnight!" Chicago.

—— (1994f) "Two Ways to Make Better Marketing Decisions While Conserving Your Research Budget," Chicago.

Market Facts—New York, Inc. (1994) "National Show Case," New York.

Market Research Corporation of America (no date) "MRCA Reporting Systems," Chicago.

—— (no date) "The National Consumer Panel," Chicago.

—— (no date) "The National Household Menu," Chicago.

Mayer, Charles S. (1967) "Evaluating the Quality of Market Research Contractors," *Journal of Marketing Research*, 4, May, 134–41.

Mediamark Research, Inc. (1987) "Mediamark Research," New York.

NFO Research, Inc. (1994a) *NFO Outlook*, 5, Spring, New York.

—— (1994b) "NFO Research, Inc.," Greenwich, Conn.

—— (1994c) "NFO's Consumer Panel Helps You . . .," Greenwich, Conn.

—— (1994d) "Targeted Copy Testing...," Greenwich, Conn.

Nielsen, A. C. (1975) "Nielsen Retail Index Services," Northbrook, Ill.

—— (1980) "Management with the Nielsen Retail Index System," Northbrook, Ill.

Nielsen Marketing Research (1986) "1986 Nielsen Business Information Manual," New York.

NPD Group (1986) "Tools for Knowledge," Port Washington, N.Y.

Quality Strategies (1994) "The Numbers Are In ... NOW WHAT?" M/A/R/C Group, Irving, Tex.

SAMI/Burke, Inc. (1985) "SAMI Reports, 1985," New York, October.

—— (1987) "SAMI Warehouse Withdrawals," New York.

ScanAmerica (1986) "Redefining the American Television Audience," New York.

Selling Areas-Marketing, Inc. (1983) "How to Use SAMI for Making More Effective Sales Presentations," New York.

—— (1985) "The Facts of SAMI, SARDI, and Market Segmentation," New York.

Shoemaker, Robert, and Lewis G. Pringle (1980) "Possible Biases in Parameter Estimation with Store Audit Data," *Journal of Marketing Research*, 17, February, 91–96.

Simmons, W. R., and Associates Research (1977) *The Study of Selective Markets and the Media Reaching Them*, New York.

Simmons Market Research Bureau, Inc. (1987) "Study of Media & Markets," New York.

—— (1994a) "Simmons," New York.

—— (1994b) "Simmons Custom Media," New York.

Starch INRA Hooper (1987) "Starch Readership Report Scope, Method and Use," Mamaroneck, N.Y.

Targetbase Marketing (1994) "Let's Get to the Point ...," M/A/R/C Group, Las Colinas, Tex.

Walsh America/PMSI (1994) promotional material, Phoenix, Ariz.

Westat, Inc. (1987a) "Crossley Surveys," New York, 1987.

—— (1987b) "Westat," Rockville, Md.

CHAPTER 5

Qualitative Research

Given the general orientation of this book toward analysis of quantitative data, the reader may wonder why we begin detailed discussion of data collection with a chapter (even a brief one) on qualitative methods. The answer is that the purpose of research is typically to gain insight rather than prove something to be true or false.

Qualitative work is ideal for both exploratory analysis and for gaining deeper and different insights into, and understanding of, key findings. Simply observing customers provides a wealth of information, though not necessarily generalizable results. Trade shows and the Sony store on Michigan Avenue in Chicago are just two examples of settings where company personnel interact with and observe customers examining and using their products. This chapter briefly discusses three popular qualitative methods: focus groups, expert observation, and in-depth interviews.

FOCUS GROUPS

As discussed in Chapter 4, focus groups have a number of uses and benefits. Basically they allow for discussion and probing within a small group to uncover a level of detail and nuances unlikely to emerge from a structured survey. They provide a manager one way to get "close to the customer" through viewing the sessions in person, by video, or at least through edited verbatim comments. The key to the success of a focus group is the group leader. The role of the leader is to gently but firmly keep the discussion moving. This requires an empathetic attitude and efforts to keep all members of the group involved. The leader should be interested in the topic and have some, but not too much, information about it so that a certain "freshness" is apparent. Possibly most important, the leader must be both prepared and flexible. Preparation includes an outline of topics to be covered and a general concept of the order in which they should be discussed. A useful outline of topics and sample questions from a focus group on cookware was provided by Lautman (1981) from ARBOR, Inc. (Table 5.1).

A somewhat less specific suggested outline for discussing new product concepts provided by McQuarrie and McIntyre (1986) is shown in Table 5.2. Flexibility means allowing the group discussion to find its own path through the topics and to accept and encourage unexpected (as opposed to totally nonsensical) comments.

The problems with focus groups are also numerous. First, the process depends heavily on the moderator's ability to direct the discussion. Second, bad group dynamics (e.g., one loudmouth) can greatly reduce the value of the results. Third, interpreting the results requires considerable skill. A corollary to this is that the buyer of research who does not observe a focus group either in person or on tape may lose much of the value of the session. For purposes of idea generation, one study indicated separate interviews produced more ideas than a focus group (Fern, 1982). The study also suggested that two focus groups of four may be more productive than one of size eight. Still, focus groups are not useful for projecting to total markets (Bellenger, Bernhardt, and Goldstucker, 1976).

Role of the Moderator

A moderator has several tasks to perform.

1. *Establish a comfortable relationship with the participants.* Unless respondents are comfortable, they will not be forthcoming in their responses. Hence, the moderator has to establish a rapport with the respondents through small talk, humor, and communicating a nonjudgmental interest in their opinions.
2. *Manage the discussion* by gently returning the group to topics of concern without stifling what they want to say.
3. *Control those members who want to dominate the discussion.*
4. *Probe both individuals making statements and other group members* to clarify and elaborate on their statements.
5. *Remember to be a neutral observer.* The moderator's opinions and knowledge are not important. The job is to uncover the respondents' opinions.

A good focus group leader is thus similar to a good case-method teacher (which MBAs at least may have some experience with), who, without appearing to inject his or her own opinion, ends up with a coherent set of class comments (and finishes within the allotted time).

Methodological Issues

The use of focus groups also generates a number of methodological issues.

1. Group membership Given a small group of size 6–12, the addition or deletion of one member can have a major impact on group dynamics and, hence, what the output will be. The decision of who to include is critical at two levels. First, you want to make sure the members are those whom you want to talk to. This obvious sampling issue is often forgotten when convenience samples are used (i.e., whoever happens to be in or willing to come to a shopping mall on a given day).

Second, you need to decide on how similar the respondents should be. The impact of group similarity has been discussed extensively (Corfman, 1994). Similar respondents will feel comfortable and may be more willing to speak and present some generally unpopular opinions (e.g., "I'm terrified of e-mail"). But similar respondents may not sufficiently challenge each others' positions to stimulate careful thought. On the other hand, using dissimilar respondents may lead to unwillingness to speak or posturing. For

TABLE 5.1 Focus Group Topics and Sample Questions

1. Definition of significant classes of the attitude object.
   What kinds of cookware are there?

2. Brand awareness.
   What brands of cookware are you familiar with?

3. Evaluation of attitude objects.
   Which brand is best, worst, and why?

4. Situational contexts/relevant others.
   How, when, and where do you use cookware?

5. Weights of situational contexts/relevant others.
   When giving cookware as a gift, what is important?

6. Evaluation of each attitude object in each situational context/relevant others.
   Which brands do you prefer as a gift, and why?

7. Attributes of the attitude object for each situational context.
   a. *Physical attributes.*
      When you think about cooking with aluminum pans, what features of the cookware come to mind?
   b. *Interpersonal.*
      Does anyone in your family care what type of cookware you use?
   c. *Affective.*
      Do you have any special feelings toward particular pots and pans?

8. Association among attributes.
   If a pot is heavy, will it be more or less likely to have even heat distribution?

9. Dimensions, levels, and range of attributes.
   When you say you want a heavy pot, what do you mean by "heavy"?

(*continued*)

example, it has been suggested that in some cultures mixing across age groups, men and women, marital and family status, and students and adults may adversely affect the group discussion.

2. Determining the Purpose   Focus groups are flexible tools and often produce unexpected results. Unless they are purely exploratory, however, it helps to have a general structure in mind. Consider a business school interested in understanding more about its curriculum that (at least somewhat enlightenedly) decided to conduct focus groups with students and alumni. Unless some direction is provided, the student discussion can degenerate into comments about individual professors and job interviews. Similarly, the alumni groups may gravitate toward general themes (e.g., analytical ability, communication skills), which often apply to all schools and even to society in general. Unless you know what you want to find out, you can end up with a lot of interesting information that may have little relevance for the question at hand. If the question is really which courses should be required, some gentle prodding is needed.

3. Conveying the Results   There are a number of ways to convey the results of a focus group. Typically, the most powerful is to have managers sit behind the infamous one-way mirror or, alternatively, to view the focus group through a remote hook-up. The

---

TABLE 5.1 *(Continued)*

10. Threshold of satisfaction.

   How long does a pot have to last for you to consider it durable?

11. Beliefs and opinions of brands on attributes, dimensions, and threshold of satisfaction.

   Are Mirro aluminum pans durable enough for you to consider buying them?

12. Latitude of acceptance of beliefs and opinions.

   Would you believe it if I said that the Teflon™ coating on a pan will last longer than the pan itself?

13. Evaluation of attributes (salience).

   For which of these things which you say you want in your next set of cookware would you be willing to pay more?

14. Determination of values.

   How would you characterize someone who is a good cook?

15. Hierarchy of values.

   Would you rather be a good cook or have a successful business outside of the home?

16. Saliency of relationships between attributes and values.

   You say you want a pot with even heat distribution. What does that affect, your health, your reputation as a cook, or what?

17. Attribute salience and latitude of acceptance as related to values.

   How much do you think easy cleaning cookware can really affect your lifestyle?

18. Category importance as related to value system.

   How much time in an average day do you spend with cookware?

Source: Martin R. Lautman, "Focus Groups: Theory and Method," from *Advances in Consumer Research* 9 (1981): pp. 55–56. Reprinted with the permission of the publisher.

advantage of concurrent viewing is not only currency, but also the ability in some cases to encourage expanded discussions in certain areas either during or immediately after the session. When managers view focus groups simultaneously at a remote location (cleverly called video focus groups), they can send information or questions that arise to the moderator as well as avoid the hassle and expense of travel.

The next most accurate method for transmitting what happened is a recorded version. Clearly, video is better than audio-only, since gestures and other physical movements are an important means of communication. Also, its impact tends to be greater.

Recorded versions have one noticeable disadvantage, the time required to view/listen to them. Six 2-hour focus groups means 12 hours of listening, something few managers seem willing to do (though that isn't much time if you truly want to be customer-oriented). As a consequence, edited versions are often prepared. The key issue here becomes the quality of the editor (censor?). Just as TV news sound bites often bear little relation to complex issues, so can highlights of focus groups inaccurately reflect the underlying discussions.

It is also possible to transcribe the discussion into a written version. This is a time-consuming task, but it has the virtue of allowing the manager rather than someone else to decide what information is relevant and how to interpret it.

TABLE 5.2 A Six-Step Procedure for Conducting Group Discussions of New Product Concepts

I. *Problem/Need Identification.*

What problems/shortcomings/unmet needs have you experienced with existing products?

What new products in this area have caught your eye/would you like to see?

II. *Presentation of Product Concept(s).*

Statement of product concept.

Detailed discussion of product features/capabilities.

III. *Evaluation of Product Concept.*

Get global reactions first.

Solicit reactions feature by feature.

Ranking of most/least attractive features.

IV. *Determination of Price Points.*

Either suggest a price to the group, *or*

Have the group suggest an appropriate price.

V. *Extensions to the Product.*

Determine whether options could enhance the product.

Address specific strategic concerns.

VI. *Suggestions for Improving the Product.*

Summarize group reactions.

Source: E. F. McQuarrie and S. H. McIntyre, "Focus Groups and the Development of New Products by Technologically Driven Companies: Some Guidelines," from *Journal of Product Innovation Management* (March 1986): 44. Reprinted with the permission of Elsevier Science, Inc., 655 Avenue of the Americas, New York, NY 10010–5107.

Typically, someone (often the moderator) prepares a summary of what happened, interspersed with quotations. This requires writing skills, perceptivity, and allied qualities—which are not in large supply in the general population. When this form of output is used, one must make sure the supplier (or whoever is designated to do this inside the firm) is up to the task.

Probably the least effective way to convey the results is through a one-page memo. While a few individuals may be able to capture the essence of a focus group session in a short statement, even they cannot deal with subtle nuances, the uncovering of which is the main benefit of focus groups.

Electronic Focus Groups

An interesting recent development is the use of electronic focus groups. In these, participants respond by typing (into a computer linked to a central server) their reactions. Participants can be in the same or different locations. Besides eliminating the need to be in the same location, electronic groups have other advantages. For example, since all participants can respond at the same time, thoughts are not lost waiting for one's turn. Also, the person with the loudest voice doesn't necessarily get to talk most. Importantly, the information is already input, so that the tedious and error-prone process of transcribing the results is eliminated. Finally, since information can be presented anonymously, sensitive subjects may be easier to explore.

There are concerns with the use of electronic focus groups. First, typing skills and basic knowledge of computers are required, and so the groups are better suited to younger, upscale participants. Second, the group dynamics change, and one wonders whether the absence of human contact alters the information generated. Also, the moderator tends to have less control.

Still, initial comparisons with in-person groups show reasonable similarity in the number of ideas and content elicited. Chakravarti et al. (1994) report a comparison between traditional and electronic groups. While similar, they found electronic groups had more even participation, produced comments that were impersonal and more negative, and generated an increased quantity of opinions relative to facts. Several online focus groups have been established as well, including Viacom's panel of 8- to 12-year-olds on CompuServe and BKG's service through America Online.

Summary

Focus groups are widely used and discussed, and many firms conduct them (see the Focus Group Directory). When dealing with consumers, the cost is fairly low (e.g., $4,000 per eight-person group). Before utilizing them, however, it is advisable to read more widely on the subject (e.g., Greenbaum, 1993; Morgan, 1988; Templeton, 1987).

OBSERVATION AND ANALYSIS

The term *qualitative research* covers a variety of different approaches, including a number that rely on in-depth observation and analysis. These tend to be case-based approaches that draw on anthropological and historical approaches. Much survey and customer data-based research focuses on describing behavior and explaining it based on either cognitive activity (when reasons for behavior are directly probed, as in the case of attribute importance ratings) or conditioning (stimulus-response, e.g., when the response to increased advertising spending or promotions is quantified). In contrast, in-depth observation and analysis looks for more complex explanations, which often emphasize social and cultural aspects of behavior.

Many terms are used to describe forms of qualitative research: hermeneutics (Arnold and Fischer, 1994); semiotics (Mick, 1986); existential-phenomenology (Thompson, Locander, and Pollio, 1989); ethnography; naturalistic inquiry (Belk, Sherry, and Wallendorf, 1988); and humanistic inquiry (Hirschman, 1986). These polysyllabic descriptors (a.k.a. big words) can be intimidating or alienating to many (e.g., the authors). Fortunately, numerous books exist on the subject (cf. Denzin and Lincoln, 1993). Therefore, this section provides a brief nontechnical discussion of some of the approaches.

One major difference between quantitatively oriented survey-based and qualitative research is the focus. For example, survey-based satisfaction studies typically focus on getting an overall satisfaction score as well as respondents' ratings of subdimensions, determinants of, and likely consequences of (e.g., complaining behavior, retention/repurchase intent) satisfaction. In contrast, one qualitative study of satisfaction with technological consumer durables (computers, answering machines) focused much more heavily on the meaning the products take on in their owners' lives (Mick and Fournier, 1995). Data consisted of loosely structured interviews with a total of 40 people and a diary kept by one of the authors. Respondents' satisfaction formulation followed a number of processes including (*a*) *expectancy-disconfirmation* (comparing expectations with performance), (*b*) *equity* (whether the exchange was perceived to be a fair transaction), and (*c*) *desires congruency* (how well the product meets or exceeds their desires). Even disconfirmation occurs in unusual ways, with one subject indicating satisfaction with a telephone answering machine because a negative expectation (concerning being forced to return calls) was not fulfilled. Perhaps most important, the study provides insights into how products become a part of the life of their owners (i.e., a phone machine was a surrogate secretary for screening calls). Attachments to and associations with the products become central output of the research rather than scores or ratings.

Windows on Meaning

Qualitative research often involves using different vantage points (windows) to uncover the meaning of various feelings and behaviors. These include

1. *Language*. The language used per se is often analyzed in detail to provide understanding (Tedlock, 1983). Basically, this requires studying an oral or written (often transcribed from oral) record and searching for understanding. One common method for studying language is content analysis (Kassarjian, 1977; Kolbe and Burnett, 1991).

2. *Symbols/myths*. Another vantage point focuses on the symbolic role behavior and products play (Levy, 1981; Mick, 1986). A superstitious athlete may go through certain rituals (activities) not because they are enjoyable or productive but because they are "good luck." The consumption of turkey and cranberries at Thanksgiving is a reflection of tradition and family more than a product attributes such as protein or taste preference. Further, possessions often take on special meanings unrelated to the attributes of alternative brands (Wallendorf and Arnould, 1991). This explanation for behavior rests on the background of the consumer rather than on the product itself.

3. *Behavior patterns*. Simple observation is a common tool of the qualitative researcher (Sherry, 1990). Unfortunately, the opportunities for misinterpretation are great, especially when the observations are collected over a short time period. More extensive observation in the tradition of anthropology (often involving a participant-observer) is thus an expensive but useful approach.

4. *Introspection*. Introspection comes in two forms: researcher-based and subject/consumer-based (Wallendorf and Brucks, 1993). Consumer-based introspection can be further subdivided by the extent to which the consumer is led/guided through a thought process by the researcher. Obviously, the more insightful (after the fact) the researcher is, the more one should rely on the researcher. Unfortunately, it is often difficult to tell a priori how insightful the researcher is, and reliance on researchers makes the results more susceptible to their own particular biases and views of the world.

5. *Pictorial representation*. Subjects are sometimes asked to bring in pictures and/or take photographs to describe their feelings, etc. (cf. Heisley and Levy, 1991). These can be analyzed directly by the researcher. More often, subjects are asked to describe why they chose the pictures and what they represent.

6. *Popular culture*. To the extent popular culture reflects consumers' behavior, it provides another basis on which to study it. Movies (Holbrook and Grayson, 1986), TV shows (Hirschman, 1988), literature (Stern, 1989), and ads (Wells and Gale, 1995) all provide a perspective on consumer behavior.

7. *History*. Historians have a long and distinguished tradition of providing interpretation and background for events and behaviors. This includes archaeological methods, study of written records, and so forth.

Data analysis for qualitative research is less clear and well prescribed than for quantitative data. Spiegel (1994) lists five basic steps:

1. Categorization—basically coding data (e.g., statements referring to time saving)
2. Abstraction—basically grouping codes into more abstract constructs (e.g., convenience)
3. Comparison of situations in which the data were collected
4. Dimensionalizing—identifying categories of response that vary by degrees (level of convenience)
5. Integration—linking constructs together (e.g., convenience to preference)

By iteratively performing these steps, the researcher converges on an organization of available qualitative data. Interpretation then gives meaning to the data from some perspective (e.g., cultural).

Consumer Contact

Customer contact makes managers de facto qualitative researchers. A number of companies now encourage/force direct contact with customers. For example, Ford places newly hired engineers in a customer service center answering customer phone calls and P&G sends chemists into homes to talk to customers. Customer visits are used to develop a common vision of the customer in business-to-business firms to help coordinate the marketing, quality, production, and R&D functions in new product development and satisfaction measurement (McQuarrie and McIntyre, 1992). Basically, most managerial "gut feel" is the result of informal qualitative research.

DEPTH INTERVIEWS

In-depth interviewing has a long tradition in marketing. Ernst Dichter popularized the method in the 1960s, which then fell into disfavor as newer quantitative procedures became popular. However, attempts to get close to customers have produced a revival of this form of information collection. Essentially, this method relies on a trained interviewer probing a respondent one-on-one (McCracken, 1988), sometimes involving projective techniques (McGrath, Sherry, and Levy, 1993). In effect, it is a focus group of size one.

Laddering/Means-Ends Chains

One popular form of depth interview focuses on uncovering consumers' means-ends chains (Gutman, 1982; Olson and Reynolds, 1983). The procedure is an extension of the Kelly Repertory Grid (Kelly, 1963). The basic approach assumes (A) product attributes (means) relate to (C) consequences, which in turn relate to (V) basic values (ends). For example, a blow-dryer dries hair—an attribute (A) that leads to looking better (C), which leads to popularity (C), which leads to self-esteem (V). Walker and Olson (1991) studied

"Thinking-of-you" cards and traced the attributes (words, pictures) to end-goals such as "express my personality" and "to make them happy." These chains often have more than three steps (e.g., one attribute may be linked to another attribute, one consequence to another consequence).

Methods for developing these ladders center on a one-on-one interview in which the interviewer continually probes with questions such as "Why is that important?" Reynolds and Gutman (1988) discuss several ways to structure an interview to uncover differences among products:

1. *Triadic comparisons.* Basically, this consists of giving respondents three products and asking them to say why two differ from the third. For example, given three beers—Bud Light, Beck's, and Sam Adams—a respondent might group Beck's and Sam Adams together and say they were higher (*a*) in alcohol, (*b*) status, or (*c*) flavor.

2. *Preference ratings.* This involves getting respondents to rank alternatives and then asking them why one brand is most preferred or why one brand is preferred to another.

3. *Different uses.* Focusing on different usage occasions helps generate more distinctions. Returning to the beer example, this could include asking which beer is preferred after a workout, at a social function, with dinner, etc.

To link the distinctions (attributes) to consequences and values, Reynolds and Gutman indicate a number of prompts are useful including (*a*) focusing on specific situations, asking (*b*) what would they do if _____ were not available?, (*c*) why wouldn't they _____?, and (*d*) how has your behavior changed?, (*e*) asking about others' (e.g., friends) behavior, and (*f*) repeating the answer to the respondent.

An Example: The Zaltman Metaphor Elicitation Technique

Individuals' decision processes are often complex and rely on metaphors and stories more than attribute-based evaluation. The Zaltman Metaphor Elicitation Technique (Zaltman and Higie, 1994) uses an extensive two-hour interview to uncover a deep understanding of decisions and behavior.

The first stage of the method involves giving the respondents a camera and asking them to take pictures or to collect pictures from magazines, etc., that are relevant to the topic in question. The interview then goes through nine stages (Zaltman and Higie, 1994):

1. *Storytelling*—describing each picture.

2. *Omitted relevant pictures*—describing what pictures they could not obtain that they would like to have.

3. *Sorting* the pictures into groups.

4. *Construct elicitation*, where key constructs are uncovered using a form of laddering and the Kelly Repertory Grid. Typically, 15 respondents are sufficient to uncover all the key constructs.

5. Indicating the *most representative picture* and why it was chosen.

6. Describing *opposite images*, pictures that represent the opposite of the task/focus.

7. Describing *sensory* associations, including color, sound, smell, taste, and touch plus emotions.

8. Arranging the constructs that have been elicited in a *mental map* by linking related constructs.

9. Developing a *summary image*, a picture that incorporates the key constructs and relations. This involves a "cut and paste" procedure, often done with multimedia technology.

Summarizing the different respondents' mental maps is a nontrivial task. Generally, it involves developing a consensus map. These summary maps seem to account for the vast majority of the constructs, and the relations among them, of the individual respondents.

SUMMARY

Qualitative research is an important source of insight. It also depends heavily on the quality of the person doing the study and the nature of the typically small sample studied; it is not easy to generalize or quantify. It is most useful for (*a*) early/exploratory work, (*b*) adding insight to more quantitative knowledge, and (*c*) uncovering an innovative new way to think. Perhaps most interesting, a little interviewing goes a long way toward uncovering the needs and ideas of an entire population. Griffin and Hauser (1993), among others, have found that 7–10 focus groups or one-on-one interviews uncover the vast majority of needs, concerns, and the like (see Figure 5.1). Thus qualitative work is an efficient way to get a sense of the issues of concern (but not necessarily their relative importance) to a population of interest.

PROBLEMS

1. Design a focus group outline to uncover reasons why consumers exercise.
2. Use a laddering procedure to explain the exercise behavior of two people.
3. Analyze (*a*) ads for exercise products and (*b*) articles about exercise to uncover reasons why they are bought.
4. Consider your own exercise behavior and describe/explain it in detail.
5. Summarize the results of problems 1–4.

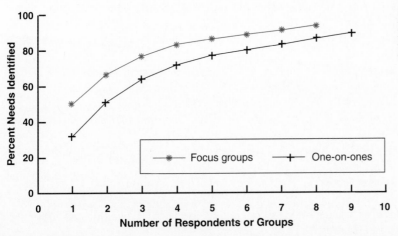

FIGURE 5.1
Focus Groups vs. On-on-One Interviews for Office Equipment
Source: Silver and Thompson, 1991.

REFERENCES

AMERICAN MARKETING ASSOCIATION (1994) *The Focus Group Directory, 3rd Edition of the 1994 GreenBook*, New York: American Marketing Association/New York Chapter, Inc.

ARNOLD, STEPHEN J., AND EILEEN FISCHER (1994) "Hermeneutics and Consumer Research," *Journal of Consumer Research*, 21, June, 55–70.

ARNOULD, ERIC J., AND MELANIE WALLENDORF (1994) "Market-Oriented Ethnography: Interpretation Building and Marketing Strategy Formulation," *Journal of Marketing Research*, 31, November, 484–504.

BELK, RUSSELL W., JOHN F. SHERRY, JR., AND MELANIE WALLENDORF (1988) "A Naturalistic Inquiry into Buyer and Seller Behavior at a Swap Meet," *Journal of Consumer Research*, 14, March, 449–70.

BELLENGER, DANNY N., KENNETH L. BERNHARDT, AND JAC L. GOLDSTUCKER (1976) *Qualitative Methods in Marketing*, Chicago: American Marketing Association.

CHAKRAVARTI, DIPANKAR, CAROL BRUNEAU, JON LAUDENBACH, AND DANIEL MITTELMAN (1994) "Electronic Focus Groups Information Technology in Qualitative Market Research," presented at Marketing Science Conference, Tucson, Ariz., March.

CORFMAN, KIM P. (1994) "The Importance of Member Heterogeneity to Focus Group Quality," working paper, New York University, August.

DENZIN, NORMAN K., AND YVONNA S. LINCOLN (1993) *Handbook of Qualitative Research*, Thousand Oaks, Calif.: Sage.

DICHTER, ERNEST (1964) *The Handbook of Consumer Motivations*, New York: McGraw-Hill.

FERN, EDWARD F. (1982) "The Use of Focus Groups for Idea Generation: The Effects of Group Size, Acquaintanceship, and Moderator on Response Quantity and Quality," *Journal of Marketing Research*, 19, February, 1–13.

GREENBAUM, THOMAS L. (1993) *The Handbook for Focus Group Research*, New York: Lexington Books.

GRIFFIN, ABBIE, AND JOHN R. HAUSER (1993) "The Voice of the Customer," *Marketing Science*, 12, Winter, 1–27.

GUTMAN, JONATHAN (1982) "A Means-End Chain Model Based on Consumer Categorization Processes," *Journal of Marketing*, 46, Spring, 60–72.

HEISLEY, DEBORAH D., AND SIDNEY J. LEVY (1991) "Autodriving: A Photoelicitation Technique," *Journal of Consumer Research*, 18, December, 257–73.

HIRSCHMAN, ELIZABETH C. (1986) "Humanistic Inquiry in Marketing Research: Philosophy, Method, and Criteria," *Journal of Marketing Research*, 23, August, 237–49.

———, ED. (1987) *Interpretive Consumer Research*, Provo, Utah: Association for Consumer Research.

——— (1988) "The Ideology of Consumption: A Structural-Syntactical Analysis of 'Dallas' and 'Dynasty,'" *Journal of Consumer Research*, 15, December, 344–59.

HOLBROOK, MORRIS B., AND MARK W. GRAYSON (1986) "The Semiology of Cinematic Consumption: Symbolic Consumer Behavior in *Out of Africa*," *Journal of Consumer Research*, 13, December, 374–81.

KASSARJIAN, HAROLD H. (1977) "Content Analysis in Consumer Research," *Journal of Consumer Research*, 4, June, 8–18.

KELLY, GEORGE A. (1963) *A Theory of Personality*, New York: Norton.

KOLBE, RICHARD H., AND MELISSA S. BURNETT (1991) "Content-Analysis Research: An Examination of Applications with Directives for Improving Research Reliability and Objectivity," *Journal of Consumer Research*, 18, September, 243–50.

KRUEGER, RICHARD A. (1994) *Focus Groups; A Practical Guide for Applied Research*, Thousand Oaks, Calif.: Sage.

LAUTMAN, MARTIN R. (1981) "Focus Groups: Theory and Method," in Andrew Mitchell, ed., *Advances in Consumer Research*, vol. 9, 55–56. Association for Consumer Research.

LEVY, SIDNEY J. (1981) "Interpreting Consumer Mythology: A Structural Approach to Consumer Behavior," *Journal of Marketing*, 45, Summer, 49–62.

MCCRACKEN, GRANT (1988) *The Long Interview*, Newbury Park, Calif.: Sage.

MCGRATH, MARY ANN, JOHN F. SHERRY, JR., AND SIDNEY J. LEVY (1993) "Giving Voice to the Gift: The Use of Projective Techniques to Recover Lost Meanings," *Journal of Consumer Psychology*, 2, 171–91.

MCQUARRIE, EDWARD F., AND SHELBY H. MCINTYRE (1986) "Focus Groups and the Development of New Products by Technologically Driven Companies: Some Guidelines," *Journal of Product Innovation Management*, March, 44.

—— (1992) "One Customer Visit: An Emerging Practice in Business-to-Business Marketing," MSI Report 92-114.

MICK, DAVID GLEN (1986) "Consumer Research and Semiotics: Exploring the Morphology of Signs, Symbols, and Significance," *Journal of Consumer Research*, 13, September, 196–213.

MICK, DAVID, AND SUSAN FOURNIER (1993) "Phenomenological and Life History Approaches to Understanding Consumers and Their Technological Products," presented at New Methods and Applications in Consumer Research Conference, Cambridge, Mass.: MSI, September.

—— (1995) "Process and Meaning in Consumer Satisfaction: A Qualitative and Longitudinal Multimethod Inquiry," MSI working paper, 95-104. Cambridge, Mass.: MSI.

MILES, MATTHEW B., AND A. MICHAEL HUBERMAN (1994) *Qualitative Data Analysis*, Thousand Oaks, Calif.: Sage.

MORGAN, ANTHONY (1984) "Point of View: Magic Town Revisited," *Journal of Advertising Research*, 24, No. 4, 49–51.

MORGAN, DAVID L. (1988) *Focus Groups as Qualitative Research*, Beverly Hills, Calif.: Sage.

OLSON, J., AND T. J. REYNOLDS (1983) "Understanding Consumers' Cognitive Structures: Implications for Advertising Strategy" in L. Percy and A. Woodside, eds., *Advertising and Consumer Psychology*, Lexington, Mass.: Lexington Books.

REYNOLDS, THOMAS J., AND JONATHAN GUTMAN (1988) "Laddering Theory, Method, Analysis, and Interpretation," *Journal of Advertising Research*, 28, February–March, 11–31.

SHERRY, JOHN F., JR. (1990) "A Sociocultural Analysis of a Midwestern American Flea Market," *Journal of Consumer Research*, 17, June, 13–30.

SILVER, JONATHAN ALAN, AND JOHN CHARLES THOMPSON, JR. (1991) "Understanding Customer Needs: A Systematic Approach to the 'Voice of the Customer,'" Master's thesis, Cambridge, Mass.: Sloan School of Management, MIT.

SMITH, RUTH ANN, AND DAVID S. LUX (1993) "Historical Method in Consumer Research: Developing Causal Explanations of Change," *Journal of Consumer Research*, 19, March, 595–610.

SPIEGEL, SUSAN (1994) "Analysis and Interpretation of Qualitative Data in Consumer Research," *Journal of Consumer Research*, 21, December, 491–503.

STERN, BARBARA B. (1989) "Literary Criticism and Consumer Research: Overview and Illustrative Analysis," *Journal of Consumer Research*, 16, December, 322–34.

STEWART, DAVID W., AND PREM N. SHAMDASANI (1990) *Focus Groups, Theory and Practice*, Thousand Oaks, Calif.: Sage.

TEDLOCK, DENNIS (1983) *The Spoken Word and the Work of Interpretation*, Philadelphia: University of Pennsylvania Press.

TEMPLETON, J. F. (1987) *Focus Groups: A Guide for Marketing and Advertising Professionals*, Chicago: Probus.

THOMPSON, CRAIG J., WILLIAM B. LOCANDER, AND HOWARD R. POLLIO (1989) "Putting Consumer Experience Back into Consumer Research: The Philosophy and Method of Existential-Phenomenology," *Journal of Consumer Research*, 16, September, 133–46.

——— (1990) "The Lived Meaning of Free Choice: An Existential-Phenomenological Description of Everyday Consumer Experiences of Contemporary Married Women," *Journal of Consumer Research*, 17, December, 346–62.

WALKER, BETH A., AND JERRY C. OLSON (1991) "Means-End Chains: Connecting Products with Self," *Journal of Business Research*, 22, 111–18.

WALLENDORF, MELANIE, AND ERIC J. ARNOULD (1988) "'My Favorite Things': A Cross Cultural Inquiry into Object Attachment, Possessiveness, and Social Linkage," *Journal of Consumer Research*, 14, March, 531–47.

——— (1991) "'We Gather Together': Consumption Rituals of Thanksgiving Day," *Journal of Consumer Research*, 18, June, 13–31.

WALLENDORF, MELANIE, AND MERRIE BRUCKS (1993) "Introspection in Consumer Research: Implementation and Implications," *Journal of Consumer Research*, 20, December, 339–59.

WELLS, WILLIAM D., AND KENDRA L. GALE (1995) "Fictional Subjects in Consumer Research," in Frank Kardes and Mita Sujan, eds., *Advances in Consumer Research*, vol. 22, 306-310. Association for Consumer Research.

ZALTMAN, GERALD, AND ROBIN A. HIGIE (1994) "Seeing the Voice of the Customer: The Zaltman Metaphor Elicitation Technique," MSI working paper 93-114, February. Cambridge, Mass.: MSI.

CHAPTER 6

Experiments

The notion of causality is both subtle and crucial. When a manager cuts price 10 percent, there is usually an implicit assumption about how this will affect sales and profits. For example, it may be assumed that sales will increase 30 percent. This assumption is based on the events that a price change precipitates (causes) in the market. Such assumptions may be intuitive or based on actual experience (e.g., "That's what happened in Des Moines in 1993"). The purpose of this chapter is (1) to indicate how important a concept causality is, (2) to indicate that causality is difficult to uncover, and (3) to discuss experiments that are the best, but far from infallible, tools for assessing certain kinds of causality.

BASIC CONCEPTS

The concept of causality implies that if I change a particular variable (e.g., advertising), then another variable (e.g., sales) will change *as a result of my actions*. Hence, almost any marketing decision (and in fact any decision) is implicitly made by considering its "consequences." If managers can develop an understanding of the causal relations in a market, then they can make "optimal" decisions. Causal inference, therefore, is essential to effective decision making.

One way to make causal inferences is deductively. For example, one can use a strong theory about the way the world behaves (e.g., Einstein's theory of relativity) to predict the consequences of various actions. Much work in mathematics and physics falls into this category, where causal inferences are deduced and then examined. Similarly, economists often deduce consequences of actions in the market based on their models. When the inferences derived from a model or theory are proved false, then a new theory is required (a process known as "falsification").

A second way to draw causal inferences is to examine data in an attempt to see what they indicate about the world. Recent developments in so-called neural networks allow the data to define the pattern of relationships that exist. Still, a pure "inductive" process is rarely practiced, since even the most naive managers or researchers have some causal notions or theories. In fact, deciding whether data or theory should come first is similar to the proverbial debate about which came first—the chicken or the egg. The crucial fact is that theory (causal notions) leads to data collection, which in turn leads to revised theory in a never-ending process.

A third way to draw causal inferences is intuitively. Experienced managers, through a process that contains elements of both deduction and induction and that is often not completely conscious, may be good at predicting the consequences of their actions. If such managers are available, they should be utilized. However, relying on this approach will have two unpleasant consequences. First, the more complex the situation, the greater the likelihood of mistakes. Second, how managers draw conclusions will remain a black box both to them and to the rest of the company. Thus when they leave, their knowledge leaves with them.

Causality can be understood on several levels. On the one hand, it is possible to construct an understanding of simple cause and effect relationships of the following type:

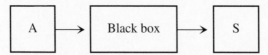

Here we understand that advertising (A) causes sales (S), but not how. While this level of understanding may be adequate for many simple decisions, it fails to consider more complex situations. For example, if our competitors' advertising and prices as well as our advertising change during a period of inflation and recession, what will happen to our sales? In this situation, one should consider both the simultaneous impact of advertising and prices as well as the competitors' reactions. Put differently, incomplete causal understanding can be misleading and even dangerous.

On the other hand, it is possible to search endlessly for a complete model of the world. While this is an (the?) appropriate goal for academic research and a worthwhile pursuit for business, it is also an expensive and time-consuming task. Hence, most businesses make the decision to operate in a world of incomplete understanding and imperfect prediction of the consequences of their actions. While this is appropriate, especially in the short run, some people (including guess who?) feel that, in the long run, firms would benefit from a more thorough attempt to explicitly examine the likely consequences of their actions.

ESTABLISHING CAUSALITY

As an example of the difficulty in deducing causality, consider the following scenario. In one of a company's eight sales districts (Cleveland), both the promotion budget and sales increased 20 percent, while in the other seven districts, promotion and sales were unchanged. A deduction one could (and, in some sense, would like to) draw is that increasing promotion 20 percent *caused* sales to increase 20 percent. Unfortunately, such a deduction is likely to be unwarranted for one of several reasons:

1. *Randomness.* To assume that the 20 percent change produced exactly a 20 percent increase ignores the essential randomness in the world. At the extreme, this may have been a fluke that would almost never recur. At the least, the conclusion that a 20 percent increase in promotion budget produces a 20 percent increase in sales ignores the need to hedge such a prediction. Put differently, given human knowledge, it is impossible to predict the consequences of an action with certainty. In business, causality is a probabilistic rather than a deterministic concept.

2. *Other explanations.* It is possible that a major competitor withdrew from the market in Cleveland and that this, not promotion, caused sales to increase. Alternatively, it may be that top management targeted Cleveland for extra effort this year, including greater advertising support, more salespeople, and so on, and that this effort caused the increase in sales. Finally, it could be that a general economic upsurge in the Cleveland district caused both promotional budgets and sales to increase.

3. *Reverse causality.* The assumption made in drawing the promotion-causes-sales deduction is that promotion precedes sales. Given that many promotional budgets are set as a percent of sales, an equally plausible explanation of the facts is that such a promotional budgeting rule was followed by the company.

In attempting to establish causality, then, several steps are required. These are generally grouped into three major categories: demonstrating concurrent variation between two variables, establishing precedence, and eliminating alternative explanations.

1. *Concurrent variation.* A necessary but insufficient condition for establishing causality between two variables (A and B) is that the two move together in a consistent pattern (i.e., when A goes up, B goes up *or* when A goes up, B goes down). Note here we generally do not require a deterministic relation between two variables, only that when one changes the other is likely to change (known unexcitingly as probabilistic causality). Returning to the promotion-sales example, consider the following two situations representing the combination of promotion and sales across 200 districts:

Case I: Positive Relation

		Sales	
		Up	Down
Promotion:	Up	80	20
	Down	20	80

Case II: No Relation

		Sales	
		Up	Down
Promotion:	Up	50	50
	Down	50	50

In case I, sales and promotion tend to move together, while in case II they are unrelated. Assuming that we are looking for a simple promotion-to-sales relationship, case I looks promising, while case II indicates that no simple causal relationship exists.

2. *Precedence.* Case I passed the concurrent variation test. The next issue is to determine which came first—promotion increases or sales increases. If sales increased first, it is clearly not appropriate to say that promotion caused sales.

The notion of precedence is conceptually clear. Unfortunately, it is often difficult to determine which came first in nonexperimental settings. For example, if the effect of promotion on sales occurs within one day, and if data on sales are available weekly, then it is very difficult to determine which change came first. This is especially true when promotions and sales are measured at the same time.

3. *Elimination of alternative explanations.* Basically, one has to examine what "else" might have occurred that could have produced the results that two variables (P and S) are related. One particularly relevant possibility is that something else that just happened to be related to P caused S to increase (Figure 6.1, Case 1). For example, in many categories price is positively related to unit sales (that is, high-priced products have higher sales). The assumption that higher price causes high sales is, however, probably not warranted. Higher-priced goods tend to be higher in quality as well as early entrants in a market. It is likely that quality and market pioneering lead to higher sales, and the relation of price to sales is circumstantial. The major advantage of laboratory experiments is that by controlling other variables, the likelihood that something else causes S to increase is greatly reduced or eliminated.

One other possible explanation for the relation between P and S is so-called "spurious correlation." It is possible that something else occurred that caused both P and S to, say, increase, thus making it appear that P causes S whereas the relation is purely coincidental/spurious (which makes one wonder why it isn't called *coincidental* instead of *spurious* correlation). Consider again the observation that where there are

FIGURE 6.1
Other Explanations for Relation
of P to S

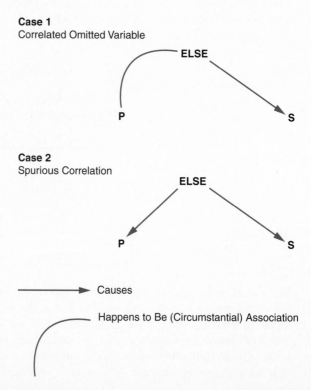

Case 1
Correlated Omitted Variable

ELSE

P   S

Case 2
Spurious Correlation

ELSE

P   S

———————▶ Causes

Happens to Be (Circumstantial) Association

more outlets, there are more sales. To some extent, additional outlets may lead to more sales (though probably not if the category is funeral homes and funerals). However, it is also likely that something else (population and income, or more generally, market potential) has driven both the number of outlets and sales. At the very least, the causal relation between outlets and sales is likely to be overstated; in the extreme, it can be completely spurious. Note also that, as in the case of omitted variables, experiments can be designed to rule out the possibility of spurious correlation.

A variety of alternative explanations may exist for a set of results—any one of which could cause one to alter the apparent causal inference from a set of data. Unless these can be ruled out, a causal relationship has not been conclusively established. Notice that it is almost always possible to come up with an essentially infinite number of alternative explanations, although not all may be particularly believable. Hence, causality can rarely be established with absolute certainty. The best we can hope for, therefore, is to establish causality beyond reasonable doubt. In general, managers and researchers settle for evidence suggesting a high probability of a causal relationship.

EXPERIMENTS

To make decisions concerning price, advertising, and so forth, a manager is concerned with how these factors influence sales and profits. In other words, the manager wants to know what will happen to sales if the price is increased 10 cents a package. The obvious way to get the answer is to raise the price 10 cents somewhere and see what happens. This straightforward experimental approach has two problems. First, most experiments have unforeseen problems that make direct causal interpretation difficult. Second, causality and certainty are not synonyms. Even if I know that a price increase will cause sales to drop, the amount of the decrease will not be known with certainty. Put differently, the best one can hope for is an estimate of the effect of price on sales with a fairly narrow range of uncertainty.

In designing experiments, concerns about the validity (usefulness) of the experiment are traditionally grouped into two categories. Internal validity refers to the experiment producing a "clean" result, which rules out competing explanations for the results. In contrast, external validity refers to the extent to which the results of an experiment are generalizable. A perpetual conflict/tension exists between these two goals. Concern about internal validity leads to strict controls in a laboratory setting, which may not bear much resemblance to the real world, whereas realistic (natural) situations have numerous competing explanations for their results. The craft of market research, therefore, involves balancing these two concerns.

Internal Validity

Interpretation of an experiment can be clouded by several factors, including the following:

Noncomparability of Groups (Selection) In many field or natural experiments, the subjects are assigned to groups (selected) after the treatment occurs. In such cases, it is not unusual for the subjects who "selected" the treatment (e.g., read the *Wall Street Journal*) to differ from those who were not exposed to the treatment in some unmeasured way (e.g., interest in reading, desire/need to keep current on topics) that could affect the results.

Lost Subjects (Mortality)   Over the course of an experiment, subjects inevitably drop out (e.g., individuals can get tired, move; businesses can fold or get new management teams who are less hospitable to the research). Dropout rates of 20 percent are not uncommon in survey research between waves of a study, and single studies often have termination rates of 10 to 30 percent, especially for long surveys. If dropouts differ from the retained subjects in their reactions to the treatments (which they often do), then the results are affected.

Exogenous Events (History)   During many experiments (especially field experiments), an event occurs outside the control of the researcher (e.g., an oil embargo, a strike, a new product introduction). This event influences the measured results and makes it hard to estimate the treatment effect. In test markets, it is not uncommon for competitors to increase advertising or reduce price, thus making interpretation of the results difficult.

Changes over Time (Maturation)   Over the course of an experiment, the subjects change. Aside from the obvious fact that respondents age over time, they can also become more expert consumers, tired, better off financially, etc.

Effect of the Experiment (Testing/Conditioning)   The fact that an experiment is being conducted often has an important effect on the subjects. The so-called Hawthorne effect is named for an experiment where workers increased productivity after a workplace redesign, not, it turned out, because of the redesign but because they felt special. Even prior measurement can, by alerting the subjects to the topic of the study, cause them to change their behavior. Hence, even a measurement can be a factor that influences results.

Instrument Variability   Any change in the measuring instrument (e.g., changing the number of scale points on a questionnaire, changing the accounting method from FIFO [first in, first out] to LIFO [last in, first out] in measuring profits) can produce a change in the results due to the instrument rather than the treatment. Consequently, it is advisable to keep the measuring device as constant as possible.

Hypothesis Guessing   Subjects in experiments may guess the purpose of a study and then try to give the researcher the responses/reactions they think the researcher wants. While opinions vary on how serious a problem this may be (cf. Sawyer, 1975; Shimp, Hyatt, and Snyder, 1991), it potentially can seriously distort any experiment.

Luck (Regression to the Mean)   A fundamental property of most data is the tendency of observations that are above the mean on one occasion to become smaller (closer to the mean) on the next occasion, and for observations below the mean to become larger. This tendency occurs for everything from stock returns and test scores to purchase rates. The reason for this is that observed values are made up of some true mean tendency (e.g., skill) and random error (luck). Even if everyone has the same mean (skill), behavior (e.g., amount of product purchased) will vary. Consequently, those who have the highest observed purchase rates will typically have positive random errors. Since, in general, they are not likely to have positive random errors on the next occasion, their purchase rate will be lower. While the phenomenon of regression to the mean generally doesn't affect experimental design (unless you use previous behavior as a treatment variable), it has obvious implications for interpretation. Basically, regression to the mean is a general problem for all measurements.

External Validity

Many of the threats to internal validity (e.g., noncomparability of groups or exogenous events) are reduced through the use of a strictly controlled environment. This makes tremendous sense in physical science studies where, for example, identically sized marbles can be subjected to various repeated tests in a closed environment. Unfortunately, people cannot be transferred to a laboratory without recognizing the change in settings and, consequently, potentially altering their behavior. External validity is the extent to which experimental results can be generalized to apply to other settings. Encouragingly, some recent evidence suggests that computer-simulated environments are reasonably accurate in predicting such things as market shares and promotion sensitivity (Burke et al., 1992).

Part of the problem with laboratory experiments is that there are limits to what one can do to human subjects. For example, assume that I were interested in determining the impact of smoking on individuals. Since smokers and nonsmokers are rarely perfectly matched, a dedicated researcher (albeit a slightly demented one) concerned with internal validity might propose an experiment in which some people were forced to smoke and others were prevented from doing so. Aside from the problems in conducting such an experiment logistically, there are certain ethical issues raised by this design. Consequently, a more likely design is to compare actual smokers and nonsmokers. Unfortunately, smokers and nonsmokers may differ on both obvious (e.g., physical) and subtle (e.g., personality) dimensions. It is possible to draw what are known as matched cohorts by pairing smokers with nonsmokers who are similar in age, lifestyle, and so on. Unfortunately, producing such a sample is difficult; and while it is a reasonable compromise between internal and external validity, it still may have some of both types of limitations. The point, therefore, is that any single experiment involves a balancing of internal and external validity concerns.

If a certain finding or area of investigation is particularly crucial, then a series of experiments is typically used. Such studies should be different in nature, ranging from those with strong internal validity (e.g., lab experiments) to those with great external validity (e.g., field experiments). Only when a result holds up across such a broad range of situations is the cautious researcher willing to claim that a causal relationship has been demonstrated.

Another issue is how well the results measured in an experiment will persist over time. To illustrate, a promotion often increases sales in the period in which the promotion takes place by cannibalizing the next period's sales. If an experiment is run for only one period, longer-term impact (which is typically crucial to decisions) must be either guessed or ignored. Obviously, running an experiment longer increases both costs and the likelihood that internal validity will be compromised. Still, the issue of what will happen over time is an area that is frequently ignored in both design and interpretation of experiments—occasionally with disastrous consequences.

DESIGN: MANAGERIAL ISSUES

Before running an experiment, it is useful to have a sense of what are the key causes of the criterion variable (e.g., sales). In general, the following types of variables should be considered:

1. General conditions (e.g., economic, regulatory)
2. Competitive actions
3. Your own marketing mix
4. Characteristics of the sample (e.g., people or markets)

In designing an experiment, carefully consider all factors that might influence results and then classify them as:

1. Those that will be ignored (hopefully because you believe they are not relevant and not just because they are hard to measure)
2. Those that will be controlled for (i.e., each treatment group will be matched in terms of these variables)
3. Those that will be monitored/measured so you can assess (statistically) if they were important after the fact
4. Those that will be manipulated in the design

Variables that are ignored can be taken care of by a randomization process, whereby subjects are randomly assigned to treatments. This process generally (but not necessarily) produces treatment groups that are nearly equal in terms of these variables. Thus average differences between the groups cannot be explained based on these "elses." Random assignment is also implicitly assumed by many of the statistical procedures used to evaluate results. When a variable is considered sufficiently crucial to the design that the researcher is not willing to risk unequal groups in terms of that variable, then assignments are made in order to "balance" the groups in terms of that variable. When a variable is considered a possible key influence, it should be measured (as well as controlled for in some situations). Finally, some key variables become the basis for the actual experimental manipulation.

Selection of Dependent (Criterion) Variables   Selection of one or more variables that measure the impact of the experiment is a more difficult task than it first appears to be. Assuming a business application, the appropriate criterion for any decision is the value of the firm's stock or at least profits. Unfortunately, if Maytag tries a different cooperative advertising program for dishwashers in Kansas City, the impact is unlikely to be found in stock price or profit statements. On the other hand, one could choose awareness of the ad as the criterion measure. Unfortunately, awareness does not guarantee either a positive reaction mentally or any increase in sales at the expense of competitors. Hence, the choice of a dependent variable is a tradeoff between measuring what is likely to change as a result of the experiment and what is likely to matter if it does vary.

Controllable versus Uncontrollable Variables   Many executives assume (somewhat egotistically) that the major causes of consequences of interest should be within their control.

They spend most of their time worrying about how their actions affect the consequences of interest and are typically frustrated by their limited impact. This is true of public policymakers as well, who are typically frustrated about their relative impotence when introducing rules (e.g., nutritional labels) in markets. The point here is that other forces (e.g., general economic trends) may be more powerful than marketing mix variables (e.g., ad copy or regulations). Any causal understanding of the world should, therefore, include uncontrollable as well as controllable variables.

Aggregation   Most studies ignore the issue of aggregation. The most common approach to causality is to assume that the same event or action should, at least on the average, produce the same consequence. This is often false, as the Lehmann family's reaction to Brussels sprouts indicates. Assume that such a typical American family of four is served this delicate vegetable at dinner. The "cause" is constant; the consequences are quite different (while the wife enjoys the treat, the other members alternate between sulking, dropping items on the floor, and questioning the sanity of the cook).

Aggregation deserves special consideration because it tends to obscure important relationships. For example, assume that feeding bulk food to weightlifters is beneficial, while feeding bulk food to white-collar workers is detrimental. If a researcher feeds bulk food to a sample made up of 50 percent weightlifters and 50 percent white-collar workers, then half would be better off and half would be worse off. In other words, on average bulk food would have no impact on people. This would lead to an incorrect and in fact harmful medical conclusion: Consumption of bulk food has no impact on health. The point here, therefore, is that the nature of the sample (people, sales districts, etc.) must be considered in searching for causal relationships. Notice also that balancing treatment groups in terms of key variables (e.g., percent of weightlifters) does not prevent aggregation from obscuring the true causal relationships. All balancing does is prevent the variable from being a cause of *average* differences.

Time Series Designs

Cross-sectional designs involve measurement at a single point in time. In contrast, time series designs measure the same phenomenon at several points in time. This allows both for the treatment to take effect and for assessing how long the effect persists. On the other hand, it also allows for a number of other factors (exogenous events) to arise, which can affect the results.

A common type of experiment involves observing behavior over time and partway through changing a key variable (e.g., price). Assuming other variables stay the same, the impact of the treatment is the difference between, for example, sales before and after the price decrease. In Figure 6.2, there is apparently an increase in sales for the first two periods after a price change, following which sales return to their prechange level. This "clean" result is more likely in a lab than in the real world, where competitors quickly match price cuts (sometimes automatically through computer programs), and other factors (advertising, distribution, new product introduction) are likely to change as well. The problem with time series designs is that over time the impacts of mortality, history, maturation, and conditioning are more likely to be important.

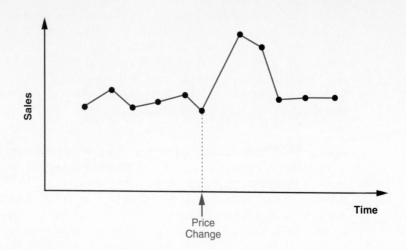

FIGURE 6.2
The Impact of a Price Decrease

Between versus Within Subjects

A major distinction exists between designs where different subjects (people, companies, regions) are exposed to different treatments and a design where the same subjects are exposed to multiple treatments. Within-subject designs run the risk of problems such as, to some extent, the time series problems of mortality, history, maturation, and particularly conditioning, whereas between-subject designs have potential problems with comparability of subjects and with the additional random component of response that occurs when analyzing differences across (heterogeneous) people. Consider response to a treatment in a between-subjects design as

Subject i's Response = Average subject's response + Subject i's unique effect
+ Experimental impacts (conditioning, etc.)

Subject i's information about the average response is confounded by subject i's unique characteristics, which can mask treatment effects. A within-subject design would allow us to estimate the difference between two treatments at the subject level, and hence the unique subject effects would drop out (be controlled for within subject). Within-subject designs are also often less expensive and easier to administer. On the other hand, conditioning effects are more likely to affect within-subject designs, especially when they occur over time (see Table 6.1).

TABLE 6.1   **Key Problems with Various Designs**

	Cross-Sectional	Time Series
Between Subjects	Noncomparability	Noncomparability
		Exogenous events
Within Subjects	Conditioning	Mortality
		Maturation
		Exogenous events

DESIGN: BASIC NOTIONS

The logic underlying a simple experiment is fairly straightforward. Assume that a company is considering changing advertising strategy from copy A to copy B. It could do the following:

1. Expose subjects to copy B.
2. Measure attitude toward the product after exposure.

This seems logical except for one point. Attitude after exposure needs to be compared with something. An attitude after exposure of 4 on a 5-point scale may sound good; but if the attitude before exposure was 4.5, it may indicate an impending disaster. The basic choices for standards of comparison are:

1. Attitude before exposure to copy B
2. Attitude after exposure to copy A

Comparing attitude after exposure to copy B with attitude after exposure to copy A gives an indication of whether copy A or copy B is better. Hence, we could design the following two treatments to test whether copy A or copy B is more effective:

	Treatment	
	1	2
Premeasure of attitude	X	X
See copy A	X	
See copy B		X
Postmeasure of attitude	X	X

Assume the results (a bigger number indicates more favorable attitude) were as follows:

	Treatment	
	1	2
Premeasure	10	10
Postmeasure	15	13

We can thus see that copy B appears effective in an absolute sense, but not as effective as copy A in a relative sense.

Alternatively, we might have been concerned about the possible effect of the premeasure on the results. Then we could have designed the following four treatments:

	Treatment			
	1	2	3	4
Premeasure of attitude	x(10)	x(10)		
See copy A	x		x	
See copy B		x		x
Postmeasure of attitude	x(15)	x(13)	x(14)	x(15)

The reason for including treatments 3 and 4 is the possibility that the premeasure could influence the results by heightening awareness of the product and, hence, either receptivity or resistance to the ads. By measuring the effect of the copy both with and without premeasures, the difference between the results gives an estimate of the effect of the premeasure.

If, as before, one only looks at treatments 1 and 2, it appears that copy A (15) is more effective than copy B (13). Looking at treatments 3 and 4, on the other hand, it appears that copy B (15) is more effective than copy A (14). In this case, the premeasure seems to have improved the effect of copy A by one (15 − 14), while the premeasure reduced the effect of copy B by two (13 − 15). However, in removing the possible effect of the premeasure in treatments 3 and 4, we have also removed the check that indicated that the groups exposed to treatments 3 and 4 had the same initial attitudes. To put it bluntly, we're not sure which ad is better.

If you are now somewhat confused as to the effect of copy A versus copy B, good. The seemingly simple problem of determining which ad is better is actually considerably harder to solve than it appears at first. While using experiments is an obvious approach, the choice of (a) which experiment to run and (b) how to interpret the results can be fairly difficult.

At this point, three things should be apparent. First, the design of an experiment depends heavily on logic and is essentially the process of deciding which factors (variables) could influence the results so that the effect of each one can be separately isolated by either manipulation or control. Second, the number of factors that could possibly influence the results is enormous. Therefore, choosing the most important variables for designing treatments and controlling and monitoring other variables that could influence results is crucial. Finally, one must be very careful in interpreting the results, since the differences may not be statistically significant. For this reason, interpretation of the results of an experiment almost always involves a statistical analysis—usually analysis of variance (see Chapter 12).

FORMAL EXPERIMENTAL DESIGNS

In the previous section, the basic notion of an experiment was introduced. In this section, some examples of experimental designs will be presented. Before proceeding, however, it is useful to adopt the following definitions:

Factor: A variable that is explicitly manipulated as a part of the experiment (e.g., price, advertising copy)

Levels: The values a factor is allowed to take on (e.g., prices of $100, $200, and $300; advertising copy A or B)

Treatment: The combined levels of the factors to which an individual is exposed (e.g., price of $200 and advertising copy A)

Control group: Subjects who are exposed to no treatment

Measurement: The recording of a response of the respondent by any means (observation, survey, etc.)

Subject: The object of the treatment, which may be a person, a district, a company, or any other unit of measure of interest

Variation in the results of an experiment can be due to several factors:

1. *Treatment effects.* These are the effects of interest, since the treatments typically vary the decision variables (price, advertising copy). While in controlled situations exposure to a treatment is usually forced, it is still often useful to use a "manipulation check" to make sure subjects were aware of the treatment (Perdue and Summers, 1986).

2. *Experimental effects.* These include the impact of a measurement on a subject's subsequent behavior, as well as the impact of being in the experiment. These are unintended/nuisance effects, which need to be measured so they can be removed.

3. *Other-variable effects.* These are the effects of ignored ("else") variables. They are assumed to be zero but, in the case of field experiments, often appear. While these variables can sometimes be measured after the fact, their effect is often so large that it obscures the impact of the treatments.

4. *Randomness.* Not every subject, or even one person on every occasion, responds the same way to a treatment. Hence, a part of the response is essentially random and, for small sample sizes, the average responses (i.e., to an ad) can be unstable, leading an inferior ad to outperform a superior one. This effect on the average response is reduced by increasing the sample size in the experiment. Basically, the weaker the treatment effect, the larger the sample size needed to establish its impact.

The trick in interpreting the results of an experiment, and therefore in designing it, is to separate these effects. In this section, we describe several simple designs and show how they can be used to estimate the treatment effect and, in some cases, to isolate some of the experimental effects.

Single-Factor Designs

These designs, which vary a single treatment variable, differ in the amount of attention they pay to the various problems and, hence, the precision with which they assess the impact of the treatment.

After-Only Without Control Group This, the simplest design, selects a single group of subjects, exposes them to a treatment (X), and then takes a measurement (O):

$$\text{Group 1} \quad X \quad O$$

For example, a group of purchasing agents might be sent to a training program and then their performance measured. If there is no premeasure or control group, it is impossible to tell if performance improved or declined. Hence, in isolation this design is essentially worthless. (Note there may be a standard of comparison for similar tests, such as Burke scores for day-after TV ad recall, which provides a useful comparison point for the observed behavior.)

Before-After Without Control Group   This adds a premeasure to the after-only design:

$$\text{Group 1} \quad O_1 \quad X \quad O_2$$

Unfortunately, this design does not allow one to separate the effect of the premeasure (the measurement effect) from the treatment effect.

After-Only with One Control Group   To measure the impact of a treatment without the confounding effect of a premeasure, two groups are needed: one exposed to the treatment and one that is not:

$$\text{Group 1} \quad X \quad O_1$$
$$\text{Group 2} \qquad\quad O_2$$

This design is often used post hoc when exposure to a treatment (e.g., an ad) is monitored after the fact. The effect of the treatment is given by $O_1 - O_2$. However, this design makes the untestable assumption that measurements would have been equal in the two groups before the study.

Before-After with One Control Group

$$\text{Group 1} \quad O_1 \quad X \quad O_2$$
$$\text{Group 2} \quad O_3 \qquad\quad O_4$$

The advantage of a premeasure is it allows for slightly unequal groups in terms of key variables, since the difference (change) in the key variable is used to estimate the effect of a treatment. Here, the effect of the treatment is given by $(O_2 - O_1) - (O_4 - O_3)$. The control group is used to estimate the maturation and testing effects.

Four-Group, Six-Study

$$\text{Group 1 (experimental)} \quad O_1 \quad X \quad O_2$$
$$\text{Group 2 (control)} \qquad\quad O_3 \qquad\quad O_4$$
$$\text{Group 3 (experimental)} \qquad\quad X \quad O_5$$
$$\text{Group 4 (control)} \qquad\qquad\quad O_6$$

The so-called four-group, six-study design is used when an interaction effect between the premeasure and the treatment is expected (e.g., when asking opinions about a topic causes a subject to begin thinking about the topic and thus to respond differently to information on the subject). The prior level of the variable of interest is estimated as the average of the two premeasures:

$$\tfrac{1}{2}(O_1 + O_3)$$

Consequently, the four groups yield estimates of the impact of the experimental treatment (E), premeasurement (M), the interaction between the premeasure and the treatment (I), and uncontrolled variables (U) as follows:

$$\text{Group 1} \quad O_2 - O_1 = M + E + I + U$$
$$\text{Group 2} \quad O_4 - O_3 = M + U$$
$$\text{Group 3} \quad O_5 - \tfrac{1}{2}(O_1 + O_3) = E + U$$
$$\text{Group 4} \quad O_6 - \tfrac{1}{2}(O_1 + O_3) = U$$

By solving these four equations in four unknowns, we can estimate each of the separate effects. For example, we can estimate the experimental effect based on groups 3 and 4 as $(O_6 - O_5)$. This design costs twice what an after-only or before-after with one control group costs, since it requires four groups instead of two. If one can assume the premeasure has no major interaction with the treatment, then the simpler design is used. Put differently, this design is elegant and thorough but rarely used.

Multiple-Factor Designs

Designs involving the monitoring of two or more factors are very common. The basic idea of such experiments is to simultaneously assess the effects of varying levels on several factors.

The most important principle involved in multifactor experiments is to make sure the factors are not confounded (that is, that they vary separately). For example, assume you were testing for the effects of advertising and promotion and had two treatments: high advertising/high promotion and low advertising/low promotion. In this case, you can estimate the impact of marketing effort (advertising plus promotion) but you cannot logically (and hence statistically) separately estimate the impacts of advertising and promotion. A number of standard designs exist for multiple factors, including:

Factorial Design The most complete information can always be obtained by means of a full factorial design. A full factorial design requires exposing two or more subjects to each of the various possible combinations of the factors. The results allow estimation of the effect of each level for each factor, as well as the interaction (synergy) between each combination of factor levels. Consider for a moment a problem involving in-store testing of four advertising strategies (A, B, C, D), three packages (I, II, III), and three colors (red, green, orange). There are $4 \times 3 \times 3 = 36$ combinations possible (see Table 6.2). To implement a full factorial design, you need at least 36 stores. To estimate interactions (e.g., the unique effect of putting package design III and red color together), 72 stores (2 per possible treatment) are needed. Factorial designs are thus essentially two things:

1. The best in terms of information attainable, since all possible combinations are examined
2. The most expensive to implement

Finding 72 stores that are both comparable and willing to participate in an experiment is often impossible; and even if it were possible, it would be a difficult-to-manage

TABLE 6.2 A Three-Factor Factorial Design Example: All Possible Treatments

Advertising Strategy	Package Design	Color	Advertising Strategy	Package Design	Color
A	I	Red	C	I	Red
A	I	Green	C	I	Green
A	I	Orange	C	I	Orange
A	II	Red	C	II	Red
A	II	Green	C	II	Green
A	II	Orange	C	II	Orange
A	III	Red	C	III	Red
A	III	Green	C	III	Green
A	III	Orange	C	III	Orange
B	I	Red	D	I	Red
B	I	Green	D	I	Green
B	I	Orange	D	I	Orange
B	II	Red	D	II	Red
B	II	Green	D	II	Green
B	II	Orange	D	II	Orange
B	III	Red	D	III	Red
B	III	Green	D	III	Green
B	III	Orange	D	III	Orange

experiment. Hence, researchers tend to use less than full factorial designs. These designs, such as the so-called fractional factorial designs (Holland and Cravens, 1973; Green, 1974), require substantially fewer data than a full factorial design.

There are a massive number of fractional factorial designs that are commonly used. All of these designs involve a "trick": in order to simplify the problem, we assume something about the way the influencing variables affect the dependent variable. Some of the most common are as follows:

1. *Independent factor testing.* In this method, we assume the factors (influencing variables) all affect the dependent variable separately. We can separately use four stores to check on the effect of advertising, three stores to check packaging, and three stores to check color, for a total of 10 instead of 72 stores.

2. *Orthogonal designs.* If it is possible to assume that certain interactions do not occur (e.g., advertising and color do not interact), subsets of the factorial array can often be used to estimate the direct effects of the influencing variables. Such designs are available in table form (Addleman, 1962; Hahn and Shapiro, 1966) and are discussed in conjunction with conjoint measurement in Chapter 15.

3. *"Logical" designs.* In many cases, it is relatively easy to eliminate several combinations as either infeasible technically (e.g., a machine that is inexpensive, has high output, and produces high-quality products), unappealing intuitively (plain packaging with a high fashion appeal item), or infeasible politically (e.g., company policy is to produce high-quality products; the boss likes TV advertising; etc.). Therefore, we can reduce many apparently factorial problems to the testing of a small number of feasible combinations.

4. *Latin square.* Latin square designs apply when two factors are involved. For example, in studying three package designs, we may wish to use actual store testing. We may also feel that store sales change over time due to seasonal demand variation. Since recruiting stores is very difficult, we attempt to use as few as possible. Basically, this is a time series design where the treatments rotate among the stores over time. The Latin square "trick" is twofold. First, assume that there is no interaction between the factors (often a reasonable assumption) and that there is no carryover effect; that is, sales in one period do not influence sales in the next. Then, use only three stores over three time periods by cycling each package through each store (Table 6.3). This allows estimation of both the time effect and the package design effect. A major problem with Latin square designs where one factor is time is the no-carryover assumption, which is clearly inappropriate for any product that either can be stockpiled (e.g., canned fruit) or satisfies a demand for a long time period (e.g., a car).

Experiments and Complex Relationships

Most relationships tend to be fairly straightforward, a combination of simple main effects (e.g., higher price leads to lower sales), and interactions (e.g., higher advertising leads to a reduced impact of price on sales). Most standard designs are developed to efficiently estimate main effects and, to some extent, interactions. Occasionally, however, the problem under consideration has a more complex nature. In these situations, a combination of logic and a specialist are required.

Consider a complex pattern such as that in Table 6.4. The only rule that is consistent with this is the dependent variable is 1 if A and B and C are 1 *or* if A or B and C and D are 1. If we select a typical orthogonal design (Table 6.5), the rule appears to be the dependent variable is 1 if C and D are 1. If we select every other observation (1, 3, . . .) from the factorial design, we conclude B and C must be 1. What this suggests is that while simple designs work well to uncover simple relationships, complex relationships require more complex designs.

Summary

Developing an ability to design successful experiments requires a combination of logic, perseverance, and experience (plus a nontrivial amount of luck). Cookbook approaches

TABLE 6.3 Latin Square Design

	Store		
Time	1	2	3
1	A	B	C
2	B	C	A
3	C	A	B

where
 A = package design A
 B = package design B
 C = package design C

TABLE 6.4 Hypothetical Relationship

Observation	Treatment Factors				Dependent Variable
	A	B	C	D	
1	1	1	1	1	1
2	1	1	1	0	1
3	1	1	0	1	
4	1	0	1	1	1
5	0	1	1	1	1
6	1	1	0	0	
7	1	0	1	0	
8	1	0	0	1	
9	0	1	1	0	
10	0	1	0	1	
11	0	0	1	1	
12	1	0	0	0	
13	0	1	0	0	
14	0	0	1	0	
15	0	0	0	1	
16	0	0	0	0	

TABLE 6.5 Partial Designs

Orthogonal Design

A	B	C	D	Dependent Variable
0	0	0	0	
0	0	0	1	
0	1	1	0	
0	1	1	1	1
1	0	1	0	
1	0	1	1	1
1	1	0	0	
1	1	0	1	

Every Other One Design

A	B	C	D	Dependent Variable
1	1	1	1	1
1	1	0	1	
0	1	1	1	1
1	0	1	0	
0	1	1	0	
0	0	1	1	
0	1	0	0	
0	0	0	1	

are useful in formulating a basic design. Still, in designing an experiment, there are a variety of considerations, including the following:

Always have a control group or other result to serve as a baseline, since absolute results are usually meaningless.

Choose a criterion variable that is both measurable and translatable to market results. The variable chosen to be measured during an experiment has to be both readily measurable and relevant. Awareness may be measurable but not closely related to market results; actual sales in stores are impractical to measure. For this reason, such intermediate measures as attitude are often used.

Calibrate before the experiment, so the translation from the experimental criterion variable (e.g., attitude) to the likely market result (e.g., share) is well established.

Be careful not to assume that the result of a one-shot treatment (e.g., price, ad copy) will be repeated with multiple exposures. Competitive reaction and boredom will both tend to affect results if a marketing program is continued over time. On the other hand, several exposures to certain advertisements may be necessary before the advertisement has an impact.

If you want to measure the effect of a particular factor or variable, make sure that it (a) varies (if I only expose subjects to diet sodas, I can't assess the effect of calories on preference) *and (b) varies in such a way that its variation is not perfectly related to the variation of other factors.* If all low-price products were also late entrants in the market, it is impossible to know whether their share is a function of late entry or price.

Be aware that the experiment itself may influence behavior by, for example, heightening awareness on the part of respondents. Even the time of day at which the experiment occurs may influence the results. (Postlunch studies about food will differ from prelunch studies, etc.)

LABORATORY EXPERIMENTS

Most people's notion of experiments comes from the natural sciences, where laboratories are used to tightly control conditions. In lab experiments, we can control the angle at which a marble hits a wall to find out that the angle of incidence equals the angle of reflection. Lab experiments are also commonly used in dealing with animals, and many psychologists are especially fond of rats. Unfortunately, consumers and businesses are both more likely to realize they are being observed and to refuse to participate than a marble or a rat. (Only on New Year's Eve do most people get sufficiently interested in cheese to crawl through a maze to get it.) In fact, lab experiments are difficult to use for a number of reasons, including the following:

"Normal" people may refuse to participate, leaving the sample stocked with "weirdos" (a problem with long jury trials as well).

Those people who participate may be more likely to game-play than respond normally.

Calories	Flavor	
	Cola	**Lemon-Lime**
Nondiet	Coke	7-Up
	Pepsi	Sprite
	Tab	Like
Diet	Diet Pepsi	Fresca

FIGURE 6.3
Brands in Soft Drink Experiment

There may be such a tremendous number of variables of interest that a manageable design for separating all their effects is impossible. Assume you believed there were eight key variables, each with three possible levels. This would produce $3^8 = 6,561$ possible combinations and, thus, 6,561 potential treatments. Unless simplifying assumptions can be made so that less than full factorial designs are employed, this is an essentially hopeless situation.

Lab conditions may be sufficiently different from the real world that laboratory results do not accurately reflect real-world results. Often this is a difference of degree, not kind, however. For example, in a lab setting everyone may see the test ad, whereas if the same ad ran on television only 20 percent of viewers might see it, with the other 80 percent busy sleeping, talking, reading, getting a snack, or going to the bathroom. Hence, it is especially crucial in the case of lab experiments to develop a way to translate (calibrate) lab results into a useful prediction of market results.

An Example

An example of a laboratory experiment concerning soft drink preference (Bass, Pessemier, and Lehmann, 1972) is instructive. This experiment involved 264 students and secretaries (your basic convenience sample) who participated in a study over a three-week period. Part of the study involved filling out questionnaires at four points during the three-week period. The other basic part of the experiment consisted of subjects selecting soft drinks on 12 occasions. All soft drinks were in 12-ounce cans and served cold. The eight soft drinks themselves were selected to reflect two dimensions: flavor and calories (Figure 6.3). As part of the experiment, subjects were denied the opportunity to purchase Coke on the fifth occasion. The purpose of this was to see if those who had bought Coke in the previous period would switch to the most similar brand, Pepsi. The results are presented in Table 6.6. The obvious conclusion from this is that the majority of individuals did indeed switch to Pepsi when Coke was out of stock.

TABLE 6.6 Percent Switching from Coke to Each Brand

	Coke	7-Up	Tab	Like	Pepsi	Sprite	Diet Pepsi	Fresca	Sample (n)
Average switching in periods 1-2, 2-3, 3-4	48	16	2	6	15	6	2	5	239
Period 4-5 switching	x	22	2	3	53	13	3	5	64

FIELD EXPERIMENTS

Field experiments are the opposite of lab experiments on the realism scale. By moving the experiment to the real world, many of the problems arising from the artificial nature of lab experiments are reduced. As a corollary, field experiments tend to be concerned with aggregate and objective data (such as sales) rather than individual and subjective data (such as attitudes).

In solving the artificiality problem, field experiments pay a heavy price. One of the major detriments is cost in terms of money, time, and aggravation. Field experiments, such as test markets in two cities, involve budgets of $700,000 or more and require a minimum of six months to complete.

The other major problem with field experiments is the lack of control. I can show an ad on network TV, but I can't control who watches it. Similarly, as a manufacturer I can cut price 5 cents but can't control competitive activity or retailer pricing practices. It would be hard to tell the effect of a price cut if simultaneously one competitor introduced a new product, a second dropped an old product, a third ran a major coupon special, and a fourth doubled advertising. Such events often happen without planning, but companies are likely to do anything possible to confuse test markets in order to deny useful information to their competitors.

NATURAL EXPERIMENTS

The standard view of an experiment is the situation in which a researcher assigns subjects to treatments in either a random or systematic manner. While this is possible in lab experiments, it is difficult in field settings. (How do I convince Mr. Smith of 123 Maple Street that he must watch channel 7 at 7:30 Monday night?) The concept of a natural experiment is to allow subjects to choose which treatment they receive. For example, some people will have been exposed to ads and some not. To measure the effect of an ad, we simply observe (after the fact) the difference in behavior between those who happened to see the ad and those who did not see it. Put differently, performing a natural experiment is treating data as though they were the output of an experiment.

The advantage of a natural experiment is that the artificial nature of a controlled experiment is circumvented. The disadvantage is that interpretation becomes a serious problem. Often, the characteristic that led the subject to select a particular treatment is related to the criterion variable. Put differently, an important covariate may exist. For example, those who saw an ad may have been exposed to the ad because they sought it out and, thus, their likelihood of buying the product after the ad is greater not because of the effect of the ad but because of greater prior interest (another example of an "else" variable). Still, post hoc experimentation is a very useful tool.

An Example

To see how a natural experiment works, consider the issue of which media, TV or magazine, is more effective in increasing perceived knowledge of a new small car. It is possible to design either a lab or field experiment and control advertising exposure to examine the effect of advertising exposure on perceived knowledge. Such experiments, however, tend to be either unrealistic or expensive.

An alternative approach is to examine the perceived knowledge of subjects based on their actual exposure. In this case, subjects were asked their perceived knowledge (on a 10-point scale) of a new car both before and after the presentation of a major introductory campaign. The subjects were also asked to report which magazines they read and which television shows they viewed. By using the actual media plan, a potential advertising exposure measure was established (Lehmann, 1977). While this measures potential rather than actual exposure (I may read a magazine and skip the ads), this objective measure seemed preferable to self-reported advertising exposure, which can be expected to be both inaccurate and contaminated by attitudes. Based on the advertising exposure measures, 622 subjects were divided into nine categories. Next, the average change in perceived knowledge was calculated for each of the nine possible combinations of TV and magazine advertising exposure. The average changes and number of subjects in each cell are shown in Table 6.7.

Ignoring issues of statistical significance and "fancy" analytical procedures, these results seem to indicate three interesting findings:

1. More exposure generally means a larger increase in perceived knowledge. The exception to this is the low-low group.
2. Both TV and magazine advertising seem to contribute (at approximately equal levels) to increased knowledge. Since the budget was split about 50:50, this suggests (albeit weakly) that both media were about equally effective.
3. Even low-exposure people become noticeably more knowledgeable, presumably due to word-of-mouth discussion, etc.

A problem exists with these results. The problem (common to all natural experiments) is that other variables are not controlled for. It is possible that, for example, all high-income people are in the high magazine–low TV exposure cell. Hence, the results in this cell could be as much or more attributable to the effect of income (and its covariates, such as education) as to advertising exposure. This problem of uncontrolled variables that are related to the measured/key variables—often called *covariates*—makes

TABLE 6.7 Average Change in Perceived Knowledge

Magazine Advertising Exposure	TV Advertising Exposure		
	Low	Medium	High
Low	1.68 (72)	1.32 (74)	1.90 (61)
Medium	1.19 (66)	1.50 (78)	1.61 (65)
High	1.89 (58)	2.30 (84)	2.70 (64)

Source: Donald R. Lehmann, "Responses to Advertising a New Car," from *Journal of Advertising Research* 17 (August 1977): 25. Copyright © 1977 by the Advertising Research Foundation. Reprinted with the permission of the publishers.

simple analysis of the results dangerous. Dealing with covariates requires analytical procedures (such as the brilliantly named analysis of covariance, which is essentially multiple regression) beyond the scope of this chapter. It is interesting to note, however, that employing "sophisticated" analytical procedures to control for the effect of these covariates did not change the findings in this case.

QUASI-EXPERIMENTS

A number of firms offer methods that blend the characteristics of controlled and natural experiments. One of the earliest field-test procedures for testing broadcast TV ads was offered by AdTel. The design utilized split-cable TV with a sample of households. Using cities that are somewhat isolated where TV viewing was mainly restricted to cable (e.g., Pittsfield, Mass.), households were divided into two groups (an A and B panel). Each group could receive different ads (or an ad vs. no ad). Panelists maintained purchase diaries, which could then be matched to TV exposure.

Currently, the best-known successor to AdTel is IRI's BehaviorScan. In addition to expanding the service to eight markets, BehaviorScan uses special shopper cards, which are scanned whenever the household shops (and remembers the card) at grocery, drug, or mass merchandise stores in the city. In this panel, households can be identified and then targeted with advertising based on purchase records (e.g., loyalty to a given brand) and demographics.

Other hybrids include various product testing methods such as BASES, ASSESSOR (M/A/R/C), LTM (Yankelovich), and COMP (Elrick and Lavidge). These simulated test markets have proven to be quite accurate and both faster and less expensive (e.g., $100,000 vs. $1,000,000) than full test markets. In general, there is a trend toward this type of research.

CONTINUOUS (ADAPTIVE) EXPERIMENTATION

As discussed earlier, marketing research is traditionally thought of as a collection of one-shot studies, each addressing a particular problem. Consistent with this perspective, this chapter has focused on the design of a single, controlled experiment. The current trend, however, suggests both market research in general and experiments in particular form a continuous series of activities aimed at learning. One example of this is advertising copy testing, which can be approached as a series of tests aimed at selecting and refining a message rather than a single go/no go decision. The best examples of continuous learning/experimentation come from direct marketing. Here, marketing and marketing research become intertwined as a customer contact program/mailing (marketing) produces a response (data), which is then analyzed (marketing research) to produce insight, which is used to produce subsequent customer contact programs (marketing).

Increasingly, the view of a company as a learning organization requires thinking of research (and experimentation) as something done in the course of business rather than solely a special event. Similarly, many (natural) experiments can be found in existing data, only a few of which are very tightly controlled. Hence, viewing marketing research and marketing as a series of analyses and adaptations is increasingly both feasible and desirable.

PLANNING FOR ANALYSIS

Since the reason for gathering data is to perform analysis, the adequacy of the data is directly tied to their value in performing the analysis. Put differently, optimal design depends on the planned analysis. In marketing, the key analysis is generally an ANOVA (analysis of variance) or regression analysis. Both procedures are more efficient when the predictor variables are not confounded (soon to be called collinear). Importantly, one can assess the efficiency of the estimates (e.g., the effect of advertising on sales) before data are collected and compare alternative designs a priori. Since these techniques have not yet been discussed, we postpone detailed discussion until later. The important point here is that you should consider the ramifications of a particular design on the ability to interpret results *before* you collect data. Anyone interested in detailed statistical discussions should consult other sources (e.g., Hahn, Meeker, and Feder, 1976; Kuhfeld, Tobias, and Garratt, 1994).

SUMMARY

Volumes can and have been written on the design and interpretation of experiments. The major point of this chapter is that experimental design is basically logic and common sense. Variables that don't matter should be ignored. Those variables that matter but are not the focus of the study should be controlled for (by making the groups equal) and/or measured so their impact can be assessed. The variables that are the focus of the study should be manipulated so that they vary and their variation is not confounded with other variables (e.g., a premeasurement).

This chapter has attempted to focus attention on the logical issues involved in deducing causality and designing experiments. Interpretation has been discussed in general terms. Specific statistical analysis of results is typically accomplished by means of analysis of variance (ANOVA), which will be discussed in chapter 12.

PROBLEMS

1. Assume I ran an experiment and got the following results:

	Treatment				
	1	*2*	*3*	*4*	*5*
Premeasure	x(10)		x(11)	x(9)	x(10)
Exposure to ad			x		x
Exposure to cents off coupon	x	x			x
Postmeasure	x(14)	x(13)	x(13)	x(11)	x(16)

a. Estimate the effects of the ad and the coupon.

b. What assumptions did you make in (a)?

c. Change one of your assumptions and see if the results change.

2. The market research department of brand A ran an experiment involving a promotion and got the following results:

First Purchase	Second Purchase A	B
Test Group		
A	.90	.10
B	.15	.85
Control Group		
A	.80	.20
B	.15	.85

Assuming brand A has a 20 percent share currently, interpret the results.

3. Write down a model of how you think people go about buying beer.

4. Get a group of friends together. Have them discuss beer purchasing. Summarize the discussion.

5. The sales levels in each of the two weeks following distribution of cents-off redeemable coupons were as follows:

Coupon	Sales After Distribution 1st Week	2nd Week
5¢ off one package	20	0
10¢ off on purchase of second package	50	10
10¢ off one package	40	40
20¢ off one package	90	70

The coupon distributions were made several months apart to allow the effects of previous coupons to die out before the next coupon was distributed. What can you conclude about the difference in sales due to the coupons?

6. In the Yuk market, there are two major brands: Awful and Bad. Currently, their shares are 40 percent and 30 percent, respectively. Traditionally, the percentage of people who repeatedly purchase these brands from one period to the next has been 80 percent and 70 percent, respectively. Also, 80 percent of the users of minor brands in one period purchase a minor brand in the following period. If a minor brand purchaser in a previous period does not buy a minor brand, he or she is equally likely to purchase Awful and Bad. Similarly, nonrepeat purchasers of Awful are equally likely to purchase Bad or a minor brand. However, purchasers of Bad that don't repeat purchase are twice as likely to buy Awful as any of the minor brands. What will be the market shares next period?

7. Assume you have 100 samples of a particular product. You wish to measure the product's ignition point at different air temperature and humidity conditions. How would you proceed?

8. You have been assigned to find out which of three advertising campaigns, which of three package designs, and which of four names are best for a particular new detergent. How would you proceed, given:

a. A budget of $5,000 and one month?

b. A budget of $30,000 and three months?

c. A budget of $500,000 and one year?

REFERENCES

ADDLEMAN, SIDNEY (1962) "Orthogonal Main-Effects Plans for Asymmetrical Factorial Experiments," *Technometrics*, 4, February, 21–46.

BANKS, SEYMOUR (1965) *Experimentation in Marketing*, New York: McGraw-Hill.

BASS, FRANK M. (1974) "The Theory of Stochastic Preference and Brand Switching," *Journal of Marketing Research*, 11, February, 1–20.

BASS, FRANK M., EDGAR A. PESSEMIER, AND DONALD R. LEHMANN (1972) "An Experimental Study of Relationships Between Attitudes, Brand Preference, and Choice," *Behavioral Science*, 17, November, 523–41.

BURKE, RAYMOND R., BARI A. HARLAM, BARBARA E. KAHN, AND LEONARD M. LODISH (1992) "Comparing Dynamic Consumer Choice in Real and Computer-Simulated Environments," *Journal of Consumer Research*, 19, June, 71–82.

CAMPBELL, DONALD T., AND JULIAN C. STANLEY (1966) *Experimental Designs for Research*, Skokie, Ill.: Rand-McNally.

CLAYCAMP, HENRY J., AND LUCIEN E. LIDDY (1969) "Prediction of New Product Performance: An Analytical Approach," *Journal of Marketing Research*, 4, November, 414–20.

COOK, THOMAS D., AND DONALD T. CAMPBELL (1979) *Quasi-Experimentation: Design and Analysis Issues for Field Settings*, Chicago: Rand-McNally.

DEY, ALOKE (1985) *Orthogonal Fractional Factorial Designs*, New York: John Wiley and Sons.

GREEN, PAUL E. (1974) "On the Design of Choice Experiments Involving Multifactor Alternatives," *Journal of Consumer Research*, 1, September, 61–68.

HAHN, GERALD J., WILLIAM Q. MEEKER, JR., AND PAUL I. FEDER (1976) "The Evaluation and Comparison of Experimental Designs for Fitting Regression Relationships," *Journal of Quality Technology*, 8, July, 140–57.

HAHN, GERALD J., AND S. S. SHAPIRO (1966) "A Catalog and Computer Program for the Design and Analysis of Symmetric and Asymmetric Fractional Factorial Experiments," Technical Report 66-C-165, General Electric Research and Development Center, Schenectady, N.Y.

HOLLAND, CHARLES W., AND DAVID W. CRAVENS (1973) "Fractional Factorial Experimental Designs in Marketing Research," *Journal of Marketing Research*, 10, August, 270–76.

KALWANI, MANOHAR U., AND DONALD G. MORRISON (1977) "A Parsimonious Description of the Hendry System," *Management Science*, 23, January, 467–77.

KERLINGER, FRED N. (1973) *Foundations of Behavioral Research*, 2nd ed., New York: Holt, Rinehart and Winston.

KUHFELD, WARREN F., RANDALL D. TOBIAS, AND MARK GARRATT (1994) "Efficient Experimental Designs with Marketing Research Applications," *Journal of Marketing Research*, 31, November, 545–57.

LEHMANN, DONALD R. (1977) "Responses to Advertising a New Car," *Journal of Advertising Research*, 17, August, 23–32.

LYNCH, JOHN G., JR. (1982) "On the External Validity of Experiments in Consumer Research," *Journal of Consumer Research*, 9, December, 225–39.

PERDUE, BARBARA C., AND JOHN O. SUMMERS (1986) "Checking the Success of Manipulations in Marketing Experiments," *Journal of Marketing Research*, 23, November, 317–26.

SAWYER, ALAN G. (1975) "Demand Artifacts in Laboratory Experiments in Consumer Research," *Journal of Consumer Research*, 2, March, 20–30.

SELLITZ, CLAIRE (1959) *Research Methods in Social Relations*, New York: Holt, Rinehart and Winston.

SHIMP, TERENCE A., EVA M. HYATT, AND DAVID J. SNYDER (1991) "A Critical Appraisal of Demand Artifacts in Consumer Research," *Journal of Consumer Research*, 18, December, 273–83.

WEBB, EUGENE J., DONALD T. CAMPBELL, RICHARD D. SCHWARTZ, AND LEE SECHREST (1966) *Unobtrusive Measures*, Skokie, Ill.: Rand-McNally.

CHAPTER 7

Survey Design

Surveys are mainstays of marketing research. Surveys are relatively cheap and easy to administer and are also the only known way to get measures of thoughts and attitudes. Of course, self-reported behaviors are often inaccurate. In spite of occasional (make that constant) problems, however, surveys remain an integral part of research.

This chapter proceeds by describing some of the choices and problems involved in developing a questionnaire. Next, choice of survey method is discussed. Finally, some issues of pretesting and control are addressed.

The best way to learn about surveys and their problems is to become involved in them. Especially useful is assuming the role of a personal interviewer so that problems such as refusal to cooperate, don't know responses, and bad respondents become real. Filling out a few questionnaires will also help hone your skills.

Before beginning to design a survey, the problem should be well defined. Moreover, information needs and more specific research objectives should be delineated. If a survey appears to be an appropriate part of the research project, two related tasks must be performed: the survey instrument must be designed, and a method of administering it (e.g., telephone) selected. This chapter discusses these two issues. Specifically, the chapter proceeds through the steps listed in Figure 7.1, beginning by considering types of information needed and specific examples. A more technical discussion of scale design, as well as a general discussion of types of errors that affect research usefulness, appears in the following chapter.

CONTENT

There is a danger that too little or the wrong information will be collected when the final version of the questionnaire is frozen before pilot tests or respondent interviews are completed. On the other hand, it is common to end up with an unwieldy document, especially if the "wouldn't it be nice to know" mentality dominates questionnaire construction. Another sure way to generate a massive, incoherent questionnaire is to allow everyone in the neighborhood to put in a few questions. This questionnaire-by-committee

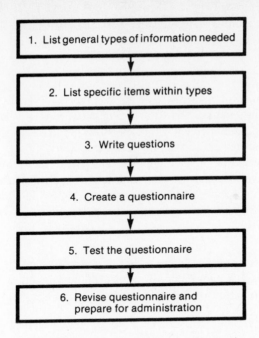

1. List general types of information needed

↓

2. List specific items within types

↓

3. Write questions

↓

4. Create a questionnaire

↓

5. Test the questionnaire

↓

6. Revise questionnaire and prepare for administration

FIGURE 7.1
Steps in Survey Design

approach may solve many individuals' data needs for no apparent additional cost (the something-for-nothing syndrome), but chances are the results will be sufficiently cumbersome or muddled that even the original sponsor of the research will be dissatisfied.

The types of information that can be collected via surveys fall into two major categories: product category variables, which relate directly to the product category under consideration; and segmenting variables, which help in describing, locating, and effectively reaching present and potential users of a product category. Generally, segmenting variables are useful predictors of product usage rates, but poor predictors of brand choice (e.g., Hunt's Catsup versus Heinz Ketchup) or individual consumer behavior. This section describes examples of the various types of information that are collected.

Segmenting Variables

Demographic   There are numerous demographic variables that are surveyed. For describing individual consumers, the following are most common:

1. Age
2. Sex
3. Marital status
4. Household size
5. Number of children
6. Region
7. Degree of urbanization

For research involving industrial products, data on the firm in terms of size (number of employees, size of plant) and type of business (often defined by SIC codes) are commonly sought. Many times data on the individual being surveyed are also collected.

Socioeconomic   These relate to the economic status of the individual or household:

1. Income
2. Education
3. Occupation

For industrial products, data on sales, market share, and profits, as well as elements of the company's general strategy (e.g., the percent of sales spent on R&D), are frequently obtained. The basic demographic and socioeconomic data that Market Facts maintained on the panelists in its Consumer Mail Panel and the categories they used are shown in Appendix 7-A. Generally, these variables have been fairly weak predictors of consumer behavior. Massy, Frank, and Lodahl (1968) found background (demographic and socioeconomic) and personality variables together account for less than 10 percent of the variation in brand choice.

Ownership   Ownership of products is frequently obtained. For individuals, these include appliances, automobiles, computers, and homes. For an industrial survey, this might include type of copying equipment, automation of the manufacturing process, or telecommunication devices on hand.

Media Exposure   Media exposure variables (e.g., TV and print) are often collected to increase the efficiency of advertising spending.

Personality   A variety of general personality variables have been applied in marketing studies for many years (Gottlieb, 1959; Robertson and Myers, 1969). The hope is to find an enduring general characteristic of a person that relates to many aspects of behavior.

In his summary, Kassarjian (1971) reviews several basic psychological theories: Freudian, social theory, stimulus-response, trait and factor theories, and self-concept. Some general personality instruments that have been used in marketing research (typically of the trait or factor theory type) include the following:

> *Gordon Personal Profile*, used by Tucker and Painter (1961) and Kernan (1968).
>
> *Edwards Personal Preference Scale*, made famous in marketing by the 1960s controversy over whether you could tell a Ford owner from a Chevy owner (Evans and Roberts, 1963). (Answer: Not very well, unless of course you observe what car they drive.)
>
> *Thurstone's Temperament Scale*, used by Kamen (1964) and Westfall (1962).
>
> *California Personality Inventory*, used for innovativeness and opinion leadership studies by Robertson and Myers (1969) and Bruce and Witt (1970), topics also investigated by King and Summers (1970) and Darden and Reynolds (1974). Also, considerable work has been done on self-concept in general (Birdwell, 1968; Grubb and Hupp, 1968) and self-confidence and risk taking in particular (Cox and Bauer, 1964; Barach, 1969; Venkatesan, 1968), as well as inner-outer directedness (Kassarjian and Kassarjian, 1966).

Some other scales that have been used include:

McClosky Personality Inventory
Dunette Adjective Checklist
Borgatta Personality Scale
Strong Vocational Interest Bank
Cattell's 16 Personality Factor Inventory

In spite of all this effort, the predictive power of these general variables has been low, typically around 5 to 10 percent of the total variation available to be explained. Both Jacoby (1971) and Kassarjian (1971) point out that, given the purposes for which general personality scales were developed, the low predictive power for brand choice decisions is quite reasonable. Product class choice seems more promising as a subject for personality variable prediction (Alpert, 1972; Bither and Dolich, 1972; Greeno, Sommers, and Kernan, 1973). Still, personality variables are generally of little value.

General Activities/Attitudes/Opinions/Interests   Generally known as lifestyle or psychographic measures, these variables are logically more closely related to product choice than personality scales. Exactly where to draw the line between personality, lifestyle, and product-related variables is somewhat unclear. Nonetheless, most researchers agree that dominance-compliance is a personality trait, love of the outdoors a lifestyle (attitude) variable, and time spent playing tennis is a product-use variable (at least if the product I'm studying is a tennis racket). Hence, we will classify a lifestyle variable as something more general than a product-related variable and something more product oriented than a personality trait. Lifestyle variables come in two major types: activities and attitudes.

> *Activities*. Measures of the actual involvement in various activities such as sports, crafts, watching TV, reading magazines, and so forth
>
> *Attitudes*. Opinions about life in general, institutions (e.g., credit, education, churches), particular issues (e.g., welfare programs), as well as activities (e.g., baking from scratch) and interests (e.g., reading)

A list of lifestyle variables taken from Plummer (1974) appears as Table 7.1.

Lifestyle measures have been used for some time (see Wells, 1974; Plummer, 1974; Reynolds, 1973; Hustad and Pessemier, 1971). A major inventory of lifestyle questions used extensively by Market Facts was reported by Wells and Tigert (1971). Reliability of lifestyle measures has been investigated and found to be reasonably good (see Pessemier and Bruno, 1971; Villani and Lehmann, 1975). Moreover, several companies have used lifestyle segmentations as the basis for developing marketing strategy (e.g., White Stag used lifestyle analysis to reposition its clothing product line). Yet here again, the predictive results have often been disappointing in spite of some reported successes. One thing that is true (and not at all surprising) is that the closer the lifestyle variables are to product variables, the better they are as predictors. An excellent review of

TABLE 7.1 A Set of Lifestyle Variables

Activities	Interests	Opinions	Demographics
Work	Family	Themselves	Age
Hobbies	Home	Social issues	Education
Social events	Job	Politics	Income
Vacation	Community	Business	Occupation
Entertainment	Recreation	Economics	Family size
Club membership	Fashion	Education	Dwelling
Community	Food	Products	Geography
Shopping	Media	Future	City size
Sports	Achievements	Culture	Stage in the life cycle

Source: Joseph T. Plummer, "The Concept and Application of Life Style Segmentation," from *Journal of Marketing* (January 1974): 34. Copyright © 1974 by the American Marketing Association. Reprinted with the permission of the publishers.

psychographics is provided by Wells (1974, 1975)—"must" reading if you are interested in using these variables.

Values   There has been considerable interest in relating behavior to basic values of individuals. Early research focused on a categorization provided by Rokeach (1973) who distinguished 18 instrumental and 18 terminal values. The VALS™ (values and lifestyles) typology of SRI International became popular in the 1980s. New York Telephone Company (predivestiture) used original VALS to segment markets for its decorator sets and to help train sales personnel (Schiffman and Jones, 1983).

In 1989 VALS was revised to focus more explicitly on explaining and understanding consumer behavior. VALS 2 classifies U.S. adults into eight consumer groups (Table 7.2) based on their answers to 35 attitudinal statements such as "I often crave excitement" and "I would rather make something than buy it" and 4 demographic questions. Integrating these statements into consumer surveys such as Simmon's *Survey of the American Household* or custom surveys provides data about product, leisure activity, and media preferences by each VALS consumer group. GeoVALS™ provides data on where to find concentrations of the desired target by ZIP code or block. iVALS is used to understand who is on the internet and what is motivating their behavior.

Other examples of general segmentation schemes include Backer Spieglvogel Bates Worldwide's GLOBAL-SCAN (which in 1989 divided consumers in different countries into Strivers, Achievers, Pressured, Adopters, and Traditionalists), CCA from Socio-Styles-Systeme of France, and RISC from the Swiss-based International Research Institute for Social Change.

Another scale, the List of Values (LOV) Scale, has been promoted as superior to VALS (Kahle, Beatty, and Homer, 1986) for predicting various behaviors. The nine basic values in that scale are:

1. Self-respect
2. Security

3. A warm relationship with others
4. A sense of accomplishment
5. Self-fulfillment
6. A sense of belonging
7. Being well-respected
8. Fun and enjoyment
9. Excitement

These values differ across regions of the United States (Kahle, Beatty, and Homer, 1986) and have been widely studied (Novak and MacEvoy, 1990; Kamakura and Mazzon, 1991; Corfman, Lehmann, and Narayanan, 1991; Kamakura and Novak, 1992).

TABLE 7.2 VALS Segments

VALS group	Self-orientation	Descriptors
Actualizers	Difficult to categorize by self-orientation because of wide experience and high self-confidence	Successful, sophisticated, daring
Fulfilleds	Principle-oriented	Mature, satisfied, knowledgeable, home-oriented, value order
Believers	Principle-oriented	Traditional, all-American, family and community oriented, brand-loyal
Achievers	Status-oriented	Relatively affluent, aware of social position, career-oriented, buy prestige products
Strivers	Status-oriented	Financially insecure, aware of social position and work to improve it, stylish
Experiencers	Action-oriented	Enthusiastic, impulsive, dislike conformity, tend to be single, impulsive
Makers	Action-oriented	Self-sufficient, independent, practical unimpressed with prestige products
Strugglers	Difficult to categorize by self-orientation because of restricted resources	Poor, concerned with security and safety, limited consumption

Source: SRI Consulting the Values and Lifestyles (VALS) Program.

Product Category Variables

Product and Brand Usage   Typically, the key variables for marketing decisions are brand choice and product usage, and considerable effort is devoted to measuring them. Common variables include:

1. Usage rate of the product class as a whole.
2. Brand used/planned to use. This includes brand bought last time, time before last, and planned to buy next time.
3. Quantity purchased.
4. Time between purchases.

Determinants of Brand Choice   A number of variables have been hypothesized to be determinants (or antecedents) of choice. Some of the most widely used are:

1. Awareness of the product class in general and of particular brands
2. Awareness and liking of advertising
3. Knowledge/understanding of the brand
4. Perception/rating of brands on specific attributes (for example, in the case of toothpaste, ratings of Crest, Colgate, etc., on such attributes as decay prevention and tooth whitening)
5. Importance of product attributes
6. Satisfaction with present product
7. Perceived risk in using the product
8. Approach used to make the choice

The last item mentioned—approach used—is generally overlooked. Still, it is often important to understand whether a respondent is just learning about the product (extensive processing), actively comparing alternatives (limited processing), or simply following a rule for making choices (routinized behavior) (Howard, 1977).

Contextual/Situational Variables   A variety of contextual/situational variables influence product and brand choice (Belk, 1975). A purchase of a sofa may depend on where it will be used (basement versus formal living room), who will use it (kids versus guests), and amount of wear you expect it to suffer. These variables break into two basic types:

> *Usage situation.* This includes place used, alternatives, time of day, social visibility, heaviness of usage, and so forth.
>
> *Influence of others* (children, spouse, etc.) on the decision.

Intention   A very common element on both consumer and industrial surveys is measuring planned or intended behavior. Such data are unreliable at the individual level (i.e., many who say they will buy won't, and vice versa), but on average, often provide a useful barometer of future prospects (Juster, 1966; McNeil, 1974). Studies of intentions data (Morrison, 1979; Kalwani and Silk, 1983; Jamieson and Bass, 1989; Morwitz and Schmittlein, 1992) indicate transformations of the data that discount intention levels are important in interpreting responses to such questions. For example, on a five-point scale, the "top box" (most favorable) intention score is likely to be converted to actual behavior between 50 and 60 percent of the time and less favorable intentions much less frequently (Infosino, 1986; Mullet and Karson, 1985). Given the error in intentions measures, it should be no surprise that questions that attempt to measure the timing of intended purchase (e.g., next 6 months, 6–12 months, etc.) are particularly unreliable (Morwitz, 1993).

Brand Equity

Brand equity has emerged as a major concern for marketers (Aaker, 1991; Aaker and Keller, 1990; Batra, Lehmann, and Singh, 1993; Keller, 1993). One view of brand equity is financial, that is, the value of the brand (trademark) itself in the financial markets. The other focuses on the value of the brand to consumers, basically how much extra (or less) they would pay to have a branded vs. unbranded product with identical physical attributes. Customer-based equity can be viewed in terms of four "A's": Awareness, Attitude, Associations, and Attachments. Awareness and attitude (general liking) are self-explanatory. Associations include quality as well as image or personality variables. Aaker (1994) describes five dimensions of personality: Sincerity, Excitement, Competence, Sophistication, and Ruggedness. Attachments relates to strength of relation, basically brand loyalty. Loyalty has a long tradition and is measured in terms of both attitudes and behavior (Jacoby and Chestnut, 1978).

Quality/Satisfaction

The quality movement and the measurement of satisfaction now play a major role in both marketing research and management. The SERVQUAL scale (Parasuraman, Zeithaml, and Berry, 1988) has been widely applied and modified (Cronin and Taylor, 1994; Teas, 1994; Parasuraman, Zeithaml, and Berry, 1994). Satisfaction measurement focuses on its three major determinants: expectations, performance, and the gap between expectations and performance (Anderson and Sullivan, 1993; Boulding et al., 1992).

Customer Focus/Market Orientation

Surveys focus on employees as well as customers. Many firms employ extensive programs to create and measure customer focus and market orientation (e.g., Dow, J.P. Morgan, USAA, Xerox). These attempt to measure the culture of the firm and its relation to customers.

Summary

The list of potential variables to include in a survey is effectively endless. Still, most of these fall into the two main categories:

    1. Descriptive variables
        a. Who are:
            (1) The purchasers
            (2) The users
        b. What they do:
            (1) What they buy
            (2) What they use it for
        c. Where they buy it:
            (1) Information sources
            (2) Shopping location
            (3) Purchase location

   d. How they buy it:
      (1) Amount
      (2) Terms (e.g., credit)
   e. When they buy it:
      (1) Time of year
      (2) Full price versus on deal
   2. Explanatory variables
      a. Why buy product category:
         (1) Alternatives considered
         (2) Needs met
      b. Why buy brand:
         (1) Benefits/attributes
         (2) Quality, satisfaction, brand equity

By considering these variables in past, present, and (most importantly) future terms, a reasonably complete assessment of customers is possible.

WRITING QUESTIONS

This section discusses some of the major issues in designing questions.

Open- versus Closed-End Questions

Data can be gathered in either open- or closed-end forms. Consider the following examples.

Brand Choice   In the case of brand choice, since the major brands are often well known, the reason for an open-ended question is unclear. Its only advantage is that users of off-brands might not feel as conspicuous as they would if they were relegated to the "other" (translation: they must be weird) category. On the other hand, for many product categories the number of people in the "other" category should be negligible, and both the respondent (because it's easier to check a space than write a word) and the analyst (because the data are precoded) will find the closed-end format better.

Open end: What brand of toothpaste do you use most often? _____

Closed end: Please indicate which brand of toothpaste you use most often:

   Aim   _____
   Colgate   _____
   Crest   _____
   Other (please specify) _____

Open end: Why do you choose a particular brand of toothpaste: _____

Closed end: Please indicate the importance of the following attributes in selecting a toothpaste:

	Very Unimportant				Very Important
Decay prevention	1	2	3	4	5
Price	1	2	3	4	5
Tooth whitening	1	2	3	4	5

Reason for Brand Choice   In the case of questions relating to reason for brand choice, the closed-end question requires more careful consideration. First, it implicitly assumes that the decision rests on attributes and their relative importances. Second, we must assume that the relevant attributes are known and included in the questionnaire. For many product categories this is a fairly believable assumption, but it does require the researcher to have either knowledge of the product or past research data. Note that the open-end question shown here is not without problems, since such incisive answers as "to put on my toothbrush" and "for brushing my teeth" are likely responses.

A serious general problem with open-ended questions is that the extent of the response depends on the glibness and interest of the respondent. Open-end answers that are the result of opinionated, glib respondents may not be representative of the total population. (This is especially true of political surveys.) Also, open-end questions do not guarantee direct comparisons between competing attributes (i.e., the relative importance of two attributes), and the relative importance must be inferred from the percent of the time each of the attributes is mentioned. While generalizations are dangerous, it is usually true that open-end questions should be restricted to the following:

1. Exploratory studies from which closed-end questions will be formed.
2. Pilot tests where they can be used to pick up missing relevant data by allowing the respondent to report them.
3. Small-sample studies of especially articulate respondents or respondents who are being surveyed by special interviewers.
4. As a final catchall question to pick up any ideas the respondent holds or provide the respondent a chance to voice his or her opinion on a subject of interest. (Many people will put up with a certain amount of pain and suffering if they have the feeling that somehow their opinions will be heard.)
5. As the first question(s) in situations where the response could be biased by responses to the closed-end questions.

An example of the value of an open-end question occurred in a study of soft drink preference. After ranking eight soft drinks on a set of prespecified attributes, respondents were asked to list other attributes that were important to their choice. Several respondents listed "aftertaste" (which they apparently distinguished from the included variable "flavor") and "packaging" (which, since all soft drinks were served cold in 12-ounce pop-top cans, suggested that some people got their jollies by looking at the designs on the cans). Since this was a multiwave study, these attributes were included in a subsequent wave of data collection.

Direct versus Indirect

In asking a question, the researcher must decide whether to ask the question directly or indirectly. The indirect method assumes that an individual will not accurately respond to a direct question because of:

Inability to understand the question if it is asked directly (e.g., Would you characterize your decision style as sophisticated or routinized?).

Inability to answer the question (e.g., you might not know how long you spend eating each day).

Unwillingness to provide the accurate response because of social pressure (e.g., nutrition is important, etc.). A favorite gambit for avoiding this problem is a projective technique where, instead of asking directly, the question is phrased in terms of the person's reference group, such as "my neighbors" (cf. Fisher, 1993). The assumption here is that you are more willing to expose undesirable traits if they are not personally attributed to you. The disadvantage is that you assume neighbors are similar (how many of your neighbors do you exactly match?), which guarantees some error in the results.

The direct method, on the other hand, assumes that the respondent can and will try to respond accurately. While indirect methods may be necessary for complex social issues or unstructured problems, most of the questions in marketing research are sufficiently straightforward that direct questions will suffice. The indirect method is also somewhat condescending, since it assumes that (*a*) the respondent isn't too bright or honest and (*b*) the respondent can be easily tricked. Actually, most normal respondents will try to respond honestly if given that opportunity, but may be offended by "tricks." Incidentally, the best respondents tend to be those who have normal profiles (high school or college graduates with a job, etc.) or grammar school students (whose interest in filling out questionnaires is remarkable). Experts (especially MBAs or market researchers) are typically poor respondents, since they spend time evaluating the questionnaire, making helpful suggestions, and trying to figure out what tricks have been employed, not to mention protesting the format.

Aided versus Unaided

Another issue is whether the responses should be aided or unaided. This is really a variation of the open- versus closed-end question theme that deals with how much information to give the respondent. A common example of this problem is the question of whether to measure aided or unaided advertising recall. Several levels of "aidedness" can be envisioned:

1. Have you heard anything lately?
2. Have you heard any ads lately?
3. Have you heard any sneaker/athletic shoe ads lately?
4. Have you heard any ads for Nike lately?
5. What is Nike's slogan?
6. Whose slogan is "Just Do It"?

Depending on what you want the percentage who are aware of Nike's slogan to be, you can use the first two (likely response less than 1 percent), the third (probably about 20 percent), or the specified aided versions 4 through 6, where the recall may be more than half. Which you use depends on what you want: top of the mind recall or to know if someone has stored the message in memory. Also, for most studies it is not the absolute value but the changes over time that matter, and so the real problem is to keep using the same scale over time.

Phraseology

Choosing a set of words to convey a construct is at best a difficult task. Words are imprecise, and most individuals' knowledge of their meanings even fuzzier. By being overly detailed, you run the risk of creating fatigue and boredom. Also, many individuals typically try to answer questions without looking at the directions (just like putting together a tool or a toy without using the directions, it seems so much easier that way). On the other hand, vague phrasing can create problems in interpreting the response. For example, I could respond affirmatively to "Do you like Rolls-Royce?" either because I like it but have no intention of buying it given my cash position, or to indicate I am considering buying it. Hence, the solution is to be "just right" in terms of detail.

Two procedures are crucial in getting good wording for a question. First, give up on the notion that the first draft of a questionnaire is the final one. During tests, continually see if respondents (*a*) answered, (*b*) answered with some reasonable dispersion, and (*c*) seemed to understand the question. Further, respondents can be asked to "think aloud" as they fill out the survey and these verbal protocols can then be used to refine the questionnaire (Bolton, 1993). Second, the translation practices used in going from one language to another can be employed in a modified fashion. (In translating questions from one language to another, it is advisable to have one person translate the question from the first language to the second and a second translator translate the translated question back to the original language. Only when the retranslated question matches the original is the question used.) Here, a researcher writes a question and a respondent then assesses what the researcher really wanted to know. Only when the researcher's problem matches the data the respondent thinks he or she is supposed to give is the question accepted. Some general tips include the following:

Be direct. Don't ask, "May I know your age?" since the correct answer is yes or no. Ask, "What is your age?"

Avoid slang and fancy/polysyllabic wording. For example, use "like" instead of "appreciate."

When rating products, specify their use/purpose. Rating products without use/situation specification can be very hard for the respondent and misleading to the researcher.

Ask questions that can reasonably be answered. Don't ask typical respondents questions that would be difficult for a Ph.D., or ask for excessive detail (e.g., number of ounces of water drunk in the last month).

Use unambiguous wording. "Do you appreciate the ad?" could be interpreted to mean you like it or understand it, two different issues.

Ask simple, not compound, questions. Don't ask, "Have you stopped eating candy?" Unless they started, the grammatically correct answer is "no"; although, given current literacy, the answer may not reflect this. Thus:

```
Do you own a summer house and a snowmo-
bile?
    Neither                         _____
    Summer house only               _____
    Snowmobile only                 _____
    Both                            _____
```

is generally inferior to:

```
Which of the following do you own:
    Summer house

         _____      _____
           Own           Do not own
    Snowmobile

         _____      _____
           Own           Do not own
```

Use nontechnical language. Too many studies go to the field in a form that is useful to engineering but meaningless to customers. For example, in one study concerning a major purchase item, a group of nontechnically trained respondents was exposed to product features developed and named by the R&D group. While the terms used were precise (e.g., response time in milliseconds, frame buffer), the typical respondent simply didn't know (or much care) what the technical features were, and hence the responses were of limited value.

Don't ask slanted questions. Don't make the correct answer obvious (e.g., don't ask, "You do care about health, don't you?").

Borrow someone else's questions. Why start from scratch if a proven alternative already exists?

Response Format

Response format determination has three main aspects: multiple measures, scale type, and provision for don't knows and refusals. A more detailed discussion appears in the next chapter.

Multiple Measures   A fundamental issue is whether a single scale or multiple items will be used to measure a construct. Using multiple items may help cancel out some errors that are idiosyncratic to a particular item. One disadvantage is that the presentation of multiple measures may either irritate the respondent (who then could retaliate by giving poor-quality responses) or convince the respondent that the survey is a consistency test and bias the responses accordingly. The main disadvantage is that it takes time and space for multiple measures, which means either extending the questionnaire, with the effect of increasing both cost and respondent fatigue, or eliminating other items from the survey. In most marketing research studies where the focus is on average rather than individual behavior, the use of 20–30 item scales to measure a single construct is not advisable. However, for key constructs, 3 to 5 measures are sometimes useful.

Scale Type   The scale type (nominal, ordinal, interval, ratio) used depends on (*a*) the analysis desired and (*b*) the amount of effort obtainable from the respondents. Most questions should be gathered on interval scales when possible. One interesting point concerns the choice between rankings (i.e., "please rank the following brands with 1 being your most preferred ...") and ratings (i.e., "please indicate how well you like each of the following scales by circling a 1 if you strongly dislike it, a 6 if you strongly like it, or somewhere in between depending on how well you like the brand."). Rankings (ordinally scaled) are usually harder to obtain than ratings and produce more refusals, bad data (i.e., incomplete rankings), and so forth. The reason for choosing a ranking over a rating is to prevent ties. Hence, if it is important to know what *the* first choice brand is, rankings may be required. Otherwise, ratings will usually suffice. The next chapter discusses specific question format in more detail.

Provision for Don't Knows and Refusals   The don't know/refusal response presents a difficult problem. In some cases it is a legitimate answer (e.g., "Do you know what the term *compact* means in numerical topology?"). In other cases, it is a convenient cop-out to avoid answering taxing or unpleasant questions. For example, I might wish to get a person's perception of a brand even though he or she had never used it to either assess its image or see if there were a reason for the nonuse. In general, experienced/involved respondents produce fewer don't know responses, and don't knows increase as the number of scale points increase (Leigh and Martin, 1987).

A key decision, therefore, is whether to formally provide the respondent with the don't know response or not. (You can be sure some respondents will leave questions blank anyway.) If the "don't know" response is meaningful data, it should be used as a response category even though some respondents will use it as an easy out. If "don't know" is an unusual response, however, providing a don't know response will generally reduce the quality of the data (Malhotra, 1986).

General Suggestions

Group Questions of Similar Types Together   It is possible to ask questions in the following manner:

	Dislike Very Much				Like Very Much
How well do you like yogurt?	1	2	3	4	5	6
	Very Infrequently				Very Frequently
How often do you watch TV?	1	2	3	4	5	6

However, it is often more efficient to get this information by combining the questions into a series of agree-disagree questions:

Please indicate your degree of agreement with the following statements:						
	Disagree Strongly					*Agree Strongly*
I like yogurt	1	2	3	4	5	6
I watch TV frequently	1	2	3	4	5	6

Use Mutually Exclusive and Exhaustive Categories for Multichoice Questions On the technical level, this means the following scale is bad:

       1–10, 10–20, 20–30,. . .

while this scale is good:

       0–9, 10–19, 20–29,. . .

On the more general level, it means you should take care to (*a*) specify all reasonable responses and (*b*) make it clear when only one answer is desired.

When Appropriate, Use Objective Rather than Subjective Scales for Key Constructs It is possible to measure TV viewing on subjective scales, such as "none" to "a great deal" or on agree-disagree scales. As long as TV viewing is not a key question, this is probably good enough. If a question is central, however, a quantitative scale is better:

How much TV do you watch on a typical night:					
None	Less than $\frac{1}{2}$ hour	$\frac{1}{2}$–1 hour	1–2 hours	2–3 hours	More than 3 hours

While this scale requires the researcher to know a priori something about typical amounts of TV viewing, the scale may actually be easier for the respondent to use than a vague agree-disagree type question.

Use Balanced Scales Unbalanced scales are generally undesirable, since they give clear indication to the respondent which end of the scale is expected to attract the majority of the responses. This is especially true of rating scales that have such categories as "poor," "satisfactory," "good," "very good," and "excellent." However, when the construct to be measured is importance or desirability, a scale such as "extremely important," "very important," "quite important," "somewhat important," "not very important," and "not at all important" may produce better information than a perfectly balanced scale, since most respondents tend to list all attributes of a product as important.

Rate Brands Attribute by Attribute   It is possible to rate all the brands on one attribute at a time or a single brand on all the attributes. The former approach is better: it reduces a respondent's tendency to "halo" ratings by responding only to overall feeling about the brand, rather than the particular attribute in question (Beckwith and Lehmann, 1975). Hence, this is better:

	Very Poor				*Very Good*
Please rate the following brands in terms of decay prevention:

	Very *Poor*				*Very* *Good*
Aim	____	____	____	____	____
Crest	____	____	____	____	____
Colgate	____	____	____	____	____

Nothing, however, can be done to totally eliminate halo effects in ratings. Also, respondents often use their assumptions about relations between attributes (e.g., price and quality) in answering questions. To illustrate, if they know a brand is high in price, they may rate (and believe) it to be high in quality (Bettman, John, and Scott, 1986). Hence, ratings on an attribute frequently contain elements of both overall attitude and ratings on other attributes.

Be Careful of the Order in which a Set of Alternatives Is Presented   Since items in the first position tend to get a disproportionate number of mentions due to heightened visibility, it is often useful to put a weak alternative in this position to force respondents to look further in the list when the responses are of the multiple-choice type. Some researchers like to randomly order lists, and others use alphabetical order. If the question asks the respondent to rate a series of alternatives on some criteria, the first alternative serves as a reference point. For this reason, some people try to put a neutral/typical alternative first on the assumption it will be rated in the middle of the scale, leaving room for both more positive and negative responses. While order bias cannot be removed on an individual question, it is possible to reduce its effect on average responses by rotating the order of the responses. This could be done for three brands (A, B, and C) by giving each third of the sample a different format:

Format 1	*Format 2*	*Format 3*
A	B	C
B	C	A
C	A	B

Don't Worry Too Much about the Physical Format for Scaled Questions   A variety of response formats can be used for scaled questions. Some of the most popular are

	Very *Sad*				*Very* *Happy*
Please circle the answer that best describes your feelings.	1	2	3	4	5
Please check the answer that best describes your feelings.	____ ○ □	____ ○ □	____ ○ □	____ ○ □	____ ○ □

Other scales have also been used. Many researchers have used three- to seven-point "smile" scales with pictures ranging from a sad to a happy face when questioning children. Format does appear to matter for special populations such as children (John and Karsten, 1993) or the elderly (Flynn, 1993). Fortunately, the choice of format is usually more a matter of aesthetic opinion than of practical importance.

On the other hand, for self-administered questions the format can affect the responses. Obviously, the question should be pleasing to the eye (which means well reproduced with adequate blank space and large typeface) and easily filled out (which means response categories should line up in columns). The examples in Figure 7.2 from Dillman (1978) illustrate several less-than-desirable formats.

Try to Get Relative Ratings   Absolute ratings of brands are interesting (i.e., brand X is good; averaging 4 on a five-point scale) but often disguise information. (If competitive brands Y and Z rate 4.5 and 4.7, 4.0 is pretty bad, whereas if the other brands rate 3.5 and 3.7, brand X is in good shape.)

Beware of Recall Data   Individuals' ability to recall data is limited (otherwise we would all have had straight As). When the question concerns an important event (e.g., marriage date), at least most people can accurately recall the information (at least when the aided "don't you remember what today is?" probe is presented). For low-salience items, in contrast, recall is subject to very severe limitations, including "telescoping" (thinking something happened more recently than it actually did). Recalling, for example, the last five brands of soft drink you purchased or the last five customers who entered your store is a difficult task. For this reason, many researchers prefer a "critical incidence" approach, where people are asked to recall a single incidence (cf. Bitner, Booms, and Mohr, 1994) or, better still, are asked to check their last MasterCard or Visa slip or monthly bill to see what they purchased.

In asking for usage data, a choice must be made between asking for usage rate (e.g., times per month) and recency data (e.g., When did you last ____?). A study involving questions about dining out showed that the way respondents answer varies with the two most prevalent approaches: actual counting (enumeration) of occurrences, and direct estimation (Blair and Burton, 1987). Actual counting was most frequent for low-incidence events, and when shorter time frames were used. Usage rate estimation is more accurate

Q–22 Your sex: _____ Male _____ Female

Q–23 Your present marital status: _____ Never Married _____ Married _____ Separated _____ Widowed

Q–24 Number of children you have in each age group: _____ Under five years _____ 5–13 _____ 14–18 _____ 19–25 and over

Q–25 Your present age: _____

Q–26 Do you own (or are you buying) your own home? _____ No _____ Yes

Q–27 Did you serve in the armed forces? _____ No _____ Yes (Year entered _____. Year discharged _____)

Q–28 Are you presently: _____ Employed _____ Unemployed _____ Retired _____ Full-time homemaker

Q–29 Please describe the usual occupation of the principal wage earner in your household, including title, kind of work, and kind of company or business (If retired, describe the usual occupation before retirement).

Q–30 What was your approximate net family income, from all sources, before taxes, in 1970?
Less than $3,000   _____   10,000 to 12,999 _____
20,000 to 24,999   _____
    5,000 to 6,999 _____   13,000 to 15,999 _____   25,000 to 29,999   _____
    5,000 to 6,999 _____   16,000 to 19,999 _____   Over $30,000   _____
    7,000 to 9,999 _____

Q–31 What is the highest level of education that you have completed?
No formal education   _____   _____ Some college
Some grade school _____   _____ Some college...major _____
Some high school _____   _____ A graduate degree...degree and major _____
Completed high school _____

Q–32 What is your religious preference? _____ Protestant denomination _____ Jewish _____ Catholic _____ Other _____ Specify _____ None

Q–33 How frequently did you attend religious services in a place of worship during the past year: _____ Regularly _____ Occasionally _____ Only on special days _____ Not at all

Q–34 Which do you consider yourself to be? _____ Republican _____ Democrat _____ Independent _____ Other _____ Specify

Q–35 Which of the best describes your usual stand on political issues? _____ Conservative _____ Liberal _____ Middle of the road _____ Radical

FIGURE 7.2
Unacceptable Formats of Commonly Asked Survey Questions
Source: D. Dillman, *Mail and Telephone Surveys,* page 134. Copyright © 1978 by John Wiley & Sons, Inc. Reprinted with the permission of the publishers.

than enumeration for frequently occurring events (Menon, 1993). Another study suggested that recency data are better than usage rate data for low-usage, low-salience events (Buchanan and Morrison, 1987). The moral of this is that even the seemingly trivial choice between asking how often something was done and how recently it was done can affect the results.

Don't Automatically Assume Literacy   Most of the world is in some sense functionally illiterate (including a substantial fraction in the United States), and most people do not speak English (again including a sizable fraction in the United States). Try to ask questions that are simple and in the appropriate language. Also be aware that, in self-administered surveys, eyesight and lack of literacy will adversely affect quality of response as well as response rate.

Key Informants May Misinform   It is often convenient to ask one person to provide data about others (e.g., family members or others in a firm). Unfortunately, they are not always accurate, especially in giving nonfactual information.

Make It Fun or At Least Painless   Respondents will produce better data if they find the task fun (as opposed to overly cute).

QUESTION SEQUENCE

The order of questions is important. Early questions set the tone of the survey by creating the mindset the respondent uses to produce answers. This is true in terms of both content and interest. For example, a series of early questions on symphony orchestra music might serve to (*a*) lead the consumer to assume that the subject matter was music preference and, thus, answer accordingly or (*b*) increase (or decrease) the subject's interest and, consequently, the likelihood the respondent will complete the questionnaire. In fact, maintaining interest is one of the largest problems in many surveys. While some topics are inherently more interesting than others, proper format (including plenty of white space) and sequencing can do a lot to maintain the respondent's concentration. Some issues include placement of hard questions, placement of sensitive or experimental questions, variety of format, and branching.

Placement of Hard Questions

Many surveys have two or three key questions that are particularly difficult (e.g., preference rankings from 1 to 20 of 20 TV shows or suppliers). When these are placed at the beginning of a study, they may convince a subject that the study is overly difficult and, hence, lead to a refusal to participate. On the other hand, placing these questions last will confront tired respondents with a difficult task, leading to either terminations or poor-quality data. The best solution is often to put difficult questions fairly early interspersed with easy questions. Many surveys begin with a simple "warm-up" question or two (the marketing research equivalent of "What color is the White House?"), then turn to the real issues.

Placement of Sensitive Questions

There is no place to hide questions that people don't want to answer (including income). Typically, however, a survey will still have some value without these responses. Therefore, it is often advisable to put these questions toward the end to avoid contaminating the other responses. Wording differences can also matter (Blair et al., 1977).

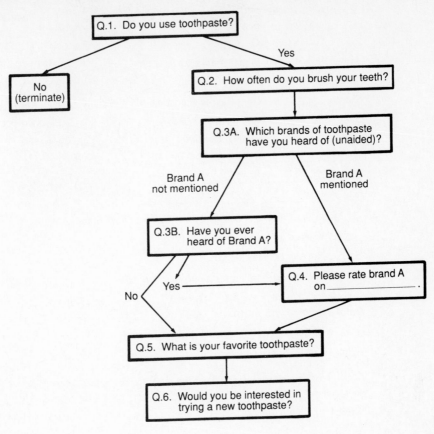

FIGURE 7.3
Flow Diagram of Question Branching

Variety of Format

To keep respondents alert, it is useful to vary the format somewhat throughout the questionnaire. Thus, when gathering data on a large number of variables of the same type (e.g., 150 lifestyle measures), some people choose to break up the section into parts (e.g., three parts of 50 each) and intersperse the parts with other questions. It is not clear, however, that this type of variety markedly improves data quality.

Branching

In many questionnaires, the questions to be asked depend on the answers to previous questions. One piece of advice is not to branch unless necessary, especially in self-administered surveys.

If branching is needed, it is useful to first set up a diagram to summarize the flow, such as Figure 7.3. Translating this into questionnaire form, we get Figure 7.4. As can be seen from this example, even simple branching instructions can be hard to follow.

1. Do you use toothpaste?

_____ Yes (go to question 2)

_____ No (terminate)

2. How often do you brush your teeth?

_____	_____	_____	_____	_____
Rarely	Weekly	A few times a week	Daily	More than once per day

3a. What brands of toothpaste have you heard of?

_____

_____

_____

3b. (If brand A is not mentioned) Have you heard of brand A?

_____ Yes (go to question 4)

_____ No (go to question 5)

4. Please rate brand A in terms of its sex appeal.

Very Ordinary				*Very Sexy*
1	2	3	4	5

5. What is your favorite toothpaste?

Aim _____

Colgate _____

Crest _____

UltraBright _____

Other (please specify) _____

6. Would you be interested in trying a new toothpaste?

Very Uninterested				*Very Interested*
1	2	3	4	5

FIGURE 7.4
A Questionnaire with Branching

Some become so elaborate that they can quickly get out of hand, although computer-controlled interviews can handle them quite well.

A related issue is whether you can ask someone to rate a product that he or she has not actually used. Some people believe in branching around such questions to avoid burdening the respondent. An alternative approach is to ask everyone to rate a product whether they have heard of it or not. The rationale for this is they have perceptions of the brand that may explain their nonuse (e.g., I can rate bank robbing as risky without doing it.) Since I can also ask (preferably later, to cut down on refusals) whether the product has been used, I have the option of looking at only those people who use the product anyway. This strong-arm approach may produce additional information while avoiding branching instructions and is typically preferable if the respondents can reasonably be expected to have some knowledge of or attitude toward the product in question.

Recent developments in computer-administered surveys have increased the feasibility of individually tailoring questionnaires. By allowing respondents to only respond to brands and features they know or care about, respondent burden and time is minimized (Kamakura and Wedel, 1995). Similarly, multi-item scales can be shortened by adapting the survey based on previous responses (Balasubramanian and Kamakura, 1989; Singh, Howell, and Rhoads, 1990). While posing difficulties for analysis, customized questionnaires seem likely to increase in usage.

PRETEST AND REVISION

The stage in the research process that is most likely to be squeezed out due to cost/time pressures is the pretest. This is unfortunate, since a pretest is also the stage in which fundamental problems in a survey can be corrected. There are an incredible number of disasters around that a pretest of 50 to 100 "real" subjects would have prevented. Pretests allow checking to see (a) whether there are a disproportionate number of nonresponses to particular questions, (b) whether the questions discriminate (respondents give different answers), and (c) whether the respondents seem to understand the questions.

Pretests can also be used to convert open-ended questions to categories for the final study. There is also no shame in using multiple pretests, especially if convenience samples are used at most of the stages. A questionnaire that does not change between initial drafting and field execution is probably one that has not been carefully examined.

CODING THE QUESTIONNAIRE

Have a clear coding scheme for inputting the data for analysis before collecting them. A discussion of coding and editing issues appears in Chapter 10.

TYPE OF SURVEY

This section focuses on alternative methods of collecting survey data from individuals. Response rates have been dropping as a result of disenchantment with unwanted solicitations. Here, eight major methods will be discussed:

1. Personal interviews
2. Telephone interviews
3. Mail surveys
4. Drop-off, callback
5. Panels
6. Group interviews
7. Location interviews
8. Information highway

Personal Interviews

One view of marketing research in the general public is a mental picture of an interviewer asking questions of an individual and recording the responses on a clipboard (Figure 7.5). Like all survey approaches, it has both advantages and disadvantages.

Advantages

Relatively complex presentations can be shown to subjects (e.g., samples of different packages, mock-ups of a new machine, descriptions of situations, slides and videotapes; Bateson and Hui, 1992).

Higher completion rates are likely, since the interviewer can urge the respondent to finish ("Just one more minute, please").

Depending on what answer a respondent gives to a particular question, the interviewer can then branch to the next appropriate question. Branching instructions are often quite complex. For example, "If it's Tuesday and the person answered '2' to question 31, go to question 34. If not, . . ." While complex branching could theoretically be done with other designs, in practice only telephone or computer-controlled surveys also do this as standard practice.

Respondents can be asked to give responses other than the multiple-choice type. For example, respondents could be asked to sort cards containing the names of different brands into piles based on some criterion.

The presence of the interviewer can help convince the respondent to answer questions he or she might otherwise leave blank. Alternatively, the interviewer may be able to deduce information such as annual income based on cues (e.g., the size of the house and type of furniture).

The interviewer can also observe the respondent and record the observations as data.

FIGURE 7.5
A Common View of Market Research

Disadvantages

The presence of the interviewer may influence the responses. This influence may be the result of the interviewer's opinions showing or the respondent giving those answers that he or she perceives will meet with approval from another human being. The ethnicity and gender of the interviewer can influence response (e.g., Webster, 1996). Even when personal interviews are not used, measuring constructs such as intent may affect behavior (Morwitz, Johnson, and Schmittlein, 1993).

Since the interviewer often is required to interpret the response and assign it to a predesignated category, there is a serious potential problem of errors in interpretation caused because of either the selective perception of the interviewer based on personal opinions, expectations of the likely response, or simply random error in recording the answer.

There is a strong possibility of interviewer cheating. Firms that offer personal interviewing services generally bid on a potential job based on the number of completed interviews. Once they get a job, there is a very obvious incentive to get the interviews completed as quickly as possible. This incentive is likely to be transferred from the project director to the interviewers, often very directly by means of a pay schedule that is based on the number of completed interviews. Hence, it is very common for interviewers to "help out" a respondent by filling in some answers without asking the questions, and not uncommon for an interviewer to dummy up an entire questionnaire. For example, they might play-act: "If I lived at 1182 Maple Avenue, how would I respond?" Besides dealing with a reputable firm or, more drastically, doing the interviewing yourself, the only alternative is to check up on the interviewers. Calling back 20 percent of the respondents and asking four to five questions to see if the responses match is a common practice. Unfortunately, even this process is inexact, since demographics may be relatively easily guessed by the interviewer and attitudes are subject to change over time. The shrewd interviewer who asks the objective questions and a few of the subjective ones and then fills out the rest is especially difficult to catch. Since the respondent may be reluctant to "rat" on the interviewer, even asking what the interviewer did may fail to uncover the cheating. In short, interviewer cheating is a difficult problem to control.

"Completion time" is fairly long. It takes several weeks for a typical personal interview study to be completed.

Costs Personal interviews are, in general, the most expensive way to collect data from individual respondents. Costs can range from about $10 per completed interview for relatively short questionnaires (those requiring about 5 minutes to complete) with simple instructions and sample designs (e.g., any warm body) to $500 or more for longer questionnaires (requiring 45 minutes to one hour to complete) and "hard-to-get" respondents, such as executives or ghetto dwellers. For a half-hour questionnaire (six to eight pages) and a sample consisting of typical consumers, the cost tends to be about $30 to $80 per completed interview. For surveys of children, $100 per interview is not uncommon—about half the $200 rate for doctors.

Response Rate The response rate to personal interviews obviously depends on many factors, including the sample chosen, the length of the questionnaires, the number of callbacks, the reward offered, and the competence of the interviewer. Nonetheless, typical response rates run between 50 and 80 percent.

Telephone Interviews

Phone interviewing, essentially a low-cost form of personal interviewing, has gained in popularity and now is the most common form of survey. As such, it shares many of the pros and cons of personal interviewing.

Advantages

Like personal interviews, phone interviews may follow fairly elaborate branching patterns.

The phone interviewer may help prod the respondent to answer questions.

Some individuals are more likely to answer a phone than to let a stranger enter their house, especially in high-crime areas and in the evening when interviewing of people who work during the day is normally done.

It can be completed quickly. Phone interviews on a topic can be ready for analysis faster than personal interviews, sometimes within 24 hours.

It can be done from a single location. By using WATS lines, all the interviewing can be conducted from a central location, simultaneously increasing control and reducing travel time.

Interviewer bias is reduced somewhat, since the interviewer is not physically present.

Disadvantages

The questions must be asked without any visual props, such as actual packages or pictures of products. While you can send material prior to the interview, you cannot guarantee that subjects will use it.

People may well respond differently to phone interviews than they do to personal interviews or, in fact, than they actually feel. In general, a person responding to a phone interview will probably concentrate less than when responding to a personal interview.

The responses are limited, in that complex response scales (such as a constant sum scale) are not practically usable. Also, it is rare for a phone interview to exceed 30 to 45 minutes in duration, and much shorter ones are the norm.

As in the case of personal interviews, there is the opportunity for the interviewer to exert influence either overtly or subconsciously, misperceive the answer given, or outright cheat.

Unless the person you are trying to contact has a phone, you can't get him or her. This is an especially serious problem when phone books are the source of the sample, since in areas like southern California half the phones are unlisted. Fortunately, studies have shown that for many responses, nonlisted phone owners are very similar to listed phone owners. However, unlisted phones are most common among the young or the very old, the poor or the very rich. The use of a technique called *random digit dialing*, which, as the name implies, dials numbers randomly and then includes the person answering the phone in the sample, circumvents the problem of only listed phone owners being available. Random digit dialing does have the disadvantage of generating a lot of worthless responses (numbers not in service, businesses, and other people outside the target population). Also, those with unlisted numbers may not respond even if you call them. After all, they have their numbers unlisted to keep from getting nuisance calls. In fact, some people have been known to complain bitterly to the phone company, which they believe has given out their number. Nothing, however, helps with the problem of reaching individuals without phones. Since, for most products, people without phones account for a very small share of the business, this is fortunately more of a theoretical than a practical problem.

People may hang up. This fact gives the respondent greater control than in the case of a personal interview. This can lead to, for example, fewer mentions of brands used; in one case, 2.5 for phone versus 4.8 for personal interviews (Telser, 1976). It also can lead to premature termination of an interview. Even when the interview is completed, distractions (TV, children, etc.) may detract from the quality of the responses.

Costs   Compared with personal interviews, phone interviews are relatively inexpensive. Although costs vary depending on the length of the interview, and so forth, costs for a completed interview tend to run between $10 and $50. A 1987 bid for a 10-minute, 25-question phone survey of 200 executives was $6,000—about $30 per completed interview.

This low cost is partly due to the existence of WATS lines, which allow unlimited calling from a particular area to another area for a fixed monthly charge. WATS lines allow interviewers in a central location to do interviewing essentially anywhere and supervisors to monitor their work. Phone interviews also eliminate the costs associated with travel between interviews, which is a part of personal interviewing costs.

The current trend is toward the use of computer-controlled telephone interviewing. This provides for easy (once programmed) branching. In fact, since the data are input during the interview, branching can be based on an analysis of responses to previous questions.

Response Rate   The response rate of phone surveys is usually slightly below that of personal interviews, ranging from 40 to 75 percent.

Mail Surveys

The third of the big-three methods of obtaining responses from individuals is the mail survey. This method, which is self-administered, provides a clear contrast with both personal and phone surveys (see Figure 7.6).

Characteristic	Personal	Mail	Phone
Usable length	Good	Fair	Poor to fair
Suitability for complex questions	Good	Poor	Fair
Minimization of process bias	Poor	Good	Fair
Cost per completed interview	High	Low	Low to moderate
Speed	Moderate	Slow	Fast

FIGURE 7.6
A Comparison of Three Survey Methods

Advantages

The respondent is allowed to work at his or her own pace in completing the questions.

No interviewer is present to bias or misinterpret the responses.

With adequate instructions, fairly complicated scales can be used to gather responses.

By receiving the responses directly, the possibility of interviewer cheating is essentially eliminated. (If you allow a firm to collect the responses for you, they could potentially "doctor" them to improve the response rate.)

Disadvantages

There is no one present to prod the respondent to complete the questions. This leads to greater numbers of partially completed questions and also to a higher rate of discontinuance in the middle of the survey (or, for that matter, before the start).

No one is available to help interpret instructions or questions. This can lead to both confusion and frustration on the part of the respondent. One partial solution is to provide an 800 telephone number for respondents with questions to call.

There is a nontrivial chance the survey will be treated as another piece of junk mail and appropriately filed (discarded). Alternatively, someone else in the household or firm may complete the survey.

Since most mail lists are at least one to two years old, many people on the list will have moved, and hence many of the respondents will be unreachable. Unlike the case in personal and phone interviews, however, this will not be immediately obvious.

Most mail surveys are left open three to four weeks, although the bulk of responses come in during the first two weeks. This means that mail surveys take longer to complete than phone or personal interviews if the latter are fully expedited.

Respondents tend to be slightly more upscale (higher income, education, etc.) than nonrespondents.

Branching instructions are not generally recommended. Respondents follow directions about as well as parents follow instructions for putting together toys on Christmas Eve.

Don't know/blank responses are more frequent. The largest fraction of don't know responses typically occurs on self-administered questionnaires (e.g., mail), with personal interviews producing possibly slightly fewer than telephone surveys.

Costs   The cost of mail surveys is similar to or somewhat smaller than that of phone surveys (e.g., $10 per completed interview). An example of the cost basis for a single mail-out is approximately as follows:

Stamp	$ .33
Envelope	.15
Return envelope and stamp	.48
Cover letter	.20
Questionnaire (6 pages)	.25
Name label	.10
Total	$1.51

While labor increases this cost, the base cost is still low compared with that of a personal interview. As in the case of phone surveys, very short (10 questions or fewer) surveys are even less expensive.

Response Rate   The response rate of mail surveys varies widely. The lower bound can be close to zero if too much is asked of the respondent. For example, direct-mail solicitations typically get 1 percent or smaller responses. On the other hand, some interesting surveys with artful cover letters have received 50 to 60 percent responses. Somewhere in the middle of these two extremes lies the most likely result. To illustrate, one survey that was six pages long, focusing on durable goods ownership plus demographics, and containing no incentive other than a cover letter penned by yet another fictitious research director, produced a response rate of 20 percent out of 100,000 mailed questionnaires.

Drop-off, Callback

A procedure designed to include the best aspects of several methods, drop-off, callback involves dropping off a questionnaire (usually after asking the respondent a few initial questions) and then returning to pick it up sometime later. This strategy allows the respondent to complete the questionnaire on his or her own time and yet has the advantage of an interviewer to build initial commitment and "check up" on the responses. This technique has been used extensively for super-long questionnaires, which often run over 100 pages and take several hours to complete (Pessemier, DeBruicker, and Hustad, 1971; Lovelock et al., 1976).

Preexisting Panels

One way to collect data is to utilize a group of individuals who have already agreed to participate. This approach includes both using commercially available panels and instituting and maintaining your own panel. There are really three major types of panels. The first is the diary panel, in which members agree to record their purchases of a variety of products in terms of brand, price, size, and so forth. M/R/C/A and NPD maintain well-known panels of this type. A second type of panel is one in which individuals' behavior is monitored by some device that does not require panel member participation. The famous Nielsen TV ratings is the prime example of this type. Monitored panels could be totally unobtrusive by basing them on credit card receipts, utility bills, and so forth. The third type of panel is simply a list of a set of individuals who agree to answer questionnaires. The mail panels of Market Facts, National Family Opinion (NFO), and NPD are examples of this type of panel. While the particulars of the panels obviously are important, some general comments about panel usage are appropriate.

Advantages

The response rate among panel members is high. Even for mail panels, the response rate to four- to six-page questionnaires is usually 70 to 80 percent.

For established panels, a great deal of other information, such as demographics, is already available on each of the respondents.

Using a panel is "easy," since the sample design issue is already taken care of.

Disadvantages

At least in one aspect, panel members are clearly not typical individuals. Recruitment is difficult, with typically 10 percent or fewer of the individuals agreeing to participate in standby panels. These panel members tend to be "questionnaire freaks."

Panels have a tendency to age. As time passes, either the average age increases or the panel must be "rolled over" by the addition of younger panel members.

Most mail panels, including those designed to represent all segments of the population, tend to underrepresent both minority groups and low-education levels. (Someone who feels alienated or can't read will hardly be likely to fill out six-page questionnaires.)

Being in a panel tends to "condition" respondents. Someone who has filled out three questionnaires about a product or seen the name of an unfamiliar product may tend to behave differently by, for example, spending more time considering the product or trying the unfamiliar product as a result of being made aware of it. Therefore, care must be taken that panel members' responses have not been conditioned by prior questionnaires or information collection.

Costs   Costs vary greatly depending on the panel in question. Six-page questionnaires sent to standby mail panels tend to cost about $15 to $20 per completed interview. Ongoing panels generally require a yearly subscription—at a price from $50,000 to $200,000.

Response Rate   The response rates of panels are very high, ranging from 70 to 80 percent for the mail panels to close to 100 percent for mechanical observation panels, such as Nielsen.

Group Interviews

Group interviews are widely used in marketing research. They are essentially a combination of "cheap" personal interviews and self-administered questionnaires. A leader administers a questionnaire to a group of individuals at one time in a single location. This technique can be very economical, especially when used with church or community groups.

Location Interviews

One of the least expensive ways to collect survey data is to station an interviewer in a central ("high traffic") location. The interviewer then "accosts" unsuspecting individuals and attempts to convince them to participate in the study. One of the most common forms of this type of study is shopping center or mall intercept interviews.

In such studies, the interviewer may conduct the interview on the spot as a personal interview. Alternatively, the interviewer will lead the respondent to a separate area, where the respondent may be treated to either a self-administered, personal, or group interview. Usually, the separate area will contain some type of demonstration of either a product or advertising. Not surprisingly, only people who are not very busy or who are intrigued by marketing research tend to be included in shopping mall studies.

Information Highway Methods

Surveys can be facilitated and conducted using so-called information technology. Faxes can be sent. Questionnaires can be made available on floppy disks, computer networks, e-mail, and via the Web on the Internet. These methods can work well with some groups (e.g., faxes with business executives; Dickson and MacLachlan, 1996), producing results similar to mail surveys. Their use is clearly increasing, due to cost, speed, and convenience. Still, these methods currently exclude most consumers (who don't own modems and fax machines).

Combination of Methods

The methods of collecting survey data described to this point are not necessarily mutually exclusive. For example, one could use a phone-screening questionnaire followed by a personal interview with a self-administered questionnaire left behind to be mailed in later. In fact, combinations of methods are often the most effective way to collect data.

With VCR penetration having passed 70 percent of U.S. households, another method for gathering data is to send to respondents both a VCR tape and a mail questionnaire. The tape allows for product descriptions and advertisements to be presented, with reactions then collected with self-administered surveys (or a follow-up phone survey). While VCR owners are different from nonowners in at least one way, this approach seems likely to gain in popularity.

FIELDING THE SURVEY

When a survey is finally deemed acceptable, it then must be implemented. Although the process is typically handled by a supplier, a few points are worth making. First, the survey should have a short but pleasing introduction, which indicates the name of the firm collecting the data (e.g., XYZ Research Corporation). In general, however, it is not advisable (and sometimes disastrous) to make known the identity of the firm that wishes to use the survey (e.g., the IRS). Similarly, a simple closing including thanks is appropriate. Finally, a well-defined sampling plan (to be discussed later) is needed.

Quality control while the study is in the field is very important. Interviewers are motivated to get completed interviews and will tend to help respondents by either suggesting answers or by simply filling in sections of the survey to ease the burden on the respondent. To control this, checking is required. Typically, this is done by recontacting 20 percent of the sample and asking (a) if they were in fact interviewed and (b) some questions to which the answers should not have changed. By comparing answers to these questions between the original and follow-up surveys, grossly disparate response patterns can be seen, which can be used to eliminate both the respondent and the interviewer.

EXAMPLES

Surveys abound. Anyone staying in a hotel/motel or attending an executive program or MBA course is likely to be given one. Examples of surveys can be misleading, since there is no such thing as a typical survey. While some are short, others are quite long (e.g., Chilton's 1995 "The Survey of American Consumers" contains 96 pages of detailed questions about product use, TV viewing, etc.). Nonetheless, Appendixes 7-B to 7-D present three examples worth studying: a personal interviewer's guide for a commercial survey, a nutritional survey, and an ownership and values survey. Note the difference in format between the personal interview and the self-administered surveys.

Commercial Survey

Appendix 7-B presents a survey which represents the format of a commercial study done by personal interviewing about a product category with several different brands (Katz, 1974). With the exception of the income categories, it is a good model/starting point for such a study. The purpose of each of the product-related questions is to measure the following:

1.	Unaided recall of brands
2.	Unaided advertising recall of brands
3–5.	Purchase
6.	Aided recall
7.	Opinion/attitude
8.	Ever tried
9.	If repeat purchase
10.	Advertising recall
11.	Copy point recall (unaided)
12.	Copy point recall (aided)
13.	Brand ratings on attributes
14–16.	Size and style used

The classification questions measure:

1-3.	Price change perceptions
4.	TV viewing
5.	Age
6.	Household size
7.	Income

Nutritional Survey

Appendix 7-C presents a questionnaire that serves as a basis for discussion later in this book. It was administered in 1975 to a mail panel and is more structured than the personal interview survey of Appendix 7-B. (It also is academic rather than commercial in purpose, and hence less tightly focused.) The questions were as follows:

Section I:		
	1–8	Food shopping habits
	9–10	Food attribute importance
	11–14	Personal food consumption
	15	Change in household consumption.
Section II:		
	Nutritional information sources and perceived needs	
Section III:		
	Background (over and above already collected demographics)	
Section IV:		
	Lifestyle	
Section V:		
	Knowledge and perception of foods	

As an aside, it is useful to remember that this questionnaire, imperfect as it is, went through five revisions, including a field pretest. The pretest found a serious problem in the wording of the final three questions, which caused 20 percent of the sample to refuse to answer the section. Consequently, the wording of question 2, section V, was changed from "Please indicate which of the nine functions of the body listed below are aided by consuming whole milk, beef, tomatoes, and enriched bread by putting a check in the appropriate box" to "For each of the nine body functions listed down the side of the page, please indicate which of the four foods contribute *importantly* to the function. *Check as many or as few* of the foods as you think apply to each function." This seemingly small change greatly reduced nonresponse and again demonstrated the value of a pretest. As a further aside, the last three questions were added (*a*) to replicate questions on a study done for the FDA and (*b*) to serve as input for the use of multidimensional scaling algorithms. Since the scaling procedures basically recovered the four basic food groups, the value of these questions is debatable after the fact. (The survey was conducted before the pyramid replaced the four food groups as the basis for nutritional education.)

Ownership and Values Survey

The focus of this study* was the relation between ownership of major products and services and basic values of customers. Data were collected in the mid 1980s. Thirty products considered to be optional purchases (e.g., VCR, piano, vacation home) were included. For each product, three separate pieces of information were sought:

1. Current ownership (question 1*a*)
2. Intention to buy (question 1*b*)
3. Importance of having (question 2)

The ownership question allowed for multiple items since, for example, the first color TV may almost always be purchased before a compact disc player and, hence, not really compete; but the second color TV and a compact disc player might compete for dollars in a person's budget. Intention was asked over a 2-year period as a compromise between "too short" a period (e.g., one month) and too long a period (e.g., 10 years). The 100-point scale was used, rather than a 6- or 7-point scale, in the hope of getting responses that could be interpreted as probabilities of purchase. The question about importance of owning was assumed to be a good way to get at basic values and, unlike ownership data, to be minimally contaminated by gifts. (However, if having a product leads one to appreciate it, the two are clearly related.)

To measure basic values, several scales were considered. The basic two scales that were chosen were the LOV (List of Values) scale and the original VALS typology. Questions pertaining to the nine LOV scales are the first nine responses in question 3 (self-respect, security, . . ., excitement). The VALS typology, even with its short form, still requires several pages in a questionnaire (Mitchell, 1983). Given page constraints, an attempt was made to provide a basic description of each of the eight basic types and then to have respondents rate how well each description described themselves (question 4). The remaining items in question 3 were other values that seemed worth investigating culled from a number of sources.

In addition to the product-based and value-based questions, a number of demographic questions ("background") were also included. The survey appears in Appendix 7-D. This self-administered study, like the nutritional survey, is used as a basis for discussion in this book.

SUMMARY

Survey design is a craft that requires balancing various sources of error and costs. It is important to recognize that many sources of error are beyond the control of the researcher, such as the respondent's lack of interest in the subject and resulting lack of care in filling out the survey. Survey execution requires effort and care. In short, survey design and execution is an area where additional effort improves results. The desire

---

* The study was developed by a market research class to serve as the common core of course projects. Each team focused on a particular product or service and collected 50 observations, which included the common core questions plus those that pertained to their particular product. This allowed each group to have a large sample to analyze and to profile those who owned and intended to buy their product.

to "get on with it" so that data can be analyzed and decisions made is understandable but, unless held in check, is often counterproductive.

This chapter has focused on a six-step process for developing a survey: listing general types of information needed, listing specific information items, writing questions, creating a questionnaire, testing the questionnaire, and revising the questionnaire. It has also discussed different means for administering a questionnaire: personal interviewing, phone interviewing, mail, drop-off, panels, group interviews, location interviews, and information highway. Those desiring more detail should consult other sources, such as Schwarz and Sudman (1995); Sudman, Bradburn, and Schwarz (1996); Sudman and Bradburn (1982); Blankenship (1977); Payne (1951); and Jacoby (1976). The next chapter discusses measurement issues that relate to writing questions in greater detail.

PROBLEMS

1. Evaluate the questionnaire in Appendix 7-B.
2. Evaluate the questionnaire in Appendix 7-C.
3. Evaluate the questionnaire in Appendix 7-D.
4. Assume you were designing a phone survey to find out how consumers choose a new appliance.
   a. Design the flow of the questionnaire (similar to Figure 7.4).
   b. Would you have a screening question?
   c. If your client were General Electric, how would the survey change?
   d. If your client were White-Westinghouse, how would the survey change?
5. Which type of survey (personal, phone, mail) would you use to get
   a. Opinions about political issues?
   b. Ratings of a new product?
   c. Ratings of a new product concept?
   d. Priority rankings of 15 goals?
6. List 10 things that you could do *wrong* in a survey.

REFERENCES

AAKER, DAVID A. (1991) *Managing Brand Equity*, New York: Free Press.

AAKER, DAVID A., AND KEVIN LANE KELLER (1990) "Consumer Evaluations of Brand Extensions," *Journal of Marketing*, 54, January, 27–41.

AAKER, JENNIFER L. (1994) "Measuring Brand Personality," working paper, Graduate School of Business, Stanford University.

ALPERT, MARK I. (1972) "Personality and the Determinants of Product Choice," *Journal of Marketing Research*, 9, February, 89–92.

ANDERSON, EUGENE W., AND MARY W. SULLIVAN (1993) "The Antecedents and Consequences of Customer Satisfaction for Firms," *Marketing Science*, 12, Spring, 125–43.

BALASUBRAMANIAN, SIVA K., AND WAGNER A. KAMAKURA (1989) "Measuring Consumer Attitudes Toward the Marketplace with Tailored Interviews," *Journal of Marketing Research*, 24, August, 311–26.

BARACH, JEFFREY A. (1969) "Advertising Effectiveness and Risk in the Consumer Decision Process," *Journal of Marketing Research*, 6, August, 314–20.

BATESON, JOHN E. G., AND MICHAEL K. HUI (1992) "The Ecological Validity of Photographic Slides and Videotapes in Simulating the Service Setting," *Journal of Consumer Research*, 19, September, 271–81.

BATRA, RAJEEV, DONALD R. LEHMANN, AND DIPINDER SINGH (1993) "The Brand Personality Component of Brand Goodwill: Some Antecedents and Consequences," in David A. Aaker and Alexander L. Biel, eds., *Brand Equity and Advertising: Advertising's Role in Building Strong Brands*, Hillsdale, N.J.: Lawrence Erlbaum Associates.

BECKWITH, NEIL E., AND DONALD R. LEHMANN (1975) "The Importance of Halo Effects in Multi-Attribute Attitude Models," *Journal of Marketing Research*, 12, August, 265–75.

BELK, RUSSELL W. (1975) "Situational Variables and Consumer Behavior," *Journal of Consumer Research*, 2, December, 157–64.

BETTMAN, JAMES R., DEBORAH ROEDDER JOHN, AND CAROL A. SCOTT (1986) "Covariation Assessment by Consumers," *Journal of Consumer Research*, 13, December, 316–26.

BIRDWELL, AL E. (1968) "A Study of the Influence of Image Congruence on Consumer Choice," *Journal of Business*, 41, January, 76–88.

BITHER, STEWARD W., AND IRA J. DOLICH (1972) "Personality as a Determinant Factor in Store Choice," *Proceedings*, Third Annual Conference, Association for Consumer Research, College Park, Md.

BITNER, MARY JO, BERNARD H. BOOMS, AND LOIS A. MOHR (1994) "Critical Service Encounters: The Employee's Viewpoint," *Journal of Marketing*, 58, October, 95–106.

BLAIR, EDWARD, AND SCOT BURTON (1987) "Cognitive Processes Used by Survey Respondents to Answer Behavioral Frequency Questions," *Journal of Consumer Research*, 14, September, 280–88.

BLAIR, EDWARD, SEYMOUR SUDMAN, NORMAL M. BRADBURN, AND CAROL STOCKING (1977) "How to Ask Questions about Drinking and Sex: Response Effects in Measuring Consumer Behavior," *Journal of Marketing Research*, 14, August, 316–21.

BLANKENSHIP, A. B. (1977) *Professional Telephone Surveys*, New York: McGraw-Hill.

BOGART, LEO (1967) "No Opinion, Don't Know, and Maybe No Answer," *Public Opinion Quarterly*, 31, Fall, 332.

BOLTON, RUTH N. (1993) "Pretesting Questionnaires: Content Analyses of Respondents' Concurrent Verbal Protocols," *Marketing Science*, 12, Summer, 280–303.

BOULDING, WILLIAM, RICHARD STAELIN, AJAY KALRA, AND VALARIE A. ZEITHAML (1992) "Conceptualizing and Testing a Dynamic Process Model of Service Quality," MSI Working Paper, Cambridge, Mass.: MSI, 92–127.

BRUCE, GRADY D., AND ROBERT E. WITT (1970) "Personality Correlates of Innovative Buying Behavior," *Journal of Marketing Research*, 7, May, 259–60.

BUCHANAN, BRUCE, AND DONALD G. MORRISON (1987) "Sampling Properties of Rate Questions with Implications for Survey Research," *Marketing Science*, 6, Summer, 286–98.

CAHALAN, DON (1968–9) "Correlates of Respondent Accuracy in Denver Validity Survey," *Public Opinion Quarterly*, 32, Winter, 607–21.

CANNELL, CHARLES F., LOIS OKSENBERG, AND JOAN M. CONVERSE (1977) "Striving for Response Accuracy: Experiments in New Interviewing Techniques," *Journal of Marketing Research*, 14, August, 306–15.

CORFMAN, KIM P., DONALD R. LEHMANN, AND SUNDER NARAYANAN (1991) "Values, Utility, and Ownership: Modeling the Relationships for Consumer Durables," *Journal of Retailing*, 67, Summer, 184–204.

Cox, Donald F., and Raymond A. Bauer (1964) "Self-Confidence and Persuasibility in Women," *Public Opinion Quarterly*, 28, Fall, 453–66.

Cronin, J. Joseph, Jr., and Steven A. Taylor (1994) "SERVPERF versus SERVQUAL: Reconciling Performance-Based and Perceptions-Minus-Expectations Measurement of Service Quality," *Journal of Marketing*, 58, January, 125–31.

Darden, William R., and Fred D. Reynolds (1974) "Backward Profiling of Male Innovators," *Journal of Marketing Research*, 11, February, 79–85.

Dickson, John P., and Douglas L. MacLachlan (1996) "Fax Surveys: Return Patterns and Comparison with Mail Surveys," *Journal of Marketing Research*, 33, February, 108–13.

Dillman, Don A. (1978) *Mail and Telephone Surveys*, New York: John Wiley and Sons.

Erdos, Paul (1970) *Professional Mail Surveys*, New York: McGraw-Hill.

Evans, Franklin B., and Harry V. Roberts (1963) "Fords, Chevrolets, and the Problem of Discrimination," *Journal of Business*, 36, April, 242–49.

Fisher, Robert J. (1993) "Social Desirability Bias and the Validity of Indirect Questioning," *Journal of Consumer Research*, 20, September, 303–15.

Flynn, Leisa Reinecke (1993) "Do Standard Scales Work in Older Samples?" *Marketing Letters*, April, 4, No. 2, 127–37.

Fornell, Claes (1992) "A National Customer Satisfaction Barometer: The Swedish Experience," *Journal of Marketing*, 56, January, 6–21.

Gottlieb, Morris J. (1959) "Segmentation by Personality Types," in Lynne H. Stockman, ed., *Advancing Marketing Efficiency*, Chicago: American Marketing Association, 148–58.

Greeno, Daniel W., Montrose S. Sommers, and Jerome B. Kernan (1973) "Personality and Implicit Behavior Patterns," *Journal of Marketing Research*, 10, February, 63–69.

Grubb, Edward L., and Gregg Hupp (1968) "Perception of Self, Generalized Stereotypes, and Brand Selection," *Journal of Marketing Research*, 5, February, 58–63.

Howard, John A. (1977) *Consumer Behavior: Application of Theory*, New York: McGraw-Hill.

Hustad, Thomas P., and Edgar A. Pessemier (1971) "Segmenting Consumer Markets with Activity and Attitude Measures," Institute Paper 298, Lafayette, Ind.: Krannert Graduate School of Industrial Administration, Purdue University.

Infosino, William J. (1986) "Forecasting New Product Sales from Likelihood of Purchase Ratings," *Marketing Science*, 5, Fall, 372–84.

Jacoby, Jacob (1971) "Personality and Innovation Proneness," *Journal of Marketing Research*, 8, May, 244–47.

   (1976) *Handbook of Questionnaire Construction*, Cambridge, Mass.: Ballinger.

Jacoby, Jacob, and Robert W. Chestnut (1978) *Brand Loyalty Management and Measurement*, New York: John Wiley and Sons.

Jamieson, Linda F., and Frank M. Bass (1989) "Adjusting Stated Intention Measures to Predict Trial Purchase of New Products: A Comparison of Models and Methods," *Journal of Marketing Research*, 26, August, 336–45.

Jaworski, Bernard J., and Ajay K. Kohli (1993) "Market Orientation: Antecedents and Consequences," *Journal of Marketing*, 57, July, 53–70.

John, Deborah Roedder, and Yvonne Karsten (1993) "Measuring Children's Preferences," presented at *New Methods and Applications in Consumer Research*, Cambridge, Mass., MSI conference, September.

Juster, F. T. (1966) "Consumer Buying Intentions and Purchase Probability: An Experiment in Survey Design," *Journal of the American Statistical Association*, 61, September, 658–96.

KAHLE, LYNN R., SHARON E. BEATTY, AND PAMELA HOMER (1986) "Alternative Measurement Approaches to Consumer Values: The List of Values (LOV) and Values and Life Style (VALS)," *Journal of Consumer Research*, 13, December, 405–09.

KALWANI, MANOHAR U., AND ALVIN J. SILK (1983) "On the Reliability and Predictive Validity of Purchase Intention Measures," *Marketing Science*, 1, Summer, 243–86.

KAMAKURA, WAGNER A., AND JOSÉ AFONSO MAZZON (1991) "Value Segmentation: A Model for the Measurement of Values and Value Systems," *Journal of Consumer Research*, 18, September, 208–14.

KAMAKURA, WAGNER A., AND THOMAS P. NOVAK (1992) "Value-System Segmentation: Exploring the Meaning of LOV," *Journal of Consumer Research*, 19, June, 119–32.

KAMAKURA, WAGNER A., AND MICHEL WEDEL (1995) "Life-Style Segmentation with Tailored Interviewing," *Journal of Marketing Research*, 32, August, 308–17.

KAMEN, JOSEPH M. (1964) "Personality and Food Preferences," *Journal of Advertising Research*, 4, September, 29–32.

KASSARJIAN, HAROLD H. (1971) "Personality and Consumer Behavior: A Review," *Journal of Marketing Research*, 8, November, 409–19.

KASSARJIAN, HAROLD H., AND WALTRAUD M. KASSARJIAN (1966) "Personality Correlates of Inner- and Other-Direction," *Journal of Social Psychology*, 70, June, 281–85.

KATZ, JERROLD P. (1974) "An Examination of Sample Survey Research in Marketing in the Context of a Buyer Behavior Model," Ph.D. dissertation, Columbia University.

KELLER, KEVIN LANE (1993) "Conceptualizing, Measuring, and Managing Customer-Based Brand Equity," *Journal of Marketing*, 57, January, 1–22.

KERNAN, JEROME (1968) "Choice Criteria, Decision Behavior, and Personality," *Journal of Marketing Research*, 5, May, 155–64.

KING, CHARLES W., AND JOHN O. SUMMERS (1970) "Overlap of Opinion Leadership Across Consumer Product Categories," *Journal of Marketing Research*, 7, February, 43–50.

KOHLI, AJAY K., BERNARD J. JAWORSKI, AND AJITH KUMAR (1993) "MARKOR: A Measure of Market Orientation," *Journal of Marketing Reseach*, 30, November, 467–77.

LEIGH, JAMES H., AND CLAUDE R. MARTIN, JR. (1987) "'Don't Know' Item Nonresponse in a Telephone Survey: Effects of Question Form and Respondent Characteristics," *Journal of Marketing Research*, 24, November, 418–24.

LOVELOCK, CHRISTOPHER H., RONALD STIFF, DAVID CULLWICK, AND IRA M. KAUFMAN (1976) "An Evaluation of the Effectiveness of Drop-off Questionnaire Delivery," *Journal of Marketing Research*, 13, November, 358–64.

MCNEIL, J. (1974) "Federal Programs to Measure Consumer Purchase Expectations, 1946–73: A Post-Mortem," *Journal of Consumer Research*, 1, December, 1–10.

MALHOTRA, NARESH K. (1986) "An Approach to the Measurement of Consumer Preferences Using Limited Information," *Journal of Marketing Research*, 23, February, 33–40.

MASSY, WILLIAM F., RONALD E. FRANK, AND THOMAS M. LODAHL (1968) *Purchasing Behavior and Personal Attributes*, Philadelphia: University of Pennsylvania Press.

MENON, GEETA (1993) "The Effects of Accessibility of Information in Memory on Judgments of Behavioral Frequencies," *Journal of Consumer Research*, 20, December, 431–40.

MENON, GEETA, BARBARA BICKART, SEYMOUR SUDMAN, AND JOHNNY BLAIR (1995) "How Well Do You Know Your Partner: Proxy-Reports and Their Effects on Convergence to Self Reports," *Journal of Marketing Research*, 32, February, 75–84.

MITCHELL, ARNOLD (1983) *The Nine American Life Styles,* New York: Warner.

MORRISON, DONALD G. (1979) "Purchase Intentions and Purchase Behavior," *Journal of Marketing*, 43, Spring, 65–74.

MORWITZ, VICKI G. (1993) "The Predictive Validity of Time Conditioned Intent Measures: Will I Buy and When Will I Buy?" working paper, Stern School, New York University, June.

MORWITZ, VICKI G., ERIC JOHNSON, AND DAVID SCHMITTLEIN (1993) "Does Measuring Intent Change Behavior?" *Journal of Consumer Research*, 20, June, 46–61.

MORWITZ, VICKI G., AND DAVID SCHMITTLEIN (1992) "Using Segmentation to Improve Sales Forecasts Based on Purchase Intent: Which 'Intenders' Actually Buy," *Journal of Marketing Research*, 29, November, 391–405.

MULLET, GARY M., AND MARVIN J. KARSON (1985) "Analysis of Purchase Intent Scales Weighted by Probability of Actual Purchase," *Journal of Marketing Research*, 22, February, 93–96.

NOVAK, THOMAS P., AND BRUCE MACEVOY (1990) "On Comparing Alternative Segmentation Schemes: The List of Values (LOV) and Values and Life Styles (VALS)," *Journal of Consumer Research*, 17, June, 105–09.

PARASURAMAN, A., VALARIE A. ZEITHAML, AND LEONARD L. BERRY (1988) "SERVQUAL: A Multiple-Item Scale for Measuring Consumer Perceptions of Service Quality," *Journal of Retailing*, 64, Spring, 12–37.

 (1994) "Reassessment of Expectations as a Comparison Standard in Measuring Service Quality: Implications for Further Research," *Journal of Marketing*, 58, January, 111–24.

PAYNE, STANLEY L. (1951) *The Art of Asking Questions*, Princeton, N.J.: Princeton University Press.

PESSEMIER, EDGAR A., AND A. BRUNO (1971) "An Empirical Investigation of the Reliability and Stability of Selected Activity and Attitude Measures," *Proceedings*, Annual Conference, Association for Consumer Research, 389–403. College Park, Maryland.

PESSEMIER, EDGAR, STEWART DEBRUICKER, AND THOMAS HUSTAD (1971) "The 1970 Purdue Consumer Behavior Research Project," Lafayette, Ind.: Purdue University.

PLUMMER, JOSEPH T. (1974) "The Concept and Application of Life Style Segmentation," *Journal of Marketing*, 38, January, 33–37.

PRESSLEY, MILTON M., ED. (1976) *Mail Survey Response: A Critically Annotated Bibliography*, Greensboro, N.C.: Faber.

PRESSLEY, MILTON M., AND WILLIAM L. TULLAR (1977) "A Factor Interactive Investigation of Mail Survey Response Rates from a Commercial Population," *Journal of Marketing Research*, 14, February, 108–11.

REYNOLDS, FRED D. (1973) *Psychographics: A Conceptual Orientation,* Research Monograph no. 6, Athens, Ga.: College of Business Administration, University of Georgia.

ROBERTSON, THOMAS S., AND JAMES H. MYERS (1969) "Personality Correlates of Opinion Leadership and Innovative Buying Behavior," *Journal of Marketing Research*, 6, May, 164–68.

ROKEACH, MILTON (1973) *The Nature of Human Values*, New York: Free Press.

SCHIFFMAN, LEON G., AND MICHAEL D. JONES (1983) "New York Telephone's Use of VALS," *Marketing Review*, 38, December–January, 25–29.

SCHUMAN, HOWARD, AND STANLEY PRESSER (1981) *Questions and Answers in Attitude Surveys*, New York: Academic Press.

SCHWARZ, NORBERT, AND SEYMOUR SUDMAN (1995) *Answering Questions*, San Francisco: Jossey-Bass.

SHAW, MARVIN E., AND JACK M. WRIGHT (1967) *Scales for the Measurement of Attitude*, New York: McGraw-Hill.

SINGH, JAGDIP, ROY D. HOWELL, AND GARY K. RHOADS (1990) "Adaptive Designs for Likert-Type Data: An Approach for Implementing Marketing Surveys," *Journal of Marketing Research*, 28, August, 304–21.

SUDMAN, SEYMOUR, AND NORMAN M. BRADBURN (1982) *Asking Questions,* San Francisco: Jossey-Bass.

SUDMAN, SEYMOUR, NORMAN M. BRADBURN, AND NORBERT SCHWARZ (1996) *Thinking about Answers: The Application of Cognitive Process to Survey Methodology*, San Francisco: Jossey-Bass.

TEAS, R. KENNETH (1994) "Expectations as a Comparison Standard in Measuring Service Quality: An Assessment of a Reassessment," *Journal of Marketing*, January, 132–39.

TELSER, EUGENE (1976) "Data Exorcises Bias in Phone vs. Personal Interview Debate, but if You Can't Do It Right, Don't Do It at All," *Marketing News*, 9, September 10, 6–7.

TORGERSON, WARREN S. (1958) *Theory and Methods of Scaling*, New York: John Wiley and Sons.

TUCKER, WILLIAM T., AND JOHN PAINTER (1961) "Personality and Product Use," *Journal of Applied Psychology*, 45, October, 325–29.

TYEBJEE, TYZOON T. (1979a) "Response Latency: A New Measure for Scaling Brand Preference," *Journal of Marketing Research*, 16, February, 96–101.

(1979b) "Telephone Survey Methods: The State of the Art," *Journal of Marketing*, 43, Summer, 68–78.

Venkatesan, M. ed. Determinant Factor in Store Choice," *Proceedings*, Third Annual Conference, Association for Consumer Research, 9–19. College Park, Maryland.

VENKATESAN, M. (1968) "Personality and Persuasibility in Consumer Decision Making," *Journal of Advertising Research*, 8, March, 39–45.

VILLANI, KATHRYN E. A., AND DONALD R. LEHMANN (1975) "An Examination of the Stability of AIO Measures," *Proceedings*, Fall Conference American Marketing Association, 484–88. Chicago, IL.

WEBSTER, CYNTHIA (1996) "Hispanic and Anglo Interviewer and Respondent Ethnicity and Gender: The Impact on Survey Response Quality," *Journal of Marketing Research*, 33, February, 62–72.

WELLS, WILLIAM D. (1974) *Life Style and Psychographics,* Chicago: American Marketing Association.

(1975) "Psychographics: A Critical Review," *Journal of Marketing Research*, 12, May, 196–213.

WELLS, WILLIAM D., AND DOUGLAS J. TIGERT (1971) "Activities, Interests, and Opinions," *Journal of Advertising Research*, 2, August, 27–35.

WESTFALL, RALPH (1962) "Psychological Factors in Predicting Product Choice," *Journal of Marketing*, 26, April, 34–40.

WHALEN, BERNIE (1983) "Ad Agency Cross-Tabs VALS with 'Nine Nations'; Results 'Unnerving,'" *Marketing News*, 16, January 21, 20.

APPENDIX 7-A

MARKET FACTS CONSUMER PANEL BASIC DATA

Sex of Panel Member
Male
Female

Panel Member Age

Family (Female Age if Present)
Under 30 years
30–39 years
40–49 years
50–59 years
60 years and older

Non Family
Male under 30 years
Male 30 years and older
Female under 30 years
Female 30 years and older

Geographic Division Code
New England
Middle Atlantic
East North Central
West North Central
South Atlantic
East South Central
West South Central
Mountain
Pacific

State Codes
(50 stated plus District of Columbia)

County Code
(3-digit code)

Metropolitan Statistical Area Code
(3-digit code)

Type of Dwelling Unit
Mobile home or trailer
1-family home detached from any other houses
1-family home attached to 1 or more houses (duplex/townhouse)
A building for 2 families
A building for 3 or more families

Other
Not specified

Ownership of Residence
Owned by you or someone else in household
Rented for cash rent
Occupied with no cash rent paid
Not specified

Total Household Income Previously Reported
Less than $7,500
$7,500–$12,499
$12,500–$17,499
$17,500–$19,999
$20,000–$22,499
$22,500–$27,499
$27,500–$34,999
$35,000–$39,999
$40,000–$49,999
$50,000–$59,999
$60,000–$74,999
$75,000 and over

Education Level of Panel Member
1–7 years grade school
8 years grade school
1–3 years high school
4 years high school
1–3 years college
4 years college
5–8 years college
Did not attend school
Not specified

Education Level of Spouse
(same as categories as Education Level of Panel Member)

Occupation of Panel Member
Professional specialty
Executive, administrative, and managerial
Administrative support, including clerical
Sales
Precision production, craft, and repair
Operator, fabricator, and laborer

Technician and related support
Farming, forestry, and fishing
Service
Not specified
Panel member not employed

Employment Status of Spouse
Works for someone else full-time
Temporarily unemployed
Self employed
Works for someone else part-time only
Retired and not employed
Disabled, student, etc., and not employed
Full-time homemaker
Not specified
No spouse

Occupation of Spouse
(same categories as Occupation of Panel
Member)

Employment Status of Panel Member
(same categories as Employment Status of
Spouse)

Household Size
One
Two
Three
Four
Five
Six
Seven
Eight or more

Year of Birth - Panel Member
(last 2 digits of year)

Age of Spouse
Under 30 years
30–39 years
40–49 years
50–59 years
60 years and older
Spouse's age not specified

Year of Birth - Spouse
(last 2 digits of year)

*Sex and Year of Birth of First Other
Household Member*
(3-digit code)

*Sex and Year of Birth of Second Other
Household Member*
(3-digit code)

*Sex and Year of Birth of Third Other
Household Member*
(3-digit code)

*Sex and Year of Birth of Fourth Other
Household Member*
(3-digit code)

*Sex and Year of Birth of Fifth Other
Household Member*
(3-digit code)

*Sex and Year of Birth of Sixth Other
Household Member*
(3-digit code)

Marital Status
Married
Widowed
Divorced
Separated
Never married
Not specified

Household Income Most Recently Reported
Less than $7,500
$7,500–$12,499
$12,500–$17,499
$17,500–$19,999
$20,000–$22,499
$22,500–$27,499
$27,500–$34,999
$35,000–$39,999
$40,000–$49,999
$50,000–$59,999
$60,000–$74,999
$75,000 and over

*Population Density and Degree of
Urbanization*
Non-MSA

Metropolitan Statistical Area
(Population 50,000–499,999)
Central City
Non-Central City

Metropolitan Statistical Area
   (Population 500,000–1,999,999)
   Central City
   Non-Central City

Metropolitan Statistical Area
   (Population 2,000,000 and Over)
   Central City
   Non-Central City

Age of Panel Member
   Under 30 years
   30–39 years
   40–49 years
   50–59 years
   60 years and older

CPM Job Number

Group Number

Control Number

Special Purpose Columns

Household Income Most Recently Reported
(21 Categories)
   Less than $5,000
   $5,000–$7,499
   $7,500–$9,999

$10,000–$12,499
$12,500–$14,999
$15,000–$17,499
$17,500–$19,999
$20,000–$22,499
$22,500–$24,999
$25,000–$27,499
$27,500–$29,999
$30,000–$32,499
$35,000–$34,999
$35,000–$39,999
$40,000–$44,999
$45,000–$49,999
$50,000–$59,999
$60,000–$74,999
$75,000–$99,999
$100,000–$124,999
$125,000 and over

Special Purpose

Sex of Selected Respondent
(if applicable)

Age of Selected Respondent
(if applicable)

Card Number

APPENDIX 7-B

COMMERCIAL PERSONAL INTERVIEW SURVEY*

DO NOT WRITE IN THIS SPACE

Study #	(1–3) X05
Respondent #	(4–7)
Area Code	(8–9)
Questre. Type	10–5
Card #	11–1

Respondent's Name _____

Address _____

City, State _____ Zip Code _____

Telephone # _____

(Area Code _____)

Interviewer's Name _____

City _____ State _____

Date _____

---

* Reprinted with permission of Professor Jerrold P. Katz, Simmons College, Boston, Massachusetts.

1. First, when you think of product 1 what brands come to mind? Any others? (CIRCLE BELOW BY ORDER OF MENTION)

2. What brands of product 1 have you seen or heard advertised recently? Any others? (CIRCLE BELOW BY ORDER OF MENTION)

3. The last time you bought product 1 what brand did you buy? (CIRCLE BELOW)

4. What other brands have you bought in the last two months? (CIRCLE BELOW)

5. And what brand do you buy most often? (CIRCLE BELOW)

INTERVIEWER: CIRCLE UNDER Q.6 "YES", EACH BRAND MENTIONED IN Q.1 THROUGH Q.5 THEN ASK Q.6 FOR EACH BRAND NOT YET CIRCLED "YES".

6. Have you ever heard of _____ product 1? (CIRCLE BELOW)

ASK Q.7 AND Q.8 FOR EACH BRAND CIRCLED UNDER Q.6 "YES".

7. Everything considered, what is your overall opinion of _____? Would you say it is one of the Best, Very Good, Good, Fair or Poor ? (CIRCLE BELOW)

8. Have you ever tried _____ product 1 (CIRCLE BELOW)

| 11-3 | Q.1 Come to mind | | | Q.2 Advertised | | | Q. 3,4,5 – Brand buying | | | Q.6 Heard Of | | Q.7 Overall Opinion | | | | | | Q.8 |
| | | | | | | | Q.3 | Q.4 | Q.5 | | | | | | | | | |
	1st	2nd	Others	1st	Others	Last	Others	Most	Yes	No	One of The Best	Very Good	Good	Fair	Poor	No Opinion	Tried
Brand E	12-1	14-1	16-1	18-1	20-1	22-1	24-1	26-1	28-1	30-1	32-1	-2	-3	-4	-5	X	45-1
Brand F	-2	-2	-2	-2	-2	-2	-2	-2	-2	-2	33-1	-2	-3	-4	-5	X	-2
Brand B1	-3	-3	-3	-3	-3	-3	-3	-3	-3	-3	34-1	-2	-3	-4	-5	X	-3
Brand B2	-4	-4	-4	-4	-4	-4	-4	-4	-4	-4	35-1	-2	-3	-4	-5	X	-4
Brand B3	-5	-5	-5	-5	-5	-5	-5	-5	-5	-5	36-1	-2	-3	-4	-5	X	-5
Brand G	-6	-6	-6	-6	-6	-6	-6	-6	-6	-6	37-1	-2	-3	-4	-5	X	-6
Brand A	-7	-7	-7	-7	-7	-7	-7	-7	-7	-7	38-1	-2	-3	-4	-5	X	-7
Brand R	-8	-8	-8	-8	-8	-8	-8	-8	-8	-8	39-1	-2	-3	-4	-5	X	-8
Brand P	-9	-9	-9	-9	-9	-9	-9	-9	-9	-9	40-1	-2	-3	-4	-5	X	-9
Brand H	-0	-0	-0	-0	-0	-0	-0	-0	-0	-0	41-1	-2	-3	-4	-5	X	-0
Brand I	13-1	15-1	17-1	19-1	21-1	23-1	25-1	27-1	29-1	31-1	42-1	-2	-3	-4	-5	X	47-1
Brand U	-2	-2	-2	-2	-2	-2	-2	-2	-2	-2	43-1	-2	-3	-4	-5	X	-2
Other	-3	-3	-3	-3	-3	-3	-3	-3	-3	-3	44-45						

9. (FOR EACH BRAND BELOW CIRCLED IN Q. 8, ASK:) Have you tried _____ just once or more than once? (CIRCLE BELOW)

10. (FOR EACH BRAND BELOW CIRCLED IN Q. 6, ASK:) Have you seen or heard of any advertising recently for _____ product 1 (CIRCLE BELOW)

11. (FOR EACH BRAND BELOW CIRCLED IN Q. 10, ASK:) a) Please describe exactly what you saw in the advertising for _____ product 1 (RECORD BELOW)
b) What else did you see? (INTERVIEWER: PROBE FOR AS MUCH DETAIL AS POSSIBLE, RECORD BELOW)

	Q.9 Tried		Q.10	Q. 10, 11 Advertising
	Once	More than once		Q. 11 a, b Exactly what was seen
Brand B1	48-3	49-3	50-3	
Brand B2	-4	-4		
Brand B3	-5	-5		
Brand G	-6	-6	-6	
Brand A	-7	-7	-7	
Brand P	-9	-9	-9	

INTERVIEWER: IF ANY OF THE Brand B PRODUCTS ARE TO BE ASKED ABOUT IN Q. 10-11, SIMPLY ASK ABOUT Brand B WITHOUT MENTIONING THE TYPES

51-
52-
53-
54-
55-
56-
57-
58-
59-
60-

12. Different brands of product I say and show different things in their advertising. I'm going to read you some of these things, and I'd like you to tell me which brand's advertising I am describing. (DO NOT READ BRANDS – CIRCLE OR WRITE IN BRANDS MENTIONED BY RESPONDENT)

```
11 – 2
12 – x
13 – x
```

	Brand B	Brand G	Brand A	Brand P	Other (SPECIFY EXACTLY)	Don't Know
a. Advertising Copy 1	14–3	-6	-7	-9	15-_____	X
b. Advertising Copy 2	16–3	-6	-7	-9	17-_____	X
c. Advertising Copy 3	18–3	-6	-7	-9	19-_____	X
d. Advertising Copy 4	20–3	-6	-7	-9	21-_____	X
e. Advertising Copy 5	22–3	-6	-7	-9	23-_____	X
f. Advertising Copy 6	24–3	-6	-7	-9	25-_____	X
g. Advertising Copy 7	26–3	-6	-7	-9	27-_____	X
h. Advertising Copy 8	28–3	-6	-7	-9	29-_____	X
i. Advertising Copy 9	30–3	-6	-7	-9	31-_____	X

ASK Q.13 FOR EACH BRAND LISTED BELOW THAT WAS CIRCLED IN Q.6.

13. Now, I'd like your opinion of a few brands of product 1 on some of their specific features. For example, would you say that _____ product 1 is one of the best, very good, fair or good, fair or poor on Attribute 1?

(CIRCLE BELOW AND REPEAT EACH FEATURE FOR EACH BRAND CIRCLED IN Q.6)

ATTRIBUTE ONE

	One of the best	Very good	Good	Fair	Poor	Have no opinion
Brand E	36-1	2	3	4	5	X
Brand F	6	7	8	9	0	Y
Brand B	37-1	2	3	4	5	X
Brand A	6	7	8	9	0	Y
Brand P	38-1	2	3	4	5	X
Brand H	6	7	8	9	0	Y
Brand I	39-1	2	3	4	5	X

ATTRIBUTE TWO

	One of the best	Very good	Good	Fair	Poor	Have no opinion
Brand E	40-1	2	3	4	5	X
Brand F	6	7	8	9	0	Y
Brand B	41-1	2	3	4	5	X
Brand A	6	7	8	9	0	Y
Brand P	42-1	2	3	4	5	X
Brand H	6	7	8	9	0	Y
Brand I	43-1	2	3	4	5	X

ATTRIBUTE THREE

	One of the best	Very good	Good	Fair	Poor	Have no opinion
Brand E	44-1	2	3	4	5	X
Brand F	6	7	8	9	0	Y
Brand B	45-1	2	3	4	5	X
Brand A	6	7	8	9	0	Y
Brand P	46-1	2	3	4	5	X
Brand H	6	7	8	9	0	Y
Brand I	47-1	2	3	4	5	X

14. As you probably know there are   size 1   and size 2 units of product 1.   About how many size 1 units   did your family use last month?

RECORD # UNITS _____ (64–65) IF NONE, CIRCLE: Y

15. About how many   size 2 units of product 1 did your family use last month?

RECORD # UNITS _____ (66–67) IF NONE, CIRCLE: Y

16. For the next few questions, please tell us how often you buy different kinds of product 1. Your answer should be either frequently, occasionally, seldom or never.
For example, how often do you buy.........(CIRCLE)

		Frequently	Occasionally	Seldom	Never
		68–1	69–1	70–1	71–1
a.	Kind 1	–2	–2	–2	–2
b.	Kind 2	–3	–3	–3	–3
c.	Kind 3	–4	–4	–4	–4
d.	Kind 4				
e.	Product 1 on special price, coupon, cents-off, or on some other special deal	–5	–5	–5	–5

CLASSIFICATION

1. Please think for a moment about your purchase of product 1 in the past six months. In general, do you seem to be buying....(CIRCLE BELOW)

2. And what about your purchase of product 2 in the past six months? In general, do you seem to be buying....(CIRCLE BELOW)

	Q.1 Product 1	Q.2 Product 2
More expensive brands	72-1	73-1
Less expensive brands or	2	2
The same priced brands that you have always bought	3	3
Don't know (DO NOT READ)	X	X

3. Generally speaking, in the next six months do you expect the price of products such as product 1, product 2, etc. ....(CIRCLE BELOW)

Go up some	74-1
Go down some or	(2)
Remain the same	3
Don't know (DO NOT READ)	X

4. In terms of a typical seven-day week, how much television do you watch at different times of the day and night? For example, during the day before 5 pm, do you watch a lot of TV, or none at all? Now in the evening.....(REPEAT FOR EACH OF THE THREE REMAINING TIME PERIODS - CIRCLE BELOW)

11-1
CONT'D

	A Lot	A Little	None	(DO NOT READ) Don't Know
During the day before 5 PM	63-1	64-1	65-1	-9
Between 5 and 7:30 PM	-2	-2	-2	-0
Between 7:30 and 11 PM	-3	-3	-3	-X
After 11 PM	-4	-4	-4	-Y

66-X

5. Which of these age groups are you in? (CIRCLE NUMBER UNDER THE GROUP)

	Under 25	25 - 34	35 - 44	45 - 54	Over 54
67	-1	-2	-3	-4	-5

6. How many members of your family are living at home now, including yourself? (CIRCLE)

68	-1	-2	-3	-4	-5	-6+

7. And to help us tabulate your answers, what is your total family income per year before taxes? (CIRCLE NUMBER TO LEFT OF GROUP)

69-1	Under $3,000	-4	$7,500 - $10,000	
-2	$3,000 - $5,000	-5	$10,000 - $15,000	70-
-3	$5,000 - $7,500	-6	Over $15,000	71-

APPENDIX 7-C ▬▬▬▬▬▬

NUTRITIONAL QUESTIONNAIRE

<u>SECTION I - FOOD AND SHOPPING HABITS</u>

1. Please check to indicate what portion
   of the food shopping for your household
   you do personally . . . .
   - ☐ None of it
   - ☐ Less than half of it
   - ☐ About half of it
   - ☐ Most of it
   - ☐ All of it

2. About how many times PER WEEK
   do you shop for food? · · · · · · · · · · · · · · ·
   - ☐ Less than once a week
   - ☐ Once a week
   - ☐ 2 - 4 times a week
   - ☐ 5 or more times a week

3. a) Do you prepare a shopping list before you go to the store?

   ☐ YES - Continue   ☐ NO - Skip to Question 4

   b) About what portion of the items that are
       purchased at the grocery store or super-
       market are on your shopping list? . . . .
       - ☐ None of them
       - ☐ Some of them
       - ☐ About half of them
       - ☐ More than half
       - ☐ Almost all of them

4. Approximately how much money
   is spent on food for your
   household in an average <u>week</u>? . . . .
   - ☐ Under $15
   - ☐ $15 - $29
   - ☐ $30 - $44
   - ☐ $45 - $60
   - ☐ Over $60

5. Approximately how much different
   is the amount you now spend on
   food each week as compared to one
   year ago at this time? . . . .
   - ☐ Spend at least $10 less than last year
   - ☐ $5 - $10 less than last year
   - ☐ About the same as last year
   - ☐ $5 - $10 more than last year
   - ☐ Over $10 more than last year

6. When you buy staple products (i.e. canned soup,
   ketchup, etc.), how many brands and sizes do you
   usually consider? (CHECK ONLY ONE) . . . .
   - ☐ Only 1 or 2
   - ☐ Many brands, one size
   - ☐ Many sizes, one brand
   - ☐ Many brands and sizes

7. Which <u>one</u> of the following <u>best</u> describes the way you shop for food?   (CHECK ONLY <u>ONE</u>)

   - ☐ I actively seek information about food in terms of nutritional value, price, etc.
   - ☐ I sometimes try new foods because of new information, but generally buy the same foods
   - ☐ The food I buy is almost always the same, and I spend very little time thinking about it

8. Have you, or any members of your immediate family, ever used food stamps?

   - ☐ Never
   - ☐ Used to, but do not use them now
   - ☐ We are presently using them

9. When deciding which foods to serve, how important are the following considerations? Indicate the degree of importance for each either by checking under the heading that describes your feelings, or by checking a box in between the headings that describe your feelings if your feelings fall somewhere between the headings.

	VERY IMPORTANT		SOMEWHAT IMPORTANT		NOT VERY IMPORTANT
Variety..	☐	☐	☐	☐	☐
Taste..	☐	☐	☐	☐	☐
Other family members' preferences..............	☐	☐	☐	☐	☐
Diet restrictions..............................	☐	☐	☐	☐	☐
Price..	☐	☐	☐	☐	☐
Availability at stores where you normally shop.	☐	☐	☐	☐	☐
Ease of preparation............................	☐	☐	☐	☐	☐
Habit (past eating patterns)...................	☐	☐	☐	☐	☐
Advertised specials............................	☐	☐	☐	☐	☐
Nutritional value..............................	☐	☐	☐	☐	☐

10. When you are deciding which brand of a particular food to purchase in the store, how much attention do you pay to the following?

	Pay a Great Deal Of Attention	Pay Some Attention	Pay Little or No Attention
Brand name.....................................	☐	☐	☐
Number of servings.............................	☐	☐	☐
Net weight or volume...........................	☐	☐	☐
Total price....................................	☐	☐	☐
Amount of ingredients..........................	☐	☐	☐
Unit price.....................................	☐	☐	☐
List of ingredients...........................	☐	☐	☐
Nutritional value.............................	☐	☐	☐
Recipes..	☐	☐	☐
Food additives and preservatives..............	☐	☐	☐
Date of manufacture or expiration.............	☐	☐	☐

11. Please check below to indicate how many times per week you, personally, eat each of the following meals.

	Never	1 - 2	3 - 4	5 - 6	Everyday
Breakfast.....................	☐	☐	☐	☐	☐
Lunch.........................	☐	☐	☐	☐	☐
Dinner........................	☐	☐	☐	☐	☐

12. How many snacks do you, personally, have in a typical day?

None..........................	☐
One...........................	☐
Two...........................	☐
Three or more.................	☐

13. How much food do you can yourself?

☐ None   ☐ A small amount   ☐ A large amount

14. How often do you personally consume each of the following?

	Never	A Few Times A Year	1 - 2 Times A Month	Weekly	Several Times A Week	Once A Day	More than Once A Day
Canned fruit................	☐	☐	☐	☐	☐	☐	☐
Fresh fruit.................	☐	☐	☐	☐	☐	☐	☐
Bread.......................	☐	☐	☐	☐	☐	☐	☐
Rice........................	☐	☐	☐	☐	☐	☐	☐
Butter......................	☐	☐	☐	☐	☐	☐	☐
Margarine...................	☐	☐	☐	☐	☐	☐	☐
Cheese......................	☐	☐	☐	☐	☐	☐	☐
Ice cream...................	☐	☐	☐	☐	☐	☐	☐
Whole milk..................	☐	☐	☐	☐	☐	☐	☐
Skim milk or low fat milk....	☐	☐	☐	☐	☐	☐	☐
Snack foods (potato chips, pretzels, etc.)..........	☐	☐	☐	☐	☐	☐	☐
Desserts....................	☐	☐	☐	☐	☐	☐	☐
Alcoholic beverages (beer, wine, liquor)...........	☐	☐	☐	☐	☐	☐	☐
Soft drinks.................	☐	☐	☐	☐	☐	☐	☐
Fish........................	☐	☐	☐	☐	☐	☐	☐
Cold cereal.................	☐	☐	☐	☐	☐	☐	☐
Frozen vegetables...........	☐	☐	☐	☐	☐	☐	☐
Fresh vegetables............	☐	☐	☐	☐	☐	☐	☐
Canned vegetables...........	☐	☐	☐	☐	☐	☐	☐
Poultry.....................	☐	☐	☐	☐	☐	☐	☐
Beef (hamburger or stew meat)	☐	☐	☐	☐	☐	☐	☐
Beef (steak or roast).......	☐	☐	☐	☐	☐	☐	☐
Pork........................	☐	☐	☐	☐	☐	☐	☐
Tuna fish...................	☐	☐	☐	☐	☐	☐	☐
Frozen dinners..............	☐	☐	☐	☐	☐	☐	☐
Hot dogs....................	☐	☐	☐	☐	☐	☐	☐
Coffee or tea...............	☐	☐	☐	☐	☐	☐	☐
Pasta (pizza, spaghetti, etc.)	☐	☐	☐	☐	☐	☐	☐
Food at "fast food" restaurant (i.e. McDonald's, etc.)....................	☐	☐	☐	☐	☐	☐	☐
Food at regular restaurants..	☐	☐	☐	☐	☐	☐	☐

15. How has the amount your household consumes of each of the following food categories changed in the past year?

	Much Less	Somewhat Less	About The Same	Somewhat More	Much More
Canned fruit............................	☐	☐	☐	☐	☐
Fresh fruit............................	☐	☐	☐	☐	☐
Bread..................................	☐	☐	☐	☐	☐
Rice...................................	☐	☐	☐	☐	☐
Butter.................................	☐	☐	☐	☐	☐
Margarine..............................	☐	☐	☐	☐	☐
Cheese.................................	☐	☐	☐	☐	☐
Ice cream..............................	☐	☐	☐	☐	☐
Whole milk.............................	☐	☐	☐	☐	☐
Skim milk or low fat milk.............	☐	☐	☐	☐	☐
Snack foods (potato chips, pretzels, etc.)...................	☐	☐	☐	☐	☐
Desserts...............................	☐	☐	☐	☐	☐
Alcoholic beverages (beer, wine, liquor).....................	☐	☐	☐	☐	☐
Soft drinks...........................	☐	☐	☐	☐	☐
Fish..................................	☐	☐	☐	☐	☐
Cold cereal...........................	☐	☐	☐	☐	☐
Frozen vegetables.....................	☐	☐	☐	☐	☐
Fresh vegetables......................	☐	☐	☐	☐	☐
Canned vegetables.....................	☐	☐	☐	☐	☐
Poultry...............................	☐	☐	☐	☐	☐
Beef (hamburger or stew meat).........	☐	☐	☐	☐	☐
Beef (steak or roast).................	☐	☐	☐	☐	☐
Pork..................................	☐	☐	☐	☐	☐
Tuna fish.............................	☐	☐	☐	☐	☐
Frozen dinners........................	☐	☐	☐	☐	☐
Hot dogs..............................	☐	☐	☐	☐	☐
Coffee or tea.........................	☐	☐	☐	☐	☐
Pasta (pizza, spaghetti, etc.)........	☐	☐	☐	☐	☐
Food at "fast food" restaurants (i.e. McDonald's, etc.)...........	☐	☐	☐	☐	☐
Food at regular restaurants...........	☐	☐	☐	☐	☐

SECTION II - NUTRITIONAL INFORMATION

1. How much information about nutrition have you gained from each of the following sources?

	None	Very Little	Some	Quite A Bit	A Tremendous Amount
Books.................................	☐	☐	☐	☐	☐
Magazines.............................	☐	☐	☐	☐	☐
Labels on the packages food comes in....	☐	☐	☐	☐	☐
Your mother...........................	☐	☐	☐	☐	☐
Other family members..................	☐	☐	☐	☐	☐
Friends...............................	☐	☐	☐	☐	☐
Doctors...............................	☐	☐	☐	☐	☐
TV programs...........................	☐	☐	☐	☐	☐
TV advertisements.....................	☐	☐	☐	☐	☐
Newspapers............................	☐	☐	☐	☐	☐
Your own experience...................	☐	☐	☐	☐	☐
Courses in school.....................	☐	☐	☐	☐	☐

2. In the past year, have you read book(s) about any of the following? . . . .

	NO	YES
Dieting.............	☐	☐
Nutrition...........	☐	☐
Cooking.............	☐	☐

3. Assume the Federal Government were about to launch a major nutrition education campaign aimed at adults. Which of the following forms would you prefer the campaign to take?

₁ ☐ Column in the newspapers
₂ ☐ TV special
₃ ☐ Special edition of a prominent magazine
₄ ☐ Government brochure
₅ ☐ Extension courses
₆ ☐ Workshops
₇ ☐ Public Service TV announcements
₈ ☐ Information on packages
₉ ☐ Information in TV advertisements
₁₁ ☐ Don't Care

4. If a service were to become available which provided specific information about the nutritional value of the brands offered in your local supermarkets, how much would you be willing to pay per week to subscribe to it?

₁ ☐ Nothing   ₄ ☐ 50¢ - 99¢
₂ ☐ 10¢ - 19¢   ₅ ☐ $1 - $2
₃ ☐ 20¢ - 49¢   ₆ ☐ Over $2

5. Have you ever had a formal nutrition course in any of the following? . . . .

	NO	YES
High School......................	☐	☐
College..........................	☐	☐
Adult Education/Workshop.........	☐	☐

SECTION III - BACKGROUND INFORMATION

1. Please indicate if any members of your household are on any of the following special diets:

CHECK HERE IF NO MEMBERS OF YOUR HOUSEHOLD ARE ON A DIET ☐

	Self-imposed		Doctor's Orders	
Low cholesterol.............	1	☐	1	☐
Low fat/calorie.............	2	☐	2	☐
Diabetic....................	3	☐	3	☐
Low salt....................	4	☐	4	☐
Vegetarian..................	5	☐	5	☐
Low triglyceride............	6	☐	6	☐

2. How often do you smoke?

☐ Never
☐ Occasionally
☐ Regularly, but light (less than 1 pack of cigarettes each day)
☐ Regularly (one pack of cigarettes a day)
☐ Heavily (more than 1 pack each day or equivalent)

3. Which of the following types of vitamin pills do you personally take?

₁ ☐ None
₂ ☐ Multiple
₃ ☐ Vitamin C
₄ ☐ Vitamin G
₅ ☐ Vitamin B-12 Complex
₆ ☐ Vitamin A
₇ ☐ Iron

National Family Opinion, Inc.

50739

4. How much time do you spend
    watching TV on an average
    day? . . . .
    ☐ None   ☐ 3 - 4 hours
    ☐ Less than 1 hour   ☐ Over 4 hours
    ☐ 1 - 2 hours

5. How has your family income
    changed in the last year? . . .
    ☐ Gone down a lot   ☐ Gone up a little
    ☐ Gone down a little   ☐ Gone up a lot
    ☐ Stayed about the same

6. How has your household size
    changed in the past year? . . .
    ☐ Decreased by two or more   ☐ Increased by one
    ☐ Decreased by one   ☐ Increased by
    ☐ Stayed the same   two or more

SECTION IV - GENERAL ATTITUDE INFORMATION

Please indicate how much you agree or disagree with each of the following statements by checking a box
under the heading that best describes your feelings.

	STRONGLY AGREE	SOMEWHAT AGREE	NEITHER AGREE NOR DISAGREE	SOMEWHAT DISAGREE	STRONGLY DISAGREE
People need to eat meat to be healthy.........	☐	☐	☐	☐	☐
A high level of consumption is necessary to maintain a high standard of living........	☐	☐	☐	☐	☐
I am personally more conscientious in conserving energy than I was 3 years ago.....	☐	☐	☐	☐	☐
The government should be more active in giving information about nutrition to consumers..	☐	☐	☐	☐	☐
I expect things to get better for my family next year...................................	☐	☐	☐	☐	☐
I feel the need for more information about nutrition.................................	☐	☐	☐	☐	☐
All people would have better diets if there were fewer mouths to feed.................	☐	☐	☐	☐	☐
All cold cereals are about the same nutritionally............................	☐	☐	☐	☐	☐
Health is more important than money...........	☐	☐	☐	☐	☐
I get more exercise than the average person...	☐	☐	☐	☐	☐
We entertain at home more than the average family..................................	☐	☐	☐	☐	☐
I am healthier than the average American......	☐	☐	☐	☐	☐
I consider myself better informed about nutrition than the average American.......	☐	☐	☐	☐	☐
National brands of food are a better buy than local brands........................	☐	☐	☐	☐	☐
Life is going well for me.....................	☐	☐	☐	☐	☐
Prices of food are so high that my nutrition is suffering..............................	☐	☐	☐	☐	☐
Television advertising has an adverse effect on diets because it encourages people to eat "junk" foods.........................	☐	☐	☐	☐	☐
I am heavier than I should be.................	☐	☐	☐	☐	☐
I would be willing to eat less if the food were sent to the poor in the United States	☐	☐	☐	☐	☐

SECTION IV - GENERAL ATTITUDE INFORMATION (Continued) Please continue to indicate how much you agree or disagree with each of the following statements by checking a box under the heading that best describes your feelings.

	STRONGLY AGREE	SOMEWHAT AGREE	NEITHER AGREE NOR DISAGREE	SOMEWHAT DISAGREE	STRONGLY DISAGREE
America has a responsibility to share our agricultural abundance with hungry people in poor countries as well as home in the United States...............................	☐	☐	☐	☐	☐
The United States Government should pass laws which would encourage and reward the farmer for full scale production....................	☐	☐	☐	☐	☐
The children in our household have a large influence on what we eat.....................	☐	☐	☐	☐	☐
Filling out this questionnaire has made me think about things which will change the types of foods I buy........................	☐	☐	☐	☐	☐

SECTION V - FOOD OPINIONS This final section deals with food opinions. I am asking questions about how you feel about certain types of foods. It would be quite unusual for a person to know the correct answers to every one of these questions. However, your feelings are very important to me, and I would like you to answer every question even if you have to guess.

1. Please answer the following questions by checking TRUE, FALSE, or DON'T KNOW.

	True	False	Don't Know
Hamburger contains substantially more protein per ounce than do soy beans....................................	☐	☐	☐
Pasta is high in cholesterol.....................................	☐	☐	☐
Poultry are more efficient than cattle as producers of protein...	☐	☐	☐
A large amount of one vitamin is sufficient to overcome deficiencies of other vitamins.............................	☐	☐	☐
Beans and rice together are a low-protein meal...................	☐	☐	☐
Eating a variety of foods from the supermarket will ensure a balanced diet......................................	☐	☐	☐
The cost of the vitamins needed to meet 100% of the minimum daily requirements is less than 10c per day..........	☐	☐	☐
Food coloring additives create hyperactivity in children.........	☐	☐	☐
Sugar causes cavities in children................................	☐	☐	☐
Whole wheat bread is healthier than enriched white bread.........	☐	☐	☐

2. For each of the nine body functions listed down the side of the page, please indicate which of the four foods contribute importantly to the function. Check as many or as few of the foods that you think apply to each function.

	Whole Milk	Beef	Tomatoes	Enriched Bread
Eyes are aided by:............................	☐	☐	☐	☐
Teeth and bones are aided by:................	☐	☐	☐	☐
Muscle tissue is aided by:...................	☐	☐	☐	☐
Repair of body tissues is aided by:.........	☐	☐	☐	☐
Blood cells are aided by:....................	☐	☐	☐	☐
Fighting infection is aided by:.............	☐	☐	☐	☐
Nervous system is aided by:.................	☐	☐	☐	☐
Skin is aided by:...........................	☐	☐	☐	☐
Proper growth of children is aided by:.......	☐	☐	☐	☐

3. For each of the nutrients listed down the side of the page, <u>check as many or as few of</u> the four foods (whole milk, beef, tomatoes, enriched bread) that you think contain <u>a lot of</u> the nutrients.

	Whole Milk	Beef	Tomatoes	Enriched Bread
There is a lot of <u>Vitamin A</u> in:..................	1 ☐	1 ☐	1 ☐	1 ☐
There is a lot of <u>Thiamin (Vitamin B₁)</u> in:........	2 ☐	2 ☐	2 ☐	2 ☐
There is a lot of <u>Riboflavin (Vitamin B₂)</u> in:.....	3 ☐	3 ☐	3 ☐	3 ☐
There is a lot of <u>Niacin</u> in:.....................	4 ☐	4 ☐	4 ☐	4 ☐
There is a lot of <u>Vitamin C</u> in:..................	5 ☐	5 ☐	5 ☐	5 ☐
There is a lot of <u>Vitamin D</u> in:..................	6 ☐	6 ☐	6 ☐	6 ☐
There is a lot of <u>Protein</u> in:...................	7 ☐	7 ☐	7 ☐	7 ☐
There are a lot of <u>Carbohydrates</u> in:.............	8 ☐	8 ☐	8 ☐	8 ☐
There is a lot of <u>Fat</u> in:.......................	9 ☐	9 ☐	9 ☐	9 ☐
There are a lot of <u>Calories</u> in:.................10 ☐		10 ☐	10 ☐	10 ☐
There is a lot of <u>Iron</u> in:.....................11 ☐		11 ☐	11 ☐	11 ☐
There is a lot of <u>Calcium</u> in:..................12 ☐		12 ☐	12 ☐	12 ☐

4. And finally, I would like you to match certain foods with others. <u>Check as many or as few</u> of the four (4) foods (whole milk, beef, tomatoes, enriched bread) that you think have <u>a lot of</u> the same benefits to the body as each of the 14 foods listed down the side of the page.

	Whole Milk	Beef	Tomatoes	Enriched Bread
<u>Oatmeal</u> provides a lot of the same benefits as:.......	1 ☐	2 ☐	3 ☐	4 ☐
<u>Fish</u> provides a lot of the same benefits as:.........	☐	☐	☐	☐
<u>Rice</u> provides a lot of the same benefits as:.........	☐	☐	☐	☐
<u>Navy beans</u> provide a lot of the same benefits as:....	☐	2 ☐	3 ☐	4 ☐
<u>Chicken</u> provides a lot of the same benefits as:.......	1 ☐	2 ☐	3 ☐	4 ☐
<u>Potatoes</u> provide a lot of the same benefits as:.......	☐	☐	☐	☐
<u>Eggs</u> provide a lot of the same benefits as:..........	☐	☐	☐	☐
<u>Macaroni</u> provides a lot of the same benefits as:......	1 ☐	2 ☐	3 ☐	4 ☐
<u>Pork and Lamb</u> provide a lot of the same benefits as:..	1 ☐	2 ☐	3 ☐	4 ☐
<u>String beans</u> provide a lot of the same benefits as:...	☐	☐	☐	☐
<u>Carrots</u> provide a lot of the same benefits as:........	☐	☐	☐	☐
<u>Bananas</u> provide a lot of the same benefits as:........	1 ☐	2 ☐	3 ☐	4 ☐
<u>Peanut butter</u> provides a lot of the same benefits as:.	1 ☐	2 ☐	3 ☐	4 ☐
<u>Cottage cheese</u> provides a lot of the same benefits as:	1 ☐	2 ☐	3 ☐	4 ☐

APPENDIX 7-D

OWNERSHIP AND VALUES SURVEY

Columbia University, New York, N.Y. 10027

GRADUATE SCHOOL OF BUSINESS   **URIS HALL**

This survey is part of an academic research project at Columbia University Graduate School of Business. It will require about 20 minutes of your time to fill out, and concerns products and services you own and/or may want to acquire as well as some general background questions. The results will be treated anonymously and used only for statistical analysis.

While we cannot offer you a large incentive other than our sincere thanks for participation, we have arranged to enter you, along with the other participants, in a lottery. The winner of the lottery will receive a check for $500. If you wish to participate in the lottery, simply put your name and address on this sheet and return it with your survey. (The cover sheet will be detached to insure anonymity.)

Thank you in advance for your cooperation.

NAME _____

ADDRESS _____

_____

PRODUCTS AND SERVICES

1. This question concerns products and services you may own and which you may plan to buy. For each product and service listed, please indicate:

   a. How many you have *in your household,* and

   b. How likely you are to buy one in the next 2 years.

   Please write a number from 0 to 100 in the space provided (0 = definitely will not buy, 100 = definitely will buy). Please fill this out even for items that you already own.

	(a) Number of Each Owned *(fill in number)*	*(b)* Likelihood of Buying in Next 2 Years *(# between 0 and 100)*
Cable TV service		
Piano		
Microwave oven		
Cat		
Dog		
Car		
VCR		
Sofa bed		
Personal computer		
Copying machine		
Fur coat		
Window air conditioner		
Downhill skis		
Cross-country skis		
Weight-lifting equipment		
Sailboat		
Original artwork		
Sports car		
Dishwasher		
Compact disc player		
Phone answering machine		
Color TV		
Wide-screen TV		
Vacation home		
Van or camper		
Food processor		
Burglar alarm/home security system		
35mm camera		
Video recorder/camcorder		
Exercise bike		

2. This question concerns how important the following products and services are to you. If you had *nothing at all* and were starting from scratch to acquire possessions, how important would it be to acquire each of these products and services? Please indicate your answer by checking "Extremely Important" for those products to which you would give the highest priority, "Not important" for those to which you give the lowest priority, and somewhere in between for the others.

	Not *Important*					*Extremely* *Important*
Cable TV service	___	___	___	___	___	___
Piano	___	___	___	___	___	___
Microwave oven	___	___	___	___	___	___
Cat	___	___	___	___	___	___
Dog	___	___	___	___	___	___
Car	___	___	___	___	___	___
VCR	___	___	___	___	___	___
Sofa bed	___	___	___	___	___	___
Personal computer	___	___	___	___	___	___
Copying machine	___	___	___	___	___	___
Fur coat	___	___	___	___	___	___
Window air conditioner	___	___	___	___	___	___
Downhill skis	___	___	___	___	___	___
Cross-country skis	___	___	___	___	___	___
Weight-lifting equipment	___	___	___	___	___	___
Sailboat	___	___	___	___	___	___
Original artwork	___	___	___	___	___	___
Sports car	___	___	___	___	___	___
Dishwasher	___	___	___	___	___	___
Compact disc player	___	___	___	___	___	___
Phone answering machine	___	___	___	___	___	___
Color TV	___	___	___	___	___	___
Wide-screen TV	___	___	___	___	___	___
Vacation home	___	___	___	___	___	___
Van or camper	___	___	___	___	___	___
Food processor	___	___	___	___	___	___
Money market account	___	___	___	___	___	___
IRA	___	___	___	___	___	___
Life insurance policy	___	___	___	___	___	___
Burglar alarm/home security system	___	___	___	___	___	___
35mm camera	___	___	___	___	___	___
Video recorder/camcorder	___	___	___	___	___	___
Exercise bike	___	___	___	___	___	___

3. Please indicate how important the following are to you by checking the appropriate spaces. As in question 2, please spread your answers out to indicate the relative importance of the items.

	Not Important					*Extremely Important*
Self-respect	____	____	____	____	____	____
Security	____	____	____	____	____	____
Warm relationship with others	____	____	____	____	____	____
Sense of accomplishment	____	____	____	____	____	____
Self fulfillment	____	____	____	____	____	____
Sense of belonging	____	____	____	____	____	____
Being well-respected	____	____	____	____	____	____
Fun & enjoyment	____	____	____	____	____	____
Excitement	____	____	____	____	____	____
Physical fitness	____	____	____	____	____	____
Being in control	____	____	____	____	____	____
Knowledge	____	____	____	____	____	____
Convenience	____	____	____	____	____	____
Owning things	____	____	____	____	____	____
Beauty	____	____	____	____	____	____
Getting a good deal	____	____	____	____	____	____
Being practical	____	____	____	____	____	____
Travel	____	____	____	____	____	____
Variety	____	____	____	____	____	____
Success	____	____	____	____	____	____
Wealth	____	____	____	____	____	____
Fame	____	____	____	____	____	____
Being unique	____	____	____	____	____	____
Personal growth	____	____	____	____	____	____
Fairness	____	____	____	____	____	____
Simplicity	____	____	____	____	____	____

4. Please indicate how well each of the following statements describes you:

	Describes Me Very Poorly					Describes Me Very Well
I seek intense personal experiences	____	____	____	____	____	____
I am worried about financial security	____	____	____	____	____	____
Fame and success are important to me	____	____	____	____	____	____
I am struggling to survive	____	____	____	____	____	____
I am individualistic	____	____	____	____	____	____
I am concerned about social issues	____	____	____	____	____	____
I try to live like the rich and successful	____	____	____	____	____	____
I seek to be part of a group	____	____	____	____	____	____

BACKGROUND

5. Which of these best describes your occupation?

_____ Professional/technical   _____ Student
_____ Managerial   _____ Homemaker
_____ Skilled worker   _____ Retired
_____ Clerical/sales   _____ Unemployed
_____ Farmer   _____ Other (please specify) _____

6. What is your sex?   _____   _____
                          male   female

7. What is your marital status?

_____   _____   _____   _____
single   married   divorced,   other
                      widowed, or
                      separated

8. How many children do you have who are under 18 and living in your home?

_____   _____   _____   _____   _____
  0   1   2   3   4 or more

9. What is your age?

_____   _____   _____   _____   _____   _____
under 25   25–34   35–44   45–54   55–64   65 or over

10. What is the highest level of school you have completed?
    _____ Elementary school   _____ Some high school   _____ High school
    _____ Some college   _____ College graduate   _____ Graduate school

11. What type of dwelling do you live in?
    _____ Studio apartment   _____ 1 bedroom apartment
    _____ 2 or more bedroom apartment   _____ House

12. Do you own or rent your home? _____   _____
                                          own   rent

13. What is your total annual household income?
    _____ Under $15,000   _____ $15,000–24,999   _____ $25,000–34,999
    _____ $35,000–49,999   _____ $50,000–99,999   _____ $100,000 or over

14. How much of your household income did you save or invest last year?

_____	_____	_____	_____	_____
None	Less than $1,000	$1,000–2,999	$3,000–9,999	$10,000 or more

15. What is your zip code?   _____

CHAPTER 8

Measurement and Scaling

Measurement involves assigning numbers to represent concepts (constructs). For example, we frequently try to quantify customers' attitudes toward and satisfaction with a product. This chapter deals with general issues of measurement and specific issues of question and scale design in survey research in some detail. In discussing the topic, the fundamental concepts of social science research are relevant. While these concepts will be introduced, however, this is an applied and analytically oriented book. Hence, those with strong interests in measurement should consult another source to fill out their study of measurement fundamentals. This chapter begins by describing the basic types of scales and what analyses can be performed on the different types of scales. Next, some fundamental concepts in measurement (e.g., validity, bias) are described, as are a series of data collection issues. Finally, a typology of errors that can occur in a study is presented.

SCALES AND SCALE TYPES

The notion of measurement assumes that there is something worth measuring. The "thing" to be measured (e.g., an attitude toward a supplier, favorite color, or sales) is referred to here as a *construct*. Many constructs are fairly complex (e.g., one's attitude toward Japanese restaurants selling liquor on Sundays includes feelings toward Japanese, restaurants, liquor, etc.) Nonetheless, in order to arrive at a bottom-line statement about such constructs, there is a strong tendency to convert/simplify these constructs into a single scale or series of scales, usually quantitative ones.

In many cases, the underlying construct may in fact be numerical (e.g., sales). In other cases, the construct is measured numerically because this proves to be a useful way to represent the construct. While quantification of some constructs, such as attitude, may lose some of the subtleties of the concept, the advantages of a quantitative representation for purposes of analysis and interpretation often outweigh the costs. One motivation for the quantification of a construct is the desire to convert a problem to a form where current computer technology and programs can deal with it. Therefore, for better or worse (and in general, for better), constructs are usually converted to quantitative scales.

Several schemes for classifying data have been proposed, most notably by Coombs (1964) and Stevens (1951). In this book, the commonly used four-part classification will be followed: nominal (categorical), ordinal, interval, and ratio.

Nominal (Categorical)

The simplest scale is nominal. A nominal scale arbitrarily assigns a number to each response, and so its only value is as an identification number. The number has no meaning in and of itself. Some obvious examples of nominal scales include Social Security numbers and the numbers on basketball players' jerseys. Put differently, there is no obvious relation between the quantity of the construct being measured and the numerical value assigned to it (as in Figure 8.1A).

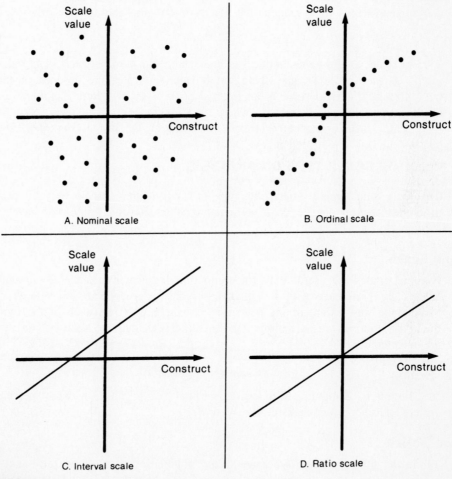

FIGURE 8.1
The Relation of Construct and Scale Values

Ordinal

In an ordinal scale, the higher the number, the more (or less) the construct exists. The absolute size of the number, however, has no meaning, nor do the differences between two scale values. Consider the most common form of an ordinal scale, a ranking. If the ranking is based on intelligence, we know that the subject ranked first is more intelligent than the person ranked second, but we have no idea how much smarter he or she is. A graphical example of an ordinal scale is shown in Figure 8.1B.

Interval

In an interval scale, differences (intervals) between scale values have meaning, but the absolute scale values do not. A good example of an interval scale is the Fahrenheit temperature scale. The difference between 41 degrees and 42 degrees is the same as the difference between 8 degrees and 9 degrees. The origin (0 degrees), however, has no particular meaning. All we can say is that 0 degrees is colder than 1 degree and warmer than −1 degree. Hence, 100 degrees is not twice as hot as 50 degrees. An interval scale can be represented as a straight line that does not pass through the origin (Figure 8.1C).

Ratio

A ratio scale, as the name implies, is one where the ratio between scale values is meaningful. A ratio scale is one where the 0 value indicates the absence of the construct; put differently, a ratio scale is an interval scale with a natural origin. A good example of this type of scale is money, where $100 is twice as much as $50. Graphically, a ratio scale would appear as a straight line through the origin (Figure 8.1D).

THE EFFECT OF SCALE TYPE ON ANALYSIS

The scale type directly affects the type of analysis that can be usefully performed. Put differently, if you plan to do a particular type of analysis, you better have data that are appropriate.

Nominal Scales

Nominal scales are useful only for computing frequencies. Hence, for a scale that indicates color preference with 1 = blue, 2 = red, 3 = green, and 4 = yellow, it is possible to compute the percent of the people in a sample who like each of the four colors and the most common response (the mode). Other calculations, such as the average value, are meaningless.

Ordinal Scales

In addition to computing frequencies, ordinal scales allow medians, percentiles, and a variety of other order statistics to be utilized.

Interval Scales

While the first two scale types are called nonmetric, interval and ratio scales are called metric. The presence of an interval scale allows computation of means and standard deviations, the use of parametric statistical tests, and the computation of product-moment correlations between two intervally scaled variables. This in turn allows the application of such "fancy" techniques as regression, discriminant, and factor analysis. In short, interval scales are highly desirable: they allow the use of most of the analytical tools common to statistics and marketing research.

Ratio Scales

Ratio scales allow, in addition to the analysis permitted by interval scales, some specialized calculations, such as a geometric mean or the coefficient of variation. They are also meaningful when multiplied together, something that is desirable in certain models.

The practical significance of scale type is fairly clear. Higher-order scales can be subjected to more analytical procedures and, hence, are easier to analyze. On the other hand, in a survey getting a higher-order scale often requires more effort on the part of the subject. Consequently, choosing a scale type involves a tradeoff between putting the burden on the respondent and putting the burden on the analyst. While no general solution is apparent, an interval scale is usually the chosen alternative in applied marketing research. It also is important to understand that some constructs are inherently only nominally scaled (e.g., color) and attempts to measure them on higher-order scales (e.g., degree of blueness) may be foolish. A more complete discussion of the relation of scale type to analysis appears in Chapter 11.

COMMON EXAMPLES

This section will provide some examples of scales used in marketing research in general and surveys in particular. The coverage is intended to be useful but not necessarily complete. Nonetheless, most types of questions used in market research studies are discussed here.

Nominal Scales

Multiple Choice   An obvious way to get a nominally scaled measure of a construct is to get a respondent to check a single answer from a set of alternatives. This type of question (known to students as multiple guess) has the following general form:

> Which of the following terms best describes inizlots?
> _____ A Riboflavit.
> _____ B Ordils and humspiels.
> _____ C Octiviniginianus.
> _____ D All of the above.
> _____ E B on alternate Tuesdays.
> _____ F None of the above.

For quantification purposes, one would typically assign a 1 to the first answer (riboflavit), a 2 to the second (ordils and humspiels), and so forth, so the "none of the above" response would be coded as a 6. These numbers would only indicate which response category was chosen, not how much of the construct was present. It is important to recognize that letters themselves differ in desirability with A, B, and S most desirable and Q, X, Z, and F least so (apparently correlated with grading systems) according to a Market Facts study (Decision Systems Group, 1985). Hence, the letters themselves can influence responses.

Some examples of multiple-choice questions are:

Region: Where do you live?			
East	Midwest	South	West
(= 1)	(= 2)	(= 3)	(= 4)

(Notice this is a poor question because the regions are not clearly defined for the respondent.)

Marital status: What is your marital status?			
Single	Married	Divorced, separated	Widowed
(= 1)	(= 2)	(= 3)	(= 4)

Occupation: What is your occupation?

Lawyer	Teacher	· · ·
(= 1)	(= 2)	

Brand choice: Which brand of soft drink did you last buy?

Coke	7-Up	Pepsi	Other
(= 1)	(= 2)	(= 3)	(= 4)

The categories used may be either given to the respondent (aided) or coded after the respondent gives a verbal/written answer (unaided). In general, the aided/structured approach is easier for both the respondent and the analyst.

Yes-No (Binary) Measures that have only two possible values are typically nominal scales. Some examples are:

Ownership: Do you own a color TV?

_____   _____
 Yes   No
(= 1)   (= 2)

Awareness: Have you heard of new Znarts cereal?

_____   _____
 Yes   No
(= 1)   (= 2)

Trait association (adjective checklist): Please indicate which of the following descriptions apply to these products. Check as many descriptions as you feel apply to each product.

	Descriptions			
Product	*Necessary*	*Fun*	*Useless*	*Good Investment*
Color TV	_____	_____	_____	_____
Snowmobile	_____	_____	_____	_____
Life insurance	_____	_____	_____	_____

Here the trait association question is presented in matrix (table) format to save space. One could repeat the traits for each product (or products for each trait). Questions like this are often called a *pick any of n* scale, since the respondent is free to check any of the n (here, 4) descriptors (necessary, fun, useless, good investment). Frequently researchers attempt to get a fixed number (k) of responses toward each object—the so-called *pick k of n* data. For example, the respondent could be given the following instruction: for each product, please indicate the two traits that best describe it (pick two of four).

Ordinal Scales

Forced Ranking   The most obvious ordinal scale is a forced ranking. One interesting application of ranking data involves the ranking of durable goods in priority order for purchase. These data are used to evaluate the appeal of new durables and to assess the value of existing ones (Hauser and Urban, 1986). A typical application involves ranking alternative brands in a product category:

Please rank the following five brands in terms of your preference by marking a 1 next to your most preferred brand, a 2 next to your second most preferred brand, and so forth:

    Coke   _____
    Pepsi   _____
    7-Up   _____
    Dr Pepper _____
    Slice   _____

Paired Comparison   Paired comparisons are a means of generating an ordinal scale without asking the respondent to consider all the alternatives simultaneously. Rather, respondents only choose the more preferred (or heavier, or prettier, or any other characteristic you wish to measure) of two alternatives at a time. Converting the previous question involving five soft drinks into a paired comparison framework, there are 10 pairs:

> Please indicate which of the following soft drinks you prefer by circling your more preferred brand in each pair:
>
>   Coke, Pepsi
>   Coke, 7-Up
>   Coke, Dr Pepper
>   Coke, Slice
>   Pepsi, 7-Up
>   Pepsi, Dr Pepper
>   Pepsi, Slice
>   7-Up, Dr Pepper
>   7-Up, Slice
>   Dr Pepper, Slice

The derived scale value for each brand is simply the number of times that the brand was preferred in comparisons involving it. The advantage of this method is that each individual decision made is as simple as possible. The method also allows for intransitivity (i.e., preferring Coke to Pepsi, Pepsi to Dr Pepper, and Dr Pepper to Coke), which is an advantage in uncovering choice processes but a disadvantage in that it sometimes raises questions about data quality that we may prefer to have hidden. The major disadvantage with paired comparisons is that they become quite cumbersome with many alternatives. If there are 15 alternatives, 105 paired comparisons are required, quite a lot of trouble to get an ordinal scale. Because of their cumbersome nature, complete paired comparisons are rarely used except in pilot studies or laboratory situations.[1]

Semantic Scale   A semantic scale obtains responses to a stimulus in terms of semantic categories. For example, we could ask:

> Do you like yogurt?
>
> | _____ | _____ | _____ | _____ | _____ |
> | Dislike tremendously | Dislike | Neutral | Like | Like tremendously |
> | (= 1) | (= 2) | (= 3) | (= 4) | (= 5) |

---

[1]A modification of this approach, called *triads*, has respondents pick the most and least favored alternative from triples. Since it works best for certain numbers of alternatives and saves space but not respondent effort, this approach is rarely used.

Respondents are instructed to check the category that best describes their feelings. Since they choose the category on the basis of the words (semantics) attached to it, this is a semantic differential scale. The scale is ordinal but not interval. For example, it is not clear how the difference between like and neutral and the difference between dislike and dislike tremendously are related (Myers and Warner, 1968; Dickson and Albaum, 1977).

The reason semantic scales are only ordinal is that the distinctions between words are rarely equal. Studies by Cliff (1959) and Howe (1966) derived interval scale values for commonly used descriptors of intensity and frequency using college students (Table 8.1).

A modification of the semantic scale is the Stapel scale, which uses a single key word (e.g., like) and gets people to rate an object (e.g., yogurt) on a scale from, for example, "does not apply" to "applies." This makes the derivation of opposites unnecessary and can also uncover complex attitudes (e.g., one could like yogurt and also dislike its consistency, so both like and dislike could be associated with it). In practice, however, there appears to be no important difference between the two scales (Hawkins, Albaum, and Best, 1974).

Picture Scales One alternative to a semantic scale is a graphical scale. Such scales are particularly useful for children and those populations where literacy is low. For example, a so-called smile scale with faces ranging from sad to happy is often used with children to derive attitudes.

Recent developments include the use of pictorial scales representing behavioral reaction to a product when encountered in a store and the willingness to share it with others (Karsten and Rhoedder-John, 1994). The five-point shopping scale ranges from likes a lot (a picture of the child asking for cereal, jumping up and down) to dislike a lot (a picture of the child throwing the cereal box on the floor). Given their effectiveness with children, one can only speculate about the effect of their equivalent form with adults, but at least the prospect of designing such scales suggests some interesting comedic approaches.

Picture scales can be utilized when an interviewer or physical questionnaire is not present. Phone surveys are typically limited in the number of scale points that can be used in response to a question. However, asking respondents to use the phone dial/push buttons as a 1-to-9 scale, a clock as a 1-to-12 scale, or a thermometer permits finer distinctions to be obtained.

TABLE 8.1 Scale Values of Intensity and Temporal Adverbs

Intensity Adverbs[a]	Scale Value	Temporal Adverbs[b]	Scale Value
Extremely	1.528	Repeatedly	0.983
Unusually	1.299	Often	0.868
Very	1.298	Frequently	0.844
Decidedly	1.204	Usually	0.829
Quite	1.066	Sometimes	0.438
Pretty	0.925	Occasionally	0.395
Rather	0.859	Seldom	− 0.498
Somewhat	0.689	Rarely	− 0.556
Slightly	0.551		

Note: Average values across three university samples.
[a]Cliff, 1959.
[b]Howe, 1966.

Summated (Likert)   A Likert scale is an extension of a semantic scale in two ways. First, rather than measure a construct by a single item, a series of items are used to measure the construct and a summed score is calculated. Second, the scales are traditionally calibrated so a neutral response is coded "0." (This difference is, however, unimportant.) For example, attitude toward yogurt might be assessed by several questions:

Do you like the taste of yogurt?				
	X			
Dislike strongly	Dislike	Neutral	Like	Like strongly
(−2)	(−1)	(0)	(+1)	(+2)
Is yogurt a healthful food?				
		X		
Extremely not healthful	Not healthful	Neutral	Healthful	Extremely healthful
(−2)	(−1)	(0)	(+1)	(+2)
Do your friends like yogurt?				
X				
Dislike strongly	Dislike	Neutral	Like	Like strongly
(−2)	(−1)	(0)	(+1)	(+2)

In this case, the summed score would be $-1 + 0 + (-2) = -3$, which indicates a negative attitude toward yogurt.

Others   There are a variety of other ordinal scales. One is the Guttman scale, which is really designed to order statements but is rarely used in marketing research. Another is the Q-sort technique, which is designed to cluster either respondents or alternatives. This works in several steps:

1. A set of items to be sorted is chosen. (Traditionally, about 100 items have been used.)
2. Subjects are required to sort the items (usually represented by cards) into piles (traditionally 11), which represent degrees on a scale, such as aesthetic beauty, value for the money, and so on.
3. The results are used to indicate similarity among either subjects (by seeing how closely subjects agree on the sorting results) or items (by seeing which items are consistently sorted into the same pile).

Unfortunately, this technique is so unwieldy that it, too, is almost never used in large-scale marketing research. It is sometimes used in small-sample studies, usually as a basis for structuring a large-scale study.

Interval Scales

Equal Appearing Interval   Thurstone (1959) proposed that an interval scale measure of an overall attitude could be constructed by a series of steps: (*a*) At least 100 statements related to the overall attitude are chosen. (*b*) A set of judges rate the statements in terms of their favorability from 1 to 11. (*c*) The 10 to 20 statements that get the most consistent ratings are selected, and they are assigned the median value from the 1 to 11 scale given them by the judges. (*d*) Subjects indicate which of the statements they agree with. (*e*) Attitude scores are created as the sum of the scale values in (*c*) for the statements that the subject checked. Given the difficulty in applying this technique, it is almost never used.

Bipolar Adjective   The bipolar adjective scale is a revision of the semantic scale with the express hope that the subjects will respond to it by giving intervally scaled data. Rather than attaching a description to each of the response categories, only the two extreme categories are labeled:

Dislike *Tremendously*					*Like* *Tremendously*
1	2	3	4	5	6

Since the scale points are equally far apart both physically and numerically, it can be assumed that the responses will be intervally scaled. Two points are worth making here. The first is that many people find this argument wanting and argue that at best the scale is somewhere in between an interval and an ordinal scale. Second, when respondents are asked to rate on both bipolar adjective and semantic scales, the results are typically almost identical. In fact, both types are commonly referred to as semantic differential scales (Osgood, Suci, and Tannenbaum, 1957). Hence, for practical purposes, either scale is equally useful if intervally scaled data are needed.

Agree-Disagree Scale   A variant of the bipolar adjective scale is an agree-disagree scale. For example, to obtain a subject's opinion of yogurt, we could ask the subject to indicate his or her agreement with the statement, "I like yogurt" on an agree-disagree scale:

Disagree *Strongly*					*Agree* *Strongly*
1	2	3	4	5	6

There is a minor logical problem with interpreting responses on the disagree end of this scale. In the case of "I like yogurt," I could disagree because (*a*) I am strongly neutral or (*b*) I dislike yogurt. However, most respondents seem to interpret a "1" as indicating strong dislike and, thus, the scale has proved to be quite useful.

Continuous Scales   It is also possible to get people to respond on a continuous scale:

Very Bad _____ Very Good

and then actually measure (usually with an optical scanner) the exact position on the scale. This is generally agreed to be an intervally scaled measure. However, results using these continuous scales are essentially identical to bipolar adjective scales. Continuous scales have recently grown in popularity in studies where subjects use a cursor or a "mouse" to give responses on a computer.

Another continuous measurement device is the attitude pollimeter, which involves filling in a circle with two colors in proportion to the degree of positive or negative attitude toward a statement (Lampert, 1979). Another continuous scale involves turning a dial to reflect reaction (e.g., attitude). Hughes and Pham (1993) have demonstrated the ability of a continuous dial-turning method to assess what parts of a TV commercial are particularly appealing (or not appealing).

Equal Width Interval   Another way to generate intervally scaled data is to ask respondents to indicate into which category they fall when the categories are quantitative groupings of equal size. The following scale is only ordinal:

| ____ | ____ | ____ | ____ | ____ |
| None | 1–2 | 3–15 | 16–99 | 100 or more |

while the next scale is more nearly interval since the category midpoints form an interval scale (2, 7, 12, 17, . . .):

| ____ | ____ | ____ | ____ | |
| 0–4 | 5–9 | 10–14 | 15–19 | . . . |

While the practical difference is small, the second approach to grouping responses has a slight advantage and no obvious cost associated with it if likely responses are fairly evenly distributed. When the vast majority of responses are likely to be 0 or 1 to 2, however, unequal-sized categories are more useful.

At this point three questions usually arise. The first is *how many scale points* to use. The number depends on the ability of respondents to make discriminations on the construct. The finer the discriminations the respondent makes, the more scale points are appropriate. For individual-level analysis, six or more scale points are usually sufficient to account for respondents' discriminatory abilities (Lehmann and Hulbert, 1972). For aggregate analysis, even fewer are needed. Most scales use between four (for phone surveys, intercept interviews, and low-commitment situations) and ten (for committed and knowledgeable respondents) scale points.

The second major question is whether there should be an *odd or even number of scale points*. Arguments can be made on either side of the issue. Proponents of odd numbers argue that the presence of a neutral point allows respondents who are neutral to quickly and easily indicate so. Proponents of even numbers argue that the neutral vote is a cop-out, that the respondent is really leaning one way or the other, and that using an even number forces the respondent to reveal which way he or she is leaning. While we in general prefer even numbers, the differences in results between well-done studies using, for example, five and six scale points are essentially unnoticeable.

A similar argument exists over whether to include a *don't know* response. Basically, the decision depends on whether you believe the respondent has a legitimate reason for giving a don't know or is likely to use it as an easy answer. The issue is particularly relevant when ratings of multiple brands on attributes are sought and respondents may not be familiar with all of them. Although it makes certain analyses more complicated (due to nonresponses), many studies allow/ask respondents to only rate those brands they know or even have used.

Another question has to do with whether a scale should be *balanced or not*. Consider these examples of balanced and unbalanced scales:

How do you rate the writing style of this book?

| ____ | ____ | ____ | ____ | ____ |
| Poor | Average | Good | Very good | Excellent |

| ____ | ____ | ____ | ____ | ____ |
| Very poor | Poor | Neutral | Good | Very good |

In the first case, the responses are stacked toward the positive. While this may be beneficial to the ego, it probably biases the results unfairly since the midpoint of the scale is "good," and many respondents will consider the position and not the semantic cues. On the other hand, balanced scales often produce highly skewed results so that almost all the responses fall in one half of the scale. This typically happens when subjects rate the importance of a list of attributes. Almost no respondents say that an attribute is unimportant. Hence, an unbalanced scale is occasionally used to increase dispersion of the responses. Unless there is a particular reason not to do so, however, balanced scales are typically employed.

Law of Comparative Judgment   Paired comparisons can be converted into intervally scaled data by means of Thurstone's law of comparative judgment. Two basic assumptions are required: (*a*) a group of respondents are homogeneous (in agreement) with respect to their ratings of the alternatives, and (*b*) individuals are uncertain about their feelings toward each alternative and respond with some random component toward it. Based on this, an interval scale is obtained. This technique is interesting (see Appendix 8-A) but infrequently used in marketing research.

Dollar Metric (Graded Paired Comparison)   One way to generate an interval scale is an extension of the paired comparison method known as the dollar metric (Pessemier, 1963).

This method works by getting paired comparison judgments of both which brand is preferred and the amount (in dollars) by which it is preferred. Returning to the example involving the five brands of soft drinks, the responses could be as follows:

Which Brand Do You Prefer?	How Much Extra Would You Be Willing To Pay To Get Your More-Preferred Brand?
Coke, Pepsi	2¢
Coke, 7-Up	8¢
Coke, Dr Pepper	5¢
Coke, Slice	12¢
Pepsi, 7-Up	6¢
Pepsi, Dr Pepper	3¢
Pepsi, Slice	10¢
7up, Dr Pepper	3¢
7-Up, Slice	4¢
Dr Pepper, Slice	7¢

By summing the values when a brand is being compared, a preference scale can be generated. Here, we have:

$$
\begin{aligned}
\text{Coke:} \quad & 2 + 8 + 5 + 12 = 27 \\
\text{Pepsi:} \quad & -2 + 6 + 3 + 10 = 17 \\
\text{7-Up:} \quad & -8 + (-6) + (-3) + 4 = -13 \\
\text{Dr Pepper:} \quad & -5 + (-3) + 3 + 7 = 2 \\
\text{Slice:} \quad & -12 + (-10) + (-4) + (-7) = -33
\end{aligned}
$$

Thus, we have an intervally scaled measure of preference. For a variety of reasons, this does not directly represent the actual strength of preference between brands. It is possible, however, to transform this scale into a predicted market share for each brand.[2]

_____

[2]This is done by first converting the dollar metric scale to a 0 to 1 adjusted scale where Coke becomes a 1, Slice a 0, and the rest of the brands in between. The formula for this is

$$
\frac{\$\,\text{Metric scale value}_i + |\text{Smallest scale value}|}{\text{Range of scale values}} = \frac{\text{Scale value} + 33}{60}
$$

The predicted share is given by

$$
\text{Predicted share}_i = \frac{\left(\text{Adjusted score}_i\right)^K}{\text{Sum of } \left(\text{adjusted score}_j\right)^K \text{ for all } j \text{ brands}}
$$

The K value is a constant (usually between 2 and 6) determined by trial and error so that the predicted share matches the actual share as closely as possible. The effect of K is to increase the predicted share of the first-choice brand and to reduce the predicted shares of the less-preferred brands.

Ratio Scales

Direct Quantification   The simplest way to obtain ratio scaled data is to ask directly for quantification of a construct that is ratio scaled. For example:

How many dress shirts do you own?_____

How old are you?_____

How many gallons of coolant did your manufacturing operation use last year?_____

The problem with this approach is that the respondent probably doesn't know (i.e., how many dress shirts do you own?) or want to reveal (e.g., age) what the exact answer is. Instead of upgrading from an intervally to ratio scaled answer, you may end up with no answer at all. Consequently, direct quantification in surveys tends to be used only in pilot/small-scale surveys or for very highly salient items that are not considered socially sensitive (e.g., number of VCRs owned). Of course, much of the data collected by standard sources (e.g., sales, price, advertising dollars) is ratio scaled.

One fairly common example of direct quantification is the so-called willingness-to-pay scale (cf. Cameron and James, 1987), which asks how much a person is willing to pay for, say, a new product. Another use of direct quantification is getting respondents to draw a line on a picture of a jar to indicate amount used. In many instances, categories (intervals) are provided to make the response task easier.

Constant Sum Scale   A very popular device in marketing research is the constant sum scale. Respondents are given a number of points (if the process is conducted in person, chips or other physical objects are often used) and told to divide them among alternatives according to some criteria (e.g., preference, importance, aesthetic appeal). Since respondents are told to allocate chips in a ratio manner (if you like brand A twice as much as brand B, assign it twice as many chips, etc.), the results are presumably ratio scaled. The ratios obtained are often related to the proportion of each alternative bought (e.g., different cereals).

For example, I might ask for 10 points to be allocated among three brands:

A	2
B	3
C	5
	10

At least two problems exist with this approach. First, respondents may mess up the allocation by not using 10 points, necessitating recalculation by the analyst. Hence, some time is often required to teach the approach to respondents. Second, determining the appropriate number of points/chips to use requires trading off between rounding error if too few are used and fatigue/frustration/refusal problems if too many are used. Still, the approach is quite useful.

Constant sums can also be applied in paired comparisons. Rather than simply getting which brand is preferred in a paired comparison, you can assess strength of preference with a constant sum scale (i.e., divide 10 points between the two alternatives).

The resulting values can then be used in Thurstone's law of comparative judgment to form a ratio scaled measure of preference.

Delphi Procedure   The Delphi procedure is a modification of the constant sum scale designed to produce agreement among judges. For a more thorough discussion, see Appendix 8-B.

Reference Alternative   Sometimes called *fractionation* or *magnitude scaling*, this approach has respondents compare alternatives with a reference alternative. Respondents are instructed to indicate how alternatives compare with the reference alternative on some criterion, such as preference, by putting down a number half as large if the alternative is half as preferred, and so on:

> Reference alternative X = <u>100</u>
> Alternative A _____
> Alternative B _____
> Alternative C _____

A respondent might then assign 50 to A, 250 to B, and 130 to C. In essence, this is a paired-comparison type method where respondents only consider two alternatives at once. Unfortunately, the choice of the reference alternative has been found to influence the results, necessitating rotating the reference alternative to remove this effect. Since this approach is somewhat more cumbersome vis-à-vis a constant sum scale, the constant sum scale is more widely used.

PRACTICAL CONSIDERATIONS

Having completed a discussion of different scaling approaches, it is interesting to consider how crucial the choice of method is. One study (Haley and Case, 1979) compared 13 disparate measures of response to a brand (Figure 8.2). Their main findings were as follows:

1. All 13 are highly correlated.
2. Awareness and brand choice are somewhat different from the other measures.
3. Acceptability, 6-point adjective, agreement, quality, 10-point numerical, thermometer, and Stapel scales tend to produce predominantly favorable readings (Figure 8.3).
4. For purposes of predicting market share, scales that restrict the number of brands getting top ratings (such as constant sum) tend to discriminate better.
5. With the exception of the constant sum scale, ratings less than the midpoint were associated with essentially a zero share, and even top-category ratings tended to be related to only about a 50 percent share (Figure 8.4).

For choice of scale wording, one study suggests semantic differential is preferable to Likert scales, which are, in turn, preferable to single-adjective scales in terms of measure reliability (Ofir, Reddy, and Bechtel, 1987). A broader range of alternatives were

Scale	Structure	Subject	Scores*		
1. Acceptability	7-point verbal balanced	Brand acceptability	Extremely acceptable (7) Quite acceptable (6) Slightly acceptable (5) Neither one nor the other (4) Slightly unacceptable (3) Quite unacceptable (2) Extremely unacceptable (1)		
2. Purchase probability	11-point numerical and verbal	Chance of buying brand next time product is purchased	100 absolutely certain 90 80 strong possibility 70 60 50 40 30 20 slight possibility 10 0 absolutely no chance	100 in 100 90 in 100 80 in 100 70 in 100 60 in 100 50 in 100 40 in 100 30 in 100 20 in 100 10 in 100 0 in 100	
3. Six-point adjective	6-point verbal unbalanced	Brand opinion	Excellent (7) Very good (6) Good (5) Fair (4) Not so good (2) Poor (1) "Don't know" permitted (3)		
4. Paired comparison	51 value positions, scores:150. constant sum	Brand liking	Possible range of brand scores: 0 to 50. Sum of six brand (Each of the 15 brand pairs compared and rated by dividing 10 points between the two brands in that pair. A brand's score is the sum of points received in the five pairs where that brand appeared.)		
5. Brand choice	3-point	Brand choice if purchased tomorrow	First choice (2) Second choice (1) No mention (0)		
6. Ten-point numerical	10-point numerical	Brand opinion	1 poor 2 : 9 10 excellent		

(continued)

FIGURE 8.2
Scales Tested

Source: Russell I. Haley and Peter B. Case, "Testing Thirteen Attitude Scales for Agreement and Brand Discrimination" from *Journal of Marketing* 43 (Fall 1979): 22. Copyright © 1979 by the American Marketing Association. Reprinted with the permission of the publishers.

Scale	Structure	Subject	Scores*
7. Thermometer	11-point numerical and verbal	Brand liking opinion	100 90 excellent 80 like very much 70 like quite well 60 like fairly well 50 indifferent 40 not like very well 30 not so good 20 not like at all 10 terrible 0 Where numbers represent degrees on a thermometer
8. Verbal purchase intent	5-point verbal unbalanced	Chance of buying brand next time product is purchased	Definitely will buy (5) Very likely will buy (4) Probably will buy (3) Might or might not buy (2) Definitely will not buy (1)
9. Agreement with strongly positive statement	5-point verbal	Brand opinion	Agree completely (5) Agree somewhat (4) Don't know (3) Disagree somewhat (2) Disagree completely (1) (Statement saying that brand "would be considered one of the best" was read for each brand.)
10. Constant sum	11 value positions, constant sum	Brand liking	Possible range of brand scores: 0 to 10. Sum of six brand scores: 10. (Respondent divided 10 pennies among brands, giving more to brands she liked.)
11. Quality	7-point verbal balanced	Brand quality	Extremely high quality (7) Quite high quality (6) Slightly high quality (5) Neither one nor the other (4) Slightly low quality (3) Quite low quality (2) Extremely low quality (1)

(continued)

FIGURE 8.2
(continued)

Scale	Structure	Subject	Scores*
12. Stapel scale	11-point numerical	Brand opinion	-5 Poor -4 $\vdots$ 0 $\vdots$ 4 5 excellent
13. Awareness	5-point	Awareness of brand names	Top of mind (4) Second unaided mention (3) Other unaided mention (2) Aided recall (1) Never heard of (0)

*Scores assigned to verbal scales are indicated in parentheses.

FIGURE 8.2
(continued)

compared for their ability to measure attribute importances: open-ended elicitation, acquisition-based information, direct ratings, conjoint measurement (discussed in Chapter 15), a subjective probability approach, and paired comparisons (Jaccard, Brinberg, and Ackerman, 1986). Here, the correlations among scales, though positive, were fairly low (e.g., 0.2), indicating that the methods had considerable impact on the results. Thus, while tending to give similar directional indications (e.g., from attitude to choice), various scales are sufficiently different that they are not interchangeable. Consequently, consistency in use of a scale is at least as important as the specific scale used.

BASIC CONCEPTS OF MEASUREMENT

There is a long tradition in measurement, especially in the psychological literature (see Torgerson, 1958; Thurstone, 1959). From this literature come two major terms which relate to measurement: *reliability* and *validity*. From statistics come the terms *bias*, *efficient*, and *consistent*. While these terms themselves have no great value, the ideas they represent are quite important.

Reliability

A measure is said to be reliable if it consistently obtains the same result. Hence, a scale that measured a weight and got 90.10 pounds, 89.95 pounds, 90.06 pounds, and 89.98 pounds in four trials would be quite reliable (the spread/range is only .15 pound) even if the true weight were 100 pounds. Conversely, a second scale that produced weights of 95 pounds, 103 pounds, 92 pounds, and 109 pounds would be less reliable than the

FIGURE 8.3

Response Distributions of Different Scales

Source: Russell I. Haley and Peter B. Case, "Testing Thirteen Attitude Scales for Agreement and Brand Discrimination," from *Journal of Marketing* 43 (Fall 1979), 24. Copyright © 1979 by the American Marketing Association. Reprinted with the permission of the publishers.

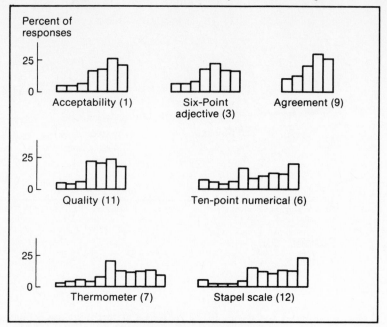

Response Distributions with Many Favorable Ratings

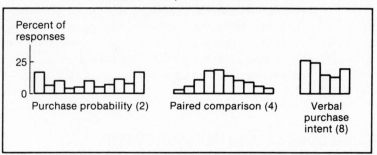

Balanced Response Distributions

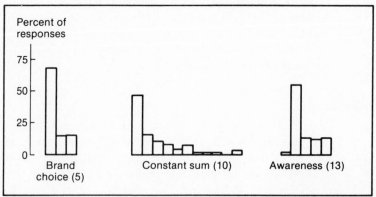

Response Distributions with Few Favorable Ratings

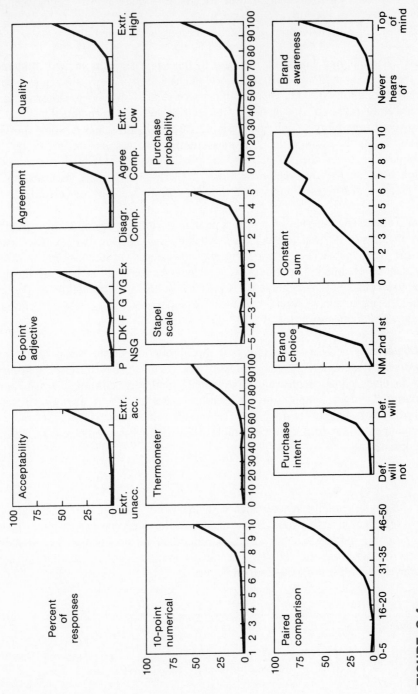

FIGURE 8.4

Brand Share by Rating Scale Point

Source: Russell I. Haley and Peter B. Case, "Testing Thirteen Attitude Scales for Agreement and Brand Discrimination," from *Journal of Marketing* 43 (Fall 1979), 30. Copyright © 1979 by the American Marketing Association. Reprinted with the permission of the publishers.

first even if in the sense of being closer to the true value it was better. Reliability is thus synonymous with repetitive consistency.

Three basic operational approaches exist to measuring reliability.

Test-Retest   By applying the same measure to the same subjects at two different points in time, we can compare the two measures and see how closely they match and what the test-retest reliability is. This is a common approach in such areas as educational testing. In marketing research, one generally expects a correlation in the range of .5 to .7. Using test-retest reliability as an indicator of true reliability makes some fairly strong assumptions. First, it assumes that the measurement process has no effect on the subject. Second, it assumes the subject's opinion/behavior has remained constant over the time period between the two measures. Since at least one of these assumptions is likely to be violated, test-retest comparisons are imperfect measures of reliability.[3]

Alternative Form   The alternative form approach to measuring reliability assumes that equivalent measuring devices (forms) are available. By applying two or more equivalent forms to the same subjects and checking the consistency of the results, a measure of reliability can be obtained. Unfortunately, this measure depends at least as much on the degree of equivalency of the alternative forms as on the true reliability of the measure. Still, some researchers have found this measure superior to test-retest or split-half sample procedures (Parameswaran et al., 1979).

Internal Consistency   Consistency refers to the ability to get the same result from different (equivalent) samples. A common way to assess this is through *split-half* tests. Often this involves giving a measure to a sample, randomly splitting the sample in half, and comparing the two samples on the measure. Alternatively it involves giving equivalent items to two samples (e.g., half a set of measures of a single construct such as attitude) and then comparing the two samples. The closeness of the results indicates the level of consistency.

Validity

The term *valid* is essentially synonymous with the word *good*. In fact, the term is loosely used in conversation as a synonym by many people. This causes purists to be unbearably uncomfortable and occasionally leads to important misunderstandings. Actually there are a variety of subclasses of validity. The most common types of validity are construct, content, convergent, discriminant, and predictive.

---

[3]It is also true that test-retest measures are heavily influenced by the heterogeneity of the sample. Reliability is often written as:

$$\frac{\text{Variance (true score)}}{\text{Variance (true score)} + \text{Variance (error)}}$$

Therefore, it is possible to increase reliability by either decreasing error or increasing the variance of the true score. For example, I can increase most measures of test-retest reliability of attitude toward yogurt by either producing a measure that yields very consistent responses over time (reducing the error) or by using a sample with big differences in attitudes toward yogurt (increasing the variability of the true score).

Construct Validity Construct validity refers to the ability of a measure to both represent the underlying construct (concept) and to relate to other constructs in an expected way. This is a fairly amorphous term; a measure has construct validity if it behaves according to existing theory. Given the relative paucity of good theory in marketing, construct validity rarely receives much attention in applied marketing research.

Content Validity Content validity refers to the logical appropriateness of the measure used. For example, one might argue that observing how much a person eats of a vegetable on his or her plate is a measure of the person's liking of the vegetable. This has logical appeal (often called *face validity*), and hence the measure would appear to have content validity. (Of course, the amount eaten might depend on how hungry the person was or some other variable.) Content validity also refers to the inclusiveness in the measure of all relevant aspects of the construct. A content valid measure of your opinion of this book should include your opinion of its topic, style, format, and so on. In order to achieve content validity, constructs often must be measured by more than one item.

Convergent Validity A measure has convergent validity if it follows the same pattern as other measures of the same construct. For example, three different measures of attitude would be said to have convergent validity if they were highly correlated with each other, and if the construct they are measuring is unidimensional. When a construct does not achieve convergent validity, either the measures are poor or the construct is multidimensional.

Discriminant Validity A construct should be sufficiently distinct from other constructs to justify its existence (see, for example, Peter, 1981). One method of examining simultaneous convergent and discriminant validity is through a *multitrait-multimethod (MTMM) matrix* (Campbell and Fiske, 1959; see Appendix 8-C). Efforts to assess convergent and discriminant validity and, more generally, to separate trait (construct), method (e.g., scale type), and error variation in responses have employed increasingly sophisticated procedures. These include factor analysis (discussed in Chapter 15) and some relatively complex analytical methods that are currently mainly employed by academic researchers (Anderson and Gerbing, 1982; Widaman, 1985; Peter and Churchill, 1986; Rentz, 1987; Cote and Buckley, 1987; and Kumar and Dillon, 1987a,b) and are beyond the scope of this section.

Predictive Validity *Criterion validity* is the ability of a variable to predict key variables (criteria). A distinction is often drawn between *concurrent validity* (when all the variables are measured at the same time) and *predictive validity* (when the criterion variable is measured after the predictor variable).

Predictive validity is the most pragmatic form of validity. In the narrow sense of the term, predictive validity is the ability of the measure to relate to other measures in a known/predicted way. Taken in its loosest form, predictive validity is synonymous with predictive usefulness/accuracy. In the extreme, predictive accuracy is an engineering (as opposed to scientific) view, which says that if a measure is useful in prediction, then use it, regardless of whether we can explain why it works. To take an extreme example, assume I predicted sales of a new product by multiplying the number of letters in the name by the weight of a package. Assume somehow this turned out to be predictive of sales. While the measure has no construct or content validity, it works and is predictively valid. Most people smirk at this point and argue they would never use such a foolish measure. Consider the following: Would you use it if it worked 10 times in a row? How about 100 times? The point is that, at some stage, the predictive accuracy of a measure will outweigh the prior theories and can, in fact, lead to the development of new theories. (If this were not true, it would imply we already perfectly understood the world, which is both scary and untrue.)

Bias

The term *biased* as used in marketing research has nothing to do with holding offensive personal opinions or prejudices. The term *bias* is borrowed from statistics, and a biased measurement is one where we expect the measured result to be different from the true value of the construct/variable. A person who consistently underestimates how long a task will take gives biased estimates. Similarly, the "reliable" scale of the previous section, which kept measuring the 100-pound weight at about 90 pounds, would also be called biased. Actually, a biased measure can be very useful if the extent of the bias can be assessed. For example, if the temperature control on an oven consistently registers 50 degrees warmer than the actual oven temperature, it is fairly simple to adjust the control to achieve the desired temperature. Similarly, panels may be biased if they overreport purchases of a certain brand; but if one looks at purchases of the brand over time, then the result can be very useful for signaling changes in sales.

Efficient

Another term borrowed from statistics, a procedure is said to be *efficient* if it gets the maximum possible information from a given sample size. In measurement terms, a simple scale may be just as accurate a measuring device as a more elaborate setup and, thus, would be chosen because of its superior efficiency.

Consistent

The third major statistical term relevant here, *consistency*, refers to the ability of a statistic to tend toward the true value of the construct/variable as more data are gathered. In measurement terms, a measure would be consistent if averaging repeated measures produced a result that approached the true value as the number of measures averaged increased.

So What?

The terms and issues just discussed are important to someone who decides to specialize in measurement theory and methods. To the applied researcher or manager, however, the terms often are either foreboding or used merely as advertising slogans. For example, "We have a valid study that . . ." Therefore, it is useful to translate these concepts into some action suggestions. At least six suggestions are relevant:

1. Select only those variables to measure that make logical sense in the context of the problem being studied.
2. Use measures that seem logically appropriate to the construct/variable to be measured.

3. Use measures that are fairly stable over time.
4. Use variables that produce similar results over related measurement methods. (If the response obtained depends heavily on the measurement method employed, chances are the information being collected is a response to the measurement method and not the construct.)
5. Select measures that are as easily usable by researcher and respondent as possible.
6. Use measures that prove to be useful in a pragmatic way. (That is, if a variable proves to be a good predictor of a key variable, use it; if a variable doesn't seem to be related to any other variables, save your effort and don't measure it).

MEASUREMENT ERROR

For quantitatively measurable constructs such as attitude, satisfaction, and so forth that can be measured on an interval (or ratio) scale, the basic measurement process can be summarized as:

$$\text{Measured value} = \text{True value} + \text{Error}$$

Further, error can be subdivided into various components. Basically, there are two types of error:

Systematic (e.g., method effects, social desirability, and yea-saying in surveys, etc.), also known as bias, and

Random (e.g., uncertainty, sloppiness, etc.)

Thus,

$$\text{Measured value} = \text{True value} + \text{Systematic error} + \text{Random error}$$

This simple model has a number of consequences.

The objective of measurement is to obtain measured values close to the true values or, put differently, to minimize systematic and random errors. The standard approach involves (a) carefully developing the measures themselves and (b) using multiple measures to average out random errors.

Sometimes you can remove the impact of systematic error at the time of analysis *if* you know how big it is (which is rarely known with certainty). For example, if you have a thermometer that constantly reads five degrees high, then it is easy to calculate the true temperature as measured temperature minus five degrees. Put differently, a known and consistent systematic bias is not a problem. Notice also that when you are interested in *differences* in measured values, systematic bias is not a problem—since when it is common to the two measured values, it cancels out. Thus, while you certainly are not happy to know you have a biased measure, it is not necessarily disastrous.

In the case of survey measures, each measure potentially has its own bias (systematic error) as well as random error. Therefore, a reasonable way to get at the true value is to average several measures of the construct and let the random and unique systematic errors "cancel out" (courtesy of the central limit theorem):

$$\sum \text{Measured values} = \sum \text{True values} + \sum \text{Systematic errors} + \sum \text{Random errors}$$

Notice that common method biases (e.g., if there is a tendency for respondents to give favorable ratings in personal interviews) will not cancel out unless different methods are used. What this means is that simply asking more, say, six-point scaled questions won't automatically help. If the bias is simply toward giving agree-type responses, however, you can reduce the bias by reverse-scaling half the questions (e.g., I like yogurt; Yogurt is unappealing; . . .).

Multiple measures do improve measurement reliability. Reliability is basically the percent of information relative to the true variation in the construct:

$$\text{Reliability} = \frac{\text{Variance (true score)}}{\text{Variance (true score)} + \text{Variance (error)}}$$

For multiple (k) item measures, reliability is typically measured by Cronbach's (1951) alpha:

$$\alpha = \frac{k\bar{r}}{1 + (k - 1)\bar{r}}$$

where $\bar{r}$ = average interitem correlation among measures of the construct.

Clearly, the larger the number of items and the higher $\bar{r}$, the higher coefficient alpha is. In terms of how high is high enough, Nunnally (1978) suggests .7 is satisfactory for preliminary/exploratory research, while .8 is needed for basic (theoretical) research, and .9 is desirable for applied work such as marketing research. By way of comparison, the mean level of alpha reported in various academic journals generally falls between .75 and .80 (Peterson, 1994).

There is, however, a major problem with using multiple measures to better measure a construct. Measures are costly and, in the case of surveys, burdensome to respondents. Increased respondent burden can lead to greater response error due to fatigue, biased responses (e.g., giving all 5s on a six-point scale to simplify/complete the task), or refusal to participate entirely.

When the objective is to assess average behavior (across respondents, etc.), the averaging process reduces random error, and so there is no real advantage to using multiple measures per construct for each respondent. If the purpose of the study is to accurately assess one or two key constructs at the individual level *and* there is reason to expect a large random error component to a response, then multiple measures may be required. Still using more than three to five measures per unidimensional construct is generally overkill (though not uncommon practice among academic researchers).

While this discussion has implicitly focused on survey measures, the same principles apply to other forms of measurement. For example, audit-based sales estimates using shipments received by a retailer minus inventory retained will overstate sales due to pilferage. Also, a person hired to count customers may both have random errors and, if they have a tendency to doze off or be distracted, a bias toward undercounting. Even scanner data is not error-free.

Nominally scaled data also has an error component, particularly when the scaling is done by human coders. When multiple coders are used, the basis for evaluating reliability is the extent of agreement among independent coders. Since the percent of agreement is naturally higher when there are fewer categories, a number of measures have been developed to take into account chance agreement. Probably the best known is Cohen's kappa, which measures agreement between two judges:

$$\frac{\text{Number of agreements} - \text{Number of agreements expected by chance}}{\text{Total number of judgments} - \text{Number of agreements expected by chance}}$$

Perreault and Leigh (1989) and Rust and Cooil (1994) discuss these and other measures at length.

Two other principles also apply:

1. *Measurement affects behavior.* In physics, the Heisenberg Uncertainty Principle suggests that measuring an object's speed influences its weight, and vice versa. In the social sciences, any obtrusive measurement can affect both response (e.g., through subjects giving responses they feel are appropriate) and behavior (by raising issues, creating curiosity about a product, etc.).

2. *Responses are context dependent.* The response to subjective questions such as "How good is ____?" depends both on the circumstances the respondent is in (e.g., mood, room comfort, recent past experiences) and the other alternatives/subjects considered (Simmons, Bickart, and Lynch, 1993; Schuman and Presser, 1981; Bradburn, 1983; Teas and Wong, 1992; Bickart, 1993). Even seemingly innocuous differences in format (Ellen and Madden, 1989) and wording can affect responses. For example, similarity and dissimilarity are logically opposites but perceptions of them differ (Tversky, 1977; Donthu and Cherian, 1993).

The consequence of this is that measurement is often a difficult task. For this reason, it is usually better to pick a scale (set of measures) someone has already developed. If a new measure absolutely must be developed, a series of steps is typically required.

Basically scale development requires thoroughness and persistence. Churchill (1979) suggests eight steps are required:

1. Defining the construct
2. Generating a list of possible measures
3. Collecting data
4. Selecting measures with good properties (high intercorrelations)
5. Collecting fresh data on the selected measures
6. Evaluating reliability (e.g., via coefficient alpha)
7. Assessing validity via MTMM analysis and predictive studies
8. Developing norms for the measured construct

Multidimensional Constructs

Many constructs have multiple components/dimensions. Attitude has cognitive (knowledge, attribute ratings), affective (liking), and behavioral (intention to buy) components. It is often also broken into hedonic (feels good) vs. utilitarian (does good) dimensions. Batra and Ahtola's (1990) results suggest measuring hedonic by:

1. Pleasant–unpleasant
2. Agreeable–disagreeable
3. Nice–awful
4. Harmonious–dissonant
5. Sociable–unsociable

The utilitarian component can be measured by:

1. Useful–useless
2. Beneficial–harmful
3. Important–unimportant
4. Meaningful–meaningless
5. Intelligent–unintelligent

Three measures relate to both components and hence measure overall attitude: (1) positive–negative, (2) like–dislike, and (3) good–bad.

Emotional responses have been broken into several typologies. Mehrabian and Russell (1974) describe three basic dimensions: (1) pleasure, (2) arousal, and (3) dominance. Plutchik (1980) describes eight dimensions:

1. Fear
2. Anger
3. Joy
4. Sadness
5. Disgust
6. Acceptance
7. Expectancy
8. Surprise

Other emotions—shame and guilt—have also been considered (Westbrook and Oliver, 1991). The two sets of dimensions are related but not equivalent (Havlena and Holbrook, 1986). Another different set of emotions has been described by Bagozzi, Baumgartner, and Pieters (1994).

The concept of *market orientation* is described in terms of three components by Kohli, Jaworski, and Kumar (1993):

1. Intelligence generation
2. Intelligence dissemination
3. Responsiveness

as well as (4) Competitor Orientation, (5) Interdepartmental Coordination (Narver and Slater, 1990; Slater and Narver, 1992), and (6) Organizational Climate and Culture (Deshpandé, Farley, and Webster, 1993).

As was suggested earlier, one of the best ways to generate a scale is to borrow one. A number have become established (e.g., VALS and LOV, as discussed in Chapter 7), although most use several items to measure a single construct. These vary considerably in content. As a sample, consider the following:

1. Customer orientation of salespeople (Saxe and Weitz, 1982; Michaels and Day, 1985)
2. Opinion leadership (Childers, 1986)
3. Consumer ethnocentrism (Shimp and Sharma, 1987)
4. Consumer response to advertising (Wells, 1964; Leavitt, 1970; Zinkhan and Fornell, 1985)
5. Basic human values (Rokeach, 1973; Munson and McIntyre, 1979)

6. Compulsive buying (Faber and O'Guinn, 1992)
7. Materialism (Richins and Dawson, 1992)
8. Emotions (Mehrabian and Russell, 1974; Plutchik, 1980; Havlena and Holbrook, 1986; Westbrook and Oliver, 1991; Bagozzi, Baumgartner, and Pieters, 1994)
9. Service quality (Parasuraman, Zeithaml, and Berry, 1988)

Fortunately, sources of existing scales exist. Bearden, Netemeyer, and Mobley (1993) present 124 scales that have appeared in the marketing literature since 1964, and Bruner and Hensel (1993) present 588. The moral of this is if you want to measure something, see if it has already been measured (hopefully successfully) and then borrow from past researchers, modifying as necessary.

OTHER ISSUES

Noncomparative versus Comparative Measures

All responses tend to be based on some frame of reference and hence are to some extent comparative. Still, a distinction exists between scales that, say, evaluate attitude for one alternative at a time (e.g., ratings on six-point semantic scales) and scales that explicitly compare two or more alternatives (paired comparisons, dollar metric, constant sum, reference alternative). The choice of scale depends on the objective of the research. Trying to estimate share or relative position on an attribute calls for comparative scaling (e.g., constant sum) of the leading competitors, or at least getting ratings of all competitors so a competitive set is implicitly established. On the other hand, basic diagnostic information can be gained from one-at-a-time *monadic* measurements.

Individual versus Aggregate

Most of the discussion presented so far is directed at accurately estimating an individual's scale value. In marketing, one typically is interested in group/average behavior for decision purposes (at least in consumer marketing). One advantage of this is that averaging results tends to cover up problems in scale type. Averages are intervally scaled even if the original scale is binary. Moreover, if you're lucky, averages reduce some measurement and response style problems as well.

There are, however, two disadvantages to grouping respondents/data points. The first is that the respondents are implicitly assumed to be homogeneous, a sometimes fallacious assumption. For example, if some people like tea hot and some cold, the average preferred temperature for tea would be lukewarm. While this suggests an interesting marketing strategy ("Try Blahz, the room temperature tea"), the strategy is likely to be a disaster (although the Snapple tea bought for lunch is often room temperature by the time it is consumed). Hence, making sure that only homogeneous data points are grouped is an important (but difficult) task.

The second disadvantage deals with the operational problem of comparing responses of different people on nonobjective questions, such as attitudes. Consider the following two respondents:

	Very Bad							Very Good
			Respondent 1					
A	1	2	3	④	5	6	7	8
B	1	2	3	4	5	⑥	7	8
C	1	2	3	4	5	6	7	⑧
D	1	2	3	4	5	⑥	7	8
E	1	2	3	④	5	6	7	8
F	1	2	3	4	5	6	7	⑧
			Respondent 2					
A	1	②	3	4	5	6	7	8
B	1	2	③	4	5	6	7	8
C	1	2	3	④	5	6	7	8
D	1	2	③	4	5	6	7	8
E	1	②	3	4	5	6	7	8
F	1	2	3	④	5	6	7	8

In considering the response to A, there are at least three pieces of information in the "4" given by respondent 1: the absolute value of the response (indicating a slightly negative attitude), the position relative to a typical response (lower, indicating a negative attitude), and the difference between "4" and a typical response (two scale points). If we believe that only relative responses matter, we could *normalize* the data to obtain relative responses. Alternatively, if we believe both the typical response and the amount of spread a respondent uses in answering are not meaningful, we can *standardize* the data to remove both effects (see Appendix 8-D). If we standardized the answers of both respondents, we would argue that both respondents view the six alternatives identically. Without any adjustment, respondent 1 appears to be favorable toward all but A and E, while respondent 2 thinks all the alternatives are bad. What you believe about the meaning of a response thus has a lot to say about how data are grouped and analyzed.

Direct versus Indirect Probing

Another issue involves whether information should be gathered directly or in a more circuitous manner. The simplest way to gather data is the obtrusive, direct method, where the subject is aware of being studied and is directly asked the question at hand. This method works quite well most of the time.

The straightforward approach runs into trouble, however, when respondents either have a reason to hide their feelings (as in the case of certain antisocial attitudes) or can't really express their feelings accurately. In these cases, indirect methods are often employed. Here, rather than asking persons what they personally do or think, the subject may be asked how friends or neighbors think or behave. The assumptions underlying this approach are that (*a*) neighbors behave the same way and (*b*) I will be more honest in revealing my neighbors' behavior patterns than my own. Another indirect method is the *projective* technique. Here, a subject is given a vague task and the response then is used to deduce the subject's feelings. This technique takes many forms, including sentence completion (e.g., "People who eat Znarts are _____"), scenario/cartoon interpretation known as TATs (thematic apperception tests), and word association (e.g., "What word do you associate with Znarts?"). Possibly the best-known projective technique is the Rorschach Inkblot Test. Interesting as these techniques are, however, they are used almost exclusively in small-scale, qualitative, or pilot studies in marketing research. Anyone interested in using projective techniques should consult another source, such as Kassarjian (1974).

Soft (Survey) versus Hard (Observed) Data

The difference between survey and hard data appears to be large. Yet on closer inspection there are more similarities than most people notice. First, much so-called hard data is estimated, projected, or fudged. (Do you really believe anyone knows exactly how many dishwashers were sold in the United States last year?) Also, with the exception of mechanical recording devices (which are far from foolproof themselves), a person gathers data either by interpreting written reports (e.g., audits) or by actually asking a question. Hence, these data are subject to many of the same sources of error (misinterpretation, expectation, etc.) as survey data.

A more meaningful distinction is between *objective* data (for which a right answer exists and is directly measurable) and *subjective* data (for which the right answer, if it exists, is not precisely measurable). For example, the number of cars I own is objective data, while my attitude toward public education is subjective. In measuring an objective variable, both survey and hard methods are applicable. For example, to measure how many cars I own, one could (*a*) ask me, (*b*) check the motor vehicle registration list, or (*c*) observe how many cars are parked at my house at night. The survey method may produce a wrong answer if I decide to hide the true number of cars owned for whatever reason. On the other hand, checking the auto registration lists may fail because (*a*) I have registered a car in another state or not at all, or (*b*) the auditor makes a mistake. Similarly, observing how many cars are at home at night may (*a*) spot a neighbor's cars, or (*b*) fail to spot a car that is in a body shop for repairs.

Subjective constructs, such as attitudes, are generally thought to be measurable mainly through questions. While observed behavior is often indicative of attitude ("actions speak louder than words," or as economists argue, "'revealed preference' is an/the appropriate measure of attitude"), the only way to directly assess attitude is through questions. However, when attitudes are either poorly formed or likely to be "hidden" by the respondents (e.g., what do you say when your professor asks how the course is going?), actual behavior may be a better measure of attitude than response to a question.

AN ERROR TYPOLOGY

Having discussed measurement methods and problems, it is useful to lay out some of the major sources of error that affect research. These sources of error, here divided into five major categories, go far beyond measurement issues (Hulbert and Lehmann, 1975). Their purpose, therefore, is to put measurement issues "in their place" (see Figure 8.5).

General Source	Type
I. Researcher/user	Myopia (wrong question)
	Inappropriate analysis
	Misinterpretation:
	Mistaken
	Researcher expectation
	Communication
II. Sample	Frame (wrong target population)
	Process (biased method)
	Response (biased respondents)
III. Measurement process	Conditioning
	Process bias
	Recording:
	Interpretation (mistaken)
	Carelessness
	Fudging
IV. Instrument	Individual scale item:
	Rounding
	Truncating
	Ambiguity
	Test instrument:
	Evoked set
	Positional (order)
V. Respondent	Response style:
	Consistency/inconsistency
	Boasting/humility
	Agreement (yea saying)
	Acquiescence
	Lying
	Extremism/caution
	Socially desirable
	Response:
	Mistakes
	Uncertainty
	Inarticulation

FIGURE 8.5
Sources of Errors

Researcher

Four errors are directly traceable to the researcher: myopia, inappropriate analysis, misinterpretation, and communication.

Myopia Research results can be reduced in value if wrong data are gathered. This is usually a manifestation of poor problem definition and research objective specification.

Inappropriate Analysis There are two major ways a researcher can err in performing analysis. The first is an error of omission: failing to perform what would be a meaningful analysis. The second is an error of commission: performing an analysis for which the data are not suited.

Misinterpretation The two kinds of misinterpretation errors are quite different. A mistaken interpretation can be the result of poor training, inability to understand the results of the analysis performed because of a technical deficiency, or just a bad day (even we brilliant researchers occasionally make an error in judgment due to time pressure, fatigue, carelessness, poor eyesight, etc.). On the other hand, misinterpretation may be the result of *researcher expectation*. When one has a strong prior feeling about the results of a study for either logical or emotional reasons, it is usually possible to find some result that supports this prior feeling. Hence, the interpretation may be unduly influenced by prior opinions.

Communication Even the most competent researcher has a serious problem in communicating results. Often the users of research are unable to correctly perceive the results because of technical deficiencies, strong prior opinions, or a general distrust of or dislike for research. Also, the technically competent researcher is frequently unable to translate results into a form that is understandable by intelligent, decision-oriented managers.

Sample

Since most data collection is partial in nature, the selection of who to analyze can greatly influence the results. There are at least three basic types of sampling error: frame, process, and response.

Frame In studying a particular problem, an early decision must be made concerning who are the relevant subjects/respondents. For example, in studying the market for TV video games, one could target male heads of households. Since others in the family, especially children, influence this decision, the target population would be defined too narrowly. Alternatively, it is possible to design the target population so broadly that the "frame" includes many irrelevant people. Matching the sampling frame to the appropriate population is very important, and erring by having too narrow a frame is especially disastrous.

Process Once the frame is chosen, a process must be chosen for selecting respondents. If, for example, a list is chosen as the source of respondents, it can be too broad and include people not in the target population. (The National Association of Retired

Persons has been trying to get Lehmann to join since he was 29, which, unless they know something he doesn't, is just a bit too premature.) This is wasteful but not necessarily destructive. On the other hand, the process may be so narrow that it excludes important segments of the target population.

Response   Even with a good frame and process, the sample may be unrepresentative because many people fail to respond to research inquiries. Response rates are rarely above 70 percent and sometimes 10 percent or less. If the nonrespondents have different characteristics than respondents, then the results can be badly distorted. One general tendency is for both old people and poor people to respond less than other groups. Also, people with strong opinions about the subject in question are more likely to respond. An example of this is a survey about school priorities undertaken in New Jersey in the late 1970s. Under both court and legislative mandates to find out what localities want in a "thorough and efficient" education, many districts mailed questionnaires to all residents in their towns. With response rates of 10 percent or less in many localities, it is hard to argue convincingly that the results are projectable to the community at large. This nonresponse problem is typically greatest when either recruitment for extended tasks (e.g., panel membership) or mail surveys are used.

Measurement Process

The measurement process itself is an important determinant of responses and, therefore, a potential source of error. Some of the major characteristics of the measurement process are conditioning, process bias, and recording.

Conditioning   Data collection processes are outside stimuli that can condition/affect responses. By exposing a subject to a topic, the subject's attention will be drawn to the topic, and consequently the subject may behave differently. This is an especially serious concern when the subject is questioned several times.

Process Bias   Respondents often are motivated by the data collection process as a "game" and respond to beat the game. The best-known example of this problem is interviewer bias, where the presence of the interviewer leads the respondents to respond to please (or occasionally, to irritate or surprise) the interviewer. For example, when the interviewer is identified as working for a particular company, the respondent often tends to give answers favorable to the company in order to please the interviewer. Also, the physical surroundings (e.g., a bright, cheerful, air-conditioned room) can affect the respondent's overall attitude and, hence, responses.

Recording   The process of recording a response is subject to many possible sources of error. The most obvious error of this type, mistaken interpretation, is usually associated with an interviewer misinterpreting a verbal response. This error can also occur when gremlins infest mechanical recording devices. A related form of error is due to simple carelessness, where the interviewer or recording device records the wrong answer due to sloppiness. A third type of recording problem is fudging. Here, answers are recorded without measurement to speed up the data collection or to make life easier for the respondent and interviewer. Given crafty interviewers, this source of error is quite hard to detect.

Instrument

The particulars of the questions/measures themselves have a strong influence on responses. Two basic sources of these problems exist: the individual question/scale and the test instrument.

The Individual Question/Scale One problem with questions is that the response categories given often *truncate* responses. Multiple-choice questions tend to limit the respondents' consideration to the listed alternatives even if an "all other" category is included. (Filling out an "other" response is more trouble than checking one of the listed alternatives and also may connote that the respondent is somehow different/weird.) In quantitatively scaled questions (e.g., rate how well you like Brussels sprouts on a six-point scale from 1 = dislike somewhat to 6 = like somewhat), especially strong feelings cannot be expressed and, hence, are truncated. (On the Brussels sprouts scale, my true feelings are about −8; but, being a good subject, I would circle a 1.)

Another major scale problem is *rounding error*. Given a multiple-choice question, a respondent will tend to choose the answer that is closest to his or her true response. The classic example is a numerical scale. For example, if I truly feel about Brussels sprouts 3.4 on a six-point scale, I would round off my response to the closest digit (3) and the rounding error would be .4. Similarly, if I were asked, "Are you going to vote in the next election?" and I were 60 percent sure I would, I would have to round my response to "yes" (100 percent certain) or "no" (no chance at all of voting).

A final type of problem is *ambiguity*. Ambiguity can occur because the underlying construct to be measured and the question are not perfectly congruent. For example, to measure attitude toward the environment one might ask, "Should pollution control standards on automobiles be relaxed?" An affirmative answer would presumably indicate a relatively low environmental concern. However, it could also indicate a great concern for jobs or for increasing the use of coal to conserve petroleum reserves. Hence, the match between the construct and the question is imperfect. Another source of ambiguity is confusion about the meaning of the particular combination of words used to define the question. Both gross lack of understanding due to poor vocabulary skills on the part of either the question writer or the respondent or more subtle, different nuances in meanings resulting from different cultural backgrounds can lead the respondent to answer a different question than the researcher wished answered.

Test Instrument In surveys, the questionnaire itself provides a context for the response and thus has an effect on the response. The items discussed bring to mind an *evoked set* of thoughts and standards of comparison that the respondent uses to determine his or her response. For example, if one designed a questionnaire concerning such leisure time activities as bridge, chess, backgammon, cribbage, and football, football would on an exertion or risk of injury scale probably be rated at the maximum. If, on the other hand, football were being compared with rugby, sword fighting, and motorcycle racing, it probably would be rated more moderately in terms of exertion or injury risk. In short, the responses depend on the bases of comparison that the test instrument (questionnaire) establishes.

The *position* (*order*) of items is also important. This is true at both the macro level (question order) and micro level (order of responses within question). At the micro level, the response category in the first possible position tends to get an inordinate number of responses simply because it is convenient to use. At the macro level, the position of an item in the test affects both the attentiveness of the respondent (one tends to be pretty casual about answering the 141st lifestyle question) and the frame of reference that the previous questions have imparted.

Respondent

Ultimate control over the quality of data is in the hands of the subject/respondent. This control is exercised in two major ways: response style and the response.

Response Style   The way a respondent approaches the data collection process influences the responses obtained. Responses may be as much the result of the respondent's response style as his or her true feelings or behavior. A variety of such styles may exist, including the following:

Consistency/Inconsistency   Many respondents give answers to questions under the assumption that their answers to the questions should be what they perceive to be consistent, even if their feelings or behavior is not (i.e., if I have previously indicated that I am in favor of equal rights, I "should," to be consistent, also indicate support of such programs as the ERA). Interestingly, some respondents give inconsistent responses to appear interesting to the researcher.

Boasting/Humility   Respondents may overstate their position (e.g., income, possessions) in order to appear superior. There also is the tendency in some individuals to state that "I can do anything better than you!" Alternatively, some humble souls may understate their accomplishments out of some form of humility. (An excellent example of this is available to anyone who plays golf and attempts to subjectively establish a handicap with three other players.)

Agreement   Some respondents have a tendency to be yea-sayers, responding positively to most questions. (Do you like to swim? *Yes.* Do you like to sit on the beach? *Yes.* Do you like to stay home? *Yes.*) This can be controlled somewhat by using multiple measures and reverse-scaling half of the questions or more elaborate analytical methods (Greenleaf, 1992).

Lying   Respondents sometimes knowingly falsify data. While some may be pathological liars, most probably lie out of self-interest. One need only observe a few individuals filling out tax returns to notice this tendency. Also, respondents will give answers they think are "right" in order to get a possible reward—a free product, a trip, and so on.

In the extreme, fear of responding honestly can lead to no response at all if the question asked is sufficiently sensitive. One way to reduce the unwillingness to answer sensitive questions is to guarantee respondent anonymity. To guarantee anonymity, administering questionnaires in a group setting (obviously without identifying the respondents) is a useful approach. When a one-on-one interview is used, one helpful technique is a *randomization procedure* (Warner, 1965; Stem and Steinhorst, 1984). For example, by having two questions (where A is sensitive and B is not) with the same answer scale (e.g., Yes-No), an interviewer can ask the respondent to *secretly* flip a coin and then answer question A if the coin is heads and B if the coin is tails:

	Yes	*No*
A. Do you beat your spouse?	☐	☐
B. Are you left-handed?	☐	☐

The respondent then reports the answer *without* indicating which question was answered. If the nonsensitive question B has a known response (e.g., the percent of left-handed people in the population), then the overall fraction of Yes and No responses can be used to derive the fraction of Yes responses to the sensitive question. For example, if the fraction of Yes responses to the question is 40 percent and we know 25 percent of the people are left-handed, then by solving

$$25(\tfrac{1}{2}) + X(\tfrac{1}{2}) = 40$$

we can see that 55 percent of the people beat their spouses. The disadvantages of this ingenious approach are twofold. First, it is relatively time consuming. Second, it does not make it possible to determine which respondents perform the sensitive behavior. If in the previous example my objective was to see if spouse-beating were related to demographic or psychographic measures (e.g., "I get frustrated when people aren't on time"), I'm out of luck.

Extremism/Caution   Some respondents tend to use extreme responses on scaled questions (i.e., 1s and 5s on a 1-to-5 scale), while others may use more moderate (i.e., 2s and 4s) responses. The tendency toward caution is generally correlated with cynical or highly educated people who do not believe in absolutes.

Socially Desirable   Many respondents feel uncomfortable admitting to unusual behavior or attitudes. As a consequence, their answers reflect as much what they perceive to be the desirable answer as their own true responses. For example, in a jury selection process, prospective jurors were asked if they liked to read. Not surprisingly, 90 percent said they did, although one suspects a smaller percentage were actually avid readers. Sudman and Bradburn (1982) report socially desirable behavior, such as voting, is overstated by about 25 percent in person, 23 percent on the telephone, and 22 percent by a mail survey. Socially desirable response bias tends to be greater in nonobjective questions (Gruber and Lehmann, 1983).

Response   The respondent is the source of the following three other errors:

Inarticulation   In responding to a question (especially an open-ended one), a respondent may be unable or unwilling to accurately articulate a response.

Mistakes   Even sincere respondents can make errors by marking the wrong response carelessly, especially if they are not committed to the task. Also, for many questions, there is a strong tendency to give a particular answer because, for example, a brand has become synonymous with the product category. (What soft drink did you last have? Coke. What kind of facial tissue do you use? Kleenex.)

Uncertainty All of the foregoing sources of error are theoretically controllable. Yet even perfect control of these (the impossible dream of researchers) would not guarantee perfect data. Individuals are often not sure exactly what their true feelings are or actual behavior has been. This underlying source of measurement error is irreducible.

Controlling Errors

A general comment about controlling errors is in order. Setting aside for the moment researcher and sampling errors, we can view the measured response as a sum of the true response plus the possible errors:

$$\text{Measured value} = \text{True value} + \text{Measurement errors}$$
$$+ \text{Instrument errors} + \text{Respondent errors}$$

While it would be convenient to assume that all the sources of error will cancel out, this approach is pure Pollyanna. To make the measured value closer to the true value, there are a variety of fairly obvious methods available, such as precise wording, which should reduce ambiguity errors and possibly general fatigue by making the task easier.

Still, three points remain:

1. Reducing one type of error will often increase another (e.g., increasing scale points reduces rounding error but increases respondent burden and, hence, respondent errors).
2. Some random error remains no matter what you do.
3. As an individual progresses through a test situation (experiment, questionnaire, etc.), the experience will change him or her by both conditioning and fatigue.

The purpose of these three points is not to discourage efforts to reduce error; rather, it is to indicate that error reduction is a vexing, complex problem. Fortunately, if one is concerned with relative, rather than absolute, values, many of these sources of error will tend to cancel out. Also, unless, for example, response style and the true value being measured are correlated, average responses will not be affected. Thus by focusing on average and relative values, many of the measurement problems become less serious.

SUMMARY

Having read (or at least turned the pages of) this chapter, someone may pose the question, "Can a few simple notions be taken from this chapter?" Put more crudely, "What good is all this?" This section is an attempt to respond to that question.

Measurement Theory

A variety of concepts have been advanced as desirable characteristics of measurement. Though the terms are formidable, the concepts are largely intuitive. Good measures are ones that produce consistent (reliable) estimates of the constructs and that are related to other measures of interest.

Scale Types

There are four basic scale types: nominal (categorical), ordinal, interval, and ratio. Whenever possible, intervally scaled data should be obtained, since they allow the more powerful statistical tools (e.g., regression analysis) to be applied. It is possible to use nonmetric data in calculations such as correlations and means. The problem is that some error is introduced by using nonintervally scaled data, such as rankings, in these calculations, which we have classified as "inappropriate analysis." As long as the data are ordinally scaled (monotonic), these calculations are, in general, not so badly distorted that they need be abandoned. While the results of such calculations are not appropriate for fine-tuning, they certainly are useful for getting a general notion about the results.

One final point is that the respondent controls the quality and scale of the data. A respondent can respond on a continuous scale as though it were ordinal, or an interval scale even if the scale appears to be only ordinal. Thus, respondent commitment is at least as important as the scale in determining the quality of data (Hauser and Shugan, 1980).

Typical Scales

In spite of the variety of scales available, a surprisingly small number form the mainstay of market research data. The following are the most commonly used:

NOMINAL (CATEGORICAL):
   1. Multiple choice (e.g., region, occupation, brand chosen)
   2. Yes-no (e.g., ownership, awareness)

ORDINAL:
   Forced ranking (e.g., brand preference)

ORDINAL-INTERVAL:
   Semantic differential/bipolar adjective (e.g., attitudes, opinions)

RATIO:
   1. Direct quantification (e.g., number of people in household)
   2. Constant sum scale

Sources of Error

There are a vast number of sources of error that *cannot* be simultaneously reduced. Many of these sources of error depend on the researcher, sample, or respondent and are beyond the control of the measurement process, which is not the major source of error in most studies. Put differently, worrying about measurement errors is productive only when problem definition and sample composition are well established.

PROBLEMS

1. How would you determine

   a. How important nutrition was to consumers in their choice of food?

b. What process consumers follow in selecting a brand of gasoline for their cars?

c. How many pairs of slacks a sample of consumers own?

d. What consumers feel is the effect of television advertising on children?

2. Write a dollar metric question to assess preference for brands of washing machines.

3. Assume you had to predict the likely winner of the next presidential election based on a single poll two weeks before the election. A good sample has already agreed to participate.

   Assume you are to ask two questions: Will you vote? and Who will you vote for? Describe

   a. The exact form of the response scale.

   b. Exactly (mathematically) how you would go about making your prediction.

4. List the major control variables a survey/question designer has at his or her disposal (e.g., number of scale points).

5. Suggest how the control variables in your answer to problem 4 relate to the sources of error in Figure 8.5.

REFERENCES

ANDERSON, JAMES C., AND DAVID W. GERBING (1982) "Some Methods for Respecifying Measurement Models to Obtain Unidimensional Construct Measurement," *Journal of Marketing Research*, 19, November, 453–60.

ANDERSON, JAMES C., DAVID W. GERBING, AND JOHN E. HUNTER (1987) "On the Assessment of Unidimensional Measurement: Internal and External Consistency, and Overall Consistency Criteria," *Journal of Marketing Research*, 24, November, 432–37.

BAGOZZI, RICHARD P., HANS BAUMGARTNER, AND RIK PIETERS (1994) "Goal-Directed Emotions," working paper, University of Michigan.

BAGOZZI, RICHARD P. AND YOUJAE YI (1991) "Multitrait-Multimethod Matrices in Consumer Research," *Journal of Consumer Research*, 17, March, 426–39.

BATRA, RAJEEV, AND OLLI T. AHTOLA (1990) "Measuring the Hedonic and Utilitarian Sources of Consumer Attitudes," *Marketing Letters*, 2, April, 159–70.

BEARDEN, WILLIAM O., RICHARD G. NETEMEYER, AND MARY F. MOBLEY (1993) *Handbook of Marketing Scales, Multi-Item Measures for Marketing and Consumer Behavior Research*, Newbury Park, Calif.: Sage.

BICKART, BARBARA A. (1993) "Carryover and Backfire Effects in Marketing Research," *Journal of Marketing Research*, 30, February, 52–62.

BRADBURN, K. (1983) "Response Effects," in P. Rossi, J. Wright, and A. Anderson, eds., *Handbook of Social Research*, New York: Academic Press.

BRUNER, GORDON C., II, AND PAUL J. HENSEL (1993) *Marketing Scales Handbook, A Compilation of Multi-Item Measures*, Chicago: American Marketing Association.

CAMERON, TRUDY A., AND MICHELLE D. JAMES (1987) "Estimating Willingness to Pay from Survey Data: An Alternative Pre-Test-Market Evaluation Procedure," *Journal of Marketing Research*, 24, November, 389–95.

CAMPBELL, DONALD T., AND DONALD W. FISKE (1959) "Convergent and Discriminant Validation by the Multitrait-Multimethod Matrix," *Psychological Bulletin*, 56, 81–105.

CHILDERS, TERRY L. (1986) "Assessment of the Psychometric Properties of an Opinion Leadership Scale," *Journal of Marketing Research*, 23, May, 184–88.

CHURCHILL, GILBERT A., JR. (1979) "A Paradigm for Developing Better Measures of Marketing Constructs," *Journal of Marketing Research*, 16, February, 64–73.

CLIFF, NORMAN (1959) "Adverbs as Multipliers," *Psychology Review*, 66, January.

COOMBS, CLYDE H. (1964) *A Theory of Data*, New York: John Wiley and Sons.

COTE, JOSEPH A., AND M. RONALD BUCKLEY (1987) "Estimating Trait, Method, and Error Variance: Generalizing Across 70 Construct Validation Studies," *Journal of Marketing Research*, 24, August, 315–18.

CRONBACH, LEE J. (1951) "Coefficient Alpha and the Internal Structure of Tests," *Psychometrika*, 16, September, 297–334.

DECISION SYSTEMS GROUP (1985) "Letter Identification in Product Testing: A Potential Source of Bias," *Marketing Review*, 40, June–July, 17–18.

DESHPANDÉ, ROHIT, JOHN U. FARLEY, AND FREDERICK E. WEBSTER, JR. (1993) "Corporate Culture, Customer Orientation, and Innovativeness in Japanese Firms: A Quadrad Analysis," *Journal of Marketing*, 57, January, 23–37.

DICKSON, JOHN, AND GERALD ALBAUM (1977) "A Method for Developing Tailormade Semantic Differentials for Specific Marketing Content Areas," *Journal of Marketing Research*, 14, February, 87–91.

DONTHU, NAVEEN, AND JOSEPH CHERIAN (1993) "Differences in Consumer Perceptions of Similarity and Dissimilarity," *Marketing Letters*, 4, January, 31–38.

ELLEN, PAM SCHOLDER, AND THOMAS J. MADDEN (1989) "The Impact of Response Format on Relations among Intentions, Attitudes, and Social Norms," *Marketing Letters*, 1, June, 161–70.

FABER, RONALD J., AND THOMAS C. O'GUINN (1992) "A Clinical Screener for Compulsive Buying," *Journal of Consumer Research*, 19, December, 459–69.

GREENLEAF, ERIC A. (1992) "Improving Rating Scale Measures by Detecting and Correcting Bias Components in Some Response Styles," *Journal of Marketing Research*, 29, May, 176–88.

GRUBER, ROBERT E., AND DONALD R. LEHMANN (1983) "The Effect of Omitting Response Tendency Variables from Regression Models," in W. R. Darden, K. B. Monroe, and W. R. Dillon, eds., *Research Methods and Causal Modeling in Marketing*, Chicago: American Marketing Association, 131–36.

HALEY, RUSSELL I., AND PETER B. CASE (1979) "Testing Thirteen Attitude Scales for Agreement and Brand Discrimination," *Journal of Marketing*, 43, Fall, 20–32.

HAUSER, JOHN R., AND STEVEN M. SHUGAN (1980) "Intensity Measures of Consumer Preference," *Operations Research*, 28, March–April, 278–320.

HAUSER, JOHN R., AND GLEN L. URBAN (1986) "The Value Priority Hypotheses for Consumer Budget Plans," *Journal of Consumer Research*, 12, March, 446–62.

HAVLENA, WILLIAM J., AND MORRIS B. HOLBROOK (1986) "The Varieties of Consumption Experience: Comparing Two Typologies of Emotion in Consumer Behavior," *Journal of Consumer Research*, 13, December, 394–404.

HAWKINS, DEL I., GERALD ALBAUM, AND ROGER BEST (1974) "Stapel Scale or Semantic Differential in Marketing Research," *Journal of Marketing Research*, 11, August, 318–22.

HEELER, ROGER M., CHIKE OKECHUKU, AND STAN REID (1979) "Attribute Importance: Contrasting Measurements," *Journal of Marketing Research*, 16, February, 60–63.

HOWE, EDMUND S. (1966) "Verb Tense, Negatives, and Other Determinants of the Intensity of Evaluative Meaning," *Journal of Verbal Learning and Verbal Behavior*, 5, April.

HUGHES, G. DAVID, AND MICHEL TUAN PHAM (1993) "Using On-Line Technology to Assess Responses to Communications," presented at MSI Conference, Cambridge, Mass., September.

HULBERT, JAMES, AND DONALD R. LEHMANN (1975) "Reducing Error in Question and Scale Design: A Conceptual Framework," *Decision Sciences*, 6, January, 166–73.

JACCARD, JAMES, DAVID BRINBERG, AND LEE J. ACKERMAN (1986) "Assessing Attribute Importance: A Comparison of Six Methods," *Journal of Consumer Research*, 12, March, 463–68.

KARSTEN, YVONNE C., AND DEBORAH RHOEDDER-JOHN (1994) "Measuring Young Children's Preferences: The Use of Behaviorally Anchored Rating Scales," Cambridge, Mass.: MSI Report 94-122.

KASSARJIAN, HAROLD H. (1974) "Projective Methods," in Robert Ferber, ed., *Handbook of Marketing Research*, New York: McGraw-Hill, 3/85–3/100.

KOHLI, AJAY K., BERNARD J. JAWORSKI, AND AJITH KUMAR (1993) "MARKOR: A Measure of Market Orientation," *Journal of Marketing Research*, 30, November, 467–77.

KUMAR, AJITH, AND WILLIAM R. DILLON (1987a) "The Interaction of Measurement and Structure in Simultaneous Equation Models with Unobservable Variables," *Journal of Marketing Research*, 24, February, 98–105.

—— (1987b) "Some Further Remarks on Measurement-Structure Interaction and the Unidimensionality of Constructs," *Journal of Marketing Research*, 24, November, 438–44.

LAMPERT, SCHLOMO I. (1979) "The Attitude Pollimeter: A New Attitude Scaling Device," *Journal of Marketing Research*, 16, November, 578–82.

LEAVITT, C. (1970) "A Multidimensional Set of Rating Scales for Television Commercials," *Journal of Applied Psychology*, 54, 427–29.

LEHMANN, DONALD R., AND JAMES HULBERT (1972) "Are Three-Point Scales Always Good Enough?" *Journal of Marketing Research*, 9, November, 444–46.

MEHRABIAN, ALBERT, AND JAMES A. RUSSELL (1974) *An Approach to Environmental Psychology*, Cambridge, Mass.: MIT Press.

MICHAELS, RONALD E., AND RALPH L. DAY (1985) "Measuring Customer Orientation of Salespeople: A Replication with Industrial Buyers," *Journal of Marketing Research*, 22, November, 443–46.

MUNSON, J. MICHAEL, AND SHELBY H. MCINTYRE (1979) "Developing Practical Procedures for the Measurement of Personal Values in Cross-Cultural Marketing," *Journal of Marketing Research*, 16, February, 48–52.

MYERS, JAMES H., AND W. GREGORY WARNER (1968) "Semantic Properties of Selected Evaluation Adjectives," *Journal of Marketing Research*, 4, November, 409–13.

NARVER, JOHN C., AND STANLEY F. SLATER (1990) "The Effect of Market Orientation on Business Performance," *Journal of Marketing*, 54, October, 20–35.

NUNNALLY, JUM C. (1978) *Psychometric Theory*, 2nd ed., New York: McGraw-Hill.

OFIR, CHEZY, SRINIVAS K. REDDY, AND GORDON G. BECHTEL (1987) "Are Semantic Response Scales Equivalent?" *Multivariate Behavioral Research*, 22, January, 21–38.

OSGOOD, C., G. SUCI, AND P. TANNENBAUM (1957) *The Measurement of Meaning*, Urbana: University of Illinois Press.

PARAMESWARAN, RAVI, BARNETT A. GREENBERG, DANNY N. BELLENGER, AND DAN H. ROBERTSON (1979) "Measuring Reliability: A Comparison of Alternative Techniques," *Journal of Marketing Research*, 16, February, 18–25.

PARASURAMAN, A., VALARIE A. ZEITHAML, AND LEONARD L. BERRY (1988) "SERVQUAL: A Multiple-Item Scale for Measuring Consumer Perceptions of Service Quality," *Journal of Retailing*, 4, Spring, 12–37.

PERREAULT, WILLIAM D., JR., AND LAURENCE E. LEIGH (1989) "Reliability of Nominal Data Based on Qualitative Judgments," *Journal of Marketing Research*, 26, May, 135–48.

PESSEMIER, EDGAR A. (1963) *Experimental Methods of Analyzing Demand for Branded Consumer Goods with Applications to Problems in Marketing Strategy*, Bulletin 39, Pullman: Washington State University Bureau of Economic and Business Research, June.

PETER, J. PAUL (1979) "Reliability: A Review of Psychometric Basics and Recent Marketing Practices," *Journal of Marketing Research*, 16, February, 6–17.

——— (1981) "Construct Validity: A Review of Basic Issues and Marketing Practices," *Journal of Marketing Research*, 18, May, 133–45.

PETER, J. PAUL, AND GILBERT A. CHURCHILL, JR. (1986) "Relationships among Research Design Choices and Psychometric Properties of Rating Scales: A Meta-analysis," *Journal of Marketing Research*, 23, February, 1–10.

PETERSON, ROBERT A. (1994) "A Meta-analysis of Cronbach's Coefficient Alpha," *Journal of Consumer Research*, 21, September, 381–91.

PLUTCHIK, ROBERT (1980) *Emotion: A Psychoevolutionary Synthesis*, New York: Harper and Row.

RENTZ, JOSEPH O. (1987) "Generalizability Theory: A Comprehensive Method for Assessing and Improving the Dependability of Marketing Measures," *Journal of Marketing Research*, 24, February, 19–28.

RICHINS, MARSHA L., AND SCOTT DAWSON (1992) "A Consumer Values Orientation for Materialism and Its Measurement: Scale Development and Validation," *Journal of Consumer Research*, 19, December, 303–16.

ROBINSON, JOHN P., AND PHILIP R. SHAVER (1973) *Measures of Social Psychological Attitudes*, rev. ed., Ann Arbor: Institute of Social Research, University of Michigan.

ROKEACH, MILTON J. (1973) *The Nature of Human Values*, New York: Free Press.

RUST, ROLAND T., AND BRUCE COOIL (1994) "Reliability Measures for Qualitative Data: Theory and Implications," *Journal of Marketing Research*, 31, February, 1–14.

SAXE, ROBERT, AND BARTON A. WEITZ (1982) "The SOCO Scale: A Measure of the Customer Orientation of Salespeople," *Journal of Marketing Research*, 19, August, 343–51.

SCHUMAN, HOWARD, AND STANLEY PRESSER (1981) *Questions and Answers in Attitude Surveys: Experiments on Question Form, Wording, and Content*, New York: Academic Press.

SEWALL, MURPHY A. (1981) "Relative Information Contributions of Consumer Purchase Intentions and Management Judgment as Explanators of Sales," *Journal of Marketing Research*, 18, May, 249–53.

SHIMP, TERENCE A., AND SUBHASH SHARMA (1987) "Consumer Ethnocentrism: Construction and Validation of the CETSCALE," *Journal of Marketing Research*, 24, August, 280–89.

SIMMONS, CAROLYN J., BARBARA A. BICKART, AND JOHN G. LYNCH, JR. (1993) "Capturing and Creating Public Opinion in Survey Research," *Journal of Consumer Research*, 20, September, 316–29.

SLATER, STANLEY F., AND JOHN C. NARVER (1992) "Market Orientation, Performance, and the Moderating Influence of Competitive Environment," Cambridge, Mass.: MSI Report 92-118.

STEM, D. E., AND R. K. STEINHORST (1984) "Telephone Interview and Mail Questionnaire Applications of the Randomized Response Model," *Journal of the American Statistical Association*, 79, September, 555–64.

STEVENS, STANLEY S. (1951) "Mathematics, Measurement, and Psychophysics," in S. S. Stevens, ed., *Handbook of Experimental Psychology,* New York: John Wiley and Sons.

SUDMAN, SEYMOUR, AND NORMAN M. BRADBURN (1982) *Asking Questions,* San Francisco: Jossey-Bass.

TEAS, R. KENNETH, AND JOHN K. WONG (1992) "Item Context and the Stability of Entity-Based and Attribute-Based Multiattribute Scaling Methods," *Journal of Consumer Research,* 18, March, 536–45.

THORNDIKE, ROBERT L., ED. (1971) *Educational Measurement,* Washington, D.C.: American Council on Education.

THURSTONE, L. L. (1959) *The Measurement of Value,* Chicago: University of Chicago Press.

TORGERSON, W. S. (1958) *Theory and Methods of Scaling,* New York: John Wiley and Sons.

TVERSKY, A. (1977) "Features of Similarity," *Psychological Review,* 84, 327–52.

"USING LETTERS TO IDENTIFY PRODUCTS OR BRANDS," (no date) *Research on Research,* No. 16, Chicago: Market Facts, Inc.

WARNER, S. L. (1965) "Randomized Response: A Survey Technique for Eliminating Evasive Answer Bias," *Journal of the American Statistical Association,* 60.

WELLS, W. D. (1964) "EQ, Son of EQ, and the Reaction Profile," *Journal of Marketing,* 28, 45–52.

WESTBROOK, ROBERT A., AND RICHARD L. OLIVER (1991) "The Dimensionality of Consumption Emotion Patterns and Consumer Satisfaction," *Journal of Consumer Research,* 18, June, 84–91.

WIDAMAN, KEITH F. (1985) "Hierarchically Nested Covariance Structure Models for Multi-trait-Multimethod Data," *Applied Psychological Measurement,* 9, March, 1–26.

WIND, YORAM, AND DAVID LERNER (1979) "On the Measurement of Purchase Data: Surveys versus Purchase Diaries," *Journal of Marketing Research,* 16, February, 39–47.

ZINKHAN, GEORGE M., AND CLAES FORNELL (1985) "A Test of Two Consumer Response Scales in Advertising," *Journal of Marketing Research,* 22, November, 447–52.

APPENDIX 8-A

LAW OF COMPARATIVE JUDGMENT

The law of comparative judgment requires that several subjects (or one subject at several points in time) perform paired comparisons on a set of alternatives.

Consider the following example:

Number of times column item
preferred to row item (n = 200)

	A	B	C	D
A	—	40	80	130
B	160	—	140	180
C	120	60	—	150
D	70	20	50	—

We next compute the percent of time each alternative is preferred to each other alternative. (Note that 50 has been put on the diagonal. This is unnecessary but traditional and has no effect on the result.)

Percent of time column item
preferred to row item

	A	B	C	D
A	50	20	40	65
B	80	50	70	90
C	60	30	50	75
D	35	10	25	50
Total	225	110	185	280

We can see that D is most preferred followed by A, C, and B (D > A > C > B). To convert this to an interval scale, we will assume the following:

1. Respondents have the same preferences on some underlying interval scale.
2. Respondents are equally uncertain about the alternatives and draw their preference feelings from a normal distribution (Figure 8A.1). Since preferences are stochastic, it is possible that a respondent will say B is preferred to A when, in fact, A is truly preferred to B. The number of times this occurs is an indication of how far apart the alternatives are on the underlying scale. The trick of the law of comparative judgment is to deduce the underlying scale from the preference data.

Consider the preference distribution for A and B (Figure 8A.2). The percent of the time A is preferred to B depends on (*a*) the difference in their preferences $P_A - P_B$, and (*b*) the amount of uncertainty in their preferences. Since the reported feelings toward A and B are assumed to be normally distributed and independent, the difference between them will also be normally distributed with mean $P_A - P_B$ and

$$\text{Standard deviation} = \sqrt{s_A^2 + s_B^2} = s\sqrt{2}$$

FIGURE 8A.1
Reported vs. True Feeling

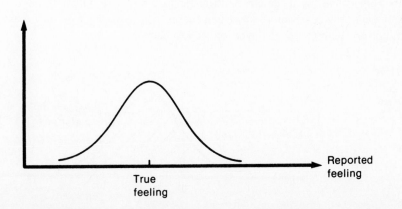

Reported
feeling

True
feeling

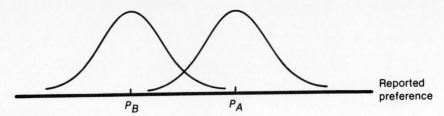

FIGURE 8A.2
Preferences for Two Alternatives

since we assume s_A and s_B are equal (Figure 8A.3). If we knew P_A, P_B, and s, we could get the percent of the time that A should be preferred to B from the standard normal table. Here we reverse that procedure, taking the percent of the time A is preferred to B to the table and deducing how far apart A and B are in standard deviations. For example, since A is preferred to B 80 percent of the time, we estimate A is .84 standard deviations above B on the preference scale. Similarly, we fill in an entire table of estimates of the number of standard deviations between pairs of alternatives:

	A	B	C	D
A	0	− .84	− .25	.39
B	.84	0	.52	1.28
C	.25	− .52	0	.67
D	− .39	− 1.28	− .67	0
Total	.70	− 2.64	− .40	2.34

Since the column sums are measured in units (standard deviations) of the underlying preference distribution, the totals form an interval scale (actually a normalized interval scale, since the scale values sum to zero).

This clever approach is perhaps most useful because of its two major assumptions. The formalized homogeneity assumption, which is used in many calculations but is usually hidden or ignored, is bothersome, as it should be. The random response notion is basic to the concept of measurement. Hence, even if the technique is not used, its two major assumptions require attention in analysis of any type of survey data.

FIGURE 8A.3
Probability as Preferred

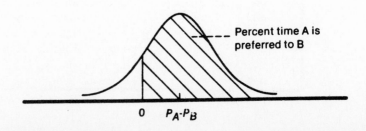

APPENDIX 8-B

THE DELPHI PROCEDURE

The Delphi procedure is designed to produce a consensus ratio-scaled evaluation of alternatives among a set of judgments. It is most commonly used in evaluating budget priorities. To see how it works, consider the following example:

Assume three trustees were assigned to allocate funds ($100) to four projects. At step 1, each would be asked to allocate the $100 among the four projects:

| | Trustee | | |
Project	A	B	C
I	40	20	15
II	10	30	50
III	20	15	10
IV	30	35	25
	100	100	100

Someone then collates the responses from the three trustees and computes the average allocation for each project. Each trustee is then given a copy of both the original allocation and the average, and he or she is asked to modify the original allocation. For example, trustee A would receive a form, such as:

Project	Original Allocation	Average Allocation	New Allocation
I	40	25	
II	10	30	
III	20	15	
IV	30	30	—
	100	100	100

By repeating the process several times, agreement (or at least near agreement) presumably can be reached. The big advantage of this technique is that it can be used for individuals who are distant geographically or who have difficulty discussing allocations amicably. It also downplays the importance of slick verbal presentations in obtaining allocations. On the other hand, several problems exist. First, participants must be sufficiently committed that they respond honestly but not so fanatical that they refuse to budge (having participated in three such studies, I found that the game could be brought to a conclusion by adopting the mean as my response by wave 3). Second, shrewd respondents can influence results by a modified "bullet-vote" technique, where they inflate the allocation to their pet project and reduce it to their main competitors, thereby biasing the averages and, they hope, the final solution. Finally, there is the implicit assumption that either the average is right (very democratic but often false) or that agreement is an end in itself (which it can become, given especially strident arguments). Consequently, the technique is very specialized and not useful for most marketing research purposes.

APPENDIX 8-C

MULTITRAIT-MULTIMETHOD MATRIX

The basic notion of a multitrait-multimethod matrix is that the correlations (or whatever measure of association is appropriate, given the scales used) among multiple measures of the same trait should be the largest correlations in the matrix. For example, if five measures (e.g., six-point bipolar adjective scales) measure two traits, then the largest correlations between the measures should be among pairs of measures of the same trait. This incorporates notions of convergent (alternate forms) and discriminant validity. Continuing with a hypothetical example, assume the two traits are "educational ability" and "ability to pay":

Trait	Measure
A. Educational ability	1. Years of school
	2. SAT score
	3. Self-reported aptitude
B. Ability to pay	1. Salary
	2. Investments

Hence, one would, under model I in Figure 8C.1, expect the correlations between years of school and SAT score and salary and investments to be higher than the correlation between SAT

FIGURE 8C.1
Alternative Relations Among Traits

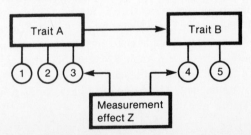

I. Three Independent Traits

II. Three Related Traits

III. Three Related Traits with a Measurement (Method) Effect

	Measurement		Measure				
Trait	Method	Measure	1	2	3	4	5
A	X	1	1	Big	Big	Small	Small
A	Y	2		1	Big	Small	Small
A	Z	3			1	Moderate	Small
B	Z	4				1	Big
B	W	5					1

FIGURE 8C.2
Multitrait-Multimethod Correlation Matrix

score and investments, which should be close to zero. If educational ability and ability to pay are related (model II, Figure 8C.1), then the correlation between SAT score and investments should be larger but still not as large as between, say, SAT score and self-reported aptitude. Also, a common measurement bias or method effect will generally increase correlations. For example, if ego boosting leads some people to overstate *both* educational aptitude and income (model III, Figure 8C.1), then measures 3 and 4 will be more highly correlated. Consequently, the relative sizes of the correlations between the five measures should be as in Figure 8C.2.

If this "relative size" tendency is not borne out in the data, one of two things must be true. First, the data themselves may be atypical. Second, the original definition of the traits or their measures may be in error. Obviously if the second is true, the constructs, at least as operationalized, are invalid.

For a more sophisticated treatment of this topic, see Bagozzi and Yi (1991).

APPENDIX 8-D ━━━━━━━━━━━━━━━━

NORMALIZING AND STANDARDIZING

NORMALIZING

Normalizing is the process of removing the mean (average) from a series of responses:

$$\text{Normalized } X = \text{Original } X - \text{Mean } X$$

$$\text{or } X_N = X - \overline{X}$$

Example

Given:

$$\underline{X}$$

4

6

8

6

4

8

Thus, $\overline{X} = 6$, and we get:

$$\underline{\overline{X}_N = X - \overline{X}}$$
$$-2$$
$$0$$
$$+2$$
$$0$$
$$-2$$
$$+2$$

STANDARDIZING

Standardizing is the process of making the mean 0 and the standard deviation 1 for a series of responses:

$$\text{Standardized } X = \frac{\text{Original } X - \text{Mean } X}{\text{Standard deviation of } X}$$

$$\text{or } X_s = \frac{X - \overline{X}}{s_X}$$

Example

Given:

$$\underline{X}$$
$$4$$
$$6$$
$$8$$
$$6$$
$$4$$
$$8$$
$$\overline{X} = 6$$

and

$$s = \sqrt{16/5} = \sqrt{3.2} = 1.79$$

Thus,

$$\underline{X_s}$$
$$-1.12$$
$$0$$
$$+1.12$$
$$0$$
$$-1.12$$
$$+1.12$$

APPLICATIONS

There are two basic applications of normalizing and standardizing. One is by variable across people to indicate which people are relatively high or low on the variable. The other is by person across response. This approach obtains, on the individual level, the relative responses to a series of questions, and it removes the tendency of individuals to generally give either high or low responses. It is also possible to double standardize by standardizing first by person across variables and then across people by variable. The purpose of all these transformations is to convert data to a form that is more useful for comparative purposes. The danger is that both normalizing and standardizing cause the loss of information (the absolute values of the variables) that may be useful. Hence, decisions concerning normalizing or standardizing should be made only if (*a*) a firm grasp of the problem and (*b*) an assumption about the meaning of the absolute level of a response are available.

CHAPTER 9

Sampling in Marketing Research

Sampling is fundamental to human behavior. When trying a new food, a person will typically eat one or two bites and then form an opinion. Similarly, a reader of this book will often sample several passages in order to make a decision about whether to continue reading. Yet somehow sampling in marketing research has achieved an aura of mystery and even science, due only in part to the formulas involved. While one approach to making sampling decisions is to call in a high priest (read Ph.D. in statistics), for most common situations a few basics plus some common sense will suffice. The purpose of this chapter is to introduce such basics. More detailed treatments are found in Hansen, Hurwitz, and Madow (1953); Deming (1960); Cochran (1977); Kish (1965); Sudman (1976); and Kalton (1983).

Sampling is often viewed as a branch of applied statistics, full of confusing formulas and complex terms. While there are formulas and statistical concepts involved, the essence of sampling for purposes of decision making is very simple:

> To *gather* information from *enough* of the *right sources* to get a *good (accurate) sense* of *what you are interested in.*

Viewed this way, comments such as "How big a sample is valid?" are basically naive/stupid. Bigger is better (it gives you a more accurate sense of what you are interested in) and there is no magic number that makes a sample good/valid. (If you can quantify what level of accuracy is good enough, then you can sometimes—as we will in this chapter—indicate how big a sample is needed.) Moreover, consulting more of the wrong sources (talking to the wrong people) will not help; it will only give a false sense of accuracy.

BASIC ISSUES

Sample design issues can be divided into three categories:

1. Identifying the *right sources*. The sample should be representative of the population of interest in terms of the key responses. A sample does not have to be typical of the general population or even the part of the population under study in terms of other characteristics. While one would expect a sample that had the same average income, age, and so forth as the population of interest to be representative in terms of purchase behavior, it may not be. Conversely, a sample can be very different demographically and still be representative of some types of behavior. Obviously, a sample that is similar to the population under study is, in general, more likely to be representative in terms of key responses than one that isn't. Equally important, the use of a matched sample increases receptivity to the results, making the information more likely to be used and hence useful.

2. Selecting a method for *gathering* information. The specific procedure used must focus on the right sources. A more subtle issue has to do with nonresponse. Even the best-designed sampling plans encounter nonresponse (information is not available from the source designated by the sample plan) and partial nonresponse (the source does not provide complete information). The method of handling nonresponses often is much more important than the particular sampling plan chosen.

3. Deciding *how many are enough* to sample. Assuming you consult the right sources, accuracy is directly related to sample size. Put differently, you can purchase accuracy. Hence, the decision involves trading off cost (both in time and money) vs. accuracy.

To cover the major aspects of sampling in a systematic way, the chapter proceeds to address the following issues:

1. Who is the target population (frame)?
2. What method (process) will be used to elicit responses?
3. How many will be sampled?
4. How will the sampling points be selected?
5. What will be done about nonresponse?

Sampling issues apply to all types of studies. Because of its prominence in survey research and in order to make the discussion as concrete as possible, however, much of the discussion implicitly focuses on survey sampling.

WHO IS THE TARGET POPULATION?

The target population, or frame, is that part of the total population (universe) to which the study is directed. For example, for a company selling automobiles in the United States, the universe could be the entire U.S. population plus foreign visitors, and the frame might be people aged 18 or over. Alternatively, for Lexus the focus could be on relatively well-off individuals, and hence the target might be those with annual incomes above $50,000. Choice of a target population that is too large leads to the collection of data from people whose responses are meaningless. For example, car preferences of 8-year-olds, assuming they are relatively uninfluential in family auto purchase decisions, are irrelevant. On the other hand, choice of an overly narrow frame will tend to exclude potentially useful responses. For example, focusing on males aged 25 to 49 might cover the majority of a market but will undoubtedly exclude some important segments. The choice of a target population, then, requires balancing between including irrelevant sampling points and excluding relevant ones. Most important, this decision is logically the responsibility of the person who requested the study and not a statistician.

WHAT METHOD WILL BE USED?

Choice of method depends on the type of information desired and, importantly, on the available budget. For example, for a survey a choice must be made between the cost and speed of a phone survey versus the personalization and detail obtainable in personal interviews. Since the advantages of various methods have already been discussed in some detail in Chapter 4, they will not be discussed further here.

HOW MANY WILL BE SAMPLED?

The decision about how many to sample can be very complex. An entire branch of Bayesian statistics is devoted to this issue (Schlaifer, 1959). For the practical marketing researcher, however, four major considerations are paramount: statistical precision (accuracy), credibility, company policy (generally accepted practice), and financial constraints.

Statistical Precision

The larger the sample, the more confident the researcher can be that the results are representative of the things being measured. In general, the accuracy/precision of an estimate (e.g., mean) is related to the square root of the sample size. In other words, to double the precision of an estimate, the sample must be quadrupled.

Once the sample is drawn, the level of precision is already determined. If the level of precision needed can be specified ahead of time, however, it is possible to determine the minimum required sample size. Here, sample size refers to the number of usable responses, not to the number of individuals in the target sample (e.g., if you expect a 50 percent response rate, the number in the target sample will be twice the number of usable responses needed, assuming equal response rates in all segments).

The formulas for precision given in this section strictly apply to probability samples where each member of the population has a known and equal probability of being selected. Also, it is important to recognize that most surveys have multiple items of interest, while the formulas that follow assume there is a single key item. Therefore, this section should be used to provide a general guideline, rather than an absolute answer, to the question of how many must be sampled when you are interested in measuring a numerical average (e.g., income) or a percent (e.g., the percent who buy a given brand).

Averages Consider the problem of estimating the average income of U.S. households from a representative sample. As you may recall from statistics (but typically do not; see Appendix 9-A), the average income generated by the sample ($\bar{x}$) is the best guess of the average income of U.S. households. However, the sample $\bar{x}$ may not exactly equal the population average due to idiosyncrasies of the sample. The most accurate statement that can be made is that the true mean is within some range about $\bar{x}$. To quantify this range, two important facts are used:

1. The sample mean $(\bar{x})$ is approximately normally distributed.
2. The standard deviation of the sample mean is the standard deviation calculated in the sample divided by the square root of the sample size:

$$s_{\bar{x}} = \frac{s}{\sqrt{n}}$$

Using these two facts, it is possible to construct a range (known to statistics students as a *confidence interval*) into which the true mean will fall with a given probability (known to statistics students as a *confidence level*). This range is given by:

$$\text{Range in which true mean falls} = \text{Sample mean} \pm z_{\alpha}\frac{s}{\sqrt{n}}$$

where z_{α} is a constant drawn from a standard normal table that depends on the level of confidence desired (Figure 9.1). For example, the commonly used 95 percent confidence interval (the range in which we are 95 percent sure the true mean falls) is given by:

$$\bar{x} \pm 1.96 \frac{s}{\sqrt{n}}$$

Hence, if we took a sample of 400 households in the United States and measured their average income as $32,172 and the standard deviation of their income as $6,216, the 95 percent confidence interval for true household average income in the United States would be:

$$32,172 \pm 1.96\left(\frac{6,216}{\sqrt{400}}\right) = 31,172 \pm 609$$

$$= \text{between } 31,563 \text{ and } 32,781$$

A slight variation on this formula can be used to determine necessary sample size in advance. First, decide on an acceptable confidence level. Second, estimate the standard deviation of income(s) in the target population. (In order to be conservative and guarantee the sample size is adequate, make sure this is a generous estimate.) This can be done either objectively (from a prior or small pilot sample) or subjectively (in other words, a guess). One useful method for estimating the standard deviation is to first estimate the range of the distribution and then divide by 6. Third, establish what is an acceptable "tolerance"—that is, how tightly/accurately you need to measure the variable of interest (e.g., if you need to measure income within $700, that means the tolerance is $700. Notice in Figure 9.1 that the tolerance is half the confidence interval.)

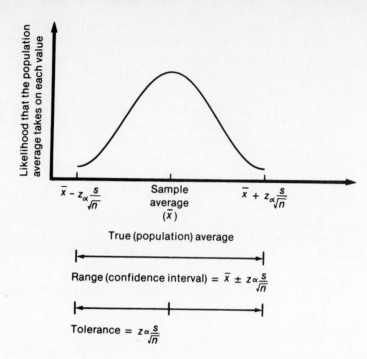

FIGURE 9.1
Estimating the True Mean from a
Sample Mean

If you know the confidence level, standard deviation, and tolerance, you can use the following formula:

$$\text{Tolerance} = z_\alpha \frac{s}{\sqrt{n}}$$

$$\text{or } n = \frac{z_\alpha^2 s^2}{(\text{Tolerance})^2} \tag{9.1}$$

For example, assuming s were 3,000, the tolerance acceptable were 100, and we wanted to be 95 percent sure that we would be within the tolerance, we would get:

$$n = \frac{(1.96)^2 (3,000)^2}{(100)^2}$$

and therefore:

$$n = 3,457.44 \Rightarrow 3,458$$

(We can't sample fractional people, and 3,457 won't give quite enough precision.) Hence, if we sample 3,458 people, we can estimate the mean within ±100.

In deciding on sample size, a researcher may be interested in relative precision. That is, the desire may be to estimate a quantity within a fixed percent (e.g., 10 percent) of the mean value. In such a case, the tolerance level acceptable would be set equal to 10 percent of the anticipated mean value. Assuming the mean was expected to be about 1,000, this leads to a tolerance level of $(.10)(1,000) = 100$. Notice that the number 3,458 is deceptively precise since it depends on exactly knowing the (unknown) standard deviation. Hence, these formulas provide more general guidance than absolute precision and in this case suggest a sample of 3,500 or even 4,000 if budget is not a major concern.

In some instances you may be interested in establishing that a particular effect (e.g., of advertising on sales) is above some standard. Recall the basic measurement model from the previous chapter:

$$\text{Measured effect} = \text{Average effect} + \text{Error}$$

where error includes both random error and variation unaccounted for across sample points. Here, the confidence interval for the true average effect is

$$\text{Average measured effect} \pm z_\alpha \frac{s}{\sqrt{n}}$$

If your goal is to "prove" an effect is not zero *and* you have a good idea what both the average effect and its standard deviation will be, the sample size needed becomes a modified form of (9.1):

$$n = \frac{(z_\alpha)^2 (s)^2}{(\text{Average measured effect})^2}$$

Thus, if you expect a small effect size of .02 and a standard error of .10, you need (at the 95 percent confidence interval):

$$n = \frac{(1.96)^2 (.10)^2}{(.02)^2} = 96.04 \Rightarrow 97$$

If your goal is to "prove" the effect is bigger than some standard (for example, the breakeven value needed to justify the proposed advertising), then the formula becomes

$$n = \frac{(z_\alpha)^2 (s)^2}{(\text{Average measured effect} - \text{Standard})^2}$$

In the previous example, if an effect size of .01 is needed to justify the advertising, then

$$n = \frac{(1.96)^2 (.10)^2}{(.02 - .01)^2} = 384.16 \Rightarrow 385$$

Percents   Assume we wish to estimate the percent of our accounts who also buy from a major competitor. If we take a sample of our accounts and calculate the percent of them who also buy from the competitor (p), the percent is approximately normally distributed. The percent of our accounts who buy from the competitor can be estimated by a confidence interval:

$$p \pm z_\alpha \sqrt{\frac{p(100 - p)}{n}}$$

For example, assume we sample 400 of our 30,000 accounts and find that 32 percent also buy from our competitor. The 95 percent confidence interval for the percent of all our accounts who buy from the competitor is given by

$$\text{Range of true percent} = \text{Sample percent} \pm z_\alpha \sqrt{\frac{p(100 - p)}{n}}$$

$$= 32 \pm 1.96 \sqrt{\frac{(32)(68)}{400}}$$

$$= 32 \pm 4.6$$

So, the range is from 27.4 percent to 36.6 percent.

As in the case of the mean, this formula can be modified to estimate the necessary sample size in advance. In this case, the required sample size can be derived from the following:

$$n = \frac{z_\alpha^2 p(100 - p)}{(\text{Tolerance})^2} \tag{9.2}$$

Assuming we wanted to be accurate within 3 percent at the 95 percent confidence interval, this reduces to

$$n = \frac{(1.96)^2 p(100 - p)}{3^2}$$

If we have a prior notion of p, we then proceed to plug it in. If, for example, we thought p were about 10 percent, then we would get

$$n = \frac{(1.96)^2 (10)(90)}{3^2}$$

Therefore,

$$n = 384.16 \Rightarrow 385$$

Alternatively, we could adopt the "conservative" procedure and assume p were 50 percent. (This produces the maximum sample size needed for a given tolerance. Actually, any p between .3 and .7 produces fairly similar results.) In this case, we would obtain

$$n = \frac{(1.96)^2 (50)(50)}{3^2}$$

Therefore,

$$n = 1,067.1 \Rightarrow 1,068$$

Notice that this result produces the "magic" sample size of between 1,000 and 1,500, which is characteristic of most national samples. In fact, this size national sample is chosen with just such notions of precision in mind.

Finite Population Correction   The previous procedures apply when the target population is essentially infinite. This is the case for most consumer goods studies. When the sample gets large in relation to the target population (over 10 percent of its size), however, these formulas will overestimate the required sample. (If the size of the target population is only 5, then clearly at most we need a sample of size 5, which would actually be a census.) The correction factor accounts for the fact that when the sample size n approaches the population size N, the uncertainty about the population average drops to zero. This converts the formula for sample size when you were interested in measuring an average to

$$n' = \frac{z_\alpha^2 s^2}{(\text{Tolerance})^2} \left(\frac{N - n'}{N - 1} \right) \tag{9.3}$$

Notice in Equation (9.3) that if N is much larger than n', then the $(N - n')/(N - 1)$ term approaches 1 and in effect drops out of the formula, leaving us with Equation (9.1). You may have also noticed that the desired sample size n' now appears on both sides of the equation. The formula to solve for n' now becomes

$$n' = \frac{\dfrac{z_\alpha^2 s^2}{(\text{Tolerance})^2}}{1 + \dfrac{1}{N} \left(\dfrac{z_\alpha^2 s^2}{(\text{Tolerance})^2} - 1 \right)} \tag{9.4}$$

Alternatively, you can compute n without the correction factor using (9.1) and then convert to the (smaller) required number n' by

$$n' = n \left(\frac{N}{N + n - 1} \right)$$

Again, however, unless the sample size is a substantial portion of the population (e.g., above 10 percent), the more complex formula makes only a minor adjustment in the suggested sample size and, hence, is typically not used.

Planning for Subsamples   In many if not most studies, a major purpose is to compare various subgroups of the population (e.g., users of our product with users of competitive products). All the formulas for sample size given previously deal with precision at the aggregate level. Hence, while a sample of 1,000 to 1,500 will produce an estimate of a percent within 2 to 3 percentage points of a true value at the aggregate level, it will be much less accurate at the subgroup level. For example, assume there are nine groups in the population. Even if the groups are equal in size (which they rarely are), this leaves only about 150 responses per group, and consequently the 95 percent confidence interval for the fraction close to 50 percent in a subgroup is about ±8 percent (e.g., 42 percent to 58 percent).

A sampling plan for studying mustard consumption might consider the following segments:

Family Size	Income		
	Under $20,000	$20,000–$50,000	Over $50,000
1–2			
3–4			
5 or more			

To accurately represent mustard consumption in each of the nine segments would require nine times as many observations as to represent mustard consumption in general. Since the costs of increasing a sample size ninefold are usually prohibitive, samples are generally allocated on a number affordable/number of segments basis. While this is reasonable, it is important to recognize that the ability to profile each of the segments is fairly weak. Put differently, it is desirable to have at least 50 to 100 observations per segment.

One useful approach for dealing with subgroups is to see whether they are, in fact, different. If certain groups are not different either importantly (e.g., average behavior is quite similar) or statistically, then the groups may be combined.

Credibility

Since the purpose of gathering data is to provide information someone else will use, it is important to have a credible sample size. Statistical issues aside, 100 is a sine qua non and 1,000 a magic cutoff among many users of research. Since marketing research is part marketing, a wise researcher takes this into account.

Company Policy (Generally Accepted Practice)

Many companies develop a sampling pattern over time that becomes a standard operating procedure. For example, for a new product 200 interviews are gathered in the Albany area during test marketing. While these policies (written or unwritten) usually have a logical basis, a different sample size may be better. Unless the sample is woefully inadequate, however, attempts to change the policy may prove more quixotic than useful (not to mention politically unwise, since your boss may have established the precedent).

Financial Constraints

When all the scientific talk subsides, someone always asks how much money is available for the study. If this is known, the easiest way to calculate the sample size is to take the budget (*SP*), subtract the fixed costs of the study (*EN*) plus any dinners, trips, or expenses we can charge to it (*D*) and then divide by the variable cost of a sample point or interview (*IT*). This leads to the very scientific formula:

$$n = \frac{SP - EN - D}{IT}$$

This formula is, in reality, every bit as important in determining sample size as those relating to the statistical precision of the results.

SELECTION OF SAMPLE POINTS: PROBABILITY SAMPLES

In deciding who to sample, one can turn to the supplier or to a firm that specializes in sampling, such as Survey Sampling, Inc. However, even if outside help is used, one should have some basic concept of the choices and issues involved. In deciding who to sample, the first step often is to see if some list or other organized breakdown (e.g., geographic) of the target population exists. If not, location sampling or random digit dialing are probably the only alternatives. In this section, we assume some list is available when it is required by the sampling procedure.

One commonly drawn distinction is between probability and nonprobability samples. In probability samples, each member of the target population has a fixed (often equal) probability of being a member of the target sample. Some of the major probability sampling approaches include simple random sampling, *n*th name (systematic) sampling, stratified sampling, universal sampling (census), cluster sampling, and replicated and sequential sampling. Nonprobability samples include convenience, quota, and snowball samples.

Simple Random Sampling

The best known and most "democratic" form of selecting a sample is random. This method gives every individual observation in the target population an equal chance of being drawn. This is commonly done by using a random number table to generate *n* (the desired number to sample) random numbers between 1 and the number of names on the list. The observations with numbers corresponding to the random numbers then become the target sample. This method is equivalent to a lottery where names are placed in a hat and drawn out randomly.

Random samples have many nice properties. They are not, however, the most efficient (either logically or in a statistical estimation sense) procedure for many situations. For example, a random sample of 20 could contain all smokers, with the resulting average opinions about the dangers of cigarettes seriously distorted. While such inhospitable results are relatively rare, they do occur (especially in small samples). For that reason, some of the subsequent procedures that guarantee the correct proportion of smokers and nonsmokers are sometimes more efficient in representing the target population (i.e., they get a closer estimate of the true population value for a given

TABLE 9.1   Data on the 50 States

	Inc.	Pop.	Popch.	Urb.	Tax	South	Govt.	Col.	Min.	For.	Mfg.	Farm
1. Alabama	4.6	3.6	0.9	62	383	1	236	136	765	21.8	5.8	1,384
2. Alaska	8.8	0.4	2.9	44	611	0	41	14	448	119.1	0.2	5
3. Arizona	5.3	2.2	4.3	74	582	0	155	132	1,562	18.6	2.4	1,232
4. Arkansas	4.4	2.1	1.8	38	384	1	120	56	407	18.3	3.2	2,547
5. California	6.6	21.2	1.1	93	762	0	1,549	1,312	2,797	42.4	30.7	8,212
6. Colorado	5.8	2.5	2.6	81	587	0	206	130	750	22.5	2.7	2,051
7. Connecticut	6.9	3.1	0.4	89	689	0	171	150	35	2.2	7.9	200
8. Delaware	6.8	0.6	1.1	68	679	0	40	29	5	0.4	1.4	257
9. Florida	5.5	8.4	4.0	84	520	1	511	277	1,044	17.9	6.5	2,029
10. Georgia	5.0	4.9	1.4	57	477	1	352	152	363	25.5	8.6	2,225
11. Hawaii	6.4	0.9	2.2	81	765	0	73	37	42	2.0	0.5	226
12. Idaho	5.0	0.8	2.7	17	479	0	59	34	209	21.6	1.0	1,425
13. Illinois	6.8	11.1	0.1	81	699	0	699	468	1,149	3.8	29.4	6,256
14. Indiana	5.6	5.3	0.4	66	547	0	314	199	441	3.9	16.4	3,250
15. Iowa	5.9	2.9	0.3	37	590	0	186	104	177	2.5	5.6	7,698
16. Kansas	6.0	2.3	0.2	43	573	0	169	111	889	1.3	3.4	4,362
17. Kentucky	4.7	3.4	1.0	47	441	1	197	108	2,563	12.0	6.5	1,587
18. Louisiana	4.7	3.8	0.8	63	496	1	243	141	8,147	15.4	4.8	1,258
19. Maine	4.8	1.1	1.2	24	597	0	68	34	36	17.7	1.6	466
20. Maryland	6.4	4.1	0.8	85	674	1	279	167	173	3.0	5.3	620
21. Massachusetts	6.2	5.8	0.5	87	767	0	377	343	62	3.5	11.7	195
22. Michigan	6.2	9.2	0.6	82	679	0	612	383	1,040	19.3	27.2	1,691
23. Minnesota	5.8	3.9	0.6	63	696	0	263	165	1,026	19.0	6.7	4,754
24. Mississippi	4.0	2.3	1.1	26	425	1	151	78	391	16.9	3.5	1,614
25. Missouri	5.4	4.8	0.3	64	501	0	310	192	691	14.9	9.1	2,849
26. Montana	5.4	0.7	1.4	24	587	0	60	28	575	22.8	0.5	1,154
27. Nebraska	6.2	1.5	0.8	44	543	0	123	64	99	1.0	2.0	4,028
28. Nevada	6.5	0.6	3.7	80	738	0	44	20	258	7.7	0.2	141
29. New Hampshire	5.2	0.8	2.0	36	483	0	55	32	14	5.1	1.5	74
30. New Jersey	6.6	7.3	0.4	93	683	0	453	263	141	2.5	17.8	342
31. New Mexico	4.5	1.1	2.3	34	484	0	97	50	1,942	18.3	0.4	733
32. New York	6.6	18.1	−0.1	89	952	0	1,320	962	441	17.4	33.6	1,525

sample size). In spite of this, however, *random* is a word close to motherhood and apple pie in the ears of many laypersons. One reason for this is that most of the statistical formulas used assume a random sample was taken. For that reason, random samples are often taken (or other sampling plans described as random) to gain credibility for the study. In fact, some researchers have been known to keep drawing random samples until the sample drawn looks good in terms of its characteristics. The resulting sample, however, is obviously neither very efficient in a practical sense nor truly random in a statistical sense.

TABLE 9.1 *(continued)*

	Inc.	Pop.	Popch.	Urb.	Tax	South	Govt.	Col.	Min.	For.	Mfg.	Farm
33. North Carolina	4.8	5.5	1.3	45	461	1	311	182	156	20.6	12.6	2,575
34. North Dakota	5.9	0.6	0.5	12	517	0	60	26	159	0.4	0.3	2,417
35. Ohio	5.9	10.8	0.2	80	497	0	632	370	1,108	6.5	31.2	2,668
36. Oklahoma	5.0	2.7	1.1	56	428	1	206	128	2,124	9.3	2.6	1,994
37. Oregon	5.6	2.3	1.7	61	570	0	173	110	104	30.4	4.3	1,119
38. Pennsylvania	5.9	11.8	0.0	81	615	0	687	423	2,375	17.8	26.8	1,500
39. Rhode Island	5.9	0.9	−0.5	91	606	0	60	59	6	0.4	1.9	25
40. South Carolina	4.5	2.8	1.6	48	422	1	182	110	105	12.5	5.9	907
41. South Dakota	5.0	0.7	0.5	14	519	0	54	27	103	1.7	0.4	1,937
42. Tennessee	4.8	4.2	1.2	63	424	1	265	164	396	13.1	8.8	1,134
43. Texas	5.4	12.2	1.7	78	467	1	779	507	9,999	24.1	17.7	5,968
44. Utah	4.8	1.2	2.5	79	472	0	111	75	952	15.3	1.2	330
45. Vermont	4.9	0.5	1.1	00	661	0	36	28	35	4.4	0.7	218
46. Virginia	5.7	5.0	1.3	66	510	1	352	205	1,058	16.4	6.9	1,031
47. Washington	6.2	3.5	0.7	71	622	0	273	164	144	23.1	5.7	1,766
48. West Virginia	4.8	1.8	0.6	37	450	1	108	67	2,403	12.2	2.9	153
49. Wisconsin	5.6	4.6	0.8	60	696	0	291	180	115	14.9	10.8	2,552
50. Wyoming	5.9	0.4	2.3	00	590	0	33	18	1,437	10.1	0.2	360
Average	5.6	4.2	1.2	58	572	0.3	283	184	1,029	15.1	8.1	1,901

Key to variable names:

Inc.: Average personal income in thousands.

Pop.: Population in millions.

Popch.: Percent change in population over the last 5 years.

Urb.: Percent of population living in metropolitan areas.

Tax: State and local taxes per capita.

South: 1 if yes, 0 if no.

Govt.: Government employees in thousands.

Col.: College enrollment in thousands.

Min.: Mineral production in millions of dollars.

For.: Forest acreage in millions.

Mfg.: Value added by manufacturers in billions of dollars.

Farm: Farm cash receipts in millions of dollars.

Source: Statistical Abstract of the U.S., 1974.

Consider the data presented in Table 9.1, which represent the 50 states in the United States, with data drawn mainly from the 1974 *Statistical Abstract of the United States*. (The interested reader will note these figures are no longer accurate; but since they are used in later examples, they are retained so the author doesn't have to redo all his calculations. The figures also are interesting in that they are about one generation old.) To draw a random sample of the states, we could use the first two columns of Appendix A. If the number is 00 or 01, we will choose Alabama, if the number is 02 or 03, Alaska, and so forth. The random numbers and the states selected along with their income and population data were as follows:

Set	Random Number	State	Income	Population
1	56	New Hampshire	5.2	0.8
	83	Tennessee	4.8	4.2
	55	Nevada	6.5	0.6
	47	Mississippi	4.0	2.3
	84	Texas	5.4	12.2
2	08	California	6.6	21.2
	36	Maine	4.8	1.1
	05	Arizona	5.3	2.2
	26	Indiana	5.6	5.3
	42	Michigan	6.2	9.2
3	95	West Virginia	4.8	1.8
	95	(West Virginia)		
	66	North Dakota	5.9	0.6
	17	Florida	5.5	8.4
	03	Alaska	8.8	0.4
	21	Hawaii	6.4	0.9

Notice that, in some sense, even the sample of size 15 does not represent the United States well since *none* of the major northeastern states (New York, Pennsylvania, Connecticut, Massachusetts) are included. Breaking the sample into three sets of five states makes this difference even more noticeable, with set 3 (West Virginia, North Dakota, Florida, Alaska, and Hawaii) especially suspect. In terms of average income and population, the three sets of five differ noticeably both among themselves and from the U.S. average:

	Average Income	Average Population
Set 1	5.18	4.02
Set 2	5.70	7.80
Set 3	6.28	2.42
15 states	5.72	4.75
50 states	5.62	4.24

The major differences occur in population due to its relatively greater variability across the states. The point is that while, *on average*, random samples will represent a population well, particular random samples and especially small random samples may not represent the general population well at all.

*n*th Name (Systematic) Sampling

An *n*th name sample is an easy way to get a quasi-random sample. The procedure generates target sample points by picking an arbitrary starting point and then picking every *n*th name in succession from a list. For example, if I wished to draw a target sample of 30 from a target population of 1,200, I might arbitrarily select the 11th individual (a number between 1 and 40) as a starting point and then individuals 51, 91, 131, ... , 1,171 as my 30 target sample points.

The major problem with nth name procedures occurs if there is a cycle in the data that is related to the interval between respondents. Especially obvious would be an nth name sample of daily sales of a particular store. If I took a seventh name sample, I would hit the same day of the week every time. If the day were Sunday and blue laws closed the store on Sundays, this would be especially unfortunate. While such cycles are obvious, occasionally a more subtle relation does appear. Assuming no cyclical problems, however, nth name samples turn out to be more efficient (give a more reliable estimate of some variable) than random samples when the underlying list used is logically ordered (e.g., from smallest to largest or by geographic area).

The major advantage of nth name sampling is its ease vis-à-vis random sampling. First, a set of random numbers does not have to be generated. Second, these random numbers do not have to be matched with individual respondents. Since some lists contain more than 80 million households, matching is inefficient unless the random numbers are arranged in order, and even then the length of time to scan the data file or tapes and pull off the names and addresses or phone numbers of the designated individuals is longer than in an nth name sample. For this reason, most consumer mail surveys are based on nth name designs.

Returning to the example of the 50 states, one nth name sample is states 2, 12, 22, 32, and 42, which turn out to be Alaska, Idaho, Michigan, New York, and Tennessee. While not a perfect sample, it seems to be as useful as any of the three pure random samples in the previous section.

Stratified Sampling

For many studies, the target population can be divided into segments with different characteristics. In this case, the information about the segments (strata) can be used to design the sampling plan. Specifically, separate sampling plans can be drawn for each stratum (segment). This guarantees that each stratum will be adequately represented, something that random sampling does not ensure.

In the example involving states, we might classify states into "big industrial" versus "other" strata. Then drawing randomly from each stratum, we could guarantee representation of each type, something random set 3 failed to provide.

Assuming different samples are drawn from each of k strata, the mean and standard deviation of a variable in the entire target population can then be estimated as follows:

Let N_i = size of the ith stratum

n_i = sample size in the ith stratum

N = size of the total target population

n = total sample size

w_i = weight of the estimate of the ith stratum = N_i/N

k = number of strata

s_i = standard deviation in the ith stratum

$\bar{x}_i$ = mean in the ith stratum

Then

$$\bar{x} = \sum_{i=1}^{k} w_i \bar{x}_i \tag{9.5}$$

and

$$s_{\bar{x}} = \sqrt{\sum_{i=1}^{k} w_i^2 s_{\bar{x}_i}^2} = \sqrt{\sum_{i=1}^{k} w_i^2 \frac{s_i^2}{n_i}} \tag{9.6}$$

Basically (9.5) provides a weighted average of the various strata where the weight represents the size of the strata. For proportions, the formulas become:

$$p = \sum_{i=1}^{k} w_i p_i \tag{9.7}$$

and

$$s_p = \sqrt{\sum_{i=1}^{k} w_i^2 \frac{p_i(1 - p_i)}{n_i}} \tag{9.8}$$

Stratified sampling actually encompasses two approaches: proportionate (where the number sampled in each stratum is proportional to the size of the stratum) and disproportionate (where the number sampled is based on something other than the sample size).

Proportionate Stratified Sampling For proportionate stratified sampling, the sample size of each stratum (n_i) is given by the proportion of the population that falls into that stratum (N_i/N). The formula for the standard deviation of the estimate of the mean (Equation 9.6) can be rewritten as:

$$s_{\bar{x}} = \sqrt{\sum \left(\frac{N_i}{N}\right)^2 \frac{s_i^2}{n_i}}$$

And since $n_i = (N_i/N) \cdot n$

$$s_{\bar{x}} = \sqrt{\frac{\sum w_i s_i^2}{n}} \tag{9.9}$$

Consider the hypothetical situation (Table 9.2) where beer consumers were divided into four segments (strata) based on demographics. A proportionate sample would be drawn with sample size in each stratum proportional to the size of the sample:

$$n_i = \frac{N_i}{N} \cdot n$$

TABLE 9.2 An Example of Proportionate Stratified Sampling

Stratum	Size of Stratum	Stratum Sample Size $= \dfrac{N_i}{N} \cdot n$	Average Beer Consumption	Standard Deviation of Beer Consumption
1	8,000	80	20	4
2	6,000	60	10	4
3	4,000	40	15	5
4	2,000	20	6	2
	20,000	200		

Hence, a proportionate sample of size 200 would consist of 80, 60, 40, and 20 people, respectively, from the four strata.

Now assume a proportionate sample of 200 were drawn from the target population and the results in Table 9.2 were obtained. Thus, my estimate of overall average beer consumption would be:

$$\bar{x} = .4(20) + (.30)(10) + (.2)(15) + (.1)(6)$$
$$= 8 + 3 + 3 + .6$$
$$= 14.6$$

Similarly, using the general formula (9.6):

$$s_{\bar{x}} = \sqrt{(.4)^2 \frac{4^2}{80} + (.3)^2 \frac{4^2}{60} + (.2)^2 \frac{5^2}{40} + (.1)^2 \frac{2^2}{20}}$$
$$= \sqrt{.032 + .024 + .025 + .002}$$
$$= \sqrt{.083} = .288$$

Alternatively, the shortcut formula (9.9) gives

$$s_{\bar{x}} = \sqrt{\frac{.4(4)^2 + .3(4)^2 + .2(5)^2 + .1(2)^2}{200}}$$
$$= \sqrt{\frac{6.4 + 4.8 + 5.0 + .4}{200}}$$
$$= .288$$

Disproportionate Stratified Sampling The reasons for disproportionate sampling are multiple. One obvious reason is that certain segments of the population may be considered key for marketing strategy, and a researcher will want a relatively large number of sample points in these segments, while at the same time other strata may be sufficiently important that they cannot be totally ignored. Another reason for disproportionate sampling is that the costs of sampling across strata may be quite different. Therefore, a fixed budget dictates both logically and statistically that a relatively large proportion of the sample be drawn from the relatively cheap-to-question strata.

There also is a statistical reason for sampling disproportionately. If the goal is to produce the most reliable estimate possible, the optimal sample size drawn from each stratum depends on both the size of the stratum and the variance within the stratum. Taking an extreme example, assume one segment has a standard deviation of 4 and another a standard deviation of 0. Here, a single observation from the second stratum will produce all the information available from the stratum (the mean) and all other sample points in this stratum will be redundant. In this case, all of the sample except one should be drawn from the first segment if the goal is to produce the minimum variance (most reliable) estimate of the overall mean. (Notice that it is the uncertainty/standard deviation and not the mean that determines sample allocation.)

The formula for optimal sampling to minimize total variance of the estimate of an average is:

$$n_i = \frac{w_i s_i}{\sum\limits_{i=1}^{k} w_i s_i} \cdot n \tag{9.10}$$

and the resulting standard error of the mean is:

$$s_{\bar{x}} = \sqrt{\frac{\left(\sum\limits_{i=1}^{k} w_i s_i\right)^2}{n}} \tag{9.11}$$

(The interested reader can prove this is a special case of the general formula in (9.6).)

Returning to our beer (example, that is), we can find the optimal sample allocations as follows:

$$n_1 = \frac{.4(4)}{.4(4) + .3(4) + .2(5) + .1(2)} \cdot 200$$

$$= \frac{1.6}{4.0} \cdot 200$$

$$= 80$$

Similarly,

$$n_2 = 60$$
$$n_3 = 50$$
$$n_4 = 10$$

It is important to notice that this procedure requires knowing the standard deviations in each stratum in advance. Since the true standard deviations are never known, we substitute either subjective estimates of the sample or the results of a prior study.

Assuming we now proceeded to take another survey of size 200 according to the disproportionate approach, the results might be as follows:

Strata Size	Size of Sample	Mean	Standard Deviation
8,000	80	20	4
6,000	60	10	4
4,000	50	15	5
2,000	10	6	2

The estimate for average beer consumption would then be, as before,

$$\bar{x} = .4(20) + .3(10) + .2(15) + .1(6)$$
$$= 14.6$$

The standard deviation would be

$$s_{\bar{x}} = \sqrt{\frac{[.4(4) + .3(4) + .2(5) + .1(2)]^2}{200}}$$

$$= \sqrt{\frac{4^2}{200}} = \sqrt{.08}$$

$$= .283$$

In this case, the standard deviation is only slightly (less than 2 percent) smaller under the disproportionate sampling plan, a surprisingly typical result. In fact, unless the standard deviations of the strata are very different, disproportionate sampling does very little to the variance estimate. For example, if 50 were sampled from each of the four strata, the standard deviation of the mean would be (assuming the estimates of the mean and standard deviations were unchanged)

$$s_{\bar{x}} = \sqrt{(.4)^2 \frac{4^2}{50} + (.3)^2 \frac{4^2}{50} + (.2)^2 \frac{5^2}{50} + (.1)^2 \frac{2^2}{50}}$$

$$= \sqrt{\frac{5.04}{50}} = \sqrt{.1008}$$

$$= .317$$

The point, therefore, is that for most marketing surveys, sampling disproportionately to get the most reliable estimates is not very useful. Since it is both troublesome and a source of headaches for certain types of analysis, such "scientific" sampling is rarely employed purely to reduce overall variance in estimates. The major reason for using a stratified sample, therefore, is to ensure adequate representation of key subgroups of the target population.

Stratified samples often are applied to situations where more than one variable serves as a basis for stratification. For example, I might be interested in a consumer product that appealed primarily to middle-aged, high-income consumers. Given a budget that allowed for a sample of 2,000, a stratified sampling plan might look like Table 9.3.

If one were interested in estimating percents via a stratified sample, then the equivalent to formula (9.10) would be found by replacing s_i with $p_i(1 - p_i)$. Notice here you would tend to allocate sample points to strata with the most uncertainty about the percents, those with p's close to 50 percent.

Often, we are more interested in estimating the total market than in estimating market share. In such cases, one often estimates the average consumption in various strata and then estimates total consumption as the sum over strata of the number of members in each stratum times the estimated average consumption in each stratum:

$$\text{Total market} = \sum_{\substack{\text{all} \\ \text{strata}}} (\text{Number of members in stratum}) \cdot (\text{Average in stratum}) \qquad (9.12)$$

The estimated standard deviation for the total market is then (assuming the number in each stratum is known)

$$\text{Standard deviation of total market} = N s_{\bar{x}} \qquad (9.13)$$

As mentioned before, these formulas are only usable if good estimates of standard deviations are available. In attempting to estimate standard deviations subjectively prior to data collection, one can take advantage of the fact that the standard deviations often are proportional to the mean. Since most managers feel more comfortable (and are better at) estimating means than standard deviations, it is possible to get subjective estimates of the means and then to use the means in place of the standard deviations in the formulas for optimal sample allocation in stratified sampling. Alternatively, one can ask for an estimate of the range of values in a stratum and (assuming the item being measured is distributed similarly in each stratum) use the range in place of the standard deviation to allocate sample points.

Pragmatically, however, these formulas often give unappealing results (e.g., sampling only three in some strata). Since an implicit goal in most research is to estimate within strata as well as for the population as a whole, the numbers tend to be adjusted anyway. Consequently, a reasonable approach is to assign more sample points to strata that (a) have more members, (b) are likely to have a larger average amount of the behavior of interest, and (c) where you are less sure what the answer is, while still guaranteeing a "reasonable" sample size in each stratum (e.g., Table 9.3). While doing this

TABLE 9.3   Stratified Sampling Plan

Income Level	Age Group		
	Under 30	30–50	51 and Over
Under $20,000	50	50	50
$20,000–$29,999	50	200	100
$30,000–$49,999	100	400	100
$50,000 and over	200	500	200
			2,000

subjectively does not guarantee a plan that is optimal statistically, it tends to produce a pretty good plan in terms of statistical efficiency. More important, the plan tends to be seen as more reasonable by users of the research.

Universal Sampling (Census)

In most consumer surveys, it is obviously overly expensive to survey all possible customers. In industrial surveys, on the other hand, there may be only 30 to 40 important customers. In these situations, sampling all the important customers is both logically and statistically desirable. It is important to note, however, that a true census is almost never obtained, as the uproar over the court challenges to the U.S. Census suggests.

Cluster Sampling

Cluster samples are exactly what the name implies, samples gathered in clusters. The basic motivation for cluster sampling is cost reduction. In the case of personal interviews, giving each interviewer a series of addresses leads to a large amount of travel time, even when an elaborate scheduling mechanism is employed. To cut this travel time (or to draw a sample when no list is available), a common approach is to draw samples in clusters. This means that areas (e.g., blocks), are selected and then interviewers are instructed to get several interviews from the same block. This type of cluster sampling is commonly known as *area sampling*. Cluster samples can also be drawn from lists. An example of this is sampling people whose names begin with a set of randomly selected letters.

Returning to the 50 states example, we could first choose five states in which to sample (e.g., Alaska, Idaho, Michigan, New York, and Tennessee). We could then proceed to choose sample points within each of the states by either taking a census (which would lead some to call this a one-stage cluster sample) or select respondents within each state based on any of the methods discussed here, such as random, nth name or convenience, (called a *two-stage cluster sample*). We could also choose a second level of cluster within each of the first-level clusters (e.g., counties within states) and then proceed. In fact, many cluster sampling plans have several stages, such as:

1. Pick states.
2. Pick counties or MSAs within states.
3. Pick census tracts, block groups, or ZIP codes within counties or MSAs.
4. Choose respondents randomly within census tract, etc.

Notice that cluster samples differ from stratified samples: in cluster sampling, many/most of the strata (e.g., states) are left out of the sampling plan. However, it is quite common to select clusters and then use stratified sampling (e.g., based on income) within each cluster.

Replicated and Sequential Sampling

The sampling plans discussed to this point all assume a single sample is taken. Two alternative approaches are possible.

One is to take several smaller samples simultaneously. Such replicated samples (e.g., 10 samples of 100) have some advantages over a single sample of equal size. They are, however, rarely used in marketing research.

The other alternative sampling approach is sequential. In this method, a small sample is drawn and the results analyzed. If the results are sufficiently clear, a decision is made and the rest of the sample is not drawn. If not, another sample is drawn subsequently. For example, if an initial sample of 100 produces an average response rate of 22 percent to a direct mail solicitation that has a break-even rate of 3 percent, it makes sense to do a mass mailing rather than test further. Sequential sampling offers potential economy by possibly reducing sample size. (Some of this economy is lost if economies of scale exist in data collection.) On the other hand, this approach takes longer than a one-shot study. Given the time pressure and fear of competitive reaction most market researchers face, sequential sampling is mainly employed when feedback from an initial sample is used to modify the study (as in the case of product concept testing).

Nonprobability Sampling

Nonprobability sampling procedures are generally used when probability samples are expensive or inefficient (i.e., when the target population is very small and there is no list or easy way to reach them). They involve researcher judgment that the sample is in fact representative and, hence, have less face credibility. In general, these methods are accepted for exploratory work but less so for descriptive or causal studies. Here, we discuss quota, convenience/location, and snowball methods.

Quota Sampling   A quota sample is based on the preconceived notion that certain individual characteristics must be adequately represented if the sample is to be projectable. It is essentially a compromise between a stratified and a convenience sample. For example, a firm may want the opinions of at least 30 housewives between the ages of 40 and 55. Hence, a quota sample may be generated by having the interviewer collect data from the first 30 women who fall into that category who agree to participate. Such a procedure obviously does not make the quota sample as good as a random sample; but it does guarantee that, in terms of some obvious characteristics, the sample will represent the target population. Whether such a sample is a "good enough" approximation of a more elaborate design is an open question. The fact that quota samples are widely used indicates that, for at least some purposes, some relatively intelligent researchers think they are. One of the major uses of quota samples is in maintaining panels. NPD concentrates on variables that relate to expenditures, including household income, household size, and employment/occupation/education, as well as market area in balancing its panel.

Convenience/Location Sampling   The cheapest form of sample design is referred to as a *convenience sample*. This translates to using any warm body that is available. It is very popular in academic research (remember reading about samples of 56 college sophomores?) but also has a useful place in "real" research. While their projectability is very questionable, convenience samples are extremely useful for hypothesis generation and initial pilot testing of surveys.

A relatively useful form of convenience sample is a central location study, such as a mall intercept survey. These take advantage of central locations where large numbers of the target population arrive (e.g., shopping malls, trade shows, conventions). Shopping mall studies have become a mainstay of consumer research and are second only to phone surveys in usage rate. By balancing respondents based on demographics or other characteristics (typically with a quota system), these produce reasonable samples at a reasonable cost. In comparing mall intercept with phone interview responses, Bush and Hair (1985) found no difference in the completeness of response (e.g., number of brands mentioned) or in lifestyle responses. In contrast, phone respondents tended to report more socially desirable behaviors (newspaper subscription, voting). Refusals to participate were also higher for the phone survey (37.1 vs. 26.5 percent). Not surprisingly, mall respondents tend to visit more stores on a shopping trip. Still, for many purposes, central location sampling is quite useful. (They do not pick up stay-at-homes, however, and hence for such purposes as assessing direct-marketing programs are not very helpful.)

Special Populations: Snowball Methods   In some instances there are very few people/data sources relevant to a study. Examples include both buying center studies in business-to-business marketing and users of specialty products. If a proportion of the general population that falls in a special population is p (e.g., 10 percent), then to get a sample from the special population of size n one can survey n/p people. Thus drawing a random sample from a target population where 1 percent or fewer are relevant is inefficient and a bit irritating.

Sometimes the special population is clustered (e.g., ethnic groups, certain industries). When a population is clustered, it is possible to screen by area, phone exchange, or the like, and then convenience sample where the special population is concentrated (Sudman, 1985). A modified stratified sampling procedure for rare subjects (e.g., business customers who plan to upgrade a phone service) can also be developed (Weerahandi and White, 1992). Sometimes, however, there is no obvious systematic way to locate the desired respondents. Therefore, many procedures rely on finding a few key contacts and then using them to identify other relevant sample points (and so on, until few new members of the population emerge). This can present a nontrivial problem of noncooperation, partly due to suspicions that the names will be used for solicitation rather than research. It also requires that the members of the population know each other. However, the procedure can be far more cost-effective than any other method, especially now when subjects are Internet users who use common bulletin boards or interest groups.

Sources of Sampling Points

Many sample designs require a list of the target population. While this may seem to be a simple requirement, finding a good list is not a trivial task. Lists are notorious for containing outdated information. Given the large fraction of people (and businesses) who move each year, this is partially inevitable. Add in copying mistakes, list inflation (the longer the list, the higher price it commands), duplicate names, and less-than-annual updates, and the portion of usable names on many lists drops to 50 percent.

There are several major sources for consumer lists. Telephone directories are a major but imperfect source. While phone penetration/ownership is 95 percent (ranging from 87.4 percent in Mississippi to 97.9 percent in Massachusetts; Survey Sampling, 1993), unlisted numbers are common and reach 64.6 percent in Las Vegas and 61.7 percent in Los Angeles–Long Beach; Survey Sampling, 1993). Magazine subscriptions form a well-known basis, as do organization membership lists and credit cards. Professional associations are another common source of lists. Lists are available for just about anything, however, including everyone from agricultural agents to zoologists. Lists of industrial concerns are also legion. Often based on trade association memberships, these lists cover almost every imaginable business. Lists are also available for associations, such as PTAs.

A major focal point for such lists is the Direct Marketing Association. A variety of companies compile "lists of lists" (catalogs). SRDS offers more than 55,000 lists of both businesses and consumers. Professional Mailing Lists offered such interesting lists as High School Bowling Coaches ($n = 1,400$) and Wholesale Confectionery Businesses ($n = 4,100$). American Business Lists' 1994 catalog provided lists of 10 million businesses compiled from the Yellow Pages, broken down by six-digit SIC code. Zeller's 1993 catalog offers such exciting lists as Abattoirs and Slaughterhouses, Meat Packers ($n = 4,800$) and a list of 31,947 trial lawyers, all for $50 per 1,000 names.

Several firms have mailing lists of more than 50 million households. In addition to addresses, the most recent census data available are so coded into each household that median income and age of the neighborhood, among other variables, are available as a basis for selectively pulling samples. For example, Burke's CMAS (Custom Market Area Sampling) used a file of 52 million listed telephone residences and drew samples based on geographic and census data at a cost of about 6 cents per mailing label. Reuben H. Donnelley (cousin of R. A. Donnelley of Yellow Pages fame and son of Dun & Bradstreet) maintains a list based on merging telephone books with the auto registration lists of the various states. (States sell these lists to help defray costs of registration.) Not surprisingly, these lists are more widely used for direct-mail solicitation than for research.

Screening Questions

Many interviews begin by screening the respondents. The basis of screening may be visual (e.g., age, make of car, whether they just bought a particular product) or verbal (asking a screening question, such as "Do you smoke?"). Screening questions are used to avoid interviewing individuals not in the target population. Only those subjects who "qualify" are then presented with the full survey. Assuming the objective is to interview respondents with incomes over $40,000, a screening questionnaire is typically used. Such a questionnaire may include two or three general questions as a warm-up to the key income question. In form, the questions used (in phone survey format) might be as follows:

> Hello, my name is J. R. Sincere from the ZYX Market Research Corporation. I would like to ask you a few questions about your opinion of the economy. Would you please help me?
>
> Before we begin, I need to ask you a few questions to help us classify your responses. Your answers are confidential, and will be used only for tabulation purposes.
>
> S1: How old are you?
>
> _____   _____   _____   _____   _____
> under 30   31–40   41–50   51–60   over 60
>
> S2: How many people live in your household? _____

S3: What is your total annual household income?

_____ _____ _____ _____

under 20,000   20,000–39,999   40,000–59,999   60,000 and over

(If the answer to question 3 is 1 or 2, terminate interview. If the answer to question 3 is 3 or 4, continue.)

Screening needs to be carefully thought out. Restricting a sample to those who recently bought a product may produce a sample that is abnormally price sensitive (Kim and Rossi, 1994). Similarly, in an ad recall study, including viewers of an ad who are not interested in the product (nonprospects) can distort measures of the impact of the ad (Wells, 1993).

One way to obtain a sample of purchase data is the purchase intercept technique (McIntyre and Bender, 1986). In this method, subjects were observed making a purchase and then immediately interviewed about their current shopping trip. This allows for data collection when the consumer is most likely to be aware of what he or she bought and why (although for low-involvement goods, recall is pretty limited even 60 seconds after product selection). One study found that only 28 percent of people queried by phone identified the brand bought "most often" as the one that their purchase diaries reported as most often bought (Wind and Lerner, 1979). Hence, using behavior as a screen has some notable advantages.

THE PROBLEM OF NONRESPONSE

Response Bias

Even the best-planned samples of researchers and statisticians generate incomplete data and nonrespondents. A major issue, therefore, is what bias does this nonresponse create? Put differently, how much of the result is attributable to which sample points responded? Obviously, the lower the response rate, the more nervous one tends to become about the representativeness of the sample. While doubling sample size may make the results seem more believable, it does nothing to reduce response bias. Response bias has two major parts: noncoverage and nonresponse.

Noncoverage Most methods of obtaining samples have an inherent noncoverage element. Personal interviews are not useful for surveying people in remote areas due to cost and in areas where door-to-door interviews are banned by local ordinance. Mail questionnaires will not be filled out by illiterates or when the occupant moves. Phone questionnaires can only contact those with phones who don't screen calls with an answering machine.

Nonresponse Nonresponse bias can occur when a target subject cannot be found. In addition to those who are *unable to respond*, there are those people who are *not at home*. A classic example of a question that would be biased by the not-at-home problem is, "What do you do during the evening?" Taking an evening survey would yield a disproportionately high "stay at home" response since those who don't stay at home are nonrespondents. A final category of nonresponse is *refusals*. A person may refuse to participate because of fear for personal safety (would you open the door at night for a stranger with a clipboard?), desire to protect privacy, lack of interest in the subject, time pressure, or a general dislike for marketing research or business. If any of these nonrespondents would have responded differently to the questions asked, the results are biased. In fact, respondents to mail surveys tend to be somewhat more upscale: younger, richer, and better educated than the total population. Similarly, phone surveys initially obtain older, poorer, less-educated, female, rural respondents (Nelson, 1982).

Studies by Walker Research suggest one in three respondents typically refuse to participate in phone surveys. When contacted, a variety of outcomes are possible (Figure 9.2). Given the risk of nonresponse bias, an obvious reaction is to minimize the nonresponse rate. A plethora of devices are used to increase the response rate. To understand how they work, consider the following typology of potential respondents:

1. Happy to respond (15 percent)
2. Willing to be convinced to respond with modest effort (50 percent)
3. Can be bought at a high price (15 percent)
4. No way to make them respond (10 percent)
5. Not even covered by the process (10 percent)

I. Respondent contacted (prescreening)
   A. Refusal (by respondent)
   B. Reject (by interviewer)
   C. Cooperating
      1. Eligible
         a. Completed
         b. Terminate
         c. Refusal
         d. Reject
         e. Not usable
      2. Eligible but over quota
      3. Ineligible
         a. Nonhousehold
         b. Did not pass screening
II. Respondent not contacted
   A. No number available
   B. No answer
   C. Not at home
   D. Household refusal
   E. Disconnected
   F. Busy
   G. Nonworking number
   H. Other

Source: Wiseman and McDonald, 1980, p. 29.

FIGURE 9.2

Possible Outcomes When Attempting to Contact Respondents for Telephone Surveys
Source: Frederick Wiseman and Philip McDonald, 1980, *Toward the Development of Industry Standards for Response and Nonresponse Rates*. Copyright © 1980. Reprinted with permission.

Looking at this typology, we see that category 1 is pretty much guaranteed. (It is possible to destroy even these respondents, however, with an especially arduous and confusing questionnaire or experiment.) On the other hand, people in categories 4 and 5 are practically unattainable. Given limited budgets, category 3 is usually conceded as well. That means the effort is usually placed on category 2 people. It also means that response rates tend to run from a low of 10 to 20 percent to a high of around 80 percent of the population of interest.

Measurement and reporting of response rate is important for interpreting the results of a study. Still, the calculation of response rate is not always simple. Table 9.4 is taken from a filing with the FCC by MCI to establish cellular mobile phone service in Pittsburgh, Pa. Households with incomes above a certain minimum were the target population. Phone interviews were done by random digit dialing and the disposition of those calls used to give a response rate estimate of 57 percent. However, different approaches are also used. Wiseman and McDonald (1980a) surveyed 40 leading marketing and public opinion research firms, leading to 29 different formulas for measuring response rate for a given set of results (Table 9.5). Consequently, one is well advised to see how reported response rates are actually calculated.

Determinants of Response Rate

A variety of factors influence the response rate. The effects of those factors under the control of the researcher have been studied extensively, especially in mail surveys (Kanuk and Berenson, 1975; Linsky, 1975; Houston and Ford, 1976; Yu and Cooper, 1983).

TABLE 9.4 Sample Disposition (Pittsburgh SMSA)

Households:

a. Completed interviews	796
b. Ineligibles	1,490
c. Eligible refusals	63
d. Undetermined refusals	365
e. Eligible callbacks	257
f. Undetermined callbacks	63
g. Language barriers, ill, etc.	21
h. No answer, busy	621

Nonhouseholds:

i. Businesses, institutions, etc.	241
j. Nonworking numbers	1,153
Total	5,070

Incidence of eligible households:

$$P_e = (a + c + e)/(a + c + e + b) = 1,116/2,606 = .428$$

Response rate: $RR = \dfrac{a}{P_e[d + f + (.4)(h)] + a + c + e} = 796/1,405 = .57$

Note: In the response rate formula, .4 is multiplied by the number of households in the no answer/busy category because the experience of previous surveys has shown that, on the average, only 40 percent of the no answer/busy numbers are actually households.

TABLE 9.5 Response Rate Calculations

The data in these tables are based on the following example, which appeared in the questionnaire with the requests indicated.

For the survey outcomes described below, please indicate the numbers that you would include in the numerator and denominator when calculating response, contact, and completion rate.

Source of Sample: Telephone Directories

Category	Frequency
Total numbers dialed	4,175
Disconnected/nonworking number	426
No answer, busy, not at home	1,757
Interviewer reject (language barrier, hard of hearing, etc.)	187
Household refusal	153
Respondent refusal	711
Ineligible respondent	366
Termination by respondent	74
Completed interviews	501

A: Response Rate Calculations for Telephone-Directory Sample

Most frequently used definitions	Value	Freq.
$\dfrac{\text{Household refusals} + \text{Rejects} + \text{Ineligibles} + \text{Terminations} + \text{Refusals} + \text{Completed interviews}}{\text{Total numbers dialed}}$	48%	3
$\dfrac{\text{Rejects} + \text{Ineligibles} + \text{Terminations} + \text{Refusals} + \text{Completed interviews}}{\text{Total numbers dialed}}$	44%	3
$\dfrac{\text{Completed Interviews}}{\text{Total numbers dialed}}$	12%	3

Sample statistics:

Mean	35%
Median	30%
Minimum	12%
Maximum	90%
Standard deviation	19
Number of different definitions reported	29

B: Contact Rate Calculations for Telephone-Directory Sample

Most frequently used definitions	Value	Freq.
$\dfrac{\text{Household refusals} + \text{Rejects} + \text{Ineligibles} + \text{Terminations} + \text{Refusals} + \text{Completed interviews}}{\text{Total numbers dialed}}$	48%	20
$\dfrac{\text{Rejects} + \text{Ineligibles} + \text{Terminations} + \text{Refusals} + \text{Completed interviews}}{\text{Total numbers dialed}}$	44%	11

(continued)

TABLE 9.5 *(continued)*

$\dfrac{\text{Household refusals + Rejects + Ineligibles +}}{\text{Terminations + Refusals + Completed interviews}}$		
Total numbers dialed − (Disconnected/nonworking)	53%	7

Sample statistics:

Mean	46%
Median	48%
Minimum	23%
Maximum	53%
Standard deviation	6
Number of different definitions reported	12

C: Completion Rate Calculations for Telephone-Directory Sample

Most frequently used definitions	Value	Freq.
$\dfrac{\text{Completed interviews}}{\text{Total numbers dialed}}$	12	13
$\dfrac{\text{Completed interviews}}{\text{Household refusals + Rejects + Ineligibles + Terminations + Refusals + Completed interviews}}$	25%	11
$\dfrac{\text{Completed interviews}}{\text{Rejects + Ineligibles + Terminations + Refusals + Completed interviews}}$	27%	7

Sample statistics:

Mean	22%
Median	25%
Minimum	12%
Maximum	61%
Standard deviation	10
Number of different definitions reported	13

Note: A comparison of the most frequently used definitions given in A and B for response and contact rate illustrates the confusion that exists among practitioners with these two terms. The first two definitions listed in both examples are identical. In a survey, the response rate should always be less than or equal to the contact rate, because the former rate takes into account refusals and terminations as well as those not contacted.

Source: Frederick Wiseman and Philip McDonald, "Movement Begins Toward Much Needed Response Rate Standards," *Marketing News* 13 (January 11, 1980): 4. Copyright © 1980 by the American Marketing Association. Reprinted with the permission of the publishers.

These factors include interest, length, opening, incentives/bribery, format, advance notice, and callback/follow-up.

Interest The greater the interest, the lower the portion of nonrespondents. In fact, interest is probably the major determinant of response rate. Unfortunately, interest is largely inherent in the topic (most people would rather answer a questionnaire about food or sports than about caskets). Nonetheless, tedious surveys dampen enthusiasm, and clever design (use of white space, pictures, etc.) may increase interest.

Length The longer the interview, questionnaire, or experiment appears to be, the less likely someone is to begin it. Also, the longer it takes to complete, the greater chance that the respondent will either terminate the survey or leave large numbers of questions unanswered. (These partial nonresponses pose a particularly difficult problem for complex forms of data analysis, such as regression analysis.) Length also noticeably increases fatigue and decreases the quality of response. While an amazing number of questions can be asked, typically a small number will suffice. While response rates drop off fairly sharply for more than a minimal 1-page survey, they are remarkably constant for 8- to 20-page questionnaires. The cost of length, then, includes both lower response quality and lower response rate.

Opening   The opening, which invites the individual to participate, is very important. Aside from the appearance of the interviewer or questionnaire (or the sound of the interviewer's voice in the case of phone interviews), the first two or three sentences must grab the prospective respondent (or in the case of an executive, the executive's assistant or secretary) much like the beginning of an ad. Appeals of many types are useful, including mercy ("I'm a poor college student . . ."), self-interest ("your opinion will count"), or duty ("you should express your views"). Guarantees of anonymity are useful in persuading reluctant individuals to participate, as are the "right" credentials for the interviewer or survey company. Use of the person's name to get a personal touch tends to increase the response rate, though it has become so common in direct marketing solicitations that it has little effect and may even be viewed suspiciously (e.g., "Dear Bob" letters to someone who calls himself Robert). In mail surveys, better responses are obtained by using a personalized letter, a return envelope with postage paid, and a classy format. Other variables, such as the color of the questionnaire, seem to have little effect.

Incentives/Bribery   The most blatant (and expensive) way to increase sample size is to buy respondents. This is commonly done by a monetary inducement. A recent analysis of past studies suggests on average these increase response rates about 20 percent, whereas nonmonetary incentives increase them 8 percent (Church, 1993). Sometimes this inducement is offered in advance to shame the individual into responding. A typical bribe in mail surveys is to include a small amount of money (the source of my current collection of Susan B. Anthony dollars and Indian Head pennies) when the questionnaire is mailed. This is designed to increase both commitment and response rate, and, even though it is usually a pittance on a per hour basis, it often helps. One problem with bribery is that the respondents may be more likely to give responses they think you want to hear, rather than true answers.

While modest monetary inducements help with some respondents, they do very little for those who can only be bought for a high monetary price. On the other hand, "end around" strategies may prove more successful than monetary rewards. For example, aesthetic appeals (stamps, pictures, etc.) may induce some to participate when money would fail. Similarly, offering to give a small sum to a favorite charity or church is often a successful inducement. In addition, some phenomenal successes have been achieved with gimmick rewards (who could refuse a Mickey Mouse ring or a yo-yo?). In general, however, incentives are not overly effective. In a study involving a survey about durable goods, three versions were sent to groups of 400 each: version 1 had just a cover letter, version 2 some mint coins (monetary), and version 3 some very attractive stamps (aesthetic). Alas, when the results came back, there was essentially no difference in the response rates, and certainly not enough to justify anything except the plain cover letter approach.

Another way to provide an incentive is to indicate that those who participate will be included in a lottery with a prize (e.g., color TV, $500). Lottery inducements seem to be quite useful. Finally, promising to send copies of the results can encourage response, especially in surveys of businesses.

Format   Using adequate white space on a mail survey, breaks in a phone or personal interview, or graphics in a computer survey helps keep the respondent fresh. Essentially, the format must make it easy (both in appearance and in fact) for the respondent to respond.

Advance Notice   To secure cooperation, it is common to give advance notice (by phone, postcard, or letter) of the impending study. This is often useful in increasing both response rate and quality.

Callback/Follow-up   Many individuals in the sample may not be home when the company makes the first attempt to contact a potential respondent. If no subsequent attempt is made to reach the individual, response rates to personal interviewing dip below 50 percent. If, on the other hand, elaborate callback plans involving six to eight callbacks at different times of the day and week (or follow-up plans, in the case of a mail study) are employed, response rates may reach 80 percent. Making two or three callbacks is fairly standard practice.

Overall   In getting a higher response rate, the cost per completed interview usually increases. This higher response rate is obtained not by magic but by work: more follow-ups, and so forth. An obvious question is, "Where does the tradeoff between response rate and cost/sample size occur?" The answer to this depends on the purpose of the study.

If the researcher is interested in studying the process/psychological phenomena on an individual level, biased samples may suffice. (How else could we publish articles based on 149 college sophomores in course X, etc.?) Similarly, the relations among variables as measured by correlations may not be sensitive to modestly biased samples. When a study is interested in estimating levels (e.g., average income), however, nonresponse bias becomes a serious problem. (I would prefer a sample of 500 and a 60 percent response rate to a sample of 800 and a 35 percent response rate *ceteris paribus* for estimating facts and opinions.)

The Problem of Dropouts

In any study where the respondents are contacted repeatedly, a certain percentage drop out between waves. This percentage ranges from less than 5 percent in specially designed panels or experiments to 25 percent in some multiwave phone surveys. Since dropouts are typically different in some way from respondents (at least in terms of interest in the study), this makes subsequent analysis difficult. The two basic approaches to analyzing multiwave data are to use only those individuals who respond to all waves and waste the other responses or use all the responses and run the risk of measuring the differences between people, rather than changes over time.

Weighting to Account for Nonresponse

There are two basic sources of bias in the final sample. The first is noncoverage of the target population by the process, and the second is the nonrespondents being different in some important way from the respondents. The problem is that, to assess the bias, the characteristics of nonrespondents must be known.

One way to treat the nonresponse bias is to logically (subjectively) adjust the results. Consider, for example, a mail survey that attempted to find the number of people who would be interested in buying a new product. There was a 30 percent response rate, and, of the respondents, 40 percent said they would buy the product. One estimate for the percent of the population who would be interested in buying (which, incidentally, would greatly overstate actual buying) would thus be 40 percent. On the other hand, we could assume that the other 70 percent did not return the survey because they were not interested in the product. In that case, the appropriate estimate would be 40 percent × 30 percent = 12 percent. Actually, the number would probably lie somewhere in between 12 and 40 percent, but 12 percent is likely to be a more accurate estimate than 40 percent.

One interesting approach for dealing with a nonresponse problem was developed by Politz and Simmons (1949; Ackoff, 1953). This procedure is designed to estimate results without callbacks and to overcome the not-at-home bias. The procedure accomplishes this by asking respondents to classify themselves in terms of how often they are home (and available to be questioned). Assume, for example, that respondents classified themselves according to three categories: at home 80 percent of the time, 50 percent of the time, and 20 percent of the time. If we call at random, we would expect to get 80 percent of group 1, 50 percent of group 2, and 20 percent of group 3, and hence, overrepresent group 1 respondents. This overrepresentation is corrected by weighting each respondent in the group by the inverse of their likelihood of being home. (That is, weight each group 1 respondent by 1/.8 = 1.25, each group 2 respondent by 1/.5 = 2, and each group 3 respondent by 1/.2 = 5.) This corrects the sample by removing the at-home bias in the original sample. Unfortunately, the accuracy depends on the (somewhat unreliable) self-reported probabilities of being home. While evidence conflicts somewhat, one study (Ward, Russick, and Rudelius, 1985) suggested that the costs of and problems with this weighting method may outweigh its benefits.

Another approach to nonresponse is to do a follow-up study on nonrespondents. Hopefully, nonrespondents reached on the second try will be similar to respondents. If the nonrespondents are different, however, the problem is which result to believe. Consider another example, this one a mail survey of 100,000 which had a 30 percent response rate. A subsequent phone follow-up study of 1,500 initial nonrespondents revealed a pattern of slight differences based on 1,000 respondents (a 67 percent response rate). The weights given to the two samples can vary greatly, depending on whether you think the 1,000 respondents to the follow-up represent (a) the 70 percent of the individuals who did not respond, (b) 67 percent of the 70 percent, or (c) just themselves. Assuming the original 20,000 were given weights of 1 each, the respective weights given to the follow-up respondents would be (a) 70, (b) 46.66, and (c) 1. Since the first alternative essentially means the first study was largely worthless, this is very unappealing. In fact, because of the problems in deciding on appropriate weights and the problems of incorporating unequal weights into subsequent analysis, the nonresponse bias is often ignored. Fortunately, as long as the bias is small, this is an acceptable alternative. Still, the problem of potential nonresponse bias and how to deal with it makes increasing the response rate a very important goal. Assessing the nonresponse bias is good practice in most studies.

Item Nonresponse

A serious problem in many studies is the tendency of certain data to be missing (e.g., some people refuse to fill out income questions). The nonresponse to particular items makes interpretation of results difficult. When item nonresponse is truly random, it poses no major problems. When nonresponse occurs disproportionately in one category (e.g., high income), however, serious problems arise in estimating the population values based on the sample. A more complete discussion of the handling of this problem occurs in Chapter 10, on coding and editing data.

SAMPLE DESIGN EXAMPLES

Random Digit Dialing

Random digit dialing is often done via a computer-controlled probability sampling system. Unfortunately, most numbers are nonworking. One approach is M/A/R/C's TELNO, which is based on a county stratification and uses only working telephone prefixes, increasing "valid" numbers from 35 to 70 percent. A working record of individual numbers called with a three-callback maximum is shown in Table 9.6. A summary of the results of a callback analysis appears in Table 9.7.

The *Literary Digest* Poll

One of the classic examples of an unfortunate choice of sample involved the 1936 U.S. presidential election. Prior to the election, the *Literary Digest*, then among the most prestigious magazines in the country, predicted that Alf Landon would beat Franklin Roosevelt. Since FDR beat Landon in a landslide (for trivia buffs, Landon carried only Maine and Vermont), this prediction seriously damaged the magazine's reputation.

The seeds of the disastrous prediction were sown in the sampling plan. In the first phase, the magazine mailed cards to 10 million subscribers and asked those who would be willing to participate to return the card along with a phone number. About 2.3 million responded. A random sample was then drawn from those who agreed to participate. The problem was that the sample was biased. The popular version of this story suggests the problem was noncoverage based on the assumption that both subscribers to the *Literary Digest* and those who had telephones tended to be Republicans. Another explanation is that those who responded to the initial request were more committed/interested in the election and those who were interested were Republicans (Bryson, 1976). Whichever is true, it is clear that a response bias affected the results. (If you think we have learned from this, try to explain the continued popularity of reader/listener call-in polls.)

The Nutrition Study

The nutrition study previously referred to required that a sample be drawn. Given a budget of $9,000, this made personal interviews too costly to get a "reasonable" sample size (800 to 1,000). On the other hand, phone interviews were deemed inappropriate because of the length of the survey (it takes about 30 minutes to complete). That left, in order to get broad geographic and demographic coverage, mail.

The choice then boiled down to a special mail-out or a mail panel. The mail panel has inherent bias in its makeup. In the case of this study, one would expect panel members to be relatively well-organized and systematic shoppers. A "blind" mail-out,

TABLE 9.6 Callback Analysis

Mon., Mar. 17, 1986, 1:24 p.m.

Shave Cream

Total Numbers in Sample	Total Numbers Finished	Total Numbers Used	Total Interviews Completed	Total Number of Dialings	Average Dialings per Interview
4232	2357	2890	400	4807	12.02

Dialing Summary					
Call Results	First Call	1st Callback	2nd Callback	3rd Callback	4th Callback	Total
---	---	---	---	---	---	---
Completed	251 (8.7)	92 (8.7)	41 (7.0)	16 (5.9)	0 (.0)	400 (8.3)
Busy	66 (2.3)	30 (2.8)	22 (3.8)	15 (5.5)	0 (.0)	133 (2.8)
No answer	1070 (37.0)	597 (56.3)	364 (62.2)	177 (65.1)	0 (.0)	2208 (45.9)
Disconnect	600 (20.8)	34 (3.2)	7 (1.2)	4 (1.5)	0 (.0)	645 (13.4)
Business	116 (4.0)	55 (5.2)	22 (3.8)	6 (2.2)	0 (.0)	199 (4.1)
Resp. not at home	161 (5.6)	87 (8.2)	53 (9.1)	20 (7.4)	0 (.0)	321 (6.7)
No eligible resp.	113 (3.9)	44 (4.2)	21 (3.6)	10 (3.7)	0 (.0)	188 (3.9)
Refusal	394 (13.6)	101 (9.5)	38 (6.5)	18 (6.6)	0 (.0)	551 (11.5)
Terminate	79 (2.7)	11 (1.0)	9 (1.5)	5 (1.8)	0 (.0)	104 (2.2)
Quota filled	0 (0.0)	0 (0.0)	0 (0.0)	0 (0.0)	0 (0.0)	58 (0.0)
Other	40 (1.4)	9 (0.8)	8 (1.4)	1 (0.4)	0 (.0)	58 (1.2)
Total	2890 (100.0)	1060 (100.0)	585 (100.0)	272 (100.0)	0 (.0)	4807 (100.0)

Final Disposition of Calls Summary					
Call Results	First Call	1st Callback	2nd Callback	3rd Callback	4th Callback	Total
---	---	---	---	---	---	---
Completed	251 (13.7)	92 (19.4)	41 (13.1)	16 (5.9)	0 (.0)	400 (13.8)
Busy	10 (0.5)	6 (1.3)	4 (1.3)	15 (5.5)	0 (.0)	35 (1.2)
No answer	192 (10.5)	93 (19.6)	149 (47.6)	177 (65.1)	0 (.0)	611 (21.1)
Disconnect	600 (32.8)	34 (7.2)	7 (2.2)	4 (1.5)	0 (.0)	645 (22.3)
Business	116 (6.3)	55 (11.6)	22 (7.0)	6 (2.2)	0 (.0)	199 (6.9)
Resp. not at home	35 (1.9)	30 (6.3)	14 (4.5)	20 (7.4)	0 (.0)	99 (3.4)
No eligible resp.	113 (6.2)	44 (9.3)	21 (6.7)	10 (3.7)	0 (.0)	188 (6.5)
Refusal	394 (21.5)	101 (21.3)	38 (12.1)	18 (6.6)	0 (.0)	551 (19.1)
Terminate	79 (4.3)	11 (2.3)	9 (2.9)	5 (1.8)	0 (.0)	104 (3.6)
Quota filled	0 (0.0)	0 (0.0)	0 (0.0)	0 (0.0)	0 (.0)	0 (0.0)
Other	40 (2.2)	9 (1.9)	8 (2.6)	1 (0.4)	0 (.0)	58 (2.0)
Total	1830 (100.0)	475 (100.0)	313 (100.0)	272 (100.0)	0 (.0)	2890 (100.0)

on the other hand, could be expected to get a relatively low response rate for the eight-page questionnaire. Nonetheless, a university cover letter and a good list could probably achieve as many respondents for the same cost. In this case, however, the advantages of the panel having already collected socioeconomic variables (age, income, etc.) and not having the hassle involved in drawing a special sample (stuffing envelopes, etc.) favored the mail panel. As usual, convenience won out. The survey was mailed to an NFO panel of 1,000, which was designed to match national percentages of age, region, and income. An additional 200 surveys were mailed to the lowest-income members of a second panel to increase representation of lower-income groups. Four weeks after the initial mailing, 940 questionnaires were returned. As is typically done, the sample was described in terms of some basic demographics (Table 9.8). The sampling

TABLE 9.7 Phone Interviewing Record

| | Telephone Household | | | | | Call Results | | | | | | |
Sequence	State Code	County Code	Area Code	Prefix	Suffix	Complete	Busy	No Answer	Disconnect Invalid	Business Number	No Eligible Respondent	Refused
80	26	161	313	475	7440			1, 2			3	
81	26	125	313	477	4067				1			
82	26	115	313	567	2453		1	2, 3, 4				3
83	26	099	313	725	1400			1, 2				
84	26	125	313	669	4638	1						
85	26	099	313	408	5644					1		
86	26	163	313	255	7478						1	
87	26	163	313	873	2933	4		1, 2, 3				
88	26	125	313	685	1204					1		
89	26	099	313	673	1510		1	2				
90	26	163	313	751	7792	1						
91	26	099	313	571	9603			1, 2, 3, 4				
92	26	099	313	758	5481	1		1, 2, 3, 4				1
93	26	151	313	791	5044							
94	26	161	313	622	8537		3	1, 2				4

TABLE 9.8 Demographic Characteristics of the Nutrition Study Sample (by percent)

	Sample	U.S.
Respondent's age:		
Under 30	19.7	23.8
30–39	17.4	20.7
40–49	18.6	20.7
50–59	19.7	18.6
60 and over	24.6	16.6
Household income:		
Under 6,000	32.9	19.3
6,000–9,999	16.9	19.9
10,000–14,999	21.5	25.5
15,000–19,999	13.9	16.7
20,000 and over	14.8	18.6
Family size:		
2	44.1	36.1
3	20.3	21.4
4	17.0	19.7
5 or more	19.6	22.8
Race:		
White	96.8	
Other	3.2	
Population density:		
Rural	18.9	15.3
2,500–49,999	11.4	11.3
50,000–499,999	19.0	18.4
500,000–1,999,999	23.3	24.6
2,000,000 and over	27.3	30.4
Education:		
Attended grade school	3.4	
Grade school graduate	4.5	
Attended high school	14.0	
High school graduate	42.1	
Attended college	19.7	
College graduate	13.4	
Graduate school	2.6	
No answer	0.2	

plan did succeed in increasing low-income respondents but left the sample relatively old and rural. Similarly, minorities were badly underrepresented.

The Ownership and Values Survey

The ownership and values survey data were gathered by a cluster sampling procedure using multiple locations and an intercept method. While that may sound good, what it means is that each of the groups in my research class was required to find 50 "real"

TABLE 9.9 Demographic Characteristics of the Durable Ownership and Values Study (*n = 796*)

Age:	
Under 25	15.2%
25–34	40.6
35–44	18.8
45–54	14.2
55–64	8.2
65 or over	3.0
Sex:	
Male	44.5%
Female	55.5
Income:	
Under $15,000	9.7%
15,000–24,999	15.6
25,000–34,999	15.6
35,000–49,999	18.8
50,000–99,999	29.8
100,000 and over	10.2
Marital status:	
Single	42.1%
Married	47.2
Other	10.7
Dwelling:	
Studio apartment	4.9%
1 BR apartment	18.0
2 or more BR apt.	27.2
House	49.9

respondents. They effectively sampled the New York area and also some other locations (including 15 respondents from Hawaii—students do enjoy vacations). The resulting sample reasonably represents most major income and age categories (Table 9.9). Still, it would be best described as an upscale convenience sample.

SUMMARY

Good sampling requires getting the *right sources* by selecting (1) the appropriate target population (frame), (2) a good method to reach them, and (3) encouraging a high response rate. *Accuracy* is enhanced both by (1) the closeness of the resulting sample to the target (including accurate responses) and (2) the sheer size of the sample.

This chapter has outlined the most widely used means of obtaining a sample. In doing so, the advantages and disadvantages of each have been briefly discussed. For those who wish to really know about sampling, this chapter is only a sketchy introduction. Anyone who began this chapter hoping to find the "right" way should by now be disillusioned. There is no simple way to make sampling decisions. Cost, reliability of the results, and convenience all affect the choice of a sample design. Often, a smaller, more costly sample may be preferred because of lower nonresponse bias or increased interviewer control. Similarly, the method of data collection used and the method of choosing sampling points are closely related. Worrying about statistical niceties will improve the quality of the results as well as making them more credible. Most serious errors in sample design, however, turn out to be errors in logic, not statistics.

PROBLEMS

1. Evaluate the quality of the sample in the nutrition study in Table 9.8.

2. Draw a random sample of 20 from a list of 83 potential respondents. (Hint: Use a table of random numbers.)

3. Assume that a customer's purchase probabilities of buying three brands (A, B, and C) are .7, .2, and .1, respectively.

   a. Using a table of random numbers, simulate 10 purchases.

   b. Simulate 10 more purchases.

   c. How representative are (a) and (b) of the customer's true purchase behavior?

4. Assume you were to take a sample of five customers for Junk, Inc. Which customers would you sample and why?

	Capital District Customer List of Junk, Inc.			
	Customer	Location	Age	Business Annually
1.	W. Rockhead	Albany, N.Y.	42	$110,000
2.	S. Blitz	Albany, N.Y.	24	32,000
3.		Albany, N.Y.	35	271,000
4.		Albany, N.Y.	57	14,000
5.		Albany, N.Y.	62	42,000
6.		Albany, N.Y.	21	5,000
7.		Albany, N.Y.	61	19,000
8.		Troy	35	41,000
9.		Troy	27	15,000
10.		Troy	51	7,000
11.		Troy	23	4,000
12.		Saratoga	34	37,000
13.		Saratoga	41	60,000
14.		Saratoga	42	15,000
15.		Schenectady	51	80,000
16.		Schenectady	41	14,000
17.		Schenectady	27	21,000
18.		Schenectady	35	87,000
19.		Schenectady	61	59,000
20.		Schenectady	58	8,000

5. Assume you had been retained to take a national sample of 1,000 to gauge opinions about food additives. Set up a plan to do personal interviewing.

   a. Use states as a starting point and draw 10 at random.

   b. Use states as a starting point and draw 10 randomly with the probability of inclusion proportional to their population.

   c. Set up a purposive plan for drawing states.

   d. Which of (a), (b), or (c) seems better?

   e. How would you go about sampling within states?

6. Assume you were going to set up a sample of 100 four-year colleges to monitor trends in undergraduate education. Which 100 would you choose?

   a. Assume cooperation is no problem.

   b. Develop a contingency procedure in the event of a refusal.

7. A mail survey produces a 43 percent response rate. Discuss potential nonresponse bias and what could be done to (*a*) assess it and (*b*) correct for it.

8. How many people in the United States must I sample to estimate preference in a two-way presidential race within 1 percent at the 95 percent confidence level?

9. Two years ago, average consumption of fingles was 23 slops/slurp. The standard deviation of fingles consumption was .6. I feel that fingle consumption has about doubled and would like a new estimate on it. If I wish to be within .2 slops/slurp, how many people do I need to sample?

10. Assume you were in charge of setting up a panel to monitor introduction of a new breakfast food. How would you proceed? (Hint: Indicate how you would select panel members and what characteristics you would control for to help ensure its representativeness.)

11. Given the following situation:

Group (stratum)	Size	Standard Deviation of Bottles of Beer Consumed
A	2,000	4
B	4,000	1
C	6,000	4
D	8,000	3
E	2,000	2

   a. How should I sample 600 people to minimize the variance of the estimate of average beer consumption?

b. If I sample and get the following results:

Group	Sample Size	Average Beer Consumption	Standard Deviation
A	100	5	4.5
B	100	1	.8
C	100	12	4.1
D	200	2	2.9
E	100	3	1.8

(1) What is your estimate of average beer consumption?

(2) What is your standard deviation of this estimate?

12. Two lists of names commonly used for obtaining samples are vehicle registration lists and telephone directory lists.

a. How would you draw a simple random sample from each list?

b. What statistical biases would you expect if your population of interest were all U.S. households?

c. What could you do to reduce these biases?

13. You wish to estimate the average consumption of caviar in the United States by interviewing a sample of 1,000 households drawn from the population of 100 million households. The research firm has proposed a stratified sample, which will "save you money." The firm said it would "oversample the high-income and urban areas where the caviar consumption variance is larger." What does this mean? In what sense does it save you money? Why would the firm oversample these groups?

14. Recent studies by the Advertising Research Foundation have suggested that about 5 to 10 percent of field interviews are not actually conducted with the respondent, and that another 30 percent of the reported interviews contain substantial inaccuracies. What can be done to reduce the risk of such interviewer "cheating" or "bias"?

15. In assessing the market for a new consumer durable, your boss plans to do a national survey using personal interviews and a probability sample. Discuss the advisability of such a course of action and suggest some feasible alternatives.

16. In 1980, two mail surveys (one about donations, one about the school in general) were taken using alumni lists of a major business school. The response rates were as follows:

	Respondents	Nonrespondents
Donation survey:		
Donors	81	154
Nondonors	71	194
General survey:		
Donors	89	71
Nondonors	89	231

Interpret.

REFERENCES

ACKOFF, RUSSEL L. (1953) *The Design of Social Research*, Chicago: University of Chicago Press.

AMERICAN BUSINESS LISTS, INC. (1994) *Lists of 10 Million Businesses,* Omaha, Neb., published annually.

ARMSTRONG, J. SCOTT, AND TERRY S. OVERTON (1977) "Estimating Nonresponse Bias in Mail Surveys," *Journal of Marketing Research*, 14, August, 396–402.

ASSAEL, HENRY, AND JOHN KEON (1982) "Nonsampling versus Sampling Errors in Survey Research," *Journal of Marketing*, 46, Spring, 114–23.

BLAIR, JOHNNY, AND RONALD CZAJA (1982) "Locating a Special Population Using Random Digit Dialing," *Public Opinion Quarterly*, 46, Winter, 585–90.

BROWN, STEPHEN W., AND KENNETH A. CONEY (1977) "Comments on 'Mail Survey Premiums and Response Bias,'" *Journal of Marketing Research*, 14, August, 385–87.

BRYSON, MAURICE C. (1976) "The *Literary Digest* Poll: Making of a Statistical Myth," *The American Statistician*, 30, November, 184–85.

BUSH, ALAN J., AND JOSEPH F. HAIR, JR. (1985) "An Assessment of the Mall Intercept as a Data Collection Method," *Journal of Marketing Research*, 22, May, 158–67.

CHILDERS, TERRY L., AND O. C. FERRELL (1979) "Response Rates and Perceived Questionnaire Length in Mail Surveys," *Journal of Marketing Research*, 16, August, 429–31.

CHURCH, ALLAN H. (1993) "Estimating the Effects of Incentives on Mail Survey Response Rates: A Meta-analysis," *Public Opinion Quarterly*, 57, 62–79.

COCHRAN, W. G. (1977) *Sampling Techniques*, 3rd ed., New York: John Wiley and Sons.

DEMING, W. E. (1960) *Sampling Design in Business Research*, New York: John Wiley and Sons.

DUKTA, SOLOMON (1983) *Notes on Statistical Sampling for Surveys*, New York: Audits and Surveys, Inc.

FORSYTHE, JOHN B. (1977) "Obtaining Cooperation in a Survey of Business Executives," *Journal of Marketing Research*, 14, August, 370–73.

FURSE, DAVID H., AND DAVID W. STEWART (1982) "Monetary Incentives versus Promised Contribution to Charity: New Evidence on Mail Survey Response," *Journal of Marketing Research*, 19, August, 375–80.

GATES, ROGER, AND PAUL J. SOLOMON (1982) "Research Using the Mall Intercept: State of the Art," *Journal of Advertising Research*, 22, September–October, 43–49.

GOODSTADT, MICHAEL S., LINDA CHUNG, REENA KRONITZ, AND GAYNOLL COOK (1977) "Mail Survey Response Rates: Their Manipulation and Impact," *Journal of Marketing Research*, 14, August, 391–95.

GROVER, ROBERT M., AND ROBERT L. KAHN (1979) *Surveys by Telephone: A National Comparison with Personal Interviews*, New York: Academic Press.

HANSEN, MORRIS H., WILLIAM N. HURWITZ, AND WILLIAM G. MADOW (1953) *Sample Survey Methods and Theory*, Vol. 1, New York, John Wiley and Sons.

HOUSTON, MICHAEL J., AND NEIL M. FORD (1976) "Broadening the Scope of Methodological Research on Mail Surveys," *Journal of Marketing Research*, 13, November, 397–402.

HOUSTON, MICHAEL J., AND JOHN R. NEVIN (1977) "The Effects of Source and Appeal on Mail Survey Response Patterns," *Journal of Marketing Research*, 14, August, 374–78.

KALTON, GRAHAM (1983) "Introduction to Survey Sampling," Quantitative Applications in the Social Sciences Series, Beverly Hills, Calif.: Sage.

KANUK, LESLIE, AND CONRAD BERENSON (1975) "Mail Surveys and Response Rates: A Literature Review," *Journal of Marketing Research*, 12, November, 440–53.

KIM, BYUNG-DO, AND PETER E. ROSSI (1994) "Purchase Frequency, Sample Selection, and Price Sensitivity: The Heavy-User Bias," *Marketing Letters*, 5, January, 57–67.

KISH, LESLIE (1965) *Survey Sampling*, New York: John Wiley and Sons.

LANDON, E. LAIRD, JR., AND SHARON K. BANKS (1977) "Relative Efficiency and Bias of Plus-One Telephone Sampling," *Journal of Marketing Research*, 14, August, 294–99.

LINSKY, ARNOLD S. (1975) "Stimulating Responses to Mailed Questionnaires: A Review," *Public Opinion Quarterly*, 39, Spring, 82–101.

LYONS, WILLIAM, AND ROBERT F. DURANT (1980) "Interviewer Costs Associated with the Use of Random Digit Dialing in Large Area Samples," *Journal of Marketing*, 44, Summer, 65–69.

MCINTYRE, SHELBY H., AND SHERRY D. F. G. BENDER (1986) "The Purchase Intercept Technique (PIT) in Comparison to Telephone and Mail Surveys," *Journal of Retailing*, 62, Winter, 364–83.

MCKENZIE, JOHN (1983) "The Accuracy of Telephone Call Data Collected by Diary Methods," *Journal of Marketing Research*, 20, November, 417–27.

National Business Lists, Inc., *Direct Mail List, Rates and Data*, Skokie, Ill.: Standard Rate and Data Service, Inc., published annually.

NELSON, JAMES E. (1982) *The Practice of Marketing Research*, Boston: Kent Publishing.

O'ROURKE, DIANE, AND JOHNNY BLAIR (1983) "Improving Random Respondent Selection in Telephone Surveys," *Journal of Marketing Research*, 20, November, 428–32.

PESSEMIER, EDGAR, STEWART DEBRUICKER, AND THOMAS HUSTAD (1971) "The 1970 Purdue Consumer Behavior Research Project," Lafayette, Ind.: Purdue University.

POLITZ, ALFRED, AND WILLARD SIMMONS (1949) "An Attempt to Get the Not-at-Homes into the Sample Without Callbacks," *Journal of the American Statistical Association*, 13, March, 9–32.

Professional Mailing Lists, *The Direct Mail Marketing Guide*, New York, published annually.

RICH, CLYDE L. (1977) "Is Random Digit Dialing Really Necessary?" *Journal of Marketing Research*, 14, August, 300–05.

SCHLAIFER, ROBERT (1959) *Probability and Statistics for Business Decisions*, New York: McGraw-Hill.

SUDMAN, SEYMOUR (1976) *Applied Sampling*, New York: Academic Press.

(1985) "Efficient Screening Methods for the Sampling of Geographically Clustered Special Populations," *Journal of Marketing Research*, 22, February, 20–29.

SURVEY SAMPLING, INC. (1993) "Telephone Ownership Continues to Increase," *The Frame*, Fairfield, Conn., March, 2. (One Post Road, 06430; Beverly Weiman, CEO.)

WAKSBERG, JOSEPH (1978) "Sampling Methods for Random Digit Dialing," *Journal of the American Statistical Association*, 73, March, 40–46.

WALKER, BRUCE J., AND RICHARD K. BURDICK (1977) "Advance Correspondence and Error in Mail Surveys," *Journal of Marketing Research*, 14, August, 379–82.

WARD, JAMES C., BERTRAM RUSSICK, AND WILLIAM RUDELIUS (1985) "A Test of Reducing Callbacks and Not-at-Home Bias in Personal Interviews by Weighting at-Home Respondents," *Journal of Marketing Research*, 22, February, 66–73.

WEERAHANDI, SAMARADASA, AND ROBERT G. WHITE (1992) "A Bayesian Survey Technique for Rare Subjects," *Marketing Letters*, 3, January, 39–47.

WELLS, WILLIAM D. (1993) "Consequences of Contamination," working paper, August.

WIND, YORAM, AND DAVID LERNER (1979) "On the Measurement of Purchase Data: Surveys versus Purchase Diaries," *Journal of Marketing Research*, 16, February, 39–47.

WISEMAN, FREDERICK, AND PHILIP MCDONALD (1979) "Noncontact and Refusal Rates in Consumer Telephone Surveys," *Journal of Marketing Research*, 16, November, 478–84.

—— (1980a) "Movement Begins Toward Much Needed Response Rate Standards," *Marketing News*, 13, January 11, 1 & 4.

—— (1980b) *Toward the Development of Industry Standards for Response and Nonresponse Rates*, Cambridge, Mass.: MSI, 29.

WISEMAN, FREDERICK, MARIANNE SCHAFER, AND RICHARD SCHAFER (1983) "An Experimental Test of the Effects of a Monetary Incentive on Cooperation Rates and Data Collection Costs in Central-Location Interviewing," *Journal of Marketing Research*, 20, November, 439–42.

YU, JULIE, AND HARRIS COOPER (1983) "A Quantitative Review of Research Design Effects on Response Rates to Questionnaires," *Journal of Marketing Research*, 20, February, 36–44.

ZELLER, ALVIN B., INC. (1993) *Catalog of Mailing Lists*, New York, published annually.

APPENDIX 9-A

REVIEW OF PROBABILITY AND STATISTICS

This appendix briefly summarizes/reviews some basic statistics concepts.

PROBABILITY DISTRIBUTION

A probability distribution indicates the relative likelihood of different possible outcomes. When there are a discrete (finite, manageable) number of possible outcomes (e.g., number of days it rains this week), the distribution attaches a probability to each of the possible outcomes, as in Figure 9A.1. Here,

$$\sum_{\substack{\text{all} \\ \text{outcomes}}} P(X) = 1$$

FIGURE 9A.1
Discrete Probability Distribution

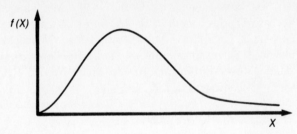

FIGURE 9A.2
Continuous Probability Distribution

When the outcomes are continuous (e.g., the diameter of a part can be infinitely many sizes), the relative likelihood of different outcomes is given by a density function (Figure 9A.2). Here $\int_{-\infty}^{+\infty} f(X)\,dx = 1$. Also, the probability of a particular result (e.g., $P(x) = 3.12471$) is 0.

SUMMARY STATISTICS

The most comprehensive information about possible occurrences is contained in the complete probability distribution or density function. Since these can be fairly unwieldy, however, measures are calculated that summarize the information contained in the distribution. The first group of measures concerns the notion of a "typical" response. Three measures are commonly calculated:

> Mode: The most likely result.
> Median: The result that lies exactly at the middle of the distribution (i.e., the score of the 49th student from a class of 99).
> Mean: The average (expected) result.

Of these three measures, the mean is the most widely used. It is calculated by:

Discrete distribution	*Continuous distribution*

$$E(X) = \mu = \sum_{all\,X} XP(X) \qquad\qquad \mu = \int_{-\infty}^{+\infty} X f(X)\,dX$$

The second group of measures deals with the dispersion/"fatness" of the distribution. These measures indicate the uncertainty inherent in the outcome. The most typical measure is the variance (σ^2):

Discrete distribution	*Continuous distribution*

$$E(X - \mu)^2 = \sigma^2 \qquad\qquad \sigma^2 = \int_{-\infty}^{+\infty} (X - \mu)^2 f(X)\,dx$$
$$= \sum_{all\,X}\left((X - \mu)^2 P(X)\right)$$
$$= \sum X^2 P(X) - \mu^2$$
$$= E(X^2) - \mu^2$$

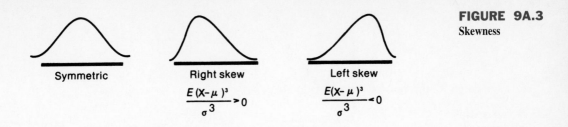

FIGURE 9A.3
Skewness

(N.B.: Variance $(a + bx) = b^2$(variance x).) Actually, the square root of the variance, σ, called the *standard deviation*, is the most commonly used measure of dispersion. Another description of a distribution is the *skewness*, which indicates whether the distribution is symmetric about the mean (Figure 9A.3).

COMMONLY USED DISTRIBUTIONS

While many distributions exist, a small number turn out to be especially useful in marketing research. Some of these are the binomial, Poisson, normal, Student's t, chi-square, and F distributions.

Binomial

The binomial is a discrete distribution that indicates the probability of X "successes" out of n trials. Binomial represents a situation in which there are (*a*) n independent trials and (*b*) exactly two possible outcomes for each trial. (This makes it a special case of the multinomial.) Its probability distribution is given by:

$$P(X) = \binom{n}{X} p^X (1 - p)^{n-X}$$

where p = probability of success on a given trial. Also,

$$\mu = np$$
$$\sigma = \sqrt{np(1 - p)}$$

It turns out that the binomial can be approximated by other distributions:

1. For p close to 0 or 1, the binomial is similar to the Poisson.

2. For p close to .5 or for large n, the binomial is close to the normal.

Poisson

Another major discrete distribution is the Poisson. It is often viewed as the distribution of the number of successes in a given time period. Its density function is given by

$$P(X) = \frac{\lambda^X e^{-\lambda}}{X!}$$

Its mean and standard deviation are

$$\mu = \lambda$$
$$\sigma = \sqrt{\lambda}$$

For large λ, the poisson becomes approximately normal.

Normal

The normal distribution is the standard bell-shaped symmetric curve, which recurs in many situations. It is continuous, and its density function is given by

$$f(X) = \frac{1}{\sqrt{2\pi}\,\sigma}\, e^{-\frac{1}{2}\left(\frac{X-\mu}{\sigma}\right)^2}$$

where

$$\mu = \text{the mean}$$
$$\sigma = \text{the standard deviation}$$

This is such a mess mathematically that calculations of probabilities are impossible. To estimate probabilities (e.g., the probability a part will be between 80 and 85 mm in length), a "scale model" approach is used. The approach is to convert to the standard normal distribution where $\mu = 0$ and $\sigma = 1$ (Figure 9A.4) and then look up the answer in a table. The conversion is achieved by

$$Z = \frac{X - \mu}{\sigma}$$

For example, assume I were interested in obtaining the probability that a certain part were between 80 and 85 mm. If $\mu = 81$ and $\sigma = 1$, this means the shaded area in Figure 9A.5. Now from the table, the area from 0 to -1 standard deviation is about .34. Similarly, the area from 0 to $+4$ is about .5. Hence, the probability the part is between 80 and 85 mm is .5 + .34 = .84.

FIGURE 9A.4
Standard Normal Distribution

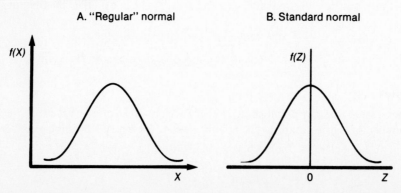

A. "Regular" normal   B. Standard normal

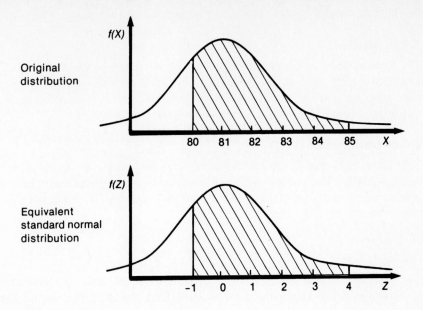

FIGURE 9A.5
Example of Conversion to Standard Normal

Student's *t*

The Student's *t* is another bell-shaped distribution; it is slightly "fatter" than the normal. Its density function is also a "mess." (Since it was developed by the employee of an Irish brewery named Gosset who used the pen name Student, its "sloppiness" is understandable.) Fortunately, the function is tabled, so that the density function is not used. The mean and standard deviation of the *t* distribution are given by

$$\mu = 0$$

$$\sigma = \sqrt{\frac{v}{v - 2}}$$

where *v* is called degrees of freedom.

For large *v*, the *t* distribution is approximately standard normal.[1]

Chi-Square ($\chi2$)

The chi-square distribution is the distribution of a sum of squared independent standard normal variables.[2] Its density function is also unwieldy. Its mean and standard deviation are given by

$$\mu = v$$

$$\sigma = \sqrt{2v}$$

---

[1] The *t* distribution is often expressed as the ratio of a standard normal to a chi-square: $t = $ [SEE P. 350] where *x* is standard normal and *y* is chi-square with *v* degrees of freedom.

[2] $\chi^2 = \sum_{i=1}^{v} X_i^2$ where X_i is standard normal.

For large v, the chi-square distribution is approximately normal.

F Distribution

The F distribution is the ratio of two chi-square variables.[3] Its density function is too messy to bother writing since it also is tabled. One interesting fact is that the F distribution has a fixed endpoint at 0 (no negative values are possible since it is made up of the ratio of squared numbers), a mean of 1, and a strong right skew (Figure 9A.6).

Other Distributions

The distributions just listed are the most commonly used for statistical testing in marketing research. Other distributions are used in special circumstances, especially stochastic modeling, including the negative binomial, exponential, gamma (of which both the exponential and chi-square are special cases), and the beta.

Estimates and Truth

The distributions just described were given in terms of their true parameters. Unfortunately, a researcher rarely knows the true parameters (μ, σ, etc.). We mortals then must estimate (guess) what the parameters are.

The estimates are typically given by the following:

	True Value	*Estimate*
Mean	μ	$\overline{X} = \dfrac{\Sigma X}{n}$
Variance	σ	$s^2 = s_X^2 = \dfrac{\Sigma(X - \overline{X})^2}{n - 1}$
Standard deviation (of population)	$\sigma = \sqrt{\sigma^2}$	$s = \sqrt{s^2}$
Standard deviation (of mean)	$\sigma_{\overline{X}} = \dfrac{\sigma}{\sqrt{n}}$	$s_{\overline{X}} = \dfrac{s}{\sqrt{n}}$
Proportion	θ	$p = \dfrac{\text{Number of successes}}{n}$

Notice that, by convention, Greek letters stand for true values and Arabic letters for approximations. (Everyone knows the ancient Greeks had truth, don't they?)

---

[3] $F = \dfrac{\dfrac{X_1}{v_1}}{\dfrac{X_2}{v_2}}$ where X_1 and X_2 are chi-square with v_1 and v_2 degrees of freedom, respectively.

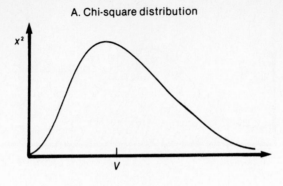

A. Chi-square distribution

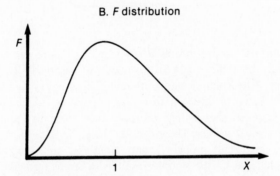

B. F distribution

FIGURE 9A.6
Two Common Distributions

Confidence Intervals

A confidence interval is a range into which we expect a value to fall. There are two types of confidence intervals:

1. Given true parameters (e.g., μ and σ), where will a measured value (e.g., $\bar{x}$) fall?

2. Given a measured value (e.g., $\bar{x}$ and s), in what range are the true values (e.g., μ) likely to be?

A confidence interval of the first type can be expressed graphically (Figure 9A.7). The confidence level $(1 - \alpha)$ is the probability that an event will fall in the confidence level. The significance level (α) is the probability an event will occur outside the confidence interval.

Sampling Distributions and Statistical Significance

A sampling distribution is the representation of the likelihood that a given value (e.g., an individual's weight, the mean diameter of a part, or the percent of a consumer sample who prefer a certain color) will occur (Figure 9A.8). The uncertainty in the results may be due to the measurement process and/or random differences among respondents. One often-asked question is whether a particular sample result is "different." In answering this question we are really addressing the question, "Is the population from which the sample result was drawn

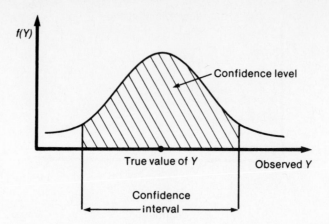

FIGURE 9A.7
Confidence Interval

different from the original population?" Consider the three situations in Figure 9A.9. In case A, the sample result is well outside the typical range of values (as described by a confidence interval) and, hence, would be called significantly different. This implies that the population from which the sample was drawn is different from the original population in terms of this particular characteristic. In case B, the sample result is very close to the expected result and well within the range of typical values. Therefore, the result in case B is not significantly different. (Put differently, this result probably came from the same population of results as did the previous results.) In case C, the sample result is different from the expected result but not so different as to be completely beyond the range of typical results. What will determine statistical significance is whether the likelihood that as "odd" a result would occur due to chance is sufficiently small to conclude the result is really different from what we expected.

The reasonable chance cutoff (α level or Type I error) can be set at any level. In social science, however, the level is typically either .1, .05, or .01, and by far the most widely used cutoff is .05. In other words, if there is less than a 5 in 100 chance that the sample result or a more extreme result would come from the hypothesized process, then the sample result is declared significantly different.

The effect of sample size on statistical significance is very important. Consider again case C. If the sample result is based on a single observation, we would conclude it is not possible to label that person as significantly different from the original population. If it is

FIGURE 9A.8
Sampling Distribution

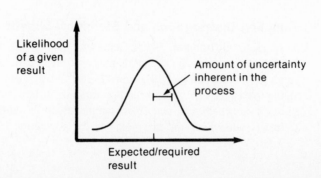

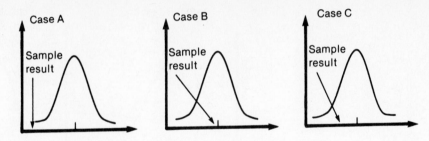

FIGURE 9A.9
Three Hypothetical Sample Results

the average of 10 observations, we are more likely to feel that the population from which the sample is drawn is different from the original population. If the sample size were 2,000, we would almost certainly feel the second population is different from the first. While it is possible to subjectively take sample size into account, a more methodical way is available in two important cases: averages and proportions.

Sampling Distributions of an Average ($\bar{x}$)

Assume the value of a particular result has mean $\bar{x}$ and standard deviation s_x (usually just written as plain s). Then the mean and standard deviation of the sampling distribution (likely results) of the average of a sample of size n are:

$$\text{Mean of sample size } n = \bar{x}$$

$$\begin{array}{l}\text{Standard deviation of} \\ \text{the mean of the} \\ \text{sample of size } n\end{array} = s_{\bar{x}} = \frac{s}{\sqrt{n}}$$

What this means is that the sampling distribution becomes tighter as sample size increases (Figure 9A.10). Consequently, a result that is not significant as an isolated instance may become significant if it occurs repeatedly.

A useful result is that the mean ($\bar{x}$) follows the normal distribution, even if the underlying distribution of x is not normal (courtesy of the central limit theorem). This means that we can use the normal distribution to check for statistical significance. Note, also, that precision increases as the square root of sample size. In other words, to be twice as confident of what the results are (cut the range in half), you need four times the sample size. (This has some strong implications for the diminishing marginal utility of increasing sample size.)

Sampling Distribution of a Proportion

The sampling distribution of the proportion of respondents exhibiting a particular behavior (i.e., owning a color TV) is given by

$$\text{Expected proportion} = p$$

$$\text{Standard deviation} = s_p = \sqrt{\frac{p(1-p)}{n}}$$

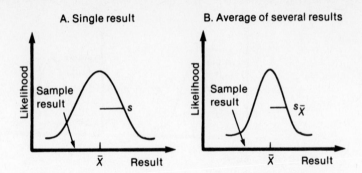

FIGURE 9A.10
Sampling Distribution of the Mean (X)

Notice that the closer p is to 50 percent, the greater the standard deviation. Since this distribution is also approximately normally distributed for n greater than 30, we can get a notion of how accurate proportions are. If we wish to get a range into which 95 percent of actual results are likely to fall (commonly known as the 95 percent confidence level), we get $p \pm 1.96 s_p$. If we think p is .50 and take a sample of 100, this becomes

$$.50 \pm 1.96 \sqrt{\frac{(.5)(.5)}{100}} = .50 \pm .10 = .40 \text{ to } .60$$

In other words, we are 95 percent sure that the results would be between 40 and 60 percent. This is a fairly broad range and brings forth an important point: apparently big differences in proportions may not be significant.

Hypothesis Testing

Hypothesis testing is the process of determining whether a result is or is not statistically significantly different from an expected result. Numerous hypotheses can be tested. For marketing research, however, a few basic tests cover the majority of the situations encountered. These commonly used tests are introduced in this book when the problems to which they apply are discussed.

CHAPTER 10

Data Coding and Editing

There are two basic stages between data collection and interpretation. The more interesting of these is analysis. However, before analysis can begin, the data must be converted into a form suitable for analysis. The conversion of the data from "raw" form—for example, questionnaires—to a form that facilitates analysis is the subject of this chapter. The problem of converting secondary data to a form ready for analysis is a much simpler but still important task. The steps include designing a data file, rough screening, coding, data input, and dealing with bad and missing responses.

DESIGNING A DATA FILE

When the number of observations is small, it is possible to do the analysis by hand (assuming no fancy analyses are desired and that there are a fairly small number of variables). Pilot studies of size 20 and industrial marketing studies of 25 purchasing agents may be analyzed without resorting to computers. Here, a combination of scanning the results and a simple question-by-question tabulation is often sufficient.

Assuming (a) there are a reasonably large number of respondents, (b) there are a large number of responses, or (c) there is a desire to get more than simple tabulations of the responses, the practical way to proceed is to prepare the data for computer analysis. By far the most popular way to do this is to create a data file or tape. Recently, it has become popular to input data directly into computer memories (e.g., by using WATS interviewing and computers).

Traditionally, the basic unit of data storage was the computer card: essentially, a table of 80 columns (the number of columns on many computer screens is also 80). Each of the 80 columns could contain a separate piece of information. For example, column 8 might be the response to a question about how well I like yogurt, column 9 a question about what type of car I own, and so forth. Groups of columns can also be used to store information (e.g., age might be in columns 19 and 20). Whenever more data exist for a respondent than fit on a single record, a second record is used. Alternatively, it is possible to specify a "record length" of other than 80 and, hence, to put all the data for one person (observation) on a single record.

	Column					
	ID			Line No.		Data
Line	1	2	3	4	5	6 · · · · · · · · · · · · · · · 80
1	0	0	0	1	1	
2	0	0	0	1	2	
3	0	0	0	1	3	
4	0	0	0	2	1	
5	0	0	0	2	2	
6	0	0	0	2	3	
7	0	0	0	3	1	
8	0	0	0	3	2	
9	0	0	0	3	3	
10	0	0	0	4	1	
11	0	0	0	4	2	
12	0	0	0	4	3	

FIGURE 10.1
Data File

To keep track of individual observations, it is desirable to keep a set of columns for identification purposes. For example, we could use columns 1 through 4 for an ID number. Assuming there is more than one line per respondent, column 5 might be used to indicate line number (actually, any column will do, and many suppliers tend to use column 80 to indicate line number).

Data are usually stored by observation (person, company). Assuming we had a sample of four people with three lines per person, the data file might look like Figure 10.1.

ROUGH SCREENING

The first thing that is typically done when a survey is completed is to do a rough screening job on the returned questionnaires. This essentially consists of looking for grossly "bad" respondents with illegible, incomplete, or inconsistent responses.

Illegible responses. This is a common problem for poorly supervised personal interviews and questionnaires with a large number of open-ended responses.

Incomplete responses. Many returned questionnaires will have a large percentage of nonresponses to individual questions.

Inconsistent responses. Sometimes, a casual glance will indicate the respondent is not very believable (e.g., income > $50,000, age < 15, loves sports, never participates in sports, etc.). Alternatively, the respondent may have given the same response to a large number of consecutive questions, indicating a certain lack of interest.

Dealing with Bad Data

Since there are inevitably some "bad" respondents, a question that immediately arises is what to do with them. The decision concerning what to do with bad respondents depends heavily on how many good respondents there are. When there are a large number of good respondents both in an absolute sense and relative to the number of bad respondents, it may be possible to ignore the bad ones. When, on the other hand, data points are expensive and many are needed for purposes of analysis and projectability, then some way must be found to "fix up" the bad responses. Three basic approaches are used in dealing with bad respondents: going back to get better information, using the data as they are, and throwing out bad respondents.

Getting More Complete Data   Assuming the individuals in question can be identified, it is possible to go back and try to get the respondent to "correct" his or her responses. This is obviously fairly expensive in the case of a large-scale national survey. If (*a*) the percentage of bad respondents is small (less than 20 percent), (*b*) the bad respondents are not different in obvious ways (e.g., income, product usage, etc.) from good respondents, and (*c*) there is a reasonably large sample size (e.g., greater than 500), then it is probably better to avoid going back for more data. In the case of either lab experiments or industrial marketing surveys of a small number of key accounts, on the other hand, it is often relatively easy to go back to collect key pieces of missing data. It is important to realize, however, that data collected the second time may be different from the data at the time of the original survey, because of both changes over time and the different means of gathering the data (e.g., phone callbacks to mail survey respondents). As an alternative to remeasuring, we can attempt to "clean up" the bad/incomplete responses. Procedures for doing this are discussed later in this chapter.

Using the Data As They Are   It is possible to use the data exactly as they are received for basic analysis. This approach is commonly used by suppliers, not surprisingly so since they are typically committed to getting a certain number of respondents. Tabulations can keep track of the nonresponses as a separate category. Inconsistent responses might be assumed to average out over the sample. As long as only simple tabulations are performed, the results may not be too badly distorted. Whenever fancy analysis (e.g., regression) is to be performed, however, this approach leads to considerable problems. Some relatively complex procedures have been developed for dealing with incomplete data (Malhotra, 1987).

Throwing Out Bad Respondents   A third alternative is to discard the bad respondents. This is the easiest thing to do and a widely followed approach, given sufficient sample size to allow it. There are, however, three main drawbacks to this approach. First is that it is an extra step not typically performed by suppliers, which requires time and effort. Second, the bad respondents may, in fact, be very meaningful in that they are in essence saying the topic of your survey is so uninteresting and irrelevant that they refuse to take the time to complete it. Finally, in deciding what a bad respondent is (especially an inconsistent one), the potential for researcher bias influencing the final results is high. Put differently, the bad respondents may be different from good respondents in terms of the variables being measured, and consequently excluding them may bias the results. While these problems discourage many researchers from discarding bad respondents, the key point to remember is that the purpose of information collection and analysis is to improve the odds of making a good decision. Hence, if the researcher believes the results will be more useful if bad respondents are removed, he or she can make the managerial decision to remove them as long as he or she carefully records and reports the procedure used.

CODING

The next step in preparing for analysis is to develop a coding scheme for the responses. Since open-ended questions require individual attention (theoretically, by multiple coders to ensure good results), generally most questions in a large-scale survey should be closed-end multiple-choice. Converting responses to a data file is essentially a two-step process: (a) converting the responses to code values (e.g., on coding sheets where the appropriate codes are placed in the appropriate columns) and (b) inputting the data. To save time and money, it is usually possible to eliminate the first step by precoding the questionnaire so that an operator can input data directly from the questionnaire or, even better, the responses can be optically scanned. It is the desire to have precoded responses that pushes market researchers into the almost exclusive use of multiple-choice questions. Notice that in computer-controlled data collection methods, coding occurs automatically during data collection.

Two standard approaches are used for coding. The first is to code possible responses from left to right beginning with "1." For example, if we asked the following question:

	Definitely Not				Definitely
Is hard work good for you?	○	○	○	○	○

it would be coded 1 through 5, with a "1" representing a "definitely not" response and so forth. The second standard approach is to treat all nonresponses the same way. Some suppliers leave nonresponses blank, others punch a "9" or a "." It is useful to code a nonresponse to a question separately from "don't know" responses. One more point is extremely important: Do not attempt to save space by "packing" data into a small number of columns. Let each piece of information have a separate column (in general, even if this requires extra records per respondent).

Coding Questionnaires

Consider the example in Figure 10.2. In this case, the first five columns are devoted to an identification field—here, the respondent number "12345."

Column 6 will be coded "1," since the first category was indicated on question 1.

Question 2 will occupy columns 7 through 14. Each separate piece of information gets its own column. In this case, the blanks checked indicate values "3, 2, 4, 3, 3, 5, 2, 4."

ID 1-5
6

1. Do you use toothpaste? ✔
   Yes   No

2. Please indicate your degree of agreement with the following statements by circling a 6 if you strongly agree, a 1 if you strongly disagree, or somewhere in between depending on your degree of agreement with the statement.

	Strongly Disagree					Strongly Agree		
Hard work is good for you.	1	2	③	4	5	6	7
I am very health-conscious.	1	②	3	4	5	6	8
I tend to be conservative in my dress.	1	2	3	④	5	6	9
I enjoy participating in vigorous exercise.	1	2	③	4	5	6	10
I am very family-centered.	1	2	③	4	5	6	11
My appearance is very important to me.	1	2	3	4	⑤	6	12
I use mouthwash often.	1	②	3	4	5	6	13
I enjoy meeting people.	1	2	3	④	5	6	14

3. Please rate each of the following brands of toothpaste by marking a 6 if you feel the brand is very good, a 1 if you feel the brand is very poor, or somewhere in between depending on how good you feel the brand is.

	Very Poor					Very Good		
Aim	1	2	③	4	5	6	15
Colgate	1	2	3	4	⑤	6	16
Crest	1	2	3	④	5	6	17
Macleans	1	②	3	4	5	6	18
UltraBright	1	②	3	4	5	6	19

4. Please rate the following brands in terms of their *breath freshening ability* by marking a 6 if you feel the brand is very good, a 1 if you feel the brand is very poor, or somewhere in between depending on how good you feel the brand is.

	Very Poor					Very Good		
Aim	1	2	3	④	5	6	20
Colgate	1	2	3	④	5	6	21
Crest	1	2	3	④	5	6	22
Macleans	1	2	3	4	⑤	6	23
UltraBright	1	2	3	4	⑤	6	24

(continued)

FIGURE 10.2
Sample Questionnaire

5. Please indicate how important each of the following features of toothpaste is to you by circling a 6 if the feature is very important, a 1 if the feature is very unimportant, or somewhere in between depending on how important the feature is to you.

	Very Unimportant				Very Important		
Breath freshening	1	2	③	4	5	6	25
Decay prevention	1	2	3	4	⑤	6	26
Taste	1	2	3	④	5	6	27
Price	1	2	③	4	5	6	28

6. How often do you brush your teeth?

Never	Rarely	Few times a day	✔ Daily	Two times a day	More than two times a day	29

7. Who makes the purchase decision concerning which brand of toothpaste your household uses?

Male head of household   ✔_____   30

Female head of household   ✔_____   31

Children   _____   32

8. What brand of toothpaste did your household last purchase?

_____CREST_____   33

9. How old would you like to be?

Under 20	✔ 21–35	36–50	Over 50	34

10. What is the highest level of education you have completed?

6th grade	High school	✔ College	Graduate school	35

11. What is your total annual household income?

Under $5,000	$5,000– $9,999	$10,000– $14,999	$15,000– $19,999	✔ Over $20,000	36

12. What is your occupation?

✔ White-collar	Blue-collar	Homemaker	Student	Other	37

13. How many people live in your household?   _____4_____   38

FIGURE 10.2
(continued)

14. What is your sex?

   ✔

_____   _____   39

Male   Female

15. What is your marital status?

             ✔

_____   _____   _____   _____   40

Single   Married   Divorced, widowed,   Other

                       or separated

16. Do you own a:

   House?   _____   ✔

                    Yes   No   41

   Car?   ✔

                    Yes   No   42

   Snowmobile?   ✔

                    Yes   No   43

   Color TV?   ✔

                    Yes   No   44

   CB Radio?   ✔

                    Yes   No   45

17. How old are you? 27   46–47

Note: The numbers down the right side of the questionnaire indicate the column in which the particular piece of data will be placed.

FIGURE 10.2
(continued)

Question 3 occupies columns 15 through 19 with numbers "3, 5, 4, 2, 2."
Question 4 occupies columns 20 through 24 with numbers "4, 4, 4, 5, 5."
Question 5 occupies columns 25 through 28 with values "3, 5, 4, 3."
Question 6 is coded into column 29 with a "4," since *Daily* is the fourth category.
Question 7 takes up three separate columns (30 through 32), since it would be possible and logical to check more than one response (as this respondent did). While we could (and would if we were old-time coders) indicate this by punching both a "1" and a "2" in column 30 (called *multiple punching*), this would play havoc with many of the analysis routines to be used later. Therefore, we use three separate columns and indicate "1," "1," blank. (If we had asked which person has the most influence, then only one answer would have been appropriate, and the data could have been coded in column 30 as a "1"—male head of household, "2"—female head of household, or "3"—child.)

Question 8 is an open-ended question, which must be manually coded. Actually, it could have been precoded by including the major brands and an "all other—please specify" category. Assuming our code were "1" = Aim, "2" = Colgate, "3" = Crest, "4" = Macleans, "5" = UltraBright, and "6" = all others, we would place a "3" in column 33.

Question 9 will produce a "2" in column 34.

Question 10 will produce a "3" in column 35.

Question 11 will generate a "5" for column 36.

Column 37 will be a "1" to represent the "white-collar" response to question 12.

Question 13 will place a "4" in column 38. Notice here that a response of 10 or more is unaccounted for. Hence, we must either collapse 10 into another value, such as 9, or save two columns (38–39) for the response.

Question 14 implies a "1" for column 39.

Question 15 implies a "2" for column 40.

Question 16 fills columns 41 through 45 with "2, 1, 1, 2, 1." Notice again that rather than collapse the information into a single column, each durable ownership response occupies a separate column.

Question 17 fills columns 46 and 47 with 27. If someone is over 100, we would punch a 99 and congratulate that person and ask for his or her secret of success. If someone is 8, we would place the 8 in column 47, a process known as *right justifying*. The reason for this is that the computer will read a ____8 as 8, and an 8____ as 80.

One other point worth mentioning is that it is highly desirable to use fixed field codes. This means that (*a*) the number of lines for each observation is the same and (*b*) the same piece of data appears in the same column for all observations. Failure to do this is disastrous for many analytical procedures. The tendency to use uneven record lengths comes from questions where the respondent lists several items (e.g., family members, cars owned, credit cards carried). Since to use fixed record lengths means the code will be determined by those with the largest number of responses, there will be a large amount of blank space on the records of those respondents with few responses. Here, the puritan ethic of not wasting space will lead to the wrong decision. The cost of the blank space is usually far smaller than the cost of uneven record length. For example, in response to a question concerning car ownership, we might leave room for four cars, which will cover over 99 percent of the responses. (While we could include the one person with 13 cars, this is such an unusual observation that, in general, it is not worth the trouble of keeping track of all 13.)

Actually, assuming you plan to use certain computer algorithms for analysis, you can also input data by leaving a blank space between consecutive pieces of data. (This also allows you to use nonfixed-length formats, so we could input 9, 90, or 109 for age. Unfortunately, this also makes it harder to check for errors, since the data no longer line up neatly in columns on a computer screen or in printed output.) Still, since this is closer to typing for people familiar with typing or word processing systems, it is often useful for the person who only occasionally inputs data.

Data entry is also possible through scanners. Though not perfect, this technology has improved substantially and offers a high level of accuracy for coded responses (e.g., SAT tests).

Coding Secondary Data

The conversion of secondary data into computer form is fairly simple. Assume I collected data on annual dishwasher sales in units and GDP:

Line	Column																		
	1	2	3	4	5	6	7	8	9	10	11	12	13	14	15	16	17	18	19
1	1	9	6	0								5	5	5		5	0	3	7
2	1	9	6	5							1	2	6	0		6	8	4	9
3	1	9	7	0							2	1	1	6		9	7	7	1
4	1	9	7	2							3	1	9	9	1	1	5	5	2
5	1	9	7	3							3	7	0	2	1	2	8	9	1

FIGURE 10.3
Coded Dishwater Sales Data

Year	Dishwasher Sales (units)	GDP ($ billion)
1960	555,321	503.7
1965	1,260,462	684.9
1970	2,116,119	977.1
1972	3,199,201	1,155.2
1973	3,701,982	1,289.1

The ID field would be year, probably in columns 1 through 4. Since plenty of space is available, we could skip some space before beginning dishwasher sales in some column, such as 11. Clearly, we could input seven columns' worth of data for dishwasher sales. However, the accuracy of the last three columns, as well as their value, given only five data points, is very questionable. It seems more reasonable to only include the data to the nearest thousands of units. Since the maximum number of columns needed is 4 (for 3,702, the largest number), we assign columns 11 through 14 for dishwasher sales (remembering they are now measured in thousands of units sold).

It is unnecessary to input a decimal point, since (*a*) we could interpret the results just as well in units of hundreds of millions as units of billions and (*b*) we can tell the computer where the decimal point belongs and have it replaced during analysis. (For FORTRAN fans, use F 5.1). Since 12,891 is the largest number, we can use five columns (15 through 19) to represent GDP. The resulting data would then be input, as is shown in Figure 10.3.

DATA INPUT

The task of inputting data, formerly called *punching data* in the card era, is straightforward and essentially the same as typing. An experienced typist can turn out 80 to 100 lines or the equivalent per hour at a cost of about 30 cents per line from a supplier. Because typists occasionally make errors, it is usually desirable to check their work.

The standard way to do this is to "verify" the work. This is done by a second typist who essentially repunches the data from the original questionnaire. If the result matches the original typist's input, nothing happens. If the input does not match, then the observation is put aside for reentry.[1]

One point of caution: If you are inputting data yourself, be sure to save the data frequently. Otherwise, hours of work can be destroyed by a power failure or the accidental striking of a wrong key. Also, never rely on a single data set. Data sets have a habit of becoming mutilated. Typically, large data sets are stored on magnetic tape, disks, or CD-ROMs. The minimum safety margin is two copies (e.g., a tape and a disk copy) stored in different places.

The increasing use of WATS phone interviewing and the advent of microcomputers has made it possible for either the interviewer or the subjects themselves to directly create a data file. Direct data entry, however, has some inherent problems. Care must still be taken to verify answers, since careless recording can produce nonsensical results. Also, care must be taken to design input routines to allow a mistaken entry to be fixed before it becomes part of a data file. For each answer, it is often desirable to give the respondent, the interviewer, or both, a printed (on the screen) summary of a response and then have the respondent verify (in which case, the next question is given) or contradict the response (in which case, the question is repeated). Also, this form of data entry tends to preclude marginal notes made by interviewers, which have on occasion been useful in interpreting results. Still, direct entry is increasing in popularity, mainly as a result of the increased usage of WATS and computer-controlled interviewing.

Code Book

Data delivered by a supplier are accompanied by a code book giving a column-by-column explanation of the relation between the codes and the responses to the questions. These can be quite extensive, as the code book from the nutrition study turned out to be. That 8-page questionnaire produced a 30-page code book, which is presented in abbreviated form in Appendix 10-A. Notice that, since this study was performed in the mid 1970s, data lines are referred to as cards. Also typically included in a code book will be information on how to access the data (where it is physically stored if it is in card form, and what instructions access it if it is stored on tape or disk).

CLEANING THE DATA

Data cleaning involves dealing with two problems: missing data and inconsistent/illogical data. Here we discuss them in the context of survey responses; the same issues are relevant to other forms of data (e.g., secondary data, sales call reports).

---

[1] This used to be done by a machine called a *verifier*. Instead of punching holes in the cards, however, the verifier shot a beam of light at the card. If the light went through (meaning there was a hole in the correct space), the card proceeded to the next column. If the light did not go through, the card remained in the same position. The verifier then tried again. If the light still failed to go through, the card was marked and returned to be repunched. This verification process essentially doubled both the time and cost of punching.

Illogical data come in three forms. First, there are *illegal codes*, that is, values that aren't part of the coding procedure. These are relatively easy to spot. Second, there are *outlier codes*, legal but unusual codes (e.g., income over $2 million). As we will see, outliers can have a disproportionate impact on results. Therefore it is often worthwhile to examine these outliers and make sure they are correctly input. Finally, there are *illogical codes*. Basically, these are codes that are not consistent with other available information (e.g., income over $2 million and receiving food stamps). These are the most difficult to spot and the most prone to researcher expectation; in fact, they are defined as inconsistent based on researcher expectation. Hence, great care is required in dealing with these.

The problem of missing data is widespread. For example, a nationwide mail panel study (Horowitz and Golob, 1979) showed that, while 60 percent of the 1,565 respondents had fewer than 1 percent of their responses blank, about 10 percent had at least 5 percent missing data. It is important to note that missing data occurs in all types of studies, and procedures for filling it in are relevant for scanner as well as survey data (Owens, 1989).

Cleaning Data Before Analysis

Cleaning the data for final analysis has several steps. First, a column-by-column count of the responses is made. Typical results are shown in Figure 10.4, taken from card 1 of the nutrition study. These results give indications of missing and illegal entries and, also, an initial glimpse at the results.

Cleaning data requires deciding what to do with isolated missing or illogical responses (e.g., questions that an otherwise good respondent left blank). There are four major choices:

> *Leaving them blank*. This is fine for tabs and cross-tabs but is a problem for many computer programs that treat blanks as zeros.
>
> *Substitute a neutral value*. Typically, this approach involves substituting a value, usually the mean response to the question, for the missing response. This approach keeps the mean constant and also tends to have a relatively small effect on calculations such as correlations. Good as this may sound, putting a 3.5 (the mean for the missing question *across all respondents*) on the card of a respondent who mainly indicated 1s and 2s seems questionable.
>
> *Assign the value the individual "would have used" if he or she had answered the question*. By looking at the individual's pattern of responses to other questions, we can try to logically deduce an appropriate answer to the missing question based on the respondents who gave the same responses to the other questions and filled in the missing/illogical response. Since these methods (*a*) require considerable effort and (*b*) may introduce researcher bias, they are not very popular. Still, it is an approach that may be useful for some situations (Madow, Nisselson, and Olkin, 1983).
>
> *Assume they were "don't know" or "not applicable" responses*. A nonresponse may mean the question does not apply (n.a.). For example, a survey may branch so that only owners of trucks fill out certain questions, meaning that truck nonowners will leave several questions blank. Alternatively, it may be that the respondent genuinely doesn't know (d.k.) the answer.

COLUMN	TOTAL CODED	-12-	-11-	-0-	-1-	-2-	-3-	-4-	-5-	-6-	-7-	-8-	-9-
						Card 1							
061	940				645	67	1	227					
062	940	3	234	135	39	109	59	41	135	113	50	3	19
063	940			407	362	171							
064	940			93	188	71	122	131	119	138	55	67	44
065	940				784	107	49						
066	940			8	758	168	6						
067	940		57	10	504	299	60	8	1	1			
068	940		478	206	226	20	8		1	1			
069	940			1	910	28	1						
070	940			367	109	59	49	77	123	102	31	23	
071	940			349	99	39	64	90	73	60	65	52	49
072	940			545	20	21	10	2	296	20	9	9	8
073	940				246	694							
074	940				53	156	186	88	142	67	96	41	111
075	940				178	107	179	219	257				
076	940				185	164	175	185	231				
077	940				309	159	202	131	139				
078	940					415	191	160	107	42	19	4	2
079	940			940									
080	940				940								

FIGURE 10.4
Sample Basic Tabs From Nutrition Study

Dealing with Missing Responses During Analysis

If missing responses are included after data cleaning, two options are used during analysis:

Deletion of the observation. Most computer programs allow the analyst to remove observations that have prespecified codes. Therefore, if a 9 indicates missing data, all observations with 9s are deleted either (a) from the entire analysis (which is expensive in terms of data) or (b) from any analysis involving that particular variable.

Pairwise deletion. Another way to deal with missing data is to utilize all available data for each calculation at the time of analysis. For a correlation coefficient, all observations with data on both variables are used, and any with missing observations on either of the variables are deleted. This procedure works well when (*a*) there is a large sample size and relatively few missing observations and (*b*) the variables are not highly related. However, it can produce unappealing results (such as an estimated correlation matrix that is "impossible"— i.e., not positive definite for linear algebra fans) for small sample sizes. Also, when the variables are highly interrelated, assuming missing data are random can distort relations. Hence, this method must be used with care.

A major problem in deciding how to "fill in" missing data or fix up illogical data is to determine whether the missing data are random or related to other variables. For example, assume income data are omitted by 10 percent of a sample. First, one must consider whether income omission is random or predominant in a particular income group (e.g., high). If high-income people have a disproportionate tendency to refuse to give income data, then randomly assigning income or putting in the average based on those who answered will produce a biased estimate of average income as well as lead to misestimation of relations between income and other variables. Second, income may be related to other variables, such as education. If the missing data follow the same relation between education and income as the obtained data (often a good assumption), then assigning a value for income without considering education will distort/bias relationships even if the mean is not affected.

To see the impact of various "data-fixing" procedures, consider the example in Figure 10.5, where income is assumed to be either $10,000 or $30,000 per year and education level either 12 years (high school) or 16 years (college). First, consider case B. Here, the mean income is $20,000 in the complete data. Substituting the mean or randomly assigning a value will not influence the mean, nor, since income and education are independent, will it change this relationship (case B'). In case C, however, missing income data come from the high-income category. The mean of the available data is $18,889, and therefore, substitution of the mean will cause an underestimation of the true mean. However, since income and education are independent, the relationship (or, in this case, perfect independence between the two) will be maintained by random assignment (case C').

If, on the other hand, income and education are positively related, as in case D (and school PR brochures), things are worse. In the case of randomly missing data (case E), substitution of the mean income ($20,000) would not affect the average-income calculations. However, random assignment of income values to the missing data points will "depress" the relationship between income and education (case E'). When the data are omitted in high-income categories (case F), the mean is again $18,889 in existing data and, hence, is biased downward. If data are assigned without regard to the relationship between income and education, then both the mean of income and the relationship between income and education are affected. It is also worth noting that, in case F, deleting observations with missing data on income will lead to an understatement of not just average income but average education as well.

One way to fill in missing data is to predict the value of the missing observation based on available data. For example, if we assume Income = $B_0 + B_1$(Education), we can fill in missing income data if education data are available. This is done by (*a*) estimating B_0 and B_1 from observations where both income and education are available and (*b*) putting education into the resulting formula. In Figure 10.5 (case F), one would predict that 80 percent 64/(64 + 16) of the 20 nonresponses to income would have an income of $30,000 and 20 percent would have an income of $10,000.

Income and education independent				
		Income		
	Education	$10,000	$30,000	No Data
A. Complete data	12 years	50	50	—
	16 years	50	50	—
B. Randomly missing data	12 years	45	45	10
(income only)	16 years	45	45	10
B′. Randomly assigning	12 years	50	50	—
missing data	16 years	50	50	—
C. High income data missing	12 years	50	40	10
	16 years	50	40	10
C′. Randomly assigning	12 years	56	44	—
missing data	16 years	56	44	—

Income and education related				
		Income		
	Education	$10,000	$30,000	No Data
D. Complete data	12 years	80	20	—
	16 years	20	80	—
E. "Randomly" missing data	12 years	72	18	10
	16 years	18	72	10
E′. Randomly assigning	12 years	77	23	—
missing data	16 years	23	77	—
F. High education causing	12 years	80	20	0
missing income data	16 years	16	64	20
F′. Randomly assigning high	12 years	82	20	—
income missing data*	16 years	27	73	—

*In proportion to 96 versus 84, the observed split on income.

FIGURE 10.5
Missing Data Patterns: Hypothetical Examples

By randomly assigning people in those proportions, we would re-create case D, the complete data.

This "bootstrapping" approach is useful if the income-education relationship is the same in respondents as in nonrespondents. It is possible that some Ph.D.s are ashamed to admit to poverty status, and this explains why they fail to give income data. If this is the reason for the nonresponse, this procedure will overestimate income for nonrespondents. The approach also requires a significant relationship between income and education (otherwise, the equation will essentially predict the average income value for all education levels). For these reasons, this approach is rarely used.

SUMMARY

Unless the data are converted accurately to a usable form, subsequent analysis will be both difficult and misleading. The secret is simply to be careful in establishing procedures for coding the data. Several key points need reiterating:

Keep an identification field that indicates both person and line number (if more than one). The ID field allows you to go back to the questionnaire if the data are incorrectly input, or to the respondent if further information is needed.

Code the data in a disaggregated form. Do not pack data in a few columns, as this is a false economy.

Don't multiple-punch. Multiple punches (inputting more than one piece of data in a column) are disastrous for most computer routines. In fact, some people strive valiantly to keep the number of possible responses to nine or fewer to reduce the tendency to multipunch. Also, take care to force suppliers into not multipunching, since, left to their own devices, some still multipunch or at least mix numeric and letter codes in a column as a carryover from the card era.

Keep fixed record lengths. Saving space is a false economy.

Keep backup data sets. Those who keep a single data set deserve the frustration of seeing it mangled.

Spend time cleaning the data. This means both throwing out hopelessly bad respondents and seeing if nonresponses can be converted to responses.

Be lucky. Those who aren't careful almost always get burned, but it helps to be lucky to avoid trouble.

The main point made here is that the treatment of missing data can affect results—especially when variables are related. Hence, the moral of the story is to (*a*) keep item nonresponse to a minimum and (*b*) consider the implications of using various data-fixing procedures before employing them.

PROBLEMS

1. Assume you wished to build a model relating GDP, Housing Starts, the Dow-Jones average, the Consumer Price Index, and automotive sales in the United States on a yearly basis from 1972 to 1988. Set up the code sheets for your data set.

2. How would you interpret nonresponse to each of the following questions?

> Do you own an air conditioner?_____   _____
>   Yes   No
>
> How many children do you have?_____
>
> | | *Dislike Very Much* | | | | | *Like Very Much* |
> |---|---|---|---|---|---|---|
> | How well do you like peas? | 1 | 2 | 3 | 4 | 5 | 6 |
>
> What is the largest selling brand of shampoo? _____

3. Set up a coding scheme for the questionnaire in problem 2.

REFERENCES

HOROWITZ, ABRAHAM D., AND THOMAS F. GOLOB (1979) "Survey Data Reliability Effects on Results of Consumer Preference Analyses," in William L. Wilkie, ed., *Advances in Consumer Research*, vol. 6., Ann Arbor, Mich.: Association for Consumer Research, 532–38.

MADOW, W. G., H. NISSELSON, AND I. OLKIN, EDS. (1983) *Incomplete Data in Sample Surveys*, 3 vols., New York: Academic Press.

MALHOTRA, NARESH K. (1987) "Analyzing Marketing Research Data with Incomplete Information on the Dependent Variable," *Journal of Marketing Research*, 24, February, 74–84.

OWENS, WILLIAM B. (1989) "Missing Data," *The Nielsen Researcher*, 2, Spring, 15–17.

PESSEMIER, EDGAR A. (1975) "Data Quality in Marketing Information Systems," in John U. Farley and John A. Howard, eds., *Control of Error in Market Research Data*, Lexington, Mass.: Lexington Books, 109–44.

SIEDL, PHILIP S. (1974) "Coding," in Robert Ferber, ed., *Handbook of Marketing Research*, New York: McGraw-Hill, 2-178–2-199.

APPENDIX 10-A

NUTRITION STUDY CODEBOOK

Column	CARD 1: Standard Family Background Codes* Code
1–6	Application number (identification)
7–8	State Codes
9–11	County codes
12–14	City codes
15	Live within city limits: 1—Inside city limits 2—Outside city limits
16	Office use
17	Marital status: 1—Now married 2—Never married 3—Divorced 4—Widowed 5—Separated 0—No answer

CARD 1 *(continued)*

Column	Code
18–19	Year married:

Last two digits of year punched actual
00—No answer

20–22	Homemaker:
20	Month of birth

1—January
2—February
3—March
4—April
5—May
6—June
7—July
8—August
9—September
0—October
X—November
+—December

21–22	Year of birth (last two digits of year punched actual)

23–25	Husband:
23	Month of birth (see codes for column 20)
24–25	Year of birth (see codes for columns 21 & 22)

X—Living away from home (service)
Blank—No husband

26–53	Other family members:
26	Month of birth (see codes for column 20)
27–28	Year of birth (see codes for columns 21 and 22)
29	Sex

1—Male
2—Female

54–56	Office Use
57	Homemaker's education:

1—Attended grade school
2—Graduated from grade school
3—Attended high school
4—Graduated from high school
5—Attended college
6—Graduated from college
7—Masters
8—Doctors
0—No answer

58	Husband's education:

1—Attended grade school
2—Graduated from grade school
3—Attended high school
4—Graduated from high school
5—Attended college
6—Graduated from college
7—Masters
8—Doctors
0—No answer
X—No husband

CARD 1 *(continued)*

Column	Code
59	Homemaker's employment:

59   Homemaker's employment:
  1—Full time
  2—Part time
  3—Not employed
  4—No answer

60   Husband's employment:
  1—Full time
  2—Part time
  3—Not employed
  0—No answer
  X—No husband

61   Principal wage earner:
  1—Husband
  2—Homemaker
  3—Other
  4—No wage earner (income derived from source other than
     employment)

62   Occupation:
  0—Professional, technical, and kindred workers
  1—Farmers and farm managers
  2—Managers, officials, and proprietors (except farm)
  3—Clerical and kindred workers
  4—Sales workers
  5—Craftsmen, foremen, and kindred workers
  6—Operative and kindred workers
  7—Service workers (including private household)
  8—Farm laborers and foremen
  9—Laborers (except farm and mine)
  X—Retired, students, disabled, unemployment, and armed forces
  +—No answer

63–64 Annual family income:
  03—Under $3,000
  04—$3,000–$3,999
  05—$4,000–$4,999
  06—$5,000–$5,999
  07—$6,000–$6,999
  08—$7,000–$7,999
  09—$8,000–$8,999
  10—$9,999–$9,999
  11—$10,000–$10,999
  12—$11,000–$11,999
  13—$12,000–$12,999
  14—$13,000–$13,999
  15—$14,000–$14,999
  16—$15,000–$15,999
  17—$16,000–$16,999
  18—$17,000–$17,999
  19—$18,000–$18,999
  20—$19,000–$19,999
  21—$20,000–$24,999
  22—$25,000–$29,999
  23—$30,000–$35,000
  24—Over $35,000

CARD 1 *(continued)*

Column	Code
65	Type of residence:

65 Type of residence:
    1—House
    2—Apartment
    3—Other
    0—No answer

66 Home ownership:
    1—Own
    2—Rent
    3—Live with relatives (in their home)
    4—Other
    0—No answer

67 Car ownership:
    1—1 car
    2—2 cars
    3—3 cars
    4—4 cars
    5—5 cars
    6—6 cars
    7—7 cars
    8—8 cars
    9—9 cars
    X—None
    0—No answer

68 Truck ownership:
    (see codes for car ownership)

69 Homemaker's race:
    1—White
    2—Negro or black
    3—Oriental
    4—Other
    0—No answer

70–72 Metropolitan area code

73 Office Use

74 Geographic divisions:
    1—New England
    2—Middle Atlantic
    3—East North Central
    4—West North Central
    5—South Atlantic
    6—East South Central
    7—West South Central
    8—Mountain
    9—Pacific

75 Population densities:
    1—Rural
    2—Cities, 2,500–49,999

    Metropolitan areas:
    3—50,000–499,999
    4—500,000–1,999,999
    5—2,000,000 and over

CARD 1 (concluded)

Column	Code
76	Homemaker's age coded:
	1—Under 30 years
	2—30 through 39 years
	3—40 through 49 years
	4—50 through 59 years
	5—60 years and over
77	Income coded:
	1—Under $6,000
	2—$6,000–$9,999
	3—$10,000–$14,999
	4—$15,000–$19,999
	5—$20,000 and over
78	Size of family
	2—2 members
	3—3 members
	4—4 members
	5—5 members
	6—6 members
	7—7 members
	8—8 members
	9—9 or more members
79	panel number
80	Card No. 1

Punch-card layout (Card 1):

Columns	Field
1–6	APPLICATION
7–8	STATE
9–12	COUNTY
13–14	CITY
15	IN-OUT
16	NFO USE
17	MARITAL
18–19	YEAR MARRIED
20–21	HMK — MONTH
22	HMK — YEAR
23–24	HUS — MONTH
25	HUS — YEAR
26–27	OFM 1 — MONTH
28	OFM 1 — YEAR
29	OFM 1 — SEX
30–31	OFM 2 — MONTH
32	OFM 2 — YEAR
33	OFM 2 — SEX
34–35	OFM 3 — MONTH
36	OFM 3 — YEAR
37	OFM 3 — SEX
38	OFM 4 — MONTH
39	OFM 4 — YEAR
40	OFM 4 — SEX
41	OFM 5 — SEX
42–43	OFM 5 — MONTH
44	OFM 5 — YEAR
45	OFM 6 — SEX
46–47	OFM 6 — MONTH
48	OFM 6 — YEAR
49	OFM 7 — SEX
50–51	OFM 7 — MONTH
52	OFM 7 — YEAR
53	SEX
54–56	NFO USE
57	HMK. EDUC.
58	HUS. EDUC.
59	HMK. EMPL.
60	HUS. EMPL.
61	PRIN. WAGE E
62	OCCUPATION
63–64	ANNUAL FAMILY INCOME
65	TYPE RES.
66	HOME OWN
67	CARS OWNED
68	TRUCKS OWNED
69	HMK. RACE
70–72	METRO AREA
73	NFO USE
74	CLASS — GEO.
75	CLASS — POP.
76	CLASS — AGE
77	CLASS — INCOME
78	CLASS — FAMILY SIZE
79–80	PANEL NUMBER

CARD 2

Column	Code
1–6	Application number
7–8	Coded income

Section I—Food and shopping habits

9	Q. 1	Portion of household food shopping done personally:
		1. None of it.
		2. Less than half of it.
		3. About half of it.
		4. Most of it.
		5. All of it.
		0. No answer.

CARD 2 *(continued)*

Column	Code		
10	Q. 2	Number of times per week shop for food:	

10   Q. 2   Number of times per week shop for food:
1. Less than once a week.
2. Once a week.
3. 2–4 times a week.
4. 5 or more times a week.
0. No answer.

11   Q. 3a   Shopping list prepared before going to the store:
1. Yes.
2. No.

12   Q. 3b   What portion of items purchased at store are on shopping list?
1. None of them.
2. Some of them.
3. About half of them.
4. More than half.
5. Almost all of them.
0. No answer.

13   Q. 4   Approximately how much money is spent on food in average week?
1. Under $15.
2. $15–$29.
3. $30–$44.
4. $45–$60.
5. Over $60.
0. No answer.

14   Q. 5   Approximately how much different is the amount spent now on food each week compared to one year ago?
1. Spend at least $10 less than last year.
2. $5–$10 less than last year.
3. About the same as last year.
4. $5–$10 more than last year.
0. No answer.

15   Q. 6   When buying staple products, how many brands and sizes do you usually consider?
1. Only 1 or 2.
2. Many brands, one size.
3. Many sizes, one brand.
4. Many brands and sizes.
0. No answer.

16   Q. 7   Which best describes the way you shop for food?
1. I actively seek information about food in terms of nutritional value, price, etc.
2. I sometimes try new foods because of new information, but generally buy the same foods.
3. The food I buy is almost always the same, and I spend very little time thinking about it.
0. No answer.

17   Q. 8   Have you or any members of your immediate family ever used food stamps?
1. Never.
2. Use to, but do not use them now.
3. We are presently using them.
0. No answer.

CARD 2 *(concluded)*

Column	Code		
18–27	Q. 9	How important are the following considerations when deciding which foods to serve?	
		1.	Very important
		2.	
		3.	Somewhat important.
		4.	
		5.	Not very important.
		0.	No answer.
28–38	Q. 10	When deciding which brand to buy, how much attention do you pay to the following?	
		1.	Pay a great deal of attention.
		2.	Pay some attention.
		3.	Pay little or no attention.
		0.	No answer.
39–41	Q. 11	Number of times per week you, personally, eat the following meals.	
		1.	Never.
		2.	1–2.
		3.	3–4.
		4.	5–6.
		5.	Every day.
		0.	No answer.
42	Q. 12	Number of snacks you, personally, have in a typical day.	
		1.	None.
		2.	One.
		3.	Two.
		4.	Three or more.
		0.	No answer.
43	Q. 13	How much food do you can yourself?	
		1.	None.
		2.	A small amount.
		3.	A large amount.
		0.	No answer.
44–73	Q. 14	How often do you personally consume each of the following?	
		1.	Never.
		2.	A few times a year.
		3.	One to two times a month.
		4.	Weekly.
		5.	Several times a week.
		6.	Once a day.
		7.	More than once a day.
		0.	No answer.
74–78	Q. 15	How has the amount your household consumed of each of the following changed in the past year?	
		1.	Much less.
		2.	Somewhat less.
		3.	About the same.
		4.	Somewhat more.
		5.	Much more.
		0.	No answer.
79	BLANK		
80	Card No. 2.		

CARD 3

Column	Code	
1–6	Application number	

Section I—Food and shopping habits (continued)

7–31	Q. 15	How has the amount your household consumed of each of the following changed in the past year?

    1. Much less.
    2. Somewhat less.
    3. About the same.
    4. Somewhat more.
    5. Much more.
    0. No answer.

Section II—Nutritional information

32–43	Q. 1	Degree of information gained from listed sources.

    1. None.
    2. Very little.
    3. Some.
    4. Quite a bit.
    5. A tremendous amount.
    0. No answer.

44–46	Q. 2	In the past year, have you read any books about any of the following?
44		Dieting:

    1. No.
    2. Yes.
    0. No answer.

45		Nutrition:

    1. No.
    2. Yes.
    0. No answer.

46		Cooking:

    1. No.
    2. Yes.
    0. No answer.

47–56	Q. 3	If government launched a major nutrition education campaign aimed at adults, which form would you prefer?
47		0. No answer.
		1. Column in newspaper.
48		1. TV special.
49		1. Special edition of a prominent magazine.
50		1. Government brochure.
51		1. Extension courses.
52		1. Workshops.
53		1. Public service TV announcements.
54		1. Information on packages.
55		1. Information in TV advertisements.
56		1. Don't care.
57	Q. 4	Amount willing to pay to subscribe to a service providing information about nutritional value of brands offered in local supermarkets.

    1. Nothing.
    2. 10¢–19¢.
    3. 20¢–49¢.

CARD 3 *(concluded)*

Column	Code	
		4. 50¢–99¢.
		5. $1–$2.
		6. Over $2.
		0. No answer.
58	Q. 5	Any formal nutrition course in any of the following?
		High school:
		1. No.
		2. Yes.
		0. No answer.
59		College:
		1. No.
		2. Yes.
		0. No answer.
60		Adult education/workshops:
		1. No.
		2. Yes.
		0. No answer.

Section III—Background information

Column	Code	
61–72	Q. 1	Any members of household on any special diet?
61–66		Self-imposed:
		0. No answer.
		+. No members of household on a diet.
		1. Low cholesterol.
62		1. Low fat/calorie.
63		1. Diabetic.
64		1. Low salt.
65		1. Vegetarian.
66		1. Low triglyceride.
67–72		Doctor's orders:
67		0. No answer.
		1. Low cholesterol.
68		1. Low fat/calorie.
69		1. Diabetic.
70		1. Low salt.
71		1. Vegetarian.
72		1. Low triglyceride.
73	Q. 2	How often do you smoke?
		1. Never.
		2. Occasionally.
		3. Regularly, but light (less than one pack of cigarettes each day).
		4. Regularly (one pack of cigarettes a day).
		5. Heavily (more than one pack each day or equivalent).
		0. No answer.
74–79	Blank	
80	Card 3	

CARD 4

Column	Code	
1-6		Application number

Section III—Background information (continued)

Section IV—General attitude information

Section V—Food opinions

7-13   Q. 3   Which of following vitamin pills do you personally take?

    7
        0. No answer.
        1. None.

    8   1. Multiple.

    9   1. Vitamin C.

   10   1. Vitamin G.

   11   1. Vitamin B-12 complex.

   12   1. Vitamin A.

   13   1. Iron.

14   Q. 4   Amount of time spent watching TV on average day—

        1. None.
        2. Less than 1 hour.
        3. 1-2 hours.
        4. 3-4 hours.
        5. Over 4 hours.
        0. No answer.

15   Q. 5   How has your family income changed in the last year?

        1. Gone down a lot.
        2. Gone down a little.
        3. Stayed about the same.
        4. Gone up a little.
        5. Gone up a lot.
        0. No answer.

16   Q. 6   How has your household size changed in the past year?

        1. Decreased by two or more.
        2. Decreased by one.
        3. Stayed the same.
        4. Increased by one.
        5. Increased by two or more.
        0. No answer.

17-39   *Section IV—General attitude information*

Indicate how much you agree or disagree with the following statements.

        1. Strongly agree.
        2. Somewhat agree.
        3. Neither agree nor disagree.
        4. Somewhat disagree.
        5. Strongly disagree.
        0. No answer.

40-77   *Section V—Food opinions*

40-49   Q. 1   Opinions about certain types of food:

        1. True.
        2. False.
        3. Don't know.
        0. No answer.

CARD 4 (concluded)

Column	Code	
50–77	Q. 2	Which foods contribute importantly to listed functions?
50–53		Eyes are aided by:
		1—Whole milk.
		0—No answer.
51		1—Beef.
52		1—Tomatoes.
53		1—Enriched bread.
54–57		Teeth and bones are aided by:
		Code same as columns 50–53
58–61		Muscle tissue is aided by:
		Code same as columns 50–53
62–65		Repair of body tissues is aided by:
		Code same as columns 50–53
66–69		Blood cells are aided by:
		Code same as columns 50–53
70–73		Fighting infection is aided by:
		Code same as columns 50–53
74–77		Nervous system is aided by:
		Code same as columns 50–53
78–79		BLANK
80		Card No. 4

CARD 5

Column	Code	
1–6		Application number

Section V—Food opinions (continued)

7–14	Q. 2	Which foods contribute importantly to listed functions?
7–10		Skin is aided by:
		1—Whole milk.
		0—No answer.
8		1—Beef.
9		1—Tomatoes.
10		1—Enriched bread.
11–14		Proper growth of children is aided by:
		Code same as columns 7–10
15–62	Q. 3	Nutrients contained in listed items:
15–26		Whole milk:
15		1—There is a lot of vitamin A in—
		0—No answer.
16		1—There is a lot of thiamin (vitamin B) in—
17		1—There is a lot of riboflavin (vitamin B2) in—
18		1—There is a lot of niacin in—
19		1—There is a lot of vitamin C in—
20		1—There is a lot of vitamin D in—
21		1—There is a lot of protein in—
22		1—There is a lot of carbohydrates in—
23		1—There is a lot of fat in—
24		1—There is a lot of calories in—
25		1—There is a lot of iron in—
26		1—There is a lot of calcium in—

CARD 5 *(concluded)*

Column

27–38   Beef:
             Code same as columns 15–26

39–50   Tomatoes:
             Code same as columns 15–26

51–62   Enriched bread:
             Code same as colmns 15–26

63–79   BLANK

80   Card No. 5

CARD 6

Column   *Code*

1–6   Application number

            Section V—Food opinions (continued)

7–62   Q. 4 Listed foods that you think have a lot of the same benefits to the body:
              1st col. 1. Whole milk
                     0. No answer
              2d col. 1. Beef
                     0. No answer
              3d col. 1. Tomatoes
                     0. No answer
              4th col. 1. Enriched bread
                     0. No answer

7–10   Oatmeal provides a lot of the same benefits as—

11–14   Fish provides a lot of the same benefits as—

15–18   Rice provides a lot of the same benefits as—

19–22   Navy beans

23–26   Chicken

27–30   Potatoes

31–34   Eggs

35–38   Macaroni

39–42   Pork and lamb

43–46   String beans

47–50   Carrots

51–54   Bananas

55–58   Peanut butter

59–62   Cottage cheese

63–79   BLANK

80   Card No. 6

CHAPTER 11

Basic Analysis

Having carefully coded and input a data set, the analyst now must decide how best to interpret it. This chapter will proceed by first describing the basic types of analyses that are appropriate for various types of data (nominal, ordinal, interval, and ratio). Next, examples of the basic procedures are described. Before beginning, however, it is useful to visualize the structure of data. Imagine a sheet of paper on which each column represents a different variable and each row a different observation:

		Variable				
		1	*2*	*3*	*. . .*	*k*
	1					
	2					
Observation	3					
	.					
	.					
	.					
	n					

If data have been collected at several points in time, then each separate data collection would produce a different sheet of paper:

Time 3

OBSER-
VATION

VARIABLE
1 2 . . . k

1
2
.
.
.
n

While it would be possible to present such a folder to a manager, in general this is not a good idea, since managers are busy and tend to prefer a somewhat more parsimonious summary. (Also, if there are, for example, 200 variables and 1,000 observations, each page in the notebook would be 9 feet wide and 28 feet long—a little difficult for the average analyst to carry.) Consequently, analysis can be viewed as the task of reducing the data to a more manageable and easily interpretable form. In this chapter, we focus on how to analyze a single time period of measurement (often known as a cross section), and on describing responses to a single variable and relations among two variables.

SCALE TYPE AND ANALYSES

Scales form a hierarchy, so that any "higher-order" scale can use procedures for a lower-order scale, but not vice versa (Figure 11.1). For example, any analysis appropriate for nominally scaled data may also be applied to intervally scaled data. Hence, having higher-order data is very desirable.

Nominally scaled data, such as region of the country or preference for furniture style, present very limited possibilities for analysis. Logically, all one can do is report on the percent who live in each region or prefer each style—often called a *tabulation* or *frequency count*. One can also report which is the most common region or most preferred style, a statistic known as the *mode*.

To relate two nominally scaled variables, the most appropriate method is to simply cross-tabulate the results:

Preferred Style of Furniture	*Region of the Country*				*Total by Style*
	East	*Midwest*	*South*	*West*	
Early American	90	5	5	0	100
Modern	5	5	10	80	100
Cheap (early grandmother)	5	90	85	20	200
Total by region	100	100	100	100	

FIGURE 11.1
Scale Types and Analysis Methods

	Single-Variable Description	**Measure of Relation Between Two Variables**
Nonmetric:		
Nominal	Frequency distribution Mode	Contingency table (cross-tab) and coefficient
Ordinal	Median	Nonparametric statistics: Spearman's R Kendall's Tau
Metric:		
Interval	Mean Standard deviation	Pearson product moment correlation
Ratio	Coefficient of variation ($S/\overline{X}$)	

In this hypothetical example, it appears obvious that Easterners like Early American, Westerners like Modern, and those in the Midwest and South prefer Cheap.

If one has ordinally scaled variables, then it is possible to describe each one via percentiles. The most common example of this is standardized testing, where we find out such fascinating facts as B.J. is in the 92nd percentile in math (i.e., of 100 people taking the test, 91 did worse), the 58th percentile in vocabulary, and the 3rd percentile in music aptitude. (Hopefully B.J. plans to be an engineer.) To relate two ordinally scaled variables, a number of so-called nonparametric measures of association are used, such as the Spearman rank correlation.

If a variable is metric (at least intervally scaled), then a number of other statistics become appropriate, such as the mean and standard deviation. Moreover, when examining the relationship between two intervally scaled variables, it is possible to use the Pearson product-moment correlation. Since the mean, standard deviation, and correlation are required for many useful procedures (e.g., regression analysis), having intervally scaled data is a big plus.

With ratio scaled data, one can compute the coefficient of variation $(S/\overline{X})$, which is a measure of the variability of a variable as a percent of its mean. Since this is not a widely used statistic, this advantage of going from an intervally scaled variable to a ratio scaled one is not overwhelming. The major advantage of ratio scaled data is that they allow one to multiply two variables (X and Y) together to form another (Z), whereas with two intervally scaled variables the coding of the variables (e.g., 1 to 5 versus -2 to $+2$) can affect the relative size of the product (Z). Consider the following example:

	Disagree				Agree
Person A: Likes yogurt	✓				
Likes diets	✓				
Person B: Likes yogurt					✓
Likes diets					✓
Person C: Likes yogurt	✓				
Likes diets					✓

If we code the two variables 1 to 5 and create the product of the two responses, we get 1, 25, and 5 for persons A, B, and C, respectively. If we code the variables -2 to $+2$, however, the products would be 4, 4, and -4, respectively. Notice that the ranking of people on the created variable has changed from B, C, A to B, A, C. Hence, the interpretation of the product depends on the arbitrary coding scheme followed.

Two important points are worth adding here. First, it is possible to violate the scale assumptions by, for example, computing averages from ordinal scales (e.g., ranking of five different package designs) or including ordinally scaled variables in regressions. Often, this produces useful insights. It does, however, violate the assumptions of the procedures themselves and affects significance tests on them. Computer programs make no check to see if your data are properly scaled and will, for example, compute correlations between nominally scaled variables. Be careful interpreting results from situations where you "dump everything in to see what happens." Therefore, to "get away" with "misusing" data, a combination of luck and experience is required.

DESCRIBING A SINGLE VARIABLE

Simple Tabulation

The simplest way to analyze data is to tabulate the responses on a question-by-question basis. This form of analyzing the data (not so ingeniously called *tabulating*) is the most common form of analysis. The only calculation involved is that, after the number of respondents who chose each of the available answers is tabulated, the percentage of the time each response is given is calculated. For example, assume the following question was asked of 940 female heads of households:

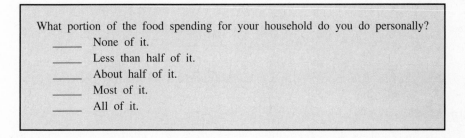

What portion of the food spending for your household do you do personally?
_____ None of it.
_____ Less than half of it.
_____ About half of it.
_____ Most of it.
_____ All of it.

The tabulated results would be in the form of Table 11.1. It takes very little statistical analysis to see what this implies. Over half the sample are doing all the shopping, and almost another one-third doing most of it. Thus, the vast majority of the sample are experienced food shoppers. It is often the case that a particular response is the key one (i.e., the proportion of people who buy our brand). The percent who give that response is frequently more important than the entire distribution. This is especially true

TABLE 11.1 Portion of Food Shopping Done

Response	Frequency	Percent
1. None	15	1.6
2. Less than half	34	3.6
3. About half	52	5.5
4. Most	295	31.4
5. All	538	57.2
6. No answer	6	.6
	940	99.9

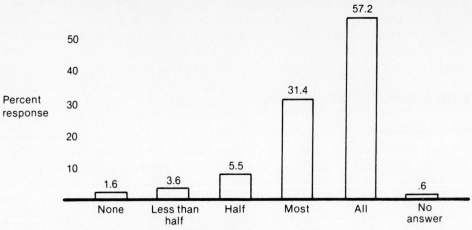

FIGURE 11.2
Bar Chart of Table 11.1 Responses

for questions such as purchase intention, where often only the most positive ("top box") response is considered to be a useful measure of intention.

Graphical Display

To highlight results, a common approach is to construct a bar chart to represent the results graphically (Figure 11.2). Other popular displays include pie charts (to indicate percents). Graphical displays are growing in popularity given available software.

Simple Calculations

Another way to indicate the pattern of responses to a single question is to compute a statistic.

Mode One common statistic is called the *mode*. This is the most frequently occurring response (in the case of Table 11.1, 5—all of it—is the most typical result).

Median Another statistic commonly calculated is called the *median*. This is the score that is exactly in the middle of the responses (in Table 11.1, this is also 5).

Mean The statistic that is most often calculated is the *mean* (average) response. This is calculated by using the code value for each response and weighting by the frequency that the response is given. In Table 11.1, if we ignore the "no answer" response, the mean is $[(15)(1) + (34)(2) + (52)(3) + (295)(4) + (538)(5)]/934 = 4.40$.

The Nonresponse Problem Consider Table 11.2. A major problem in analyzing these results is the nonresponses. There are three major choices: do nothing with nonresponses, convert the no-answer response, and exclude no-answer responses.

Do Nothing with Nonresponses   If we do nothing, most computer programs will, by default, count nonresponses as whatever code they were given. In this case, that would mean the following:

Code	Frequency	Code × Frequency
1	425	425
2	61	122
3	11	33
4	340	1,360
9	83	747
	920	2,687

Hence the mean = 2,687/920 = 2.92. Putting the 9s in implies that no-answer means the person would have responded much more than 5. This is clearly ridiculous, and the mean of 2.92 is biased. However, if the number of nonresponses to all the questions is small (less than 1 to 2 percent), their effect on the mean will be slight and thus unlikely to change any significant conclusions.

Convert the No-Answer Response   Sometimes it is possible to logically assign no-answers to a category. In this case, we might assume that nonresponses were some respondents' way of saying the question was irrelevant and they were really responding "none." Thus, we could add them into the "none" category (code = 1). The results would then be

Code	Frequency	Code × Frequency
1	508 (425 + 83)	508
2	61	122
3	11	33
4	340	1,360
	920	2,023

Here the mean = 2,023/920 = 2.20.

TABLE 11.2 Sample Response Pattern

Response	Code	Frequency
None	1	425
1–2	2	61
3–4	3	11
5 or more	4	340
No answer	9	83

Delete No-Answer Responses It is possible to simply exclude no-answer respondents from each calculation. This is both easy, given current computer algorithms, and popular. One source of its popularity is that, in excluding these respondents, it appears that we are getting a "good" answer. Actually, the answer is good only if the nonresponses would, if we were able to convert them to responses, follow the same pattern as the responses. Since this is often not the case, converting no-answers may be better than ignoring them. The results of ignoring the nonresponses for our example would be as follows:

Code	Frequency	Code × Frequency
1	425	425
2	61	122
3	11	33
4	340	1,360
	837	1,940

Now the mean = 1,940/837 = 2.32.

Usefulness of Averages Averages (means) are a popular measure. They are only useful, however, when the following conditions are met:

The data should be intervally scaled. If the codes (Table 11.2) indicated favorite color (1 = blue, 2 = red, 3 = green, 4 = yellow), then the data say that blue and yellow are popular and red and green are not. Calculating an average of 2.3 could be misleading. (In this case, the median, 2 = red, would also be misleading.) When the data constitute an ordinal scale, it is also theoretically incorrect to compute an average. Nonetheless, since most ordinal scales are fairly close to interval scales in their composition, and since respondents may well respond to an ordinal scale as though it were an interval scale, calculation of averages on ordinal scales is a widely accepted practice in marketing research, where the tradeoff between simplification and theoretical correctness often leans toward simplification.

The data should have some central tendency. In other words, most responses should be clustered around the mean. In this example, a mean of 2.3 is misleading since almost the entire sample checked 1 or 4. The irrelevance of the mean can be seen by considering the temperature people prefer for tea. Most people either like tea hot or iced. Averaging the preferred temperatures produces room temperature, which represents no one's preference very well.

Sensitivity of the mean. It is also interesting to note how insensitive the mean is to fairly large changes in the response distribution. In the previous example, when we added the nonrespondents (10 percent of the original sample) to the extreme of the distribution (code = 1), the mean only changed from the 2.32 obtained by excluding them to 2.20. Given the importance of top box responses (e.g., "definitely will buy the product" responses), the average is a fairly insensitive measuring device and small changes in it may be very important managerially.

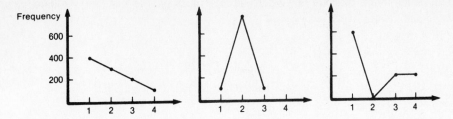

FIGURE 11.3
Three Distributions with Equal Means

Standard Deviation

To assess the accuracy of the mean in representing responses, a measure of central tendency is helpful. Consider the following three (hypothetical) response distributions:

Code	A	B	C
1	400	100	600
2	300	800	0
3	200	100	200
4	100	0	200

In each case, the mean response is 2. Yet obviously the distributions are very different. In fact, only in case B does the mean represent a typical response well, and in case C, the mean response of 2 was given by none of the 1,000 respondents. By graphing the three distributions (Figure 11.3), we see that a major difference is spread (width) of the response patterns about the mean. The difference in spread is sometimes easier to see in a continuous case (Figure 11.4). Here, both cases have means of 2, but in case A there is more spread about the mean than in case B.

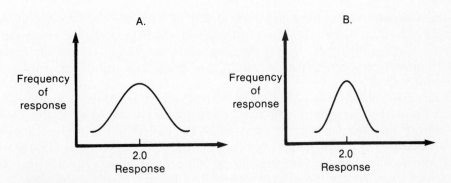

FIGURE 11.4
Two Response Definitions

To have an index that captures this spread, most people use the standard deviation. It is estimated as follows:

$$s_x = s = \sqrt{\dfrac{\displaystyle\sum_{\substack{\text{all} \\ \text{observations}}} \left(X - \overline{X}\right)^2}{\text{Number of observations} - 1}} \cdot \sqrt{\dfrac{N - n}{N - 1}}$$

$$= \sqrt{\dfrac{\displaystyle\sum_{j=1}^{n} \left(X_j - \overline{X}\right)^2}{n - 1}} \cdot \sqrt{\dfrac{N - n}{N - 1}}$$

When the sample size n is small in relation to the population size N (which it typically is), the $(N - n)/(N - 1)$ term (the finite population correction factor) is close to 1 and the formula reduces to

$$s = \sqrt{\dfrac{\displaystyle\sum_{j=1}^{n} \left(X_j - \overline{X}\right)^2}{n - 1}}$$

When data are grouped into categories (as they usually are in survey data), this formula reduces to

$$s = \sqrt{\dfrac{\displaystyle\sum_{j=1}^{c} f_i\left(X_j - \overline{X}\right)^2}{n - 1}}$$

where

$$f_i = \text{frequency of the } i\text{th response}$$
$$c = \text{number of response codes}$$

Using this formula on the three hypothetical sets of data, we find standard deviations of 1, .45, and 1.27, respectively. The smaller the standard deviation, the closer the actual responses are to the mean. In this case, we again see that in case B the mean is a relatively good representation and in case C the mean is a particularly terrible representation of responses.

At this point, it is worth noting (as the careful reader no doubt has) that case C is different from the other two in that it is bimodal—that is, the most likely results are either high or low, but not near the mean of 2. The easiest way to recognize this is to observe the frequency distribution. Since computing frequencies or even looking at them is somewhat tedious, however, the standard deviation is useful as a tip-off/signal to look at responses more closely. Specifically, when the standard deviation becomes large in relation to the range of the variable (in case C, 1.43 is almost half the possible range), then we may have bimodal responses. On the other hand, when the standard deviation is small in relation to the range (in case B, .45 vs. 3), then most of the information about responses is likely to be "captured" by the mean.

To give an example of the calculation of a standard deviation, we return to the example in Table 11.2. Assuming nonresponses were excluded (and, therefore, the mean was 2.32), we get the following:

Frequency Code	(f_i)	$(X_i - \overline{X})^2$	$f_i(X_i - \overline{X})^2$
1	425	1.74	739.50
2	61	.10	6.10
3	11	.46	5.06
4	340	2.82	959.62
	837		1,710.28

Thus,

$$s = \sqrt{\frac{1,710.28}{836}} = 1.43$$

When data are collected on limited range scales, the standard deviation and mean are related. For example, on a five-point scale the only way to get a mean of 1 or 5 is to have a standard deviation of 0 (all ratings = 1 or 5). By contrast, for a mean of 3, the standard deviation can range between 0 (all ratings = 3) and 1.414 (half the ratings = 1, the other half = 5). Practically what this means is that one or two outliers can make a huge difference in means when they are high (as any person or company being rated by a number of sources realizes).

COMPARING VARIABLES

Until now, this chapter has been devoted to analyzing variables one at a time. This section, by contrast, discusses techniques for comparing several variables if the data are intervally scaled.

Consider, for example, ratings of a series of attributes in terms of their importance. Typically, most of the attributes will be rated as important. The key is to uncover the most important attributes. Hence, we must look at responses across attributes.

Plotting

Consider Table 11.3, taken from question 9 in the nutrition study which rated importance of attributes of food on a five-point scale from 1 (very important) to 5 (very unimportant). We can construct a plot of these results to highlight them (Figure 11.5). It is obvious from this plot that taste is the key attribute, with other family members' preferences, price, and nutritional value all closely bunched as next most important. (Given that the socially correct answer favors nutrition, one might suspect that it is the fourth most important attribute.)

TABLE 11.3 Importance of Attributes in Choosing Food

Attribute	Mean Importance (1 = very important, 5 = not very important)
Variety	2.02
Taste	1.24
Other family members' preferences	1.71
Diet restrictions	2.98
Price	1.74
Availability	2.16
Ease of preparation	2.78
Habit	2.82
Advertised specials	2.26
Nutritional value	1.66

We can augment the profile chart by plotting, for each variable, both its mean and some indication of the range of responses. For example, you could display the 10th and 90th percentile values:

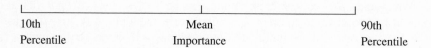

10th Percentile	Mean Importance	90th Percentile

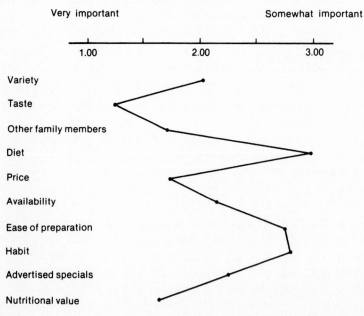

FIGURE 11.5
Food Attribute Importances

Notice this elegantly simple presentation immediately conveys information about the distribution and its shape without plotting all the responses. Further, the degree of overlap between different attribute importances gives an indication of how different they are.

Ranking

Another way to analyze the results is simply to rank the attributes by the mean response. In this case, results are

1. Taste
2. Nutritional value
3. Other family members' preferences
4. Price
5. Variety
6. Availability
7. Advertised specials
8. Ease of preparation
9. Habit
10. Diet restrictions

This ranking has several shortcomings. First, there is no significance in some of the differences, such as between 3 and 4, and 8 and 9. Presentation of rankings (and to a lesser extent, the profile chart) tends to downplay this point. Second, the attribute "diet restrictions" intuitively is not the tenth most important. This is because it is essentially a binary attribute: either you have a diet restriction, or you do not. Therefore, for those who think it is very important (26.7 percent), it may well be the most important attribute. Since we are ranking average importance, however, it appears unimportant, and we could falsely conclude that it can be ignored.

Indexing

A third approach for indicating relative scores is to recalibrate the scale. This approach is related to the process of normalizing and standardizing discussed in Chapter 8. We first find the typical average important score for an attribute by taking the average of the average importance scores:

$$
\begin{array}{r}
2.02 \\
1.24 \\
1.71 \\
2.98 \\
1.74 \\
2.16 \\
2.78 \\
2.82 \\
2.26 \\
\underline{1.66} \\
\overline{21.37}
\end{array}
$$

$$
\text{Overall Average} = \frac{21.37}{10} = 2.14
$$

TABLE 11.4 Attribute Importance Indexes

Attribute	Difference	Ratio
Variety	− .12 (2.02 − 2.14)	.94 (2.02/2.14)
Taste	− .90	.58
Other family members' preferences	− .43	.80
Diet restrictions	.84	1.39
Price	− .40	.81
Availability	.02	1.01
Ease of preparation	.64	1.30
Habit	.68	1.32
Advertised specials	.12	1.06
Nutritional value	− .48	.78

We then recompute average importance scores either in terms of differences from this average value, or as the ratio of the average on the particular attribute to the overall average (Table 11.4). The advantage of these indexes is that they highlight extreme cases and quickly indicate relatively important and unimportant attributes.

BASIC ANALYSIS EXAMPLES

Typically, analysis by a supplier is simply a series of tabulations. If a more elaborate form of presentation is desired, one would expect to see some interpretation interspersed with a question-by-question reporting of basic analyses. While there is no standard format, the report of the nutrition study in Appendix 11-B provides, in addition to some interesting results, a basic format for preparation of such reports.

Another example of basic analyses can be found in a study of purchasing agents. Lehmann and O'Shaughnessy (1974) reported an attempt to assess which product attributes are most important for different types of products. Forty-five purchasing agents were asked to rate the importance of 17 product attributes for the following four situations:

Type I: Routine order product.

Type II: Procedural problem products (where the principal user must be taught to use the product).

Type III: Performance problem products (where there is some question about whether the product will perform adequately).

Type IV: Political problem products (where there is an extremely large capital outlay or several departments are involved in the decision, or both).

Importances were rated on six-point bipolar adjective scales from 1 = very unimportant to 6 = very important. Ignoring the real question of representativeness given a sample size of 45 (26 in the United States and 19 in the United Kingdom), the average results were computed (Table 11.5).

Looking at the averages leads to several interesting conclusions. First, almost all the attributes are rated in the important half of the scale for all product types. (This

TABLE 11.5 Average Attribute Importance for the Four Product Types

| | Product Type | | | | | | | |
| | I | | II | | III | | IV | |
Attribute	Mean	Rank	Mean	Rank	Mean	Rank	Mean	Rank
1. Reputation	4.84[a]	4	5.33	7	5.29	5	5.53	2
	(1.09)		(.80)		(.82)		(.69)	
2. Financing	4.51	9	4.07	16	3.91	16	4.91	13
	(1.39)		(1.29)		(1.31)		(1.24)	
3. Flexibility	5.07	3	5.40	5	5.42	2	5.51	5
	(1.12)		(.62)		(.62)		(.59)	
4. Past experience	4.71	6	4.93	13	5.07	9	5.04	10
	(.94)		(.86)		(.69)		(.93)	
5. Technical service	4.36	12	5.53	1	5.38	3	5.40	7
	(1.28)		(.66)		(.89)		(.62)	
6. Confidence in	3.96	14	4.73	15	4.42	15	4.58	16
salespersons	(1.35)		(1.23)		(1.20)		1.20	
7. Convenience in	3.80	15	3.73	17	3.71	17	4.08	17
ordering	(1.32)		(1.29)		(1.34)		(1.24)	
8. Reliability data	4.47	11	5.16	11	5.33	4	5.53	3
	(1.24)		(1.07)		(.67)		(.59)	
9. Price	5.60	2	5.29	8	5.18	8	5.56	1
	(.62)		(.70)		(.94)		(.69)	
10. Technical	4.73	5	5.22	9	5.27	6	5.42	6
specifications	(1.25)		(.67)		(.69)		(.72)	
11. Ease of use	4.51	10	5.53	2	5.24	7	5.18	8
	(1.29)		(.59)		(.80)		(.83)	
12. Preference of user	4.00	13	4.76	14	4.53	13	4.84	14
	(1.19)		(1.11)		(1.14)		(.90)	
13. Training offered	3.22	16	5.42	3	4.73	12	5.00	11
	(1.18)		(.87)		(1.19)		(.83)	
14. Training required	3.22	17	5.11	12	4.44	14	4.69	15
	(1.22)		(1.23)		(1.22)		(1.02)	
15. Reliability of	5.64	1	5.42	4	5.44	1	5.53	4
delivery	(.53)		(.72)		(.66)		(.69)	
16. Maintenance	4.60	8	5.20	10	4.82	11	5.00	12
	(1.05)		(.69)		(.96)		(.74)	
17. Sales service	4.64	7	5.36	6	5.07	10	5.09	9
	(1.25)		(.77)		(.84)		(.70)	
Product type mean	4.46		5.07		4.90		5.11	

[a]Mean (standard deviation).
Source: Donald R. Lehmann and John O'Shaughnessy, "Differences in Attribute Importance for Different Industrial Products" from *Journal of Marketing* 38 (April 1974): 39–42. Copyright © by the American Marketing Association. Reprinted with the permission of the publishers.

is a typical result for importance questions, since individuals seem averse to indicating anything is unimportant, especially when the attributes have been selected to be potentially important; and in any event, they don't often distinguish between degrees of unimportance.) Second, as expected, more complex problems produced higher importance ratings on all attributes. In terms of seeing which were the most important attributes, however, the means alone are not easily interpretable. Hence, the attributes were ranked in terms of average importance for each of the four product types. Reliability of delivery is always one of the most important attributes—not surprising given the criticism a purchasing agent has to endure when deliveries are late. For the routine order product, price, flexibility, and reputation also rank high. For the procedural problem product, technical service, ease of use, and training offered rank highest. For the performance problem product, flexibility, technical service, and reliability data are the other most important attributes. The unexpected results were those dealing with the political problem product. Here, the high importance attributed to price and reliability data was contrary to prior expectations. One explanation for this is that purchasing agents aren't involved in such decisions and, hence, the results are not meaningful. Alternatively, it may be that political problems are so amorphous and difficult that decision makers search for something they can evaluate, and look to such concrete attributes as price and reliability data to make, or at least justify (especially if something goes wrong), the appropriateness of their choice.

Another way to look at the data is to recalibrate the importance scale by subtracting the mean importance for the product type from the average importance for each attribute. For example, the recalibrated score for the attribute reputation for Type I products is $4.84 - 4.46 = .38$. This gives a quick partitioning of the attributes into relatively more important (positive values) and relatively less important attributes (Table 11.6).

It is possible to compare the average importance of each of the attributes across the four product types. When significance tests are performed (see Chapter 12 for an explanation of how the tests are done), the original attribute ratings are found to change significantly at the .05 significance level in 13 of the 17 attributes and in 10 of the 17 attributes at the .01 significance level. This establishes beyond reasonable doubt that the ratings did change. However, we know that much of the change is due to the increasing importance of all attributes as the product becomes more complex. To see if relative importance changes, we need to test for significant changes in the adjusted scores. Six of the 17 attributes change significantly across the four product types. Two of these are price and reliability of delivery, which are by far the most important for Type I and are about equally important for the other three product types. The other significant changes were for training offered and required (highest for Type II products), financing (highest for Type I products), and technical service (highest for Type II and III products). These results are all perfectly reasonable. (Notice that the seemingly counterintuitive result previously discussed for Type IV products is not significant when the results are viewed in this way.)

In summary, it often takes some manipulation to get data in the form best suited for interpretation. Also, it is very desirable to check for statistical significance before interpreting results. This avoids the difficult and often misleading task of inventing explanations for what could well be chance results.

RELATIONS BETWEEN VARIABLES: CROSS-TABS

Two Variables

The question of how variables are related is crucial to most research. For example, I might like to see how heaviness of usage of a product category, region of the country, and household income relate to each of the questions in a survey. This is commonly done by specifying usage, region, and income as what are known as *banner points*. As the survey results are tabulated question by question, each question is tabulated and percentaged both in total and by each banner point. A typical page of the output might look like Table 11.7. From this table, one would probably conclude that most people are pretty neutral toward Znarts, that heavy users of the product category (which also includes such well-known brands as Whafles, Splibles, and Snuzzles) are somewhat more favorable toward it but not wildly so, that the brand is strongest in the Midwest and East, and that the brand appeals to high-income consumers.

In drawing conclusions from such pages, the key element of analysis is the cross-tabulation between two variables. For example, we tabulated purchase level versus region for a sample of 1,000 people as shown in Table 11.8. This raw tabulation is interesting

TABLE 11.6 Significance of Differences in Mean Importance across Product Types

Attribute	Significance[b] Raw	Adjusted Average Importance[a]				Adjusted Significance[c]
		I	II	III	IV	
Reputation	.01	.38	.26	.39	.42	—
Financing	.01	.05	− 1.00	− .99	− .20	.01
Flexibility	—	.61	.33	.52	.40	—
Past experience	—	.25	− .13	.17	− .07	—
Technical service	.01	− .10	.46	.48	.29	.01
Confidence in salespersons	.05	− .50	− .34	− .48	− .53	—
Convenience in ordering	—	− .60	− 1.34	− 1.19	− 1.03	—
Reliability data	.01	.01	.09	.43	.42	—
Price	.05	1.14	.22	.28	.45	.01
Technical specifications	.01	.27	.15	.37	.31	—
Ease of use	.01	.05	.46	.34	.07	—
Preference of user	.01	− .46	− .31	− .37	− .27	—
Training offered	.01	− 1.24	.35	− .17	− .11	.01
Training required	.01	− 1.24	.04	− .46	− .42	.01
Reliability of delivery	—	1.18	.35	.54	.42	.01
Maintenance	.05	.14	.13	− .18	− .11	—
Sales service	.01	.18	.29	.17	− .02	—

[a]For each product type, the mean product importance across the 17 attributes was subtracted from the importance for each of the 17 attributes.
[b]Significance of difference among product types based on raw average importance.
[c]Significance of difference among product types based on adjusted average importance.
Source: Donald R. Lehman and John O'Shaughnessy, "Differences in Attribute Importance for Different Industrial Products" from *Journal of Marketing* 38 (April 1974): 36–42. Copyright © 1974 by the American Marketing Association. Reprinted with the permission of the publishers.

TABLE 11.11   Relation of Purchase Level and Region

| | Purchase Level | | | | Row |
Region	0–1	2–3	4 or more	Total	Probability
A	200	140	60	400	.4
B	60	80	60	200	.2
C	140	180	80	400	.4
Total	400	400	200	1,000	
Column probability	.4	.4	.2		1.0

times the total number of people in the table: $.08(n) = .08(1,000) = 80$. Hence, we can derive an expected table from[1]

$$\text{Number expected in cell } i, j = (\text{Probability of being in row } i)$$
$$\cdot (\text{Probability of being in row } j)$$
$$\cdot (\text{Number of people in the table}) \qquad (11.1)$$

Here, we get the expected numbers as in Table 11.12.

Building an Index   The index used measures the difference between the expected and actual number of observations in each cell of the table. The index is the sum of the squared differences between expected and observed numbers divided by the expected number in each cell (to keep the numbers a manageable size) for all cells:

$$\text{Index} = \sum_{\text{all cells}} \frac{(\text{Observed number in cell } i, j - \text{Expected number in cell } i, j)^2}{\text{Expected number in cell } i, j}$$

$$= \sum_{i=1}^{r} \sum_{j=1}^{c} \frac{(f_{\text{obs}} - f_{\text{exp}})^2}{f_{\text{exp}}} \qquad (11.2)$$

---

[1]For hand computational purposes, it is possible to use a short form of either (probability of being in row i) · (number of people in column j) or (number of people in row i) · (probability of being in column j). While mathematically identical, these formulas do not convey as clearly the role of the independence assumption in generating the expected values and, hence, were not used in the main presentation.

[2]The degree of freedom notion is fairly subtle. The basic idea is that an observation is "free" if its value is unconstrained. Since in calculating the expected cell sizes we "rigged" the data so that the number in each row was equal to the actual number, there is one degree of freedom lost. (In other words, if you tell me all but one of the expected values, the other can be found.) Since this is true for each row and column, we are left with the following table without the bordering row and column in terms of free observations:

		X
		X
X	X	X

Hence, there are $(r - 1)(c - 1)$ "free" observations left. (If this brief explanation is unappealing, either (a) see a statistics book or (b) memorize $(r - 1)(c - 1)$, an inelegant but effective approach.)

TABLE 11.12   Expected Cell Sizes

| | Purchase Level | | |
Region	0–1	2–3	4 or More
A	160	160	80
B	80	80	40
C	160	160	80

where r is the number of rows and c the number of columns. The larger the index, the more different the observed and expected values are. In this case, by comparing Tables 11.8 and 11.12, we get:

$$\text{Index} = \frac{(200 - 160)^2}{160} + \frac{(140 - 160)^2}{160} + \frac{(60 - 80)^2}{80} + \frac{(60 - 80)^2}{80}$$

$$+ \frac{(80 - 80)^2}{80} + \frac{(60 - 40)^2}{40} + \frac{(140 - 160)^2}{160}$$

$$+ \frac{(180 - 160)^2}{160} + \frac{(80 - 80)^2}{80}$$

$$= 10 + 2.5 + 5 + 5 + 0 + 10 + 2.5 + 2.5 + 0$$

$$= 37.5$$

Evaluating the Index   The standard of comparison for this index is the chi-square (χ^2) table. Specifically, the index is χ^2 with $(r - 1)(c - 1)$ degrees of freedom.[2] In this case, the χ^2 value has $(3 - 1)(3 - 1) = 4$ degrees of freedom.

Remembering the way the index was constructed, we are only willing to reject the independence assumption if the index is large. (Hence, it is almost universally accepted that a one-tail test is appropriate.) Therefore, for this case and the .05 significance level, we get from a table $\chi^2_{4, .05} = 9.49$. Since 37.5 is larger than 9.49, we reject the independence hypothesis and conclude that region and purchase level are related and, hence, that the contingency table percentages are worth studying.

At this point, a comment about statistical significance is in order. Statistical testing generally focuses on determining whether a result is "unusual," that is, whether it is noticeably different from what you expect. Basically there are two kinds of mistakes one can make: declaring a result "unusual" (significant) when it is not really so (called a Type I or α error) and declaring a result normal when it is unusual (called a Type II or β error). Hence declaring a result "significant" involves a tradeoff between doing so too easily (leading to a Type I error) and too stringently (leading to a Type II error). The appropriate cutoff depends on the relative costs of the two errors and the degree of confidence you have a priori that the result either should or should not be unusual. For a number of reasons, in the social sciences (including business) testing tends to focus on Type I errors. Further (for no particularly good reason), many people use the .05 level as a cutoff (though .20, .10, and .01 are also used). Consequently, in this book we often (arbitrarily) refer to significant as different/unusual at the .05 level.

TABLE 11.13 Code Values for Food Survey

Code	Meaning
Weekly food expenditures:	
13	Less than $15
23	$15–$29
38	$30–$44
53	$45–$59
70	$60 or more
Income:	
1	Under 10,000
2	10,000–20,000
3	Over 20,000

Example

Income versus Food Expenditures   Returning again to the nutrition data, an interesting issue is the relation between household income and weekly food expenditures. To investigate this, data were categorized according to the scheme in Table 11.13. A cross-tab between food expenditures and income was then completed, using the SPSS computer program. The results appear in Table 11.14. Each cell contains four numbers:

1. *Count.* The number of people in the cell (e.g., 33 people had incomes under $10,000 and spent less than $15 per week on food).
2. *Row percent.* The percent of the people in the row who are in the column (e.g., 33/464 = 7.1 percent of the people with incomes under $10,000 spent less than $15 per week on food).
3. *Column percent.* The percent of the people in the column who are in the row (e.g., 33/39 = 84.9 percent of the people who spent less than $15 per week on food had incomes under $10,000).
4. *Total percent.* The percent of the total sample in the particular cell (e.g., 33/933 = 3.5 percent).

While somewhat overwhelming, the table indicates that income and food expenditures are positively related (high income tends to go with high food expenditures, and low income with low food expenditures). This is confirmed by the χ^2 statistic of 167.2, a huge value for $(5 - 1)(3 - 1) = 8$ degrees of freedom.[3] Notice, however, that the relationship between income and food expenditure does not "leap out" of the table. Since income and food expenditure are both ordinally (and close to intervally) scaled variables, more efficient means for describing the relationship may be appropriate.

---

[3] A useful fact is that the mean of the chi-square is the number of degrees of freedom and, as the number of degrees of freedom increases, the test statistic becomes approximately normally distributed, with a standard deviation equal to the square root of two times the number of degrees of freedom. This fact makes it possible to quickly tell when something is clearly significant, as well as to estimate significance if table values are not available.

TABLE 11.14 Cross-Tabulation of Income versus Food Expenditures

COUNT I ROW PCT I COL PCT I TOTAL PCTI	13. I	23. I	FOOD EXPENDITURES 38. I	53. I	70. I	ROW TOTAL
1. I I I I	33 7.1 84.6 3.5	226 48.7 70.2 24.2	149 32.1 47.8 16.0	45 9.7 23.1 4.8	11 2.4 16.9 1.2	464 49.7
2. I I I I	5 1.5 12.8 0.5	73 22.0 22.7 7.8	121 36.4 38.8 13.0	102 30.7 52.3 10.9	31 9.3 47.7 3.3	332 35.6
3. I I I I	1 0.7 2.6 0.1	23 16.8 7.1 2.5	42 30.7 13.5 4.5	48 35.0 24.6 5.1	23 16.8 36.4 2.5	137 14.7
Column I Total I	39 4.2	322 34.5	312 33.4	195 20.9	65 7.0	933 100.0

You may notice that a variety of other statistics appear in computer output besides chi-square. Basically, these attempt to measure the strength of the relationship between the variables. These statistics are sometimes useful in specific situations. Nonetheless, most researchers and all managers can get along just fine without using them.

Multiway Tables

In many cases, it is desirable to consider three or more variables simultaneously. In such instances, it is customary to break the data into multiple tables. For example, assume I wished to simultaneously study the effect of income and education on food expenditures. Hence, I might first remove the effect of income on expenditures by separating the sample into low- and high-income consumers and then doing a two-way cross-tab of education and expenditures for the two samples. The results would look something like the following:

	Low Income		*High Income*	
	Low Ed.	*High Ed.*	*Low Ed.*	*High Ed.*
Low expenditures				
High expenditures				

Often, three-way and higher tabulations reveal interesting results. Consider, for example, the study by Dr. Edwin Salzman and associates concerning the effect of aspirin on reducing blood clotting following major surgery for 95 patients (Lublin, 1977). In this case, aspirin appeared to be useful when the total sample was used. Breaking the sample by sex, however, revealed that aspirin seemed to be very useful for men ($\chi^2 = 7.62$) and not at all useful for women ($\chi^2 = .01$) (Table 11.15). Here, the simple two-way results were misleading.

TABLE 11.15   Relation between Aspirin Therapy and Blood Clots after Surgery

	Clot	No Clot
Total sample:		
Aspirin	11	33
Placebo	23	28
Men:		
Aspirin	4	19
Placebo	14	11
Women:		
Aspirin	7	14
Placebo	9	17

Source: Lublin, 1977.

Cross-Tabs: Pros and Cons

Cross-tabs are a very useful tool. They have the following advantages:

1. *They present results in a simple tabular form* that is easy to communicate to management.
2. *They work on nominal scale (categorical) data*, something that most of the "fancy" analyses do not do.
3. *They make no assumption about the form of the relationship.* In the purchase level versus region example, the relationship between purchase level and region was not a simple monotonic one (i.e., as region gets "bigger," so does purchase level). While the χ^2 analysis uncovered this relation, analysis based on such measures as a correlation coefficient might not have. It is important to recognize, however, that 2×2 cross-tab tables will also hide nonlinear relationships. One classic example of this was a study by Cox (Buzzell, Cox, and Brown, 1969, pp. 174–75) on the relation between the persuadability of 121 shoppers and their self-confidence. The original 2×2 table made the two variables appear unrelated. When self-confidence was broken into three categories, however, the results changed (Table 11.16). Now we see a nonlinear relationship between persuadability and self-confidence. (The relationship has an interesting implication for salespersons: Concentrate your efforts on those who have moderate self-confidence—those with high self-confidence can't be influenced and those with low self-confidence can't make up their minds.)

In spite of these advantages, there are some problems in using cross-tabs:

1. *There should be at least five expected observations in each cell.* When less than five appear in a cell, the χ^2 value becomes unreliable.[4] Hence, it is often

---

[4]Assume one cell had two observations and an expected size of .3 observations. This one cell would contribute $(2 - .3)^2/.3 = 9.6$ to the total χ^2 value, which alone is enough to make it significant at the .05 level for four degrees of freedom.

Table 11.16 Persuadability versus Self-Confidence

Self-Confidence	Persuadability	
	Percent Persuaded	Percent Unpersuaded
Original results:		
Low	47	53
High	45	55
Revised results:		
Very low	37	63
Moderately low	62	38
High	45	55

Source: Robert D. Buzzell, Donald F. Cox, and Rex V. Brown, Marketing Research and Information Systems: Text and Cases (New York: McGraw-Hill, 1969), pp. 174–75 © 1969 by McGraw-Hill Book Company. Used with permission.

necessary to collapse categories together to get sufficient *expected*[5] size in each cell. For example, we might have to combine the "fairly strongly" and "strongly" categories to get sufficient representation in those cells.

2. *Cross-tabs are not an efficient way to search for results.* If there are 100 variables, there are 4,950 possible two-way cross-tabs to perform. Looking at all these is a huge chore, and generating them mainly creates a big pile of scrap paper. (It also is interesting to notice that you would expect at the .05 level to get .05(4950) = 248 "significant" results due to chance alone.) The portrayal of the results is also fairly cumbersome: a table of conditional probabilities is less parsimonious than a correlation coefficient.

3. *Cross-tabs burn up sample size.* An obvious extension of two-way cross-tabs is to sort the observations based on three or more variables at a time. Unfortunately, we soon find cells with few people in them. Assuming there are six categories for the first variable, four for the second, and five for the third, there are (6)(4)(5) = 120 different cells. Even with big sample sizes (e.g., 1,000), this is likely to leave small cell sizes. (How many green-eyed Midwesterners bought Bufferin last time?) Consequently, the procedure tends to break down when complex relations are being studied.

4. *The size of the chi-square value depends on the number of degrees of freedom and, hence, is a poor index of association.* For example, a chi-square value of 42 would indicate no significant relationship if there were 48 degrees of freedom, and a value of 12 would show a significant relationship if there were only

---

[5]The reason the expected size is the key, and not the observed size, is that the expected size is the denominator of the fraction.

2 degrees of freedom. Put differently, the chi-square value does not indicate the strength of the relationship between the two variables.[6]

5. *Spurious correlation is a problem.* Contingency tables are particularly susceptible to spurious correlation. Relations that appear in two-way tables may disappear when a third variable is added, or vice versa.

In summary then, cross-tabs are an extremely useful tool. They are well suited to initial investigation of the relation between a few key variables and the other variables. They are not particularly well suited to searching for relations among many variables. If results are uncovered, however, they often serve as a convenient format for conveying the results to "normal" people.

CORRELATION COEFFICIENTS

Probably the most popular method for quickly summarizing the degree of relation between two variables is a correlation coefficient. The essence of a correlation coefficient is that it is an index that ranges from +1 (the two variables are perfectly positively related—they both get larger together) to −1 (the two variables are perfectly negatively related; as one gets larger the other gets smaller).[7]

Pearson (Product-Moment) Correlation Coefficient

The most common correlation coefficient is the Pearson product-moment correlation (better known as *r*). This is the coefficient found in essentially all canned computer output and assumes both variables are intervally scaled. The formula for the correlation between two variables X_i and X_j is:

$$r = \frac{\sum_{i=1}^{n} \left(X_i - \overline{X}_i \right)\left(X_j - \overline{X}_j \right)}{\sqrt{\sum_{i=1}^{n} \left(X_i - \overline{X}_i \right)^2} \sqrt{\sum_{i=1}^{n} \left(X_j - \overline{X}_j \right)^2}}$$

$$= \frac{\sum_{i=1}^{n} \left(X_i - \overline{X}_i \right)\left(X_j - \overline{X}_j \right)}{n\left(s_{X_i} \right)\left(s_{X_j} \right)} \tag{11.3}$$

---

[6]Since χ^2 depends on both the sample size *n* (the bigger the sample size, the bigger χ^2 even for a constant relationship) and the number of categories, it is not a particularly useful measure of association. A variety of measures have been devised to overcome some of these problems. Specifically, the contingency coefficient attempts to remove the effect of sample size:

$$C = \sqrt{\frac{\chi^2}{n + \chi^2}}$$

Unfortunately, this measure still depends on the number of rows and columns in the table. As a general rule, it is difficult to compare the level of association between two pairs of nominally scaled variables.

[7]In contrast, the size of the chi-square value depends on the number of degrees of freedom and, hence, is a poor index of association.

FIGURE 11.6
Food Expenditure vs. Income

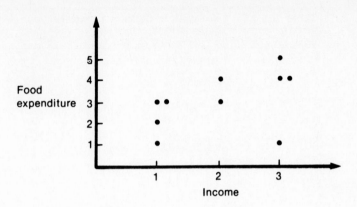

For example, assume we had the following 10 observations:

Person	X_i (income)	X_j (food expenditures)
1	1	2
2	3	4
3	3	1
4	3	4
5	1	3
6	2	3
7	1	1
8	1	3
9	3	5
10	2	4

When we plot these, as in Figure 11.6, there appears to be a positive relation between income and food expenditure. The computations would proceed as follows:

Find the means:

$$\sum X_j = 20, \quad \therefore \overline{X}_j = 2$$
$$\sum X_j = 30, \quad \therefore \overline{X}_j = 3$$

Compute the correlations using Equation (11.3) (see Table 11.17):

$$r = \frac{5}{\sqrt{8}\sqrt{16}} = .44$$

The correlation coefficient can be tested for statistical significance using the following statistic:

$$\frac{r\sqrt{n-2}}{\sqrt{1-r^2}}$$

Table 11.17   Calculations to Obtain a Correlation

X_i	X_j	$X_i - \bar{X}_i$	$X_j - \bar{X}_j$	$(X_i - \bar{X}_i)^2$	$(X_j - \bar{X}_j)^2$	$(X_i - \bar{X}_i) \cdot (X_j - \bar{X}_j)$
1	2	− 1	− 1	1	1	+ 1
3	4	+ 1	+ 1	1	1	+ 1
3	1	+ 1	− 2	1	4	− 2
3	4	+ 1	+ 1	1	1	+ 1
1	3	− 1	0	1	0	0
2	3	0	0	0	0	0
1	1	− 1	− 2	1	4	+ 2
1	3	− 1	0	1	0	0
3	5	+ 1	+ 2	1	4	+ 2
2	4	0	+ 1	0	1	0
				8	16	5

This statistic is approximately distributed according to the t distribution with $n - 2$ degrees of freedom. The t distribution looks like the normal distribution but is somewhat "fatter" for a small number of degrees of freedom. When the degrees of freedom exceed 30, the t distribution is essentially the same as the normal distribution, and hence values from the normal table can be substituted for the t values.

In the previous example, which had a sample of size 10 and $r = .44$, that means comparing a table value of $t_{.05, 8} = 2.31$ with:

$$\frac{(.44)\sqrt{8}}{\sqrt{1 - (.44)^2}} \quad \frac{.44(2.83)}{.90} = 1.38$$

Since 1.38 is less than 2.31, the correlation is not significant at the .05 level. (In other words, the apparent relation may be due to chance and, hence, misleading.) Obviously, as the sample size gets bigger, the chance for a particular size correlation being significant increases. (In fact, a correlation of .001 is statistically significant given a large enough sample size.) Also, the t distribution is approximately normal for large (greater than 30) sample sizes. Hence, if we use the .05 significance level to quickly filter out important linear relations, for samples above 30 in size we can simply look for t values above 2 in absolute value.

Limitations   There are two major limitations on the value of a correlation coefficient:

Both Variables Are Assumed to Be Intervally Scaled and Continuous Actually, for most purposes, this is an overly rigid assumption. Ordinally scaled data may be used if you recognize the resulting correlation will be biased downward slightly. Consider the following data:

X_1	X_2 (rank)
1	1
3	2
4	3
8	4
9	5

Obviously, the ordinal (rank) measure X_2 is not an accurate reflection of the true value X_1. Still, the correlation between the true and rank values of X_1 is high ($r = .98$), and thus the correlation between the ordinal measure of X_1 and anything that the true X_1 is correlated with will also tend to remain high. In short, the coefficient is very robust (stands up well) to modest violations of this assumption (Morrison, 1972).

The Relationship Between the Variables Is Linear   Consider the cases in Figure 11.7. In case A, there is a strong positive correlation (i.e., $r = +.9$). In case B, there is a negative relation ($r = -.6$), albeit weaker than case A. In case C, there is a clear relationship, but the simple correlation coefficient would be 0 ($r = 0$). This is because the simple correlation does not detect severely curvilinear (nonmonotonic) relations. In case D, we have a nonlinear relation; but since the relation is monotonic (as X_1 gets bigger so does X_2), the correlation will still be positive enough to indicate a substantial relationship ($r = +.7$). Case E gives an example where there is genuinely no relation between X_1 and X_2.

Correlation for Ranked (Ordinal) Data

When data are ordinally rather than intervally scaled, the following two choices appear:

Use the Product-Moment Correlation as an Approximation   While this would make a purist cringe, it is often a good approximation. Similarly, binary scales (e.g., yes-no) can be used to compute correlations that indicate whether the construct (e.g., the taking of aspirin) is related to another variable.

Use a Special Correlation that Takes the Ordinal Nature of the Data into Account   There are many such coefficients, including the coefficient of concordance, the coefficient of consistency, and Kendall's tau. As an example of this type of correlation, Spearman's rank correlation coefficient computes the correlation between two sets of rankings using the following formula:

$$R = 1 - \frac{6 \sum_{i=1}^{n} d^2}{n^3 - n} \tag{11.4}$$

where
d = number of places that an object differs in the two rankings
n = number of objects ranked

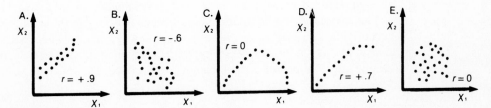

FIGURE 11.7
Sample Correlations

Table 11.18 Calculation of Spearman Rank Correlation Coefficient

First Person's Ranking	Second Person's Ranking	Difference in Rankings (d)	d^2
3	2	1	1
5	5	0	0
6	1	5	25
2	6	4	16
1	3	2	4
4	4	0	0
			46

$$R = 1 - \frac{6(46)}{6^3 - 6} = 1 - \frac{276}{210} = -.31$$

An example of the use of this formula[8] appears in Table 11.18.

DATA ADJUSTMENT PROCEDURES

In analyzing a set of data, various procedures are sometimes used. Two of the most common are recoding and weighting for unequal response rates.

Recoding

Data are often recoded for two major reasons:

To produce simplified results. For example, frequently examining the initial tabs indicates several responses (e.g., brand used last) receive a very small percentage of mentions. In such cases, it is often desirable to combine infrequent responses into an "all other" category to simplify the analysis.

To make the top end of the scale "up." Data can be collected in many different ways. For example, importances can be collected on five-point scales with "5" representing very important or, alternatively, "5" representing very unimportant. This means that it is impossible to interpret a result (e.g., a score of 4) without knowing which end of the scale is "up." The problem is compounded when two variables are combined, as in a correlation coefficient. A numerical correlation may be positive and the relation between the underlying constructs negative, or vice versa. For example, assume importance placed on money were coded 1 through 5 with a low number indicating great importance, and income was coded 1 through 6, with 6 being

---

[8]Interestingly, when there are no ties in the rankings, formulas (11.3) and (11.4) will produce the same number.

the highest category. If we assume that the importance of money would decrease as income increases, we would expect the basic concepts to be negatively related. Given this coding scheme, however, the correlation would be positive. Unless carefully interpreted, this positive number could lead to mistakenly concluding that the importance of money and income were positively related. To avoid such possible confusion, it is often desirable to recode all variables so that a bigger code value means more of the variable.

Weighting for Unequal Response Rates

Given a sample that truly represents the frame, analysis can proceed directly. When the sample does not match the frame, however, the question arises of how to adjust the results. Consider again the nutrition example that consciously oversampled lower-income respondents:

Income	Sample	Population
Less than $10,000	49.7%	39.2%
$10,000–$19,999	35.6%	42.2%
$20,000 or more	14.7%	18.6%

In general, relationships among variables (e.g., correlations) are not affected by unequal sampling. The levels (means) of other variables, however, may be. In fact, for any variable that is related to income, a direct projection will be erroneous, although not necessarily greatly in error. The issue then becomes, "How can I weight responses to get a useful projection?" The procedure utilized is based on the stratified sampling formulas of Chapter 9. In this case, we can weight people in different income classes as follows:

Income	Weight
Less than $10,000	392/497 = 0.789
$10,000–$19,999	422/356 = 1.185
$20,000 or more	186/147 = 1.265

This weighting scheme will ensure that people in the less than $10,000 income category account for 39.2 percent of the responses, and so forth. (Actually, the weights should be calculated to more significant digits, but these are enough to demonstrate the process.) To show the effect of this weighting, assume that income was related to food expenditures, as in Table 11.19. Assume we coded the expenses as $13, $23, $38, $53, and $70, respectively, for the five categories (essentially substituting the category median). The estimated unweighted mean expenditures would then be $13(.042) + $23(.345) + $38(.334) + $53(.209) + $70(.070) = $0.55 + $7.94 + $12.69 + $11.08 + $4.90 = $37.16.

Alternatively, we could reweight the data, producing Table 11.20. This implies a mean consumption of $13(.035) + $23(.315) + $38(.337) + $53(.233) + $70(.080) = $0.46 + $7.25 + $12.81 + $12.35 + $5.60 = $38.47. Hence, failure to weight the data would produce a noticeable but small (about 3.5 percent) error in the estimate of consumption expenditures. Obviously, had the sample been closer to the actual income distribution, this error would have been reduced.

Table 11.19   Raw Cross-Tabs

Income	Expense per Week					
	Under $15	$15–$29	$30–$44	$45–$60	Over $60	Total
Under $10,000	33	226	149	45	11	464
$10,000–$19,999	5	73	121	102	31	332
$20,000 and over	1	23	42	48	23	137
Total	39	322	312	195	65	933
	4.2%	34.5%	33.4%	20.9%	7.0%	100%

The weighting problem can be further complicated if the sample is off in terms of two or more variables. In this case, the weights must be developed to simultaneously account for two or more characteristics (e.g., income and age) that are disproportionately represented. In such a case, use (*a*) common sense and (*b*) a consultant.

Given the need to weight, a mundane question arises about how to do it. The dominant solution is to use software that allows unequal weights. If such a program is unavailable, the alternatives are the following:

Write your own routine (a tedious solution).

Adjust your sample. This can be done by reducing the sample to match the cell that is the most underrepresented. Assume, for example, we have the following results:

Income Group	Original Sample Size	Sample Percent	"Correct" Percent
A	500	50	50
B	400	40	30
C	100	10	20

We can now adjust the sample to match income group C, the most underrepresented. Since group C should represent 20 percent of the population, we will take all 100 respondents in group C for our new sample. The resulting reduced sample, thus, will be as follows:

Income Group	Original Sample Size	Reduced Sample Size
A	500	250
B	400	150
C	100	100

The 250 people in group A will be chosen randomly from the original 500; similarly, the 150 in group B will be chosen from the 400 originals in group B.

Table 11.20 Weighted Cross-Tabs

Income	Under $15	$15–$29	$30–$44	$45–$60	Over $60	Total
			Expense per Week			
Under $10,000	26.0	178.3	117.6	35.5	8.7	366.1
$10,000–$19,999	5.9	86.5	143.4	120.9	36.7	393.4
$20,000 and over	1.3	29.1	53.1	60.7	29.1	173.3
Total	33.2	293.9	314.1	217.1	74.5	932.8
	3.5%	31.5%	33.7%	23.3%	8.0%	100%

As can be seen from this example, this procedure is fairly inefficient in that 500 responses, half the original sample, are unused. Because of this (and a penchant for big sample sizes), many researchers will blow up, rather than reduce, a sample. This is done by increasing the results to match the overrepresented cell. In this case, we would match group B as the most overrepresented group. The resulting "sample" would then be:

Income Group	Original Sample Size	Blown-up Sample Size
A	500	667
B	400	400
C	100	267
Total	1,000	1,334

The new group A would consist of the original 500 plus 167 of the original 500 reproduced at random. The 267 of group C would consist of two duplicate sets of the original 100 plus 67 of the 100 chosen at random. While this method will produce an unbiased estimate of the means of variables, the increased sample size is deceiving. Hence, while this method may "trick" computer programs into weighting responses, it may also trick researchers into thinking they have a better sample than they really do.

The weighting of unequal responses is, thus, a nontrivial problem. It also makes statistical interpretation of the results much more difficult. The dominant solution is to get a good sample. Failing that, the researcher must choose between somewhat biased results and the prospect of some gyrations to overcome the unfortunate sampling result.

One final point is worth mentioning. Weighting can be used to cover up a poor job of sampling. In the previous example, income group C was underrepresented. Once the data were weighted, however, this fact was not obvious. Therefore, make sure you know what weighting scheme was employed and that the weights are not grossly different (e.g., weight in one stratum = 1 and weight in another stratum = 40). If the weights are grossly different *and* this is not by design, as in the case of a disproportionate stratified sample, then additional sampling may be required. Put differently, some suppliers in effect cover up their inability to obtain respondents in hard-to-reach segments of the population by weighting the data.

SUMMARY

This chapter has presented a variety of ways for analyzing data: tabulations, means, cross-tabulations, and correlations. As the book proceeds to more complicated analyses, remember that in most studies the majority of the results can be deduced from or at least reported in the form of such mundane but understandable procedures.

It is also worth emphasizing that cross-tabs and correlations are not causal. Cross-tabulation and the associated χ^2 statistic and correlations make no assumptions about how two variables are related. For example, we might find occupation and preference for type of painting are related. This does not say that occupation causes preference or that preference causes occupation. In fact, it may be that a third variable (e.g., education) affects both income and preference for type of painting. Thus, the relationships uncovered by a chi-square or a correlation are just that: observed association, which is why these methods can be thought of as means for relationship portrayal. In the next chapters we discuss methods that are designed to assess the impact (effect) of one variable on another.

PROBLEMS

1. A judge admonishes the jury: "I want you to be absolutely certain before you return a guilty verdict." What will the outcome be?

2. Given

x	8	1	4	2	3	6	5	7
y	7	2	3.5	1	3.5	8	5	6

What is

a. The Pearson correlation?

b. The Spearman rank correlation?

3. How can I test to see if two nominally scaled variables are related?

4. I sample 800 people to determine their cereal preferences. The results of the study are as follows:

		Brand		
Preference	He-Man	Supa-Sweet	Little Crispies	Slush Puppies
Like	90	100	90	120
Dislike	110	100	110	80

Are preferences and brands related?

5. To ascertain preferences for three new package designs, prototypes of each of the packages were shown to some people, who then classified them as superior, average, or inferior. Interpret these results:

		Rating		
Design	Inferior	Average	Superior	Total
1	60	80	60	200
2	160	140	100	400
3	80	80	40	200
Total	300	300	200	800

6. Interpret the following tabulation of 2,500 responses:

Number of Contacts by School	Contributions to Alumni Fund			
	None	Small	Large	Total
1	150	150	200	500
2–3	350	200	450	1,000
4 or more	500	150	350	1,000

7. In estimating the demand for a new household appliance, the following table was compiled:

	Definitely Would Buy					
	Version A ($400)		Version B ($200)		Version C ($200)	
	No.	%	No.	%	No.	%
Under 25	211	23.8	964	17.2	240	13.3
25–34	253	28.5	1,916	34.2	606	33.5
35–44	34	3.8	906	16.2	166	9.2
45–54	279	31.1	1,324	23.6	615	34.0
55 and over	115	13.0	490	8.7	181	10.0

Interpret.

8. Are region and sales significantly related?

	Region		
Brand	A	B	C
1	40	50	60
2	20	40	90
3	30	60	150

9. In a blind test, 100 respondents tested our brand of detergent and rated its bleach content as follows:

16%	Too little bleach
12	Almost enough
36	Just right
20	Slightly too much
16	Too much bleach
100%	

Another 200 respondents tested our main competitor's detergent and rated its bleach content as follows:

8%	Too little bleach
12	Almost enough
60	Just right
12	Slightly too much
8	Too much bleach
100%	

Should we be concerned about the bleach level in our detergent since only 36 percent of the respondents rated ours "Just right"?

10. The sale of beer to relatively few heavy users accounts for a large portion of the sales volume of Suds brand beer. The brand manager of Suds would like to expand the distribution but does not know which city should be selected to expand ("roll out") into. Three cities are being considered: Bluelaw, Wasdry, and Spilltown. The affluence of the citizens varies greatly among the towns. A survey of 200 Suds purchasers indicated that 70 percent of the purchasers were light users, and 50 percent had high incomes, as shown in the following table of percentages:

	High Income	Low Income
Heavy user	20%	10%
Light user	30	40

If the usage rate and income are not related, then the Suds brand manager will try to expand into Spilltown; but if they are related, then the manager will select the town with a favorable income distribution. What advice would you give the Suds brand manager?

11. A sample of 200 persons revealed that 55 percent of the sampled people who shop regularly in our chain of supermarkets usually buy our private brand of coffee. However, 63.3 percent of the sampled people who shop regularly in competing supermarkets usually buy the private label coffee in those stores. The sample included 80 persons who regularly shop in our stores and 120 persons who regularly shop in competing stores. We make more money on private brand coffee than on other coffee. The difference between 55 percent and 63.3 percent seems like a lot, especially when you consider all our millions of customers. Does the sample indicate that our private brand coffee sales are significantly lower than competitors', or should we not worry?

12. The sales of baby food to elderly people accounts for a significant portion of the sales volume. A canner has developed a line of "adult" mushy, easily digestible foods and tried selling the new products to older customers in a store in Retirement Village. Sampling 50 shoppers in the store, the canner found that 20 percent had no money worries, 20 percent get along OK, and 60 percent are financially insecure. Also, 30 percent of the shoppers indicated that they had tried the new brand, as shown in the following table of percentages:

	Tried	Did Not Try
No money worries	12%	8%
Get along OK	2	18
Financially insecure	16	44

If trial and income are not related, then the food canner feels the distribution of the product can be increased quickly. However, if they are related, then perhaps the effect of income should be studied before distribution is expanded. What advice would you give the food canner?

13. A prestigious East Coast research house conducted a national telephone survey. The firm had been hired partly because of its sophisticated sampling capability. The final report indicated the following number of interviews in each geographic area, compared with the 1970 Census breakdown for the same areas:

	Sample Size	Percent of U.S. Population
Northeast	125	24.4%
South	171	30.4
North Central	155	27.6
West	145	17.6
Total	597	100%

Is the geographic distribution of interviews consistent with the firm's contract to obtain a simple random sample of the U.S. population with telephones? What weighting of observations would you use in computing statistics from these interviews?

14. Four different BLUGOS price promotions have been advertised in successive Wednesday night newspapers. The sales (cases) of BLUGOS during the following three days were recorded each week:

Promotion	Sales
16¢ off, no coupon	105
18¢ off, no coupon	95
20¢ off, 5¢ coupon	113
25¢ off, 8¢ coupon	89

How much time should you spend understanding this data and determining the implications for our BLUGOS promotions?

15. Given the following situation where the population is divided into two strata:

Stratum	Stratum Size (million)	Sample Size	Average Consumption
A	20	900	48
B	80	100	3

What is your best estimate for overall average consumption?

16. Consider again the nutrition study described in Table 9.8. If income and family size were the two main determinants of weekly food expenditures, how would you weight the sample to produce an accurate representation of average food expenditures?

17. A distribution of the responses to a survey of 681 users of the product class is displayed here for the following measures:

> Preferred brand (A–D)
> Income level (under or over $18,000 for family)
> City (E–H)
> Marital status (M,S,O)

Respondents in City E or F	Respondents in City G or H
Low income—married;	Low income—married;
45 prefer A; 7, B; 8, C; 8, D	40 prefer A; 11, B; 13, C; 11, D
Low income—single:	Low income—single:
50 prefer A; 9, B; 8, C; 7, D	35 prefer A; 13, B; 11, C; 11, D
Low income—other:	Low income—other:
23 prefer A; 4, B; 4, C; 3, D	28 prefer A; 5, B; 5, C; 7, D
High income—married;	High income—married;
16 prefer A; 13, B; 12, C; 16, D	30 prefer A; 12, B; 13, C; 14, D
High income—single:	High income—single:
17 prefer A; 15, B; 13, C; 12, D	28 prefer A; 15, B; 13, C; 11, D
High income—other:	High income—other:
9 prefer A; 7, B; 7, C; 8, D	17 prefer A; 5, B; 6, C; 7, D

Use contingency tables to evaluate the difference in effect between the advertising theme "value" (which has been played for years in cities E and F) and the theme "style" (which has been played for years in cities G and H).

18. Over the past year, a manufacturer has increased advertising by 50 percent in city B. To assess the effectiveness of this move, the manufacturer has surveyed 300 people in city B and 300 people in city A, where the advertising has remained at the lower level.

The respondents have been broken down by income and marital status:

Respondents in City A	Respondents in City B
Married—low income:	Married—low income:
39 preferred our brand	19 preferred our brand
20 preferred their brand	40 preferred their brand
Married—high income:	Married—high income:
48 preferred our brand	94 preferred our brand
92 preferred their brand	47 preferred their brand
Single—low income:	Single—low income:
1 preferred our brand	46 preferred our brand
10 preferred their brand	23 preferred their brand
Single—high income:	Single—high income:
22 preferred our brand	11 preferred our brand
48 preferred their brand	20 preferred their brand

Interpret.

Section I—Shopping Habits

1. Portion of shopping done by the respondent:

	Percent
No answer	.6
None of it	1.6
Less than half	3.6
About half	5.5
Most of it	31.4
All of it	57.2

Interpretation: The respondents are, as expected, the principal food shoppers for their households.

2. Number of times they shop for food each week:

	Percent
No answer	.5
Less than once	12.8
Once a week	49.1
2–4 times a week	35.7
5 or more times a week	1.8

Interpretation: Most of this sample shop for food about once a week.

3. Portion of the items purchased which are on a shopping list:

	Percent
No answer	.7
None (no list)	19.0
Some	3.3
About half	5.1
More than half	14.0
Almost all	57.8

Interpretation: While most people prepare a fairly complete list before shopping, almost 20 percent go to the store with no list at all.

4. Amount of money spent on food per week:

	Percent
No answer	.7
Under $15	4.1
$15–$29	34.3
$30–$44	33.2
$45–$60	20.7
Over $60	6.9

Interpretation: A "typical" family spends $35–$40 per week on food.

5. Change in weekly spending from last year:

	Percent
No answer	.9
Spend at least $10 less than last year	2.6
$5–$10 less than last year	3.6
About the same as last year	13.2
$5–$10 more than last year	48.7
Over $10 more than last year	31.1

Interpretation: The typical household is spending $5–$10 more per week for food this year than last. This implies an increase of about 20 percent.

6. Number of brands and sizes considered in buying staple products (soup, ketchup, etc.):

	Percent
No answer	.3
Only 1 or 2	49.5
Many brands, one size	8.6
Many sizes, one brand	3.3
Many brands and sizes	38.3

Interpretation: This question was intended to find out the number of people who actively shop for a product versus the number who have previously decided which alternative to select. Interestingly, about half the people have predetermined choices and, hence, are presumably very insensitive to new offerings, point of purchase materials, and specials.

7. Approach to food shopping:

	Percent
No answer	1.0
I actively seek information about food in terms of nutritional value, price, etc.	29.0
I sometimes try new foods because of new information, but generally buy the same foods	53.1
The food I buy is almost always the same, and I spend very little time thinking about it	16.9

Interpretation: This question was intended to find out how many people actively seek information about food. The 29 percent who say they do is probably biased upward since it is in some sense the "right" answer. The fact that 70 percent are not very interested in new information suggests that attempts to change behavior through "rational" appeals will not be easy, as food manufacturers can no doubt attest.

Section I (continued)

8. Use of food stamps by the immediate family:

	Percent
No answer	.1
Never used	87.9
Used to, but do not use them now	6.9
We are presently using them	5.1

Interpretation: Food stamp usage has occurred among 12 percent of the sample with 5.1 percent currently using them.

9. Importance of attributes in the decision about which food to serve:

Attribute	No Answer	Very Important	Important			Not very Important	Average Importance	Rank of Average Importance
Variety	4.5%	38.8%	21.0%	32.2%	2.0%	1.5%	2.02	5
Taste	3.9	79.1	11.7	4.7	.2	.3	1.24	1
Other family members' preferences	5.2	51.5	23.5	16.8	1.6	1.4	1.71	3
Diet restrictions	6.8	26.7	10.5	21.1	7.6	27.3	2.98	10
Price	3.6	54.6	16.8	22.2	1.2	1.6	1.74	4
Availability at stores where you normally shop	6.1	35.4	21.6	28.9	2.9	5.1	2.16	6
Ease of preparation	5.9	18.4	17.6	36.6	9.5	12.1	2.78	8
Habit (past eating patterns)	7.9	13.0	20.3	40.1	10.5	8.2	2.82	9
Advertised specials	4.0	38.2	18.9	23.8	6.2	8.8	2.26	7
Nutritional value	3.2	55.5	21.9	16.6	2.0	.7	1.66	2

Interpretation: The importance of diet restrictions divides the sample in thirds: 27 percent find them very important, 46 percent somewhat important, and 27 percent find them completely unimportant. In terms of relative importance, taste is by far the most important variable. Nutrition is maintained to edge out price and other family members' preferences as second most important, although this is an obvious "right" answer, and hence, the stated importance of nutrition is inflated. Overall, it appears that taste and price dominate food selection decisions.

10. Attention paid to different product features.

		Amount of Attention Paid				
	No Answer	Great Deal	Some	Little or None	Average	Rank
Brand name	2.8%	38.5%	51.2%	7.6%	1.68	7
Number of servings	4.5	43.2	40.2	12.1	1.68	6
Net weight or volume	3.8	48.1	36.0	12.1	1.63	5
Total price	2.0	80.6	15.2	2.1	1.20	1
Amount of ingredients	4.9	39.6	40.3	15.2	1.74	8
Unit price	4.8	51.5	32.7	11.1	1.58	4
List of ingredients	4.7	33.4	46.3	15.6	1.81	9
Nutritional value	3.7	50.0	39.1	7.1	1.56	3
Recipes	4.8	13.9	41.8	39.5	2.27	11
Food additives and preservatives	3.7	31.3	37.2	27.8	1.96	10
Date of manufacture or expiration	2.8	65.5	26.4	5.3	1.38	2

Interpretation: Total price is by far the most salient characteristic of the purchase event. Freshness comes second with nutritional value third and unit price a close fourth. Recipes seem to be largely overlooked as are food additives and preservatives, possibly because few people (experts included) know what they really do.

Section I (continued)

11. Number of times per week the respondent eats different meals:

	No Answer	Never	1–2	3–4	5–6	Everyday
Breakfast	1.7%	10.1%	13.9%	8.9%	6.0%	59.4%
Lunch	2.4	1.6	7.3	12.4	11.3	64.9
Dinner	1.7	.3	1.3	1.6	6.1	89.0

Interpretation: One third of the population eats breakfast irregularly. Surprisingly, lunch is more often consumed than breakfast. Not surprisingly, dinner is almost universally eaten at least six days a week.

12. Number of snacks consumed per day:

	Percent
No answer	1.5
None	18.0
One	44.6
Two	27.9
Three or more	8.1

Interpretation: Less than 20 percent of the sample avoids snacks. On the other hand, only 8.1 percent and the author admit to three or more snacks per day.

13. Amount of food canned:

	Percent
No answer	2.0
None	39.7
Small amount	36.3
Large amount	22.0

Interpretation: About 60 percent of the sample indicated that they can food. This seems very high and suggests that this may have been a bad question.

14. Frequency of consumption of different foods:

	No Answer	Never	A Few Times a Year	1-2 Times a Month	Weekly	Several Times a Week	Once a Day	More than Once a Day	Mean	Rank
Canned fruit	2.1%	1.2%	18.5%	34.1%	20.2%	20.3%	2.9%	.6%	3.52	16
Fresh fruit	2.0	.7	4.1	12.7	22.4	30.3	19.0	8.6	4.73	4
Bread	2.0	.5	.9	2.2	6.0	18.4	36.3	33.7	5.90	2
Rice	1.9	5.3	19.8	45.3	22.2	4.8	.1	.5	3.04	23
Butter	5.4	30.3	17.7	6.9	4.0	9.0	12.3	14.3	3.40	20
Margarine	4.0	4.8	3.0	2.7	8.6	19.1	23.1	34.7	5.53	3
Cheese	3.3	1.4	2.2	12.7	25.4	44.6	7.8	2.7	4.48	5
Ice cream	1.8	3.4	15.6	35.4	21.9	18.9	2.3	.5	3.47	17
Whole milk	4.3	27.0	9.5	8.4	5.7	10.4	17.1	17.6	3.88	11
Skim milk or low fat milk	6.2	34.3	10.5	6.1	4.8	10.6	13.2	14.4	3.47	18
Snack foods (potato chips, pretzels, etc.)	2.6	9.4	15.5	28.4	20.7	18.0	3.8	1.6	3.41	19
Desserts	2.9	1.5	6.0	18.3	21.9	28.9	16.0	4.6	4.41	7
Alcoholic beverages (beer, wine, liquor)	1.9	35.4	21.4	16.5	10.0	8.6	5.2	1.0	2.54	29
Soft drinks	2.4	9.8	13.3	21.6	16.6	19.4	8.4	8.5	3.84	13
Fish	1.9	4.4	17.7	41.9	28.7	5.1	.2	.1	3.14	22
Cold cereal	2.0	12.6	13.9	19.9	15.6	22.9	12.1	1.0	3.64	15
Frozen vegetables	1.9	4.5	10.0	20.1	21.8	32.8	8.2	.7	3.98	10
Fresh vegetables	2.1	1.5	5.7	14.5	22.9	38.7	11.3	3.3	4.42	6
Canned vegetables	2.3	2.7	5.3	13.6	23.4	41.2	10.1	1.4	4.34	9
Poultry	1.5	.5	3.7	32.3	52.3	8.5	.9	.2	3.69	14
Beef (hamburger or stew meat)	1.2	.5	.4	7.3	47.4	40.6	2.1	.3	4.37	8
Beef (steak or roast)	3.0	1.0	3.9	24.5	48.0	18.6	1.0	.1	3.85	12
Pork	3.2	6.8	21.1	39.6	23.2	5.0	1.2	.0	3.02	24
Tuna fish	2.1	8.1	21.0	40.3	20.4	7.8	.3	.0	3.00	25
Frozen dinners	1.7	35.2	39.3	18.1	4.4	1.4	.0	.0	1.96	30
Hot dogs	2.6	7.6	24.6	40.9	19.9	3.4	.3	.9	2.91	26
Coffee or tea	3.2	4.7	1.6	2.1	2.8	5.5	14.9	65.2	6.19	1
Pasta (pizza, spaghetti, etc.)	2.4	6.5	13.2	43.1	28.9	5.9	.0	.0	3.15	21
Food at "fast food" restaurant (i.e. McDonald's, etc.)	2.3	12.8	35.1	35.2	12.0	2.1	.3	.1	2.56	28
Food at regular restaurants	1.8	7.7	42.8	31.0	14.1	2.3	.3	.0	2.61	27

Interpretation: Coffee and tea are the most widely consumed food followed closely by bread. Frozen dinners are the least frequently consumed followed by alcoholic beverages and food eaten at restaurants. Overall, "junk" food is rated as relatively little consumed although here again this is obviously the socially accepted response. Interestingly, margarine is consumed more frequently than butter and skim milk as often as whole milk.

Section I *(concluded)*

15. Change in consumption of different foods in the past year:

	No Answer	Much Less	Somewhat Less	About the Same	Somewhat More	Much More	Mean	Rank
Canned fruit	1.5%	8.9%	15.4%	64.8%	7.2%	2.1%	2.78	18
Fresh fruit	1.7	3.2	9.5	57.9	22.3	5.4	3.18	3
Bread	1.8	2.8	11.5	66.0	13.7	4.3	3.05	8
Rice	2.3	8.4	14.4	64.3	9.5	1.2	2.80	16
Butter	7.1	24.0	13.6	47.3	6.3	1.6	2.44	28
Margarine	2.4	3.9	7.3	66.2	15.7	4.4	3.10	7
Cheese	2.1	1.8	7.4	59.6	24.3	4.8	3.23	1
Ice cream	2.8	7.6	21.3	53.7	12.0	2.7	2.80	15
Whole milk	4.4	15.6	13.5	51.9	9.4	5.2	2.74	20
Skim milk or low fat milk	8.7	16.7	7.2	45.2	16.0	6.2	2.87	13
Snack foods (potato chips, pretzels, etc.)	3.1	16.5	24.6	46.6	7.4	1.8	2.52	26
Desserts	3.4	9.9	26.0	53.7	5.6	1.4	2.61	23
Alcoholic beverages (beer, wine, liquor)	9.5	21.1	11.5	53.0	4.7	.3	2.47	27
Soft drinks	3.2	13.6	18.8	50.3	11.6	2.4	2.70	22
Fish	2.9	5.9	14.8	63.6	11.4	1.5	2.88	12
Cold cereal	2.8	6.4	12.8	59.4	15.9	2.9	2.96	9
Frozen vegetables	1.9	5.5	11.8	68.5	10.6	1.6	2.91	11
Fresh vegetables	1.9	2.3	6.9	69.6	16.6	2.7	3.11	6
Canned vegetables	1.9	4.7	10.9	72.0	9.0	1.5	2.92	10
Poultry	1.8	2.3	8.1	67.2	17.6	3.0	3.11	5
Beef (hamburger or stew meat)	1.3	1.6	5.0	65.3	22.6	4.3	3.23	2
Beef (steak or roast)	2.4	7.2	19.7	59.5	9.3	1.9	2.78	17
Pork	3.6	20.6	26.8	44.4	3.2	1.4	2.36	29
Tuna fish	3.6	11.0	14.4	59.4	10.5	1.2	2.76	19
Frozen dinners	5.1	25.6	17.3	46.7	4.9	.3	2.34	30
Hot dogs	2.8	11.1	19.1	54.4	11.2	1.5	2.72	21
Coffee or tea	3.0	3.3	5.6	68.1	13.8	6.1	3.14	4
Pasta (pizza, spaghetti, etc.)	3.5	9.5	13.1	61.3	11.2	1.5	2.82	14
Food at "fast food" restaurants (i.e., McDonald's, etc.)	3.6	18.0	17.6	49.9	9.5	1.5	2.57	24
Food at regular restaurants	2.7	19.9	17.9	47.4	10.1	2.0	2.55	25

Interpretation: Frozen dinner consumption decreased the most followed by pork, butter, and alcoholic beverages. Cheese consumption increased the most followed by beef, fresh fruit, and coffee or tea. On balance, people seem to have cut back on food consumption of most items with 22 of the 30 products showing decreased average consumption.

Section II—Nutritional Information Sources

1. Amount of information gained from various sources:

	No Answer	None	Very Little	Some	Quite a Bit	A Tremendous Amount	Mean	Rank
Books	3.7%	20.6%	21.0%	35.3%	14.9%	4.5%	2.60	5
Magazines	3.2	8.7	12.6	44.9	26.3	4.4	3.05	3
Labels on the packages food comes in	3.7	5.7	16.5	43.6	26.4	4.0	3.07	2
Your mother	7.3	38.7	16.4	21.8	12.0	3.7	2.20	10
Other family members	6.0	34.7	23.8	26.7	7.2	1.6	2.12	11
Friends	5.5	22.4	26.5	36.8	8.1	.6	2.34	8
Doctors	5.0	29.6	22.4	28.8	11.2	3.0	2.32	9
TV programs	4.9	19.6	25.0	38.8	10.3	1.4	2.46	7
TV advertisements	4.8	17.8	27.1	39.1	10.1	1.1	2.47	6
Newspapers	5.2	12.9	20.7	44.1	15.5	1.5	2.71	4
Your own experience	4.1	4.3	6.2	35.4	39.3	10.7	3.48	1
Courses in school	5.4	50.9	9.1	16.1	11.1	7.4	2.10	12

Interpretation: Personal experience is by far the most important source of nutritional information with labels on packages and magazines next most important. The importance of school courses, other family members, doctors, and friends is rated very low. Whether this reflects unavailability or lack of expertise is not clear.

2. Books read in the past year:

	No Answer	No	Yes
Dieting	5.5%	51.7%	42.8%
Nutrition	8.0	58.7	33.3
Cooking	4.1	35.2	60.6

Interpretation: People read more to make gourmet treats or to solve a specific problem than to learn about nutrition in general. Still, one third of the sample claim to have read a book about nutrition this year.

Section II (concluded)

3. Preferred sources of information from a federal government campaign:

	Percent	Rank
Column in the newspapers	39.1	2
TV special	36.1	3
Special edition of a prominent magazine	15.9	7
Government brochure	19.8	6
Extension courses	11.1	9

	Percent	Rank
Workshops	9.9	10
Public service TV announcements	25.0	4
Information on packages	39.8	1
Information in TV advertisements	22.1	5
Don't care	11.3	8

Interpretation: No source of information is favored by a majority. Information on packages edges out column in newspaper and TV special as most preferred. Workshops and extension courses inspire only about 10 percent of the sample's interest. The author's favorite, a government brochure, finished a dismal sixth.

4. Amount willing to pay per week for a service providing nutritional information about available brands:

	Percent
No answer	3.3
Nothing	48.2
10¢–19¢	25.3
20¢–49¢	17.1
50¢–99¢	5.3
$1–$2	.7
Over $2	.0

Interpretation: Half the sample is unwilling to pay anything to find out nutritional information about available brands, and only 6 percent is willing to pay over 50 cents per week. If this is not an artifact of the question, it suggests that consumers would not support such a service in the free market.

5. Formal courses in nutrition:

	No Answer	No	Yes
High school	6.1%	62.2%	31.7%
College	17.3	71.9	10.7
Adult education/workshop	18.5	74.6	6.9

Interpretation: Very few of this sample have taken a formal nutrition course.

Section III—Background

1. Diets any member of the household is on:

Diet	Self-Imposed	Doctor's Orders	Total
Low cholesterol	7.3%	13.1%	20.4%
Low fat/calorie	17.0	11.3	28.3
Diabetic	1.5	9.6	11.1
Low salt	5.0	13.0	18.0
Vegetarian	1.3	.3	1.6
Low triglyceride	1.0	1.7	2.7

Interpretation: A substantial fraction of the households sampled have a member on one diet or another with self-imposed low fat/calorie most prevalent followed by doctor-imposed low cholesterol, low salt, low fat/calorie, and diabetic. Very few low triglyceride and vegetarian diets were in evidence.

2. Smoking frequency:

	Percent
No answer	1.2
Never	70.2
Occasionally	5.0
Regularly, but light (less than one pack of cigarettes each day)	8.6
Regularly (one pack of cigarettes a day)	9.1
Heavily (more than one pack each day or equivalent)	5.9

Interpretation: Over two thirds of this sample were nonsmokers with 15 percent heavy smokers.

3. Vitamin pills taken personally:

	Percent
No answer	1.9
None	48.9
Multiple	29.7
Vitamin C	17.3
Vitamin G	.0
Vitamin B-12 complex	8.9
Vitamin A	3.7
Iron	15.7

Interpretation: Half the sample take no vitamins at all. The most prominent vitamin is multiple followed by vitamin C and iron. Surprisingly, no one claimed to be taking vitamin G which indicated the sample was still awake at this point in the questionnaire.

Section III *(concluded)*

4. Time spent watching TV per day:

	Percent
No answer	.7
None	3.0
Less than 1 hour	10.0
1–2 hours	33.6
3–4 hours	35.4
Over 4 hours	17.2

Interpretation: The typical respondent watches 2–3 hours of TV daily and only 3 percent abstain entirely.

5. Change in family income:

	Percent
No answer	.9
Gone down a lot	11.4
Gone down a little	11.6
Stayed about the same	30.7
Gone up a little	41.4
Gone up a lot	4.1

Interpretation: Most people's incomes have stayed the same or increased slightly. On the other hand; 11.4 percent have experienced a large drop in income compared to only 4.1 percent who experienced a large increase.

6. Change in family size:

	Percent
No answer	1.4
Decreased by two or more	2.4
Decreased by one	9.7
Stayed the same	77.6
Increased by one	8.0
Increased by two or more	1.0

Interpretation: More of these families decreased in size than increased, a result of their age and tendency to enter the "empty nest" stage of the life cycle. Over three fourths, however, remained unchanged.

Section IV—General Attitudes

	No Answer	Strongly Agree	Some- what Agree	Neither Agree nor Disagree	Some- what Disagree	Strongly Disagree	Average Response	Rank
People need to eat meat to be healthy	1.0%	23.8%	38.2%	17.6%	13.7%	5.7%	2.39	8
A high level of consumption is necessary to maintain a high standard of living	2.6	3.0	11.0	17.9	29.1	36.5	3.87	23
I am personally more conscientious in conserving energy than I was 3 years ago	1.8	55.0	33.6	6.3	2.2	1.1	1.58	2
The government should be more active in giving information about nutrition to consumers	1.6	32.6	36.4	22.9	4.3	2.3	2.06	4
I expect things to get better for my family next year	1.5	16.6	34.5	34.4	10.4	2.7	2.47	9
I feel the need for more information about nutrition	1.6	20.1	37.0	32.1	6.3	2.9	2.34	7
All people would have better diets if there were fewer mouths to feed	2.3	7.9	14.8	25.5	23.6	25.9	3.46	20
All cold cereals are about the same nutritionally	2.3	7.7	24.5	19.9	26.5	19.0	3.25	18
Health is more important than money	1.3	83.6	11.1	2.6	.4	1.1	1.22	1
I get more exercise than the average person	1.7	12.2	25.4	33.0	20.6	7.0	2.85	13
We entertain at home more than the average family	2.8	2.7	9.9	23.6	29.5	31.6	3.80	22
I am healthier than the average American	2.8	7.3	23.6	43.0	15.6	7.7	2.93	15
I consider myself better informed about nutrition than the average American	1.5	5.6	21.4	43.6	18.4	9.5	3.05	17

Section V—Food Perceptions

1. Knowledge questions:

	No Answer	True	False	Don't Know
Hamburger contains substantially more protein per ounce than do soy beans	1.4%	13.8%	[54.7]%	30.1%
Pasta is high in cholesterol	1.7	31.8	[31.0]	35.5
Poultry are more efficient than cattle as producers of protein	1.8	[37.4]	35.4	25.3
A large amount of one vitamin is sufficient to overcome deficiencies of other vitamins	1.4	2.2	[85.2]	11.2
Beans and rice together are a low-protein meal	1.7	17.7	[59.6]	21.1
Eating a variety of foods from the supermarket will ensure a balanced diet	1.5	32.1	58.0	8.4
The cost of the vitamins needed to meet 100 percent of the minimum daily requirements is less than 10 cents per day	1.4	[38.1]	16.7	43.8
Food coloring additives create hyperactivity in children	1.9	[25.1]	33.3	39.7
Sugar causes cavities in children	1.6	[73.8]	15.5	9.0
Whole wheat bread is healthier than enriched white bread	.9	[69.6]	17.0	12.6

Interpretation: Many respondents have a reasonable knowledge of nutrition but a disconcertingly large fraction are unsure or even worse, incorrect in their opinions. For four of the questions, less than half the sample knew the correct answer ("correct" answers are in brackets).

2. Which foods aid which functions:

	Whole Milk	Beef	Tomatoes	Enriched Bread
Eyes	49.4%	31.3%	37.0%	22.6%
Teeth and bones	[96.3]	33.3	13.4	27.4
Muscle tissue	46.1	[80.2]	14.5	32.4
Repair of body tissues	[57.9]	[65.6]	25.5	31.9
Blood cells	37.4	[76.8]	26.1	21.3
Fighting infection	47.7	41.1	45.9	25.7
Nervous system	[56.7]	44.3	26.4	36.3
Skin	[70.3]	36.6	37.0	27.7
Proper growth of children	[93.3]	[69.1]	49.8	[67.3]

Interpretation: As expected, whole milk is thought to be a "super" food. Beef is also very highly regarded by the sample; especially for muscle and blood. Interestingly, enriched bread is perceived to be more related to proper growth of children than tomatoes which seem to be perceived of as relatively nonbeneficial (answers above 50 percent are in brackets).

Section V (continued)

3. Which foods contain a lot of different nutrients?

	Whole Milk	Beef	Tomatoes	Enriched Bread
Vitamin A	[58.8]%	16.9%	31.5%	25.3%
Thiamin (vitamin B_1)	28.4	31.6	13.0	48.8
Riboflavin (vitamin B_2)	31.3	32.3	10.5	44.5
Niacin	22.7	23.4	15.5	45.2
Vitamin C	19.8	4.6	[76.0]	9.6
Vitamin D	[63.4]	11.8	11.2	13.7
Protein	41.7	[81.9]	3.4	22.0
Carbohydrates	28.4	14.0	9.9	[72.7]
Fat	[71.4]	49.1	.7	27.9
Calories	[56.9]	38.6	3.7	[73.9]
Iron	26.3	[64.0]	21.4	23.6
Calcium	[91.0]	6.1	4.9	18.7

Interpretation: More than half the sample felt whole milk had a lot of vitamin D, fat, calories, and calcium and over 40 percent listed protein. For beef, protein and iron were the main characteristics followed by fat. Tomatoes are perceived to mainly have vitamin C, while enriched bread is associated with carbohydrates and calories followed by vitamins A, B_1 and B_2 (answers above 50 percent are in brackets).

4. Foods similar in benefits to the body:

	Whole Milk	Beef	Tomatoes	Enriched Bread
Oatmeal	22.6%	14.6%	2.2%	[75.6]%
Fish	21.3	[76.1]	6.3	7.6
Rice	11.1	12.1	3.4	[78.8]
Navy beans	10.9	[59.1]	8.3	37.8
Chicken	14.6	[82.4]	3.0	11.2
Potatoes	11.0	6.6	14.4	[77.1]
Eggs	44.4	[61.0]	2.9	11.4

Macaroni	9.6	6.9	1.3	[83.3]
Pork and lamb	11.4	[82.9]	2.8	6.7
String beans	7.3	9.2	[73.5]	6.3
Carrots	17.9	5.9	[72.4]	6.3
Bananas	24.8	11.1	43.2	24.5
Peanut butter	26.0	[73.8]	4.0	19.9
Cottage cheese	[76.7]	36.3	4.8	10.7

Interpretation: People seem to group foods based on the four basic food groups (answers above 50 percent are in brackets).

Accuracy of Nutritional Knowledge

In order to get some overall indication of the accuracy of people's nutritional knowledge, a summed score was developed based on some of the answers to Section V, question 1 (the true-false questions). Specifically, a summed score was developed as follows:

	Answer		
	True	False	Don't Know
Hamburger contains substantially more protein per ounce than do soy beans	-.25	+1	0
Pasta is high in cholesterol	-.25	+1	0
Poultry are more efficient than cattle as producers of protein	+1	-.25	0
A large amount of one vitamin is sufficient to overcome deficiencies of other vitamins	-.25	+1	0
Beans and rice together are a low protein meal	-.25	+1	0
The cost of the vitamins needed to meet 100% of the minimum daily requirements is less than 10¢ per day	+1	-.25	0
Sugar causes cavities in children	+1	-.25	0

Section V (concluded)

The distribution of this "Nutritional Knowledge Score" was as follows:

Score	Absolute Frequency	Adjusted Frequency	Cumulative Frequency
−1.25	1	.1%	.1%
−1.00	1	.1	.2
−.75	2	.2	.4
−.50	4	.4	.9
−.25	.0	1.1	1.9
.0	17	1.8	3.7
.25	6	.6	4.4
.50	10	1.1	5.4
.75	17	1.8	7.2
1.00	27	2.9	10.1
1.25	25	2.7	12.8
1.50	32	3.4	16.2
1.75	36	3.8	20.0
2.00	33	3.5	23.5
2.25	37	3.9	27.4
2.50	57	6.1	33.5
2.75	51	5.4	38.9
3.00	22	2.3	41.3
3.25	29	3.1	44.4
3.50	81	8.6	53.0
3.75	83	8.8	61.8
4.00	34	3.6	65.4
4.50	49	5.2	70.6
4.75	88	9.4	80.0
5.00	41	4.4	84.4
5.75	55	5.9	90.2
6.00	50	5.3	95.5
7.00	42	5.4	100.0
Total	940	100.0	

Interpretation: The average score was 3.465, and the standard deviation, 1.786. Nutritional knowledge varies widely across the sample with very few people extremely knowledgeable in an objective sense. Put differently, a substantial fraction of the sample is misinformed about nutrition.

APPENDIX 11-B

SAMPLE CROSS-TAB OUTPUT

```
STATISTICAL PACKAGE FOR THE SOCIAL SCIENCES SPSS-1 - VERSION 6.00          10/05/76          PAGE 1

  SPACE ALLOCATION FOR THIS RUN..

    TOTAL AMOUNT REQUESTED                         80000 BYTES

    DEFAULT TRANSPACE ALLOCATION                   10000 BYTES

      MAX NO OF TRANSFORMATIONS PERMITTED    100
      MAX NO OF RECODE VALUES                400
      MAX NO OF ARITH.. OR LOG.. OPERATIONS  300

    RESULTING WORKSPACE ALLOCATION                 70000 BYTES


      FILE NAME       LEHNLTRI
      VARIABLE LIST   INCOME,FAMSIZE,EXPENSE
      INPUT MEDIUM    DISK
      N OF CASES      UNKNOWN
      INPUT FORMAT    FIXED(76X,2F1.0/12X,F1.0////)

    ACCORDING TO YOUR INPUT FORMAT, VARIABLES ARE TO BE READ AS FOLLOWS

      VARIABLE    FORMAT    RECORD    COLUMNS
      INCOME      F 1. 0      1       77- 77
      FAMSIZE     F 1. 0      1       78- 78
      EXPENSE     F 1. 0      2       13- 13

THE INPUT FORMAT PROVIDES FOR  3 VARIABLES.  3 WILL BE READ
IT PROVIDES FOR  6 RECORDS ('CARDS') PER CASE.  A MAXIMUM OF  78 'COLUMNS' ARE USED ON A RECORD.

      RECODE          FAMSIZE (2=1)(3,4=2)(5 THRU 9=3)/
                      INCOME (1,2=1)(3,4=2)(5=3)/
                      EXPENSE (1=12.5)(2=22.5)(3=37.5)
                      (4=52.5)(5=75C)

      MISSING VALUES EXPENSE (0)
      READ INPUT DATA

AFTER READING  500 CASES FROM SUBFILE LEHNLTRI, END OF FILE WAS ENCOUNTERED ON LOGICAL UNIT # 8
```

STATISTICAL PACKAGE FOR THE SOCIAL SCIENCES SPSSH - VERSION 6.00   10/05/76

CATA TRANSFORMATION DONE UP TO THIS POINT..

          NO OF TRANSFORMATIONS   0
          NO OF RECODE VALUES   0
          NO OF ARITHM. OR LOG. OPERATIONS   0
     THE AMOUNT OF TRANSPACE REQUIRED IS   0 BYTES

          CROSSTABS   TABLES= INCOME BY EXPENSE
          STATISTICS   ALL

***** GIVEN WORKSPACE ALLOWS FOR   4374 CELLS AND   2 DIMENSIONS FOR CROSSTAB PROBLEM *****

STATISTICAL PACKAGE FOR THE SOCIAL SCIENCES SPSSH - VERSION 6.00   10/05/76   PAGE 7

FILE LFHVLTRI (CREATION DATE = 10/05/76)

* * * * * * * * * * * * * * *   C R O S S T A B U L A T I O N   O F   * * * * * * * * * * * * * * *
INCOME   BY EXPENSE
*   PAGE 1 OF 1

EXPENSE

COUNT / ROW PCT / COL PCT / TOT PCT	13.	23.	38.	53.	70.	ROW TOTAL
INCOME 1.	33 / 7.1 / 84.6 / 3.5	226 / 48.7 / 70.2 / 24.2	149 / 32.1 / 47.8 / 16.0	45 / 9.7 / 23.1 / 4.8	11 / 2.4 / 16.9 / 1.2	464 / 49.7
2.	5 / 1.5 / 12.8 / 0.5	73 / 22.0 / 22.7 / 7.8	121 / 36.4 / 38.8 / 13.0	102 / 30.7 / 52.3 / 10.9	31 / 9.3 / 47.7 / 3.3	332 / 35.6
3.	1 / 0.7 / 2.6 / 0.1	23 / 16.8 / 7.1 / 2.5	42 / 30.7 / 13.5 / 4.5	48 / 35.0 / 24.6 / 5.1	23 / 16.8 / 35.4 / 2.5	137 / 14.7
COLUMN TOTAL	39 / 4.2	322 / 34.5	312 / 33.4	195 / 20.9	65 / 7.0	933 / 100.0

CHI SQUARE = 167.23213 WITH 8 DEGREES OF FREEDOM   SIGNIFICANCE = 0.0
CRAMER'S V = 0.29937
CONTINGENCY COEFFICIENT = 0.38987
LAMBDA (ASYMMETRIC) = 0.16418 WITH INCOME DEPENDENT.   = 0.11948 WITH EXPENSE DEPENDENT.
LAMBDA (SYMMETRIC) = 0.13889
UNCERTAINTY COEFFICIENT (ASYMMETRIC) = 0.09231 WITH INCOME DEPENDENT.   = 0.06745 WITH EXPENSE DEPENDENT.
UNCERTAINTY COEFFICIENT (SYMMETRIC) = 0.07820
KENDALL'S TAU B = 0.36468 SIGNIFICANCE = 0.0
KENDALL'S TAU C = 0.36058 SIGNIFICANCE = 0.0
GAMMA = 0.53056
SOMERS'S C (ASYMMETRIC) = 0.33443 WITH INCOME DEPENDENT.   = 0.39767 WITH EXPENSE DEPENDENT.
SOMERS'S D (SYMMETRIC) = 0.36332
ETA = 0.40195 WITH INCOME DEPENDENT.   = 0.41076 WITH EXPENSE DEPENDENT.

NUMBER OF MISSING OBSERVATIONS = 7

CHAPTER 12

Comparing Differences in Key Variables

This chapter is the first of several devoted to analytical methods. Since these methods are borrowed from statistics, there are a number of "technical" aspects to their use. Recall, however, that the purpose of marketing research is to gain understanding and help make good decisions. Hence while we cover statistical issues, we try to emphasize interpretation and use more than statistics. Often, one is interested in the association between group membership (nominally scaled) and an intervally scaled "criterion" variable (e.g., attitude or sales). For example, one might be interested in whether per capita consumption of a particular product differs by region, or if advertising copy produces a different attitude toward a product. In these situations, one generally has a conception that the criterion (key) variable (e.g., sales, attitude) depends on/is caused by the nominal variable (e.g., region, advertising copy). This chapter focuses on examining whether means or percentages differ across categories of the (causal) variable.

THE NOTION OF STATISTICAL INFERENCE

A basic purpose of statistical analysis is to detect significantly unusual behavior. It is possible for two numbers to be different mathematically but not be different significantly. For example, one person might weigh 180.23 pounds and another 180.12. While these weights are different, for most decisions (a) the difference is unimportant and (b) the difference is well within the range of accuracy of most measuring devices and probably insignificant statistically. Hence, it is useful to distinguish between three kinds of differences:

1. *Mathematical.* If numbers are not exactly the same, they are different. (In marketing research, two results are almost always mathematically different.)
2. *Important/practically significant.* If the numerical difference would matter in a managerial sense, then the difference is important.
3. *Statistically significant.* If the difference is big enough to be unlikely to have occurred due to chance, then the difference is statistically significant.

In this chapter, we spend some time on statistical issues. Still, practical significance is more important. Consider two situations. In the first, we purchase a tool that we expect to last 20 years. It last six months. Obviously, the difference is both numerically and practically significant. However, since there is only one data point, we cannot say the product *in general* (on average) produces results statistically significantly different from 20 years. In the second situation, we observe the average weight in a 16-ounce package of Super Low-Fat Munchos is 15.97 ounces. If the average is based on enough packages, then we could establish that the difference is statistically significant. Statistical significance is thus a complement to, not a substitute for, practical significance.

In determining if differences are statistically significant, one must make a tradeoff between two extremes:

> *Calling every difference, no matter how small, significant.* For example, someone with a weight fetish might weigh herself at 8 P.M. after a huge pasta dinner and again at 8 P.M. the next night immediately after a fish dinner. If the weights were 121 and 119 pounds respectively, she could think she had lost 2 pounds. Alternatively, however, she could think (*a*) that fish is lighter than pasta, (*b*) that she exercised differently, or (*c*) that the accuracy of the scale, given changes in temperature, humidity, and position of the scale in the bathroom, is insufficient to call a 2-pound difference statistically significant. Calling a difference significant when it is not is traditionally called a *Type I* or α *error*.

> *Requiring absolute proof that a difference is significant.* Carrying the weight example further, it is possible to argue that any change might have been due to a fluke measurement. Hence it is possible that a weight change from 121 to 110 is not important or significant. (However, anyone with the 24-hour flu would strongly disagree.) Calling a difference insignificant when it is significant is called a *Type II* or β *error*.

The problem of detecting significant results involving trading off these two considerations arises in many contexts:

1. *Machine retooling.* A machine in the middle of an assembly line has to produce parts within a given tolerance. To retool the machine, the assembly line must be stopped, which is costly. On the other hand, if the machine produces bad parts, considerable repair costs are required. Based on a sample of parts from the machine, do I retool or not?

2. *Evaluating a taste testing result.* In a blind test between two versions of the same product (one less costly), 37 prefer version A and 43 version B. Is the difference significant, or can I use the cheaper version without sacrificing sales?

3. *Judicial decisions.* In rendering a decision, a judge or jury must implicitly decide between two risks: putting an innocent person in jail, or letting a guilty person go free.

Interestingly, most of the basic literature on statistics, the practices of marketing research, and the legal system in the United States focuses on the Type I (α) error. This places the burden of proof on the data to disconfirm a hypothesis. (In the previous examples, the hypotheses are that the machine is okay, the two products are equal, and the defendant is innocent.) While this makes sense when the hypothesis is strongly maintained, it is somewhat senseless if the hypothesis is arbitrary. Still, the use of statistical inference in this and subsequent chapters will maintain the tradition of focusing on Type I (α) errors, and therefore a result said to be statistically significant will generally be one that differs from a null hypothesis beyond "reasonable doubt." The astute reader may also notice that most null hypotheses implicitly assume there is nothing interesting in the data (e.g., two means are equal, two variables are unrelated). Consequently, statistically significant results will tend to be those that are "interesting" in the sense that a relationship is uncovered in the data.

TESTS CONCERNING ONE SAMPLE, ONE VARIABLE

Concept

Assume that the average consumption of beer in bottles per month was collected from a sample of 289 consumers. Since these consumers were rugby players, it seemed interesting to examine the theory that rugby players are heavy consumers of beer. Assume the data were as follows:

$$\text{"Typical" beer consumption} = 59.8$$
$$\text{Sample result: Average beer consumption} = 76.2$$

Given this result, it seems pretty obvious that rugby players are indeed heavy beer consumers. This managerial result/conclusion requires nothing more than the eyeball comparison of the sample mean with the standard. Unfortunately, results are not always this clear-cut. For example, if the average beer consumption in the sample of 289 rugby players had been 61.1 rather than 76.2, it is unclear whether the extra 1.3 bottles are the result of a "true" difference between rugby players and the general population or merely the result of having chosen a particularly heavy drinking sample of rugby players. Similarly, if the sample size had been 9 instead of 289, we again become unsure about the meaningfulness of the difference. In both cases, obviously the *sample* of rugby players differs from the typical consumer. The issue, however, is whether rugby players *in general* differ.

Approach

Whether a difference in a mean is significant or not depends on three things:

1. The standard of comparison (μ)
2. The sample mean ($\bar{x}$)
3. The degree of uncertainty concerning how well the sample mean represents the mean of the population of interest (in the previous example, all rugby players), which is related to both the consistency of the results across the sample and the sample size (n)

We can build an index as follows:

$$\text{Index} = \frac{\text{Sample mean} - \text{Standard}}{\text{Uncertainty}}$$

This index increases as the difference between the sample mean and the standard increases, and decreases as the uncertainty increases.

Drawing on our statistics training (or asking someone who knows what to do), we recall that the uncertainty of our estimate of the sample mean is quantified by its standard deviation, the standard error of $\bar{x}$:

$$s_{\bar{x}} = \frac{s}{\sqrt{n}}$$

Hence, the index becomes

$$t_{n-1} = \frac{\bar{x} - \mu}{s/\sqrt{n}} \tag{12.1}$$

This is the well-known (if you've recently taken a statistics course) t statistic. It tests the null hypothesis:

> H_0 = The mean of the population represented by the sample is equal to the standard
> $(\bar{x} = \mu)$

A large value for the index would reject the null hypothesis and, consequently, imply that the population represented by the sample differs from the standard in terms of average behavior. The values can be checked for significance against the values in a t table with $n - 1$ degrees of freedom. Whenever the index is larger than the appropriate table value, the null hypothesis is rejected. For large sample sizes, t is approximately normally distributed. Combining these two points, we can see that (using the .05 significance level as a crude screen), in general, t values above 2 will be significant and those less than 2 not significant.

Examples

Example A Applying this test to the beer consumption example, we get the following results. Given:

$$\mu = 59.8$$
$$\bar{x} = 76.2$$
$$n = 289$$
$$s = 34$$

Thus, the index becomes:

$$t = \frac{76.2 - 59.8}{\frac{34}{\sqrt{289}}} = \frac{16.4}{2} = 8.2 > 2$$

and the difference is, as we thought, statistically significant. This means in general that rugby players consume more beer than typical consumers.

Example B Now assume the sample mean had been 61.1, instead of 76.2. Given:

$$\mu = 59.8$$
$$\bar{x} = 61.1$$
$$n = 289$$
$$s = 34$$

The index would now be:

$$t = \frac{61.1 - 59.8}{\dfrac{34}{\sqrt{289}}} = \frac{1.3}{2} = .65 < 2$$

This is not significant. Hence, in this case, there is a reasonable chance that the difference between the sample mean and the standard does not represent a "true" difference in average consumption between rugby players and the typical person.

Example C Finally, assume we had a sample mean of 76.2, but only a sample size of 9. The results would now be as follows. Given:

$$\mu = 59.8$$
$$\bar{x} = 76.2$$
$$n = 9$$
$$s = 34$$

Therefore,

$$t = \frac{76.2 - 59.8}{\dfrac{34}{\sqrt{9}}} = \frac{16.4}{11.33} = 1.45 < 2$$

Hence, in this case, the difference is not significant. While this may seem surprising given the large difference in mean values, there is a nontrivial chance that the difference is a fluke due to the small sample size. (A general corollary to this result is that given a large enough sample size, even the smallest numerical difference becomes significant.)[1]

Assume we are interested in deciding whether upgraded packaging is worth its cost. If the upgraded packaging costs 20 percent of the purchase price (which we have decided not to change) and our gross margin is 40 percent, then sales must double (to account for the new 20 percent gross margin instead of the old 40 percent) in order to break even. Assume we are certain sales with the old package would be 59.8. We could run a test with the new package. Assume the results were

$$\bar{x} = 76.2$$
$$n = 81$$
$$s = 34$$

---

[1] It should also be pointed out that for very small sample sizes, unknown standard deviations, and nonnormally distributed variables, the t distribution is only an approximation of the true sampling distribution.

Therefore, the standard t test shows a significant increase in sales:

$$t = \frac{76.2 - 59.8}{\frac{34}{\sqrt{81}}} = 4.34$$

However, introducing the new package would result in sales far (as well as statistically significantly) short of the 118.6 level needed to break even:

$$t = \frac{118.6 - 76.2}{\frac{34}{\sqrt{81}}} = 11.2$$

Here automated statistical significance testing (that is, seeing if 76.2 differed from 59.8) would produce potentially misleading results, and the appropriate statistical test (comparing 76.2 with 118.6) only confirms the obvious result that the new package doesn't double sales. The most useful managerial conclusion is that the new packaging leads to a (statistically significant) 27 percent increase in sales but that this is well (and statistically significantly) short of the 100 percent increase needed to break even.

TESTS CONCERNING ONE SAMPLE, ONE PERCENTAGE

Approach

When the key variable is binary, such as a yes-no question, the percent of respondents (p) who answer yes can be compared with a standard (θ) as follows:

$$\text{Index} = \frac{\text{Sample percent} - \text{Standard}}{\text{Uncertainty}}$$

$$= \frac{p - \theta}{\sqrt{\frac{\theta(1 - \theta)}{n}}} \qquad (12.2)$$

As n increases, this index[2] becomes approximately normally distributed. The bigger n is and the closer p is to .5, the better the approximation. When n is above 30 and p between .1 and .9, this index is approximately normally distributed.

Here the null hypothesis is that the percent answering yes in the population represented by the sample is the same as the standard: H_0: $p = \theta$. A big index value

---

[2]Some people use

$$\frac{p - \theta}{\sqrt{\frac{p(1 - p)}{n}}}$$

For practical purposes, the two formulas are usually equivalent because of the insensitivity of $p(1 - p)$ to p.

(one greater than 2 for the .05 significance level) indicates the difference is statistically significant.

Since in many cases we are only concerned about values that exceed (or fall short of) the standard, the test may be set up as a one-tail test as follows: H_0: $p \geq \theta$ (or H_0: $p \leq \theta$) and hence, for n above 30, an index value greater than 1.64 (or less than -1.64) will be necessary to statistically reject the null hypothesis at the .05 significance level.

Examples

Example A Given

$$\text{Standard } \theta = 20\%$$
$$\text{Sample } p = 30\%$$
$$n = 100$$

Question: Does the sample group differ from the standard? To answer this, we test H_0: $p = \theta$. The index (test statistic) becomes

$$\frac{30 - 20}{\sqrt{\dfrac{(20)(80)}{100}}} = \frac{10}{\dfrac{40}{10}} = 2.5$$

Since $2.5 > 2$, the results in the sample group differ significantly from the standard.

Example B Given

$$\theta = 20\%$$
$$p = 28\%$$
$$n = 100$$

Question: Are the results significantly greater in the sample group? (H_0: $p \leq \theta$)
Test statistic:

$$\frac{28 - 20}{\sqrt{\dfrac{(20)(80)}{100}}} = \frac{8}{\dfrac{40}{10}} = 2$$

Since $2 > 1.64$ (this is a one-tail test), H_0 is rejected, and we conclude that the percent in the sample group is greater than 20 percent.

TESTS CONCERNING TWO MEANS

Concept

In many circumstances, measurements may be taken on a key variable in samples of two different populations (e.g., experimental and control groups, product users and nonusers, etc.). An obvious question that can be asked, therefore, is whether the two populations represented by the samples are significantly different in terms of some key variable.

Approach

We can, again, build an index of the significance as follows:

$$\text{Index} = \frac{\text{Difference in means}}{\text{Uncertainty about difference in means}}$$

Let

$$\bar{x}_1 = \text{mean in first sample}$$
$$n_1 = \text{size of first sample}$$
$$s_1 = \text{standard deviation of first sample}$$

Then we get

$$\text{Index} = \frac{\bar{x}_1 - \bar{x}_2}{s_{\bar{x}_1 - \bar{x}_2}} \tag{12.3}$$

which is t distributed with $n_1 + n_2 - 2$ degrees of freedom. The null hypothesis is H_0: $\mu_1 = \mu_2$ (or, alternatively, $\mu_1 \geq \mu_2$ or $\mu_1 \leq \mu_2$ if we are doing a one-tail test). The formula for $s_{\bar{x}_1 - \bar{x}_2}$ comes in two forms:

1. If we do not assume $s_1 = s_2$, we have

$$s_{\bar{x}_1 - \bar{x}_2} = \sqrt{\frac{s_1^2}{n_1} + \frac{s_2^2}{n_2}} \tag{12.4}$$

2. If we make the assumption that $s_1 = s_2$, we get

$$s_{\bar{x}_1 - \bar{x}_2} = \hat{s}\sqrt{\frac{1}{n_1} + \frac{1}{n_2}} \tag{12.5}$$

where

$$\hat{s}^2 = \frac{(n_1 - 1)s_1^2 + (n_2 - 1)s_2^2}{n_1 + n_2 - 2}$$

The advantage of assuming $s_1 = s_2$ is that the test is slightly more powerful: we become more likely to detect a significant difference between the two means if, in fact, one exists and $\sigma_1 = \sigma_2$. Practically, however, the difference is minimal when s_1 and s_2 are close in size.

Example

Given

$$\bar{x}_1 = 20 \qquad \bar{x}_2 = 22$$
$$s_1^2 = 3.78 \qquad s_2^2 = 10.44$$
$$n_1 = 10 \qquad n_2 = 10$$

the two samples, the difference is enough to alter the results from nonsignificant to significant at the .05 level. The point is that it is incorrect to treat matched samples as independent, and some significant changes may be lost if the incorrect procedure is applied.

TESTS CONCERNING TWO PERCENTAGES

Approach

Just as it is possible to test two means to see if they differ significantly, so is it possible to compare two percentages. The formula for this is

$$\text{Index} = \frac{p_1 - p_2}{s_{p_1-p_2}}$$

where

p_1, p_2 = percents having the characteristic in the first and second samples, respectively;

n_1, n_2 = sizes of the first and second samples, respectively;

$s_{p_1-p_2}$ = standard deviation of the difference in percents.

This index is approximately normally distributed for large sample sizes. A pooled estimate of the overall percent is derived by assuming the percents are equal in the two groups:

$$\pi = \frac{n_1 p_1 + n_2 p_2}{n_1 + n_2} \tag{12.8}$$

Thus,

$$s_{p_1-p_2} = \sqrt{\frac{\pi(100 - \pi)}{n_1} + \frac{\pi(100 - \pi)}{n_2}} = \sqrt{\frac{n_1 + n_2}{n_1 n_2}} \sqrt{\pi(1 - \pi)} \tag{12.9}$$

Example

Given

First Sample	Second Sample
$n_1 = 100$	$n_2 = 150$
$p_1 = 20\%$	$p_2 = 30\%$

and H_0: $p_1 = p_2$ (no significant difference)

Therefore, the test statistic is

$$\text{Index} = \frac{20 - 30}{s_{p_1-p_2}}$$

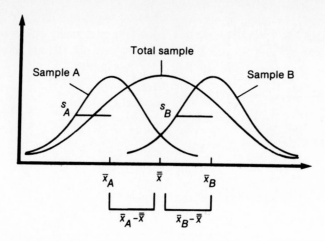

FIGURE 12.3
Overall and by Sample Distributions

ONE-WAY ANOVA

Formulas

Mathematics often is so formidable that it inhibits understanding. Also, since practical applications of ANOVA generally are done on computers, knowledge of the algebra used is unnecessary to use the procedure for detecting significant influences. Nonetheless, in this case some derivations are very useful for explaining the "magic" formulas used. Hence, this section attempts to briefly delineate the formulas used for one-way ANOVA.

Each observation differs in value from the overall mean by some amount $(x - \bar{x})$. Some of this difference may be attributable to the influence of another variable (e.g., color A, B, or C). The rest is essentially random/unexplained. The procedure followed in ANOVA attempts to partition the variance $(x - \bar{x})^2$ in the dependent variable (e.g., sales) into two subsets: that attributable to the influence of another (independent) variable (commonly called the *treatment effect*), and the rest. The model that underlies this analysis is, in words

Value of dependent variable $= f$ (levels of independent variables) + random element

The dependent variable is assumed to be intervally scaled, and the independent variables are treated as though they were categorical (nominally scaled), For one-way ANOVA, the model becomes

$$x_{jk} = \bar{\bar{x}} + C_j + e_{jk} \tag{12.10}$$

where

x_{jk} = value of the dependent variable for the kth person in the jth sample (exposed to the jth level of the independent variable)

$\bar{\bar{x}}$ = overall mean

C_j = treatment effect of the jth level of the independent variable $= \bar{x}_j - \bar{\bar{x}}$

e_{jk} = random part of the kth observation in the jth sample

Consider again our original example for one-way ANOVA with three colored packages (Table 12.4). In this case, the overall mean $(\bar{\bar{x}})$ is 8. The treatment effect of the first level (C_1) is +3. Similarly, C_2 and C_3 are 0 and −3, respectively. To see how the model works, consider the second observation in the color A sample:

$$x_{12} = \bar{\bar{x}} + C_1 + e_{12}$$

or

$$10 = 8 + 3 + e_{12}$$

Hence,

$$e_{12} = -1 \text{ to "balance" the books}$$

(Equivalently, $e_{12} = x_{12} - \bar{x}_1 = 10 - 11 = -1$.)

Statistical Test

The statistical test for significant differences is based on the relative size of the C_js and the e_{jk}s. The test takes the total variance in the x values and partitions it into two parts: that due to the differences between group means and the overall mean $(C_j$s), and that due to the "residual" error $(e_{jk}$s):

$$\text{Total variation} = \sum_{j=1}^{c} \sum_{k=1}^{n_j} (x_{jk} - \bar{\bar{x}})^2 \tag{12.11}$$

where

c = number of categories of the independent variable (e.g., three colors)

n_j = number of observations of the dependent variable when exposed to level j of the independent variable

x_{jk} = value of the dependent variable in the kth observation in the jth sample

$\bar{\bar{x}}$ = overall mean

This can be rewritten as the sum of two parts[4]:

"Between" sum of squares (treatment):

$$\sum_{j=1}^{c} \sum_{k=1}^{n_j} \left(\bar{x}_j - \bar{\bar{x}}\right)^2 = \sum_{j=1}^{c} n_j \left(\bar{x}_j - \bar{\bar{x}}\right)^2 \tag{12.12}$$

---

[4]This can be derived from

$$\sum\sum\left(x_{ijk} - \bar{\bar{x}}\right)^2 = \sum\sum\left(x_{ijk} - \bar{x}_j + \bar{x}_j + \bar{\bar{x}}\right)^2$$

$$= \sum\sum\left(x_{ijk} - \bar{x}_j\right)^2 + 2\sum\sum\left(x_{ijk} - \bar{x}_j\right)\left(\bar{x}_j - \bar{\bar{x}}\right) + \sum\sum\left(\bar{x}_j - \bar{\bar{x}}\right)^2 = \cdots$$

"Within" sum of squares (unexplained):

$$\sum_{j=1}^{c} \sum_{k=1}^{n_j} \left(x_{jk} - \bar{x}_j \right)^2 \tag{12.13}$$

Two assumptions are necessary:

1. The variances in the separate samples are equal $(s_1^2 = s_2^2 = \ldots = s_c^2)$.

2. The dependent variable (x) is normally distributed.

The key issue in ANOVA is whether the differences in means between the groups are large in relation to the uncertainty/variability within the groups on the dependent variable. Consequently, we develop an index as follows:

$$\text{Index} = \frac{\sum_{j=1}^{c} n_j \left(\bar{x}_j - \bar{\bar{x}} \right)^2 \Big/ (c - 1)}{\sum_{j=1}^{c} \sum_{k=1}^{n_j} \left(x_{jk} - \bar{x}_j \right)^2 \Big/ (n - c)} \tag{12.14}$$

This index can be compared with the F table with $c - 1$ and $n - c$ degrees of freedom. The calculation steps for obtaining this statistic are often summarized in a table (Table 12.5). The null hypothesis is that all the treatment groups have equal means $(H_0: \bar{x}_1 = \bar{x}_2 = \cdots = \bar{x}_c)$.

TABLE 12.5 One-Way ANOVA

Source	Sum of Squares	Degrees of Freedom	Mean Square (SS/d.f.)	F
Treatment (influencing variable)	$\sum_{j=1}^{c} n_j \left(\bar{x}_j - \bar{\bar{x}} \right)^2$	$c - 1$	$\dfrac{\sum_{j=1}^{c} n_j \left(\bar{x}_j - \bar{\bar{x}} \right)^2}{c - 1} = A$	$\dfrac{A}{B}$
Unexplained	$\sum_{j=1}^{c} \sum_{k=1}^{n_j} \left(x_{jk} - \bar{x}_j \right)^2$	$n - c$	$\dfrac{\sum_{j=1}^{c} \sum_{k=1}^{n_j} \left(x_{jk} - \bar{x}_j \right)^2}{n - c} = B$	
Total	$\sum_{j=1}^{c} \sum_{k=1}^{n_j} \left(x_{jk} - \bar{\bar{x}} \right)^2$	$n - 1$		

Numerical Example

Returning again to the packaging example (Table 12.4), we have

$$\text{Total sum of squares} = \sum_{j=1}^{3}\sum_{k=1}^{4}\left(x_{jk} - \bar{\bar{x}}\right)^2$$

$$= (14 - 8)^2 + (10 - 8)^2 + (11 - 8)^2 + (9 - 8)^2$$
$$+ (8 - 8)^2 + (14 - 8)^2 + (3 - 8)^2 + (7 - 8)^2$$
$$+ (8 - 8)^2 + (6 - 8)^2 + (5 - 8)^2 + (1 - 8)^2$$
$$= 174$$

$$\text{Treatment sum of squares} = \sum_{j=1}^{3}\sum_{k=1}^{4}\left(\bar{x}_j - \bar{\bar{x}}\right)^2$$

$$= \sum_{j=1}^{3} 4\left(\bar{x}_j - \bar{\bar{x}}\right)^2$$

$$= 4(11 - 8)^2 + 4(8 - 8)^2 + 4(5 - 8)^2$$
$$= 72$$

$$\text{Unexplained sum of squares} = \sum_{j=1}^{3}\sum_{k=1}^{4}\left(x_{jk} - \bar{x}_j\right)^2$$

$$= (14 - 11)^2 + (10 - 11)^2 + (11 - 11)^2 + (9 - 11)^2$$
$$+ (8 - 8)^2 + (14 - 8)^2 + (3 - 8)^2 + (7 - 8)^2$$
$$+ (8 - 5)^2 + (6 - 5)^2 + (5 - 5)^2 + (1 - 5)^2$$
$$= 102$$

(Alternatively: Unexplained sum of squares = Total sum of squares − Treatment sum of squares = 174 − 72 = 102.)

Interpretation

By using either the formulas just discussed or a computer program, we can construct an ANOVA table (Table 12.6). The key to interpretation is the test statistic F of 3.18. This statistic follows the F distribution with 2, 9 degrees of freedom. Going to the F table, we see that at the .05 significance level, $F_{2,9} = 4.26$. Since $3.18 < 4.26$, we fail to reject the null hypothesis of equal mean response to the three package colors. In

TABLE 12.6 ANOVA Table

Source	Sum of Squares	Degrees of Freedom	Mean Square	F
Treatment (colors)	72	2	36	3.18
Unexplained	102	9	11.33	
Total	174	11		

other words, the differences are not statistically significant. The reason for this is that the variation within the three samples "swamps" the differences in means among the three samples. Note, for example, the range of observations in group B is from 3—lower than the smallest mean—to 14—higher than the largest mean. Consequently, the evidence is not sufficiently consistent to conclude that the means are different.

TWO-WAY ANOVA

A logical extension of the ANOVA method is to the case where there are two influencing variables. For example, assume that, in addition to varying package color, we also changed advertising strategy, as in Table 12.7. This is a factorial design: all possible combinations ($2 \times 3 = 6$) of package color and advertising strategy are tested. There are also samples of size 2 in each of the six possible treatments. The possible treatments are often called *cells*. Having equal cell sizes is common to many experiments and is, where feasible, a desirable situation.

Examining the relative effects of the two variables is done by extending the one-variable procedure. We redefine the model as follows:

$$x_{ijk} = \bar{\bar{x}} + R_i + C_j + I_{ij} + e_{ijk} \tag{12.15}$$

where

x_{ijk} = kth observation in the sample with the ith level of the row variable and the jth level of the column variable

R_i = average effect of the ith level of the row variable
$= \bar{x}_i - \bar{\bar{x}}$

C_j = average effect of the jth level of the column variable
$= \bar{x}_j - \bar{\bar{x}}$

I_{ij} = interaction effect of combining the ith level of the row variable with the jth level of the column variable
$= \bar{x}_{ij} - \bar{x}_i - \bar{x}_j + \bar{\bar{x}}$

$\bar{x}_{ij}$ = mean of the dependent variable cell defined by the ith level of the row variable and the jth level of the column variable

TABLE 12.7 Sales Results as a Function of Package Color and Advertising Strategy

	Package Color			Average Sales for Each Advertising Strategy	Effect of Advertising Strategy (R_i)
	A	B	C		
Advertising	14	8	8	10	+ 2
strategy I:	10	14	6		
Advertising	11	3	5	6	− 2
strategy II:	9	7	1		
Average sales for					
each color	11	8	5		
Effect of color (C_j)	+ 3	0	− 3		

Conceptually, an interaction is the extra effect due to putting two or more features in combination that cannot be predicted by knowing the effects of the two features separately. Hence, it is related to the notion of synergy and the discovery of particularly felicitous (or disastrous) combinations of factors in terms of their effect on the key (dependent) variable. Besides such obvious examples as nitro and glycerin, a variety of examples can be cited. Aesthetic items (music, paintings, etc.) are obvious examples of cases in which the whole is not simply the sum of the parts. For example, a blue color package combined with an advertising strategy using mood images and jazz music might be more effective than we would expect from the addition of a blue color and mood advertising effects. Put differently, red might be the best color and factual the best advertising strategy when studied separately, but the combination of blue and mood advertising might be better than the combination of red and factual advertising, as in Table 12.8. The importance of the interaction term is that its significance indicates that there is a synergistic/nonadditive combination of the two variables that is particularly effective (or ineffective). If an interaction term is not significant, it means that optimum overall strategy may be obtained by separately choosing the best level of the two variables and then using them in combination. To estimate interactions, there must be at least two observations per cell.

Statistical Formulas: Unrelated Treatment Variables

The formulas for ANOVA when the treatment variables are related are complex. Since the purpose here is to understand ANOVA, we present the formulas for unrelated treatment variables. Dealing with related treatment variables is discussed via an example.

The partitioning of the variance in the two-variable case with equal cell sizes can be viewed as a sequential process of continually pulling apart (decomposing) the "unexplained" variance into that part attributable to some variable and that part which is not. By first removing the variance attributable to the column variables as in one-way ANOVA, one can proceed to pull out the variance attributable to the row variables and then the variance attributable to the interactions as follows:

$$\text{Total variance:} \quad \sum_{i=1}^{r} \sum_{j=1}^{c} \sum_{k=1}^{n_{ij}} \left(x_{ijk} - \bar{\bar{x}} \right)^2 \tag{12.16}$$

$$\text{Column variance:} \quad \sum_{i=1}^{r} \sum_{j=1}^{c} \sum_{k=1}^{n_{ij}} \left(\bar{x}_j - \bar{\bar{x}} \right)^2 = \sum_{j=1}^{c} n_j \left(\bar{x}_j - \bar{\bar{x}} \right)^2 \tag{12.17}$$

$$\text{Row variance:} \quad \sum_{i=1}^{r} \sum_{j=1}^{c} \sum_{k=1}^{n_{ij}} \left(\bar{x}_i - \bar{\bar{x}} \right)^2 = \sum_{i=1}^{r} n_i \left(\bar{x}_i - \bar{\bar{x}} \right)^2 \tag{12.18}$$

$$\text{Residual variance:} \quad \sum_{i=1}^{r} \sum_{j=1}^{c} \sum_{k=1}^{n_{ij}} \left(x_{ijk} - \bar{x}_i - \bar{x}_j + \bar{\bar{x}} \right)^2 \tag{12.19}$$

$$\text{Interactions:} \quad \sum_{i=1}^{r} \sum_{j=1}^{c} \sum_{k=1}^{n_{ij}} \left(\bar{x}_{ij} - \bar{x}_i - \bar{x}_j + \bar{\bar{x}} \right)^2$$

$$= \sum_{i=1}^{r} \sum_{j=1}^{c} n_{ij} \left(\bar{x}_{ij} - \bar{x}_i - \bar{x}_j + \bar{\bar{x}} \right)^2 \tag{12.20}$$

$$\text{Within variance:} \quad \sum_{i=1}^{r} \sum_{j=1}^{c} \sum_{k=1}^{n_{ij}} \left(x_{ijk} - \bar{x}_{ij} \right)^2 \tag{12.21}$$

TABLE 12.8 Average Responses ($\bar{x}_{ij}$)

Ad Type	Color			$\bar{x}_i$	R_i
	Red	Blue	Yellow		
Mood	7	11	3	7	.33
Factual	10	4	10	8	1.33
Scare	7	3	5	5	− 1.67
$\bar{x}_j$	8	6	6	6.67	
C_j	1.33	− .67	− .67		

where

c = number of categories (levels) in the column variable

r = number of categories (levels) in the row variable

n_{ij} = number of observations exposed to the ith level of the row variable and the jth level

of the column variable

This process can be viewed graphically in Figure 12.4. Notice that the within variance is the difference between the cell mean and the individual values in the cell. This is, in essence, the irreducible variance that is unexplained and unexplainable, given the two variables. (You may also notice that, unless there is more than one observation per cell, there is no way to calculate the within variance and, hence, no way to separate the interaction effect from within the variance.) The other three variances (column, row, and interaction) divide up the explainable variance by assigning it to its "cause."

Examples

Two-Way ANOVA with No Interactions   The simplest form of two-way ANOVA assumes no interactions. Thus, the variance is partitioned into three parts (see Table 12.9):

Column variance: Equation (12.17)
Row variance: Equation (12.18)
Residual variance:[5] Equation (12.19)

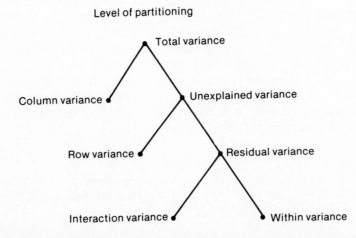

Level of partitioning

Total variance

Column variance

Unexplained variance

Row variance

Residual variance

Interaction variance

Within variance

FIGURE 12.4
Variance Decomposition in Two-Way ANOVA

[5]It is easier to compute the Residual variance as Total variance − Column variance − Row variance.

TABLE 12.9 Two-Way ANOVA without Interactions

Source	Sum of Squares	Degrees of Freedom	Mean Square	F
Column	$\sum_{j=1}^{c} n_j \left(\bar{x}_j - \bar{\bar{x}} \right)^2 = ①$	$c - 1$	$\dfrac{①}{c - 1} = A$	$\dfrac{A}{C}$
Row	$\sum_{i=1}^{r} n_i \left(\bar{x}_i - \bar{\bar{x}} \right)^2 = ②$	$r - 1$	$\dfrac{②}{r - 1} = B$	$\dfrac{B}{C}$
Residual	$\sum_{i=1}^{r} \sum_{j=1}^{c} \sum_{k=1}^{n_{ij}} \left(x_{ijk} - \bar{x}_i - \bar{x}_j + \bar{\bar{x}} \right)^2 = ③$	$n - r - c + 1$	$\dfrac{③}{n - r - c + 1} = C$	
Total	$\sum_{i=1}^{r} \sum_{j=1}^{c} \sum_{k=1}^{n_{ij}} \left(x_{ijk} - \bar{\bar{x}} \right)^2$	$n - 1$		

To see how to apply these formulas, again return to the package color and advertising strategy example (Table 12.7). First, calculate the sums of squares:

$$\text{Column sum of squares} = 4(11 - 8)^2 + 4(8 - 8)^2 + 4(5 - 8)^2$$
$$= 72$$
$$\text{Row sum of squares} = 6(10 - 8)^2 + 6(6 - 8)^2$$
$$= 48$$
$$\text{Residual[6] sum of squares} = 174 - 72 - 48 = 54$$

The resulting ANOVA table then becomes Table 12.10.

The test for column effects (H_0: all $\bar{x}_j$s are equal) is F with $c - 1$ and $n - r - c + 1$ degrees of freedom; it compares the column and residual variances. Similarly, the test for row effects (H_0: all $\bar{x}_i$s are equal) is F with $r - 1$ and $n - r - c + 1$ degrees of freedom, and compares the row and residual variances. Here, the test for the significance of the column effect at the .05 level is to compare 5.33 with $F_{2,8} = 4.46$. Since 5.33 > 4.46, we reject the null hypothesis that the column means are equal. In other words, the package colors produce significantly different sales. Similarly, we can test the rows by comparing 7.11 with $F_{.05, 1, 8} = 5.32$. Since 7.11 > 5.32, we conclude that advertising also significantly influences sales. (Put differently, we can predict sales significantly more accurately from $\bar{\bar{x}} + c_j + r_i$ than we can from $\bar{\bar{x}}$ alone.)

It is interesting to note that the column effects now appear to be significant, whereas in the simple one-way analysis they were not. The explanation for this is that the row effects, which were not accounted for in the one-way ANOVA, inflated the unexplained variance sufficiently to mask the effect of package color.

---

[6] To calculate the residuals directly, we first generate a table for $\bar{x}_i + \bar{x}_j - \bar{\bar{x}} = \bar{\bar{x}} + r_i + c_j$. We then get the residual sum of squares as $= (14 - 13)^2 + (10 - 13)^2 + (8 - 10)^2 + (14 - 10)^2 + (8 - 7)^2 + (6 - 7)^2 + (11 - 9)^2 + (9 - 9)^2 + (3 - 6)^2 + (7 - 6)^2 + (5 - 3)^2 + (1 - 3)^2 = 54$.

TABLE 12.10 Two-Way ANOVA without Interactions

Source	Sum of Squares	Degrees of Freedom	Mean Square (SS/d.f.)	F
Columns (colors)	72	2	36	5.33
Rows (advertising)	48	1	48	7.11
Residual	54	8	6.75	
Total	174	11		

Two-Way ANOVA with Interactions The same data just analyzed can be examined for the presence of interactions (Table 12.11). The column, row, and total variance formulas are identical to those of the two-way without interaction formulas. The interaction and within formulas are those of (12.20) and (12.21):

$$\text{Interaction variance: } \sum_{i=1}^{r}\sum_{j=1}^{c} n_{ij}\left(\bar{x}_{ij} - \bar{x}_i - \bar{x}_j + \bar{\bar{x}}\right)^2$$

$$\text{Within variance: } \sum_{i=1}^{r}\sum_{j=1}^{c}\sum_{k=1}^{n_{ij}}\left(x_{ijk} - \bar{x}_{ij}\right)^2$$

Returning to our example, we calculate the interaction variance as follows:

First, produce a table of cell means ($\bar{x}_{ij}$s) as in Table 12.12. (Notice that for managerial interpretation purposes, this table is the most useful output.) Second, produce the following $\bar{\bar{x}} + r_i + c_j = \bar{x}_i + \bar{x}_j - \bar{\bar{x}}$ table:

13	10	7
9	6	3

TABLE 12.11 Two-Way ANOVA without Interactions

Source	Sum of Squares	Degrees of Freedom	Mean Square	F
Column	$\sum_{j=1}^{c} n_j\left(\bar{x}_j - \bar{\bar{x}}\right)^2 = ①$	$c - 1$	$\dfrac{①}{c-1} = A$	$\dfrac{A}{D}$
Row	$\sum_{i=1}^{r} n_i\left(\bar{x}_i - \bar{\bar{x}}\right)^2 = ②$	$r - 1$	$\dfrac{②}{r-1} = B$	$\dfrac{B}{D}$
Interaction	$\sum_{i=1}^{r}\sum_{j=1}^{c} n_{ij}\left(\bar{x}_{ij} - \bar{x}_i - \bar{x}_j + \bar{\bar{x}}\right)^2 = ③$	$rc - c - r + 1$	$\dfrac{③}{rc - c - r + 1} = C$	$\dfrac{C}{D}$
Within	$\sum_{i=1}^{r}\sum_{j=1}^{c}\sum_{k=1}^{n_{ij}}\left(x_{ijk} - \bar{x}_{ij}\right)^2 = ④$	$n - rc$	$\dfrac{④}{n - rc} = D$	

TABLE 12.12 Cell Means

Ad Strategy	Color		
	A	B	C
I	12	11	7
II	10	5	3

The differences between the values in the two tables are the interactions (I_{ij}s):

$$
\begin{array}{rrr}
-1 & 1 & 0 \\
1 & -1 & 0
\end{array}
$$

Hence, the interaction variance is given by

$$2(-1)^2 + 2(1)^2 + 2(0)^2 + 2(1)^2 + 2(-1)^2 + 2(0)^2 = 8$$

To calculate the within variance, we compare the values of each observation with the cell means $\bar{x}_{ij}$:

$$
\begin{aligned}
\text{Within variance} = {} & (14 - 12)^2 + (10 - 12)^2 + (8 - 11)^2 \\
& + (14 - 11)^2 + (8 - 7)^2 + (6 - 7)^2 \\
& + (11 - 10)^2 + (9 - 10)^2 + (3 - 5)^2 \\
& + (7 - 5)^2 + (5 - 3)^2 + (1 - 3)^2 \\
= {} & 46
\end{aligned}
$$

The resulting ANOVA table is shown as Table 12.13. The table values with which we compare the computed Fs are $F_{.05, 2, 6} = 5.14$ for both the column and interaction effects and $F_{.05, 1, 6} = 5.99$ for the row effects. This implies that only the row effects are significant. The column effects now appear to be insignificant (at the .05 level). While the "right" way to interpret this depends on the purpose of the analysis, it would be appropriate to return to the simple two-way without interaction analysis and conclude that both color and advertising influence sales and that they can be considered independently of each other.

TABLE 12.13 Two-Way ANOVA with Interactions

Source	Sum of Squares	Degrees of Freedom	Mean Square	F
Column	72	2	36	4.69
Row	48	1	48	6.26
Interaction	8	2	4	.52
Within	46	6	7.67	
Total	174	11		

Managerial Interpretation

Academics have a tendency to report ANOVA results in statistical shorthand (e.g., the two-way interaction among advertising and price was significant, $F = 6.13$, $p = .03$). Unfortunately, this format is essentially worthless for managers who care about practical significance—that is, differences in average behavior. Statistical significance is merely an indicator, although an important one, of whether we can be reasonably certain that the averages really differ. Moreover, since different advertising expenditure levels, prices, etc., have different profit implications, simply demonstrating a statistically significant difference does not answer the question of which advertising strategy, etc., to follow. It is quite possible, for example, for an advertising strategy to produce significantly greater sales and not be worth pursuing, or vice versa. Hence while statistical tests should be reported, the basic focus should be on the results (e.g., different averages of the criterion variable).

Interpretation is facilitated by the inelegant but effective method of plotting the results. The mean sales for the different package designs and ads from Table 12.12 are shown in Figures 12.5 and 12.6. Let us first make two rather broad assumptions: that (*a*) all the colors are equally costly, as are the advertising strategies, and (*b*) the short-run experiment will be projectable both to the total market and over time. Faced with these results, any manager (or person with an IQ above that of a kumquat) would decide to use color A and advertising strategy I—exactly the correct decision. One need only compute conditional means to draw this conclusion, and it is, in fact, the correct decision regardless of whether the differences are statistically significant or not. What checking for statistical significance does is provide a "flag" to indicate whether you are reasonably certain the best guess (e.g., color A) is really better than the other choices so that it is worth arguing for.

The interaction concept is only slightly more involved. Recall that the average sales for each of the cells were those in Table 12.12. Faced with this, the manager would again select the combination of color A and advertising strategy I. Conceivably, however, a slight change could have made color B and advertising strategy I best, even though on average color A and advertising strategy I were best when color and advertising strategy were considered separately. The flag for this situation would be a significant interaction term in the analysis. In fact, all possible combinations of significant interactions

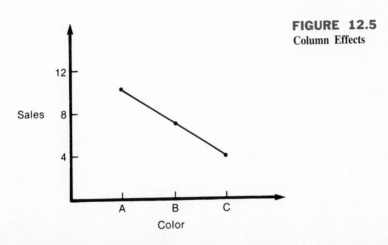

FIGURE 12.5
Column Effects

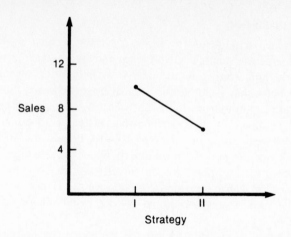

FIGURE 12.6
Row Effects

and row or column variables are possible. These possible combinations can be displayed graphically (Figure 12.7).

The managerial value of ANOVA, then, is obtained by observing the average response to different combinations of the influencing variables. The statistical tests indicate whether the differences are real or illusory.

If statistically significant differences occur, then a cost/benefit analysis is needed to determine whether the improved results of using the best mix are worth the cost. In practice, the mix that maximizes sales is rarely justified on a cost/benefit basis. Consequently, the key is to compare the costs and benefits (e.g., sales) of various combinations and choose the best one on a "net," rather than "gross" (i.e., unadjusted for cost), basis.

Referring back to the example of Table 12.4, it is clear that, in a gross sense, color A is best. If we assume sales generate profit according to the formula Profit = 6(Sales) − 30, then the profits of the three colors are 36, 18, and 0. If the costs of using the three colors are 30, 5, and 10, however, then the net profits become 6, 13, and −10, indicating that color B is best. It is possible (and in the "real world," essential) to complicate this analysis by taking into account (a) the fact that the test area may be a small fraction (e.g., 1 percent) of the total market, and therefore the numbers need to be multiplied by a constant (e.g., 100) to convert to market-level data, (b) the impact over time, properly discounted, and (c) competitive reaction. Thus, the choice of the best color depends on many factors other than statistical significance.

MORE GENERAL ANOVA

When there are more than two influencing (independent) variables that may affect the key (dependent) variable, the algebra gets extremely difficult. The concept, fortunately, remains the same: assessing which variables are significantly related to the key dependent variable. Practically, more general ANOVA is performed by using computer programs, typically via dummy variable regression.

An important source of variation in many results can be the subject of the observation itself (e.g., respondent, store). In some cases, it may be possible to perform an

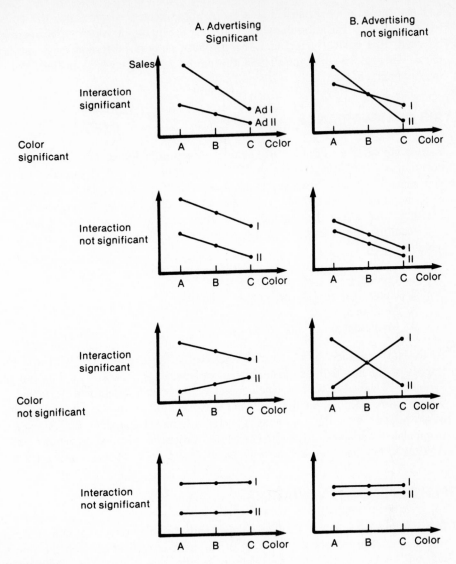

FIGURE 12.7
Sales as a Function of Color and Advertising

ANOVA *within subject*, meaning, for example, using all the observations on a single respondent or store. More typically, however, the design will be *between subjects*, where each respondent or store furnishes a single observation.

When dealing with between-subject designs where each subject provides multiple observations, it is advisable to account for the subject (respondent, store) effect in the analysis by removing its average level. This can be done by estimating the subject effect (if there are multiple observations per subject) by removing each subject's mean from the data (i.e., normalizing within subject). Alternatively, you can choose variables that account for the differences across subjects (e.g., income or store size) and use those as covariates. (This is an imperfect approach, since the covariates rarely explain all the variation between subjects.) Finally, a *repeated measures* design can be used; this basically includes the subjects as a variable and each subject as a treatment. (In essence, this generalizes the paired *t* test discussed earlier.) We discuss these in the next chapter.

ANALYSIS OF COVARIANCE

Rarely are all the variables of interest only nominally scaled (categorical). Analysis of covariance (ANCOVA) extends ANOVA to account for both continuous (intervally scaled) and categorical data. Frequently, the categorically scaled variables are manipulated in an experiment (e.g., advertising copy and color) and the intervally scaled ones are other measures that affect the dependent variable (e.g., store size or total sales).

Recalling the discussion in Chapter 5 concerning experimental design, we classified variables as

1. Ignored
2. Controlled for in the sample selection
3. Monitored
4. Manipulated

Analysis of variance as we have discussed it in an experimental situation focuses on the impact of the fourth type, manipulated variables (e.g., package color), on the dependent variable. If we also wish to include intervally scaled monitored variables (e.g., average weekly store volume) in the analysis, these are often called *covariates*. Hence, analysis of covariance uses the following general scheme: Dependent variable = *f*(Experimental/manipulated variables, Monitored/covariate variables). Special programs exist to perform ANCOVA, but one can satisfactorily handle most such situations using regression analysis.

MULTIPLE DEPENDENT VARIABLES

In some instances, more than one dependent variable may be important. For example, I might be concerned about the effect of different advertisements on the ratings of a product on several attributes. One way to handle this situation is to perform a separate ANOVA for each attribute. Alternatively, it is possible to simultaneously test the notion that all the attribute ratings remained constant. This second approach is beyond the scope of this book. Practically, it is carried out by using a computer program such as MANO-VA—multivariate analysis of variance.

A NUTRITION EXAMPLE

To see how ANOVA can be applied to nonexperimental data, consider again the nutritional study that has been mentioned throughout this book. In this case, assume we want to examine the effect of family size and household income on weekly food expenditures. The original data on 933 respondents (7 failed to answer all three questions) were coded as in Table 12.14. As you may notice, this categorization is somewhat unusual since both

TABLE 12.14 Coding Method

Family Size	
Actual Number	Category
2	1
3 or 4	2
5 or more	3

Income	
Actual Answer	Category
Under $10,000	1
$10,000–$20,000	2
Over $20,000	3

Food Expenditure	
Answer	Value
Under $15	$12.50
$15–$29	22.50
$30–$44	37.50
$45–60	52.50
Over $60	70.00

family size and income are variables that could be considered intervally scaled. Similarly, the use of median category values to represent food expenditure on an interval scale is not without error. Suffice it to say that such recoding is both pedagogically and practically useful, in this case mostly the former. The computer output on which this analysis is based is found in Appendix 12-A. Notice that, in most statistical packages, the useful/managerial data on the averages in cells must be requested separately from the statistical analysis. (No pain, no gain?)

It is possible to look at the variables separately. Studying the effect of family size, we find that average expenditures vary by family size (Table 12.15). Obviously, this difference is very substantial. One-way ANOVA (Table 12.16) clearly confirms this. The F of 222.4 is very significant at any reasonable significance level. Food expenditures also vary by income category (Table 12.17). This difference, though not quite as massive as that due to family size, is still clearly significant (Table 12.18).

Since both of these variables are significant, an obvious extension of the analysis is to perform a two-way ANOVA with interactions. In this case, however, we no longer have an equal number of observations per cell. Put differently, family size and income are related. In contrast to the previous example, the sequential partitioning formulas for the variance no longer apply here. Fortunately, someone programmed the computer with

TABLE 12.15 Family Size versus Expenditure

Family Size Category	Number in Category	Average Expenditures	Effect
1 (2)	411	$28.17	– $ 8.51
2 (3 or 4)	350	39.70	3.02
3 (5 or more)	172	50.86	14.18

TABLE 12.16 One-Way ANOVA for Family Size

Source	d.f.	Sum of Squares	Mean Squares	F
Between (family size)	2	67,535	33,767.5	222.4
Within (unexplained)	930	141,190	151.8	
Total	932	208,725		

the correct formulas (we hope). The average expenditure pattern shows substantial variation between cells (Table 12.19). Again, it is obvious that both income and family size affect food expenditures. The ANOVA results (Table 12.20) confirm this. Even without resorting to the F table, we can see that family size and income have significant effects on expenditures. Also clearly, the interactions are not significant.

Notice that the sum of squares attributed to family size and income separately is less than that attributed to both row and column effects. This is due to the unequal cell sizes, which make part of the explained variance common to both variables. To understand where the 44,696.1 comes from, recall that income alone accounted for 35,217.0 in the one-way ANOVA. Hence, the marginal contribution of family size is 79,913.4 − 35,217.3 = 44,696.1. Similarly, the marginal contribution of income is given by 79,913.4 − 67,535.0. The variance partitioning[7] can be seen in Figure 12.8.

SUMMARY

This chapter has discussed how to compare means and percentages. It also discussed analysis of variance. While the basic idea of looking at conditional means is straightforward, assessing statistical significance using formulas based on interminable squaring of numbers is fairly foreboding. Fortunately, computers have made the algebraic manipulations a nonissue.

ANOVA's major strengths are the ability to uncover a lot of information from relatively few observations and the fact that the influencing variables need only be categorical. Useful as analysis of variance can be, it is possible for a manager and even a market researcher to survive and prosper knowing very little about it. There are two major reasons for this. The first is that the conditional means, the basis for managerial

Table 12.17 Income versus Expenditure

Income Category	Number in Category	Average Expenditure	Effect
1	464	$30.64	− $6.04
2	332	41.47	4.79
3	137	45.51	8.83

---

[7] It is interesting to note that a large fraction of the variance in food expenditure is explained by the model. This fraction is:

$$\frac{79,913.4 + 355.5}{208,724.3} = 38.5 \text{ percent}$$

and is what will be subsequently called R squared (R^2) in the regression in chapter 13.

TABLE 12.18 One-Way ANOVA for Income

Source	d.f.	Sum of Squares	Mean Squares	F
Between (income)	2	35,217	17,608.5	94.4
Within (unexplained)	930	173,507	186.6	
Total	932	208,724		

TABLE 12.19 Average Food Expenditures

Family Size	Income		
	1	2	3
1	26.03	32.47	34.11
2	35.39	40.85	46.32
3	44.51	52.07	56.50

interpretation, can be calculated without knowing much about ANOVA. The second is that the technique we will take up in the next chapter—regression analysis—can do essentially everything ANOVA does.

PROBLEMS

1. MESS, a manufacturer of specialty steel products, traditionally held a 20 percent share of a market. After introductions of new products by both the company and a major competitor, the company called 100 potential customers and found 28 had purchased from MESS.

   a. Has anything significant happened?
   b. What could explain the change?

2. Using a random digit phone survey, a company surveyed potential customers in two regions. In region A, 46 of 100 were aware of the company, while in region B, 104 of 200 were aware of the company.

   a. Is the difference significant?
   b. What could explain the difference?

Table 12.20 Two-Way ANOVA with Interactions

Source	Sum of Squares	d.f.	Mean Square	F
Main effects				
(row and column)	79,913.4	4	19,978.3	143.7
Family size	44,696.1	2	22,348.1	160.8
Income	12,377.6	2	6,188.8	44.5
Interactions	355.5	4	88.9	0.6
Residual (within)	128,435.4	924	139.0	
Total	208,704.3	932		

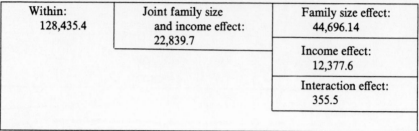

Total variance: 208,704.3

Within: 128,435.4	Joint family size and income effect: 22,839.7	Family size effect: 44,696.14
		Income effect: 12,377.6
		Interaction effect: 355.5

FIGURE 12.8
Variance Partitioning: Food Expenditures

3. A large packaged goods manufacturer tried out a new package design in several stores. The results were as follows:

Store	Sales with Old Design	Sales with New Design
1	137	152
2	573	581
3	490	480
4	102	95
5	87	120
6	237	252
7	81	98
8	123	140

a. How should I interpret the change?

b. What besides package design might have caused a change?

4. In region A, managed by M. B. Alright, average sales were $11,200 per account, with a standard deviation of $3,400 based on a sample of 100 accounts. In region B, managed by I. M. Dropout, average sales were $12,100, with a standard deviation of $2,800 based on a sample of 64 accounts.

a. Is there a difference?

b. What could explain the difference?

5. A company claims to produce a product with an average weight of at least 2,100 kilograms. Having bought five products recently, a client finds they weigh 2,060, 2,090, 2,050, 2,060, and 2,040 kilograms, respectively.

a. Is there a reason to complain?

b. Assume the client publicly claims the company is short-weighting its products and sues. The company countersues for libel. Who should win? Does the matter depend on who has the burden of proof?

6. Given the following test-market results for two stores in each cell (i.e., the two stores in Peoria exposed to strategy A sold 110 and 90 units, respectively):

	Display A	Strategy B
Peoria, Ill.	110, 90	40, 80
Springfield, Mass.	140, 100	60, 100
Gainesville, Fla.	60, 80	40, 60

What can I conclude about the display strategies?

7. Interpret the following results of a two-way ANOVA:

	d.f.	F
Advertising	1	1.31
Price	4	5.68
Interactions	4	7.26
Residual	10	

8. The All-Thumbs Hardware Store advertised outdoor grills, using three different advertising copy versions. The sales of their downtown store and suburban store following each ad are shown in the following:

Ads	Downtown	Suburban
"Smokey"	1	5
"Hot Dogs"	2	2
"Summer Evening"	3	5

Is the "Summer Evening" copy significantly better than the other advertising copy?

9. Smith's Department Store ran two advertisements, one featuring men's suits, the other featuring sports clothes. The two salespersons Al and Bob sold the following number of suits during each of the two weekends while each ad version ran:

Ads	Al	Bob
Men's suits	3, 5	5, 7
Sports clothes	2, 2	4, 4

(For example, during the two weekends when the men's suits version was playing, Al sold three suits one weekend and five on the other weekend.) Is there any real difference between the salespersons? Between the ad versions?

10. The DSNOB clothing store ran two different advertising campaigns: one an on-price promotion, and the other an off-price promotion. Salespersons Jones and Smith both worked during the test period for both campaigns. During the two weekends when the off-price commercials were playing, Jones sold one men's suit each weekend. However, Smith sold four suits one of these weekends and six the other. Similarly, during the two weekends

when the on-price ads were playing, Jones sold zero and two suits, while Smith sold one and one. What can you conclude about the campaigns? Does Smith really do unusually well with the off-price campaign, or could it have been just luck that Smith sold 10 suits on those two weekends?

11. Three different detergent brands were tested for whitening effectiveness at three different water temperatures using a full factorial design. The measured whiteness of each of the three replications for each combination of detergent and temperature was as follows:

Water	Detergent Brand		
Temperature	Jiff-O	All-Temp	Hill Fresh
45°F	47, 48, 52	50, 50, 53	54, 56, 58
95°F	48, 49, 47	45, 46, 44	49, 46, 49
145°F	56, 51, 52	49, 53, 51	47, 48, 52

a. What do you conclude about the whitening effectiveness of these detergents?

b. The present All-Temp advertising claim is "All-Temp washes equally well in hot or cold water." Could the claim be changed to "All-Temp washes equally well in any temperature water"?

12. The distributor of a perishable good ran an experiment to explore the differences among three advertising executions, Grabber, Holder, and Interest, and among three promotional deals denoted simply A, B, and C. The experiment was run in three test cities—Denver, Elmira, and Fort Wayne—using a Latin square design. The test weeks were spaced about four weeks apart to lessen the order effects of previous promotions and deals. No other advertising or promotion was conducted in these cities during the three-month test. The number of cases sold during the week of the advertising and promotion plus the number sold in the following two weeks are shown in the table below.

a. If you had to select one advertising copy and one promotional deal for national use, which would you select?

b. How confident are you that you have made the correct choices?

Advertising	City		
Copy	Denver	Elmira	Fort Wayne
Grabber	A 16	B 21	C 23
Holder	B 16	C 24	A 20
Interest	C 16	A 21	B 23

13. An experiment was performed by a local retailer in which the price of an item was varied between 30 cents and 40 cents during eight weekly periods. During some of these periods, an advertisement was also run. The sales of the product in each period were:

				Week				
	1	2	3	4	5	6	7	8
Price	30	40	30	40	30	40	30	40
Ad run	Yes	No	Yes	No	No	Yes	No	Yes
Sales	7	7	4	5	1	13	8	11

What can you conclude about the sales response to the different prices?

14. The Hardsell Company tried two different sales pitches for its door-to-door salespersons. The old pitch was basically a demonstration. The new pitch is basically a verbal sales pitch. One of the salespersons, Smith, used the new pitch and the old pitch in two suburbs of Denver, which is a popular city for test marketing. Smith makes 200 calls each week. During the eight weeks Smith was selling in Denver, the following numbers of units in the two suburban areas, known locally as Rockview and Plainview, were sold:

	Rockview	Plainview
Demonstration	90, 100	70, 60
Verbal	80, 90	80, 70

(For example: Using the demonstration pitch in Rockview, Smith sold 90 units one week and 100 units another week.) What advice would you give Smith?

15. Assume you have just taken a job as assistant brand manager for General Products, Inc. Your first assignment is to help your boss decide which of three package designs and four advertising campaigns should be used next year for one of the company's major products. Your boss wants to do this by getting the opinions of a sample of 200 individuals from the panel that G.P.I. maintains.

a. What alternatives (and their pros and cons) to the approach your boss has suggested should he or she be made aware of before making a decision?

b. Assume your boss decided to use the following test and got the following sales reports:

San Antonio, TX	Albany, NY	Muncie, IN	Portland, OR
Package design 1	Package design 2	Package design 3	Package design 3
Ad campaign 1	Ad campaign 2	Ad campaign 3	Ad campaign 4
Sales:	Sales:	Sales:	Sales:
A&P 4	A&P 6	Kmart 7	A&P 10
X-Mart 5	Grand Union 8	A&P 5	Fred's 11

(1) Is there any difference?

(2) Assume there is a statistical difference. How should I interpret it?

REFERENCES

BANKS, SEYMOUR (1965) *Experimentation in Marketing*, New York: McGraw-Hill.

COCHRAN, W., AND G. COX (1957) *Experimental Designs*, 2nd ed., New York: John Wiley and Sons.

GREEN, PAUL E. (1974) "On the Design of Choice Experiments Involving Multifactor Alternatives," *Journal of Consumer Research*, 1, September, 61–68.

HICKS, CHARLES R. (1964) *Fundamental Concepts in the Design of Experiments*, New York: Holt, Rinehart and Winston.

HOLLAND, CHARLES W., AND DAVID W. CRAVENS (1973) "Fractional Factorial Experimental Designs in Marketing Research," *Journal of Marketing Research*, 10, August, 270–76.

WINER, B. J. (1971) *Statistical Principles in Experimental Design*, New York: McGraw-Hill.

APPENDIX 12-A

SAMPLE ANOVA OUTPUT

```
STATISTICAL PACKAGE FOR THE SOCIAL SCIENCES SPSSH - VERSION 6.00          10/04/76          PAGE

         SPACE ALLOCATION FOR THIS RUN..

            TOTAL AMOUNT REQUESTED                          80000 BYTES


            DEFAULT TRANSPACE ALLOCATION                    10000 BYTES


               MAX NO OF TRANSFORMATIONS PERMITTED    100
               MAX NO OF RECODE VALUES                400
               MAX NO OF ARITHM.OR LOG.OPERATIONS     800

            RESULTING WORKSPACE ALLOCATION                  70000 BYTES

               FILE NAME        LEHNUTRI
               VARIABLE LIST    INCOME,FAMSIZE,EXPENSE
               INPUT MEDIUM     DISK
               N OF CASES       UNKNOWN
               INPUT FORMAT     FIXED(76X,2F1.0/12X,F1.0/////)


            ACCORDING TO YOUR INPUT FORMAT, VARIABLES ARE TO BE READ AS FOLLOWS

            VARIABLE   FORMAT   RECORD      COLUMNS

            INCOME     F 1. 0      1        77- 77
            FAMSIZE    F 1. 0      1        78- 78
            EXPENSE    F 1. 0      2        13- 13

THE INPUT FORMAT PROVIDES FOR    3 VARIABLES.    3 WILL BE READ
IT PROVIDES FOR  6 RECORDS ('CARDS') PER CASE.  A MAXIMUM OF   78 'COLUMNS' ARE USED ON A RECORD.

               RECODE           FAMSIZE (2=1)(3,4=2)(5 THRU 9=3)/
                                INCOME (1,2=1)(3,4=2)(5=3)/
                                EXPENSE (1=12.5)(2=22.5)(3=37.5)
                                (4=52.5)(5=70)
               MISSING VALUES EXPENSE (0)
               READ INPUT DATA

AFTER READING    940 CASES FROM SUBFILE LEHNUTRI,  END OF FILE WAS ENCOUNTERED ON LOGICAL UNIT # 8
```

```
STATISTICAL PACKAGE FOR THE SOCIAL SCIENCES SPSSH - VERSION 6.00          10/04/76     PAGE   2

      BREAKDOWN       TABLES=EXPENSE BY FAMSIZE BY INCOME/
                      EXPENSE BY FAMSIZE/EXPENSE BY INCOME

***** GIVEN WORKSPACE ALLOWS FOR  2915 CELLS AND   2 DIMENSIONS FOR SUBPROGRAM BREAKDOWN *****


STATISTICAL PACKAGE FOR THE SOCIAL SCIENCES SPSSH - VERSION 6.00          10/04/76     PAGE   3

FILE  LEHNUTRI (CREATION DATE = 10/04/76)

- - - - - - - - - -   D E S C R I P T I O N   O F   S U B P O P U L A T I O N S   - - - - - - - - - - -

CRITERION VARIABLE   EXPENSE
BROKEN DOWN BY       FAMSIZE
             BY      INCOME
- - - - - - - - - - - - - - - - - - - - - - - - - - - - - - - - - - - - - - - - - - - - - - - - - - - -

VARIABLE      CODE   VALUE LABEL              SUM           MEAN       STD DEV     VARIANCE        N

FOR ENTIRE POPULATION                     34220.000       36.6774     14.9651     223.9528     (  933)


FAMSIZE       1.
INCOME        1.                          11577.500       28.169      10.274      105.557      (  411)
INCOME        2.                           7417.500       26.026       8.747       76.518      (  285)
INCOME        2.                           2727.500       32.470      11.774      138.030      (   84)
INCOME        3.                           1432.500       34.107      11.789      138.970      (   42)

FAMSIZE       2.
INCOME        1.                          13895.000       35.100      13.572      184.186      (  350)
INCOME        1.                           4530.000       35.351      13.174      173.567      (  128)
INCOME        2.                           6822.500       40.853      12.923      167.001      (  167)
INCOME        3.                           2542.500       46.227      13.315      177.286      (   55)

FAMSIZE       3.
INCOME        1.                           8747.500       50.858      14.024      196.660      (  172)
INCOME        1.                           2270.000       44.510      13.304      177.006      (   51)
INCOME        2.                           4217.500       52.068      13.612      185.281      (   81)
INCOME        3.                           2260.000       56.500      12.920      166.923      (   40)

TOTAL CASES =    940
MISSING CASES =    7 OR   0.7 PCT.
```

```
STATISTICAL PACKAGE FOR THE SOCIAL SCIENCES SPSSH - VERSION 6.00          10/04/76          PAGE  4
FILE  LEHNUTRI (CREATION DATE = 10/04/76)

CRITERION VARIABLE   EXPENSE    - - -   D E S C R I P T I O N   O F   S U B P O P U L A T I O N S   - - -
   BROKEN DOWN BY   FAMSIZE

VARIABLE             CODE   VALUE LABEL        SUM          MEAN        STD DEV      VARIANCE        N

FOR ENTIRE POPULATION                      34220.0000     36.6774      14.9651      223.9539      ( 933)

FAMSIZE               1.                    11577.500     28.169       10.274       105.557       ( 411)
FAMSIZE               2.                    13855.000     39.700       13.572       184.186       ( 350)
FAMSIZE               3.                     8747.500     56.858       14.024       196.666       ( 172)

   TOTAL CASES  =   940
   MISSING CASES =    7 OR   0.7 PCT.


STATISTICAL PACKAGE FOR THE SOCIAL SCIENCES SPSSH - VERSION 6.00          10/04/76          PAGE  5
FILE  LEHNUTRI (CREATION DATE = 10/04/76)

CRITERION VARIABLE   EXPENSE    - - -   D E S C R I P T I O N   O F   S U B P O P U L A T I O N S   - - -
   BROKEN DOWN BY   INCOME

VARIABLE             CODE   VALUE LABEL        SUM          MEAN        STD DEV      VARIANCE        N

FOR ENTIRE POPULATION                      34220.0000     36.6774      14.9651      223.9528      ( 933)

INCOME                1.                    14217.500     30.641       12.417       154.191       ( 464)
INCOME                2.                    13767.500     41.468       14.544       211.527       ( 332)
INCOME                3.                     6235.000     45.511       15.364       236.043       ( 137)

   TOTAL CASES  =   940
   MISSING CASES =    7 OR   0.7 PCT.
```

STATISTICAL PACKAGE FOR THE SOCIAL SCIENCES SPSSH - VERSION 6.00   10/04/76   PAGE   6

    DATA TRANSFORMATION DONE UP TO THIS POINT..

        NO OF TRANSFORMATIONS   0
        NO OF RECODE VALUES   0
        NO OF ARITHM. OR LOG. OPERATIONS 0
    THE AMOUNT OF TRANSPACE REQUIRED IS   0 BYTES

            ONEWAY   EXPENSE BY FAMSIZE(1,3)/
                            RANGES=SCHEFFE(.05)/

***** ONEWAY PROBLEM REQUIRES   128 BYTES WORKSPACE *****

STATISTICAL PACKAGE FOR THE SOCIAL SCIENCES SPSSH - VERSION 6.00   10/04/76   PAGE   7
FILE   LEHNUTRI (CREATION DATE = 10/04/76)

- - - - - - - - - - - - - - - - - O N E W A Y -

    VARIABLE EXPENSE

                            ANALYSIS OF VARIANCE

        SOURCE   D.F.   SUM OF SQUARES   MEAN SQUARES   F RATIO   F PROB.
        BETWEEN GROUPS   2   67535.0000   33767.5000   222.422   0.000
        WITHIN GROUPS   930   141190.0000   151.8172
        TOTAL   932   208725.000

STATISTICAL PACKAGE FOR THE SOCIAL SCIENCES SPSSH - VERSION 6.00   10/04/76   PAGE   8

FILE   LEHNUTRI (CREATION CATE = 10/04/76)

- - - - - - - - - - - - - - - - - - - O N E W A Y -

        VARIABLE EXPENSE

MULTIPLE RANGE TEST

SCHEFFE PROCEDURE
RANGES FOR THE 0.100 LEVEL -

        3.02   3.02

HOMOGENEOLS SUBSETS   (SUBSETS OF GRCUPS, NC PAIR CF WHICH HAVE MEANS THAT DIFFER BY MCRE THAN THE SHORTEST
                         SIGNIFICANT RANGE FOR A SUBSET OF THAT SIZE)

SUBSET 1

GROUP   GRPO1
MEAN   28.1691
- - - - - - - - - -

SUBSET 2

GROUP   GRPO2
MEAN   39.7000
- - - - - - - - - -

SUBSET 3

GROUP   GRPO3
MEAN   5C.8575
- - - - - - - - - -

STATISTICAL PACKAGE FOR THE SOCIAL SCIENCES SPSSH - VERSION 6.00   10/04/76   PAGE   9

        CNEWAY   EXPENSE BY INCOME (1,3)/
                        RANGES=SCHEFFE(.10)/

***** ONEWAY PROBLEM REQUIRES   192 BYTES WORKSPACE *****

STATISTICAL PACKAGE FOR THE SOCIAL SCIENCES SPSSH - VERSION 6.00   10/04/76   PAGE   10
FILE   LEHNUTRI (CREATION DATE = 10/04/76)
- C N E W A Y -

VARIABLE EXPENSE

                        ANALYSIS OF VARIANCE

     SOURCE   D.F.   SUM OF SQUARES   MEAN SQUARES   F RATIO   F PROB.
     BETWEEN GROUPS   2   35217.0000   17608.5   94.382   0.000
     WITHIN GROUPS   930   173507.000   186.5667
     TOTAL   932   208724.000

STATISTICAL PACKAGE FOR THE SOCIAL SCIENCES SPSSH - VERSION 6.00   10/04/76   PAGE 11

FILE   LEHNUTRI (CREATION DATE = 10/04/76)

- - - - - - - - - - - - - - - O N E W A Y - - - - - - - - - - - - - - - - -

VARIABLE EXPENSE

MULTIPLE RANGE TEST

SCHEFFE PROCEDURE
RANGES FOR THE 0.100 LEVEL -

    3.94   3.94   3.94   3.94

HOMOGENEOUS SUBSETS   (SUBSETS OF GROUPS, NO PAIR OF WHICH HAVE MEANS THAT DIFFER BY MORE THAN THE SHORTEST
                        SIGNIFICANT RANGE FOR A SUBSET OF THAT SIZE)

SUBSET 1

GROUP   GRP01
MEAN   30.6412
- - - - - - - -

SUBSET 2

GROUP   GRP02
MEAN   41.4684
- - - - - - - -

SUBSET 3

GROUP   GRP03
MEAN   45.5109
- - - - - - - -

STATISTICAL PACKAGE FOR THE SOCIAL SCIENCES SPSSH - VERSION 6.00   10/04/76   PAGE 12

ANOVA   EXPENSE BY FAMSIZE (1,3) INCOME (1,3)

'ANOVA' PROBLEM REQUIRES 1995 BYTES OF SPACE.

STATISTICAL PACKAGE FOR THE SOCIAL SCIENCES SPSSH - VERSION 6.00   10/04/76   PAGE 13

FILE   LEHNUTRI (CREATION DATE = 10/04/76)

* * * * * A N A L Y S I S   O F   V A R I A N C E * * * * * * * * * *

          EXPENSE
    BY FAMSIZE
       INCOME

* *

SOURCE OF VARIATION	SUM OF SQUARES	DF	MEAN SQUARE	F	SIGNIF OF F
MAIN EFFECTS	79913.375	4	19978.344	143.730	0.001
FAMSIZE	44696.141	2	22348.070	160.778	0.001
INCOME	12377.625	2	6188.812	44.524	0.001
2-WAY INTERACTIONS	355.500	4	88.875	0.639	0.999
FAMSIZE INCOME	355.470	4	88.867	0.639	0.999
RESIDUAL	128435.375	924	138.999		
TOTAL	208704.250	932	223.932		

940 CASES WERE PROCESSED.
7 CASES (0.7 PCT) WERE MISSING.

CHAPTER 13

Regression Analysis

Regression analysis is by far the most widely used multivariate procedure in marketing research. While many people find it useful for forecasting, its applicability extends to problems such as market segmentation and estimating the effects of elements of the marketing mix.

The basic purpose of regression analysis is to estimate the relationship between variables. To use regression, a researcher must specify which variable (e.g., sales) depends on which other variable(s) (e.g., GDP, price). The procedure then calculates estimates of the relationship between the independent variables (GDP, price, etc.) and the dependent variable (sales).

This chapter first discusses the simple case of regression analysis, in which there is only one independent variable, to introduce and explain the procedure. The more realistic case of multiple independent variables is discussed next. After describing some of the problems that affect interpretation, applications of regression analysis to several situations are described. Finally, the important distinction between correlation and causation is addressed.

Before proceeding, one comment about the name *regression analysis* is appropriate. Like so many terms in our language, the term *regression analysis* bears no useful relationship to the technique. While the story of "how the technique got its name" is culturally interesting, suffice it to say that the title is a historical anachronism based on a plot of parent and child IQ data. The discovery that parents with high IQs tended to have children with lower IQs and parents with low IQs tended to have children with higher IQs seemed to indicate that the species was regressing toward the mean (Galton, 1889). The analysis of the relations between two variables then somehow got to be known as regression analysis. Having saved you innumerable hours of frustration in attempting to understand the name of the technique, this chapter now turns to the real business of understanding how to use it.

SIMPLE (TWO-VARIABLE) LINEAR REGRESSION ANALYSIS

Basic Concept

The simplest case of regression analysis is the situation where one variable is presumed to depend on only one other variable. For example, assume that sales depend solely on

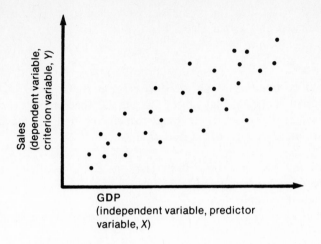

FIGURE 13.1
Sales vs. GDP

GDP. While this is not realistic, it serves as a useful example to introduce the method. In such a case, the researcher might gather data on sales and GDP for several different time periods or countries. As a first means of analyzing the relationship, the data should be plotted (Figure 13.1). Simple observation of the data indicates that, as GDP increases, so do sales. To summarize the relationship, one would tend to draw a straight line through the data points (Figure 13.2). The line summarizes, in some average sense, the relationship between GDP and sales. Hence, we could express the relationship between GDP and sales mathematically as

$$\text{Estimated sales} = B_0 + B_1 \text{ GDP}$$

The term B_0 is the constant, or intercept. This might be interpreted literally as the predicted level of sales if GDP dropped to zero. However, since such a level of GDP has not recently been experienced, extrapolating to this level is foolish. (Also, if GDP goes to zero we'll all be dead, so who cares what sales would be?) The term B_1 is the slope of the line (soon to be called the *regression coefficient*) and is interpreted as the amount sales would increase if GDP increased one (in whatever units the original data were

FIGURE 13.2
Regression of Sales vs. GDP

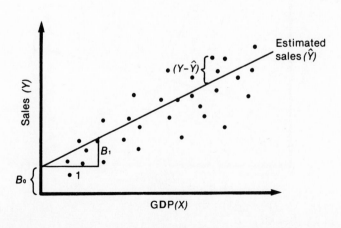

measured, e.g., billions of dollars). The error in prediction, calculated as $Y - \hat{Y}$, is simply the difference between estimated and actual sales.

Estimation

A variety of straight lines could be drawn through the data (Figure 13.3), some (A and B) that obviously do not represent the data, and others (C and D) that seem to represent the data fairly well. A problem, therefore, is to decide which line best fits the data. The following procedures exist for deciding on the best line:

1. *Graphical eyeball: Pick the line that looks best.* This procedure is often useful. Unfortunately, it breaks down when there are either numerous data points or more than one independent variable.
2. *Find the line that optimizes some criterion measure of a good fit.* Two of these criteria are
   a. The sum of the absolute differences between the predicted sales and actual sales ($\Sigma \, |Y - \hat{Y}|$)
   b. The sum of the squared differences between the predicted and actual sales values ($\Sigma(Y - \hat{Y})^2$)

The absolute differences, unfortunately, turn out to be relatively cumbersome mathematically. The generally accepted method is to minimize the sum of the squared errors (often called *least squares estimation*). One property of the squared differences is that they give slightly more weight to "far out" data points than does the absolute difference criterion. (For example, the least squares criterion would favor a line that produced four differences of size 2 as opposed to a line that produced three of size 1 and one of size 4.) Simple linear regression analysis calculates the coefficients of the line (B_0 and B_1) that minimize the sum of the squared differences between the actual value of the dependent variable and the value predicted by the line $\hat{Y} = B_0 + B_1X$.

FIGURE 13.3
Which Representation is Best?

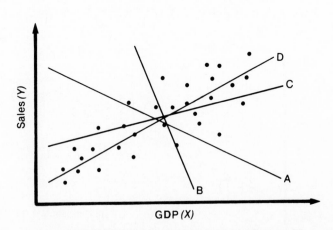

The Regression Coefficients   To find the B_0 and B_1 that thus generate the "best" line, one need only plug into two formulas (see Appendix 13-B for their derivation):

$$B_1 = \frac{\Sigma(X - \overline{X})(Y - \overline{Y})}{\Sigma(X - \overline{X})^2} = \frac{\Sigma XY - n\overline{X}\overline{Y}}{\Sigma X^2 - n\overline{X}^2} \tag{13.1}$$

and

$$B_0 = \overline{Y} - B_1\overline{X} \tag{13.2}$$

While these formulas can be used manually, generally analysis is done on a computer, especially for problems with more than 8 to 10 data points. The following two measures are often also calculated.

The Standard Error of Estimate ($S_{Y.X}$)   This is a measure of the typical deviation of the predictions from the actual values of the dependent variable (Y). It is analogous to the standard deviation (thus, the term *standard error*) and is calculated as:

$$s_{Y.X} = \sqrt{\frac{\Sigma(Y - \hat{Y})^2}{n - 2}} = \sqrt{\frac{\Sigma(Y - \overline{Y})^2 - B_1 \Sigma(X - \overline{X})(Y - \overline{Y})}{n - 2}} \tag{13.3}$$

The Coefficient of Determination (r^2)   While the standard error of estimate provides one measure of the accuracy of prediction, it is not particularly easy to interpret, much less compare across different analyses, because it depends on the units in which Y is measured. (Is a fit with a standard error of two cartons better or worse than one with a standard error of three dollars?) The correlation coefficient (r) measures the closeness of the relation between the predicted and actual values of the dependent variable. In regression, r^2, known as the *coefficient of determination*, is often used. Recall that

$$r = \frac{\Sigma(X - \overline{X})(Y - \overline{Y})}{\sqrt{\Sigma(X - \overline{X})^2}\sqrt{\Sigma(Y - \overline{Y})^2}} = \frac{\Sigma XY - n\overline{X}\overline{Y}}{ns_X s_Y} \tag{13.4}$$

We can also compute r^2 directly from

$$r^2 = 1 - \frac{\Sigma(Y - \hat{Y})^2}{\Sigma(Y - \overline{Y})^2}$$

$$= 1 - \frac{\text{Unexplained variance in } Y}{\text{Total variance in } Y}$$

$$= \text{percent of the variance in } Y \text{ explained by } X$$

A sample application of these formulas is shown in Appendix 13-A.

Interpretation

The previous section dealt with a description of the mechanics of how regression coefficients are derived. The key issue for a user, however, is how to interpret the results. There are three major elements that are especially important outputs of a regression analysis: the regression coefficients, the standard error of estimate ($S_{Y.X}$), and the coefficient of determination.

The Regression Coefficients   The *constant* or *intercept*, B_0, is interpreted as the value Y would take on if X were zero. Since many situations exist where the X values are unlikely to approach zero (e.g., a sales versus GDP equation), this interpretation is often either unnecessary or inappropriate.

The *regression coefficient* or *slope*, B_1, is interpreted as the amount Y would increase if X increased one unit. A negative regression coefficient means that as X goes up, Y decreases in value. For example, in the equation

$$\text{Sales} = B_0 + B_1 \text{ (price)}$$

we would expect B_1 to be negative, since the slope is a measure of the marginal sensitivity of sales to changes in price. Consider, for example, the equation

$$\text{Sales in cartons} = 2.5 + 2 \text{ (advertising in \$)}$$

Assuming for a moment that the relationship is causal, this implies that increasing advertising one dollar would increase sales by two cartons. This suggests that if the marginal profit of two cartons of sales were greater than a dollar, then increasing advertising would increase profits in the short run. Conversely, if two cartons of sales produced less than one dollar of profit, then reducing advertising might improve profits.

The Standard Error of Estimate ($S_{Y.X}$)   One use of regression is as a predictive tool. Continuing the sales versus advertising example, a manager might ask, "What if advertising were set at \$10?" Using the equation, the forecast would be

$$\text{Sales in cartons} = 2.5 + 2(10) = 22.5$$

This is the best guess available. In planning, however, it is necessary to know the range of likely outcomes as well as the most likely result in order to make production scheduling and the like more efficient. Consider the three cases in Figure 13.4. In case A, the past data seem to fall exactly on the line. If the rather heroic assumption that nothing is changing in the market can be made, we would be fairly confident in the prediction of 22.5. Put differently, we would tend to hedge the prediction very little, possibly using as the forecast $22.5 \pm .5$. In case B, the data fall less closely to the line and the prediction would be hedged to a greater extent, leading to a forecast more like 22.5 ± 2. Case C shows a situation where the spread of data points about the line is much greater; hence, the forecast might be 22.5 ± 14.

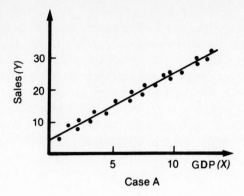

Case A

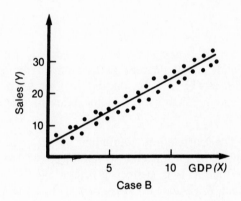

Case B

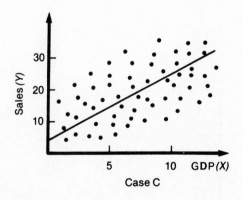

Case C

FIGURE 13.4
Different Relationship Strengths

Since deciding on the range of a forecast by graphing the data is both tedious and inexact, an efficient procedure is to use the standard error of estimate as a measure of the likely accuracy of the prediction. To be 95 percent sure that actual sales fall within the range, this suggests predicting sales will be approximately $22.5 \pm 2S_{Y.X}$ (for large n, actually $\pm 1.96S_{Y.X}$). This can be represented graphically as in Figure 13.5. As long as a reasonably large sample size were used and the advertising figures used were within the range of past experience, this would be a reasonable prediction. Should either the sample size (n) get small or the value of the dependent variable be well outside the range of past data (sometimes called the *relevant range*), however, a forecaster would correctly feel more squeamish about his or her estimates and, consequently, want to give a larger range of possible outcomes. The formula that quantifies this squeamishness is

$$\text{Forecast of } Y = \hat{Y} \pm t_{n-2, \alpha}S_{Y.X}\sqrt{1 + \frac{1}{n} + \frac{\left(X' - \bar{X}\right)^2}{\Sigma\left(X - \bar{X}\right)^2}} \tag{13.5}$$

where X' is the value of X for which the forecast is being generated. Since $t_{n-2, \alpha}$ is the number from the t distribution with $n - 2$ degrees of freedom at the $1 - \alpha$ confidence level, this reduces to approximately $\hat{Y} \pm 2S_{Y.X}$ (at the famous 95 percent confidence level) for large sample sizes and predictions within the relevant range.

The Coefficient of Determination   The correlation coefficient is an index of the fit between the predicted and actual values of the dependent variable. A value of ± 1 indicates "perfect" correlation, meaning that X is a perfect predictor of Y. A value of 0 indicates no correlation between X and Y. (Practically, this means X is useless as a predictor of Y.) A value between 0 and ± 1 indicates somewhere between no and perfect correlation.

FIGURE 13.5
Forecast Confidence Interval

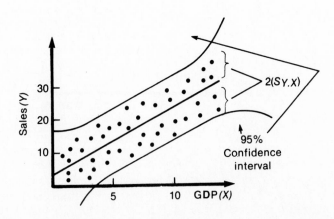

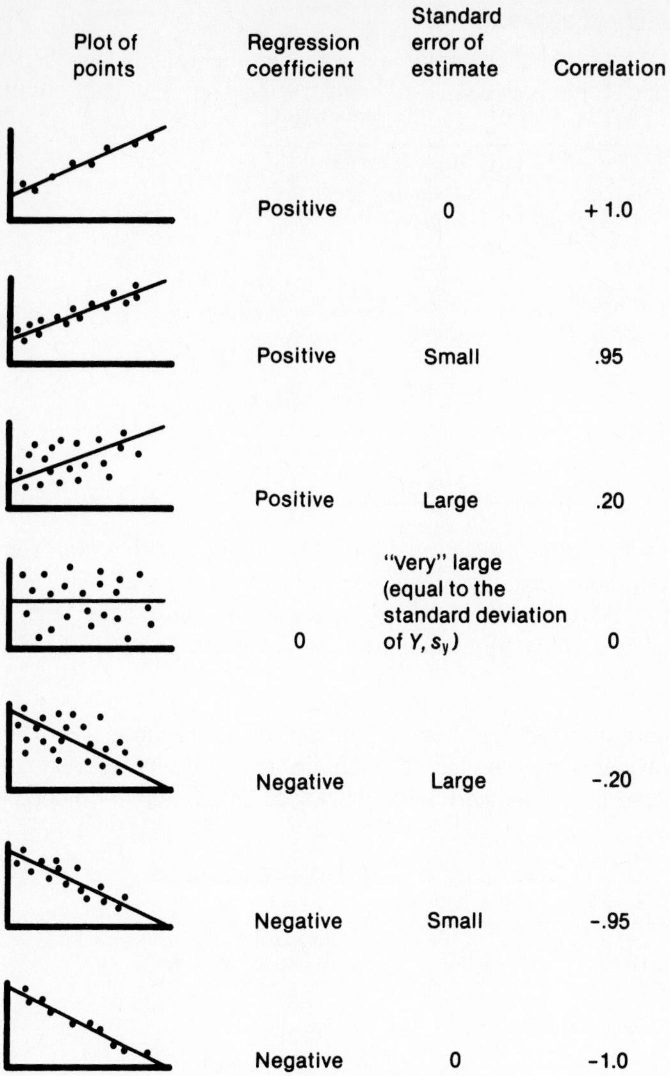

Plot of points	Regression coefficient	Standard error of estimate	Correlation
	Positive	0	+ 1.0
	Positive	Small	.95
	Positive	Large	.20
	0	"Very" large (equal to the standard deviation of Y, s_y)	0
	Negative	Large	-.20
	Negative	Small	-.95
	Negative	0	-1.0

FIGURE 13.6
Correlations and Regression Lines

The value of r^2, the coefficient of determination, is the percent of the variance in the values of Y accounted for by (predictable by, explained by, associated with) the variance in X. Therefore, an r of .7 means an r^2 of .49, which in turn indicates that about half the variance in Y is accounted for by variance in X.

The size of the correlation is related to both the regression coefficient B_1 and the standard error. This relationship is summarized in Figure 13.6.

Two Examples of Simple Linear Regression

Motor Vehicle Registrations   In the first example, we consider the relationship between motor vehicle registrations and time between 1961 and 1968. The raw data, used as input, are as follows:

Year (X)	U.S. Motor Vehicle Registrations (Y) (millions)
1	63.2
2	65.8
3	68.8
4	71.7
5	74.9
6	77.8
7	80.0
8	83.2

Plotting these data shows a very strong linear relation between time and motor vehicle registrations. Obviously, registrations are increasing at about 3 million a year, and in year 0 (in this case, equal to 1960), a shade over 60 million cars must have been registered. Performing the appropriate calculations leads to the results in Table 13.1. Hence, we conclude the following:

1. Motor vehicle registrations = 60.3 + 2.87 · (Number of years since 1960).
2. The relationship between time and motor vehicle registrations is very close ($r^2 = .999$, $S_{Y.X}$ is 210,000, compared with values of Y of about 70,000,000).

TABLE 13.1   Motor Vehicle Regression

Variable	Mean	Standard Deviation
X	4.5	2.29
Y	73.2	6.58

Constant $(B_0) = 60.3$
Slope $(B_1) = 2.87$
Standard error $(S_{Y.X}) = .21$
Coefficient of determination $(r^2) = .999$

X	Y	Estimated Y ($\hat{Y}$)	$Y - (\hat{Y})$
1	63.2	63.1	.1
2	65.8	66.0	− .2
3	68.8	68.9	− .1
4	71.7	71.7	0
5	74.9	74.6	.3
6	77.8	77.4	.4
7	80.0	80.4	− .4
8	83.2	83.2	0

Predicted 1969 registrations based on this model would then be:

$$60.3 + 2.87(9) \pm t_{6,.05}(.21)\sqrt{1 + \frac{1}{8} + \frac{(4.5)^2}{\Sigma(X - \overline{X})^2}} = 86.1 \pm .65$$

Since actual 1969 registrations turned out to be 86.4 million, this was a "good" prediction. Extrapolating far in the future is hazardous. For example, the forecast for 1992 is 152.24 million, not too far from the actual 144.213 million, but outside the range provided by formula (13.5), which is ±2.248.

MBA Salaries Now consider the relation between the salary an MBA received in 1972 and the number of years that had elapsed since he or she graduated. (Ancient history is used to prevent invidious comparisons.) Using a sample of more than 4,000 graduates of the "big name" schools, the following results were obtained:

$$\text{Intercept} = \$19,650$$
$$\text{Slope} = \$630$$
$$r^2 = .184$$
$$S_{Y.X} = \$10,440$$

We therefore conclude a typical MBA's salary would be $19,650 + $630 · (Number of years since graduation). However, the relationship between years since graduation and salary, though significant, is subject to wide variation, as indicated by the r^2 of .184 and the standard error of estimate of $10,440. This means that the forecast of the 1972 salary of an MBA 10 years after graduation would be approximately:

$$19,650 + 630(10) \pm 2(10,440) = 25,950 \pm 20,880$$

To be 95 percent confident of including an individual's actual salary, a prediction would have to be between $5,000 (Peace Corps, unemployment) and $47,000 (corporate stardom).

Three factors contribute to this large uncertainty. The first is that the relation between salary and years since graduation is likely to be somewhat nonlinear. For example, the true relation might be that of Figure 13.7. Since most of the individuals in the sample had between 5 and 15 years experience, this is the relevant range for the regression results. A nonlinear model would presumably improve the fit. It also would change the intercept to a lower figure than the implausible $19,650 (starting salaries for MBAs in 1972 were lower).

A second contributor to the low predictive value is the omission of other key variables. One would presume other variables such as school attended, major, and industry employed in would all affect salary. Inclusion of multiple variables will be discussed in another section.

The final explanation for the large variation of the predicted results is the possibility that salaries are uncertain. This uncertainty may stem from two sources. The first source is essentially noise in the data, consisting of such problems as the inaccuracy of the reported salary (how honest would you be in disclosing your salary?), the exclusion of bonuses and commissions from the salary measure of compensation, and any of a variety of coding and processing errors. The second source of uncertainty is essentially

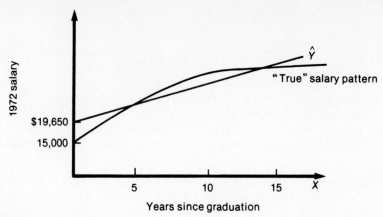

FIGURE 13.7
Salary vs. Years Since Graduation

pure randomness, which stems from the fact that a large component of salary depends on unpredictable "luck."

MULTIPLE REGRESSION

Basic Concept

The basic concept of multiple regression is the same as that of simple regression: to find the relation between independent and dependent variables. In multiple regression, however, there are several independent variables. In other words, we might assume that sales depend not just on GDP but also on price, advertising, and distribution. The model, assuming there are k independent variables, is:

$$Y = B_0 + B_1X_1 + B_2X_2 + \cdots + B_kX_k + \mu$$

Estimation

The estimation procedure developed for multiple regression is analogous to that for simple regression. The objective is to minimize the sum of the squared deviations between the actual and predicted values of the dependent variable. The regression coefficients for the k predictor variables are obtained from a mathematical formula that simultaneously estimates all the coefficients (see Appendix 13-B). In practice, the results are always found via computer programs. In addition to the regression coefficients, the other two measures that are most useful are, as in the case of simple regression, the standard error of estimate and the coefficient of determination (R^2), which are direct extensions of the simple regression counterparts. The standard error of estimate is

$$S_{Y.X} = \sqrt{\frac{\Sigma\left(Y - \hat{Y}\right)^2}{n - k}}$$

and

$$R^2 = 1 - \frac{S_{Y.X}^2}{S_Y^2} = 1 - \frac{\text{Unexplained variance}}{\text{Total variance}} = \frac{\text{Percent of the total variance}}{\text{in } Y \text{ explained by } X}$$

At this point one might ask, "Why not run a series of simple regressions and use the coefficients from each of the separate regressions?" There are three reasons for not doing this:

1. It is difficult to decide what the intercept B_0 should be, since each separate regression would produce a different intercept.
2. If some of the independent variables are related, then the estimates obtained from the simple regressions may be "bad." That is, the coefficients from the simple regressions may either over- or understate the effect of these independent variables on the dependent variable. This is due to what is called *omitted variable bias*, which will be discussed later.
3. It is inefficient. For example, 20 independent variables would require 20 separate regressions.

General Interpretation

Interpretation of the results of multiple regression is similar to that of simple regression. The three major elements to consider are the regression coefficients, the standard error of estimate, and the coefficient of multiple determination (R^2).

The Regression Coefficients

The *constant*, B_0, is the "baseline" value of Y, which is interpreted as the value Y would take on if all the independent variables were zero. As in the case of simple regression, this is rarely a meaningful interpretation, since in most marketing models the only way for all the independent variables to go to zero is for the world to end (which is well outside the relevant range of the data and tends to make the interpretation meaningless).

The *regression coefficients* (B_1 through B_k). A particular regression coefficient, B_i, is interpreted as the amount by which the dependent variable would change if the ith independent variable increased by one unit and all the other variables remained unchanged. In other words, a regression coefficient is the marginal influence of a single independent variable on the dependent variable. For example, suppose we obtained:

$$\text{Sales in cartons} = 1.2 + 1.3 \,(\text{advertising \$}) - .2 \,(\text{price in \$})$$
$$+ .1 \,(\text{GDP in billions of dollars})$$

Then, on average, when advertising increased one dollar while holding price and GDP constant, sales increased by 1.3 cartons. In general, both the sign (indicating the direction of the effect) and the absolute size (indicating the magnitude of the effect) of a coefficient should be examined.

Notice the results only describe the relation in the data used in the analysis; whether the relationship is causal—as in advertising caused sales—or will occur in other situations is a separate issue. Basically, the evidence for causality is circumstantial.

The Standard Error of Estimate   As in simple regression, the standard error of estimate quantifies the amount a prediction must be hedged. Assuming that $S_{Y.X}$ was 15 in the previous example, the best estimate of sales given advertising of $20, price of $60, and GDP of $1,000 billion would be:

$$\text{Sales} = 1.2 + 1.3(20) - .2(60) + .1(1,000)$$
$$= 115.2$$

The confidence interval for a prediction, assuming the values of the independent variables in the forecast were similar to those used to build the model, would be:

$$Y \pm t_{n-k-1,\,\alpha}\left(S_{Y.X}\right)$$

Assuming a large sample size, the 95 percent confidence interval in this case would be approximately:

$$115.2 \pm 2(15) = 115 \pm 30$$

The Coefficient of Determination (R^2)   The coefficient of determination is interpreted as the percent of the variance in the dependent variable predicted by variation in all the independent variables. The coefficient of multiple correlation (R) is an index of the closeness of the relation between the dependent variable and the independent variables. It is calculated as the square root of the coefficient of determination, R^2. For the special case of only one independent variable, the multiple correlation coefficient is equal to the simple correlation coefficient.[1]

Statistical Interpretation

Interpretation of the results of regression is often aided by the following two types of statistical tests.

---

[1]Since R^2 is based on the data used to construct the model, it only indirectly assesses the value of the model for predicting new observations. Therefore, especially when the sample size is small, many researchers will do some form of "cross-validation" (cf. Cooil, Winer, and Rados, 1987; Steckel and Vanhonacker, 1993), where a model is built on some of the data and then used to predict other observations (e.g., splitting the sample into halves; one for estimating the model and the other for assessing predictive power). Such procedures tend to favor simple models but are not used by most applied researchers.

The Individual Coefficients (B_is)   The individual coefficient estimates, the B_is, are obviously subject to error. Since the errors are usually assumed to be normally distributed, we can estimate the true value of a particular coefficient as:

$$\text{"True" value of } B_i = \text{Estimated value of } B_i \pm t_{n-k-1,\,\alpha} \begin{pmatrix} \text{standard} \\ \text{deviation} \\ \text{of } B_i \end{pmatrix}$$

One interesting question is whether the true B_i is really different from zero. (In other words, does the ith variable really influence the dependent variable?) This can be tested by either a t or F test (some computer outputs use each of these equivalent tests) as follows:

Hypothesis	t Test Statistic	F Test Statistic
The true value of the ith regression coefficient is zero $(B_i = 0)$	$\dfrac{B_i - 0}{S_{B_i}}$	$\left(\dfrac{B_i}{S_{B_i}}\right)^2$

Ignoring degrees of freedom and using the 95 percent confidence level, this means that to be significant, the t ratio must be greater than about 2 and the F ratio greater than 4. (Actually, the t test statistic is t with $n - k - 1$ degrees of freedom, and the F test statistic is F with 1 and $n - k - 1$ degrees of freedom.) Failure to be significant indicates that, although the independent variable may be related to the dependent variable, the independent variable fails to marginally affect the dependent variable (and thus aid predictions) when the effects of the other independent variables are removed. Variables with nonsignificant coefficients may be eliminated from the equation (as long as you rerun the regression with these variables removed) without greatly harming predictions. Interpretation, on the other hand, may be more difficult as the variables are removed.

The Coefficient of Determination (R^2)   The tests on the individual coefficients address the question of whether a particular variable improves prediction. A test of R^2, on the other hand, addresses the question of whether the independent variables as a group are significantly related to the dependent variable. The test is based on an analysis of variance table (Table 13.2). The F test is:

$$\dfrac{\dfrac{\text{Explained sum of squares}}{k}}{\dfrac{\text{Unexplained sum of squares}}{n - k - 1}} = \dfrac{\dfrac{\Sigma\left(Y - \bar{Y}\right)^2 - \Sigma\left(Y - \hat{Y}\right)^2}{k}}{\dfrac{\Sigma\left(Y - \bar{Y}\right)^2}{n - k - 1}}$$

TABLE 13.2 Regression ANOVA Table

	SS	d.f.	MSS
Explained variation	$\Sigma(Y - \overline{Y})^2 - \Sigma(Y - \hat{Y})^2 = ESS$	k	ESS/k
Unexplained variation	$\Sigma(Y - \hat{Y})^2 = USS$	$n - k - 1$	$USS/(n - k - 1)$
Total variation in Y	$\Sigma(Y - \overline{Y})^2 = TSS$	$n - 1$	

where k is the number of independent variables. This can be shown to be equivalent to:

$$\frac{\dfrac{R^2}{k}}{\dfrac{1 - R^2}{n - k - 1}} , \text{ which is } F_{k, n-k-1}$$

When the F test on R is insignificant, the entire regression is essentially worthless (unless, of course, a negative finding is what the researcher wanted in the first place).[2]

NUTRITION SURVEY EXAMPLE

In analyzing the data from the nutrition study, one objective was to build a model that explained different levels of expenditures on food based on other variables. Food expenditures were regressed against 15 other variables:

1. Income (coded 1–6)
2. Age of respondent (in years)
3. Family size
4. Number of brands and sizes shopped for (coded 1–4)
5. Habitual buying versus information seeking (coded 1–3)
6. Importance of variety (coded from 1 = very important to 5 = very unimportant)
7. Importance of taste
8. Importance of other family members' preferences
9. Importance of diet restrictions
10. Importance of price
11. Importance of availability
12. Importance of ease of preparation
13. Importance of habit
14. Importance of specials
15. Importance of nutritional value

---

[2]The more independent variables you have, the higher R^2 will be. Consequently, many researchers prefer to use a criterion that takes the number of independent variables into account. Hence, an adjusted R^2 is often used as follows:

$$\text{Adjusted } R^2 = 1 - \left(1 - \text{unadjusted } R^2\right)\frac{n - 1}{n - k - 1}$$

The weekly expenditure variable was recoded into dollar terms in the following manner:

Response	Recode
Under $15	$12.50
$15–$29	22.50
$30–$44	37.50
$45–$60	52.50
Over $60	70.00

The 762 (of 940) individuals who provided usable responses to all 16 variables were then chosen for analysis. The means of all the variables are shown in Table 13.3. While looking at the means may seem trivial, it is a good way to make certain that the data were input accurately. For example, had the mean of the diet importance variable been less than 1 or more than 5, the data would obviously have been input incorrectly. This check for reasonable means (or actual ones, if they are known) should always be made.

The 15 independent variables were regressed against food expenditures. The results (Figure 13.8) were obtained from the SPSS program (Appendix 13-C).

Overall Predictive Power

The R^2 is .43, a moderate value indicating that the independent variables help predictively but are not overly accurate in predicting individual household food consumption

TABLE 13.3 Food Expenditure Variables

Variable	Mean	Standard Deviation
Food expenditures	37.52	15.12
Income (coded 1–6)	2.75	1.42
Age of respondent (in years)	43.70	16.54
Family size	3.29	1.38
Number of brands and sizes shopped for (coded 1–4)	2.34	1.42
Habitual buying versus information seeking (coded 1–3)	1.87	.65
Importance of variety (coded from 1 = very important to 5 = very unimportant)	2.04	.96
Importance of taste	1.24	.57
Importance of other family members' preferences	1.70	.90
Importance of diet restrictions	3.04	1.57
Importance of price	1.75	.96
Importance of availability	2.17	1.13
Importance of ease of preparation	2.75	1.22
Importance of habit	2.79	1.14
Importance of specials	2.26	1.25
Importance of nutritional value	1.67	.88

Variable	Regression Coefficient	Beta	F	t
Importance of nutrition	.47	.03	.76	.87
Income	2.89	.27	80.11	8.95
Age	.08	.09	8.85	2.97
Family size	5.86	.53	313.61	17.71
Brands shopped	.01	.00	.00	.00
Information sought	− 1.09	− .05	2.43	1.56
Importance of variety	.02	.00	.00	.00
Importance of taste	− 1.40	− .05	2.82	1.68
Importance of others' preferences	− .28	.02	.32	.57
Importance of diet	− .46	− .05	2.65	1.63
Importance of price	.29	.02	.33	.57
Importance of availability	− .24	− .02	.35	.59
Importance of ease of preparation	.28	.02	.59	.77
Importance of habit	− 1.07	− .08	7.18	2.68
Importance of specials	.49	.04	1.82	1.35

Constant	12.76
R squared	.43
Adjusted R^2	.42
Standard error	11.53

Analysis of Variance

	d.f.	Sum of Squares	Mean Square	Overall F
Regression	15	74,667.73	4,977.85	37.43
Residual	746	99,200.62	132.98	

FIGURE 13.8

Regression Results for Predicting Food Expenditures

expenditures. The test for the null hypothesis—that all the regression coefficients are zero (and that the independent variables are worthless as predictors)—is:

$$F = \frac{\dfrac{R^2}{\text{No. independent variables}}}{\dfrac{1 - R^2}{n - \text{No. independent variables} - 1}}$$

$$= \frac{4,978}{133} = 37.4$$

This compares with a "table" $F_{15,746}$ of about 2.1 at the 1 percent significance level and indicates that the null hypothesis is convincingly rejected. The independent variables definitely help in predicting food consumption expenditures.

The overall predictive power can also be seen in terms of the size of the standard error of estimate, $11.53. This is obviously fairly large but noticeably smaller than the $15.12 standard deviation of food consumption expenses. This also suggests that 95 percent of household weekly food consumption expenditures in the United States in 1975 could be predicted within (1.96)($11.53), or about $23.

Key Determinants

An obvious question is which of the independent variables are the most useful predictors of the dependent variable. Four basic approaches are used.

The Absolute Size of the Regression Coefficients The size of the regression coefficient indicates how much an increase of one unit of the independent variable would increase the dependent variable, assuming all the other independent variables remained unchanged. The results indicate that an increase of one in family size would increase weekly consumption expenditures by $5.86, whereas movement to the next income category would increase expenditures by $2.89 per week.

The Beta Coefficients One problem with looking at the regression coefficients is that they depend on the scale of the variables. If income had been measured in dollars, the regression coefficient would have been much smaller. For this reason, many researchers (especially those in psychology) prefer to use *beta coefficients*, which are the regression coefficients that would have been obtained if the regression had been performed on standardized (standard deviation equal to 1) variables. Hence, a beta of .27 between income and expense indicates that if an individual's income increased by 1 standard deviation (1.42 scale points), then food expenses would increase by .27 standard deviations. In general,

$$\text{Beta} = B \frac{\text{Standard deviation of independent variable}}{\text{Standard deviation of dependent variable}}$$

$$\left(\text{In this example, } .27 = 2.89 \frac{1.42}{15.12} \right)$$

Elasticities Economists, among others, prefer to think in terms of elasticities. These measures indicate the percent change in the dependent variable for a 1 percent change in the dependent variable:

$$\text{Elasticity} = \frac{\Delta Y / Y}{\Delta X / X} = \frac{\Delta Y}{\Delta X} \frac{X}{Y} = B \frac{X}{Y}$$

In a linear model, the elasticity depends on the values of X and Y. Hence, a popular convention is to evaluate elasticities at the means of the variables:[3]

$$\text{Elasticity} = B \frac{\overline{X}}{\overline{Y}}$$

---

[3]A little-known (and relatively useless) fact: If the ratio of the standard deviations and the ratio of the means of the variables are equal (or equivalently, the standard deviations are proportional to the means), then the beta coefficients and elasticities from the linear model estimated at the mean will be equal.

which in this case is $(2.89)\left(\dfrac{2.75}{37.52}\right) = 0.22$

The Marginal Significance of the Variable   Each independent variable can be separately examined for the marginal contribution it makes to predicting the dependent variable. To do that, we estimate how much variation in Y can be explained by each variable which is unexplained when the other independent variables are used alone. This is tested by an F statistic (here, the statistic is $F_{1,746}$). The bigger the F, the greater the significance. In this case, family size is the most significant ($F = 314$), with income also very significant and both age and habit significant at the 5 percent level. Notice here, as is often but not always the case, the same variables with high betas (or elasticities) are also those that are the most statistically significant predictors.

ISSUES IN USING REGRESSION ANALYSIS

Users of multiple regression often encounter a variety of problems. Few managers and not all market researchers are experts on these problems. Still, because of their effect on interpretation, it is important to be able to recognize when the problems occur, understand their effect on interpretation, and have a general idea of what to do next. (Calling in a statistician without a specific assignment often creates more problems than it solves.)

These issues fall into two basic categories: issues that affect the quality of estimates of the regression, and issues that primarily affect the interpretation of the regression co-efficients.

Issues Affecting Estimation Quality

Dealing with these concerns often requires modifying the regression model. The modifications are usually designed to "trick" the regression into getting better estimates of the model, rather than implemented to better capture the phenomenon of interest and hence change the model form.

Multicollinearity   One of the most common problems encountered in regression is the result of strong interrelations among the independent variables. This does not violate any assumptions (the independent variables do not have to be independent of each other), nor does it affect predictions. It does, however, make the estimates of the regression coefficients unreliable.

The logical importance of the problem caused by correlated independent variables can be seen by considering a flawed experiment. Assume I were testing two tire brands, Goodgrief and Fireside, and that I took two cars and placed Goodgrief tires on the front and Fireside tires on the back of each. Also assume I ran the cars and then found that the sets of front tires lasted 20,000 and 30,000 miles on the two cars and the back tires ran 12,000 and 14,000 miles, respectively. However, since Goodgrief tires were never on the back and Fireside never on the front, it is impossible to separate logically the effect of brand from the effect of location on the car.

If we coded the data to run a regression, the data would be as follows:

Y (miles)	D_1 (1 if Goodgrief, 0 otherwise)	D_2 (1 if Front, 0 otherwise)
20	1	1
30	1	1
12	0	0
14	0	0

In this case, D_1 and D_2 are perfectly collinear (and equal). Attempting to run a regression program to estimate $Y_1 = B_0 + B_1D_1 + B_2D_2$ will produce no results (albeit some funny language, such as "matrix singular," may appear).

Multicollinearity thus is correlation (confounding) among the independent variables. In its most severe case, it makes estimation impossible. In less severe cases, it damages the efficiency of the estimates. Put more bluntly, it makes one less certain what the individual regression coefficients are. Therefore, having independent variables that are not highly correlated is beneficial.

If we have two variables (X_1 and X_2), the level of correlation has a direct impact on the standard deviation of the regression coefficients. Assume the correlation between X_1 and X_2 was 0, .1, .5, or .9. The relative sizes of the standard deviations of the coefficients of X_1 and X_2 become 1, 1.01, 1.33, and 5.26, respectively. Hence, for the last case a coefficient would have to be 5.26 times as large as in the first case to appear as significant. Put differently, collinearity makes it difficult to find significant relations. (It also makes the coefficients themselves intercorrelated and thus less stable.) Thus, collinearity can be a serious problem when correlations among the independent variables are large. (*Large* is an intentionally vague term. Still, most people consider correlations above .7 large.)

Another way to view collinearity is to compare the correlations among the independent variables to the correlation between the independent and dependent variables. When collinearity is high relative to the predictive power of the variables, estimation will be a problem, especially for small sample sizes (Mason and Perreault, 1991).

Detection   The most obvious way to detect collinearity is to check the simple correlations among the independent variables. When collinearity is the result of complex relations among several variables, this simple approach may fail to uncover the collinearity. Alternatively, large standard errors of the coefficients (leading to insignificant coefficients) are often a sign that serious collinearity may be present. Similarly, implausible coefficients may be a sign of collinearity. A number of other signals are used, including the ratio of the largest to the smallest eigenvalue in a principal components analysis of the independent variables (over 100 is considered fairly large). For a more thorough discussion of these analyses, see Belsley, Kuh, and Walsh (1980), Judge et al. (1985), and Ofir and Khuri (1986).

Cure   One cure for collinearity is to reduce the variables to a set that are not collinear. This is best done on the basis of judgment, but many researchers employ factor analysis or stepwise regression as a means of deciding which variables to retain.

or idiotic, can see that in the old Oolitic Silurian Period, just a million years ago next November, the lower Mississippi River was upward of one million three hundred thousand miles long, and stuck out over the Gulf of Mexico like a fishing rod. And by the same token any person can see that seven hundred and forty-two years from now the lower Mississippi will be only a mile and three-quarters long, and Cairo and New Orleans will have joined their streets together, and be plodding comfortably along under a single mayor and a mutual board of aldermen. There is something fascinating about science. One gets such wholesale returns of conjecture out of such a trifling investment of fact."

(Mark Twain, *Life on the Mississippi*)

For a regression to be used predictively, it is important that the observation for which the forecast is to be made be similar to the observations used to build the model. Put simply, if you build a model of weight versus age on 3- to 7-year-olds, it will not give good predictions of the weight of 60-year-olds. Yet in spite of the apparent obviousness of this, the concept of the relevant range often is ignored. Thus, before using a model, a good rule is to ask, "Does it make sense to apply this model here?"

The Use of Categorical Variables: Dummy Variables   A lot of data available to marketing researchers is categorical in nature (e.g., sex, occupation, region of the country). Since such variables are often presumed to be related to the dependent variables, it is obvious that it would be advantageous if such nominally scaled variables could be used in regressions. Four basic approaches are possible:

1. *Ignore the fact that the variables are categorical and run the analysis anyway*: Sales = B_0 + B_1 · (Advertising) + B_2 · (Region). This strategy is foolish (but may be used inadvertently by anyone who simply "throws the data in and lets the computer decide what's important"). Consider the variable "Region," where New England is coded 1, the West 2, Midwest 3, and South 4. It seems unlikely that the Region variable would be related to anything. Even if it were, how would we interpret a significant coefficient?
2. *Ignore the variable*. This is the easy way out but is not much better than the first approach.
3. *Use the variable as a means of segmenting the sample*. This would mean running a separate analysis for each region: Sales = B_0 + B_1 · (Advertising). Both the constant and the slope could vary across regions (Figure 13.11). This is the best method in terms of prediction and understanding. Unfortunately, it is also the most expensive in terms of sample requirements. If there are four regions, five occupations, and three marital statuses under consideration, the original sample must be divided into (4)(5)(3) = 60 subsamples. Even given an original sample size of 1,000, this is likely to lead to inadequate sample sizes in many of the 60 categories, not to mention a fairly unwieldy collection of results.
4. *Use dummy variables*. This procedure is somewhat of a compromise between strategies 2 and 3. One common assumption is that the effect of the other variables (e.g., advertising) is the same in all the regions but the constant differs across the regions.

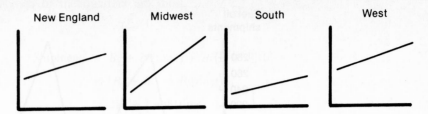

FIGURE 13.11 Regional Differences

Consider the following data on quarterly fuel oil shipments to the United Kingdom in 1964–66 (Table 13.4). In plotting this data, we see that there is, as expected, a very strong seasonal effect (Figure 13.12). Clearly, ignoring the seasonal effect would be a major error. (It would also produce significant autocorrelation.) Running four separate regressions is impractical because there would only be three observations per regression. It would be possible to deseasonalize the data before performing the regression using an adjustment factor for each quarter, such as

$$\frac{\text{Average sales for the particular quarter}}{\text{Average sales for all quarters}}$$

Possibly the most appealing approach, however, is to employ dummy variables. This would consist of first creating (dummying up) a variable for each of the four quarters (Table 13.5). The following equation would then be estimated by regression:

$$\text{Shipments} = B_0 + B_1(\text{time}) + B_2(\text{winter}) + B_3(\text{spring}) + B_4(\text{summer})$$

Note that one of the possible dummy variables must be left out so the computer program will run. If all the independent variables are included, they are perfectly multicollinear. In this case, it is impossible to invert a key matrix, and the program won't

TABLE 13.4   Fuel Oil Shipments to the United Kingdom

Quarter	Year	Sales
1	1964	210
2		120
3		140
4		260
1	1965	220
2		125
3		145
4		270
1	1966	225
2		128
3		149
4		275

If this model were used to predict shipments in the second quarter of 1968, the "best guess" prediction would then be

$$\text{Predicted shipments} = 115.5 + 1.468(18) = 142$$

Dummy variables can be used to represent several independent variables (e.g., season and region). For *each* of the independent variables, one of its dummy variables must be left out of the equation to permit estimation.

In essence, dummy variables perform analysis of variance. In fact, if all the variables are dummy variables, analysis of variance and regression are essentially equivalent. An example and discussion of this appears in Appendix 13-F.

Nonlinear Relations   The relation between the independent and dependent variables may be nonlinear. In such situations, the researcher has a choice between using a search procedure for estimating the relationship or somehow utilizing the linear regression procedure to estimate the parameters of a nonlinear model. Practicality and laziness usually dictate the latter approach.

Using regression programs to generate nonlinear parameters basically involves "tricking" the computer. Consider the following data concerning registered small aircraft versus time (Figure 13.14). The decline appears to be of the logarithmic/

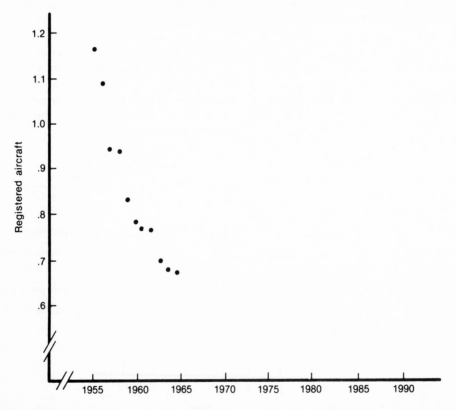

FIGURE 13.14 Registered Small Aircraft (three seats and less) per Hundred Thousand Residents Plotted Against Time

exponential variety. By plotting the logarithms of the number of registered aircraft versus time, the plot appears to be closer to linear (Figure 13.15). Mathematically, we are saying

$$\text{Log}(\text{registered aircraft}) = a + b(\text{time})$$

By simply inputting the log of registered aircraft as the dependent variable and time as the independent variable, estimates of a and b are obtained.

As another example, consider the following multiplicative model:

$$Y = B_0 X_1^{B_1} X_2^{B_2}$$

By taking logarithms of both sides, the model becomes

$$\log Y = \log B_0 + B_1 \log X_1 + B_2 \log X_2$$

By setting:

$$Y^* = \log Y$$
$$X_1^* = \log X_1$$
$$X_2^* = \log X_2$$

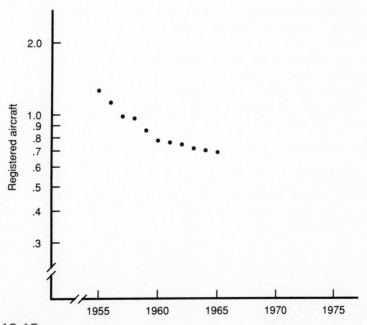

FIGURE 13.15

Registered Small Aircraft (three seats and less) per Hundred Thousand Residents Plotted Against Time-Logarithmic Scale

and running the linear regression

$$Y^* = A_0 + A_1 X_1^* + A_2 X_2^*$$

we can deduce the original parameters as:

$$B_0 = \log^{-1} A_0$$
$$B_1 = A_1$$
$$B_2 = A_2$$

Nonlinear forms involving a single variable are equally easy to handle. Consider $Y = B_0 + B_1 X_1 + B_2 X_1^2$. By submitting X_1 and X_1^2 as the two independent variables to a standard linear regression program, estimates of B_0, B_1, and B_2 can be directly obtained.

There are two problems with the process of using linear regression programs to estimate nonlinear models. First, the estimates obtained are not exactly those that would have been obtained by a specially designed procedure and are, in some sense, inferior. Given the precision in most marketing data, however, this is not typically a major problem. Second, estimation may be difficult under certain circumstances. For example, an equation involving X and X^2 terms can be tremendously unstable due to high collinearity. (One way to circumvent this is to regress X^2 on X and then use the residuals of this regression plus X in a regression to predict Y.)

One final point worth making concerns why linear models are so widely used. Three major reasons exist:

1. Computer programs do linear regression. This may be a bad normative reason, but it is a key descriptive explanation.
2. Linear models are usually good approximations of nonlinear models, especially over a small range. This is particularly true when there is noise in the data, as in the case of survey research.
3. There is one linear model for a set of variables but an infinite number of nonlinear ones. This makes trying to find an appropriate nonlinear model hazardous and time consuming.

Some good advice, therefore, is to always try a linear model unless

a. The predictive power of the linear model is inadequate.
b. Some theory or simple results (e.g., data plots) exist that suggest nonlinearity.

Stepwise Regression   When faced with a large number of potential independent variables, a researcher often wishes to let the computer select those variables that are in some sense best. One popular approach is stepwise regression. This procedure begins by selecting the independent variable that is most correlated with the dependent variable; then, a regression is performed. Next, the variable that makes the greatest marginal improvement in prediction is added and a second regression run, and so forth.

The basic criterion used by most programs is the correlation between each independent variable not in the equation and that portion of the variance in the dependent variable unexplained by variables currently in the equations (known as the *partial correlation*).

Whichever independent variable has the largest partial correlation with the dependent variable is entered next. The procedure continues checking partial correlations, adding variables, and performing regressions until (*a*) it reaches a specified number of variables or (*b*) adding variables ceases to achieve a specified level of improvement in prediction.

Consider the following example based on a sample of 513 housewives taken in 1968. To profile Gleem toothpaste preferrers, Gleem preference was regressed against seven other variables. The simple correlations among the variables are typical of the correlations among demographics, preferences, and importances (Table 13.6). Steps 1, 2, and 7 are summarized in Table 13.7. Examining these steps indicates that, in step 1, the procedure selected the variable that had the greatest (absolute) simple correlation with Gleem, importance of price. In the second step, however, the procedure found that the importance of taste was most helpful marginally, even though Cepacol preference had a larger simple correlation (.13 versus .10). The final step, which includes all the independent variables, indicates that, in spite of the model's relatively small overall predictive power ($R^2 = .1$), many of the variables are significantly related to Gleem preference (*F* ratios > 4). This is typical of segmentation type regression results, which often uncover key correlates and tendencies but rarely predict individual consumer behavior well.

The advantages of stepwise regression are essentially twofold:

1. It produces a parsimonious model.
2. The resulting model usually has relatively little multicollinearity among the independent variables.

Unfortunately, there are some important disadvantages to stepwise regression:

1. The results are notoriously unstable in split-half checks where each half of the data is analyzed separately. (The variables often enter differently in the two halves of the sample, thus making interpretation hazardous.)
2. The technique increases the odds of omitting a key variable. For example, assume that the correlations between education and income with the dependent variable were .71 and .70, respectively. A stepwise procedure would then enter education first. If education and income were fairly highly correlated, however, income might never be brought in. Hence, an apparent interpretation of the results would be that education influenced the dependent variable but income did not, while income could be an important determinant.
3. Stepwise regression is inferior methodology if any prior model or theory exists. Most studies are more useful if a logical model is first constructed (how else do I know what variables to measure?) and then examined, rather than if the results depend on some search algorithm.
4. The statistical tests reported in the output are inaccurate, since the procedure selects variables that maximize those tests (McIntyre et al., 1983).

Hence, stepwise regression must be used with great care. While it may be an easy way to select variables, it is not clear that it is a good one.

Interaction Effects   The effect of one variable X_1 on Y may depend on the level of another variable X_2. Such "interactions" are included as the product of two (or more)

TABLE 13.6 Correlation Matrix

	Preference for Gleem	Importance of Nutritional Value (orange juice)	Importance of Taste Flavor (toothpaste)	Importance of Price (toothpaste)	Cepacol Preference	Lavoris Preference	Like "Hawaii 5-0"	Own Residence
Preference for Gleem	1.00	.12	.10	-.15	.13	.09	.09	-.08
Importance of nutritional value (orange juice)		1.00	.22	-.03	.02	.04	-.13	.10
Importance of taste/flavor (toothpaste)			1.00	.13	-.05	.02	-.09	.07
Importance of price (toothpaste)				1.00	-.08	-.05	-.03	-.03
Cepacol preference					1.00	-.28	-.03	.01
Lavoris preference						1.00	-.04	.11
Like "Hawaii 5-0"							1.00	-.09
Own residence								1.00

TABLE 13.7 Stepwise Results

Variable	Coefficient	F Ratio
Step 1:		
Constant	3.52	
Importance of price (toothpaste)	− .11	5.9
$R = .15$		
Step 2:		
Constant	3.31	
Importance of taste/flavor (toothpaste)	.11	4.0
Importance of price (toothpaste)	− .13	7.2
$R = .19$		
Step 7:		
Constant	2.20	
Importance of nutritional value (orange juice)	.14	3.2
Importance of taste/flavor (toothpaste)	.11	3.7
Importance of price (toothpaste)	− .11	5.7
Cepacol preference	.14	7.2
Lavoris preference	.11	4.4
Like "Hawaii 5-0"	.08	2.8
Own residence	− .21	3.5
$R = .3190$		

variables in the model. For example, one argument for the benefit of advertising is that it makes consumers less price sensitive. This suggests a model:

$$\text{Sales} = B_0 + B_1(\text{Advertising}) + B_2(\text{Price}) + B_3(\text{Advertising})(\text{Price})$$

Here, we expect B_1 to be positive, B_2 negative, and B_3 positive.[6]

Dummy variables can also be used to allow the effect of one independent variable on the dependent variable to change depending on the value of the dummy variable. For example, assume we were predicting sales based on advertising and whether a certain law had been passed. If we ran a regression,

$$\text{Sales} = B_0 + B_1\big(\text{Advertising}\big) + B_2\big(\text{Advertising}\big)\big(\text{If law passed}\big)$$

we would interpret B_1 as the effect of advertising before the law was passed and $B_1 + B_2$ as the effect of advertising on sales after the law was passed.

SOME USES OF REGRESSION ANALYSIS

Given the aggravation associated with understanding regression analysis, a reasonable question is whether the benefits outweigh the costs. Regression is an extremely useful tool for a variety of purposes. This section will delineate three major areas of applicability that highlight some of the benefits of regression.

Forecasting

Regression analysis is a widely used forecasting tool, which is applied in two basic ways:

1. Using time as the key independent variable

---

[6]Since the impact of price on sales varies depending on advertising, this is referred to as a "varying parameter" model. It is also said that advertising "moderates" the impact of price on sales.

2. Using other variables (such as price and competitive advertising) as the independent variables

In both cases, the objective is a good prediction—which means a big R^2 and a small standard error of estimate. The coefficients themselves are used for generating predictions but are not important in their own right. Many time series regressions and regressions involving aggregate economic data produce R^2s over .99.

Segmentation

Regression is often used to define segments of customers in terms of demographics, lifestyles, or general attitudes (Massy, Frank, and Lodahl, 1968; Frank, Massy, and Wind, 1972). This typically produces an R^2 of .1 or smaller. If the goal were prediction of individual behavior, this would be poor. The goal of segmentation, however, is to find general tendencies, not to predict individual behavior. Since marketing strategy for frequently purchased products is directed at groups (e.g., high income), the basic goal is to find groups of consumers where concentrating effort would bring a greater average response. Consider the results from a study of 513 housewives. Obviously, knowing a person's income would not make possible an accurate prediction of the amount of time that particular individual spends watching TV. In fact, the R^2 was .048. On the other hand, it is obvious that average behavior is related to income (Figure 13.16). In fact, a regression between income level and average TV viewing behavior produced an R^2 of

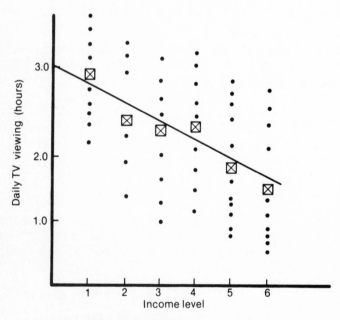

- •   Individual data point

- ⊠   Average TV viewing for all individuals in a particular income level

FIGURE 13.16
TV Viewing vs. Income
Source: Donald R. Lehmann, "Validity and Goodness of Fit in Data Analysis," in *Advances in Consumer Research*, ed. Mary Jane Schlinger (Ann Arbor, Mich.: Association for Consumer Research, 1975), p.746.

.878 (Lehmann, 1975). Practically, this shows that very low income people watched, on average, twice as much TV as high income people.

Various examples concerning the use of regression as a tool for identifying market segments appear in Bass, Tigert, and Lonsdale (1968). Using *Milwaukee Journal* diary panel data, the authors found the typical low R^2s using demographic variables (age, income, occupation, number of children, education, and TV viewing) as predictors of various frequently purchased products. The differences in average consumption, however, were very noticeable (Figure 13.17). The point, then, is low R^2s mean that individual predictions cannot be made accurately, not that the results are worthless. In fact, when using survey data, R^2s above .6 usually mean that either the equation is essentially a tautology or that the data were incorrectly analyzed.

Another example comes from the Durable Ownership and Values Study. Here, we profile fur coat ownership in terms of some basic demographics. The sample of 796 claimed to own 293 fur coats (one person owned eight—an important outlier). The output generated by SAS using the PROC REG command appears as Figure 13.18. The results are typical of segmenting regressions: low R^2 (.07) and a few significant variables (age and income, both positively related). The LOV variables failed to be individually significant, due partly to collinearity among themselves. Interestingly, eight of the nine are positively related to ownership, suggesting people who rate values as important in general tend to own fur coats. An appropriate next step would be to factor analyze the LOV variables and use the factors in the regression. (The use of factor analysis to simplify regression will be discussed in Chapter 16.)

Parameter Estimation and Model Evaluation

In certain circumstances, a model is relatively well established and regression is employed to estimate its parameters. In such a case, R^2 is of only limited interest. The major concern is with the sign and size of the coefficients. If a prior theory gives a range of acceptable values for the coefficients, then the estimated coefficients may be used as a basis for accepting or rejecting the model.

For example, one might assume (based on some theory or analysis) that the effect of raising price one dollar would be to decrease sales by between one and three units. Hence, in a regression with sales as the dependent variable and price as one of the independent variables, we would expect the regression coefficient relating price to sales to be between −1 and −3. If the estimated coefficient fell outside the range, then the model would be rejected.

In deciding what model to use to represent a situation, one less "pure" approach is to try several alternatives and see which produces the "best" result (high R^2s, plausible and significant coefficients, etc.). While this application of regression is theoretically inferior, in practice it is widely used.

Consider the level of MBA salaries. *Business Week*'s rankings of business schools are a prominent, imperfect, and popular (as measured by sales of the issue containing them) topic of conversation (at least in business schools). One suspects that the quality of some of the numbers, including average starting salaries (when not all students are placed) and acceptance rates, are questionable. One interesting analysis of the salary data was a regression by Tracy and Waldfogel (1994). As preparation for analysis, they adjusted salaries

TABLE 13.8 Regression of Salary on Student Characteristics

Variable	(1)	(2)
Constant	470.987	521.811
	(211.717)	(179.046)
GMAT	− 1,632.50	− 1,791.81
	(758.07)	(607.84)
GMAT squared	1.49	1.64
	(0.65)	(0.52)
Percent with at least one year of full time work experience	106.99	101.10
	(55.16)	(49.71)
Undergraduate grade point average	2,281.78	
	(6,655.90)	
Percent with a graduate degree	35.73	
	(179.27)	
Ratio of acceptances to applications	− 16.13	
	(65.86)	
Number of Observations	63	63
R^2	0.565	0.563

Notes: Standard errors are given in parentheses. We measure student quality (value added) using the fitted values (residuals) from specification (2).
Source: Joseph Tracy and Joel Waldfogel, "The Best Business Schools: A Market Based Approach," NBER Working Paper #4609. Reprinted by permission.

CAUSATION VERSUS CORRELATION

Regression analysis does not directly address the issue of causality. Low R^2s or insignificant regression coefficients may indicate weak causality, bad data, or a poor mathematical representation of the relation among variables. Similarly, high R^2s or significant regression coefficients may indicate bad data or tautologies. Even with good data, a high R^2 can mislead a researcher into imputing causality where none exists. For example, assume a researcher ran the following regression:

$$\text{Fertilizer applied} = B_0 + B_1(\text{crop yield})$$

Presumably both R^2 and B_1 would be significant. If the data were based on an experiment using equally productive fields, however, the conclusion that crop yield caused fertilizer application would be exactly wrong.

Numerous examples of strong correlation not necessarily indicating causation can be found, such as the stork population and the human birth rate. While the most popular explanation is that more people mean more houses, more houses more chimneys, and more chimneys more storks, the alternatives are quite interesting.

Probably the classic example of correlation is the result attributed to Jevons, who found that sunspot activity was strongly related to business cycles. This seems purely coincidental. On the other hand, it is conceivable that the relationship is causal. Sunspots change the gravitational pull of the sun, which in turn affects the orbit of the earth and its rotation. Changing the rotation of the earth then affects its electromagnetic field. Since individuals' nervous systems function by a type of electricity, this would affect the way people think and behave and, consequently, conduct business. While this may seem like a far-out explanation (or possibly a false one, if you know much about physics), the point is that it is difficult to differentiate causality and correlation. It would not be surprising if astrology turned out to be related to changing gravitational pulls "when Jupiter aligns with Mars," and so forth.

The point of this section, therefore, is that causality is essentially impossible to determine from regressions. Any causal implications must be the result of prior knowledge and judgment. What regression can do for someone interested in causality is to estimate the strength of causality that has been correctly prespecified by the researcher.

Consider again the data on the 50 states (Table 9.1). Assuming one were interested in profiling average income per capita, one might run a regression with average income versus the other available variables (population, etc.). Notice this is a "fishing expedition"—which means we may catch an old shoe rather than a prize trout.

The results, presented in the order of a typical computer output, are shown as Table 13.9. The correlations indicate income is positively related to taxes, percent in urban areas, and forest acreage, and negatively related to being in the South. The regression results bear this out, with all the coefficients except South being significant. The failure of the South to be significant can be explained by its collinearity with taxes ($r = -.60$).

The R^2 of .72 is substantial. A causal implication of the model would be that, to increase income, you increase taxes, put more people in the city, and leave more land as forests. Unsurprisingly, this is not likely to work. Also, the coefficient of the forest variable bears further discussion. In fact, it could be called the Alaska result, since Alaska had both the highest average income and the most forest acreage. Hence, this regression appears to have been influenced by one unusual data point. This emphasizes the crucial role that a few outliers (unusual data points) can play in influencing the results of a regression. In summary, then, regression fishing expeditions may find significant coefficients and big R^2s. If not interpreted carefully, however, these results can be misleading—especially if the individual coefficients are interpreted as causal relations.

Simultaneous Causality

In many circumstances, two variables might both cause each other. For example, consider the relation between advertising and sales. Sales is generally thought to depend on advertising. On the other hand, advertising budgets are often set as a percent of sales, and therefore sales affect advertising. This means that a single regression of sales versus advertising based on annual data would produce an aggregate summary of the advertising to sales and the sales to advertising relations and, hence, be relatively useless. To get around this problem of joint effects, one alternative is to construct two equations:

$$\text{Sales} = f(\text{Advertising, other variables})$$

$$\text{Advertising} = f(\text{Sales, other variables})$$

By estimating the two equations simultaneously, it is sometimes possible to estimate the separate effects of advertising on sales and sales on advertising. While simultaneous procedures are fairly technical and beyond the scope of this book (see Appendix 13-D), the recognition of the problem of joint causation and the realization that procedures exist for dealing with this problem are very useful. If you think you have encountered such a problem, call an expert.

TABLE 13.9 Regression of Average Income

Variables:

Inc.: Average personal income in thousands.

Pop.: Population in millions.

Popch.: Percent population change over last five years.

Urb.: Percent living in metropolitan areas.

Tax: State and local taxes per capita.

South: 1 if yes; 0 otherwise.

Govt.: Government employment in thousands.

Col.: College enrollment in thousands.

Min.: Mineral production in millions of dollars.

For.: Forest acreage in millions.

Mfg.: Value added by manufacturers in billions of dollars.

Farm: Farm cash receipts in millions of dollars.

Simple Correlations

Variable	Inc.	Pop.	Popch.	Urb.	Tax	South	Govt.	Col.	Min.	For.	Mfg.	Farm
Inc.:	1.00	0.24	− 0.10	0.42	0.70	− 0.51	0.25	0.28	− 0.17	0.32	0.28	0.08
Pop.:	0.24	1.00	− 0.29	0.56	0.37	0.03	0.99	0.96	0.33	0.10	0.94	0.52
Popch.:	− 0.08	− 0.29	1.00	− 0.09	− 0.16	0.08	− 0.27	− 0.25	0.03	0.35	− 0.42	− 0.26
Urb.:	0.42	0.56	− 0.09	1.00	0.42	− 0.02	0.55	0.53	0.14	− 0.02	0.54	0.09
Tax:	0.70	0.37	− 0.17	0.42	1.00	− 0.60	0.41	0.45	− 0.20	− 0.03	0.38	0.04
South:	− 0.51	0.03	0.08	− 0.02	− 0.60	1.00	0.01	− 0.05	0.35	0.03	− 0.09	− 0.03
Govt.:	0.25	0.99	− 0.27	0.55	0.41	0.01	1.00	0.98	0.31	0.12	0.91	0.52
Col.:	0.28	0.96	− 0.25	0.53	0.65	− 0.05	0.98	1.00	0.28	0.13	0.87	0.51
Min.:	− 0.17	0.33	0.03	0.14	− 0.20	0.35	0.31	0.28	1.00	0.12	0.20	0.29
For.:	0.32	0.10	0.35	− 0.02	− 0.03	0.03	0.12	0.13	0.12	1.00	0.03	− 0.00
Mfg.:	0.28	0.94	− 0.42	0.54	0.38	− 0.09	0.91	0.87	0.20	0.03	1.00	0.46
Farm:	0.08	0.52	− 0.25	0.09	0.04	− 0.03	0.52	0.51	0.29	− 0.00	0.46	1.00

Regression Results

Variable	B	Beta	S_B	F
Pop.	0.16	0.84	0.24	0.47
Popch.	− 0.10	− 0.12	0.09	1.21
Urb.	0.10	0.30	0.00	7.02
Tax	0.47	0.65	0.00	19.77
South	− 0.25	− 0.13	0.26	0.95
Govt.	− 0.25	− 0.90	0.00	0.42
Col.	− 0.94	− 0.25	0.00	0.17
Min.	− 0.24	− 0.05	0.00	0.24
For.	0.23	0.46	0.00	23.46
Mfg.	− 0.33	− 0.04	0.04	0.01
Farm	0.84	0.19	0.00	2.83

Constant: 2.29

R^2: 0.73

Adjusted R^2: 0.65

Standard error: 0.51

	Analysis of Variance			
	d.f.	Sum of Squares	Mean Square	F
Regression	11	26.71	2.43	9.24
Residual	38	9.95	0.26	

MAKING REGRESSION USEFUL

A key question is, "How can a researcher use regression without 'putting off' potential users?" This question raises two issues. The first issue concerns how to go about building a useful model. In deciding what variables to include, a variety of considerations/criteria must be weighed:

1. *Parsimony.* The boss is a busy person; don't overtax his or her brain with complicated models.
2. *Data availability.* Use what is readily available, because data collection is both expensive and tedious.
3. *Plausibility.* Try to use variables that are logically related to the dependent variables (sunspots are a no-no).
4. *Goodness of fit.* Try to get a big R^2. Low R^2s may be significant but are hard to sell.
5. *Good coefficients.* Use only variables whose coefficients are significant with plausible signs and coefficients.
6. *Technical limitations.* The entire range of technical issues (multicollinearity, autocorrelation, heteroscedasticity, omitted variables, etc.) should be considered.

Since many of these criteria conflict (e.g., parsimony versus goodness of fit), the researcher must exercise judgment. Building a regression model is thus as much a craft as a science.

The other major issue in making regression useful is in communicating the results. In this regard, remember that F tests and Durbin-Watson statistics may be important aids to interpretation but usually become barriers to communication. With rare exceptions, the users of regressions are, quite properly, not statisticians. Hence, they do not understand or care about statistical jargon and tend to be irritated by it (sometimes as a defense against feeling inadequate). The wise researcher, therefore, attempts to simplify the results. One especially effective trick is the "what if" approach. Rather than simply presenting the resulting equation, calculate estimates for different levels of the key variables by plugging the values into the equation and discuss these estimates (i.e., if we spend $100,000 on advertising, then sales will be X, whereas if we spend $200,000, sales will be Y). In short, never forget that, for marketing research, regression is only a means to the end of providing more useful information on which to base real decisions.

PROBLEMS

1. The frequency of purchase of a luxury nondurable may be a function of a person's income. The following sample has been obtained:

Income	Purchases Per Year	Income	Purchases Per Year
10	1	15	3
15	2	15	2
20	2	5	2
15	1	10	2
20	3	25	3
20	4	10	3
25	5	10	2
5	0	5	2
5	1	15	4
20	3	15	3

a. Estimate the regression line graphically.

b. Examine the plot of purchase rate versus income to determine if the assumption of homoscedasticity seems warranted. That is, does the variance of the disturbance term appear to be independent of income?

c. Examine the plot of mean purchases for each income level. Does the linear model appear to be adequate, or should a nonlinear model be used?

2. In a study, 155 full-page magazine ads were used. The percent of the people who read the ads (as measured by Starch scores) was regressed against a variety of mechanical layout variables, copy/message variables, and product class. The sixth step of a stepwise regression was as follows:

Variable	B	S_B
Bleed	4.05	1.00
Product category 11	− .48	.13
Product category 12	.51	.22
Size	− .40	.22
Product category 5	− 1.44	.84
Product category 17	− .24	.16
Constant		10.19

$$R^2 = .24$$
Standard error = 5.87

a. Interpret the results statistically.

b. What managerial conclusions can you draw?

3. Assume that we analyzed the number of Ph.D. degrees awarded by U.S. universities and GDP in the United States over the years from 1961 to 1980.

a. What do you feel the approximate value of the correlation will be (both magnitude and sign)? Justify your answer.

b. What can be said about the causal effect of Ph.D.s on GDP?

4. In using multiple regression, when is collinearity (high correlation among the independent variables) a problem and when is it not a problem?

5. Assume I am interested in the relationship of income to age and height for a sample of 10 males. The data are as follows:

Income	Age	Height (inches)
$13,000	29	69
20,000	35	76
40,000	37	70
15,000	21	73
8,000	18	64
19,000	29	71
31,000	42	67
5,000	17	72
29,000	45	75
32,000	31	68

Interpret

a. By tabular analysis.

b. By graphical analysis of the two independent variables separately.

c. By using multiple regression.

6. How might I use regression analysis to estimate b and c if I think $Y = kX^b Z^c$, given a set of measurements on Y, X, Z?

7. Is it possible for all the individual regression coefficients to be nonsignificant and R^2 to be significant? Why not *or* what would it mean?

8. When will omitted variable bias occur in regression analysis?

9. The following regression model was estimated to explain the annual sales of a mail-order house:

$$S_t = 105 + 3.0\ A_t + 12.0M_t + .5\ C_t; R^2 = .95$$
$$(4.2)\quad (1.0)\quad (1.1)$$

where

S_t = $ sales in year t;

A_t = $ advertising expenditure in year t;

M_t = $ merchandise mailing expenditures in year t;

C_t = number of catalogs distributed in year t.

The estimated standard errors are in parentheses below the coefficient estimates. The customer service manager suggests that we should increase our mailing expenditures next year by sending more shipments first class, rather than parcel post, since the mailing expenditures coefficient is "significant" in the regression. What would you advise?

10. Joe Planner is in charge of sales forecasting for Trinket Company. He collected 20 monthly variables that he thought might be related to Trinket Company sales. The first was U.S. automobile sales (seasonally adjusted). The twentieth was monthly rainfall in Morningside Heights. Joe ran a regression using the 20 monthly variables to explain the monthly sales (in dollars) of Trinket Company for the last 96 months. The regression had an R^2 of .95. Joe is predicting sales for this month of $100, based on this regression model.

   a. Interpret his work. Joe thinks that the R^2 is a good measure of his model's performance. Is it?

   b. You now find that the third variable in Joe's regression was the monthly expenditure (dollars) for salespersons entertaining customers. The coefficient of this variable was 5.2, with an estimated standard error of .2. Joe figures that, since we make 40 percent gross margin on sales, it would be profitable to increase the entertaining budget:

Spend	$ 1	more on entertaining
	× 5	(minimum sales increase/$) from regression
	$ 5	sales increase
	× 40%	gross margin
	$ 2	increase in contribution to profits
	– 1	recover added entertaining cost
	$ 1	leaves $1 profit improvement

   Is Joe's conclusion correct? Why?

   c. Joe's rival suggests that the monthly entertaining budget should be changed monthly and set randomly, based on the last digit of the winning number in the New Jersey State Lottery. Interpret the recommendation of Joe's rival. What would this recommendation gain us?

11. If my independent variables in a regression are highly correlated,

   a. Are the regression assumptions violated?

   b. What will happen to my coefficient estimates?

   c. What will happen to R^2?

12. What is a way to detect if the disturbances (errors) in regressions are correlated?

13. What is the difference between predictive, causal, and correlational relationships?

REFERENCES

BARON, REUBEN M., AND DAVID A. KENNY (1986) "The Moderator-Mediator Variable Distinction in Social Psychological Research: Conceptual, Strategic, and Statistical Considerations," *Journal of Personality and Social Psychology*, 51, 1173–82.

BASS, FRANK M., DOUGLAS J. TIGERT, AND RONALD T. LONSDALE (1968) "Market Segmentation Group versus Individual Behavior," *Journal of Marketing Research*, 5, August, 264–70.

BASS, FRANK M., AND DICK R. WITTINK (1975) "Pooling Issues and Methods in Regression Analysis with Examples in Marketing Research," *Journal of Marketing Research*, 12, November, 414–25.

BELSLEY, D., E. KUH, AND R. E. WALSH (1980) *Regression Diagnostics*, New York: John Wiley and Sons.

COOIL, BRUCE, RUSSELL S. WINER, AND DAVID L. RADOS (1987) "Cross-Validation for Prediction," *Journal of Marketing Research*, 24, August, 271–79.

DRAPER, N., AND H. SMITH (1966) *Applied Regression Analysis*, New York: John Wiley and Sons.

FRANK, RONALD E., WILLIAM F. MASSY, AND YORAM WIND (1972) *Market Segmentation*, Englewood Cliffs, N.J.: Prentice-Hall.

GALTON, F. (1889) *Natural Inheritance*, London: Macmillan.

HOERL, ARTHUR E., AND ROBERT W. KENNARD (1970) "Ridge Regression: Biased Estimation for Nonorthogonal Problems," *Technometrics*, 12, 55–67.

JOHNSTON, J. (1984) *Econometric Methods*, 3rd ed., New York: McGraw-Hill.

JUDGE, GEORG G., W. E. GRIFFITHS, R. CARTER HILL, HELMUT LUTKEPHOL, AND TSOUNG-CHAO LEE (1985) *The Theory and Practice of Econometrics*, New York: John Wiley and Sons.

KRISHNAMURTHI, LAKSHMAN, AND ARVIND RANGASWAMY (1987) "The Equity Estimator for Marketing Research," *Marketing Science*, 6, Fall, 336–57.

LEHMANN, DONALD R. (1975) "Validity and Goodness of Fit in Data Analysis," in Mary Jane Schlinger, ed., *Advances in Consumer Research*, Ann Arbor, Mich.: Association for Consumer Research, 741–49.

MCINTYRE, SHELBY H., DAVID B. MONTGOMERY, V. SRINIVASAN, AND BARTON A. WEITZ (1983) "Evaluating the Statistical Significance of Models Developed by Stepwise Regression," *Journal of Marketing Research*, 20, February, 1–11.

MASON, CHARLOTTE H., AND WILLIAM D. PERREAULT, JR. (1991) "Collinearity, Power, and Interpretation of Multiple Regression Analysis," *Journal of Marketing Research*, 28, August, 268–80.

MASSY, WILLIAM F., RONALD E. FRANK, AND THOMAS M. LODAHL (1968) *Purchasing Behavior and Personal Attributes*, Philadelphia: University of Pennsylvania Press.

NETER, JOHN, WILLIAM WASSERMAN, AND MICHAEL H. KUTNER (1983) *Applied Linear Regression Models*, Homewood, Ill.: Richard D. Irwin.

OFIR, CHEZY, AND ANDRE KHURI (1986) "Multicollinearity in Marketing Models: Diagnostics and Remedial Measures," *International Journal of Research in Marketing*, 3, 181–205.

RANGASWAMY, ARVIND, AND LAKSHMAN KRISHNAMURTHI (1991) "Response Function Estimation Using the Equity Estimator," *Journal of Marketing Research*, 28, February, 72–83.

STECKEL, JOEL H., AND WILFRIED R. VANHONACKER (1993) "Cross-Validating Regression Models in Marketing Research," *Marketing Science*, 12, Fall, 415–27.

TRACY, JOSEPH, AND JOEL WALDFOGEL (1994) "The Best Business Schools: A Market Based Approach," NBER working paper 4609.

WILDT, ALBERT R. (1993) "Equity Estimation and Assessing Market Response," *Journal of Marketing Research*, 30, November, 437–51.

APPENDIX 13-A

HAND CALCULATION

Hand calculations of regression coefficients are rarely made. Nonetheless, to see how these estimation formulas can be applied is useful. Consider the following data:

X	Y
1	8
3	16
5	19
7	25
9	36
11	34

Assuming we were forced to solve this problem by hand, we could set up Table 13A.1 and get:

$$B_1 = \frac{196}{70} = 2.8$$

$$B_0 = 23 - \frac{196}{70}(6) = 23 - 16.8 = 6.2$$

$$r = \frac{196}{\sqrt{70}\sqrt{584}} = .969$$

Alternatively, we could use the raw data in Table 13A.2. Here, the results would be:

$$B_1 = \frac{1,024 - 6(6)(23)}{286 - 6(6)^2} = \frac{196}{70} = 2.8$$

$$B_0 = 23 - 2.8(6) = 6.2$$

$$r = \frac{1,024 - 6(6)(23)}{\sqrt{286 - 6(6)^2}\sqrt{3,758 - 6(23)^2}} = \frac{196}{\sqrt{70}\sqrt{584}} = .969$$

TABLE 13A.1

	X	Y	$(X - \overline{X})$	$(Y - \overline{Y})$	$(X - \overline{X}) \cdot (Y - \overline{Y})$	$(X - \overline{X})^2$	$(Y - \overline{Y})^2$
	1	8	−5	−15	75	25	225
	3	16	−3	−7	21	9	49
	5	19	−1	−4	4	1	16
	7	25	1	2	2	1	4
	9	36	3	13	39	9	169
	11	34	5	11	55	25	121
Sum	36	138	0	0	196	70	584
Average	6	23					

TABLE 13A.2

	X	Y	XY	X²	Y²
	1	8	8	1	64
	3	16	48	9	256
	5	19	95	25	361
	7	25	175	49	625
	9	36	324	81	1,296
	11	45	374	121	1,156
Sum	36	138	1,024	286	3,758
Average	6	23			

TABLE 13A.3

X	Y	$\hat{Y}$	$Y - \hat{Y}$	$(Y - \hat{Y})^2$
1	8	9	−1	1.00
3	16	14.6	1.4	1.96
5	19	20.2	−1.2	1.44
7	25	25.8	−.8	.64
9	36	31.4	4.6	21.16
11	34	37.0	−3.0	9.00
				35.20

To calculate the standard error of estimate, we can calculate the values of $\hat{Y} = 6.2 + 2.8X$ (Table 13A.3). Thus,

$$S_{Y.X} \sqrt{\frac{35.20}{4}} = 2.97$$

APPENDIX 13-B

FORMULA DERIVATION

This appendix presents a brief outline of the derivation of the formulas used in regression analysis. As such, it assumes a knowledge of basic matrix algebra. A reader unfamiliar with it should skip this (and most of Appendix 13-E as well). For a more complete treatment, see Johnston (1984).

GENERAL LINEAR MODEL

Model:

$$Y_i = B_0 + B_1 X_{1i} + B_2 X_{2i} + \cdots + B_k X_{ki} + \mu_i$$

Matrix notation:

$$Y = XB + \mu$$

where

$$Y = \begin{bmatrix} Y_1 \\ Y_2 \\ \vdots \\ Y_n \end{bmatrix} \qquad X = \begin{bmatrix} 1 & X_{11} & \cdots & X_{k1} \\ 1 & X_{12} & \cdots & X_{k2} \\ \vdots & \vdots & & \vdots \\ 1 & X_{1n} & \cdots & X_{kn} \end{bmatrix} \qquad B = \begin{bmatrix} B_0 \\ B_1 \\ B_2 \\ \vdots \\ B_k \end{bmatrix} \text{ and } \quad \mu = \begin{bmatrix} \mu_1 \\ \mu_2 \\ \vdots \\ \mu_n \end{bmatrix}$$

Procedure: Select $\hat{\beta}$ so as to minimize

$$\sum_{i=1}^{n} \left(Y_i - \hat{Y}_i \right)^2$$

In matrix form, this becomes

$$\left(Y - X\hat{\beta} \right)' \left(Y - X\hat{\beta} \right) = e'e$$

In order to

$$\text{Min} \sum_{i=1}^{n} \left(Y_i - \hat{Y}_i \right)^2 = \text{Min} \left[Y'Y - 2\hat{\beta}X'Y + \hat{\beta}X'X\hat{\beta} \right]$$

we take the first derivative with respect to the vector $\hat{\beta}$.

Therefore,

$$\frac{\partial e'e}{\partial \hat{\beta}} = -2X'Y + 2X'X\hat{\beta}$$

Setting this equal to 0 and solving, we get

$$\hat{\beta} = \left[X'X \right]^{-1} X'Y$$

APPENDIX 13-C

SAMPLE REGRESSION OUTPUT

```
STATISTICAL PACKAGE FOR THE SOCIAL SCIENCES SPSSH - VERSION 6.00                06/27/77      F

    SPACE ALLOCATION FOR THIS RUN..

        TOTAL AMOUNT REQUESTED                        80000 BYTES


        DEFAULT TRANSPACE ALLOCATION                  13000 BYTES


            MAX NO OF TRANSFORMATIONS PERMITTED    100
            MAX NO OF RECODE VALUES                400
            MAX NO OF ARITHM.OR LCG.OPERATIONS     600

        RESULTING WORKSPACE ALLOCATION                70000 BYTES

                VARIABLE LIST   YRBORN,INCOME,FAMSIZE,EXPENSE,
                                BRAND,INFO,VARIETY,TASTE,OTHERS,DIET,PRICE,
                                AVAIL,EASE,HABIT,SPECIAL,NUTRI
                INPUT MEDIUM    DISK
                N OF CASES      UNKNOWN
                INPUT FORMAT    FIXED(20X,F2.0,54X,2F1.0/12X,F1.0,1X,
                                2F1.0,1X,10F1.0/////)


                ACCORDING TO YOUR INPUT FORMAT, VARIABLES ARE TO BE READ AS FOLLOWS

                VARIABLE  FORMAT  RECORD    COLUMNS

                YRBORN    F 2. 0     1      21-  22
                INCOME    F 1. 0     1      77-  77
                FAMSIZE   F 1. 0     1      78-  78
                EXPENSE   F 1. 0     2      13-  13
                BRAND     F 1. 0     2      15-  15
                INFO      F 1. 0     2      16-  16
                VARIETY   F 1. 0     2      18-  18
                TASTE     F 1. 0     2      19-  19
                OTHERS    F 1. 0     2      20-  20
                DIET      F 1. 0     2      21-  21
                PRICE     F 1. 0     2      22-  22
                AVAIL     F 1. 0     2      23-  23
                EASE      F 1. 0     2      24-  24
                HABIT     F 1. 0     2      25-  25
                SPECIAL   F 1. 0     2      26-  26
                NUTRI     F 1. 0     2      27-  27

    THE INPUT FORMAT PROVIDES FOR  16 VARIABLES.   16 WILL BE READ
    IT PROVIDES FOR  6 RECORDS ('CARDS') PER CASE.   A MAXIMUM OF   78 'COLUMNS' ARE USED ON A RECORD.

                RECODE       EXPENSE(1=12.5)(2=22.5)(3=37.5)
                             (4=52.5)(5=70)
                COMPUTE      AGE=75-YRBORN
                MISSING VALUES EXPENSE(0),YRBORN(00),FAMSIZE(0),INCOME(0)/
                             BRAND,INFO,VARIETY,TASTE,OTHERS,DIET,PRICE,
                             AVAIL,EASE,HABIT,SPECIAL,NUTRI(0)
                REGRESSION   VARIABLES=EXPENSE,INCOME,AGE,FAMSIZE,
```

570

STATISTICAL PACKAGE FOR THE SOCIAL SCIENCES SPSSH - VERSION 6.00   06/27/77   PAGE   2

BRAND, INFO, VARIETY, TASTE, OTHERS, DIET, PRICE,
AVAIL, EASE, HABIT, SPECIAL, NUTRI/
REGRESSION=EXPENSE WITH INCOME TO NUTRI(2)/
REGRESSION=EXPENSE WITH INCOME TO NUTRI(1)/
STATISTICS   ALL

***** REGRESSION PROBLEM REQUIRES   5120 BYTES WORKSPACE, NOT INCLUDING RESIDUALS *****

READ INPUT DATA

AFTER READING   940 CASES FROM SUBFILE NCNAME   , END OF FILE WAS ENCOUNTERED ON LOGICAL UNIT # 8

STATISTICAL PACKAGE FOR THE SOCIAL SCIENCES SPSSH - VERSION 6.00   06/27/77   PAGE   3
FILE   NONAME   (CREATION DATE = 06/27/77)

VARIABLE	MEAN	STANDARD DEV	CASES
EXPENSE	37.5230	15.1153	762
INCOME	2.7520	1.4208	762
AGE	43.7008	16.5416	762
FAMSIZE	3.2674	1.3756	762
BRAND	2.3425	1.4150	762
INFO	1.8740	0.6504	762
VARIETY	2.0407	0.9603	762
TASTE	1.2362	0.5656	762
OTHERS	1.6955	0.8578	762
DIET	3.0433	1.5749	762
PRICE	1.7520	0.9619	762
AVAIL	2.1654	1.1285	762
EASE	2.7546	1.2245	762
HABIT	2.7927	1.1390	762
SPECIAL	2.2559	1.2511	762
NUTRI	1.6745	0.8800	762

STATISTICAL PACKAGE FOR THE SOCIAL SCIENCES SPSSH - VERSION 6.00   06/27/77   PAGE   4

FILE   NONAME   (CREATION DATE = 06/27/77))

CORRELATION COEFFICIENTS

A VALUE OF 99.00000 IS PRINTED
IF A COEFFICIENT CANNOT BE COMPUTED.

	EXPENSE	INCOME	AGE	FAMSIZE	BRAND	INFO	VARIETY	TASTE	OTHERS	DIET	PRICE	AVAIL
EXPENSE	1.00000	0.41605	-0.08544	0.57810	0.03172	-0.01307	0.00627	-0.02907	-0.01740	0.01793	0.08422	-0.04510
INCOME	0.41605	1.00000	-0.12226	0.27252	-0.05005	-0.03244	0.02474	0.04357	0.01180	0.06882	0.25973	-0.01045
AGE	-0.08544	-0.12226	1.00000	-0.27220	-0.10060	0.06135	-0.02248	-0.01154	-0.02234	-0.15224	0.02787	-0.04620
FAMSIZE	0.57810	0.27252	-0.27220	1.00000	0.09856	0.03318	0.05480	0.03592	0.04967	0.11919	-0.01359	-0.02050
BRAND	0.03772	-0.00606	-0.10006	0.09856	1.00000	-0.14867	0.05480	0.02355	0.04289	-0.05148	-0.14218	0.00563
INFO	-0.01307	-0.03244	0.06135	0.03318	-0.14867	1.00000	0.11131	0.00956	0.03999	0.10925	0.12432	-0.01097
VARIETY	0.00627	0.02474	-0.01154	0.05480	-0.01897	0.11131	1.00000	0.32582	0.20949	0.14394	0.05362	0.10292
TASTE	-0.02907	0.04357	-0.01154	0.03592	-0.04235	0.00956	0.32582	1.00000	0.33071	0.04455	0.04020	0.12194
OTHERS	-0.01740	0.01180	-0.02234	0.04967	-0.02355	0.03999	0.20949	0.33071	1.00000	0.13573	0.02808	0.07829
DIET	0.01790	0.06882	-0.15224	0.11919	-0.05148	0.10925	0.14394	0.04455	0.13573	1.00000	0.10772	0.07803
PRICE	0.08422	0.25973	0.02787	-0.01359	-0.14218	0.12432	0.05362	0.04020	0.02808	0.10772	1.00000	0.20125
AVAIL	-0.04510	-0.01045	-0.04620	-0.02050	0.00563	-0.01097	0.10292	0.12194	0.07829	0.07803	0.20125	1.00000
EASE	-0.01904	-0.01162	-0.00577	-0.02516	-0.04099	-0.11477	0.05362	0.12194	0.04455	0.07803	0.12452	0.30326
HABIT	-0.12929	-0.08542	-0.04843	-0.05753	0.04413	-0.16303	0.08822	0.08001	0.12709	0.02868	0.05854	0.23015
SPECIAL	-0.02835	0.03206	-0.00964	-0.00843	0.13456	0.13496	0.08648	0.09273	0.07531	0.03578	0.32362	0.17289
NUTRI	0.03267	0.05937	0.00070	0.03938	-0.05916	0.28807	0.25361	0.22594	0.16054	0.27946	0.22741	0.08470

	EASE	HABIT	SPECIAL	NUTRI
EXPENSE	-0.01904	-0.12929	-0.02835	0.03267
INCOME	-0.01162	-0.08542	0.03206	0.05937
AGE	-0.00577	-0.00964	-0.04843	0.00070
FAMSIZE	-0.02516	-0.05753	-0.00843	0.03938
BRAND	0.04099	0.04413	0.13456	-0.05916
INFO	-0.11477	-0.16303	0.13456	0.28807
VARIETY	0.05097	0.08822	0.25361	0.25361
TASTE	0.08001	0.11692	0.09273	0.22594
OTHERS	0.05865	0.12709	0.07531	0.14054
DIET	0.02868	0.03578	0.02238	0.27946
PRICE	0.12452	0.23015	0.32342	0.22741
AVAIL	0.30326	0.05854	0.17289	0.08470
EASE	1.00000	0.28569	0.06163	-0.00837
HABIT	0.28569	1.00000	0.09907	0.02305
SPECIAL	0.06163	0.09907	1.00000	0.18079
NUTRI	-0.00837	0.02305	0.18079	1.00000

STATISTICAL PACKAGE FOR THE SOCIAL SCIENCES SPSSH - VERSION 6.00   06/27/77   PAGE   5

FILE   NGMAPE   (CREATION DATE = 06/27/77)

* * * * * * * * * * * * * * * * * *   M U L T I P L E   R E G R E S S I O N   * * * * * * * * * * * * * * *   VARIABLE LIST 1
                                                                                                            REGRESSION LIST 1

DEPENDENT VARIABLE..   EXPENSE

VARIABLE(S) ENTERED ON STEP NUMBER 1..   NUTRI
                                            INCOME
                                            AGE
                                            FAMSIZE
                                            BRAND
                                            INFO
                                            VARIETY
                                            TASTE
                                            OTHERS
                                            DIET
                                            PRICE
                                            AVAIL
                                            EASE
                                            HABIT
                                            SPECIAL

			ANALYSIS OF VARIANCE	DF	SUM OF SQUARES	MEAN SQUARE	F
MULTIPLE R	0.65532	REGRESSION	15.	74667.73002	4977.84867	37.43394
R SQUARE	0.42945	RESIDUAL	746.	99200.61808	132.97670	
ADJUSTED R SQUARE	0.41876					
STANDARD ERROR	11.53155					

---------- VARIABLES IN THE EQUATION ----------   ---------- VARIABLES NOT IN THE EQUATION ----------

VARIABLE	B	BETA	STD ERROR B	F	VARIABLE	BETA IN	PARTIAL	TOLERANCE	F
NUTRI	0.42245	0.02750	0.54198	0.700					
INCOME	2.88617	0.27128	0.32247	80.108					
AGE	0.07983	0.08737	0.02663	8.851					
FAMSIZE	5.85584	0.53293	0.33067	313.636					
BRAND	0.00635	0.00099	0.30618	0.000					
INFO	-1.08607	-0.04673	0.69705	2.428					
VARIETY	-0.02149	0.00137	0.47587	0.002					
TASTE	-1.35632	-0.05225	0.83160	2.818					
OTHERS	-0.28381	-0.01686	0.50323	0.318					
DIET	-0.46426	-0.04837	0.28534	2.647					
PRICE	-0.28637	-0.01822	0.49960	0.329					
AVAIL	-0.24058	-0.01796	0.40468	0.353					
EASE	0.28449	0.02305	0.37152	0.586					
HABIT	-1.06932	-0.08058	0.39900	7.182					
SPECIAL	0.49106	0.04064	0.36442	1.616					
(CONSTANT)	12.76075								

ALL VARIABLES ARE IN THE EQUATION

STATISTICAL PACKAGE FCR THE SOCIAL SCIENCES SPSSH - VERSION 6.00   06/27/77   PAGE   6

FILE   AGNAME   (CREATION CATE = 06/27/77)

* M U L T I P L E   R E G R E S S I O N * * * * * * * * * * * * * * * * *   VARIABLE LIST 1
                                                                                                                    REGRESSION LIST 1

CEPENDENT VARIABLE..   EXPENSE

SUMMARY TABLE

VARIABLE	MULTIPLE R	R SQUARE	RSQ CHANGE	SIMPLE R	B	BETA
NUTRI	0.03267	0.00107	0.00107	0.03267	0.47245	0.02750
INCOME	0.41612	0.17316	0.17209	0.41605	2.88617	0.27128
AGE	0.41759	0.17438	0.00122	-0.08544	0.07983	0.08737
FAMSIZE	0.64368	0.41429	0.23992	0.57810	5.85584	0.53293
INFO	0.64367	0.41431	0.00001	0.03772	0.00635	0.00059
VARIETY	0.64425	0.41506	0.00075	-0.01307	-1.08607	-0.04673
TASTE	0.64473	0.41574	0.00067	0.00627	0.02149	0.00137
OTHERS	0.64720	0.41887	0.00313	-0.02907	-1.39632	-0.05225
CIET	0.64772	0.41954	0.00067	-0.01740	-0.28381	-0.01686
PRICE	0.64953	0.42197	0.00243	0.01790	-0.46426	-0.04837
AVAIL	0.64991	0.42239	0.00042	0.08422	0.28637	0.01822
EASE	0.65029	0.42288	0.00049	-0.04510	-0.24058	-0.01796
HABIT	0.65032	0.42292	0.00004	-0.01904	0.28649	0.02305
SPECIAL	0.65426	0.42806	0.00514	-0.12929	-1.06932	-0.08058
(CONSTANT)	0.65534	0.42945	0.00139	0.02835	12.76075	0.04064

STATISTICAL PACKAGE FOR THE SOCIAL SCIENCES SPSSH - VERSION 6.00

FILE NONAME (CREATION DATE = 06/27/77)   06/27/77   PAGE 7

* * * * * * * * * * * * * * * M U L T I P L E   R E G R E S S I O N * * * * * * * * * * * * * *

DEPENDENT VARIABLE..   EXPENSE   VARIABLE LIST 1
                                                                               REGRESSION LIST 2

VARIABLE(S) ENTERED ON STEP NUMBER 1..   FAMSIZE

MULTIPLE R   0.57810   ANALYSIS OF VARIANCE   DF   SUM OF SQUARES   MEAN SQUARE   F
R SQUARE   0.33420   REGRESSION   1.   58106.10040   58106.10040   381.47701
ADJUSTED R SQUARE   0.33423   RESIDUAL   760.   115762.24769   152.31875
STANDARD ERROR   12.34175

------------ VARIABLES IN THE EQUATION ------------

VARIABLE	B	BETA	STD ERROR B	F
FAMSIZE	6.35215	0.57810	0.32523	381.477
(CONSTANT)	16.64090			

------------ VARIABLES NOT IN THE EQUATION ------------

VARIABLE	BETA IN	PARTIAL	TOLERANCE	F
INCOME	0.27925	0.32927	0.92573	92.298
AGE	0.07767	0.09159	0.92591	6.421
BRAND	-0.01944	-0.02371	0.99029	0.427
INFO	-0.03229	-0.03955	0.99890	1.189
VARIETY	-0.02548	-0.03119	0.99700	0.739
TASTE	-0.04990	-0.06111	0.99871	2.845
OTHERS	-0.04622	-0.05658	0.99753	2.438
DIET	-0.05174	-0.06296	0.98579	3.021
PRICE	0.09209	0.11285	0.99982	9.790
AVAIL	-0.03326	-0.04076	0.99958	1.263
EASE	-0.00450	-0.00551	0.99937	0.023
HABIT	-0.09635	-0.11789	0.99669	10.697
SPECIAL	0.03323	0.04072	0.99993	1.261
NUTRI	0.00992	0.01215	0.99845	0.112

STATISTICAL PACKAGE FOR THE SOCIAL SCIENCES SPSSH - VERSION 6.00

FILE   NONAME   (CREATION DATE = 06/27/77)   06/27/77   PAGE   8

* * * * * * * * * * * * * * * * * * * M U L T I P L E   R E G R E S S I O N * * * * * * * * * * * * * * *
                                                                                          VARIABLE LIST   1
DEPENDENT VARIABLE..   EXPENSE   REGRESSION LIST 2

VARIABLE(S) ENTERED ON STEP NUMBER 2..   INCOME

MULTIPLE R   0.63748   ANALYSIS OF VARIANCE   DF   SUM OF SQUARES   MEAN SQUARE   F
R SQUARE   0.40638   REGRESSION   2.   70657.10393   35328.55197   259.80087
ADJUSTED R SQUARE   0.40560   RESIDUAL   759.   103211.24416   135.98319
STANDARD ERROR   11.66118

------------- VARIABLES IN THE EQUATION -------------   ----------- VARIABLES NOT IN THE EQUATION ------------

VARIABLE   B   BETA   STD ERROR B   F   VARIABLE   BETA IN   PARTIAL   TOLERANCE   F

FAMSIZE   5.51597   0.50200   0.31938   298.281   AGE   0.09242   0.11527   0.92341   10.207
INCOME   2.97087   0.27925   0.30923   92.298   BRAND   -0.01017   -0.01313   0.98912   0.131
(CONSTANT) 11.21403   INFO   -0.02073   -0.02687   0.99704   0.548
                                                                  VARIETY   -0.02823   -0.03659   0.99689   1.016
                                                                  TASTE   -0.05942   -0.07702   0.99748   4.523
                                                                  OTHERS   -0.04574   -0.05929   0.99753   2.674
                                                                  DIET   -0.06213   -0.08000   0.98437   4.883
                                                                  PRICE   0.02001   0.02498   0.92485   0.473
                                                                  AVAIL   -0.03190   -0.04140   0.99955   1.301
                                                                  EASE   -0.00317   -0.00411   0.99934   0.013
                                                                  HABIT   -0.07722   -0.09979   0.99144   7.625
                                                                  SPECIAL   0.02367   0.03069   0.99865   0.715
                                                                  NUTRI   -0.00369   -0.00478   0.99589   0.017

STATISTICAL PACKAGE FOR THE SOCIAL SCIENCES SPSSH – VERSION 6.00   06/27/77   PAGE   9

FILE   NONAME   (CREATION DATE = 06/27/77)

* * * * * * * * * * * * * * * *   M U L T I P L E   R E G R E S S I O N   * * * * * * * * * * * * * *   VARIABLE LIST   1
                                                                                                                        REGRESSION LIST 2

DEPENDENT VARIABLE..   EXPENSE

VARIABLE(S) ENTERED ON STEP NUMBER 3..   AGE

MULTIPLE R   0.64364   ANALYSIS OF VARIANCE   DF   SUM OF SQUARES   MEAN SQUARE   F
R SQUARE   0.41427   REGRESSION   3.   72028.40852   24009.46951   178.70374
ADJUSTED R SQUARE   0.41273   RESIDUAL   758.   101839.93958   134.35348
STANDARD ERROR   11.59109

-------- VARIABLES IN THE EQUATION --------   ----------- VARIABLES NOT IN THE EQUATION ------------

VARIABLE	B	BETA	STD ERROR B	F		VARIABLE	BETA IN	PARTIAL	TOLERANCE	F
FAMSIZE	5.77801	0.52585	0.32789	310.535		BRAND	-0.00313	-0.00406	0.98294	0.012
INCOME	3.02193	0.28405	0.30779	96.396		INFO	-0.02719	-0.03539	0.99200	0.949
AGE	0.08445	0.09242	0.02643	10.207		VARIETY	-0.02758	-0.03598	0.99684	0.981
(CONSTANT)	6.52153					TASTE	-0.05941	-0.07754	0.99748	4.578
						OTHERS	-0.04492	-0.05862	0.99744	2.610
						DIET	-0.05185	-0.06670	0.96931	3.383
						PRICE	0.01626	0.02041	0.92330	0.316
						AVAIL	-0.02717	-0.03545	0.99662	0.952
						EASE	-0.00198	-0.00258	0.99916	0.005
						HABIT	-0.07459	-0.09700	0.99053	7.190
						SPECIAL	0.02827	0.03686	0.99606	1.030
						NUTRI	-0.00495	-0.00650	0.99568	0.032

. STATISTICAL PACKAGE FCR THE SOCIAL SCIENCES SPSSH - VERSION 6.00   06/27/77   PAGE 10

FILE   NGNAME   (CREATION DATE = 06/27/77)

* * * * * * * * * * * * * * * * * * * M U L T I P L E   R E G R E S S I O N * * * * * * * * * * * * * *   VARIABLE LIST 1
                                                                                                             REGRESSION LIST 2

DEPENDENT VARIABLE..   EXPENSE

VARIABLE(S) ENTERED ON STEP NUMBER 4..   HABIT

MULTIPLE R   0.64791
R SQUARE   0.41978   ANALYSIS OF VARIANCE   DF   SUM OF SQUARES   MEAN SQUARE   F
ADJUSTED R SQUARE   C.41748   REGRESSION   4.   72986.62405   18246.65601   136.91993
STANDARD ERROR   11.54405   RESIDUAL   757.   100881.72405   133.26516

--------- VARIABLES IN THE EQUATION ---------

VARIABLE	B	BETA	STD ERROR B	F
FAMSIZE	5.74100	0.52240	0.32685	308.531
INCOME	2.96080	0.27830	0.30759	92.783
AGE	0.08232	0.09008	0.02634	9.767
HABIT	-0.98909	-0.07459	0.36916	7.190
(CONSTANT)	9.66870			

--------- VARIABLES NOT IN THE EQUATION ---------

VARIABLE	BETA IN	PARTIAL	TOLERANCE	F
BRAND	0.00028	0.00036	0.98090	0.000
INFO	-0.04046	-0.05220	0.96547	2.065
VARIETY	-0.02089	-0.02726	0.98831	0.562
TASTE	-0.05109	-0.06649	0.98257	3.357
OTHERS	-0.03584	-0.04659	0.98050	1.645
DIET	-0.04873	-0.06293	C.96756	3.006
PRICE	0.02278	0.02864	0.91703	0.621
AVAIL	-0.01075	-0.01371	0.94461	0.142
EASE	0.02088	0.02626	0.91803	0.522
SPECIAL	0.03609	0.04705	0.98604	1.677
NUTRI	-0.00279	-0.00365	0.99481	0.010

STATISTICAL PACKAGE FOR THE SOCIAL SCIENCES SPSSH - VERSION 6.00   06/27/77   PAGE 11

FILE   NONAME   (CREATION DATE = 06/27/77)

* * * * * * * * * * * * * * * * * * M U L T I P L E   R E G R E S S I O N * * * * * * * * * * * * * * * *   VARIABLE LIST 1
                                                                                                           REGRESSION LIST 2

DEPENDENT VARIABLE..   EXPENSE

VARIABLE(S) ENTERED ON STEP NUMBER   5..   TASTE

MULTIPLE R	0.64988	ANALYSIS OF VARIANCE	DF	SUM OF SQUARES	MEAN SQUARE	F
R SQUARE	0.42235	REGRESSION	5.	73432.55368	14686.51074	110.54026
ADJUSTED R SQUARE	0.41929	RESIDUAL	756.	100435.79442	132.85158	
STANDARD ERROR	11.52613					

------------------ VARIABLES IN THE EQUATION ------------------   ----------- VARIABLES NOT IN THE EQUATION -----------

VARIABLE	B	BETA	STD ERROR B	F		VARIABLE	BETA IN	PARTIAL	TOLERANCE	F
FAMSIZE	5.75675	0.52409	0.32646	311.129		BRAND	0.00110	0.00143	0.98065	0.002
INCOME	2.98583	0.28065	0.30721	94.462		INFO	-0.03893	-0.05030	0.96457	1.915
AGE	0.08249	0.09028	0.02650	9.540		VARIETY	-0.00527	-0.00654	0.88911	0.032
HABIT	-0.90670	-0.06837	0.37137	5.961		OTHERS	-0.02174	-0.02684	0.88073	0.544
TASTE	-1.36528	-0.05109	0.74520	3.357		DIET	-0.04700	-0.06079	0.96639	2.800
(CONSTANT)	10.98957					PRICE	0.02398	0.03021	0.91657	0.690
						AVAIL	-0.00566	-0.00721	0.93542	0.039
						EASE	0.02351	0.02961	0.91585	0.662
						SPECIAL	0.04048	0.05271	0.97960	2.104
						NUTRI	0.00891	0.01140	0.94593	0.098

STATISTICAL PACKAGE FOR THE SOCIAL SCIENCES SPSSH - VERSION 6.00   06/27/77   PAGE 19

FILE   NCNAME   (CREATION CATE = 06/27/77)

* * * * * * * * * * * * * * * *   M U L T I P L E   R E G R E S S I O N   * * * * * * * * * * * * * *   VARIABLE LIST 1
                                                                                                      REGRESSION LIST 2

DEPENDENT VARIABLE..   EXPENSE

VARIABLE(S) ENTERED ON STEP NUMBER 13..   PRICE

MULTIPLE R	0.65532		
R SQUARE	0.42945		
ADJUSTED R SQUARE	0.42031		
STANDARD ERROR	11.51614		

ANALYSIS OF VARIANCE	DF	SUM OF SQUARES	MEAN SQUARE	F
REGRESSION	13.	74667.40535	5743.64657	43.30854
RESIDUAL	748.	99200.94275	132.62158	

--------- VARIABLES IN THE EQUATION ---------

VARIABLE	B	BETA	STD ERROR b	F
FAMSIZE	5.65684	0.53302	0.32893	317.038
INCOME	2.88617	0.27128	0.32202	80.331
AGE	0.07979	0.08732	0.02672	8.920
HABIT	-1.06634	-0.08050	0.39797	7.206
TASTE	-1.33708	-0.05191	0.80594	2.962
DIET	-0.46374	-0.04832	0.28384	2.670
SPECIAL	0.49058	0.04060	0.36205	1.836
INFO	-1.08545	-0.04671	0.69056	2.471
NUTRI	0.47603	0.02771	0.53588	0.789
EASE	0.28493	0.02438	0.37081	0.590
OTHERS	-0.28140	-0.01671	0.50019	0.317
AVAIL	-0.23969	-0.01790	0.40374	0.352
PRICE	0.28491	0.01813	0.49667	0.329
(CONSTANT)	12.79161			

--------- VARIABLES NOT IN THE EQUATION ---------

VARIABLE	BETA IN	PARTIAL	TOLERANCE	F
BRAND	0.00058	0.00073	0.93130	0.000
VARIETY	0.00136	0.00164	0.83697	0.002

F-LEVEL OR TOLERANCE-LEVEL INSUFFICIENT FOR FURTHER COMPUTATION

STATISTICAL PACKAGE FOR THE SOCIAL SCIENCES SPSSH - VERSION 6.00   06/27/77   PAGE   20

FILE   NONAME   (CREATION DATE = 06/27/77)

*   MULTIPLE   REGRESSION   * * * * * * * * * * * * * * * * * * *   VARIABLE LIST   1
                                                                                                          REGRESSION LIST   2

DEPENDENT VARIABLE..   EXPENSE

SUMMARY TABLE

VARIABLE	MULTIPLE R	R SQUARE	RSQ CHANGE	SIMPLE R	B	BETA
FAMSIZE	0.57810	0.33420	0.33420	0.57810	5.85684	0.53302
INCOME	0.63748	0.40638	0.07219	0.41605	2.88617	0.27128
AGE	0.64364	0.41427	0.00789	-0.08544	0.07979	0.08732
HABIT	0.64791	0.41978	0.00551	-0.12929	-1.06834	-0.08050
TASTE	0.64980	0.42235	0.00256	-0.02937	-1.38708	-0.05191
DIET	0.65152	0.42448	0.00213	0.01790	-0.46374	-0.04832
SPECIAL	0.65278	0.42612	0.00164	0.02835	0.49058	0.04060
INFO	0.65338	0.42769	0.00157	-0.01307	-1.08545	-0.04671
NUTRI	0.65449	0.42835	0.00066	-0.03267	0.47603	0.02771
EASE	0.65475	0.42873	0.00038	-0.01904	0.28493	0.02308
OTHERS	0.65497	0.42899	0.00025	-0.01740	-3.28140	-0.01671
AVAIL	0.65513	0.42920	0.00021	-0.04510	-0.23969	-0.01790
PRICE	0.65532	0.42945	0.00025	0.08422	0.28491	0.01813
(CONSTANT)					12.79161	

APPENDIX 13-D

SIMULTANEOUS EQUATION REGRESSION

PROBLEM

The basic regression model assumes there is one dependent variable, which is affected by a set of independent variables. This is often not an accurate assumption about the way the world operates. Consider the issue of the influence of advertising on sales. If we plotted sales versus advertising, we might get Figure 13D.1. It is easy to assume that these data can be approximated by a line that indicates the effect of advertising on sales. Presumably, advertising does indeed affect sales. On the other hand, advertising budgets are traditionally set as a percentage of anticipated sales. Hence, the observed points could well be a set of intersections of lines that indicate how advertising affects sales and how sales affects advertising (Figure 13D.2). In this case, the simple plot of sales versus advertising produces some weighted average of the advertising-to-sales and sales-to-advertising effects.

METHOD

A basic method for disentangling two-way effects among variables is simultaneous equation regression. The trick is to specify one equation for each direction of causation. In the sales-advertising example, that means two equations:

$$\text{Sales} = f(\text{Advertising})$$

$$\text{Advertising} = f(\text{Sales})$$

The method is then to simultaneously estimate coefficients of both equations.

The key to the success of simultaneous equation estimation is the presence of other (exogenous) variables which act only as independent variables. If these other independent

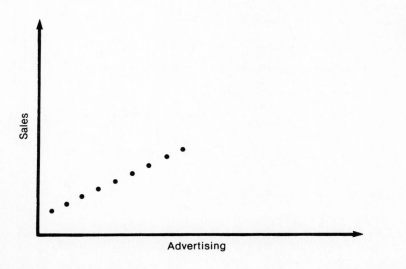

FIGURE 13D.1
Sales vs. Advertising

FIGURE 13D.2
Simultaneous Effects

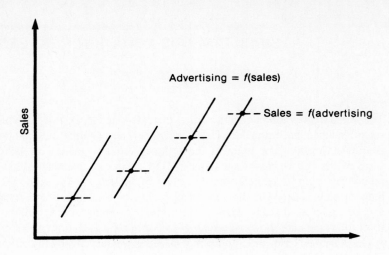

variables are fortuitous, then their influences can be used to disentangle the two-way relations among the basic (endogenous) variables. The ability of a system of equations to separate two-way relations is tied to the concept of identification. There are three types of identification: under, exact, and over.

Underidentification

Underidentification is the situation where the "other" variables are insufficient to separate the two-way effects. For example, Sales = B_1 · (Advertising), and Advertising = B_2 · (Sales). In this case, which comes first (sales or advertising) becomes a chicken-and-egg argument with no solution. Unless the model can be logically altered, no estimates can be obtained.

Exact Identification

The "neatest" situation is so-called exact identification. In this case, the estimates of the two-way relations are derived in a straightforward two-step process. Assume:

$$\text{Sales} = B_1(\text{advertising}) + \gamma_1(\text{GDP})$$

$$\text{Advertising} = B_2(\text{advertising}) + \gamma_2(\text{Competitive advertising})$$

Call

$$\left.\begin{array}{r}\text{GDP} = X_1 \\ \text{Competitive advertising} = X_2\end{array}\right\} \text{Exogenous variables}$$

$$\left.\begin{array}{r}\text{Sales} = Y_1 \\ \text{Advertising} = Y_2\end{array}\right\} \text{Endogenous variables}$$

We can now write the two equations in matrix form as:

$$\begin{bmatrix} -1 & B_1 \\ -B_2 & -1 \end{bmatrix} \begin{bmatrix} Y_1 \\ Y_2 \end{bmatrix} + \begin{bmatrix} \gamma_1 & 0 \\ 0 & \gamma_2 \end{bmatrix} \begin{bmatrix} X_1 \\ X_2 \end{bmatrix} = \begin{bmatrix} \mu_1 \\ \mu_2 \end{bmatrix}$$

or

$$BY + \Gamma X = \mu$$

To solve for Y, we multiply both sides by B^{-1}:

$$B^{-1}BY + B^{-1}\Gamma X = B^{-1}\mu$$

or

$$Y = -B^{-1}\Gamma X + B^{-1}\mu$$

Since we assume $B^{-1}\mu = 0$,

$$Y = -B^{-1}\Gamma X$$

Hence, we now have the endogenous variables as a function of the exogenous variables, often called the reduced form equations. The two-step process first requires one to run regular regression (ordinary least squares—OLS) on the reduced form equations:

$$Y_1 = a_1 X_1 + a_2 X_2$$
$$Y = a_3 X_3 + a_4 X_4$$

The next step is to deduce the β_is and γ_is from the a_is:

$$\begin{bmatrix} a_1 & a_2 \\ a_3 & a_4 \end{bmatrix} = -B^{-1}\Gamma$$

$$= \frac{-1}{1 - \beta_1\beta_2} \begin{bmatrix} -1 & -\beta_1 \\ -\beta_2 & -1 \end{bmatrix} \begin{bmatrix} \gamma_1 & 0 \\ 0 & \gamma_2 \end{bmatrix}$$

$$= \frac{-1}{1 - \beta_1\beta_2} \begin{bmatrix} -\gamma_1 & -\beta_1\gamma_2 \\ -\beta_2\gamma_1 & -\gamma_2 \end{bmatrix}$$

Thus,

$$a_1 = \gamma_1$$
$$a_2 = \beta_1\gamma_2$$
$$a_3 = \beta_2\gamma_1$$
$$a_4 = \gamma_2$$

Therefore, $\beta_1 = a_2/a_4$, and so forth. This process is called *indirect least squares* (ILS).

Logically, this "trick" works because each of the exogenous variables influences one and only one of the endogenous variables. Here, we can view this as an experiment where we know that changes in gross domestic product first affect sales and that changes in competitive advertising first affect advertising. Hence, by varying GDP and advertising (or by observing how they vary naturally), we can separate the sales-to-advertising and advertising-to-sales effects. If, for example, GDP affects both sales and advertising, we can no longer logically determine both its impact on sales and advertising, and sales and advertising's effects on each other. Thus, the key to simultaneous equation methods is the appropriateness and predictive ability of the exogenous variables.

Overidentification

Overidentification is the situation where the exogenous variables are more than sufficient to identify the two-way causations. For example,

$$\text{Sales} = \beta_1(\text{Advertising}) + \gamma_1(\text{GDP}) + \gamma_3(\text{CPI})$$
$$\text{Advertising} = \beta_2(\text{Sales}) + \gamma_2(\text{Competitive advertising})$$
$$+ \gamma_4(\text{Share}) + \gamma_5(\text{Media rates})$$

Here, no simple solution can be traced from the reduced form back to the original coefficients.

One common estimation procedure in this case is two-stage least squares (TSLS). The steps are

1. Find A from $Y = AX$ (run the reduced form equations by OLS).
2. Set $Y^* = AX$ (replace the actual values of Y with their predicted values from AX) and then run $BY^* + \Gamma X = \mu$ by OLS.

Identification Checking

In checking for identification, there are the following two common approaches:

> *Order condition.* The order condition is a necessary but not sufficient condition for identification. It is a counting rule that says, for each equation,
>
> > Number of endogenous variables included $- 1$
> > $\leq$ Number of exogenous variables excluded

> *Rank condition.* The rank condition is a sufficient condition for identification. It requires one to form the augmented ß, Γ matrix: ßΓ. Now for each equation (e.g., the second), remove the row of that equation (e.g., second row) and any column where the equation removed had a nonzero element. If the rank of the reduced matrix is equal to the number of original equations minus 1, then the equation is identified. If the rank is less than that, then the equation is not identified.

Consider the example in the exact identification case. Here, the ßΓ matrix is:

$$\begin{bmatrix} -1 & \beta_1 & \gamma_1 & 0 \\ -\beta_2 & 1 & 0 & \gamma_2 \end{bmatrix}$$

To check on the second equation, remove the second row and all columns with a nonzero value in the second row. This leaves

$$[\gamma_1]$$

Since the reduced matrix is of order $2 - 1 = 1$, the equation is identified.

Identification by Temporal Order

One clever way to produce an identified model is to use temporally prior variables as the independent variable:

$$\text{Sales}_t = f\left(\text{Advertising}_{t-1}\right)$$
$$\text{Advertising}_t = f\left(\text{Sales}_{t-1}\right)$$

If this is in fact true and you have time series data, you can simply estimate the two equations with standard (OLS) regression.

There are, however, cases where this can be illusory. For example, assume sales are fairly constant. We can estimate $\text{Sales}_t = f(\text{Advertising}_{t-1})$ and will probably find a significant relation. Given budget performance and the impact of the level of available funds, however, it is probably true that:

$$\text{Adv}_t = f\left(\text{Adv}_{t-1}, \text{Sales}_{t-1}\right)$$

Hence, the temporal order may be reversed. The point is that care must be taken in specifying causal order; significant coefficients are no guarantee that the model is correct.

ESTIMATION

Estimation problems in simultaneous equation models get very complex. The problem is that all the nice assumptions about the error terms are often false and, hence, OLS may not be the best approach. On the other hand, for recursive[7] models, OLS is the best, and it does quite well in many other situations as well. In short, simultaneous equation estimation is a technical problem that calls for technical help.

---

[7]A recursive model is one in which the causation is in one direction only (no feedback exists), such as awareness → attitude → intention → choice. If choice were assumed to influence attitude also, the model would then be nonrecursive.

APPENDIX 13-E

THE EFFECT OF COLLINEARITY ON THE STANDARD ERROR OF A REGRESSION COEFFICIENT

TWO INDEPENDENT VARIABLES

The standard error of a regression coefficient (S_{B_i}) is the product of the standard error of estimate $(S_{Y.X})$ times the ith diagonal element in the inverse of the covariance matrix $([X'X]_{ii^{-1}})$.

For two independent variables, we know:

$$[X'X] = \begin{bmatrix} S_1^2 & S_{12} \\ S_{12} & S_2^2 \end{bmatrix}$$

Consequently,

$$[X'X]^{-1} = \frac{1}{S_1^2 S_2^2 - S_{12}^2} \begin{bmatrix} S_2^2 & -S_{12} \\ -S_{12} & S_1^2 \end{bmatrix}$$

Thus, the most efficient set of data has $S_{12} = 0$, and the ratio $(S_1^2 S_2^2 - S_{12}^2)/S_1^2 S_2^2$ measures the efficiency of two correlated independent variables versus the efficiency had they been uncorrelated.

ORTHOGONAL AND NONORTHOGONAL DESIGNS

Another way to view the effect of collinearity is to consider the difference between orthogonal and nonorthogonal designs. Here, we use three independent dummy variables in a factorial design of eight observations as the "population," and we contrast an orthogonal and a nonorthogonal sample of size four.

	Observation	X_1	X_2	X_3
Factorial design:	1	1	1	1
	2	1	1	0
	3	1	0	1
	4	0	1	1
	5	1	0	0
	6	0	1	0
	7	0	0	1
	8	0	0	0
Orthogonal design:	1	1	1	1
	2	0	1	0
	3	1	0	0
	4	0	0	1
Nonorthogonal design:	1	1	1	1
	2	0	1	1
	3	1	0	1
	4	0	0	0

Putting the data in deviation form, we get:

	Observation	X_1	X_2	X_3
Factorial design:	1	.5	.5	.5
	2	.5	.5	− .5
	3	.5	− .5	.5
	4	− .5	.5	.5
	5	.5	− .5	− .5
	6	− .5	.5	− .5
	7	− .5	− .5	.5
	8	− .5	− .5	− .5
Orthogonal design:	1	.5	.5	.5
	2	− .5	.5	− .5
	3	.5	− .5	− .5
	4	− .5	− .5	.5
Nonorthogonal design:	1	.5	.5	.25
	2	− .5	.5	.25
	3	.5	− .5	.25
	4	− .5	− .5	− .75

Thus, for $[X'X]$ and $[X'X]^{-1}$ we get:

$$[X'X] \qquad\qquad [X'X]^{-1}$$

Factorial design:

$$\begin{bmatrix} 2 & & \\ & 2 & \\ & & 2 \end{bmatrix} \qquad \begin{bmatrix} \frac{1}{2} & & \\ & \frac{1}{2} & \\ & & \frac{1}{2} \end{bmatrix}$$

Orthogonal design:

$$\begin{bmatrix} 1 & & \\ & 1 & \\ & & 1 \end{bmatrix} \qquad \begin{bmatrix} 1 & & \\ & 1 & \\ & & 1 \end{bmatrix}$$

Nonorthogonal design:

$$\begin{bmatrix} 1 & 0 & .5 \\ 0 & 1 & .5 \\ .5 & .5 & .75 \end{bmatrix} \qquad \begin{bmatrix} 2 & 1 & -2 \\ 1 & 2 & -2 \\ -2 & -2 & 4 \end{bmatrix}$$

The orthogonal design produces, with a sample half the size, an estimate half as accurate as that from the full factorial design—exactly what we would expect. In contrast, the nonorthogonal design produces an estimate of the coefficient of the third independent variable one-eighth as accurate as that from the factorial design and one-fourth as accurate as that from the orthogonal design. Notice that the estimates of the coefficients of the first and second independent variables are also damaged. In summary, nonorthogonal designs hurt the accuracy of regression estimates.

APPENDIX 13-F

ANOVA AND REGRESSION

Having seen how categorical variables can be introduced in regression, the astute (i.e., fanatical) reader may notice a similarity between ANOVA and regression with categorical variables. To make clear the general equivalence, consider again the problem from Chapter 12 of the effect of package color on sales:

Advertising	Package Color		
Strategy	A	B	C
I	14	8	8
	10	14	6
II	11	3	5
	9	7	1

These data can be analyzed via regression by first creating a data set with dummy variables to represent the colors and strategies:

$$D_1 = 1 \text{ if package color } = \text{ A, } 0 \text{ otherwise}$$

$$D_2 = 1 \text{ if package color } = \text{ B, } 0 \text{ otherwise}$$

$$D_3 = 1 \text{ if advertising strategy } = \text{ I, } 0 \text{ otherwise}$$

The simple two-way without interaction model can then be estimated from:

$$Y = B_0 + B_1 D_1 + B_2 D_2 + B_3 D_3$$

If both B_1 and B_2 are not significantly different from zero, package color doesn't matter. Similarly, if B_3 equals zero, advertising strategy has no impact on sales. We can also add interaction terms ($D_1 D_3$, $D_2 D_3$) to parallel the two-way with interaction model:

$$Y = B_0 + B_1 D_1 + B_2 D_2 + B_3 D_3 + B_4 (D_1 D_3) + B_5 (D_2 D_3)$$

Here, if B_4 and B_5 equal zero, then no significant interactions exist.

We can then perform ANOVA-like analysis of the following types:

ANOVA Model	Regression Equivalent
"One-way" color only	$Y = B_0 + B_1 D_1 + B_2 D_2$
"One-way" advertising only	$Y = B_0 + B_1 D_3$
"Two-way" without interaction	$Y = B_0 + B_1 D_1 + B_2 D_2 + B_3 D_3$
"Two-way" with interactions	$Y = B_0 + B_1 D_1 + B_2 D_2 + B_3 D_3 + B_4 D_1 D_3 + B_5 D_2 D_3$

The model of two-way with interactions will exactly predict the group means as follows:

Advertising Strategy	Package Color		
	A	B	C
I	$B_0 + B_1 + B_3 + B_4$	$B_0 + B_2 + B_3 + B_5$	$B_0 + B_3$
II	$B_0 + B_1$	$B_0 + B_2$	B_0

"Standard" dummy variable coding (1–0) requires interpretation of the coefficients as the mean difference between the category of the dummy and the category that is omitted. Hence, in this example, the coefficient of D_1 is interpreted as the difference in means between color A and color C (here, $11 - 5 = 6$).

It is also possible to use so-called effect coding. This codes each dummy 1, 0, or -1, where the dummies are coded -1 if the variable falls in the omitted category. Here, if color C is used, D_1 and D_2 are coded -1 instead of the standard 0. The advantages of effect coding are that (1) the resulting coefficients can be interpreted directly as the effect of the particular dummy variable (i.e., the difference in means for that category from the grand mean), and (2) collinearity is sometimes reduced amoung the predictor variables. Under effect coding, the coefficient of D_1 becomes the difference between the mean of color A and the grand mean (here, $11 - 8 = 3$).

Furthermore, it is possible to perform analysis directly on the group means, instead of the individual observations, as long as the interactions are not used. (If they are, there are no degrees of freedom left, and the regression cannot be run.) This will not affect the coefficients if the cell sizes are equal, but it will increase R^2 by removing the within-cell variation from consideration.

Alternative coding schemes for raw and group mean data are shown in Table 13F.1. To demonstrate the essential equivalence of ANOVA and regression, several models are shown in Table 13F.2. The "interested reader" can verify that the results are equivalent by simple inspection.

SYSTEMATIC EFFECTS OF SAMPLING POINTS

Recall the basic measurement model is:

Measured value = True value + Systematic error + Random error

For methods that attempt to predict one variable based on another, an analogous model is involved:

Predicted value = Base value + Systematic effects + Random error

or

$$Y = f(x, \ e)$$

Sometimes, the systematic effects are related to a particular sampling point. For example, in a repeated measures design, the same respondent receives multiple treatments. In a so-called blocking design, sample points are grouped into categories called blocks (e.g., high-, average-, and low-sales stores) and then each block receives multiple treatments (e.g., a promotional display).

TABLE 13F.1   Coding Schemes

I. Dummy variable coding: Raw data.

	Y	D_1	D_2	D_3	D_1D_3	D_2D_3
1	14	1	0	1	1	0
2	8	0	1	1	0	1
3	8	0	0	1	0	0
4	10	1	0	1	1	0
5	14	0	1	1	0	1
6	6	0	0	1	0	0
7	11	1	0	0	0	0
8	3	0	1	0	0	0
9	5	0	0	0	0	0
10	9	1	0	0	0	0
11	7	0	1	0	0	0
12	1	0	0	0	0	0

II. Effect Coding: Raw data.

	Y	D_1	D_2	D_3	D_1D_3	D_2D_3
1	14	1	0	1	1	0
2	8	0	1	1	0	1
3	8	− 1	− 1	1	− 1	− 1
4	10	1	0	1	1	0
5	14	0	1	1	0	1
6	6	− 1	− 1	1	− 1	− 1
7	11	1	0	− 1	− 1	0
8	3	0	1	− 1	0	− 1
9	5	− 1	− 1	− 1	1	1
10	9	1	0	− 1	− 1	0
11	7	0	1	− 1	0	− 1
12	1	− 1	− 1	− 1	1	1

III. Dummy variables: Group means.

Y	D_1	D_2	D_3
12	1	0	1
11	0	1	1
7	0	0	1
10	1	0	0
5	0	1	0
3	0	0	0

IV. Effect coding: Group means.

Y	D_1	D_2	D_3
12	1	0	1
11	0	1	1
7	− 1	− 1	1
10	1	0	− 1
5	0	1	− 1
3	− 1	− 1	− 1

TABLE 13F.2   ANOVA via Regression

Column effect model color only (raw data):

		Dummy Variable Coding		Effect Coding	
		Coefficient	t	Coefficient	t
D_1:	package color A	6	2.52	3	2.18
D_2:	package color B	3	1.26	0	0
Constant		5		8	
R^2		.41		.41	
F		3.18		3.18	
ESS		72		72	
TSS		174		174	

Color and advertising without interactions:

		Raw Data				Group Means			
		Dummy Variable Coding		Effect Coding		Dummy Variable Coding		Effect Coding	
		Coefficient	t	Coefficient	t	Coefficient	t	Coefficient	t
D_1:	package color A	6	3.27	3	2.83	6	4.24	3	3.67
D_2:	package color B	3	1.63	0	0	3	2.12	0	0
D_3:	advertising strategy	4	2.67	2	2.67	4	3.46	2	3.46
Constant		3		8		3		8	
R^2		.69		.69		.94		.94	
F		5.93		5.93		10.00		10.00	
ESS		120		120		60		60	
TSS		174		174		64		64	

Color and advertising with interactions (raw data):

		Dummy Variable Coding		Effect Coding	
		Coefficient	t	Coefficient	t
D_1:	package color A	7	2.53	3	2.65
D_2:	package color B	2	0.72	0	0
D_3:	advertising strategy	4	1.44	2	2.50
$D_1 D_3$		− 2	− 0.51	− 1	− 0.88
$D_2 D_3$		2	0.51	1	.88
Constant		3		8	
R^2		.74		.74	
F		3.34		3.34	
ESS		128		128	
TSS		174		174	

In both cases, some of the variation in the variable of interest will depend on the sample points (respondents, blocks), as well as on the treatments:

Predicted value = Base value + Treatment effects + Sample point differences + Error

There are four methods for accounting for sample point effects.

1. *Include dummy variables for sampling points.* Within regression, the most direct way to deal with these effects is to include a dummy variable for each sampling point (actually all the sampling points minus 1 to permit estimation):

$$Y = BX + \sum_{\substack{\text{sample} \\ \text{points}}} C_i \big(\text{Sample point dummy variable}_i\big) + e$$

This method works well (if imperfectly) even if not all sample points receive all treatments. Its disadvantage is the potentially large number of parameters that must be estimated.

2. *Include the sample point average as a variable.* Another way to deal with sample point effects is to add a single variable to the regression that represents the average of each sample point:

$$Y = BX + C(\text{Sample point average})$$

This is more parsimonious than the first approach and will produce the same coefficients of the X variables (Bs) *if* all sample points have been exposed to all treatments. The approach breaks down, however, if all the sample points do not receive the same treatments. In this case, the sample points and treatments become correlated, so that the sample point averages are "contaminated" by the particular treatments to which they were exposed (basically, an omitted variable bias). Here, some special calculations are required.

If there is a treatment that all sample points received, then it can be used as a basis for estimating average sample point effects. That is, the value on that treatment minus the mean of the values on that treatment is an estimate of the subject effect. This method is simple and often applied, and the effect can then be subtracted from all the subjects' data before running the regression.

3. *Normalizing within sample point.* Instead of including the sample point average in the analysis, we can remove its effect by normalizing (see Appendix 8-D) within sample point, that is, subtracting the sample point average from each of the sample point's observations. This removes the average differences among sample points before the main analysis.

4. *Use differences.* Using time series data has many advantages, such as the ability to track changes and establish causal priority. However, when cross-sectional (observations across sample points) and time series data are mixed, some problems arise.

In particular, in many time series the same sample points (stores, companies, customers) are monitored over time. One way to deal with this is in a carryover model:

$$Y_t = BX_t + CY_{t-1} + e$$

To account for the sample point (fixed) effects, you can use a dummy variable for each sample point. Alternatively, many prefer to use a first-difference model:

$$Y_t - Y_{t-1} = BX_t + e$$

Here, any sample point specific effects are removed by taking the difference, so that the X variables explain change in the Y values.

APPENDIX 13-G

TESTING FOR SIGNIFICANT IMPROVEMENT

A larger regression model (one that contains more parameters/variables) will outperform a simpler one in terms of R^2. When the larger model contains the smaller one, it is possible to test for the statistical significance of the improvement due to adding the variables. This appendix presents two examples of such tests.

TESTING FOR THE SIGNIFICANCE OF A SET OF VARIABLES

In many situations, it is desirable to examine whether a category of variables as a group adds significantly to prediction. For example, one might wonder whether adding general attitudes or values improves prediction over simply using demographics. Because the values may be correlated among themselves as well as with some of the demographics, collinearity makes examination of the individual t statistics of these variables inadequate to determine whether they add anything.

What is needed is to examine the set of variables as a whole. This is done by running the analysis with and without the set of variables as a group and comparing the predictive power of the models/analyses. Consider the following example: Based on a sample of 1,000, we predicted sales of a product based on 7 demographic variables alone with an R^2 of .1. When we added 10 values, R^2 increased to .15. In this case, we can compare the R^2s and note that we increase it 5 percent (or alternatively, that we explained 5 percent of the 90 percent that needed to be explained). To see if the difference/improvement is statistically significant, we compare the errors in prediction, assuming we use both the 7 demographic and the 10 values variables, with the improvement in prediction resulting from adding the 10 values variables. Specifically, we build a test statistic (index):

$$\frac{\left(\displaystyle\sum_{\substack{\text{Demographics} \\ \text{only}}} \text{errors}^2 - \displaystyle\sum_{\substack{\text{Demographics} \\ \text{plus values}}} \text{errors}^2 \right)\Big/ 10}{\left(\displaystyle\sum_{\substack{\text{Demographics} \\ \text{plus values}}} \text{errors}^2 \right)\Big/ (1000 - 17 - 1)}$$

or equivalently,

$$\frac{\left(R^2_{\substack{\text{Demographics} \\ \text{plus values}}} - R^2_{\substack{\text{Demographics} \\ \text{only}}} \right)\Big/ 10}{\left(1 - R^2_{\substack{\text{Demographics} \\ \text{plus values}}} \right)\Big/ 982}$$

This index follows the F distribution with 10 and 982 degrees of freedom. If the test statistic is greater than the value in the F table, then we say that the added variables significantly improve prediction. Here, the test statistic is equal to:

$$\frac{.15 - .10/10}{.85/982} = 5.78$$

Since $F_{.05, 10, \infty} = 1.83$, this difference is statistically significant at the .05 level. This test, sometimes referred to as a *nested model* test, is in general given by:

$$\frac{\left(\sum_{\substack{\text{Nested} \\ \text{model}}} \text{errors}^2 - \sum_{\substack{\text{Full} \\ \text{model}}} \text{errors}^2 \right) \Big/ k}{\sum_{\substack{\text{Full} \\ \text{model}}} \text{errors}^2 \Big/ (n - m - 1)}$$

where

n = number of observations
m = number of parameters (variables) in the full model
k = number of parameters added to the nested (reduced, smaller) model by the full model

Equivalently, this can be written as:

$$\frac{\left(R^2_{\substack{\text{Full} \\ \text{model}}} - R^2_{\substack{\text{Nested} \\ \text{model}}} \right) \Big/ k}{\left(1 - R^2_{\substack{\text{Full} \\ \text{model}}} \right) \Big/ n - m - 1}$$

TESTING FOR DIFFERENCES ACROSS SEGMENTS

In many cases, you may be interested in whether a model applies to all segments or whether the segments differ. For example, you may wonder if the effects of price (X_1) and shopping convenience (X_2) in a regression model,

$$Y = B_0 + B_1(\text{Price}) + B_2(\text{Shopping convenience})$$

are the same for low-, middle-, and high-income customers:

Total	Income Segments		
Sample	Low	Middle	High
B_0	B_{L0}	B_{M0}	B_{H0}
B_1	B_{L1}	B_{M1}	B_{H1}
B_2	B_{L2}	B_{M2}	B_{H2}

Obviously, you need to run the analyses for the three segments separately and then examine the results. Beyond eyeballing the results (a fairly imprecise approach), if you also run the model for the entire sample the following test can be constructed:

$$\sum_{\substack{\text{In} \\ \text{segments}}} \text{errors}^2 = \sum_{\substack{\text{Low-income} \\ \text{regression}}} \text{errors}^2 + \sum_{\substack{\text{Middle-income} \\ \text{regression}}} \text{errors}^2 + \sum_{\substack{\text{High-income} \\ \text{regression}}} \text{errors}^2$$

Then we can compare the errors in the separate models with the errors in the model run on the full sample:

$$\frac{\left(\displaystyle\sum_{\substack{\text{Full sample} \\ \text{model}}} \text{errors}^2 - \sum_{\substack{\text{In} \\ \text{segments}}} \text{errors}^2\right)\Big/(g-1)k}{\displaystyle\sum_{\substack{\text{In} \\ \text{segments}}} \text{errors}^2 \Big/(n-gk-1)}$$

where

$$g = \text{number of segments;}$$
$$k = \text{number of parameters in the model.}$$

Here, $g = 3$ and $k = 3$. Thus, if the sum of the errors squared were 20, 30, and 15 within the three segment regressions and 100 in the full sample regression, we would have

$$\frac{100 - (20 + 30 + 15)/2(3)}{(20 + 30 + 15)/(n - 9 - 1)}$$

If the total sample size were 130, this would become

$$\frac{35/6}{65/120} = 10.77$$

Since $F_{.05, 6, 120} = 2.18$, this would indicate that the segments were significantly different.

Another way to run this test is to use dummy variables in what is sometimes called a *varying parameter model* and perform a nested model test. First, create two dummy variables: Z_1 if the person is middle income, and Z_2 if he or she has high income. Then, run the following regressions:

Full sample model:

$$Y = B_0 + B_1 X_1 + B_2 X_2$$

Segment model:

$$Y = B_0 + B_0' Z_1 + B_0'' Z_2 + B_1 X_1 + B_1'(Z_1 X_1)$$
$$+ B_1''(Z_2 X_1) + B_2 X_2 + B_2'(Z_1 X_2) + B_2''(Z_2 X_2)$$

Now, since the segmented model nests (includes) the full sample model, simply compare the results from the two regressions via a nested model test:

$$\frac{\left(R^2_{\substack{\text{Segmented} \\ \text{model}}} - R^2_{\substack{\text{Full sample} \\ \text{model}}}\right)\Big/6}{\left(1 - R^2_{\substack{\text{Segmented} \\ \text{model}}}\right)\Big/(n - 9 - 1)}$$

CHAPTER 14

Conjoint Analysis

One of the basic tenets of marketing is that firms should be customer oriented, offering products and services that provide value to customers. This raises an obvious question—how do we assess customers' perceived value for various products? Conjoint analysis is one method to answer the question, providing quantitative guidelines for addressing the following:

a. What are the perceived values or utilities that customers attach to different product attributes? When buying a notebook computer, for example, what values do customers attach to such attributes as processing speed, hard drive, and memory?

b. Do all customers value product attributes in a similar fashion, or are there segments of customers with different preferences? For example, some customers may consider the processing speed of a computer more important than its memory, while others may think just the opposite.

c. If segments exists, how big are these segments?

d. How are customer preferences and purchase intentions likely to change with changes in product design?

THE CONJOINT MODEL

Conjoint is a compensatory multiattribute model—it assumes that weakness on one attribute can be compensated for by strength in another. More specifically, conjoint analysis assumes that the utility or value for a product, U, can be expressed as a sum of utilities[1] for its features or attributes, $u(a_j)$, that is,

$$\text{Utility for an alternative} = \sum_{\substack{\text{all} \\ \text{attributes}}} \left(\begin{array}{c} \text{Utility for level of the} \\ \text{alternative on an attribute} \end{array} \right)$$

or

$$U = u(a_1) + u(a_2) + \cdots$$

---

[1]One can also include interactions in the model such as $u(a_1 \text{ and } a_2)$. For both the sake of simplicity and because such interactions are rarely significant, we focus on the simple additive model here.

Users of conjoint also generally assume the following:

> *Utilities can be measured by customers' overall evaluation of products where customers make tradeoffs among attributes.* When customers make tradeoffs in choosing among products, these trade-offs give us information about customers' value for different attributes. Unlike the compositional multiattribute models, which ask customers to rate each attribute and then create a "composite" preference score for a product, conjoint uses an approach where customers are asked to give their overall preference for a product, which is then "decomposed" into the values customers appear to have attached to various attributes or features of that product.

> *Customers differ in their preferences and the value they place on different attributes.* Differences (heterogeneity) in customer preferences can be explicitly accounted for by conducting the analysis at an individual level. This in turn provides a powerful means for benefit or need-based segmentation.

> *Estimates of the utilities can be used to make market share predictions about new products.*

In sum, conjoint analysis assumes that both the attributes and the positions of the alternatives on the attributes are known. The procedure then attempts to attach values (utilities) to the levels of each of the various attributes. Input data are typically ratings of various combinations of attribute levels, and the output is the utility of the different levels on the various attributes.

Consider the problem of assessing how customers trade off price and performance. Obviously, customers prefer the lowest price and the highest performance. To make intelligent marketing decisions, however, we need to know how much extra customers are willing to pay to get a given improvement in performance. This is exactly what conjoint analysis attempts to uncover based on customers' evaluation of various alternatives that vary in price and performance.

A NUMERICAL EXAMPLE

An example should help clarify the key ideas. Suppose that you are shopping for a notebook computer. Further assume that the notebooks you are considering differ on the following attributes:

    a. *Processing speed.* You can either get a notebook with 100mHz speed or one with a 133mHz speed.

    b. *Hard drive.* You can either get a notebook with 2GB (gigabytes) or 3GB.

    c. *Memory.* You can get a notebook with 32MB or 64MB random access memory (RAM).

Although in reality there are many features of notebook computers, including price, we restrict our example to only three attributes, each at two levels. With these features, we can create eight different combinations of notebooks (called product profiles) as in Table 14.1.

TABLE 14.1   Ranking (Value) of Different Notebook Profiles

Rankings

	HARD DRIVE			
	2GB MEMORY		4GB MEMORY	
	32MG	64MG	32MG	64MG
PROCESSOR 100mHz	8(1)	7(2)	6(3)	5(4)
133mHz	4(5)	2(7)	3(6)	1(8)

Data Coded for Analyses

Product Profile[a]	Processor[b]	Hard Drive[b]	Memory[b]	Rank[c]	Product Utility[d]
1	0	0	0	8	1
2	1	0	0	4	5
3	0	1	0	6	3
4	0	0	1	7	2
5	1	1	0	3	6
6	0	1	1	5	4
7	1	0	1	2	7
8	1	1	1	1	8

[a] Column 1 gives the eight different combinations or product profiles.
[b] Different levels of attributes with the following coding:

Processor   = 0 if speed is 100mHz,
                   = 1 if speed is 133mHz;

Hard Drive = 0 if hard drive is 2GB,
                   = 1 if hard drive is 3GB;

Memory   = 0 if memory is 32MG,
                   = 1 if memory is 64MG.

[c] Ranking of the product profiles.
[d] Column 6 reverses the scale of column 5, so that larger numbers reflect higher utility or preference—e.g., if rank is 8, utility is 1; if rank is 1, utility is 8. Note that although preference ranks are ordinal data, for illustrative purposes we assume that the scale of utility is interval scaled (you can obtain ratings instead of rankings to avoid this assumption).

We would next ask customers to rank or rate these combinations. Table 14.1 gives such a ranking for a hypothetical customer. Not surprisingly, this customer has the highest preference for a notebook with 133mHz speed, which comes with 3GB of hard drive and 64MB of memory, and has the lowest preference for the notebook with 100mHz speed, 2GB of hard drive, and 32MB of memory. It is the ranking of other combinations that reveals this customer's preference for various attributes. A casual inspection tells us that this customer attaches higher value to processing speed than to hard drive or memory. Conjoint analysis formalizes this intuition.

Uncovering Attribute Utilities from Overall Utility

Since utility for a product is assumed to be the sum of the utilities for its attributes, we can write:

$$U = a + b_1 \cdot \text{Processor} + b_2 \cdot \text{Hard drive} + b_3 \cdot \text{Memory} \qquad (14.1)$$

where Processor, Hard drive, and Memory are dummy variables (0, 1) as coded in Table 14.1, and b_1, b_2, and b_3 are the unknown utilities (also called part-worths) of each of the attributes. Using only product profiles 1 to 4, we have:

$$U_1 = a + b_1 \cdot 0 + b_2 \cdot 0 + b_3 \cdot 0 = a$$
$$U_2 = a + b_1 \cdot 1 + b_2 \cdot 0 + b_3 \cdot 0 = a + b_1$$
$$U_3 = a + b_1 \cdot 0 + b_2 \cdot 1 + b_3 \cdot 0 = a + b_2$$
$$U_4 = a + b_1 \cdot 0 + b_2 \cdot 0 + b_3 \cdot 1 = a + b_3$$

Therefore, knowing the utilities of products 1 to 4 and assuming that the ratings are accurate (i.e., they contain no error), we can calculate the values of a, b_1, b_2, and b_3:[2]

$$a = U_1 = 1$$
$$b_1 = U_2 - U_1 = 5 - 1 = 4$$
$$b_2 = U_3 - U_1 = 3 - 1 = 2$$
$$b_3 = U_4 - U_1 = 2 - 1 = 1$$

In practice, utilities for the attributes are derived by means of a computer algorithm. In general, dummy variable regression analysis is used.

Uses of Attribute Level Utilities

We can use these estimates in several ways. First, the estimates or part-worths tell us the relative value our customer attaches to different attributes. In this example, the customer values processing speed ($b_1 = 4$) more than hard drive capacity ($b_2 = 2$) or memory ($b_3 = 1$). In fact, for this customer higher processing speed is more important than an additional 1GB of hard drive and an additional 32MB of memory combined ($b_1 > b_2 + b_3$).

Second, we can use the part-worths to forecast the preferences of this customer for other notebook computers. Notice in our example we have used only the first four profiles to estimate the part-worths. To see how these part-worths predict the preferences of this customer for the last four profiles, we simply plug the appropriate dummy values in Equation (14.1) to get:

$$U_5 = a + b_1 \cdot 1 + b_2 \cdot 1 + b_3 \cdot 0 = 1 + 4 \cdot 1 + 2 \cdot 1 + 1 \cdot 0 = 7$$
$$U_6 = a + b_1 \cdot 0 + b_2 \cdot 1 + b_3 \cdot 1 = 1 + 4 \cdot 0 + 2 \cdot 1 + 1 \cdot 1 = 4$$
$$U_7 = a + b_1 \cdot 1 + b_2 \cdot 0 + b_3 \cdot 1 = 1 + 4 \cdot 1 + 2 \cdot 0 + 1 \cdot 1 = 6$$
$$U_8 = a + b_1 \cdot 1 + b_2 \cdot 1 + b_3 \cdot 1 = 1 + 4 \cdot 1 + 2 \cdot 1 + 1 \cdot 1 = 8$$

These predicted values are similar to the actual utilities of 6, 4, 7, and 8, respectively, given by the customer (which, since we made up the numbers, is not surprising).

Third, we can simulate the impact of new product introductions. Consider a market with two existing brands A and B with the attributes as given in Table 14.2. Using the

---

[2]For now, we are ignoring two aspects: (*a*) the number of observations should be greater than number of parameters, and (*b*) the utilities are measured, and hence the parameters are estimated, with some error (as in a regression model).

TABLE 14.2 Existing and New Brands

Brand	Processor	Hard Drive	Memory
A	1	0	1
B	1	1	0
New	0	1	1

dummy coding from Table 14.1, brand A has a 133mHz processor (Processor = 1), with 2GB of hard drive (Hard drive = 0) and 64MB of memory (Memory = 1). Brand B has a 133mHz processor with 3GB of hard drive, but only 32MB of memory. Let us assume that a company wants to introduce a new notebook with 100mHz speed, 3GB of hard drive, and 64MB of memory. A critical question to assess is what share can the new brand obtain and where (i.e., which competing brands) will this share come from?

To address this question, you could first obtain ranking or ratings for different product profiles from a sample of customers. Next, using the approach described earlier, you obtain the part-worths (a's and the b's) for various attributes for each customer separately. Table 14.3 presents the attribute utilities of 10 customers. From these, you can estimate the overall brand utilities (from Equation (14.1)) that each customer will assign to the existing brands (A and B), and your new brand. Assuming that each customer chooses the brand that provides the maximum utility, you can then forecast customers' brand choice with and without the introduction of the new brand. For our hypothetical market, Table 14.3 presents these estimates. The results show that before the introduction of the new brand, the market shares of the two brands are expected to be $A = 0.4$, and $B = 0.6$. When the new brand is introduced, the market shares are expected to be $A = 0.2$, $B = 0.5$, and New = 0.3. In other words, the new brand is expected to draw 20 percent share from brand A and 10 percent from brand B.

Using the attribute utilities, we can assess the relative importance of each attribute as:

$$\text{Relative importance of an attribute} = \frac{\text{Utility range of that attribute}}{\text{Sum of the utility ranges for all attributes}}$$

TABLE 14.3 Ratings of 10 Customers

| Customer | Attribute Utilities | | | | Brand Utilities[a] | | | Brand Choice | |
	a	b_1	b_2	b_3	A	B	New	w/o New Brand	with New Brand
1	1	2	4	1	4	7	6	B	B
2	0	5	1	2	7	6	3	A	A
3	2	2	3	1	5	7	6	B	B
4	1	0	3	4	5	4	8	A	New
5	0	2	1	5	7	3	6	A	A
6	1	6	1	0	7	8	2	B	B
7	0	1	3	4	5	4	7	A	New
8	1	2	5	0	3	8	6	B	B
9	1	0	6	1	2	6	8	B	New
10	2	4	2	0	6	8	4	B	B

[a] $U = a + b_1 \times \text{Processor} + b_2 \times \text{Hard Drive} + b_3 \times \text{Memory}$.

TABLE 14.4 Relative Importance of Attributes

Customer	Relative Importance of		
	Processor	Hard Drive	Memory
1	29%	57%	14%
2	63	12	25
3	33	50	17
4	0	43	57
5	25	12	63
6	86	14	0
7	13	37	50
8	29	71	0
9	0	86	14
10	67	33	0

For example, relative importance of processing speed for a customer is $b_1/(b_1 + b_2 + b_3) = 4/7$. The relative importances are given in Table 14.4.

We can also group customers with similar importance weights to form benefit segments. For example, Table 14.4 shows that customers 1, 3, and to some extent customer 8, have similar preferences. Customers 6, 10, and to a lesser extent customer 2, can also be grouped together. Customers 4 and 7 form a third group, and customer 9 stands alone in his/her preferences. Methods for grouping customers are discussed in detail in Chapter 15. The point here is that part-worths (utilities) and relative importances derived from them provide a basis for creating benefit segments.

DISJOINT ANALYSIS

Conjoint analysis essentially decomposes ratings data to find the utility (part-worth) values. An alternative approach is to ask subjects to directly rate importances or part-worths one attribute at a time. For example, we could get constant sum scale ratings for the three notebook attributes:

Processing Speed	100 mHz	_____
	133 mHz	_____
		100
Hard Drive	2GB	_____
	3GB	_____
		100
Memory	32MB	_____
	64MB	_____
		100

and also get ratings on the relative importances of the attributes on either, say, a 10-point importance scale or a constant sum scale. Such ratings have appeal (Akaah and Korgaonkar, 1983) and are useful for clustering subjects with similar preferences (Green, Carroll, and Goldberg, 1981). Unfortunately, they are not likely to work well for some attributes (e.g., price, where the low price will tend to get all 100 points), and hence trade-off questions are still needed. Still, *self-explicated* weights have been combined with conjoint results in an attempt to get better estimates of the part-worths (Cattin, Gelfan, and Danes, 1983; Green, Goldberg, and Montemayor, 1981).

STEPS IN CONJOINT ANALYSIS

In this section, we provide a more thorough discussion of the steps to follow in doing a conjoint analysis study.

1. Determine Attributes and Attribute Levels

The first task in conjoint analysis is to identify the attributes of a product or service that customers consider in making their choices. If one is not sure what the relevant attributes are, methods such as focus group or pilot studies may be necessary to ensure that no important aspects are ignored. Once the attributes are determined, we must decide which levels of the attributes to study. In our previous example, all attributes were at two levels (e.g., 100mHz or 133mHz processor). Attribute levels should be chosen to cover a range similar to that actually observed in the marketplace. The more levels an attribute has, the more complex the design but also the better the accuracy of the estimates and the more chance to detect nonlinear relations between attribute level and utility. Thus, a complexity versus accuracy trade-off guides the selection of attribute levels. In practice, most attributes are presented at two to four levels.

2. Select Attribute Profiles to Be Measured

The actual combinations of attributes to be given to respondents must be selected. There are two broad options. We can choose a *full factorial* design, which effectively gives us all possible combinations of various attributes at different levels. In our example, we had two levels of three attributes, giving $2^3 = 8$ possible combinations; thus, it was feasible to use a full factorial design. However, in most realistic applications there are many more attributes at many more levels. If we wish to study seven attributes at three levels each, we will have $3^7 = 2,187$ possible combinations. Clearly, it is not feasible to ask a respondent to rate these 2,187 profiles or combinations. One way to reduce the number of combinations is to use a *fractional factorial* design. This approach chooses a "fraction" of all possible combinations in some specific way. One common approach is to use *orthogonal* designs with the assumption that there are no interactions between attributes. For example, if we believe that the processor speed does not have any synergistic effect with hard drive capacity, then it may be reasonable to ignore any interaction between them. If we use an orthogonal design for the seven attributes at three levels each, we could use as few as 18 combinations (a.k.a. profiles) to get part-worths. An excellent source of how to choose these fractional factorial designs (e.g., how to choose 18 profiles out of a total possible of 2,187) is provided by Addleman (1962). Table 14.5 reproduces a few of these orthogonal designs.

It is common to add to the orthogonal design a few particularly interesting combinations (e.g., the ones the boss favors or ones that allow the estimation of interactions). It also makes sense to remove from the design combinations that make little sense (e.g., 200 percent increase in output at no additional cost) and hence could lead respondents to take the study less seriously. Put differently, an orthogonal design is statistically efficient and thus is a good starting point but not necessarily a requirement for the design phase.

3. Choose a Method for Stimulus Representation

The next task is to choose which way these combinations or stimuli are presented to respondents. The options include verbal description, pictures, multimedia presentations, and actual products or prototypes. Clearly, the more realistic the stimulus, the better the quality of data gathered. Also, the attributes should be described in customer- rather than engineer-oriented language. This is especially true for new products where advanced features may not convey benefits to potential customers.

TABLE 14.5 Some Orthogonal Designs

BASIC PLAN 7:3^7; 2^7; 18 trials		BASIC PLAN 8:2^{19}; 20 trials			
1234567	1234567	00000 12345	00001 67890	11111 12345	1111 6789
0000000	0000000	00000	00000	00000	0000
0112111	0110111	11001	11101	01000	0110
0221222	0001000	01100	11110	10100	0011
1011120	1011100	10110	01111	01010	0001
1120201	1100001	11011	00111	10101	0000
1202012	1000010	01101	10011	11010	1000
2022102	0000100	00110	11001	11101	0100
2101210	0101010	00011	01100	11110	1010
2210021	0010001	00001	10110	01111	0101
0021011	0001011	10000	11011	00111	1010
0100122	0100100	01000	01101	10011	1101
0212200	0010000	10100	00110	11001	1110
1002221	1000001	01010	00011	01100	1111
1111002	1111000	10101	00001	10110	0111
1220110	1000110	11010	10000	11011	0011
2010212	0010010	11101	01000	01101	1001
2122020	0100000	11110	10100	00110	1100
2201101	0001101	01111	01010	00011	0110
		00111	10101	00001	1011
		10011	11010	10000	1101

Source: Sidney Addleman, "Orthogonal Main-Effect Plans for Asymmetrical Factorial Experiments," *Technometrics* 4 (February 1962), pp. 21–46.

4. Select a Response Method and Collect Data

The options here include asking respondents to:

a. Rank the products in order of their preference.

b. Rate product profiles. These ratings could be on a like–dislike scale, a purchase intention scale (e.g., 1–5), or a purchase probability scale (e.g., 0–100).

c. Conduct pairwise comparisons, where two product profiles are given at a time and respondents are asked to choose one of them or rate their relative preference for the two products (Johnson, 1974).

d. Choose a product from a set of product profiles (this is the approach used in choice-based conjoint; see Louviere and Woodworth, 1983).

The choice of response type depends on the ease of response for the customers and the analysis approach the researcher wishes to employ. Still product profiles (*b*) seem to be both the most popular and a reasonable approach.

It is possible to use computer-aided interviewing for conjoint analysis, which allows for instant data coding and reduces missing data, and this is a common approach in many new product concept testing studies (e.g., Design Lab). Notice also that part-worths can be computed after data are partially gathered, and the design can be altered so that respondents make judgments or trade-offs where part-worths are least certain.

5. Choose a Method of Data Analysis

The most common approach for analyzing ratings data is dummy variable regression (see Appendix 14-A). Other approaches are monotone regression (for rank order data) and logit models (for choice data). It is also possible to estimate the part-worths by mathematical programming (cf. LINMAP—Srinivasan and Shocker, 1973). As suggested earlier, we recommend dummy variable regression, partly because you can perform it on a spreadsheet program.

The major decision in the analysis phase involves the level of aggregation. Moore (1980) found that treating all subjects as having the same part-worths greatly reduced both predictive power (R^2) and interpretability. In general, different individuals have different part-worths. Analyzing each person separately is inefficient in terms of both analysis and interpretation (how does one summarize 1,127 conjoint analyses?). Consequently, segmentation is typically performed by clustering respondents together (cf. Hagerty, 1985). This can be done based on (*a*) other characteristics (e.g., income) or (*b*) attribute importances either as measured by self-ratings or derived from conjoint analysis. The results are then derived for each of the segments.

6. Analyze the Data

Data analysis typically involves the following:

a. Where feasible, for each respondent estimate utilities for each attribute level. Our previous example illustrated this idea.

b. Create benefit segments by grouping customers based on their part-worth utilities. (If individual-level analysis is not feasible, then segments are often formed on a priori bases such as age, income, etc.)

c. See if there are demographic differences among the benefit segments (or differences in benefit valuation over demographic segments).

d. Determine the relative importance of each attribute for each segment. Again, assume that the utility ranges (i.e., maximum utility (for some level) of an attribute minus the minimum utility (for another level) of the same attribute) for each of three attributes are 5, 3, and 2, respectively. Then the relative importance of the first attribute is 5/(5 + 3 + 2) or 50 percent, the second attribute 30 percent, and the third attribute 20 percent. Note that the relative importance of an attribute depends both on the range of the levels used in the analysis and the number of levels used to divide up that range (Wittink, Krishnamurthi, and Reibstein, 1990). For example, a study that uses price in the range $10–$100 will find price to be more important than will an otherwise identical study that uses price in the range $10–$20. In spite of this caveat, the relative importance of attributes can be very helpful in product design (suggesting which attributes to focus on) as well as in product positioning (identifying which attributes to highlight).

7. Use the Results

Market simulation can provide share estimates for new concepts, and it can also assess the sources (i.e., competitive brands) of this share. The latter helps in anticipating competitive reactions. Comparing the utilities within and across attributes helps identify particularly important attributes and desirable levels, which in turn affect advertising and product development.

EXAMPLES

Household Cleaner

A classic example (Green and Wind, 1975) involves preference for spot removers for upholstery and carpets. The following attributes were analyzed:

> Package design (A, B, C)
> Brand names (K2R, Glory, Bissell)
> Price ($1.19, $1.39, $1.59)
> Good Housekeeping seal (yes or no)
> Money-back guarantee (yes or no)

Since there are $3 \times 3 \times 3 \times 2 \times 2 = 108$ possible combinations, it seemed infeasible to test all possible products. Hence, an orthogonal array of 18 combinations was used (translation: a representative subset of the original 108 products was selected). The design used in the cleaner example comes from columns 1, 2, and 3 for the three-level attributes and columns 4 and 5 for the two-level attributes in Basic Plan 7 in Table 14.5.

The data from one subject appear in Table 14.6. The resulting utilities appear in Table 14.7 (see Appendix 14-A for details).

The design values are converted into product attribute levels as follows:

	Design Value	Product Attribute Level
Three-level Attributes	Column 1 = 0	Package design = A
	= 1	= B
	= 2	= C
	Column 2 = 0	Brand name = K2R
	= 1	= Glory
	= 2	= Bissell
	Column 3 = 0	Price = 1.19
	= 1	= 1.39
	= 2	= 1.59
Two-level Attributes	Column 4 = 0	Seal = No
	= 1	= Yes
	Column 5 = 0	Guarantee = No
	= 1	= Yes

TABLE 14.6 Data Collected

Product					Respondent's Evaluation (ranking)
Package Design	Brand Name	Price	Good Housekeeping Seal?	Money-Back Guarantee?	
A	K2R	1.19	No	No	13
A	Glory	1.39	No	Yes	11
A	Bissell	1.59	Yes	No	17
B	K2R	1.39	Yes	Yes	2
B	Glory	1.59	No	No	14
B	Bissell	1.19	No	No	3
C	K2R	1.59	No	Yes	12
C	Glory	1.19	Yes	No	7
C	Bissell	1.39	No	No	9
A	K2R	1.59	Yes	No	18
A	Glory	1.19	No	Yes	8
A	Bissell	1.39	No	No	15
B	K2R	1.19	No	No	4
B	Glory	1.39	Yes	No	6
B	Bissell	1.59	No	Yes	5
C	K2R	1.39	No	No	10
C	Glory	1.59	No	No	16
C	Bissell	1.19	Yes	Yes	1

Source: Paul Green and Yoram Wind, "New Way to Measure Consumers' Judgments," *Harvard Business Review* 53 (July–August 1975), p. 108. Copyright ©1975 by the President and Fellows of Harvard College; all rights reserved.

TABLE 14.7 Utilities for Spot Remover Attributes

Feature	Utility
Package design:	
A	.1
B	1.0
C	.6
Brand name:	
K2R	.3
Glory	.2
Bissell	.5
Price:	
1.19	1.0
1.39	.7
1.59	.1
Good Housekeeping seal:	
Yes	.3
No	.2
Money-back guarantee:	
Yes	.7
No	.2

Source: Paul Green and Yoram Wind, "New Way to Measure Consumers' Judgments," *Harvard Business Review* 53 (July–August, 1975), p. 110. Copyright ©1975 by the President and Fellows of Harvard College; all rights reserved.

The results indicate a strong preference for package design B and a low price (surprise) as shown in Figure 14.1. A money-back guarantee also seems to help, while the brand name and Good Housekeeping seal seem to be relatively unimportant.

Rechargeable Batteries

To protect the confidentiality of the company involved, certain information (e.g., company name, product category, and attributes) are disguised.

Problem Castle Batteries is one of the largest manufacturers of batteries with worldwide operations. Fast growth of the computer industry prompted the company to consider entering the market for portable computer batteries in the early 1990s. The market segment was dominated by three existing players. The problem facing management was to select the best product to introduce and the appropriate price to charge. The company also had to decide if it should introduce different products in the United States and Europe.

First Steps Using its own knowledge of the market as well as focus groups, management decided that six attributes (including price) were important to customers. These six attributes and their levels that management decided to test are

Brand name: A, B, C, D. Branding is very critical in this market. Castle Batteries had a very strong brand name, although in a related market, and

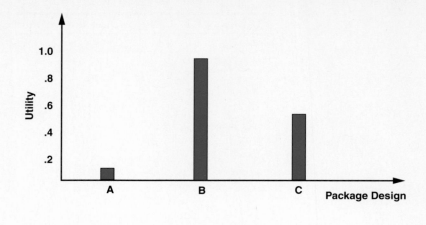

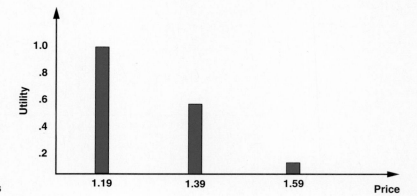

FIGURE 14.1
Cleaner Attribute Utilities

management wanted to see if the company could command a price premium. The three existing brands were labeled B, C, D, and the new product to be introduced by Castle Batteries labeled A.

Price: Current price, 25% higher, 50% higher. Management made a strategic decision to produce premium products. However, it wished to find what market shares it could expect with different price points.

Built-in charge meter: No, Yes. The purpose of this product feature was to have an easy way for customers to find how many hours of battery life are left before it needs recharging. Clearly adding this feature would enhance the appeal of the product, but it was not clear whether it was worth the cost, or what price premium customers were willing to pay for such a feature.

Environmental safety: No, Yes. With the increasing concern for the environment, the company was contemplating adding environmental safety features. Once again, the cost/benefit trade-off was the issue.

Rapid recharge: No, Yes. Another feature that could be provided to customers was an ability to rapidly recharge the batteries. With the frequent use of computer batteries, this feature could be potentially useful to many customers.

TABLE 14.8 Part-Worth Estimates

Attributes	Part-Worth Estimates			
	Aggregate	Segment 1	Segment 2	Segment 3
Brand B	0.37	1.15	− 0.28	− 0.44
Brand C	− 0.31	1.18	− 0.10	− 0.51
Brand D	0.97	2.13	0.25	− 0.01
Price + 25%	− 2.52	− 2.08	− 4.85	− 1.40
Price + 50%	− 5.42	− 4.29	− 7.20	− 2.63
Built-in meter	1.52	1.11	0.69	1.37
Envir. safety	1.53	1.10	0.78	1.24
Rapid charge	1.20	1.23	0.47	1.06
Longer life	2.04	1.53	1.11	2.15
Segment size	100.0%	22.2%	29.4%	48.3%

50% Longer life: No, Yes. Replacing old batteries is not only expensive, but also inconvenient. An extra long life could therefore be potentially valuable to customers.

Clearly, the more features a product has, the more desirable it would be. However, these features come at a cost to the customers. The key issue, therefore, was to find the trade-offs that customers were likely to make when buying this product. For example, were customers willing to pay a 50 percent higher price for a battery with the features of rapid recharge and 50 percent longer life? Are these features more valuable to customers than the built-in charge meter and environmental safety? What market shares could the company expect for various combinations of product features? Given this information and its own cost structure, the company could then conduct a profit analysis and select the best option.

Study Design With six attributes at the levels shown above, it is possible to generate 192 combinations or product profiles. Due to the large number of combinations, a fractional factorial design was used. An orthogonal design that captures the main effects needs only 16 profiles. However, the company used 32 profiles to test some interactions and also conduct validation tests. A random sample of 400 customers was selected, half of them from the United States and the other half from Europe. Each customer was asked a set of questions (including qualifying questions, demographics, etc.) and asked to rate these 32 profiles on a 0–100 probability of buying scale. The data were then used for conjoint analysis.

Analysis Two types of analyses were conducted—aggregate and disaggregate. Aggregate analysis assumes all customers have the same preferences and may be useful to provide an overall picture. Results for the aggregate analysis from a simple regression are given in Table 14.8. The following insights emerge from these results:

a. On average, customers preferred brands B and D to Castle Company's brand A.
b. Customers' preference declined almost linearly with price increases of 25% and 50%.

   c. Customers evaluated all product features (built-in meter, environmental safety, rapid recharge, long life) similarly, with longer life preferred slightly.

   d. Customers were willing to pay an additional 25% in price for two additional product features. For example, additional utility from the built-in meter and rapid recharge would be 1.52 + 1.20 = 2.72, which is approximately the same as disutility of 2.52 from an increase of 25% in price.

Disaggregate analysis provides more in-depth understanding of customer purchase behavior. This involves estimation of part-worths for each individual, and grouping or clustering individuals into segments based on their part-worths. Three groups were identified based on cluster analysis (see Chapter 15 for details of this method). The mean part-worths for each of these three groups are also reported in Table 14.8. Comparing these means across groups, we note that group 2 (29.4% in size) was the most price-sensitive group and cared the least about additional product features, while group 3 (48.3% in size) was the least price-sensitive and placed heavy importance on long battery life.

Further analysis (not presented here) was conducted to identify the demographics of these groups. This allows for efficient targeting by media and direct-marketing methods.

The next step was to conduct market simulation to assess the market share of various product designs. Table 14.9 presents the attribute composition of the three existing brands B, C, and D, as well as two product designs (A1 and A2) that Castle Company was considering. Aggregate market simulation results (Table 14.10) suggested that without the introduction of Castle Company brands, the expected shares of brands B, C, and D in a three-brand market would be 52.3, 30.6, and 17.1 percent, respectively. If brand A1 were introduced, it would get a share of 3.7 percent, whereas brand A2 would draw a share of 16.9 percent. This can be further broken down by the three segments.

TABLE 14.9 Current and Proposed Battery Products

| | Brands | | | | |
Attributes	B	C	D	A1	A2
Price	Low	Low	Med	Med	High
Built-in meter	No	Yes	Yes	No	Yes
Envir. safety	Yes	No	No	Yes	Yes
Rapid recharge	No	Yes	No	No	Yes
Long life	Yes	No	Yes	Yes	Yes

TABLE 14.10 Simulated Battery Shares

| | | Aggregate Results | | Results for A2 by Segment | | |
Brands	Current	With A1	With A2	Seg. 1	Seg. 2	Seg. 3
A	—	3.7%	16.9%	0.1%	0.1%	34.9%
B	52.3%	50.0	45.7	50.0	60.3	34.9
C	30.6	30.1	26.0	30.0	39.7	16.0
D	17.1	16.2	11.4	20.0	0.1	14.2

This segment-level analysis shows that almost all the share for brand A2 would come from the third (the least price-sensitive) segment. These results were combined with the cost information to arrive at profit estimates and the selection of the appropriate design. (The interested reader should be able to guess whether the larger selling, higher-priced model A2 was selected over the lower-priced, lower selling model A1).

ACTUAL USE OF CONJOINT

Conjoint analysis has been widely used in market research in all fields: consumer, industrial, services, and so forth (Green and Srinivasan, 1978; Page and Rosenbaum, 1987). Studies of commercial use (Cattin and Wittink, 1982; Wittink and Cattin, 1989) have produced the following highlights:

1. The most common purposes were new product/concept identification (47 percent), competitive analysis (40 percent), and pricing (38 percent).
2. Most studies used the full-profile approach, as opposed to trading off two attributes at a time.
3. Verbal descriptions of the alternatives and paragraphs account for 70 percent of the applications, with less than 10 percent using actual products.
4. Subjects are asked for preference (41 percent) or intention to buy (39 percent) most often.
5. Rating scales are used more often than rankings (49 versus 36 percent).
6. Regression/ANOVA or logit are the most common approaches to analysis.
7. A typical study uses a sample of about 300.

PROS AND CONS

The advantages of conjoint measurement include the following:

1. The data explicitly require respondents to consider trade-offs on attributes.
2. The results are easy to interpret, and the key attributes readily established.
3. The attributes can be categorical (e.g., colors, styles) as well as intervally scaled constructs.

The major disadvantages are:

1. *The relevant attributes and key levels must be known in advance.* This means not just the physical attributes that are important to engineers, but also the attributes customers actually use to make decisions need to be specified. Choosing the correct levels may seem trivial, but one author encountered a study involving prices of 5, 7, and 9 when the actual price tended to be less than 2. This cast serious doubt on the interpretation of the whole study. Also, the attributes should probably be objective rather than subjective (e.g., horsepower rather than power) whenever possible, since they directly link to product design. Unfortunately, objective attributes may be interpretable only by experts and for mature products. In such situations, "soft" attributes are needed and a separate analysis is required to link engineering characteristics to customer benefits.

2. *The additive utility function may not be appropriate.* At least for objects of art, one could question whether the "whole is the sum of its parts."

3. *The approach gets messy with many attributes and levels.* Since the alternatives are essentially factorial combinations of the attributes, the number of possible alternatives quickly gets out of hand. This has led researchers like Green to use orthogonal subsets of the possible alternatives (Green, 1974). As long as there is no complex interaction effect, this approach works quite well. Also, it appears that respondents may focus on one or two key attributes as a means of completing the task when more attributes are actually important (Huber, 1987).

4. *Market share estimates obtained from conjoint analysis differ from actual shares* due to marketing activities such as advertising and distribution, which affect awareness and availability. Appropriate adjustments are therefore needed to account for the effect of these marketing actions.

CHOICE-BASED CONJOINT

Traditional conjoint analysis consists of pairwise comparisons, rankings, or ratings of product profiles. In choice-based conjoint, proposed by Louviere and Woodworth (1983), a set of products are offered to customers, who are asked to choose one product out of this set. This task is repeated several times with a different set of product alternatives each time. The choice set and its composition are determined according to a fractional factorial design. The analysis is often done using logit (see Chapter 19).

Choice-based conjoint is used in both fixed and variable choice set scenarios. Fixed choice set scenarios use a constant choice set size (e.g., consumer always chooses among five alternatives), but change one or more attributes of a fixed number of alternatives. A variable choice set allows for the number of alternatives to vary (e.g., consumer may be faced with a choice among three, four, or five products).

We illustrate a fixed choice set study for vacation destination choice.[3] The purpose of this study was to understand the choice of vacation destinations as a function of destination and air travel costs. Five destinations and three destination-specific air travel costs were selected for the study:

New Zealand	$200	$350	$400
Japan	$600	$850	$1,100
U.K.	$1,600	$2,000	$2,400
U.S. (West Coast)	$1,650	$1,800	$2,150
Italy	$1,200	$1,500	$1,800

These alternatives and price levels form a 3^5 factorial design. An orthogonal main effects fractional factorial design from these can be selected to create 18 choice sets based on Table 14.5. Table 14.11 provides an illustration of the selected choice sets. For example, choice set 1 offered consumers a choice among New Zealand for $200, Japan for $600, the U.K. for $1,600, the United States for $1,450, and Italy for $1,200. Each

---

[3] This example is adapted from Louviere and Woodworth (1983).

TABLE 14.11 Fractional Design for Fixed Choice Set Study

Choice Set Composition

Choice Set	NZ	Japan	UK	U.S.	Italy
1	$200	$ 600	$1,600	$1,450	$1,200
2	200	850	2,000	2,150	1,500
3	200	1,100	2,400	1,800	1,800
4	350	600	2,000	1,800	1,500
5	350	850	2,400	1,450	1,800
6	350	1,100	1,600	2,150	1,200
7	400	600	2,400	2,150	1,500
8	400	850	1,600	1,800	1,800
9	400	1,100	2,000	1,450	1,200
10	200	600	2,400	1,800	1,200
11	200	850	1,600	1,450	1,500
12	200	1,100	2,000	2,150	1,800
13	350	600	1,600	2,150	1,800
14	350	1,100	2,400	1,450	1,500
15	350	1,100	2,400	1,450	1,500
16	400	600	2,000	1,450	1,800
17	400	850	2,400	2,150	1,200
18	400	1,100	1,600	1,800	1,500

choice set also included an "other/none" option, which provided a base against which all alternatives were evaluated. Consumers were asked to choose one of the five alternatives or another/none option for each of the 18 choice sets.

Information from all consumers was aggregated, and data were analyzed by a logit model. The results indicated the following price coefficients:

New Zealand	− .003
Japan	− .002
U.K.	− .0005
U.S.	− .0005
Italy	− .0009

This suggests that respondents were more sensitive to airfare costs to New Zealand and Japan than to the costs to other destinations. (Since New Zealand and Japan have the lowest mean airfare, perhaps there is a pattern here.) It is possible to use this analysis for strategic pricing decisions by predicting changes in market share resulting from changes in airfares. That is, a country/airline could estimate the difference in shares for current and alternative fares.

This approach has two key advantages. First, compared with the rating or ranking of products (the approach used in traditional conjoint), it is often easier and more realistic for customers to choose one product out of a set of product offerings. Second, choice-based conjoint experiments also typically include a no-choice option, which permits the modeling of consideration sets (an item being selected only if its utility exceeds the utility of not choosing any item from the set). The major limitation of this approach is that, unlike traditional conjoint, the analysis cannot be conducted at an individual level (primarily arising from a limited number of observations per person), thus precluding individual-level or segment-level insights. Some recent advances (e.g., latent class analysis—discussed next) have attenuated this limitation.

RECENT ADVANCES IN CONJOINT ANALYSIS

Latent Class Analysis

Latent class analysis creates segments such that customers in a segment have the same responses or utility. For example, price-sensitive customers could form one segment. In traditional conjoint analysis, these groups are formed by first conducting the analysis at the individual level, and then grouping (e.g. through cluster analysis) customers into homogeneous segments. However, if choice-based conjoint is used, it is difficult to conduct an individual-level analysis. Latent class analysis uses an iterative process where (*a*) customers are initially assigned to a group (e.g. price-sensitive), (*b*) the group- or segment-level utilities are estimated, and (*c*) based on the actual purchase behavior of each customer, he or she is reassigned to the same or the other groups (e.g., if a person frequently chooses a brand with high price, then it tells us that this person is not likely to be price sensitive, in which case he or she will be reassigned to the price-insensitive group). This process is repeated until it converges. Details of this methodology can be found in DeSarbo, Ramaswamy, and Cohen (1995).

Consideration Sets in Conjoint Analysis

Traditional conjoint assumes that customers consider all the product profiles presented to them. In most consumer and industrial settings, this is a bad assumption. For example, consumers do not consider all models of cars before making their final choice. Similarly, industrial buyers screen suppliers on many factors before doing any kind of "trade-off" in their minds. This has been incorporated in conjoint analysis in the following ways.

- Several commercially available software packages (e.g., ACA or adaptive conjoint analysis) ask *screening questions* before presenting product profiles to customers. For example, in the case of a car purchase, respondents may answer screening questions about the price range of the car they are looking for, whether they want to consider only a sedan or a sports car, and so on. The profiles are then designed within these parameters.
- A second approach, used by choice-based conjoint analysis, is to offer respondents a *no-choice option*. As we have discussed, this option permits consumers to not buy any product unless it meets their minimum requirement (e.g., car price is below the threshold).
- A third approach, recently proposed by Jedidi, Kohli, and DeSarbo (1996), uses sophisticated models to uncover consumer *thresholds for considering products*. Essentially, this approach suggests that even if ratings are obtained only on products considered by consumers, the alternatives not considered provide useful

information about each consumer's threshold on various attributes. A model is then used to uncover these thresholds.

SUMMARY

Conjoint analysis is useful in assessing the values consumers place on various attributes of a product. It is based on the premise that a product is a bundle of attributes and consumers make trade-offs among these attributes in their choice of a product. Using the rating or ranking for overall product profiles, conjoint uncovers the value that consumers implicitly place on these attributes. This in turn can help in pricing, designing products, creating benefit segments, and forecasting market shares of new products.

PROBLEMS

1. Assume you had to design the data collection instrument to do conjoint analysis in a situation where there were two attributes, both with three levels. What would the instrument be?

2. Assume you were to analyze the results of a conjoint analysis on a single subject (the chief executive officer) for type of desk preferred. Two attributes were employed: size (regular, massive) and material (plastic, metal, wood). The six combinations were as follows:

	Size	Material
A	Regular	Plastic
B	Regular	Metal
C	Regular	Wood
D	Massive	Plastic
E	Massive	Metal
F	Massive	Wood

The data were ranked by your boss from most to least preferred, as F, E, C, B, D, A. Try to deduce the boss's utility function.

3. Assume you were to design a conjoint study on home stereo systems. How would you proceed?

REFERENCES

ACITO, FRANKLIN, AND ARUN K. JAIN (1980) "Evaluation of Conjoint Analysis Results: A Comparison of Methods," *Journal of Marketing Research*, 17, February, 106–12.

ADDLEMAN, SIDNEY (1962) "Orthogonal Main-Effect Plans for Asymmetrical Factorial Experiments," *Technometrics*, 4, February, 21–46.

AKAAH, ISHMAEL P., AND PRADEEP K. KORGAONKAR (1983) "An Empirical Comparison of the Predictive Validity of Self-Explicated, Huber-Hybrid, Traditional Conjoint, and Hybrid Conjoint Models," *Journal of Marketing Research*, 20, May, 187–97.

CARROLL, J. DOUGLAS, AND JIH-JIE CHANG (1970) "Analysis of Individual Differences in Multidimensional Scaling Via an N-Way Generalization of 'Eckart-Young' Decomposition," *Psychometrika*, 35, January, 283–320.

CARROLL, J. DOUGLAS, PAUL E. GREEN, AND CATHERINE M. SCHAFFER (1986) "Interpoint Distance Comparisons in Correspondence Analysis," *Journal of Marketing Research*, 23, August, 271–80.

CATTIN, PHILIPPE, ALAN E. GELFAN, AND JEFFREY DANES (1983) "A Simple Bayesian Procedure for Estimation in a Conjoint Model," *Journal of Marketing Research*, 20, February, 29–35.

CATTIN, PHILIPPE, AND DICK R. WITTINK (1982) "Commercial Use of Conjoint Analysis: A Survey," *Journal of Marketing*, 46, Summer, 44–53.

DESARBO, WAYNE S., VENKATRAM RAMASWAMY, AND STEVEN COHEN (1995) "Marketing Segmentation with Choice-Based Conjoint Analysis," *Marketing Letters*, 6, April, 137–48.

GREEN, PAUL E. (1973) "On the Analysis of Interactions in Marketing Research Data," *Journal of Marketing Research*, 10, November, 410–20.

——— (1974) "On the Design of Choice Experiments Involving Multifactor Alternatives," *Journal of Consumer Research*, 1, September, 61–68.

GREEN, PAUL E., J. DOUGLAS CARROLL, AND STEPHEN M. GOLDBERG (1981) "A General Approach to Product Design Optimization via Conjoint Analysis," *Journal of Marketing*, 45, Summer, 17–37.

GREEN, PAUL E., STEPHEN M. GOLDBERG, AND MILA MONTEMAYOR (1981) "A Hybrid Utility Estimation Model for Conjoint Analysis," *Journal of Marketing*, 45, Winter, 33–41.

GREEN, PAUL E., ABBA M. KRIEGER, AND MANOJ K. AGARWAL (1991) "Adaptive Conjoint Analysis: Some Caveats and Suggestions," *Journal of Marketing Research*, 28, May, 215–22.

GREEN, PAUL E., AND V. SRINIVASAN (1978) "Conjoint Analysis in Consumer Research: Issues and Outlook," *Journal of Consumer Research*, 5, September, 103–23.

——— (1990) "Conjoint Analysis in Marketing: New Developments with Implications for Research and Practice," *Journal of Marketing*, 54, October, 3–19.

GREEN, PAUL E., AND YORAM WIND (1975) "New Way to Measure Consumers' Judgments," *Harvard Business Review*, 53, July–August, 107–17.

GROVER, RAJIV, AND V. SRINIVASAN (1987) "A Simultaneous Approach to Market Segmentation and Market Structuring," *Journal of Marketing Research*, 24, May, 139–53.

HAGERTY, MICHAEL R. (1985) "Improving the Predictive Power of Conjoint Analysis: The Use of Factor Analysis and Cluster Analysis," *Journal of Marketing Research*, 22, May, 168–84.

HUBER, JOEL (1987) "Conjoint Analysis: How We Got Here and Where We Are," *Proceedings of the Sawtooth Software Conference on Perceptual Mapping, Conjoint Analysis, and Computer Interviewing*, 237–52.

HUBER, JOEL, DICK R. WITTINK, JOHN A. FIEDLER, AND RICHARD MILLER (1993) "The Effectiveness of Alternative Preference Elicitation Procedures in Predicting Choice," *Journal of Marketing Research*, 30, February, 105–14.

JEDIDI, KAMEL, RAJEEV KOHLI, AND WAYNE S. DESARBO (1996) "Consideration Sets in Conjoint Analysis," *Journal of Marketing Research*, 33, August, 364–72.

JOHNSON, RICHARD M. (1974) "Trade-off Analysis of Consumer Durables," *Journal of Marketing Research*, 11, May, 121–27.

KALISH, SHLOMO, AND PAUL NELSON (1991) "A Comparison of Ranking, Rating and Reservation Price Measurement in Conjoint Analysis," *Marketing Letters*, 2, November, 327–35.

LOUVIERE, JORDAN J., AND GEORGE WOODWORTH (1983) "Design and Analysis of Simulated Consumer Choice on Allocation Experiments: An Approach Based on Aggregate Data," *Journal of Marketing Research*, 20, November, 350–67.

MEHTA, RAJ, WILLIAM L. MOORE, AND TERESA M. PAVIA (1992) "An Examination of the Use of Unacceptable Levels in Conjoint Analysis," *Journal of Consumer Research*, 19, December, 470–76.

MOORE, WILLIAM L. (1980) "Levels of Aggregation in Conjoint Analysis: An Empirical Comparison," *Journal of Marketing Research*, 17, November, 516–23.

OPPEWAL, HARMEN, JORDAN J. LOUVIERE, AND HARRY J. P. TIMMERMANS (1994) "Modeling Hierarchical Conjoint Processes with Integrated Choice Experiments," *Journal of Marketing Research*, 31, February, 92–105.

PAGE, ALBERT L., AND HAROLD F. ROSENBAUM (1987) "Redesigning Product Lines with Conjoint Analysis: How Sunbeam Does It," *Journal of Product Innovation Management*, 4, 120–37.

SRINIVASAN, V., ARUN K. JAIN, AND NARESH K. MALHOTRA (1983) "Improving Predictive Power of Conjoint Analysis by Constrained Parameter Estimation," *Journal of Marketing Research*, 20, November, 433–38.

SRINIVASAN, V., AND A. D. SHOCKER (1973) "Linear Programming Techniques for Multidimensional Analysis of Preferences," *Psychometrika*, 38, September, 337–69.

STEENKAMP, JAN-BENEDICT E. M., HANS C. M. VAN TRIJP, AND JOS M. F. TEN BERGE (1994) "Perceptual Mapping Based on Idiosyncratic Sets of Attributes," *Journal of Marketing Research*, February, 15–27.

STEFFLER, VOLNEY (1968) "Market Structure Studies: New Products for Old Markets and New Markets (Foreign) for Old Products," in Frank M. Bass, Charles W. King, and Edgar A. Pessemier, eds., *Applications of the Sciences in Marketing Management*, New York: John Wiley and Sons, 251–68.

WINER, B. J. (1973) *Statistical Principles in Experimental Design*, New York: McGraw-Hill.

WITTINK, DICK R., AND PHILIPPE CATTIN (1981) "Alternative Estimation Methods for Conjoint Analysis: A Monte Carlo Study," *Journal of Marketing Research*, 18, February, 101–06.

———— (1989) "Commercial Use of Conjoint Analysis: An Update," *Journal of Marketing*, 53, July, 91–96.

WITTINK, DICK R., LAKSHMAN KRISHNAMURTHI, AND DAVID J. REIBSTEIN (1990) "The Effect of Differences in the Number of Attribute Levels on Conjoint Results," *Marketing Letters*, 1, July, 113–23.

APPENDIX 14-A

DERIVATION OF ATTRIBUTE UTILITIES IN CONJOINT ANALYSIS

Conjoint analysis really consists of two stages. The first stage is data collection, which attempts to efficiently uncover utilities for attribute levels using as few alternatives as possible. The trick to doing this is to understand experimental design well, and to have a copy of a book such as Winer (1973) readily available.

The second stage of conjoint analysis involves estimating the utilities for each level of each attribute. This is usually done by dummy variable regression. To do this, the attribute levels are converted into a series of dummy variables. The stated ranking is then inverted so that a big number indicates high utility. For example, the cleaning product example of Green and Wind (1975) can be converted to a regression problem with 18 observations (one for each alternative) and eight dummy variables (Table 14A.1). By running a regression on this data, utilities can be estimated. (Notice also that, if the data are sufficient, dummy variables representing interactions can also be created and estimated.)

Assuming no interactions, the regression model becomes:

$$\text{Rating} = B_0 + B_1(\text{Package A}) + B_2(\text{Package B}) + B_3(\text{K2R})$$
$$+ B_4(\text{Glory}) + B_5(\text{Price 1.19}) + B_6(\text{Price 1.39})$$
$$+ B_7(\text{Good Housekeeping seal}) + B_8(\text{Money-back guarantee})$$

B_1 then becomes the difference in utility between Package A and Package C (the "left out" package), and so forth. If we thought that a particular combination of attributes was particularly effective (e.g., Package design A and Glory), we could add an interaction term to the regression model to estimate it [e.g., $B_9(\text{Package A})(\text{Glory})$]. Generally, however, researchers have not found interaction terms to be particularly useful in most conjoint studies.

TABLE 14A.1 Dummy Coding Scheme

Dependent Variable (19-ranking)	Package Design		Brand		Price		Good House-keep-ing Seal	Money-back Guar-antee
	A	**B**	**K2R**	**Glory**	**1.19**	**1.39**		
6	1	0	1	0	1	0	0	0
8	1	0	0	1	0	1	0	1
2	1	0	0	0	0	0	1	0
17	0	1	1	0	0	1	1	1
5	0	1	0	1	0	0	0	0
16	0	1	0	0	1	0	0	0
7	0	0	1	0	0	0	0	1
12	0	0	0	1	1	0	1	0
10	0	0	0	0	0	1	0	0
1	1	0	1	0	0	0	1	0
11	1	0	0	1	1	0	0	1
4	1	0	0	0	0	1	0	0
15	0	1	1	0	1	0	0	0
13	0	1	0	1	0	1	1	0
14	0	1	0	0	0	0	0	1
9	0	0	1	0	0	1	0	0
3	0	0	0	1	0	0	0	0
18	0	0	0	0	1	0	1	1

In the special case where the alternatives are derived according to a full factorial design or an orthogonal array, it is possible to estimate the utilities by hand calculation using the following steps:

1. Estimate the average value of the dependent variable for each level of each attribute. For example, Package design A appears in six combinations, and the average score is given by $(6 + 8 + 2 + 1 + 11 + 4)/6 = 5.33$ (Table 14A.2).
2. If you wish to place utilities on a particular scale, convert the average scores to a utility scale. In this case, the averages were rescaled from their range of 5.3 to 13.33 to a range of .1 to 1.0.[4] The results appear in Table 14A.3, along with the results presented by Green and Wind (1975) using MONANOVA and dummy variable regression on the data in Table 14A.1. Notice the close correspondence between the results, especially in terms of the range of utilities on each attribute.

The regression results suggest that package design is important, with a range of 8 (−4.5 to + 3.5), as is price with a range of 7.67. Some people prefer to rescale the data so that all the coefficients are positive. You can also do this by leaving the least popular level of each attribute—here Package A, Brand name Glory, Price 1.59, no Good Housekeeping seal, and no Money-back guarantee—out of the regression and running it on the remaining levels

TABLE 14A.2   Average Score for Attribute Levels

	Score
Package design:	
A	5.33
B	13.33
C	9.83
Brand name:	
K2R	9.17
Glory	8.67
Bissell	10.67
Price:	
1.19	13.00
1.39	10.17
1.59	5.33
Good Housekeeping seal:	
Yes	10.50
No	9.00
Money-back guarantee:	
Yes	12.50
No	8.00

[4]This was done by linear interpolation so that 5.33 = .1, 6.22 = .2, 7.11 = .3, and so forth.

TABLE 14A.3 Estimated Attribute Utilities

	Simple Sums	MONANOVA	Dummy Variable Regression Coefficients[a]	Recoded Regression Coefficients
Package design:				
A	.1	.1	− 4.5	0
B	1.0	1.0	3.5	8
C	.6	.6	0	4.5
Brand name:				
K2R	.5	.3	− 1.5	.5
Glory	.5	.2	− 2.0	0
Bissell	.7	.5	0	2.0
Price:				
1.19	1.0	1.0	7.67	7.67
1.39	.6	.7	4.83	4.83
1.59	.1	.1	0	0
Good Housekeeping seal:				
Yes	.7	.3	1.5	1.5
No	.5	.2	0	0
Money-back guarantee:				
Yes	.9	.7	4.5	4.5
No	.4	.2	0	0

[a]Constant = 4.83, R^2 = .98.

(Packages B and C, Brand names K2R and Bissell, Prices 1.19 and 1.39, Good Housekeeping seal, and Money-back guarantee).

Using the coefficients, we can predict the value of any combination. For example, a K2R using Package B with a Good Housekeeping seal and no Money-back guarantee priced at 1.39 would be rated as

$$4.833 - 1.5 + 3.5 + 4.83 + 1.5 + 0 = 13.16$$

and preferred to anything rated less than this.

CHAPTER 15

Cluster Analysis

Cluster analysis refers to a collection of techniques that take a set of objects (e.g., consumers, brands) and divide them into groups so that the objects in each group are similar to each other. Cluster analysis is an important tool in many academic fields such as biology (grouping animal species) and linguistics (grouping dialects). There is even a professional society (the Classification Society) and an academic journal (*Journal of Classification*) devoted to the study of cluster analysis techniques. These fields often refer to cluster analysis with more arcane names such as numerical taxonomy (Sneath and Sokol, 1973), automatic classification, or typological analysis (Chandon and Pinson, 1981).

Marketers are most interested in cluster analysis for the grouping of customers and brands. For example,[1] an antifungal medication had 14 percent of the market. To determine the effects of various improvements, as well as to identify potential switchers, the firm commissioned a conjoint analysis study.[2] Part-worth utilities were estimated for each of the 320 individual physicians in the sample.

Having 320 different sets of part-worths made managerial analysis and the development of intuition difficult. One could take the average of the individual utility functions to see what the "average" physician wants, but this would mask any differences in the population (i.e., if half the sample prefers that the treatment be cold and the other half prefers it to be hot, the average suggests an ideal of lukewarm, which satisfies nobody). In this situation, finding groups of physicians (i.e., market segments) where part-worths are similar among members of a group and different from those in other groups can be accomplished by a cluster analysis of part-worths.

CLUSTER ANALYSIS BASICS

Figure 15.1 presents a plot of the responses of about 40 hypothetical consumers to two statements about hair care on 10-point agree–disagree scales. These consumers fall into

---

[1]This example is adapted from Green and Krieger (1991).
[2]If you skipped the chapter on conjoint analysis, (*a*) shame on you and (*b*) all you need to know here is that it derives the values ("part-worths") respondents place on various levels of product attributes (e.g., 30 mpg for a car, an output rate of 2,000 parts per hour for an industrial machine).

two distinct groupings or clusters. About half of the respondents agreed with both state-ments, and about half disagreed with both. No one needs a formal statistical methodol-ogy or a computer to classify these consumers into clusters. Unfortunately, classification in real-world applications is seldom this easy (Figure 15.2). What cluster analysis attempts is to make similar inferences when they are not so obvious to the naked eye.

FIGURE 15.1

Two Clusters of Respondents

Source: James H. Myers, *Segmentation and Positioning for Strategic Marketing Decisions*, page 82. Copyright © 1996 by the American Marketing Association. Reprinted with the permission of the publishers.

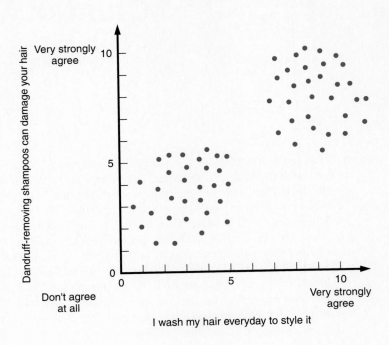

FIGURE 15.2

More "Typical" Observations on Two Variables

Source: James H. Myers, *Segmentation and Positioning for Strategic Marketing Decisions*, page 72. Copyright © 1996 by the American Marketing Association. Reprinted with the permission of the publishers.

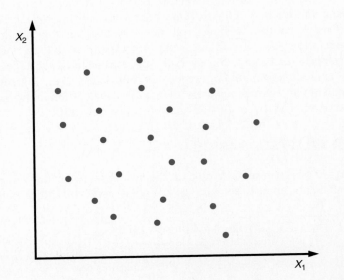

The steps involved in cluster analysis are:

a. Deciding which variables to use as bases for clustering
b. Selecting measures of similarity
c. Choosing an algorithm to group similar objects
d. Creating clusters
e. Deciding how many clusters to have
f. Defining and naming clusters
g. Testing the system

This chapter proceeds by describing the major approaches to each step.

DECIDING WHICH VARIABLES TO USE AS BASES FOR CLUSTERING

Cluster analysis groups objects together based on a particular set of variables. For example, in grouping customers one could base the groups (a.k.a. segments) on individual characteristics such as demographics, market characteristics such as products purchased, or responsiveness to changes in the marketing mix (as in the pharmaceutical example). Further, the particular variables chosen will typically affect the results. Thus the choice of variables on which to base the cluster analysis is a critical decision. Unfortunately it is rarely treated that way, and a combination of intuition and data availability lead to variable selection. Clusters based on demographics only rarely differ in terms of the benefits sought by a set of customers, and vice versa. Since we have no magic way to select good variables, we merely point out the obvious but often overlooked fact that choice of data determines the type of clusters that will emerge.

SELECTING MEASURES OF SIMILARITY

Suppose there are N objects to be clustered. These objects can be consumers, brands, markets, or whatever. Cluster analysis programs use one of two types of input structures. The first is raw data on N objects, each measured on p dimensions, attributes, or variables (e.g., survey responses or purchase patterns for consumers, product characteristics or marketing variables for brands, and demographic composition and product usage patterns for markets). The second structure is an $N \times N$ table of similarities in which the r, cth entry is a measure of how similar the object in the rth row is to the one in the cth column. If the raw data are used, the first computational step in cluster analysis is to compute similarities. If the second type of input is used, we can proceed directly to choosing an algorithm.

Selecting a measure of similarity depends on the type of data. We describe similarity measures for interval, categorical, ordinal, and ratio scaled data.

We can, and often will, speak of measures of *dis*similarity rather than measures of similarity, since their computation is often more natural and a measure of similarity can always be taken as the negative of a measure of dissimilarity. We use the notation $S(i, j)$ to denote the similarity between objects i and j and the notation $D(i, j)$ to denote the dissimilarity between them.

We assume that the raw data is in the form of an N objects by p variables table, where the rows correspond to the objects and the columns correspond to the variables. If the fth variable $(f = 1, 2, \ldots, p)$ measured for the ith object $(i = 1, 2, \ldots, N)$ is x_{if}, the table looks like the following:

		p variables	
	x_{11}	x_{1f}	x_{1p}
	....	....	
N objects	x_{i1}	x_{if}	x_{ip}
	....	....	
	x_{N1}	x_{Nf}	x_{Np}

Intervally Scaled Data

If the p variables are intervally scaled, a popular measure of dissimilarity is Euclidean distance:

$$D(i, j) = \sqrt{\sum_{f=1}^{p} \left(x_{if} - x_{jf} \right)^2}$$

This is a natural choice because if we plot the N objects in p-dimensional space, the Euclidian distance between any pair of objects is the length of the line that connects them, as in Figure 15.1.

For example, consider the data in Table 15.1. Variables 1 through 3 are attitudes measured on a seven-point scale, and variable 4 is an interest scale that ranges between 11 and 40. In this case,

$$D(1, 2) = \sqrt{(2 - 5)^2 + (4 - 2)^2 + (6 - 5)^2 + (32 - 38)^2} = \sqrt{50} = 7.07$$

$$D(1, 3) = \sqrt{7}, \text{ and so forth.}$$

An Important Property   Some researchers are not comfortable with raw Euclidean distance because it depends on the units of measurement. Suppose we are interested in clustering the Mouse family of Disneyland on the basis of age and income. We have the following data:

Name	Income (in dollars)	Age (in years)
Minnie	$55,000	55
Mickey	50,000	50
Goofy	55,000	50
Pluto	50,000	55

Figure 15.3A plots the data as is. It shows a very obvious cluster structure: Minnie and Goofy belong to one cluster, and Mickey and Pluto to another. Suppose now we measure income in thousands of dollars instead of just dollars. The plot in Figure 15.3B shows no cluster structure whatsoever. Finally, suppose we measure age in months. Figure 15.3C shows a very different, but just as obvious, cluster structure as that in Figure 15.3A: Minnie and Pluto in one, and Mickey and Goofy in the other! Depending on how you measure the variables, you obtain different sets of dissimilarities.

TABLE 15.1 Sample Data

Object Observation Person	Variable/Characteristic			
	1	2	3	4
1	2	4	6	32
2	5	2	5	38
3	3	3	7	30
4	1	2	3	16
5	4	3	2	30

To remove the effect of how variables are measured (e.g., age in years or months), some researchers standardize data with the formula $z_{if} = (x_{if} - m_f)/s_f$, where m_f and s_f are the mean and standard deviation respectively of the fth variable in the data matrix. The transformed Euclidean distance,

$$D(i, j) = \sqrt{\sum_{f=1}^{p} \left(z_{if} - z_{jf}\right)^2}$$

then becomes the dissimilarity measure. This transformation has the effect of making the data "unitless," since all variables will have a standard deviation of 1. The transformed Mouse family data will have coordinates Minnie (.707, .707), Mickey (−.707, −.707), Goofy (.707, −.707), and Pluto (−.707, .707) and be arranged in a picture most like that of Figure 15.3B. The transformed picture also seems to capture the essence of the raw data.

Note, however, that research recommends against standardizing unless the units of different variables are not comparable (Funkhouser, 1983), since putting all variables on the same scale eliminates information. For example, if everybody in a given sample is approximately the same age, then age simply is not something that discriminates among any clusters within the sample. Standardizing age would inflate its importance relative to other variables that may be useful in discrimination. So the moral is do not standardize unless the variables are measured on different scales and would potentially create artificial variable importances.

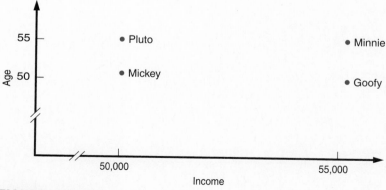

FIGURE 15.3A
Dependence of Euclidean Distance on Units of Measurement-Graphical Illustration

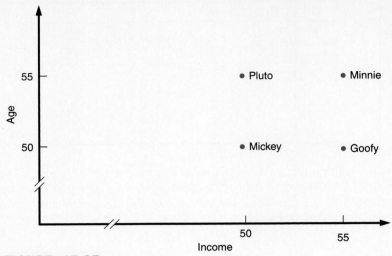

FIGURE 15.3B

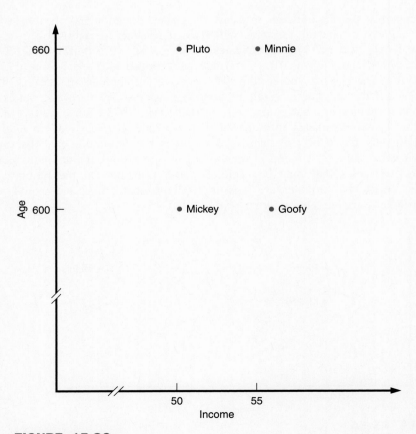

FIGURE 15.3C

In many cases, a researcher may not want the variables to be of equal importance, even if they are measured on the same scale. For example, suppose a real estate developer believes that income is much more important (say, 10 times as important) in determining housing purchase behavior than age is. One way to account for this would be to impose weights, w_f, on the (potentially standardized) variables and use one of the following measures:

$$D(i, j) = \sqrt{\sum_{f=1}^{p} w_f \left(x_{if} - x_{jf}\right)^2}$$

or

$$D(i, j) = \sqrt{\sum_{f=1}^{p} w_f \left(z_{if} - z_{jf}\right)^2}$$

City Block Distance   City block distance, defined by

$$D(i, j) = \sum_{f=1}^{p} \left|x_{if} - x_{jf}\right|$$

has its origins in the following logic. Suppose you lived in a city where the streets only run north–south and east–west (like Manhattan, for the most part). To get to a point one block north and one block east of where you are, you would have to walk two blocks (Figure 15.4A). You could not go in a straight line because buildings would be in the

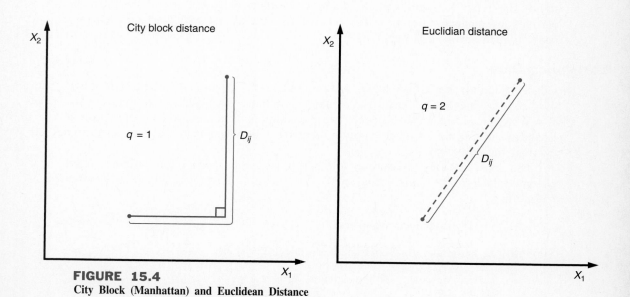

FIGURE 15.4
City Block (Manhattan) and Euclidean Distance

way. Euclidean distance would only be relevant to birds and Superman. City block distances for the data in Figure 15.2 are

$$D(1, 2) = |2 - 5| + |4 - 2| + |6 - 5| + |32 - 38| = 12$$

$$D(1, 3) = 5, \text{ and so forth.}$$

Minkowski Distance   Minkowski distance is defined by

$$D(i, j) = \sqrt[q]{\sum_{f=1}^{p} \left| x_{if} - x_{jf} \right|^q}$$

where q is any number (not necessarily an integer) greater than or equal to 1. Both city block and Euclidean distances are special cases of Minkowski distance ($q = 1$ for city block and $q = 2$ for Euclidean). The earlier comments on standardization and weighting also apply to the city block and Minkowski distances.

Correlation   A final measure of similarity between two objects is the correlation between them. For example, suppose one respondent rated the relative importance of brand name, style, and economy in choosing a car on a five-point scale (1 = not important at all; 5 = very important) as 4, 3, and 5. Suppose a second respondent gave ratings of 2, 1, and 3 and a third gave 4, 4, and 4. Euclidean, city block, and Minkowski distances all imply that the first respondent's ratings are more similar to the third's than to the second's. Yet one could convincingly argue that the first respondent's ratings are really more similar to the second's. They both rate economy as the most important attribute and brand name as the least. Correlation picks this up. The correlation between {4, 3, 5} and {2, 1, 3} is one while that between {4, 3, 5} and {4, 4, 4} is 0. In effect, the correlation standardizes data within respondent and then computes a distance measure. Whether to use correlation or one of the distance measures depends on whether one thinks the relative magnitudes of different variables *within* a respondent (which favors correlation) matters more than the relative magnitudes of each variable *across* respondents (which favors distance).

Categorical Data

Gender and last brand purchased are examples of categorical variables. If coded with numerical values (e.g., sex: 1 = female, 2 = male; last brand purchased: 1 = Tide, 2 = Wisk, etc.), Euclidean distances are meaningless. Since many computer programs use Euclidean distance as a default option, care must be taken to make sure appropriate categorical measures are used.

   The most obvious measure of similarity is the proportion of variables where two objects fall into the same category (i.e., "match"). A simple matching coefficient is therefore:

$$S(i, j) = (\# \text{ matches})/(\# \text{ variables})$$

Similarly, a "nonmatching" coefficient of dissimilarity is:

$$D(i, j) = (\# \text{ variables} - \# \text{ matches})/(\# \text{ variables}) = 1 - S(i, j)$$

Several circumstances lead to modifications of the basic measure. Often, all variables are not equally important to the research problem and managerial question at hand. This can be handled, as in the case of Euclidean distance, by weighting the variables unequally.

Asymmetric categories arise when the possible categorical outcomes are not equally important. Matches on last brand purchased may be much more important if they occur on the firm's brand. One solution to asymmetry is to count a coincidence of categories as a match only if the match is on the important category. Matches on the unimportant categories are treated as if the variable were never measured. The measure, proposed by Jaccard (1908), is essentially

$$S(i, j) = M/(M + \mathrm{MM})$$

where M = the number of matches on the important categories for variables with important categories, and MM = the number of mismatched variables. The number of matches on nonimportant categories for variables with important categories are not included. Such matches do have an impact on increasing similarity, however, since more of them implies a lower denominator M + MM and, consequently, a higher similarity.

Other potential modifications of the simple matching coefficient to account for the number of categories and their frequency of occurrence exist (Hyvarian, 1962; Lingoes, 1967).

Ordinal Data

Discrete ordinal variables are very much like nominal variables. The only difference is that the categories can be arranged in a meaningful sequence. For example, respondents are often asked to respond to a product, description, or attitude statement with a number from one to five with the following meanings:

1—definitely will not buy		1—disagree strongly
2—probably will not buy		2—disagree somewhat
3—may or may not buy	or	3—neither agree nor disagree
4—probably will buy		4—agree somewhat
5—definitely will buy		5—agree strongly

In most cases, these data can be effectively treated as intervally scaled. However, a few (and becoming increasingly fewer) researchers question this practice. They point out that no one tells the respondents to treat a purchase intentions scale as "probability of purchase" (e.g., 1 = probability of 0; 2 = .25; 3 = .50; 4 = .75; 5 = 1.00).

If (perhaps too) cautious researchers do not want to treat these data as intervally scaled, they can use matching coefficients. However, it would be a shame to waste the information contained in the order of the categories. A consumer that "probably will buy" is closer to a consumer that "definitely will buy" than a consumer that "may or may not buy" is. Furthermore, a difference of two scale points between objects means a lot more when there are only three categories than when there are (say) nine.

Ratio Scaled Data

Most statistical methods only require that data be intervally scaled. The extra properties of ratio scaled data are generally superfluous. Therefore, we can treat these data as if they were intervally scaled.

Mixed Data

Most data sets contain data of multiple types. A market research questionnaire will often request a person's age, income, last brand purchased, product ratings, and ranking of attribute importances: two ratio scaled variables, a categorical one, a set of intervally scaled variables, and a set of ordinal ones. Following Gower (1971), we suggest that the similarity between two objects simply be the *average of the similarities for each of the variables taken alone*.

To make this definition meaningful, each variable must follow the same scale. The natural one to use is 0 to 1. Logic suggests that the similarity on nominal variables be 1 or 0 depending on whether or not the categories match. For ordinal variables, one can replace the scale value with

$$z_{if} = \frac{x_{if} - 1}{M_f - 1}$$

where M_f is the number of (ordered) categories for the fth variable. This has the effect of placing all values between 0 and 1 and eliminating any artifacts created by the number of categories. Finally, the following transformation places intervally scaled variables on a comparable 0 to 1 scale:

$$S(i, j) = 1 - \frac{|x_{if} - x_{jf}|}{R_f}$$

where R_f is the difference between the maximum and minimum values of the fth variable across all objects (i.e., its range).

CHOOSING A CLUSTERING ALGORITHM TO GROUP SIMILAR OBJECTS

The literature on algorithms that group objects is enormous. To give the reader a full understanding of it is well beyond the scope of this book. The reader is referred to Bock (1974), Hartigan (1975), Jain and Dubes (1988), Arabie and Hubert (1992, 1994), and Arabie, Hubert, and DeSoete (1994). The intelligent user only need understand the basic logic behind the approaches, and can leave the technical details to the computer. Arabie and Hubert (1995) classify methods according to three major categories defined by the degree of "allowable overlap" permitted among the clusters. From least to most overlap allowed, these are partitioning methods, hierarchical methods, and fully overlapping methods. The vast majority of approaches fall into the first two categories; the third has recently emerged.

Partitioning Methods

A partitioning method classifies objects into K clusters such that each cluster contains at least one object and each object belongs to one and only one cluster. Obviously, the number of clusters cannot exceed the number of objects. Computer algorithms will construct a partitioning for any user-supplied value of K. Not all values of K will produce clusterings that look nice or are easily interpretable. Thus, one should try several values of K and compare solutions according to visual and conceptual interpretability as well as some numerical criterion. Each clustering algorithm has its own goodness of fit measure; most are based on the ratio of the average distance (dissimilarity) between all pairs of objects within clusters to the average distance between clusters.

In marketing research, the most common partitioning method is the K-means approach (MacQueen, 1967), included in most widely available software packages. K-means clustering begins with an initial random partitioning of the objects into K groups or clusters. The "means" of the clusters, also called *centroids*, are computed and used as *seed* points for later work. Each object is then (potentially re)assigned to the cluster with the nearest seed point. Each time an object is reassigned, the centroids are recomputed and new seed points are computed. This process continues cycling through all objects until one full cycle has been completed without any reassignment.

Hierarchical Methods

Hierarchical cluster analysis does not produce one set of K clusters. Rather, it builds a hierarchy of possible solutions. Most hierarchical approaches fall into a category called *agglomerative* methods because the starting point of the algorithm is a separate cluster for each individual ($K = N$) and the objects are sequentially combined ("agglomerated") into a hierarchy according to similarity.[3] The two most similar objects are combined first and linked at the bottom rung of the hierarchy; the next two most similar objects are combined next and linked at the second rung, and so forth.

The critical component of hierarchical clustering outputs is a tree diagram, called a *dendrogram*, such as that in Figure 15.5. This demonstrates how objects link together at various levels of similarity. The lower down the hierarchy two objects are linked, the more similar they are. For example, 1 and 3 are much more similar than 1 and 5. The dendrogram can also be used to assign objects to clusters by slicing it at the appropriate level. For example, the two-cluster solution, {1, 3, 16, 2, 4, 5, 7, 14, 9, 6, 8, 10, 11, 15, 12} and {13}, has object 13 in one cluster and all other objects in the other; the three-cluster solution, {1, 3, 16, 2, 4, 5, 7, 14, 9, 6, 8, 10, 11, 15}, {12}, and {13}, has object 13 in one cluster, object 12 in a second, and all others in a third. The four-cluster solution is {1, 3, 16, 2, 4, 5, 7, 14, 9}, {6, 8, 10, 11, 15}, {12}, and {13}; the five-cluster solution is {1, 3, 16, 2, 4, 5}, {7, 14, 9}, {6, 8, 10, 11, 15}, {12}, and {13}; and so forth.

---

[3] Another class of clustering algorithms, called hierarchical *divisive*, begins with the cluster of the whole and divides it up.

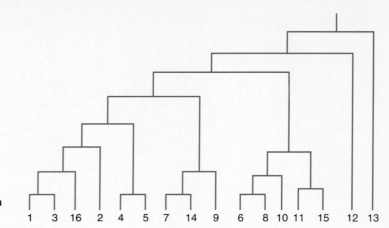

FIGURE 15.5
A Sample Dendrogram from a
Hierarchical Clustering

1   3   16   2   4   5   7   14   9   6   8 10 11   15   12   13

Calculation of Similarity Between Clusters   To proceed, we need to define the similarity between an object and a cluster and the similarity between clusters. The following basic approaches exist:

> *As similar as the most similar object (single linkage).* This approach says that an object is as similar to a cluster as it is to the nearest object in the cluster. The similarity between two clusters then is the similarity between the most similar pair of objects, one from each cluster.

> *As similar as the least similar object (complete linkage).* The polar opposite of the first approach is to assume that an object is as similar to a cluster as it is to the farthest (least similar) object in the cluster. The similarity between two clusters is the similarity between their least similar pair.

> *Average linkage.* This approach assumes that the similarity of an object to a cluster is the average of the individual similarities of the object to each of the objects in that cluster. The similarity between two clusters becomes the average of all the similarities between all possible pairs of objects, one from each cluster.

> *Centroid method.* Here, once two objects are grouped together, their values on the variables are averaged and the two objects replaced by a new "object" (their centroid), which is the average of the objects included in the cluster.

Another common hierarchical clustering approach in marketing research is Ward's (1963) method. Although it comes closest to the centroid method, it is somewhat different. Its focus is to minimize the sum across clusters of the total squared distances from the centroid in each cluster to the objects in the cluster.

Average linkage, centroid-based, single linkage, and complete linkage clustering can give rise to very different clusters on the same set of data. The centroid and average linkage methods tend to find ball-shaped clusters as they average the distances between all objects in a pair of clusters. Two clusters can have objects far from each other if they are balanced by objects near each other. Single linkage methods tend to produce elongated snakelike clusters. With single linkage rules, clusters that are close to each other at even a single point can merge, even if some objects are extremely far apart. An object can be added to a cluster that has other objects very far from it. As long as the nearest neighbors are close, nothing else matters. Finally, complete linkage clusters are the opposite. They tend to be fairly compact. Every member of a cluster must be close to every other member. Two clusters can merge only if all members of both are close to each other. These characteristics are shown in Figure 15.6.

Illustrative Example   To get a better feel of how hierarchical methods work, consider the collection of five objects in Table 15.2. Using the squared Euclidean distance, we get the distance or dissimilarity matrix in Table 15.3.[4]

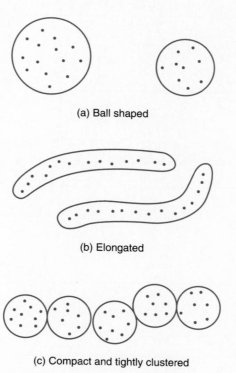

(a) Ball shaped

(b) Elongated

(c) Compact and tightly clustered

FIGURE 15.6
Types of Clusters (a) Ball shaped; (b) Elongated; (c) Compact and tightly clusterered
Source: Leonard Kaufman and Peter J. Rousseeuw, *Finding Groups in Data: An Introduction to Cluster Analysis*, page 48. Copyright © 1990 by John Wiley & Sons, Inc. Reprinted with the permission of the publishers.

---

[4]We use the squared Euclidean distance in this example rather than the Euclidean distance to eliminate the nuisance of the square root sign. If A is closer to B than it is to C in terms of Euclidean distance, it will also be closer in terms of squared Euclidean distance.

TABLE 15.2 More Sample Data		
	Variable	
Object	1	2
1	2	4
2	5	2
3	3	3
4	1	2
5	4	3

TABLE 15.3 Distance Matrix for Table 15.2					
Object	1	2	3	4	5
1	0	13	2	5	5
2		0	5	16	2
3			0	5	1
4				0	10
5					0

A "most similar" single linkage hierarchical procedure would proceed as follows:

Step 1. Objects 3 and 5 (the most similar pair) are combined.

Step 2. A new distance matrix is formed:[5]

	Object			
Object	1	2	3, 5	4
1		13	2	5
2			2	16
3, 5				5
4				

Step 3. Add either object 1 or object 2 (or both) to cluster {3, 5}.

Step 4. Assuming we add object 1 to cluster {3, 5}, we get a new distance matrix:

	Object		
Object	2	1, 3, 5	4
2		2	16
1, 3, 5			5
4			

Step 5. Add object 2 to cluster {1, 3, 5}.

	Object	
Object	1, 2, 3, 5	4

Step 6. Form the new distance matrix:

Step 7. Group 1, 2, 3, 4, and 5 together.

---

[5]Since object 1 is 2 from object 3, and 5 from object 5, its distance from the closest object in the cluster is 2.

Output. The output would then be as follows:

Number of Clusters	Cluster 1	Cluster 2	Cluster 3	Cluster 4	Cluster 5	Distance Level
5	1	2	3	4	5	0
4	1	2	3, 5	4		1
3	1, 3, 5	2	4			2
2	1, 2, 3, 5	4				2
1	1, 2, 3, 4, 5					5

Notice that if you graph the two-cluster solution, you get the classic snakelike structure (Figure 15.7).

In contrast, a "least similar" hierarchical procedure would produce the following result:

Number of Clusters	Cluster 1	Cluster 2	Cluster 3	Cluster 4	Cluster 5	Distance Level
5	1	2	3	4	5	0
4	1	2	3, 5	4		1
3	1, 4	2	3, 5			5
2	1, 4	2, 3, 5				5
1	1, 2, 3, 4, 5					16

Notice the two-cluster solution here is more appealing graphically (Figure 15.8).

The centroid method would begin as follows:

Step 1. Group 3 and 5 together (as before).
Step 2. To calculate distance, we must first replace objects 3 and 5 with their average:

	Variable	
Object	1	2
1	2	4
2	5	2
3, 5	3.5	3
4	1	2

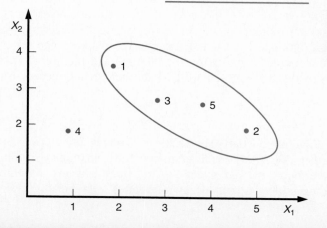

FIGURE 15.7
Two-Cluster Solution for a Single Linkage Processing of Sample Data

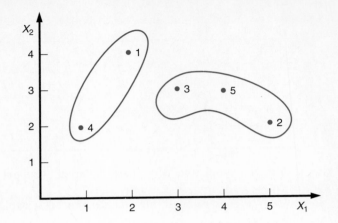

FIGURE 15.8
Two-Cluster Solution for Complete
Linkage Processing of Sample Data

The distances thus become:

			Object	
Object	1	2	3, 5	4
1		13	3.25	5
2			3.25	16
3, 5				7.25
4				

The remaining steps simply repeat 1 and 2. The final result is:

Number of Clusters	Cluster 1	Cluster 2	Cluster 3	Cluster 4	Cluster 5	Distance Level
5	1	2	3	4	5	0
4	1	2	3, 5	4		1
3	1	2, 3, 5	4			3.25
2	1, 4	2, 3, 5				5
1	1, 2, 3, 4, 5					6.36

A Final Comment   Given hierarchical clustering produces results for all values of *K*, one might wonder why partitioning methods continue to be used. Selecting the best clustering with *K* groups is not necessarily the goal of hierarchical clustering. On the other hand, it *is* the goal of partitioning methods. In hierarchical clustering, the three- and four-cluster solutions are intimately related. Hierarchical clustering can never repair what (perhaps foolish) agglomerations come before in building the hierarchy. Rigidity is hierarchical clustering's main disadvantage as well as the key to its success (in that it limits computation time).

Overlapping Clusters

Partitioning methods allow no overlap. Hierarchical methods allow overlap only to the extent that clusters farther down the dendrogram are fully contained within those above it. However, it is not difficult to find situations in which clusters *should* overlap. For example, suppose customers obtain both decay prevention and breath freshening from a toothpaste.[6] Gum can also freshen breath, and fluoridated water can also prevent tooth decay. But they also provide benefits very different from toothpaste. Gum can be a taste treat; fluoridated water can be a thirst-quencher. Toothpaste can do neither of these. So, in a clustering of N products, each measured on p benefits offered, one might desire a cluster that contains toothpaste overlap but does not coincide with others containing fluoridated water and gum. Arabie et al. (1981) describe an algorithm called MAPCLUS that allows objects to belong to more than one cluster simultaneously. However, it has not diffused down to common marketing research practice due to lack of software availability.

Choosing a Clustering Method

The spectrum of methods described in this chapter suggests that the choice of method requires careful thought. Unfortunately, most choices are based on whatever software the firm has on hand (Wind, 1978). In these cases, this chapter can give the user an understanding of what is going on within his or her computer.

In those circumstances when the researcher does indeed make a choice, the following thoughts seem to be appropriate:

a. In a variety of simulation studies, K-means, Ward's method, and the average linkage approach seem to outperform other methods in reproducing known structures. Furthermore, Ward's method outperforms the average linkage method, except in the presence of outliers (Punj and Stewart, 1983).

b. Studies show that the choice of algorithm is much more critical than the choice of similarity/dissimilarity measure in determining the final cluster structure (Punj and Stewart, 1983).

c. Partitioning methods seek to find the *best* K-group classification of the objects in question. Hierarchical clustering seeks to uncover a nested pattern or grouping of the objects. Its structure resembles an evolutionary tree and provides a more dynamic picture of the data. Use the approach most consistent with your research objectives.

d. The potentially erratic behavior of single and complete linkage methods would seem to recommend against their use unless the research or managerial objective was consistent with elongated or compact clusters. For example, the latter might be very appropriate in modern direct marketing, where appeals can be targeted to a narrower set of potential customers.

All the methods described so far require computers. Appendix 15-A presents a computer output for a hierarchical clustering of business schools. In case a researcher and client are out at lunch without a notebook computer, Appendix 15-B presents a back of the envelope approach called "quick clustering" (Kamen, 1970) that can be used to give preliminary insight until they get back to the office.

An Example: Breakfast Foods

Table 15.4 contains a matrix of dissimilarities among 15 different breakfast foods. Green and Rao (1972, p. 26) provide more details on the the data. Using a hierarchical agglomerative approach (sounds impressive, doesn't it?), we see the smallest dissimilarity is

---

[6]This example is adapted from Arabie et al. (1981).

TABLE 15.4 Dissimilarity Data for Breakfast Food Items

	TP	BT	EMM	JD	CT	BMM	HRB	TMd	BTJ	TMn	CB	DP	GD	CC
BT	59.13													
EMM	62.42	30.79												
JD	43.64	83.89	82.37											
CT	36.01	44.15	57.76	65.46										
BMM	60.21	60.94	23.80	53.33	64.11									
HRB	78.01	27.02	26.85	93.71	72.92	50.49								
TMd	34.57	36.36	52.44	55.35	32.87	59.96	64.23							
BTJ	32.10	32.29	50.18	49.11	36.29	55.83	61.55	5.52						
TMn	61.52	8.46	25.29	85.64	48.96	58.73	31.52	37.94	38.32					
CB	51.26	78.35	72.21	32.68	21.65	47.42	78.21	64.23	61.30	80.14				
DP	46.65	84.55	76.14	21.40	49.30	46.98	83.70	59.80	57.48	86.42	20.31			
GD	55.17	83.82	78.07	7.83	55.70	55.00	88.85	60.38	65.85	92.86	23.33	20.54		
CC	53.67	83.01	70.68	30.56	49.87	47.08	78.13	63.77	65.56	84.24	23.10	10.70	24.76	
CMB	72.17	48.13	21.87	73.62	62.49	15.25	33.37	63.52	64.49	52.93	58.26	62.46	66.77	54.17

Food Item	Plotting Code Used in Figures
1. Toast pop-up	TP
2. Buttered toast	BT
3. English muffin and margarine	EMM
4. Jelly donut	JD
5. Cinnamon toast	CT
6. Blueberry muffin and margarine	BMM
7. Hard rolls and butter	HRB
8. Toast and marmalade	TMd
9. Buttered toast and jelly	BTJ
10. Toast and margarine	TMn
11. Cinnamon bun	CB
12. Danish pastry	DP
13. Glazed donut	DG
14. Coffee cake	CC
15. Corn muffin and butter	CMB

Source: Paul E. Green and Vithala R. Rao, *Applied Multidimensional Scaling: A Comparison of Approaches and Algorithms*, page 26. Copyright © 1972 by Paul E. Green and Vithala R. Rao. Reprinted with the permission of Holt, Rinehart & Winston, Inc.

between buttered toast and jelly (BTJ) and toast and marmalade (TMd). This becomes the first pair linked in the hierarchy.

The (complete linkage–farthest neighbor) dissimilarity between, for example, cinnamon toast (CT) and the cluster {BTJ, TMd} is 36.29: the greater of the distances between CT and BTJ (36.29) and between CT and TMd (32.87). Similarly, the distance between the cluster {BTJ, TMd} and each of the remaining individual foods is

TP = 34.57	BT = 36.36
EMM = 52.44	JD = 55.35
BMM = 59.96	HRB = 64.23
TMn = 38.32	CB = 64.23
DP = 59.80	GD = 65.85
GC = 65.56	CMB = 64.49

Substituting these into the dissimilarity table and removing the CT and TMd singletons gives us the revised dissimilarities in Table 15.5.

The smallest remaining dissimilarity is now between jelly donuts (JD) and glazed donuts (GD). This becomes the second link in the hierarchy. Continuing this process eventually produces the dendrogram in Figure 15.9.

HOW MANY CLUSTERS?

Often the answer to the question of how many clusters is a matter of taste. Having clusters that are interpretable and are of sufficient size to be worth tracking are two key criteria for determining which cluster solution to use. A manager may simply prefer to work with a given number. Occasionally, some prior theory or knowledge will determine the answer. While there is no formal statistical test for number of clusters, numerical guidance can be provided by goodness of fit statistics. Part of the output of Ward's method is the total squared distance of the objects from the centroid of each object's cluster. Usually a table of these for all values of K is available. Table 15.6 presents such a table for a clustering of conjoint relative importances for $N_. = 100$ respondents in a study on 35mm cameras.

Since $N = 100$, the complete table would have entries from 1 to 100. We examine just a portion. As the number of clusters increases, the total squared distances and the amount of variability within the segments decreases. In the limit, $N = 100$, each object is its own cluster and is identical to its centroid, and the total distance is zero. One approach is to look for the place where the distances start decreasing at a smaller rate, a so-called "elbow" in the distance curve. Unfortunately, as the example demonstrates, it is not always clear where the elbow occurs. Here, both $N = 3$ and $N = 6$ are defensible choices.

The same elbow-based logic applies to partitioning-based clusters such as K-means. The only difference is that the goodness of fit measure is based on the ratio of total within-group variance about their centroids to total between-group variance of the centroids.

In cases like that in Table 15.6 where the elbow is not clear, one might start with the smaller number of clusters and move to the larger if the solution is not interpretable.

TABLE 15.5   Revised Dissimilarities for Breakfast Foods

	TP	BT	EMM	JD	CT	BMM	HRB	{BTJ, TMd}	TMn	CB	DP	GD	CC
BT	59.13												
EMM	62.42	30.79											
JD	43.64	83.89	82.37										
CT	36.01	44.15	57.76	65.46									
BMM	60.21	60.94	23.80	53.33	64.11								
HRB	78.01	27.02	26.85	93.71	72.92	50.49							
{BTJ, TMd}	34.57	36.36	52.44	55.35	36.29	59.96	64.23						
TMn	61.52	8.46	25.29	85.64	48.96	58.73	31.52	38.32					
CB	51.26	78.35	72.21	32.68	21.65	47.42	78.21	64.23	80.14				
DP	46.65	84.55	76.14	21.40	49.30	46.98	83.70	59.80	86.42	20.31			
GD	55.17	83.82	78.07	7.83	55.70	55.00	88.85	65.85	92.86	23.33	20.54		
CC	53.67	83.01	70.68	30.56	49.87	47.08	78.13	65.56	84.24	23.10	10.70	24.76	
CMB	72.17	48.13	21.87	73.62	62.49	15.25	33.37	64.49	52.93	58.26	62.46	66.77	54.17

Source: Paul E. Green and Vithala R. Rao, *Applied Multidimensional Scaling: A Comparison of Approaches and Algorithms, page 26. Copyright © 1972 by Paul E. Green and Vithala R. Rao. Reprinted with the permission of Holt, Rinehart & Winston, Inc.*

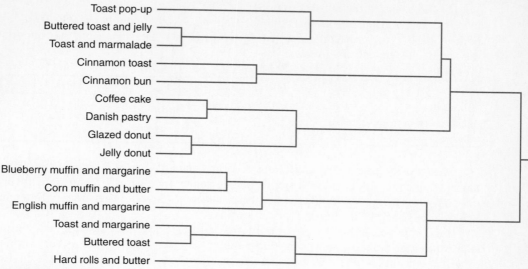

FIGURE 15.9
Complete Linkage Clustering Solution for Green-Rao (1972) Data
Source: Phipps J. Arabie and Lawrence Hubert, "Combinational Data Analysis" from *Annual Review of Psychology* 43 (1992): 162–203. Copyright © 1992 by Annual Reviews, Inc. Reprinted with the permission of the publishers.

DEFINING AND NAMING CLUSTERS

The key to describing clusters is the cluster centroids: namely, the means of all objects in the cluster for intervally scaled variables and the most common categories for nominally scaled ones. These are usually part of the output of any computer routine. Often, visual inspection of the centroids gives the researcher enough insight to give clusters names and labels.

TABLE 15.6	Selecting the Number of Clusters
# Clusters	Distance
2	44,560,850,944.000
3	71,823,864.000
4	10,015,321.000
5	1,919,148.500
6	174,971.172
7	63,479.957
8	39,869.785
9	33,049.777
10	8,397.862
11	2,617.952
12	2,039.591
13	588.102
14	490.045
15	296.331

Source: *Conjoint Segmenter Manual* (Morristown, New Jersey: Bretton-Clark, 1993), page 7. Reprinted with the permission of the publishers.

Consider the three-cluster solution for the camera study of Table 15.6. The study involved four attributes: brand (Minolta, Canon, Nikon), interchangeable lenses (yes, no), built-in flash (yes, no), and price ($100, $200, $400). The mean relative importances for the three clusters are as follows:

	Brand	*Interchangeable Lenses*	*Built-in Flash*	*Price*
Cluster 1	0.99%	26.36%	35.64%	37.01%
Cluster 2	15.71	46.71	4.47	33.11
Cluster 3	28.36	14.29	20.88	36.47

Cluster 1 is essentially indifferent to brand name; Cluster 2 gives little or no importance to built-in flash; and Cluster 3 places importance on all features, with brand second only to price. We could name these clusters "Brand insensitive," "Interchangeable lens wanters," and "Brand and price sensitive."

It is often desirable to go beyond the variables used in the original cluster analysis. Studying demographics, psychographics, media habits, and other variables that describe consumers enables marketers to characterize the people who are in each cluster and to target marketing efforts. For example, Anderson, Cox, and Fulcher (1976) found that bank customers sensitive to a convenience positioning are more likely to have fewer children, lower incomes, and unemployed spouses than those sensitive to a service positioning.

Visual inspection of cluster means provides the main insights required here as well. More formal analyses include analysis of variance testing for the difference among clusters on some descriptor variables and discriminant analysis to uncover which descriptor variables are useful in predicting group membership.

TESTING THE CLUSTER SYSTEM

The final step in a cluster analysis is to test the solution. This is the step most people skip because it both is a bother and has no standard way of being done. However, it is important that clusters be stable. Unless "sharply differing, relatively homogeneous groups of consumers exist in the respondent population," cluster analyses would only reveal "adventitious bleeps," which in reality do not justify the development of "products, messages, or media schedules" (Wells, 1975, p. 205). In other words, we need to assess the reliability and validity of the clusters we derive.

While there is no standard approach, a few ad hoc procedures provide further (tentative) insight into the reliability and validity of the clusters. The researcher might apply different similarity measures or clustering algorithms to the same data set and compare the solutions. Any agreements seen across algorithms and/or similarity measures would be a positive sign. Another possibility is for the researcher to split the data set in half randomly and perform cluster analyses on each half. The profiles of the centroids of the clusters could then be compared for the two half data sets. Again, agreement to any extent is a positive sign. One final procedure is to delete randomly chosen variables (columns) from the data set, recompute similarities, recluster, and compare solutions to those from the full set of data. Hopefully, some agreement will be found.

USES OF CLUSTER ANALYSIS

Market Segmentation

The primary application of cluster analysis in marketing is, has been, and will likely continue to be market segmentation. Marketers have long sought groups that respond homogeneously to given marketing stimuli (e.g., product attributes, product positioning, price, promotions, or some combination thereof). This was the focus of the pharmaceutical example and the 35mm camera clustering discussed earlier.

The approach begins by assembling a set of available (and hopefully relevant) product-related variables (e.g., brand preferences, benefits sought, responses to lifestyle questions) on a sample of customers (e.g., by means of a survey or through secondary data sources). If there are many variables, an attempt is often made to reduce the number (e.g., through factor analysis, which we discuss in the next chapter). The variables are then input into a cluster algorithm.

The clusters are then compared/profiled in terms of the variables that were used to form them (e.g., by simple analysis of means, ANOVAs, or discriminant analysis—another topic we discuss in a later chapter). The clusters are also compared in terms of other variables that can be used to describe them and provide managers with a path to reach them (e.g., benefits-based clusters are compared in terms of demographics).

The alternative to cluster-based segmentation is a classification of customers on the basis of a set of a few chosen variables (Wind, 1978). The groups so obtained are then profiled and compared on a full complement of variables in the same way as cluster-based segments. While not elegant, a priori clusters are often just as useful as those based on cluster analysis because they are usually readily identifiable and, if the clustering is based on some consumer behavior (e.g., favorite brand), obviously have responded differently to the product offering. However, a priori analyses are limited by the creativity of the researcher in dividing up the sample. The computational power of cluster analysis makes it likely that more distinct segments which differ on one or more of the clustering variables can be found. Nevertheless, it is usually advisable to perform at least one a priori segmentation, even if simply as a basis for comparison.

Market Structure Analysis

Market structure analysis is concerned with identifying products that compete with each other. Rao and Steckel (1995) make a compelling argument that brands or products are competitors *only if* consumers say they are. Since consumers exercise their voice by buying one instead of the other, it seems likely that brands are more competitive if there is a lot of switching between them (Lehmann, 1972). Scanner panel data makes investigating brand switching fairly easy.

Rao and Sabavala (1981) performed a market structure analysis using cluster analysis and panel data. They use a market-level switching matrix, M, where the i, j-th entry is the number of times a brand j purchase followed a brand i purchase in the data set. If a large proportion of brand i purchases are followed by brand j purchases (or vice versa), these two brands can be interpreted as competitive or, in the language of cluster analysis, similar.

To be more precise, let

N_{ij} = the number of consumers who switched from brand i on one choice occasion to brand j on the next

$N_{i.}$ = number of consumers who purchased brand i on the first choice occasion

$N_{.j}$ = number of consumers who purchased brand j on the second choice occasion

$N_{..}$ = number of purchases in the sample

One similarity measure is

$$S(i, j) = \frac{\left(N_{ij} + N_{ji} \right) N_{..}}{2 N_{i.} N_{.j}}$$

This measure is equal to 1 if i and j are independent, and it is greater than 1 if switching between them is greater than would be expected if the brands were independent.

Figure 15.10 depicts the solution to a hierarchical clustering of similarities constructed from soft drink panel data. The diagram contains paths that link each brand with every other brand. More switching occurs between pairs of brands that are linked with a path toward the bottom of the diagram. For example, there is more switching between Diet Pepsi and Tab than between Tab and Diet-Rite; there is also more switching between Tab and Diet-Rite than there is between Tab and Coca-Cola.

Products that are closer together at the base of the hierarchy, or are connected at a lower node in the hierarchy, are more competitive with each other. In particular, national brands (left-hand side of the tree) have a greater degree of competitiveness (i.e., exhibit more intragroup switching) with each other than they do with regional brands (right-hand side of the tree), regardless of flavor. Additionally, within regional brands, brand name forms a strong basis of competition (i.e., there is more intrabrand switching than intraflavor switching among regional brands).

Figure 15.11 provides a summary interpretation of Figure 15.10. National/regional distribution (or perhaps price) is the most important attribute (that is, what consumers use first). The subtree for the "National" brands has diet/nondiet as the next most important feature, followed by flavor.

Identifying Potential Test Markets

Managers contemplating test-market experiments search for markets that are relatively similar to each other so that comparisons of results achieved with different marketing programs will be meaningful. Cluster analysis of potential candidates on appropriate characteristics is one way to uncover similar markets.

General Data Reduction

Marketing involves many miscellaneous situations where a simplified view of the data is desirable. Cluster analysis is one item in the marketer's toolbox that can enable him/her to learn about the world.

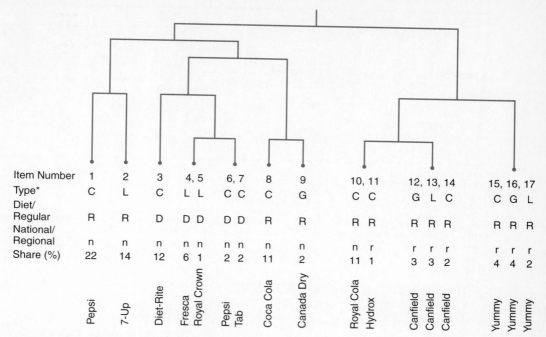

* C = Cola, L = Lemon/Lime, and G = Ginger ale.

FIGURE 15.10
Market Structure (Cluster) Analysis of Soft Drinks

One interesting application of cluster analysis in the marketing literature attempted to develop a typology of grocery product categories with respect to promotion styles generally practiced (Fader and Lodish, 1990). The authors found four pervasive styles (Table 15.7), which were related to structural characteristics of consumer behavior (e.g., household penetration, interpurchase times, purchase frequency). For example, products in cluster 4 were infrequently purchased, had low penetration, and few private labels. On the other hand, cluster 2 products were frequently purchased, had high penetration, and many private labels. Clusters 1 and 3 were between the extremes.

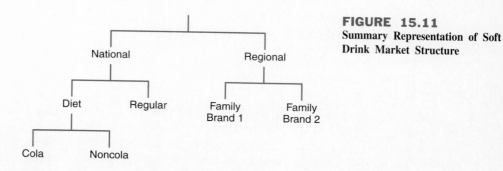

FIGURE 15.11
Summary Representation of Soft Drink Market Structure

TABLE 15.7 Description of Promotion Clusters (% of Volume)

	Cluster 1 Feature, No Display (N = 80)	Cluster 2 Display and Feature (N = 28)	Cluster 3 Manufacturer Couponing (N = 77)	Cluster 4 Low Promotion (N = 146)
Feature	16.8	21.6	7.7	5.6
Display	8.4	26.4	7.1	3.4
Manufacturers coupons	7.3	6.7	26.1	4.2
Price cut	20.3	25.1	10.8	7.9
Store coupons	1.3	1.9	0.5	0.3

Typical members in cluster
1: butter, eggs, frankfurters, bacon, cake mix, ice cream.
2: soda, tuna fish, paper towels, crackers, salted snacks, toilet paper.
3: disposable diapers, coffee, cereal, pet foods/supplies, detergents.
4: ammonia, sleeping pills, horseradish, lard, disposable foil pans.
Source: Peter S. Fader and Leonard M. Lodish, "A Cross-Category Analysis of Category Structure and Promotional Activity for Grocery Products" from *Journal of Marketing* 5 (October 1990) by the American Marketing Association. Reprinted with permission of the publishers.

THE PHARMACEUTICAL EXAMPLE REVISITED

A *K*-means cluster analysis was performed on the part-worths of the 320 physicians in the sample. A two-cluster solution was chosen. While the average part-worths for each of the two segments are confidential, the analysis recommended two products for introduction, one directed toward each segment (Table 15.8).

The two segments were compared on three background characteristics: type of practice, physician specialty, and a psychographic composite identified as "primary interest in drug efficacy, information seeker, and proneness to brand switch." Segment 1 physicians were more likely to be in group practice, whereas segment 2 members were more likely to specialize in internal medicine and score highly on the psychographic composite.

SUMMARY

As its name implies, cluster analysis aggregates individual objects (e.g., consumers, products) into groups (clusters) in which the objects are more similar to each other than they are to those in other groups. There are several steps involved in conducting cluster analyses. These are:

  a. Deciding which variables to use as bases for clustering
  b. Selecting measures of similarity
  c. Choosing an algorithm to group similar objects
  d. Creating clusters
  e. Deciding how many clusters to have
  f. Defining and naming clusters
  g. Testing the system

Similarity measures depend on the type of data being used. For example, a different similarity measure is needed for intervally scaled variables (e.g., age) than for categorical variables (e.g., favorite brand). Objects can be partitioned such that N objects are divided into K clusters, or they can be grouped in a hierarchy such that objects

TABLE 15.8 Profiles of Pharmaceutical Products

	Current Product	New Product 1	New Product 2
Clinical cure rate relative to market leader	10% below	Equal	20% above
Rapidity of relief relative to market leader	1 day slower	2 days faster	2 days faster
Recurrence rate relative to market leader	15% above	Equal	Equal
Incidence of burning/itching	17%	2%	17%
Dosage: 1 dose per	14 days	10 days	10 days

Source: Paul E. Green and Abba M. Krieger, "Segmenting Markets with Conjoint Analysis" from *Journal of Marketing* 55 (October 1991): 24, 26. Copyright © 1991 by the American Marketing Association. Reprinted with the permission of the publishers.

linked at lower levels of the hierarchy are identified as more similar than objects linked at higher levels. Judgment comes into play in deciding how many clusters to have and in identifying or naming them.

The output of a cluster analysis depends on the similarity measure and the grouping algorithm. Research suggests that the final cluster solution depends more on the algorithm leading to it than on the similarity measure used. The uses of cluster analysis in marketing research include uncovering market segments, investigating market structure, general data reduction, and identifying potential test markets.

PROBLEMS

1. Indicate on a quantitative 1 to 10 scale how similar the following pairs are:
   a. The words *pretty* and *happy*.

      The words *ugly* and *homely*.

      The words *big* and *important*.

   b. The following people: Walter Mondale, George Bush, wife, mother-in-law.
2. Using Table 15.3 as a starting point, produce a graphical summary of the steps in clustering the five objects using the "least similar" method.
3. How would you go about clustering counties in the United States?
4. Assume you were national sales manager for Xerox. How would you proceed to cluster present and potential accounts?
5. Assume a large security dealer asked you to help segment its accounts by means of cluster analysis. What would you do?
6. Get the *Business Week* issue with the latest MBA program ratings. Cluster analyze the data in the article. Do the results agree with those from the *U.S. News & World Report* study in the appendix?

REFERENCES

ANDERSON, THOMAS W., JR., ELI P. COX III, AND DAVID G. FULCHER (1976) "Bank Selection Decisions and Market Segmentation," *Journal of Marketing*, 40, January, 40–45.

ARABIE, PHIPPS, J. DOUGLAS CARROLL, WAYNE DESARBO, AND JERRY WIND (1981) "Overlapping Clustering: A New Method for Product Positioning," *Journal of Marketing Research*, 18, August, 310–17.

ARABIE, PHIPPS, AND LAWRENCE HUBERT (1992) "Combinatorial Data Analysis," *Annual Review of Psychology*, 43, 169–203.

——— (1994) "An Overview of Combinatorial Data Analysis," in Phipps Arabie, Lawrence Hubert, and Gert DeSoete, eds., *Clustering and Classification*, River Edge, N.J.: World Scientific.

——— (1995) "Cluster Analysis in Marketing Research," in Richard P. Bagozzi, ed., *Advanced Methods in Marketing Research*, Cambridge, Mass.: Blackwell Business, 160–89.

ARABIE, PHIPPS, LAWRENCE HUBERT, AND GERT DESOETE, EDS. (1994) *Clustering and Classification*, River Edge, N.J.: World Scientific.

ARNOLD, STEVEN J. (1979) "A Test for Clusters," *Journal of Marketing Research*, 16, November, 545–51.

BOCK, H. H. (1974) *Automatische Klassifikation*, Studia Mathematica, Göttingen: Vandenhoek and Ruprecht.

BRETTON-CLARK (1993) Conjoint Segmenter Manual, Morristown, N.J.: Bretton-Clark.

CHANDON, J. L., AND S. PINSON (1981) *Analyse typologique: Theories et applications*, Paris: Masson.

FADER, PETER S., AND LEONARD M. LODISH (1990) "A Cross-Category Analysis of Category Structure and Promotional Activity for Grocery Products," *Journal of Marketing*, 54, October, 52–65.

FUNKHOUSER, G. RAY (1983) "A Note on the Reliability of Certain Clustering Algorithms," *Journal of Marketing Research*, 20, February, 99–102.

GOWER, J. C. (1971) "A General Coefficient of Similarity and Some of Its Properties," *Biometrika*, 27, 857–71.

GREEN, PAUL E., AND ABBA M. KRIEGER (1991) "Segmenting Markets with Conjoint Analysis," *Journal of Marketing*, 55, October, 20–31.

GREEN, PAUL E., AND VITHALA R. RAO (1972) *Applied Multidimensional Scaling: A Comparison of Approaches and Algorithms*, New York: Holt, Rinehart and Winston.

HARTIGAN, JOHN A. (1975) *Clustering Algorithms*, New York: Wiley.

HYVARIAN, L. (1962) "Classification of Qualitative Data," *Nord. Tidskr. Info. Behandling*, 2, 83–89.

JACCARD, P. (1908) "Nouvelles recherches sur la distribution florale," *Bull. Soc. Vaud. Sci. Nat.*, 44, 223–70.

JAIN, A. K., AND R. C. DUBES (1988) *Algorithms for Clustering Data*, Englewood Cliffs, N.J.: Prentice-Hall.

KAMEN, JOSEPH M. (1970) "Quick Clustering," *Journal of Marketing Research*, 7, May, 199–204.

KAUFMAN, LEONARD, AND PETER J. ROUSSEEUW (1990) *Finding Groups in Data: An Introduction to Cluster Analysis*, New York: Wiley.

KLASTORIN, T. D. (1983) "Assessing Cluster Analysis Results," *Journal of Marketing Research*, 20, February, 92–98.

LEHMANN, DONALD R. (1972) "Judged Similarity and Brand-Switching Data as Similarity Measures," *Journal of Marketing Research*, 9, August, 331–34.

LINGOES, J. C. (1967) "The Multivariate Analysis of Qualitative Data," in M. Lovi and S. B. Lyerly, eds., *Conference of Cluster Analysis of Multivariate Data*, Springfield, Va.: U.S. Department of Commerce.

MACQUEEN, J. (1967) "Some Methods for Classification and Analysis of Multivariate Observations," in L. M. Le Cam and J. Neyman, eds., *Proceedings of the Fifth Berkeley Symposium on Mathematical Statistics and Probability*, vol. 1, Berkeley: University of California Press, 281–97.

MOORE, WILLIAM L., EDGAR A. PESSEMIER, AND DONALD R. LEHMANN (1986) "Hierarchical Representations of Market Structures and Choice Processes Through Preference Trees," *Journal of Business Research*, 14, November, 371-86.

MYERS, JAMES H. (1996) *Segmentation and Positioning for Strategic Marketing Decisions*, Chicago: American Marketing Association.

PUNJ, GIRISH, AND DAVID W. STEWART (1983) "Cluster Analysis in Marketing Research: Review and Suggestions for Application," *Journal of Marketing Research*, 20, May, 134–48.

RAO, VITHALA R., AND DARIUS J. SABAVALA (1981) "Inference of Hierarchical Choice Processes from Panel Data," *Journal of Consumer Research*, 8, June, 85–96.

RAO, VITHALA R., AND JOEL H. STECKEL (1995) *The New Science of Marketing*, Chicago: Irwin Professional.

SNEATH, P. H. A., AND R. R. SOKOL (1973) *Numerical Taxonomy*, San Francisco: Freeman.

SOKAL, R. R., AND C. D. MICHENER (1958) "A Statistical Method for Evaluating Systematic Relationships," *Univ. Kansas Sci. Bull.*, 38, 1409–38.

U.S. NEWS AND WORLD REPORT (1996) March 18, p. 90.

WARD, J. (1963) "Hierarchical Grouping to Optimize an Objective Function," *Journal of the American Statistical Association*, 58, 236–44.

WELLS, WILLIAM D. (1975) "Psychographics: A Critical Review," *Journal of Marketing Research*, 12, May, 196–211.

WIND, YORAM J. (1978) "Issues and Advances in Segmentation Research," *Journal of Marketing Research*, 15, August, 317–37.

APPENDIX 15-A ▬▬▬▬▬▬▬

SAMPLE SPSS OUTPUT

This appendix presents part of a sample SPSS output for a hierarchical cluster analysis. The objective of the analysis was to understand the structure of the top 25 business schools in 1996 according to the *U.S. News and World Report*. Table 15A.1 presents the raw data. The analysis was performed using Euclidean distance on unstandardized data with the centroid method of linking objects to clusters, and clusters to clusters. All variables except "Score" in Table 15A.1 were used. Since the data were not standardized, the variables with the largest numerical ranges, tuition and salary, were (perhaps inappropriately, perhaps not) the most influential variables in the analysis.

The first part of the output (Figure 15A.1), labeled page 3, gives the agglomeration schedule of the hierarchy. In particular, it tells us that the two most similar schools were 6 and 8 (Chicago and Columbia). These are joined in the lowest link of the hierarchy. The next two most similar objects were 4 and 13 (Northwestern and NYU), and so forth. Single objects are joined in the third and fourth stage. Finally, the fifth stage joins the (Chicago, Columbia) cluster with Duke. The culmination of the process described on page 3 is graphically depicted in the dendrogram in the last part of the output on page 5.

The second part of the output gives the details of the three-, four-, five-, and six-cluster solutions. SPSS provides the user with the option of printing out the solution derived by slicing the dendrogram at any level. We briefly describe the five-cluster solution as an illustration. Cluster 1 contains several private elite schools,{Stanford, MIT, Harvard, Penn (Wharton), Northwestern, NYU}, which are expensive, get good students, and whose graduates command high salaries. Cluster 2 is a second group of excellent schools: {Chicago, Columbia, Dartmouth, Duke, Virginia, Michigan, Carnegie Mellon, Berkeley, UCLA, Cornell}. Their students have slightly lower test scores and grades, and they command slightly lower salaries when they graduate. These schools are also expensive. Even the state schools have private-school-level tuitions. Cluster 3 consists of an excellent set of state

TABLE 15A.1 Graduate Business Schools with Highest Ranks in *U.S. News and World Report* Survey

Rank/School	Overall Score	Reputation Rank by Academics	Reputation Rank by Recruiters	Student Selectivity Rank	Placement Success Rank	Average 95 GMAT Score	95 Average Undergrad GPA	95 Acceptance Rate	95 Median Starting Salary	Employed 3 Mos. After Graduation	95 Out-of-State Tuition
1. Stanford	100.0	1	4	1	4	690	3.50	7.5%	$73,500	98.0%	$22,215
2. MIT	99.9	1	7	4	1	650	3.50	19.6	75,000	100.0	22,700
3. Wharton	99.8	6	3	2	2	660	3.51	16.8	75,000	99.0	22,228
4. Northwestern	99.3	1	1	8	5	646	3.40	16.2	70,000	98.0	21,774
5. Harvard	99.1	1	2	11	3	635	3.40	14.8	75,000	98.0	26,320
6. Chicago	98.4	1	8	7	7	656	3.40	27.7	65,000	98.5	22,668
7. Dartmouth	97.1	10	12	6	8	657	3.38	16.9	67,000	96.0	22,500
8. Columbia	96.7	7	10	10	10	650	3.30	19.2	65,000	97.0	22,700
9. Duke	96.1	10	5	18	9	630	3.25	23.3	64,250	98.2	22,900
10. Berkeley	96.0	7	15	9	12	652	3.31	16.8	64,000	96.0	16,095
11. Virginia	95.9	10	9	14	11	345	3.20	24.1	62,000	99.0	19,137
12. Michigan	95.5	7	5	13	18	643	3.32	29	62,000	95.0	22,475
13. New York Univ	94.9	16	19	16	6	638	3.24	26.9	70,000	97.0	21,542
14. Carnegie Mellon	93.6	15	17	19	13	640	3.20	37.6	61,800	96.7	21,400
15. Cornell	96.4	10	13	20	19	634	3.22	32.5	60,000	92.0	21,530
16. UCLA	93.3	10	16	3	30	650	3.50	18.3	63,000	86.0	16,185
17. North Carolina	92.7	16	11	28	15	613	3.20	18.7	59,000	97.0	10,831
18. Texas	91.3	19	14	22	24	622	3.27	24.6	55,000	95.0	10,654
19. Yale	91.3	19	21	5	32	664	3.40	31.6	63,000	88.2	22,555
20. Indiana	91.2	16	18	32	17	620	3.20	47.2	57,200	95.3	14,784
21. Purdue	90.2	21	20	39	14	600	3.20	30.3	57,000	98.0	11,125
22. Emory	89.7	33	25	21	20	626	3.30	34.7	58,000	93.0	20,140
23. Rochester	88.9	24	27	30	22	620	3.16	34.1	55,000	93.0	20,100
24. Maryland	87.8	33	43	12	27	630	3.40	1735	50,000	98.0	12,147
25. Georgetown	87.4	33	24	25	31	624	3.19	33.3	55,000	94.0	20,694

Source: *U.S. News and World Report* (March 18, 1996): 90. Copyright © 1998 by U.S. News and World Report. Reprinted with the permission of the publishers.

schools that are distinguished primarily by the fact that they are less expensive: {Chapel Hill, Texas, Indiana, Purdue}. Cluster 4, {Emory, Rochester, Georgetown}, are schools the are ranked at the lower part of the top tier. Their graduates command less money in the job market, but the schools are still expensive. Maryland is in a cluster by itself (cluster 5). What makes Maryland unique is its combination of low cost and extreme selectivity, making it seem like a great bargain.

```
* * * * * * H I E R A R C H I C A L   C L U S T E R   A N A L Y S I S * * * * * *

Agglomeration Schedule using Centroid Method
```

Stage	Clusters Combined Cluster 1	Cluster 2	Coefficient	Stage Cluster 1st Appears Cluster 1	Cluster 2	Next Stage
1	6	8	34.532738	0	0	5
2	4	13	233.703903	0	0	19
3	2	3	472.164001	0	0	9
4	23	25	594.179810	0	0	16
5	6	9	772.459106	1	0	12
6	12	19	1003.769897	0	0	8
7	10	16	1004.278992	0	0	20
8	12	14	1128.823120	6	0	10
9	1	2	1420.668579	0	3	18
10	12	15	1977.623535	8	0	13
11	17	21	2021.625244	0	0	15
12	6	7	2087.989990	5	0	14
13	11	12	2388.125977	0	10	14
14	6	11	2505.459961	12	13	20
15	17	18	2524.038818	11	0	17
16	22	23	2876.979248	0	4	21
17	17	20	3331.393799	15	0	22
18	1	5	3633.259277	9	0	19
19	1	4	4095.941650	18	2	24
20	6	10	4592.301758	14	7	21
21	6	22	5216.463867	20	16	23
22	17	24	5966.074707	17	0	23
23	6	17	7131.740234.	21	22	24
24	1	6	8806.812500	19	23	0

FIGURE 15A.1
SPSS Output for Cluster Analysis of Business Schools

Cluster Membership of Cases using Centroid Method

Number of Clusters

Label	Case	6	5	4	3
1. Stanford	1	1	1	1	1
2. MIT	2	1	1	1	1
3. Penn	3	1	1	1	1
4. Northwestern	4	1	1	1	1
5. Harvard	5	1	1	1	1
6. Chicago	6	2	2	2	2
7 Dartmouth	7	2	2	2	2
8. Columbia	8	2	2	2	2
9. Duke	9	2	2	2	2
10. Berkeley	10	3	2	2	2
11. Virginia	11	2	2	2	2
12. Michigan	12	2	2	2	2
13. New York Univ	13	1	1	1	1
14. Carnegie Mellon	14	2	2	2	2
15. Cornell	15	2	2	2	2
16. UCLA	16	3	2	2	2
17. Chapel Hill	17	4	3	3	3
18. Texas	18	4	3	3	3
19. Yale	19	2	2	2	2
20. Indiana	20	4	3	3	3
21. Purdue	21	4	3	3	3
22. Emory	22	5	4	2	2
23. Rochester	23	5	4	2	2
24. Maryland	24	6	5	4	3
25. Georgetown	25	5	4	2	2

FIGURE 15A.1
(continued)

Dendrogram using Centroid Method

Rescaled Distance Cluster Combine

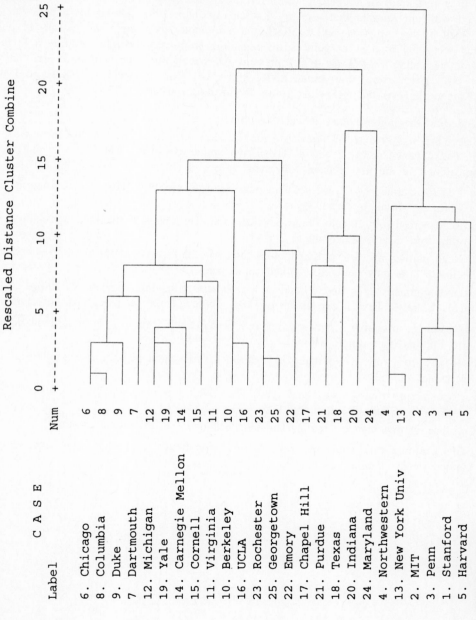

FIGURE 15A.1
(*continued*)

APPENDIX 15-B

QUICK CLUSTERING

We do not present quick clustering as an alternative to the formal procedures discussed earlier. However, quick clustering is a useful tool that can be invoked on the back of an envelope in a restaurant or to gain preliminary insight at a business meeting. We illustrate the method with an example first used by Kamen (1970, p. 199). As part of a periodic survey conducted by the American Oil Company, several motorists were asked to rate 11 gasoline brands according to a seven-point scale extending from very favorable (rating = 7) to very unfavorable (rating = 1). Table 15B.1 presents the correlation matrix of the overall ratings of every brand with every other brand in Rockford, Ill., from a survey conducted in 1965.

Kamen suggests the following recipe for forming clusters:

1. Underline the highest entry in each column.
2. Select the highest entry in the entire matrix. Here it is .640, the correlation between Martin and Owens, brands 2 and 8. These two brands constitute what we will call the reciprocal pair in the first cluster. Join them with a double arrow. See Table 15B.1.
3. a. Reading across row 2, we see that one brand, Clark (brand 10) is also underlined. Join Clark to Martin by a single arrow.
    b. Read across row 10. No brand is underlined. The chain of maximal correlations beginning from Martin is complete.
    c. Read across row 8. No brand other than Martin is underlined. Stop. The first cluster, cluster I, is now defined as brands 2, 8, and 10.
4. Excluding brands 2, 8, and 10, select the highest remaining correlation. Phillips and D-X, brands 5 and 7, have a correlation of .484. These are the reciprocal pair of cluster II.
5. a. Reading across row 5, we see that one brand, Shell (brand 3) is underlined. Join Shell to Phillips by a single arrow.
    b. Read across row 3. No brand is underlined. The chain beginning from Phillips is now complete.
    c. Read across row 7. No brand other than Shell is underlined. Stop. Cluster II is now defined as Shell, Phillips, and D-X.
6. Continue in this manner until all brands have been placed into a cluster.

This example was conducted with a correlation matrix of brands. The same recipe can be applied to any similarities matrix.

TABLE 15B.1 Correlations Among Gasoline Brands in Rockford, Illinois, in Terms of General Attitude

	Standard 1	Martin 2	Shell 3	Texaco 4	Phillips 5	Mobil 6	D-X 7	Owens 8	Skelly 9	Clark 10	Gulf 11
Standard 1	—	.006	.358	.382	.325	.289	.262	.108	.368	.178	.404
Martin 2	.006	—	.157	.088	.134	.161	.130	.640	.184	.360	.200
Shell 3	.358	.157	—	.337	.375	.343	.340	.057	.322	.256	.336
Texaco 4	.382	.088	.337	—	.430	.452	.326	.053	.357	.266	.337
Phillips 5	.325	.134	.375	.430	—	.445	.484	.170	.432	.325	.281
Mobil 6	.289	.161	.343	.452	.445	—	.358	.119	.454	.177	.322
D-X 7	.262	.130	.340	.326	.484	.358	—	.110	.393	.300	.230
Owens 8	.108	.640	.057	.053	.170	.119	.110	—	.349	.301	.180
Skelly 9	.368	.184	.322	.357	.432	.454	.393	.349	—	.238	.307
Clark 10	.178	.360	.256	.266	.325	.177	.300	.301	.238	—	.208
Gulf 11	.404	.200	.336	.337	.281	.322	.230	.180	.307	.208	—

CHAPTER 16

Factor Analysis

In the so-called information age we are constantly bombarded with numbers, be they stock prices, baseball statistics, consumer prices, changes in the economy, or measures of customer satisfaction. It is simply not feasible to use 317 variables in most analyses or presentations. To avoid information overload and to make coherent sense of the data, it is not uncommon to rely on a variety of indexes (e.g., the Dow Jones Index, the Consumer Price Index, the Index of Leading Economic Indicators). These indexes summarize information concisely. For example, the Dow Jones summarizes the movement of the stock market, and the Consumer Price Index reflects the prices of consumer products and is used to monitor inflation in the economy. An obvious question is how to create such an index that appropriately summarizes the data with the minimum loss of information.

A widely used procedure for doing this is factor analysis. In essence, factor analysis is a type of cluster analysis which attempts to cluster variables (as opposed to objects/observations); as we will see, it uses correlation between variables as a similarity measure.

BASIC NOTION

The basic purpose of factor analysis is to group together variables that are highly correlated (and thus, to some extent, redundant). There are two basic reasons for doing this. First, there is the desire for simplification. For example, while it is possible to analyze 67 variables in detail, it would be much easier, for both analyzing and communicating the results of the study, if only, say, 15 (or even better 3) variables were used. One use of factor analysis is to reduce the 67 variables to 15 (or 3) with the minimum possible loss of information (and the resulting relatively uncorrelated variables retained for further analysis). The reduced set of variables is then used (*a*) to more efficiently analyze the results of a given study by reducing the number of variables considered or (*b*) to reduce the amount of data needed in subsequent studies by reducing the number of pieces of information (e.g., responses to questions) collected. The second reason for using factor analysis is to uncover underlying structure in the data. This use of factor analysis assumes that the 67 variables are manifestations of a small number (e.g., 10) of key

TABLE 16.1 Hypothetical Correlations among Four Variables

Variable	Variable			
	1	2	3	4
1	1.0	.9	.7	.2
2		1.0	.8	.05
3			1.0	.1
4				1.0

but unmeasured constructs. It then attempts to deduce what the underlying constructs are by examining the relations among the 67 measured variables. These two uses for factor analysis place different emphasis on how the results are interpreted and used. First, a relatively mechanistic use of factor analysis is a means to an end and uses the factors as input into another analysis (e.g., regression) or decision (e.g., questionnaire design). In contrast, the second use focuses on interpreting the factors.

Consider the correlation matrix of Table 16.1. Here we have four variables, which were questions on a pilot study. Assume we need to reduce these four questions to two questions (there is only room for two questions on the next wave of the study, or the computer algorithm we want to use can only handle two variables).

The best way to simplify is to have a theory dictating which variables to retain. Absent theory (which is hard to have when the variables aren't even named, as is the case here), common sense suggests that I discard those variables that give me the least additional information value if retained. To do this, I might find out which variables are most correlated with each other. In this example, variables 1, 2, and 3 all are fairly highly correlated with each other, and 4 seems to be different. Hence, I might classify 1, 2, and 3 as type A variables and 4 as a type B variable, and then pick a representative of each type. What factor analysis essentially does (when all the theory is stripped away) is to group together those variables that are highly correlated.

To better understand the intuition behind factor analysis, consider Table 16.2, which gives the scores of students on algebra, spelling, etc. If John gets a score of 90 (out of 100) in algebra, what do you think will be his score on the geometry and numerical tests? Does his score on algebra give us any indication of his score on writing and reading? Intuition suggests that if John gets a high score on algebra, he is likely to also get a high score on geometry and numerical tests, since they all measure (an underlying construct of) analytical ability. In other words, algebra, geometry, and numerical skills, and hence the scores, are likely to be (cor)related.

TABLE 16.2 Students' Test Scores

	Score on					
	Algebra	Geometry	Numerical	Spelling	Writing	Reading
John	90			10		
Jack	30			95		
Jane	96			98		
.						
.						
.						

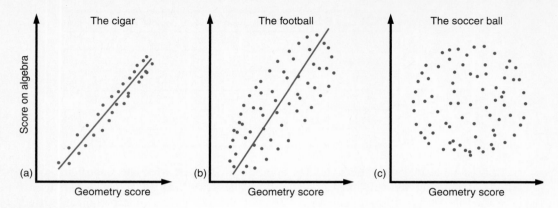

FIGURE 16.1

(a) The cigar; (b) The football; (c) The soccer ball

Figure 16.1 gives pictorial representations of three different correlations, where each point represents a student. In a three-dimensional space (e.g., algebra, geometry, and numerical), the cloud of points looks like a cigar, a football, and a soccer ball, respectively, in these three figures. For ease of illustration, consider only two variables—algebra and geometry.

In Figure 16.1A, algebra and geometry scores are very highly correlated. In other words, if we know the score of a student on algebra, we can predict his or her score on geometry fairly accurately. In this scenario, we do not need two "variables" called algebra and geometry; either one would suffice. Alternatively, we can describe everything with one "factor," which is basically the sum of the algebra and geometry scores and can be represented as a straight line through the data points as shown in Figure 16.1a.

In Figure 16.1b, the correlation between algebra and geometry scores is lower than in the first case. If we were to predict a person's geometry score from his algebra score, we would do this by drawing a straight line through the cloud of points as done in Figure 16.1b. Note two things. First, this single line represents one "factor" which captures most but not all of the information in the data. Second, this line is drawn in the direction of maximum variance, that is, through the larger axis of the cloud of points. This is exactly what factor analysis does in combining variables to obtain factors.

In Figure 16.1c, there is no correlation between the scores on algebra and geometry. In this case one factor will not capture all the information available in the data; in fact, it could capture only half of it (e.g., either algebra or geometry skill).

The key output of factor analysis is the *loadings (assignment) matrix*. This matrix indicates which variables go with which factors and "assigns" variables to factors. In our example, if (*a*) the analytical variables (algebra, geometry, numerical) were perfectly correlated with each other, (*b*) the language skills (spelling, writing, reading) were perfectly correlated with each other, and (*c*) analytical and language skills were uncorrelated as in Table 16.3, then the loadings matrix would appear as in Table 16.4A. In reality the world is never quite this simple. Table 16.4B presents a more typical loadings matrix. Although the correlations in this matrix are not 1 or 0, the pattern is similar to that of Table 16.4A (i.e., variables 1–3 have high correlation, and therefore, go with factor 1, while variables 4–6 go with factor 2).

TABLE 16.3 Two Independent Factors—Correlation Data

	A	G	N	S	W	R
Algebra	1	1	1	0	0	0
Geometry	1	1	1	0	0	0
Numerical	1	1	1	0	0	0
Spelling	0	0	0	1	1	1
Writing	0	0	0	1	1	1
Reading	0	0	0	1	1	1

THE FACTOR ANALYSIS MODEL

Factor analysis is a formal multivariate statistical procedure. While managers don't need to know much about this, we present it briefly (a) for cultural purposes and (b) because some of the terminology analysts use is based on the model.

The model underlying factor analysis is that observed data (Xs) are really "produced" by some underlying and unobserved factors (fs). This model is essentially adapted from psychology. The objective in psychology is often to understand the structure of the data (e.g., to uncover the basic determinants of individual scores on an aptitude test), and the method deduces the structure indirectly by naming the factors (e.g., quantitative ability, analytical skill). Believing this model is not necessary for using factor analysis for some purposes, such as removing redundant variables. Nonetheless, much of the "flavor" of the interpretation of factor analysis for both construct derivation and variable reduction comes from this model. The basic form of the model is

Observed value of the kth person on the ith variable	=	f(kth person's "true" scores on the underlying factors and a random element)

Put mathematically, this becomes

$$X_{ik} = \lambda_{i1}F_{1k} + \lambda_{i2}F_{2k} + \cdots + \lambda_{im}F_{mk} + e_{ik} \tag{16.1}$$

TABLE 16.4 Two-Factor Loadings Matrix

A. Extreme Scenario			B. More Typical Scenario		
Variable	Factor 1	Factor 2	Variable	Factor 1	Factor 2
Algebra	1	0	Algebra	.92	.02
Geometry	1	0	Geometry	.83	.05
Numerical	1	0	Quantitative	.76	.13
Spelling	0	1	Spelling	.11	.72
Writing	0	1	Writing	.16	.95
Reading	0	1	Reading	.09	.67

TABLE 16.5		**Assignment (Loading) Matrix**		
	Factor			
Variable	**1**	**2**	**. . .**	**m**
1	λ_{11}	λ_{12}	. . .	λ_{1m}
2	λ_{21}	λ_{22}	. . .	λ_{2m}
⋮	⋮	⋮		⋮
p	λ_{p1}	λ_{p2}	. . .	λ_{pm}

where

X_{ik} = value of variable i for the kth observation

F_{jk} = value of the jth factor for the kth observation (commonly called *factor scores*)

λ_{ij} = relation of the ith variable with the jth common factor; there are m factors and p variables, $m \leq p$

e_{ik} = error

The λ_{ij}s (often called *loadings*) indicate how the underlying constructs (factors) are related to the measured variables. More specifically, the loadings are correlations between the factors and the variables. The loadings thus form the assignment matrix (Table 16.5).

Note that if we knew the factor scores (F), we could run regressions of each of the Xs versus all the Fs to obtain the factor loadings (λ), which would be the regression coefficients. Since we don't know the factor scores, the key objective of factor analysis is to obtain both the factor scores and the loadings in such a way that the we capture most of the information available in the original variables in as few factors as possible.

HOW FACTOR ANALYSIS WORKS: METHOD AND APPLICATION

We outline various steps of the factor analysis procedure and illustrate them with an application. Our illustration shows the use of factor analysis in data reduction, and its marketing application in creating perceptual maps. We will also include typical output obtained from the statistical package SAS.

Consider the situation where a car manufacturer is trying to understand consumer perceptions of cars in order to find gaps in the marketplace and better position its own new car. Since an essentially infinite number of attributes exist on which cars differ, we need a simplified picture of the car market. We address this problem with factor analysis as follows.

1. Choose the Variables to Analyze (Manager)[1]

A crucial (but often overlooked) step is the selection of variables to be analyzed. Management typically uses some combination of past research, its own judgment, focus

---

[1]There are several steps in factor analysis where managers' input is critical, while in other steps computer programs automatically perform the task. At each step, we indicate whether the manager or the computer program is responsible for the task.

groups, or other special studies to decide which variables or attributes are important to customers in forming perceptions about their products or services. Factor analysis only reduces data present in the original variables; it does not indicate what important variables have been omitted. Therefore if you don't include variables such as car style or design, these will not emerge as important factors. Factor analysis also often reproduces obvious results. For example, if someone factor analyzed participation in two sports, consumption of two wines, and reading of two magazines, such as *Time* and *Newsweek*, he or she might get an interesting cross-fertilization (e.g., *Time*'s readers consume a certain kind of wine). More likely, however, they would obtain three factors: sports, wine consumption, and magazine readership. In our application, the managers decided to collect data on 15 attributes for the 10 cars listed in Table 16.6.

2. Obtain Data on the Variables (Manager)

The next step is to obtain perceptions/ratings (e.g., on a 0–10 scale) of the various cars included in the study on the 15 attributes.[2] To reduce the burden on consumers and to improve the quality of the data, some researchers collect data on only a few cars from any one consumer (e.g., those cars that a consumer is familiar with). Of course then you need to decide how to deal with missing data, so many researchers prefer getting ratings on all the cars. In our example, customers rated all 10 cars on all 15 attributes. It is also useful to obtain data on consumers' *preferences* (overall liking) of each car. The resulting data would look like Table 16.7.

TABLE 16.6 Attributes and Cars

Attributes		Cars	
A1	Appeals to other people	1.	Buick Century
A2	Attractive looking	2.	Ford Taurus
A3	Expensive looking	3.	Oldsmobile Cutlass Supreme
A4	Exciting	4.	Ford Thunderbird
A5	Very reliable	5.	Chevrolet Celebrity
A6	Well engineered	6.	Honda Accord
A7	Trend setting	7.	Pontiac Grand Am
A8	Has all the latest features	8.	Chevrolet Corsica
A9	Luxurious	9.	Ford Tempo
A10	Distinctive looking	10.	Toyota Camry
A11	Nameplate you can trust		
A12	Conservative looking		
A13	Family vehicle		
A14	Basic transportation		
A15	High quality		

[2]Strictly speaking, all the variables in factor analysis should be intervally scaled. In practice, inclusion of ordinally scaled variables generally produces reasonable results.

TABLE 16.7 Consumers' Ratings

Respondent	Brand	Preference	Attribute[a] 1	2	3	4	5	6	7	8	9	10	11	12	13	14	15
1	1	4	5	7	7	8	5	6	8	5	6	8	6	4	5	4	6
1	2	8	4	6	5	6	5	6	4	5	5	5	4	4	3	4	5
1	3	7	3	6	7	8	5	5	8	7	8	6	5	5	3	2	5
1	4	9	6	5	5	5	6	5	3	5	5	4	4	6	7	7	4
1	5	6	4	4	5	4	7	7	4	5	5	6	7	5	3	7	7
1	6	4	7	6	6	4	4	5	6	5	5	4	4	5	7	5	4
1	7	9	4	6	5	5	5	4	7	5	5	6	6	5	5	4	5
1	8	2	5	8	6	7	5	6	8	7	7	8	6	5	5	4	7
1	9	4	5	7	6	5	9	8	5	6	5	7	9	5	6	4	9
1	10	9	6	6	6	6	4	5	5	6	5	5	4	5	4	4	5
2	1	4	6	6	6	6	6	5	7	8	7	6	5	5	7	7	4
2	2	5	5	6	6	7	5	6	7	8	7	6	5	4	5	5	4
2	3	5	4	5	7	6	4	6	6	8	8	7	4	4	4	3	4
2	4	2	7	5	5	4	5	6	6	7	6	7	5	7	8	8	4
2	5	7	8	8	6	5	8	8	7	8	7	5	7	5	6	5	8
2	6	9	3	8	8	8	4	4	9	8	6	7	4	3	3	4	4
2	7	3	7	6	5	5	5	6	6	6	4	5	4	7	8	8	4
2	8	8	7	6	7	6	6	6	7	7	5	5	5	5	7	7	5
2	9	9	9	7	6	6	0	0	8	7	6	6	0	6	7	4	0
2	10	7	7	5	6	5	4	4	5	8	8	6	3	8	6	4	4
⋮	⋮	⋮	⋮	⋮	⋮	⋮	⋮	⋮	⋮	⋮	⋮	⋮	⋮	⋮	⋮	⋮	⋮

[a]The first column is the respondent or consumer ID, the second column is the brand rated, the third column gives a consumer's preference for that brand, and columns 4–18 show consumers' perceptions of a car on each of the 15 attributes.

3. Develop a Correlation Matrix from the Data (Computer)

Table 16.8 gives the correlation matrix for the 15 attributes used in this study.[3] (For simplicity, we only include a single significant digit.) This correlation matrix is the key input to factor analysis. Recall that high correlations among certain attributes suggest that they can be combined into a factor. For example, Table 16.8 shows that attributes 3 (expensive) and 9 (luxurious) have a correlation of 0.7 and hence are candidates for grouping together into a factor.

4. Find Factors and Factor Loadings (Computer)

Usually factors are chosen such that the first factor explains as much of the total information in all the original variables as possible, the second factor is orthogonal to (i.e.,

---

[3]It is possible to use a covariance, instead of a correlation, matrix. If the scales of various attributes are quite different, it is desirable to use a correlation matrix. We use the correlation matrix in the examples throughout this chapter. Note also that we only present one significant figure in the correlation matrix. This is done to simplify presentation, but may often reflect the accuracy of the underlying data (e.g., .039271 is usually silly precision).

TABLE 16.8 Attribute Correlation Matrix

		A1	A2	A3	A4	A5	A6	A7	A8	A9	A10	A11	A12	A13	A14	A15
A1.	Appeals to others	1	.2	.1	.2	.3	.2	.1	.2	.3	.2	.2	.2	.5	.2	.2
A2.	Attractive looking		1	.6	.2	.4	.3	.4	.3	.5	.5	.3	−.1	0	−.3	.4
A3.	Expensive looking			1	.6	.3	.3	.6	.4	.7	.6	.4	−.1	.2	−.3	.6
A4.	Exciting				1	.3	.3	.7	.4	.6	.3	.4	−.1	.3	−.2	.4
A5.	Very reliable					1	.6	.3	.3	.4	.2	.5	.2	.1	−.1	.7
A6.	Well engineered						1	.2	.1	.4	.3	.6	.2	.2	0	.5
A7.	Trend setting							1	.5	.5	.5	.4	−.1	.2	−.2	.5
A8.	Has latest features								1	.6	.2	.2	−.1	.2	−.2	.4
A9.	Luxurious									1	.5	.4	0	.3	−.2	.5
A10.	Distinctive looking										1	.3	0	.1	−.2	.4
A11.	Name you can trust											1	0	.1	0	.6
A12.	Conservative looking												1	.2	.3	0
A13.	Family car													1	.4	.1
A14.	Basic transportation														1	−.2
A15.	High quality															1

has zero correlation with) the first factor and contains as much as possible of the remaining information, and so forth.[4] If one views the cloud of data as a football (see Figure 16.1b), then graphically the first factor is a line (or a plane) that passes through the major (longest) axis of the football, the second factor is the line that is perpendicular to the first factor and passes through the next longest axis of the football, and so forth.

For our automobile application, the results of factor analysis (using SAS) are given in Table 16.9. The top of the table shows 15 factors, labeled 1 through 15. (The maximum number of factors is equal to the number of original variables.) The table also shows the *eigenvalues* associated with each factor. These eigenvalues have the following features:

a. The sum of the eigenvalues is the number of variables used in the analysis.[5] In our application we used 15 variables, which is also the sum of all the eigenvalues. This property provides an intuitively appealing way to understand what an eigenvalue represents. Loosely speaking, an eigenvalue of 5.55 for factor 1 suggests that factor 1 contains information equivalent to the information in 5.55 variables. Put differently, in terms of information content the first factor is equal to more than five uncorrelated variables. Many computer programs (including SAS) have a default option of keeping only those factors with eigenvalue greater than 1. The intuition behind this is to keep only those factors that contain information of at least one uncorrelated variable. In our application, this criterion led to the selection of three factors.

---

[4]This initial step is referred to as a *principal components* analysis. These components are uniquely derived mathematically through an "eigenvalue decomposition."

[5]If a covariance matrix is used, the sum of eigenvalues is equal to the sum of the variances of all the original variables. Since variances can be arbitrarily influenced by the scale used (e.g., thousands vs. millions), we restrict our discussion to correlation matrices only.

TABLE 16.9 Output of Car Factor Analysis

Initial Factor Method: Principal Components
Prior Communality Estimates: ONE
Eigenvalues of the Correlation Matrix: Total = 15 Average = 1

	1	2	3	4	5
Eigenvalue	5.551485	2.137958	1.503064	0.986959	0.909806
Proportion	0.3701	0.1425	0.1002	0.0658	0.0607
Cumulative	0.3701	0.5126	0.6128	0.7393	

	6	7	8	9	10
Eigenvalue	0.766337	0.57664	0.556800	0.459823	0.419628
Proportion	0.0511	0.0384	0.0372	0.0307	0.0280
Cumulative	0.7004	0.8288	0.8659	0.8966	0.9246

	11	12	13	14	15
Eigenvalue	0.366926	0.296028	0.186919	0.160394	0.121210
Proportion	0.0245	0.0197	0.0125	0.0107	0.0081
Cumulative	0.9490	0.9677	0.9812	0.9919	1.0000

3 factors will be retained by the MINEIGEN criterion.

Factor Pattern

	FACTOR 1	FACTOR 2	FACTOR 3
V1	0.34500	0.542110	0.28214
V2	0.62319	−0.19421	−0.15148
V3	0.83430	−0.21481	0.12101
V4	0.71783	−0.08673	0.35063
V5	0.62923	0.27653	−0.48664
V6	0.58628	0.40348	−0.49426
V6	0.73028	−0.24129	0.27258
V8	0.56366	−0.21881	0.29272
V9	0.82139	−0.03726	0.20562
V10	0.63698	−0.11927	0.06120
V11	0.64070	0.21370	−0.34536
V12	0.00656	0.65710	0.05607
V13	0.31392	0.59498	0.56403
V14	−0.23790	0.74703	0.18888
V15	0.78018	0.04140	−0.31559

Variance explained by each factor

	FACTOR 1	FACTOR 2	FACTOR 3
	5.551485	2.137958	1.503064

Final Communality Estimates: Total = 9.192506

V1	V2	V3	V4	V5
0.492503	0.449033	0.757269	0.645747	0.709215

V6	V7	V8	V9	V10
0.750886	0.665829	0.451276	0.718347	0.423710

V11	V12	V13	V14	V15
0.562726	0.434964	0.770684	0.650328	0.709992

b. The eigenvalue of a factor divided by the sum of the eigenvalues of all factors represents the percent variance (loosely speaking, the percent of total information) explained by that factor:

$$\begin{array}{l}\text{Percent total variation in}\\ p \text{ variables accounted for}\\ \text{by } j\text{th principal component}\end{array} = \frac{\text{Eigenvalue}_j}{\sum\limits_{i=1}^{p}\text{Eigenvalue}_i} \qquad (16.3)$$

When (as is typically done) the correlation matrix is used as the basis for factoring, this becomes:

$$\begin{array}{l}\text{Percent total variation in}\\ p \text{ variables accounted for}\\ \text{by } j\text{th principal component}\end{array} = \frac{\text{Eigenvalue}_j}{\text{Number of variables}} \qquad (16.4)$$

For example, in Table 16.9, the eigenvalue of the first factor is 5.55, and the sum of the eigenvalues is 15. Therefore, the proportion of the variance explained by the first factor is 5.55/15 = 0.37 (as shown in the second row in the top half of Table 16.9). Similarly, factor 2 explains 2.13/15 = 14 percent of the total variance. Collectively, factors 1 and 2 explain 37 + 14 = 51 percent of the variance (given in the row labeled "Cumulative"). The first three factors collectively capture almost 61 percent of the total information in the original 15 variables. This data reduction is the main objective of factor analysis. Notice that the first factor has the largest eigenvalue, the second factor has the next largest eigenvalue, and so on.

For purposes of interpretation, the most useful output is the factor pattern or the *loadings matrix*. As indicated earlier, these loadings are the correlations between a factor and a variable. For example, the loading of 0.345 represents the correlation between variable (or attribute) 1, "Appeals to other people," and factor 1.

The loadings and eigenvalues have an interesting relationship (although admittedly not one that is very useful managerially). Specifically,

$$\text{Eigenvalue}_k = \lambda_{1k}^2 + \lambda_{2k}^2 + \cdots + \lambda_{nk}^2 \qquad (16.5)$$

where λ_{pk} = loading of variable p on factor k. In our application, for factor 1 we have:

$$5.55 = (.345)^2 + (.623)^2 + \cdots + (.780)^2$$

This relationship is easy to understand if we recall that the square of the correlation is the explained variance (remember the famous R^2 of regression?). Since each variable is a linear combination of the orthogonal factors, the sum of the squares of the loadings or correlations is equal to the total variance explained by (or the eigenvalue of) that factor.

So-called *communalities* represent the proportion of the variance of each variable that is explained by the selected factors. In our application, we selected three factors.

Communalities are related to the loadings. Specifically, the sum of squares for a row in the loadings matrix is equal to the communality of a variable (as long as the factors are orthogonal). For example, for variable 1, the communality is

$$0.4925 = (.345)^2 + (.542)^2 + \cdots + (.282)^2$$

This tells us that these three factors capture .4925 of the variance (or information) in attribute 1.[6]

5. Select the Appropriate Number of Factors (Manager/Computer)

How many factors from the original 15 variables should we retain? This question can be answered in a variety of ways.

Prior Theory   The best way to determine how many factors exist in the data is to employ prior theory.

Parsimony   Limitations of a computer program or available space in a questionnaire also guide the selection of factors. Here, fewer is better.

Statistical Criteria   Three empirical criteria are typically used to select the appropriate number of factors. These are:

1. Proportion of variance explained. Generally, you want this to be large (e.g., 60–80%). The objective here is to capture most of the information available in the original data.
2. Number of factors with eigenvalues greater than 1. As explained earlier, an eigenvalue of, say, 5 represents the amount of information contained in five independent variables. Therefore, this criterion suggests that a factor that does not even contain information equivalent to one original variable should be dropped.
3. Scree plot. This is a plot of the eigenvalues (or variance explained by each factor) and the number of factors. Figure 16.2 shows the Scree plot for our application. This plot effectively shows the tradeoff between the cost (in terms of complexity) of retaining additional factors versus the benefit (explaining additional variance in the data). Not surprisingly, there are diminishing marginal returns as we increase the number of factors. Where to draw the line is a matter of judgment. In general, people look for an "elbow" in the plot, that is, a point at which the improvement in variance explained levels off. In our example, an elbow appears after four factors. (Of course in many applications the plot is smooth, with no clear elbow.)

Managerial Usefulness   The purpose of analytical techniques is to help in decision making. Therefore, one of the key decision criteria should be the ease of interpretation and understanding. For example, if a manager finds it easier to understand and interpret a

---

[6]Had we selected all 15 factors, these communality proportions would be 1 for each of the variables. However, keeping 15 factors would defeat the data reduction objective of factor analysis. Note: Some users assume the total communality is less than 1, essentially allowing for error in measurement. While interesting to multivariate statistics students, this issue is, fortunately, not central to managerial use.

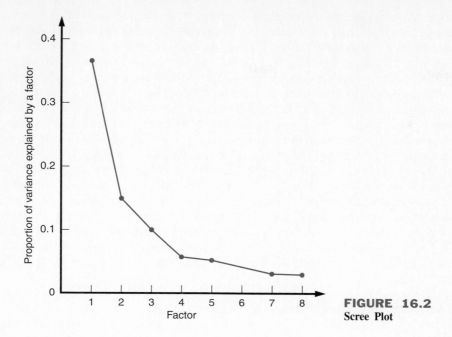

FIGURE 16.2
Scree Plot

three-dimensional factor space than a five-dimensional space, the former may be prefer-able even if the last two factors have eigenvalues greater than 1.

6. Modify the Initial Factor Analysis Solution (Computer)

The purpose of this step is to simplify interpretation and modify the original solution. Many procedures produce initial solutions (i.e., principal components/eigenvectors) that have unclear assignment matrices. In particular, almost all the variables sometimes load on the first fac-tor at a moderate level, and some variables seem to be related to more than one factor. This step "cleans up" the interpretation by getting the loadings (λ) close to 1 or 0, thereby making interpretation easier.

The modification is achieved in a factor analysis program by rotating the original factor analysis solution. There are two common rotation methods—varimax (which pre-serves the orthogonality among factors) and oblique (which permits some correlation among factors). Varimax is the standard (default) option in most programs and works well in most situations. Table 16.10 provides varimax rotated factors and the corre-sponding loadings matrix for the car example. Note that after rotation the variance explained by factor 1 has gone down from 5.55 to 4.18. What the rotation does is redis-tribute variance among the chosen factors to ease interpretation.

7. Use the Factors (Manager)

Factor analyses are used in at least six ways.

Interpreting the Underlying Constructs ("Insight")   Here, the purpose is to understand the major determinants of variation in the data. For example, in the car study we want to understand which key factors influence consumers' perceptions of cars. We have already obtained three factors. To facilitate interpretation, we use the rotated factor loadings matrix to interpret/name the factors (notice which variables belong to the third factor is noticeably clearer after rotation). The basic idea is to see which variables "load heavily" on which factors. Exactly what "load heavily" means is somewhat vague and really depends on the study. However, many people choose an arbitrary cutoff level, such as .5 for the loadings, so that each variable tends to load on exactly one factor. For example, a factor that includes income, education, and occupational status might be called "well-offness." The naming of factors is subjective but also fun and occasionally produces an interesting insight. Moreover, in some cases, such as segment development, the names themselves may be the key result of the analysis. In Table 16.10, to facilitate naming of the car factors, we have highlighted the loadings above .5 for each of the three factors for the car study. The variables that load heavily on factor 1 are attractive looking, expensive, exciting, trend setting, has latest features, luxurious, and distinctive looking. Based on these attributes, we could name the first factor "trendy".[7] Similarly, the second factor could be called "quality and reliability," and the third factor could be denoted as "basic transportation." Once we understand that these three factors drive (no pun intended) consumers' perceptions of cars, it can help us in designing and/or positioning our own car.

Reducing Variables to a More Manageable Number   Early in the study of a problem, a large number of variables (e.g., 70) may appear as candidates for study. Yet such a large number will encumber both survey and analysis. There is a strong incentive, therefore, to reduce the 70 variables to a more manageable number. The obvious place to start is to require the variables to be theoretically/logically useful and measurable. Beyond that, it is generally agreed that reducing redundancy is an efficient way to improve the variable set. Since factor analysis groups variables into factors so that all the variables in a factor are correlated with each other, it is clearly a useful technique for this problem. There are at least three major approaches for deciding how to eliminate variables.

- *Pick one variable to represent each factor.* The representative should be both a well-measured and well-understood variable and have a high loading on the factor. It is also beneficial to retain variables that do not load highly on any factor. This is the easiest approach and for many reasons preferable to the more complicated methods. Using the representative method of variable selection, however, is likely to create an omitted variable/specification problem. Assume that I use only husband's education in a regression, but that the wife's education is really the key variable. In this case, the coefficient of husband's education could well lead me to falsely conclude that it is the key variable.
- *Build an index based on the major variables on each factor.* This index could be a simple sum or some weighted combination of the "big loading" variables. The index method is basically a way to increase reliability by the use of multiple measures of a construct.

---

[7]Note we could also call it "Upscale," "Luxury," and so forth. The naming process is imprecise and can lead to either novel insights, confirmation of prior expectations, or meaningless misinterpretations if, for example, we named the first factor "Trendy" and it was really "Luxury."

TABLE 16.10 **Rotated Factor Pattern**

Rotation Method: Varimax
Orthogonal Transformation Matrix

	1	2	3
1	0.80299	0.58937	0.08858
2	−0.32599	0.30992	0.89313
3	0.49893	−0.74605	0.44099

Rotated Factor Pattern

		FACTOR 1	FACTOR 2	FACTOR 3
Appeals to other people	V1	0.24108	0.16085	0.63915
Attractive looking	V2	**0.48815**	0.42012	−0.18506
Expensive looking	V3	**0.80066**	0.33455	−0.06549
Exciting	V4	**0.77963**	0.13460	0.14075
Very reliable	V5	0.17323	**0.81961**	0.08811
Well engineered	V6	0.09261	**0.83935**	0.19442
Trend setting	V7	**0.80106**	0.15227	−0.03061
Has latest features	V8	**0.66999**	0.04601	−0.01641
Luxurious	V9	**0.77431**	0.31915	0.13015
Distinctive looking	V10	**0.58090**	0.29279	−0.02311
Name you can trust	V11	0.26447	**0.69560**	0.09443
Conservative looking	V12	−0.24745	0.24161	**0.56157**
Family vehicle	V13	0.33954	−0.05137	**0.80793**
Basic transportation	V14	−0.34032	−0.04961	**0.72942**
High Quality	V15	0.45552	**0.70809**	−0.03309

Variance explained by each factor

FACTOR 1	FACTOR 2	FACTOR 3
4.180932	2.970304	2.041271

- *Use the factor scores.* The scores of each observation on the underlying factors can be estimated and used to represent each factor (see Appendix 16-A). This can guarantee truly uncorrelated variables. It is common to use these factor scores as independent variables in a regression since they reduce multicollinearity. Unfortunately, this approach does not reduce variables to be measured for future studies, since it requires all of them to be included in the score. It also is harder to interpret a factor score than a single variable or a simple sum of two or three variables. Given the choice between known variables with uncertain coefficients and unknown variables with certain coefficients, many people prefer known variables.

Hence, all three methods reduce redundancy—but not without cost. While none of the methods is universally the best, the index method often proves the most useful.

In using factor analysis to reduce a data set, two other points are crucial. First, if there is a key factor, it is often desirable to retain several variables that are closely related to it to obtain an accurate measure of the factor. Second, there is nothing inherently important about the first few factors. They are first because they represent a large number of redundant variables, not because those variables are important or useful per se. Basically, the first factor represents the underlying construct the manager chose to collect the most measures of.

Simplifying Future Data Collection Efforts In many cases, factor analysis is used to simplify future data collection efforts. For example, based on the results of the car study, we could reduce the 15 original attributes into three factors that capture more than 61 percent of the variance in the data. If we were to conduct another survey of car buyers, we could then ask consumers their perceptions on only these three key factors instead of the 15 attributes we used earlier. This both significantly simplifies the data collection and provides us opportunities to explore other critical areas. Since many studies begin with lists of 60–100 attributes, simplification is frequently required and is not just an academic exercise (anyone who has dealt with a real-life study can testify how hard it is to ask managers to limit themselves to a short list of important attributes—usually you get a sense that everything is important).

Creating Perceptual Maps One common use of factor analysis is the creation of perceptual maps that are useful for addressing product positioning issues. Here, two steps are involved.

1. Obtain Factor Scores Knowing the loadings (Λ), it is possible to obtain *scoring coefficients* (cs).[8] These coefficients multiplied by the original variables (Xs) produce *factor scores* (Fs) as follows:

$$F_k = c_{k1}X_1 + c_{k2}X_2 + \cdots + c_{kp}X_p$$

For our application, the scoring coefficients are given in Table 16.11 and the mean of the factor scores for each of the 10 brands of cars is given in Table 16.12.

2. Plot the Factor Scores The factor scores obtained represent the coordinates of various cars in the three-dimensional factor space. We can plot these scores to obtain the *perceptual map* (Figure 16.3). The map summarizes consumers' perceptions of various cars and is helpful in understanding competitive structure and new product introduction.

This perceptual map provides several insights.[9]

- Cars on the right side of the map (e.g., Ford Taurus, Toyota Camry, Honda Accord) appear to be more luxurious or trendy than the cars on the left side of the map (e.g., Chevrolet Corsica, Ford Tempo).
- Cars on the top of the map (e.g., Ford Taurus) are generally more reliable than cars on the bottom of the map (e.g., Ford Thunderbird).

---

[8] Mathematically, the matrix of scoring coefficients is usually $C = S^{-1}\Lambda$, where S^{-1} is the inverse of the covariance matrix of original variables, and Λ is the matrix of loadings. In practice, one finds these in the output of the factor analysis.

[9] Note that these conclusions are illustrative only. For a true understanding of the car market, a large sample of consumers and cars may be needed.

TABLE 16.11 Standardized Scoring Coefficients

	Factor 1	Factor 2	Factor 3
V1	0.06090	−0.02483	0.31475
V2	0.06947	0.11320	−0.11563
V3	0.19375	−0.00277	−0.04134
V4	0.23344	−0.11040	0.07810
V5	−0.11269	0.34843	−0.01722
V6	−0.14080	0.36607	0.03294
V7	0.23290	−0.09274	−0.00917
V8	0.21206	−0.11717	0.00347
V9	0.19275	−0.02026	0.05787
V10	0.13064	0.01996	−0.02171
V11	−0.05600	0.26936	−0.00199
V12	−0.11975	0.12239	0.25795
V13	0.14191	−0.16038	0.41904
V14	−0.08562	−0.01072	0.36369
V15	0.00178	0.24547	−0.06285

- The closer two cars are in this map, the greater the competition between them is likely to be, since they are similar in basic attributes. For example, consumers of Toyota Camry are more likely to switch to Honda Accord than to Pontiac Grand Am, ceteris paribus (i.e., assuming distribution, price, etc., are similar).
- It is possible to obtain a perceptual position of the product and a separate position of its advertising campaign. If the two positions are far apart, it suggests either a possible misalignment of the ad campaign or a campaign designed to alter perceptions (typically a difficult task for established brands).
- A map can also be used to track the movement of brand positions over time.[10] This can, for example, help a manager assess whether a repositioning strategy is working.

TABLE 16.12 Mean Factor Scores for Cars

Car	Factor 1	Factor 2	Factor 3
1. Buick Century	.265	.017	.157
2. Ford Taurus	.233	.474	.299
3. Oldsmobile Cutlass	.536	−.037	−.736
4. Ford Thunderbird	−.302	−.456	.513
5. Chevrolet Celebrity	−.393	.194	−.078
6. Honda Accord	.434	−.139	−.835
7. Pontiac Grand Am	−.584	.197	.196
8. Chevrolet Corsica	−.407	.004	.056
9. Ford Tempo	−.125	−.168	−.074
10. Toyota Camry	.343	−.088	.502

---

[10]Considerable caution should be exercised here, because factor analysis solutions have no natural origin and can be rotated arbitrarily.

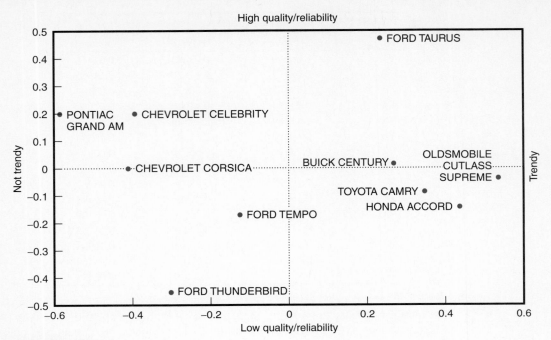

FIGURE 16.3
Perceptual Map for Cars

Creating Preference Maps   A perceptual map gives us useful insights for brand positioning and for introducing new products. We can identify "holes" in the map which are areas where few or no products exist. However, before introducing a brand to fill this gap, we must assess if consumers really want a product in that gap. In other words, a perceptual map tells us consumers' perceptions of brands (how they think of existing products), but it does not tell us about their preferences (what they like).

In the data collection phase, we collected consumers' preference/liking for these brands as their perceptions (see Table 16.7). We can use this information to locate each consumer's "ideal" car in the perceptual map.[11] Clearly, different consumers have different ideal points. We can also group consumers with similar ideal points to form segments and then estimate the size of these segments. Once we know the positions of existing brands and consumers' and/or consumer segments' ideal points, we are in position to assess the positioning strategy for a new brand (or repositioning of an existing brand).

Grouping Observations   One can infer groups of observations based on the factors that emerge. Alternatively, one can directly utilize factor analysis to group observations (known to techies as Q-type factor analysis). To do this, we first transpose the n-observation-by-k-variable data matrix into a k-variable-by-n-observation matrix. By inputting this to a factor analysis, we generate factors based on an $n \times n$ correlation matrix where the correlations are between pairs of observations. The "factors," then, are

---

[11]The idea here is to locate a consumer's ideal point closest to his/her most preferred car and farthest from his/her least preferred car.

groups of observations (i.e., the loadings indicate which observations belong to each of the factors). This method has been less widely applied recently, with most researchers preferring to use cluster analysis.

OTHER EXAMPLES

Nutritional Example

One of the questions on the now infamous food survey dealt with actual consumption of 30 foods. Specifically, frequency of consumption was asked for these foods (section I, question 14). An obvious question that arises is whether there are patterns of consumption that occur across people. To examine this notion, a factor analysis of the 30 variables was performed. The basic input data were the reported consumption of the 30 foods for the 940 respondents.

There were seven eigenvalues greater than 1, and the first seven factors accounted for 49.2 percent of the variance in the original 30 variables. This indicated a generally low level of collinearity among the variables. These seven factors were then rotated to produce a more interpretable pattern. The results are shown in Table 16.13. To name the factors, we examine those variables with the largest loadings on each factor. The factors appear to be:

1. Junk/convenience foods
2. Calories/desserts
3. Skim versus whole milk
4. Meat substitutes

5. Alcohol
6. Beef
7. Margarine versus butter

Exactly what this means is unclear. The skim versus whole milk and margarine versus butter factors represent obvious conscious choices. The junk/convenience food, meat substitute, and beef factors are also obvious groupings, as are the desserts. The fact that alcoholic beverages seem to have their own factor is only mildly interesting.

Notice that some of the communalities (portion of variance in each of the variables accounted for by the factors) are extremely low, indicating, for example, that only 15 percent of the variance in consumption of frozen dinners is accounted for by the seven factors. This suggests that either (*a*) the data are very noisy/unreliable or (*b*) the seven factors are not adequate to explain all consumption. In fact, one might want to add frozen dinners (and any other low-communality variable) to the seven factors in any subsequent analysis or data collection.

A Lifestyle Example

Another example of a use of factor analysis involved a study of lifestyle measures (Villani and Lehmann, 1975). A set of 504 housewives had been asked to indicate their degree of agreement with a series of 153 statements both in 1971 and in 1973. One issue in the study was whether the structure/pattern of responses remained constant. To measure structure, factor analyses were employed.

Comparing the 1971 and 1973 factor analyses showed a high degree of stability in the structure. Using the eigenvalue-greater-than-1 rule, both 1971 and 1973 data sets produced 51 factors accounting for 67 percent of the variance in the original 153 variables. The factors themselves also seemed to be quite stable. The first four factors

TABLE 16.13 Food Consumption Factor Loadings

Food	Factor							Communality
	1	2	3	4	5	6	7	
Canned fruit	−.12	.46	.04	.06	.00	.30	−.02	.32
Fresh fruit	−.10	.41	.22	.15.	.23	.30	−.15	.41
Bread	.07	.52	−.10	.01	.13	.15	.15	.36
Rice	.06	.17	−.00	.16	.34	.10.	.03	.18
Butter	.10	.13	.18	.00	.12	.04	−.49	.32
Margarine	.11	.31	.02	.00	.23	.13	.65	.60
Cheese	.13	.18	−.00	.11	.35	.21.	.08	.23
Ice cream	.21	.51	−.05	.01	.08	.05	−.06	.32
Whole milk	.07	.21	−.67	.09	−.02	.05	−.06	.52
Skim milk	.07	.15	.70	.18	.03	.08	.13	.58
Snack foods (potato chips, pretzels)	.62	.11	−.07	.11	.04	.02	.04	.41
Desserts	.22	.58	−.06	.06	.09	−.08	−.01	.40
Alcoholic beverages	.14	−.12	−.04	.07	.52	−.01	−.04	.31
Soft drinks	.56	−.06	−.03	.06	.01	.16	−.04	.35
Fish	.00	.16	.14	.41	.34	.22	−.13	.40
Cold cereal	−.03	.43	.03	.14	.02	.07	.05	.22
Frozen vegetables	.05	.18	.13	.05	.31	.27	−.01	.22
Fresh vegetables	−.09	.30	.10	.11	.32	.45	−.04	.43
Canned vegetables	.18	.18	.02	.28	−.04	.39	−.11	.30
Poultry	.10	.15	.00	.41	.26	.30	−.01	.36
Beef (hamburger)	.25	.25	.00	.25	.14	.46	−.12	.43
Steak or roast beef	.24	.09	−.03	.00	.21	.48	−.01	.34
Pork	.32	.12	−.09	.01	.15	.36	−.05	.28
Tuna fish	.20	.01	.08	.49	.25	.09	−.04	.36
Frozen dinners	.30	.06	.03	.22	.07	−.03	.06	.15
Hot dogs	.33	.07	−.07	.38	−.04	.03	.06	.27
Coffee or tea	.04	.18	−.01	.09	.30	.21	.11	.19
Pasta	.43	.14	−.01	.21	.15.	.14	.08	.33
Food at fast food restaurants	.66	.02	.10	.04	−.07	.10	−.10	.50
Food at regular restaurants	.30	.12	.14	−.1	.34	.15	−.15	.30

(subjectively named "creative cook," "attitude toward television," "home cleanliness," and "religious practices and attitudes") were essentially identical (Table 16.14).[12] In all, 34 of the 51 factors appear to be unchanged in content (but did not necessarily appear in the same order). The 17 factors that do not match consist of factors with only one or two variables in them, and hence are inherently less stable. The conclusion one can draw is that there are underlying lifestyle patterns that do endure over

---

[12]Notice that all the signs in the fourth factor change between 1971 and 1973. Since the sign is arbitrary (the 1971 factor might be called proreligious and the 1973 factor antireligious), this is unimportant.

TABLE 16.14 Lifestyle Factors

	Factor Loadings	
	1971	1973
Creative cook:		
I look for ways to prepare fancy meals	.62	.74
I like to try new recipes	.66	.62
I think of myself as a creative cook	.70	.69
I am more interested in new food products than most people	.56	.56
I like to make gourmet dishes	.70	.73
Attitude toward television:		
Television has added a great deal of enjoyment to my life	.70	.69
I don't like watching television and so I rarely do	−.73	−.64
Television is a friendly companion when I am alone	.75	.62
I watch television to be entertained	.56	.66
I watch television more than I should	.53	.40
I like having television on while I do other things around the house	.57	.27
I watch television in order to quietly relax	.39	.67
I watch television to get away from the ordinary cares of the day	.28	.56
Home cleanliness:		
I try to wash the dishes promptly after each meal	.55	.62
I usually keep my house very neat and clean	.58	.68
I am uncomfortable when my house is not completely clean	.73	.66
My idea of housekeeping is "once over lightly"	.−55	−.66
A house should be dusted and polished at least three times a week	.51	.46
I usually have regular days for cleaning, cooking, and shopping	.51	.33
Religious practices and attitudes:		
I pray several times a week	.73	−.75
I go to church regularly	.78	−.80
Women should be allowed to have an abortion they feel necessary	−.56	.50

Source: Kathryn Villani and Donald Lehmann, "An Examination of the Stability of AIO Measures" from *1975 Combined Proceedings,* Fall Conference (American Marketing Association), page 486. Copyright © 1975 by the American Marketing Association. Reprinted with the permission of the publishers.

a reasonable length of time. A similar finding of stability exists across geographic areas within the United States (Lesser and Hughes, 1986).

Fifty States Data Example

In previous analyses, it has been clear that various measures of a state (e.g., income, taxes) are correlated. To portray the relation among variables, a factor analysis was performed.[13] Three eigenvalues are greater than 1, and in total they account for $(5.05 + 2.26 + 1.46)/12 = 73.1$ percent of the variance in the original 12 variables. After various iterations and varimax rotation, the factor loading matrix is that of Table 16.15.

In naming the factors, it is useful to underline the largest loadings. This can entail picking an arbitrary cutoff or underlining the largest number in each row. Here, we

---

[13]The results are taken from an SPSS run of type PA2.

TABLE 16.15 Rotated Factor Matrix

	1	2	3	Communality
Income	.23	<u>.77</u>	.28	.73
Population	<u>.99</u>	.05	−.01	.00
Population change	−.29	−.10	<u>.56</u>	.41
Percent urban	<u>.54</u>	.28	.07	.37
Tax per capita	.31	<u>.82</u>	−.04	.78
If South	.06	−<u>.74</u>	.11	.57
Government expenditures	<u>.99</u>	.07	.01	.99
College enrollment	<u>.96</u>	.13	.02	.95
Mineral production	.36	−.40	.16	.32
Forest acreage	.10	.04	<u>.70</u>	.50
Manufacturing output	<u>.92</u>	.15	−.17	.90
Farm output	<u>.53</u>	−.09	−.13	.31
"Name"	Size	Wealth	Population density	
Original eigenvalues	5.05	2.26	1.46	

chose to underline loadings above .5. Examining the table, it is clear that the first factor is basically size. This factor almost always appears when comparing regions or countries. (In fact, if none of the variables were on a per capita basis, this factor would be even more dominant.) The second factor is clearly a wealth factor and shows that, in 1975, the South was a relatively poor region. The third factor is essentially a single variable—forest acreage—although by combining forest acreage with population change (which can be greater in the smaller, less densely populated states) we could "creatively" name this factor as population density. If we were to reduce the number of variables, one strategy would be to choose one variable to represent each of the factors (we prefer population, income per capita, and forest acreage) and retain those variables with small communalities (here, using .5 as a cutoff, population change, percent urban, mineral production, and farm output). Therefore, we could reduce the 11 variables to 7 with little loss of information and to 3 (population, income per capita, and forest acreage) with only moderate information loss.

CONFIRMATORY FACTOR ANALYSIS

This chapter has focused on the use of factor analysis to discover patterns of redundancy. It is also possible to use something known as confirmatory (as opposed to exploratory) factor analysis to examine whether a prior expectation of the variable grouping is consistent with the data (often using the LISREL package). This essentially requires predicting the assignment (loading) matrix and seeing how well it fits the data. That is, we assume we know what the factors are and which variables relate to which factors. Occasionally this may be so. For example, pharmaceuticals generally can be profiled in terms of efficacy, side effects, and (sometimes) dosage/ease of administration. Still, the procedure is not widely used in applied research—partly due to the lack of strong prior expectations—and consequently it will not be discussed further.

SUMMARY

The purpose of factor analysis is to group correlated variables into a small number of factors. As such, factor analysis is a data reduction method that helps (*a*) improve interpretation (by focusing on a few major factors) and (*b*) simplify tasks (e.g., future surveys can use the key factors only). It is also useful in substantive applications such as constructing perceptual and preference maps for new product positioning strategies.

PROBLEMS

1. Interpret the following factor analysis of the importance of 17 attributes used by purchasing agents in making decisions about suppliers:

Rotated Factor Matrix					
	Factor				
Attribute	*1*	*2*	*3*	*4*	*5*
Supplier reputation	.16	.04	.89	.09	−.10
Financing	.15	.79	.08	−.10	−.12
Flexibility	.11	.72	.02	.12	.43
Past experience	.17	.15	.03	.07	.85
Technical service	.47	.42	.22	−.27	.39
Confidence in salespersons	.60	.27	.27	.14	.40
Convenience in ordering	.33	.67	−.20	.03	.14
Reliability data	.57	.02	.29	.21	.46
Price	.08	.06	.03	.84	−.01
Technical specifications	.49	−.03	.07	.43	.59
Ease of use	.52	.19	−.13	−.30	.52
Preference of user	.13	.33	.57	−.43	.38
Training offered	.87	.18	.23	−.12	.06
Reliability of delivery	−.16	.61	.29	.05	.13
Maintenance	.25	.12	−.07	−.18	77
Sales service	.75	.09	−.28	.29	.13
Training required	.78	.02	.12	−.01	.34
Unrotated eigenvalues	6.30	2.02	1.44	1.37	1.08

2. How would you go about reducing a set of 150 candidate variables for a model of consumer satisfaction to a more manageable number?

3. You have designed a new product and want to advertise its introduction. You want to place advertisements in several different magazines. Your job is to select the particular set of magazines in which the ads should run. Your researcher wants to help you by running a factor analysis of your data. You know which of the 100 largest circulation magazines was read by each person in a sample of 1,000 people during the last month. That is, you have a data matrix that is 100 magazines by 1,000 people in size. Each cell has either 0 (person did not read last issue of this magazine) or 1 (person did read the last issue of this magazine).

   a. If you believe your ad must be seen many times to have any effect, then how can your researcher help you select the magazines? Please be specific about the factor analysis you want the researcher to run and how you will use the results.

   b. If you believe, instead, that your ad is so great that people who see it will instantly recognize the benefits of your new product, then how can your researcher use factor analysis to help you select the magazines? Again, please be specific.

   c. For your analyses in parts (*a*) and (*b*), would you prefer that your researcher provide you the principal components unrotated factor loadings or the rotated factor loadings? Why?

   d. If your researcher found that three factors explained 98 percent of variance in the readership data for the 100 magazines, what would you conclude? If only 5 percent?

4. Suppose that you have been collecting opinions about many various aspects of a new product. You notice that people seem to respond similarly to many of the questions.

   a. How would you determine which questions are related to each other?

   b. How would you select the questions that are redundant, so that they could be eliminated from future studies without loss of most of the information in the original set of questions?

5. You have a set of 38 time series variables, which you wish to use to explain the sales of heavy-duty machine tools. Describe two ways you might use factor analysis before running your regression. What are the advantages and disadvantages of each of these approaches?

6. The following rotated factor matrix was based on a sample of people who indicated how likely they were to drink wine coolers (measured on a five-point scale) on a number of occasions. Interpret.

	Factor		
	1	*2*	*3*
At lunch	.79	−.03	.02
Between meals	.78	30	.02
While watching TV	.77	.21	.19
At picnics	.76	.42	.16
At a beach	.73	.37	.18
At dinner	.67	.50	−.04
At cocktail parties	.24	.84	.00
At business meetings	10	.79	.02
At bars	.31	.79	.21
At restaurants	.31	.77	.16
At breakfast	.04	.03	.92
At sporting events	.44	.41	.50
Original eigenvalue	6.18	1.35	1.07
Rotated eigenvalue	3.85	3.45	1.30

7. Data on the values of a sample of customers were analyzed via factor analysis. Specifically, the responses to questions 3 and 4 on the Ownership and Values Survey (Appendix 7-D) were analyzed for some of the respondents. Interpret the results, shown here:

	Factor					
	1	2	3	4	5	6
SREPECT	.68	.00	.03	.10	.04	−.09
SECURE	.54	.17	−.03	.25	.27	.26
WARMREL	.59	−.19	.30	.09	−03	−.28
ACCOMP	.80	.16	.10	.10	−.03	−.09
SLFFIL	73	.10	.17	.12	.04	−.01
BELONG	.55	.08	.25	−.19	.20	.41
WRNSPECT	.55	.27	.11	−.12	.17	.20
FUN	.28	.15	.71	−.01	.08	−.01
EXCITE	.18	.24	.71	.00	.03	−.04
PHSFIT	.35	.15	.39	.05	.26	−.14
CONTROL	.30	.50	.05	.01	.31	−.06
KNOW	.56	.16	.04	.21	.34	−.21
COVEN	.22	.31	.26	.16	.49	.21
OWN	.12	.65	.13	−.21	.21	.19
BEAUTY	.11	.50	.25	.18	.03	.11
GDDEAL	.06	.47	.12	.05	.56	.04
PRACTL	.14	.11	.03	−.00	.76	.06
TRAVEL	.03	.06	.63	.18	.06	.07
VARIETY	.13	.13	.66	.26	.19	−.01
SUCCESS	.32	.67	.13	.11	.09	−.04
WEALTH	.06	.79	.04	−.02	.03	.07
FAME	−.12	.60	.15	.28	.13	.06
UNIQUE	.11	.30	.17	.62	.07	−.02
PGROWTH	.50	.03	.19	.46	.13	−.01
FAIR	.51	−.19	.13	.28	.38	.06
SIMPLE	.11	−.17	.20	.24	.63	.14
PEREXP	−.01	.15	.37	.48	−.09	.26
FINSEC	.00	.17	−.14	.04	.05	.65
FFAME	.01	.65	.04	.29	−.12	.16
STRUGGL	−.00	.07	−.13	.32	.15	.55
INDIV	.05	.16	.00	.71	−.01	−.06
SOCIALLY	.23	−.19	.17	.52	.16	.17
LKRICH	−.10	.52	.13	−.02	−.33	.22
PGROUP	.02	.13	.22	−.06.	02	.55
Varience explained	4.34	3.98	2.80	2.44	2.41	1.77

8. Interpret the following factor analysis of 10 attributes of cars:

Car Attribute Loading Matrix

Attributes	Factor 1	Factor 2	Factor 3	Communality
Resale value	.13	.12	.91	.850
Gas economy	.29	.73	.26	.688
Value for money	.42	.58	.50	.756
Exterior appearance	.74	.04	.44	.736
Easy and fun to drive	.65	.38	.15	.586
Easy maintanance	.43	.52	.41	.618
Reliability and constrution	.67	.21	.51	.752
Pickup	.77	.18	.15	.652
Inexpensive	.07	.89	−.03	.793
Features	.81	.21	.02	.706
				7.144

REFERENCES

ACITO, FRANK, AND RONALD D. ANDERSON (1980) "A Monte Carlo Comparison of Factor Analytic Methods," *Journal of Marketing Research*, 17, May, 228–36.

———— (1986) "A Simulation Study of Factor Score Indeterminacy," *Journal of Marketing Research*, 23, May, 111–18.

BABAKUS, EMIN, CARL E. FERGUSON, JR., AND KARL G. JÖRESKOG (1987) "The Sensitivity of Confirmatory Maximum Likelihood Factor Analysis to Violations of Measurement Scale and Distributional Assumptions," *Journal of Marketing Research*, 24, May, 222–28.

BAGOZZI, RICHARD P. (1980) *Causal Models in Marketing*, New York: John Wiley and Sons.

FORNELL, CLAES, AND FRED L. BOOKSTEIN (1982) "Two Structural Equation Models: LISREL and PLS Applied to Consumer Exit-Voice Theory," *Journal of Marketing Research*, 19, November, 440–52.

FORNELL, CLAES, AND DAVID F. LARCKER (1981) "Evaluating Structural Equation Models with Unobservable Variables and Measurement Error," *Journal of Marketing Research*, 18, February, 39–50.

HARMAN, HARRY H. (1967) *Modern Factor Analysis*, Chicago: University of Chicago Press.

JÖRESKOG, KARL G., AND DAG SÖRBOM (1982) "Recent Developments in Structural Equation Modeling," *Journal of Marketing Research*, 19, November, 404–16.

LEHMANN, DONALD R. (1974) "Some Alternatives to Linear Factor Analysis for Variable Grouping Applied to Buyer Behavior Variables," *Journal of Marketing Research*, 11, May, 206–13.

LEHMANN, DONALD R., AND DONALD G. MORRISON (1977) "A Random Splitting Criterion for Selecting the Number of Factors," working paper, Columbia University Graduate School of Business.

LESSER, JACK A., AND MARIE A. HUGHES (1986) "The Generalizability of Psychographic Market Segments Across Geographic Locations," *Journal of Marketing*, 50, January, 18–27.

STEWART, DAVID W. (1981) "The Application and Misapplication of Factor Analysis in Marketing Research," *Journal of Marketing Research*, 18, February, 51–62.

VILLANI, KATHRYN E. A., AND DONALD R. LEHMANN (1975) "An Examination of the Stability of AIO Measures," *Proceedings*, Fall Conference, American Marketing Association, 484–88. Chicago, Ill.

APPENDIX 16-A

FOUNDATIONS OF FACTOR ANALYSIS

This appendix provides a simple (six-variable) factor analysis example so that facility in interpreting results may be improved by careful study of a manageable problem. The basic data and outputs were as follows:

1. Education of wife
2. Education of husband
3. Age

4. Income
5. Family size
6. Weekly food expenditures

Correlations

	Variable					
Variable	1	2	3	4	5	6
1		61	−.30	.42	.12	.17
2			−.42	.50	.20	.25
3				−.30	−.44	−.27
4					.31	.43
5						.57

Eigenvalues

Eigenvalue	Percent Variance	Cumulative Percent
2.78	46.4	46.4
1.23	20.5	66.9
.76	12.8	79.7
.50	8.3	88.0
.38	6.3	94.3
.34	5.7	100.0

Principal Components

	Component					
Variable	1	2	3	4	5	6
1	.65	.57	.04	.39	.23	−.21
2	.75	.46	−.03	.03	−.32	.34
3	−.66	.08	.67	.22	.06	.21
4	.74	.10	.41	−.48	.21	−.01
5	.63	−.63	−.14	.19	.28	.28
6	.65	−.53	.35	.16	−.31	−.23

Two-Factor (Unrotated) Solution with Communality ≠ 1

	Factor	
Variable	1	2
1	.58	.41
2	.75	.45
3	−.55	.05
4	.64	.07
5	.63	−.61
6	.57	−.36

Here interpretation is very difficult, because all six variables appear to load on factor 1.

Squared Loadings

	Factor		
Variable	1	2	Communalities
1	.34	.17	.51
2	.56	.20	.76
3	.30	.00	.30
4	.41	.00	.41
5	.40	.37	.77
6	.32	.13	.45
Eigenvalue	2.33	.87	3.20
Percent explained	2.33/6 = 38.8%	.87/6 = 14.5%	53.3%

Notice that the 38.8 percent is really the average squared correlation between factor 1 and each of the six original variables. You can also note that the reason the percent of variance explained in the first variable (51 percent) is the sum of the percent explained by the first factor (34 percent) plus the percent explained by the second factor (17 percent) is that the two factors are orthogonal.

Two-Factor (orthogonally rotated) Solution ("loadings")

	Factor	
Variable	*1*	*2*
1	.71	.08
2	.86	.16
3	−.38	−.40
4	.53	.37
5	.07	.88
6	.19	.64

After rotation the interpretation is much easier. Factor 1 is apparently largely education, while factor 2 is mainly family size. Income tends to go with education, and age really doesn't fit either category well.

Squared Loadings

	Factor		
Variable	*1*	*2*	*Communality*
1	.50	.01	.51
2	.74	.03	.77
3	.14	.16	.30
4	.28	.14	.42
5	.00	.77	.77
6	.04	.41	.45
Eigenvalue	1.70	1.52	3.22
Average percent of variance explained	28.3%	25.3%	53.6%

Notice here that the effect of the rotation is to redistribute much of the variance from the first to the second factor. The total variance explained and the communalities, however, are unaffected.

Factor Score Coefficients

	Factor	
Variable	*1*	*2*
1	.27	−.06
2	.64	−.07
3	−.06	−.04
4	.13	.10
5	−.15	.73
6	.01	.20

TABLE 16A.1 Alternative Ways to Deal with Collinear Variables in Regression

Approach	Model	Pros	Cons
Use all variables	$Y = B_0 + B_1X_1 + B_2X_2 +$ $B_3X_3 + B_4X_4 + B_5X_5 + B_6X_6$	Easy to do	Collinearity, need all variables
Representative method	$Y = C_0 + C_1X_2 + C_2X_5$	Simple model	Omitted variable bias
Index method	$Y = D_0 + D_1(X_1 + X_2) + D_2(X_5 + X_6)$	Understandable	Still need four variables
Factor scores	$Y = E_0 + E_1(f_1) + E_2(f_2)$	Directly obtainable from computer analysis	Identity of fs unclear. No reduction in variables

Notice that these coefficients mean that the first factor score will be largely determined by the value of variable 2 while the second factor is dominated by variable 5, which turn out to be the variables with the biggest loadings on each factor.

Factor scores are estimates of the position of each observation on each unmeasured factor. Several methods of estimation are available (e.g., Harman, 1967). The most widely used form is

$$f = XS^{-1}\Lambda$$

where

> f = matrix of factor scores (an $n \times m$ matrix);
> X = raw data (an $n \times p$ matrix);
> S^{-1} = inverse of covariance matrix of the original p variables (a $p \times p$ matrix);
> Λ = estimated loadings (a $p \times m$ matrix).

To use the variables as predictors in a regression model, we can either use them all or try to reduce the number by picking a representative of each factor, using a simple index for each factor, or using the factor scores. The alternatives are summarized in Table 16A.1.

APPENDIX 16-B

SOURCES OF CORRELATION AND SEGMENTATION

Why are variables correlated? In survey data, correlations arise from people tending to answer several questions in a consistent pattern. That is, to pick a stereotypical example, when asked about leisure activities the same people who rate the ballet highly also rate opera and art museums highly and, conversely, rate football, chain sawing, and weightlifting as unappealing. Similarly those who rate football highly also like to chain saw and weightlift but not attend ballet, opera, or art museums (see Table 16B.1).

TABLE 16B.1   Source of Correlations among Variables

Example A: Survey Data

Respondent	Liking of Activities (1–6)					
	Opera	Ballet	Art Museum	Football	Chain Sawing	Weight Lifting
1. High-brow type	5	6	4	2	3	3
2. High-brow type	6	5	6	3	2	2
3. High-brow type	5	5	6	2	2	1
4. Jock type	1	2	3	6	4	6
5. Jock type	3	2	1	4	6	6
6. Jock type	2	2	2	5	5	5

Of course correlation occurs in nonsurvey data as well. For example, in data on regions or countries, many variables are correlated with size (e.g., population, manufacturing output). Scanner data, customer databases, and sales records are filled with correlated variables.

One objective is to uncover the groups (segments) whose behavior generated the correlations. Here, we use the correlations to deduce the general pattern of responses and hence respondents. In the preceding example, this suggests if you know high-brow and jock activities are positively correlated within activity type and negatively correlated between them, then it is fairly easy to deduce what the different types (segments) of respondents are.

CHAPTER 17

Geometric Representation of Objects

In the previous chapter, we used similarity between objects to form clusters. Another approach for analyzing similarity data is to display them graphically. Multidimensional scaling does exactly that. In this chapter, we first explore how one goes from similarity data to a map (picture) of the objects such as in Figure 17.1, and then discuss some alternative ways to get a similar picture.

MULTIDIMENSIONAL SCALING

Multidimensional scaling was developed by psychometricians, notably Shepard (1962) and Kruskal (1964), and received great attention in marketing (Green and Carmone, 1970; Green and Rao, 1972; Cooper, 1983). Its purpose is to deduce indirectly the dimensions a respondent uses to evaluate alternatives. The reason for using the indirect approach is that, in many cases, the attributes may be unknown and respondents unable (what attributes do you use to evaluate paintings?) or unwilling (why do you yell at your kids?) to represent their reasons accurately.

FIGURE 17.1
Brand Locations in Two Dimensions

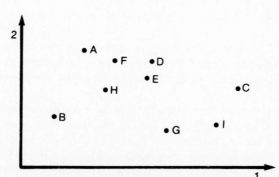

Input Data

As already mentioned, multidimensional scaling (MDS) requires an object-by-object similarity matrix as input. Thus the methods discussed in Chapter 15 on cluster analysis for generating similarity measures from object-by-variable data apply here as well.

When initially popularized, however, MDS relied on judged similarity. That is, respondents indicated how similar pairs of objects were directly (e.g., on a 1–10 or 0–100 scale). This can be a burdensome task, since for p objects, $p(p-1)/2$ judgments are needed (e.g., for 11 objects, $(11)(10)/2 = 55$). Still, the use of similarity judgments is relatively easy for respondents, especially when they can't or won't reveal the basis for their opinions.

The results of MDS depend on (a) the sample chosen to judge similarity and (b) the objects whose similarity is judged as well as the quality of the input data. MDS derives dimensions that appear to be used by those rating a particular set of objects. As in any situation, the results may or may not pertain to other (in some way fundamentally different) samples. Further, the results depend on the objects chosen. Getting similarity ratings on movies will only uncover the attribute of action if the movies differ in the amount of action and will never uncover an attribute like physical exertion or risk of injury since no movie requires either. And, of course, poor quality data (with errors, omissions, etc.) makes good quality results extremely unlikely.

Simple Space

The basic type of multidimensional scaling involves deducing graphical models of alternatives (e.g., brands) alone (hence, simple space) from similarity data. Here, we ask a respondent to rate pairs of objects in terms of their overall similarity. For three objects, this requires the following as input:

Pair	Similarity Rating
A, B	3 (most similar)
A, C	1
B, C	2

The procedure then deduces the positions of the alternatives on a prespecified number of attributes as output. The purpose of the next two sections is to give an indication of how this "magic" (translation: computer program) works.

Initial Solution   Simple space analysis proceeds in two basic stages. The first is to develop an initial solution. One alternative is to place points randomly on the desired number of dimensions. This, however, is so horribly inefficient that other procedures are used.

An intuitively appealing starting rule is a variation on the old navigation by triangulation trick. Consider Figure 17.2. If distance data were generated from this figure, we might have the input data of Table 17.1. The question addressed by multidimensional scaling is how to go from data, such as that in Table 17.1, to a picture, such as Figure 17.2.

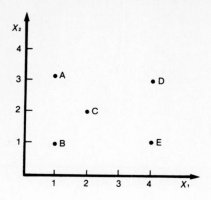

FIGURE 17.2
Initial Solution

To get an initial solution, we can arbitrarily pick any two points, preferably two which are fairly far apart. Here, we use A and D and plot them (Figure 17.3). Now choose one more point (C) by drawing circles around A and D of radii 1.4 and 2.4, respectively (Figure 17.4). Notice that these circles meet in two places. Arbitrarily choose one point and label it C. Now add the next point (B) by drawing arcs around A, C, and D of appropriate lengths and see where they intersect (Figure 17.5). If the input measures are perfect, they will meet in one point. If the input data contain some error, then the three arcs will almost meet and will form a small area. Choose the center of the area for the point's location and continue. Finally, adding E we have Figure 17.6. Notice that this configuration is approximately the original one, the difference being due to the error in the input data, although the picture has been rotated 90 degrees and reflected (the mirror image to Figure 17.2 appears in Figure 17.6). Hence, we see that what is preserved is the original orientation among the points, not their exact positions.

Second Stage   Stage two consists of taking the initial solution and trying to improve it. This is accomplished by a procedure known as the *gradient* (for math fans) or

TABLE 17.1 Input Data

Pair	Approximate Distance
A, B	2
A, C	1.4
A, D	3.0
A, E	3.6
B, C	1.4
B, D	3.5
B, E	3.2
C, D	2.4
C, E	2.3
D, E	2

FIGURE 17.3
Initial Points

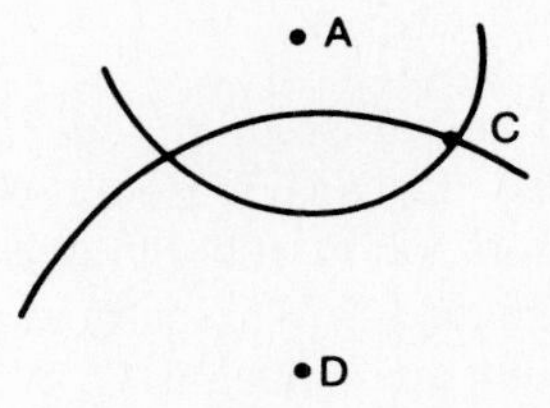

FIGURE 17.4
Third Point Added

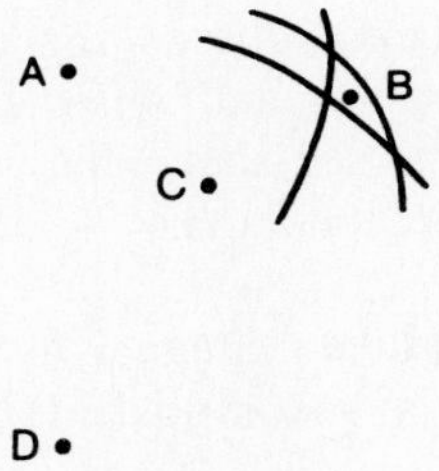

FIGURE 17.5
Four-Point Solution

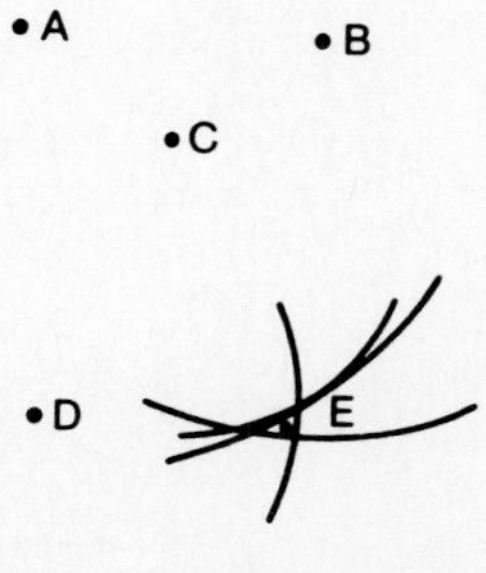

FIGURE 17.6
Five-Point Solution

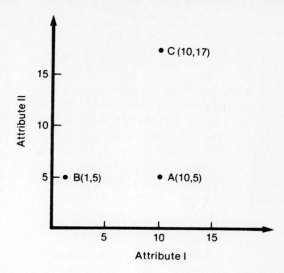

FIGURE 17.7
Three-Brand Model

hill-climbing (for poets) approach. To see how this works, return to the original three-alternative example:

Input:

Pair	Similarity Rating
A, B	3 (most similar)
A, C	1
B, C	2

Assume the initial solution is that of Figure 17.7. At this point, one might wish to evaluate how good a solution this is. One way to do this is to calculate the distances between points and see if they match the original input data, in that the most similar pair of alternatives should have the smallest distance between them and so forth. Here we obtain the following:

Pair	Similarity	Distance	"Error"
A, B	3	9	0
A, C	1	12	−1.5
B, C	2	15	+1.5

As hoped, the most similar pair (A,B) is closest together. The other two pairs, unfortunately, are "messed up" since B,C should be closer together than A,C. One way to see how bad the solution is is to try to "fudge" the distance data so that the similarity data and the derived distances are consistent. The easiest way to do this would be to move both the A,C and B,C distances to 13.5, and hence the error terms are 0, −1.5, and +1.5, respectively. To see how much fudging was required, we can construct an error index:

$$\frac{\sum \text{Errors squared}}{\sum \text{Distances squared}} = \frac{(0)^2 + (1.5)^2 + (1.5)^2}{81 + 225 + 144} = .01$$

This index can then be used as a criterion for when a new solution is better or worse than the old solution (the smaller the index, the better the solution).

One way to improve the original solution in this example is to move alternative C a little to the left, making it simultaneously closer to B and farther from A. The second stage of an MDS program would do this. Next, the program recomputes the index and again moves points to improve the index. Thus, stage two consists of moving the points around until the distances match the original similarity data well enough or the maximum number of iterations is reached.

Output

The results that are output and interpreted are the positions of the alternatives on the attributes. Assuming the initial picture (Figure 17.7) represented the final output, we would get as the output Table 17.2.

The results are missing one very important fact: the names of the dimensions. Developing the names of the dimensions is an art form akin to labeling factors in factor analysis. Here, we look for a common characteristic of alternatives that fall on the extremes of a dimension. In this example, whatever dimension I is, A and C have a lot of it and B has very little of it. Similarly, C has a lot of whatever is represented by dimension II and A and B not much of it. One popular "trick" for aiding in naming the dimensions is to also collect similarities between the alternatives and various key words that are thought to be related to the major dimensions. By scaling both alternatives and words simultaneously, the words then appear in the picture and may facilitate the task of naming the dimensions.

It is also possible to collect ratings of the brands on prespecified attributes separately. These ratings can then be correlated with the positions of the brands on the derived dimensions. If ratings on a particular attribute are highly correlated with positions on a derived dimension, that helps "name" the dimension.

Some Semitechnical Issues

In using MDS, several points are important to keep in mind.

TABLE 17.2 Output of Multidimensional Scaling

Alternative	Dimension	
	I	II
A	10	5
B	1	5
C	10	17

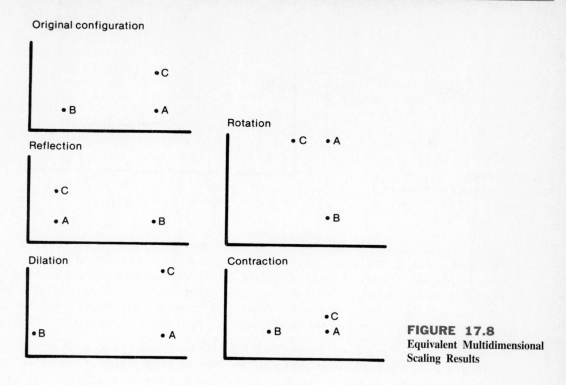

FIGURE 17.8
Equivalent Multidimensional Scaling Results

The Results Are Tentative, Not Conclusive Some early applications of MDS accepted the apparent dimensions as "truth" without question or validation, which often proved to be disastrous. It is advisable to use MDS as a generator of hypotheses, rather than as a final model of a market. Any important result should be confirmed on a separate sample with a separate method, such as direct questioning, before the results are given too much credence.

The Dimensions Are Not Unique MDS generates a configuration in which the relative positions of the brands are unique. The picture can be changed by several operations without changing the relationship among the interpoint distances in some of the algorithms (assuming Euclidean distance is used, which it almost always is). These operations are portrayed in Figure 17.8. Hence, the dimensions that appear in the output are not unique. (Still, it is fortunate how often the dimensions that are output from the analysis turn out to be useful/interpretable ones.)

Determining the Number of Dimensions Is Sometimes Difficult A prior theory about the number of dimensions is the best place to start. Absent a good theory, the most common approach is to examine the results of solutions in several dimensions (e.g., 2, 3, 4) and choose the best one. There are two basic criteria for best. The first involves getting the index used as a criterion for fit to some predetermined level. (When Kruskal's stress is used (essentially $1-R^2$), many researchers attempt to get stress below .05, with anything above .1 being unacceptable.) The second approach involves plotting the stress values and seeing where the addition of a dimension no

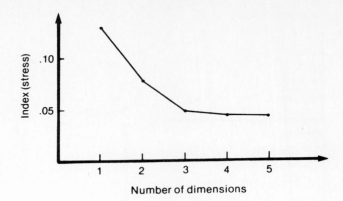

FIGURE 17.9
Badness of Fit Index vs. Number
of Dimensions

longer significantly (in a visual sense) improves the index. Look at the example shown in Figure 17.9. In this case, the index seems to improve substantially going from a one- to two-dimensional solution. Similarly, the index improves going from a two- to three-dimensional solution. The addition of a fourth dimension, on the other hand, seems to aid the solution very little. Consequently, most researchers would say there are three dimensions for this set of alternatives. The point where the plot of the index turns flat is often called the "elbow."

Collection of Similarity/Distance Data Can Be Done in Many Ways   A variety of means have been used for collecting similarity data (McIntyre and Ryans, 1977). The following are among the most useful.

Card Sorting   A common approach used in personal interviewing is to produce a separate card physically for each possible pair of alternatives (e.g., for 10 alternatives, there will be 10(9)/2 = 45 cards). Subjects are then asked to go through a two-step process. First, they are asked to sort the cards into a small number of piles, based on the similarity between the pair of alternatives (e.g., very similar, somewhat similar, somewhat dissimilar, very dissimilar). Next, they are asked to rank pairs within each pile in terms of similarity. By picking up the cards in order (and not dropping them), the researcher obtains a ranking of all pairs of alternatives in terms of similarity.

Ratings   For situations where card sorting is impractical (e.g., mail surveys), respondents are asked to rate pairs of brands on a scale (e.g., an eight-point scale from "very similar" to "very dissimilar"). Alternatively, some researchers prefer to get similarity ratings with respect to a reference brand. By rotating the reference brand, all pairs can be obtained.

Derived Similarity Data   In many studies, similarity measures are derived from other data. For example, ratings of a series of brands on a set of attributes (e.g., rating G.E., Sony, and other TVs on quality of picture, service, style, etc.) can form the basis of a similarity measure. The basic method of deriving similarity is to compute a distance measure that assesses the similarity of the different brand profiles on the attributes. Any of the similarity or distance measures discussed in the cluster analysis chapter can be used, although the two most commonly used are a matching coefficient (when the attributes are categorical) or Euclidean distance (when the attribute ratings are intervally scaled).

Burden on Respondents   A major problem in data collection is the burden on respondents as the number of alternatives increases (e.g., 20 alternatives requires 190 pairs). If respondents are "homogeneous" (have the same similarity perceptions), however, it is possible to have different subjects rate different pairs. For example, in a sample of 1,000, we could divide the 190 pairs into 10 subsets of 19 pairs and have one-tenth of the sample (100 subjects) rate each subset.

The Results Depend on the Alternatives   The dimensions that appear are a direct function of the alternatives used in the study. Leaving out an important set of alternatives (e.g., unsweetened cereal from a study of breakfast foods) means that a key dimension (e.g., sweetness) may not appear in the results. Similarly, defining the competition too broadly will result in trivial solutions. For example, studying cereals, dinner entrees, and drinks together will generally produce three clusters of alternatives: cereals, dinner entrees, and drinks. Hence, care must be taken to include (or represent) all "real" competitive alternatives if the results are to be useful (cf. Malhotra, 1987).

The Number of Alternatives Needed Is Substantial   The number of alternatives needed to produce a certain dimensional solution is much greater than the number of dimensions. While a variety of rules exist, a useful requirement[1] is

$$\text{Number of alternatives} > 3(\text{Number of dimensions})$$

This suggests (as one may have suspected) that there are an infinite number of "perfect" solutions for the three-alternative, two-dimensional example used here for pedagogical purposes.

Some Examples

The best way to get a grasp of how MDS works is to examine several examples. The solutions shown tend to be two-dimensional, since (*a*) many of them actually appear to be two-dimensional and (*b*) it is hard to draw three-dimensional solutions on a piece of paper.

Figure 17.10 comes from one of Green's earliest published examples and is based on ratings of breakfast foods. In playing the name-the-dimensions game, we might call the horizontal dimension *preparation time*. The vertical dimension could well be called *nutritional value*. On the other hand, it could also be called *hot–cold*. Hence this brings up a crucial point: many names may fit the same dimension. It is important to use other methods (e.g., focus groups, ratings on prespecified attributes) to check which name is really appropriate. Otherwise we might spend our entire advertising budget stressing how

---

[1]The reason for this requirement is that there are $\binom{n}{2} = \dfrac{n(n-1)}{2}$ pairs of alternatives, and hence $\dfrac{n(n-1)}{2} - 1$ constraints on the solutions. The solution has $n(d)$ degrees of freedom. Therefore, to get a constrained solution, $\dfrac{n(n-1)}{2} - 1 > n(d)$. Hence, $n \geq 3d$ allows a safety margin to get a well-constrained solution.

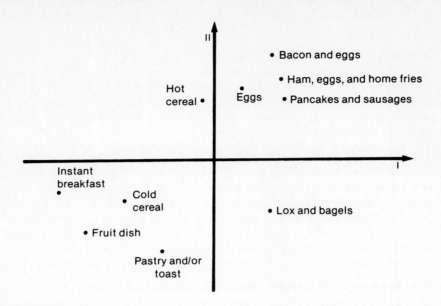

FIGURE 17.10
Breakfast Foods Map
Source: Paul E. Green, Wharton School, University of Pennsylvania.

nutritional our brand was when all consumers care about is its temperature. Assuming advertising copy matters, this is a good way to get burned.

Figure 17.11 was based on similarity judgments of 264 subjects. The purpose of the analysis was to confirm the design of an experiment that included two each of the four possible combinations of lemon-lime versus cola and diet versus nondiet soft drinks (Bass, Pessemier, and Lehmann, 1972). The results clearly indicate cola versus lemon-lime as the horizontal and dominant dimension. The vertical dimension is calories (diet versus nondiet), with one key exception. Like, the name of a diet lemon-lime soft drink at the time, was positioned with the nondiet lemon-limes. Given this mispositioning, it is not surprising that the product failed. It is also not surprising that the product was reintroduced as Sugar-Free 7-Up, making such a misperception highly unlikely.

In the same set of data, respondents were also asked to rate how similar the eight brands were to their ideal brand. Using these data, nine alternatives (the eight brands plus the ideal) were scaled. The results are shown in Figure 17.12. This figure indicates several interesting things. First, to get a "proper" interpretation, the dimensions must be rotated to reproduce the lemon-lime versus cola and diet versus nondiet dimensions. Second, the position of the ideal brand suggests that the ideal soft drink would be cola with some lemon-lime added. This may well be the result of an averaging fallacy. Compute the average temperature that tea should be served from those who drink hot tea and those who drink iced tea and you will find that room temperature tea is "best"— not a very appealing result. On the other hand, given products like Dr Pepper (cherry coke taste with prunes as content) and cream soda (basically vanilla soda), it is conceivable that such a product could succeed. The 1976 introduction of Pepsi-Lite was

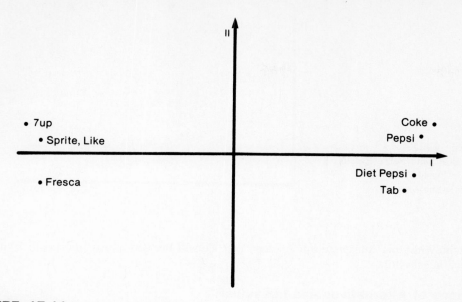

FIGURE 17.11
Soft Drinks: Judges Similarity Based MDS Output
Source: Donald R. Lehmann, "Judged Similarity Based MDS Output" from *Journal of Marketing Research* 9 (August 1972): 332. Copyright © 1972 by the American Marketing Association. Reprinted with permission of the publishers.

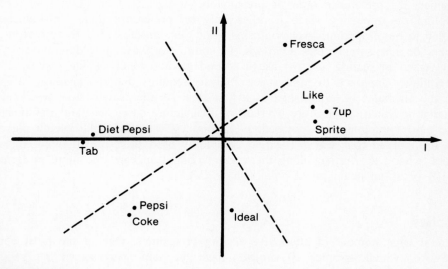

FIGURE 17.12
Soft Drinks with Ideal Brand

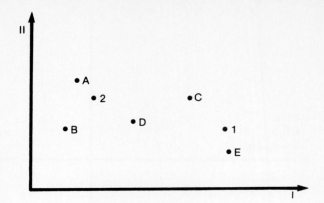

FIGURE 17.13
Hypothetical Joint Space Results
(Letters = Brands:
Numbers = Subjects)

consistent with this interpretation (except that Pepsi-Lite was partly diet), albeit it was not very successful.

Representations of Alternatives and Individuals

The approach for jointly positioning subjects and alternatives in the same map is known as *joint space analysis*. The direct method of getting such a space is known as *unfolding* and requires that respondents rank the alternatives in terms of preference. The procedure then attempts to place both alternatives and subjects in a given dimensional space simultaneously so that people are close to their preferred alternatives and far from their nonpreferred alternatives. Consider the hypothetical example of Figure 17.13, where brands are represented by letters and subjects by numbers. This picture suggests that person 1 would rank E most preferred, C second, D third, and so forth. On the other hand, subject 2's preference order is presumably A, then B, then D, and so forth.

Unfolding is appealing since it relies only on preference data. Unfortunately, the results tend to be disappointing or confusing—and very unstable. For these reasons, many researchers do not employ this approach. In short, don't use unfolding unless you (*a*) are well versed in scaling and (*b*) use a second method to check the results.

The indirect approach to joint space analysis requires that the positions of alternatives on the attributes be established as a first step. As the second step, preference data are gathered and then subjects are overlaid on the picture based on their preference ranking. The most commonly used procedure of this type is PREFMAP, which places subjects on the map in four ways. The two commonly used ways are to represent subjects as vectors, where, the further along the vector a brand appears, the more preferred it is (Phase III) or as an actual ideal point (Phase IV).

Other Approaches

There are a large number of alternative scaling procedures. One of the most appealing is INDSCAL, which assumes all subjects have the same perceptions but weight the dimensions differently. The derived weights can then be used to cluster subjects.

ALSCAL (included in the SAS system) includes a variety of options. It can handle individual differences (à la INDSCAL), asymmetric data (e.g., similarity of A to B not equal to the similarity of B to A), unfolding analysis, missing observations, and nominal, ordinal, interval, or ratio scaled input data. It can also take data that consist of ratings of alternatives on attributes and create a similarity measure from them.

ATTRIBUTE-RATING BASED MAPS

The major alternative to similarity-judgment-based maps uses direct ratings of alternatives on attributes as the key input data. These ratings can be directly plotted on a graph. The main steps involved are attribute identification, obtaining ratings, and, when the number of attributes is large, creating a parsimonious result.

Attribute Identification

Identification of the relevant attributes can be done in many ways. Since multidimensional scaling is essentially a dimension discovery procedure, a MDS study based on similarity judgments can be used to uncover key dimensions. The most commonly used commercial approach is to begin with focus groups. The focus groups are used to generate a list of potential attributes. This list of attributes is then submitted to a sample of customers, who indicate the important attributes. An alternative approach is the so-called protocol procedure. In a protocol procedure, customers are asked to describe in detail the steps they went through in buying a particular product. Attributes mentioned are then recorded and compiled as the relevant attributes. It is also common to have subjects list attributes in response to an open-ended question (often called *free elicitation*). A less elegant but useful alternative is to have the researcher and/or manager specify the attributes based on experience. This method is (*a*) inexpensive and (*b*) full of researcher bias.

Deriving Positions of Alternatives on the Attributes

The positions of the alternatives on the attributes are obtained by direct ratings. These ratings are typically done on 6- to 10-point bipolar adjective scales, although more elaborate graphical scales are occasionally used. Ratings can be obtained in two basic ways:

Rating a single alternative on all the dimensions at one time:

	Very Low					Very High
Crest:						
Decay prevention	1	2	3	4	5	6
Tooth whitening	1	2	3	4	5	6
. . .						
Colgate:						
Decay prevention	1	2	3	4	5	6
Tooth whitening	1	2	3	4	5	6

Rating all the alternatives on a single dimension:

	Very Low					Very High
Decay prevention:						
Crest	1	2	3	4	5	6
Colgate	1	2	3	4	5	6
. . .						
Tooth whitening:						
Crest	1	2	3	4	5	6
Colgate	1	2	3	4	5	6

There is strong evidence that respondents tend to "halo" their responses toward brands by rating the brands they like high on all attributes, and vice versa (Beckwith and Lehmann, 1975). Hence the first approach is not desirable because it makes it very easy for the respondent to think only of the alternative and not about the attribute; thus, all the ratings may be repeated measures of how well the respondent likes the alternative. The second approach makes the attribute the focus of attention. This causes (hopefully) a respondent to place his or her rating of an alternative in the context of the rating of other alternatives on the attribute. It also may be less boring (McLauchlan, 1987). Hence it makes it less likely that alternative A will be rated higher on the attribute than alternative B unless it really is higher (at least in the view of the respondent).

Factor Analysis

As previously discussed, it is possible to produce dimensional representations based on factor analyses. This approach often seems to work as well or better than similarity scaling or discriminant analysis (e.g., Hauser and Koppelman, 1979).

Discriminant Analysis

An alternative way to generate a perceptual map is to use discriminant analysis. The attributes derived via factor analysis tend to be those on which there is the most variance in ratings across brands, whereas those based on discriminant analysis are those that distinguish among brands (Huber and Holbrook, 1979). We give an example of this in Chapter 18.

Derived-Distance-Based MDS

One approach to deriving maps is to use ratings on attributes as the input data, but to then use derived distances between the alternatives as input into a MDS routine. This is typically done by computing the average distance between the brands on the attributes.

For example, consider again data from the food consumption survey discussed frequently in this book. Specifically, the final question dealt with how similar various pairs of foods are perceived to be. The percent of the sample who checked each pair

TABLE 17.3 Foods Similar in Benefits to the Body

	Whole Milk	Beef	Tomatoes	Enriched Bread
A. Oatmeal	22.6%	14.6%	2.2%	75.6%
B. Fish	21.3	76.1	6.3	7.6
C. Rice	11.1	12.1	3.4	78.8
D. Navy beans	10.9	59.1	8.3	37.8
E. Chicken	14.6	82.4	3.0	11.2
F. Potatoes	11.0	6.6	14.4	77.1
G. Eggs	44.4	61.0	2.9	11.4
H. Macaroni	9.6	6.9	1.3	83.3
I. Pork and lamb	11.4	82.9	2.8	6.7
J. String beans	7.3	9.2	73.5	6.3
K. Carrots	17.9	5.9	72.4	6.3
L. Bananas	24.8	11.1	43.2	24.5
M. Peanut butter	26.0	73.8	4.0	19.9
N. Cottage cheese	76.7	36.3	4.8	10.7

as similar appear in Table 17.3. Simple inspection of the results indicates that the foods were rated according to the four basic food groups. (Actually, this result could have been at least partially influenced by the design, where the four column-heading foods represent the four basic food groups.)

To use multidimensional scaling on the data, it was necessary to build an index of similarity between all pairs of food. As a first pass, the four reference foods were ignored and the 14 other foods used as alternatives. Distances between pairs of brands were defined based on the difference in the percent who rated the brands similar to each of the 4 reference foods. For example, the distance between oatmeal and fish was derived based on the difference in the percent who rated each similar to whole milk, beef, tomatoes, and enriched bread.[2] The resulting distance measures were then input to the KYST program, and the output indicated the following:

Number of Dimensions	Stress
4	.010
3	.018
2	.071

This seems to suggest a three-dimensional solution, since the fourth dimension does not improve stress noticeably. Since the third dimension was not easily interpretable, the two-dimensional solution is shown as Figure 17.14.

The exact names of these dimensions are unclear, but the horizontal attribute appears to be a protein content dimension. The vertical dimension seems to separate dairy products and fruits and vegetables from meat and starch. Hence, the four basic food groups do seem to be the basis of this sample's food similarity judgments.

---

[2]The distance from oatmeal to fish was given by $(|226 - 213| + |146 - 761| + |22 - 63| + |756 - 76|)/4$.

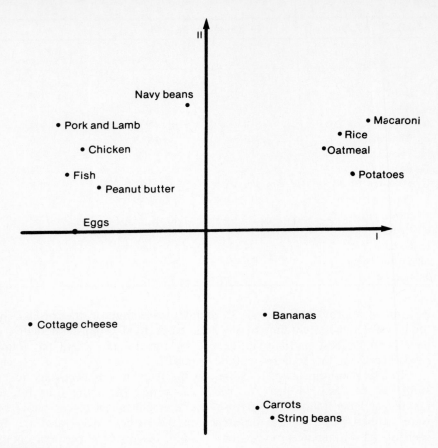

FIGURE 17.14
Map of Different Foods

As another example of this approach, the data on the 50 states (Table 9.1, with the exception of the variable "South") were used as a basis for forming distances between the 50 states. Each variable was first standardized to remove the effects of differences in their scales from the analysis. Next, Euclidean distance was computed between each pair of states and input to the ALSCAL routine in SAS.

A one-dimensional solution produced a squared correlation between input and derived distances of .875, while a two-dimensional solution increased the squared correlation to .925. The two-dimensional solution is shown in Appendix 17-A and Table 17.4. The first dimension separates states such as Alaska, Idaho, Nevada, New Hampshire, Vermont, and Wyoming from California, Illinois, New York, Ohio, Pennsylvania, and Texas, and it appears to reflect the industrial versus rural character of the states. The second dimension separates Louisiana, Mississippi, South Dakota, and Texas from Alaska, California, and New York; it appears to be an income dimension.

While such subjective naming of dimensions is appropriate, both as a check and as a means of actually developing the names, it is often useful to use a more formal

TABLE 17.4 Two-Dimensional MDS for 50 States Data

State Name	Plot Symbol	Dimension 1	Dimension 2	State Name	Plot Symbol	Dimension 1	Dimension 2
Alabama	1	0.22	0.40	Montana	Q	0.84	0.13
Alaska	2	3.08	−2.11	Nebraska	R	0.29	0.16
Arizona	3	0.72	0.03	Nevada	S	1.13	−0.29
Arkansas	4	0.72	0.70	New Hampshire	T	1.03	0.47
California	5	−5.32	−1.90	New Jersey	U	−0.63	−0.47
Colorado	6	0.15	−0.29	New Mexico	V	0.89	0.60
Connecticut	7	0.06	−0.51	New York	W	−3.35	−1.80
Delaware	8	0.77	−0.16	North Carolina	X	−0.22	−0.06
Florida	9	−0.39	−0.42	North Dakota	Y	0.86	0.55
Georgia	A	−0.13	−0.17	Ohio	Z	−1.18	−0.20
Hawaii	B	0.76	−0.30	Oklahoma	1	0.15	0.41
Idaho	C	1.14	0.45	Oregon	2	0.30	−0.28
Illinois	D	−1.68	−0.46	Pennsylvania	3	−1.15	−0.37
Indiana	E	−0.52	−0.10	Rhode Island	4	0.60	0.32
Iowa	F	−0.38	0.65	South Carolina	5	0.46	0.47
Kansas	G	−0.05	0.18	South Dakota	6	0.87	0.74
Kentucky	H	0.11	0.48	Tennessee	7	0.01	0.16
Louisiana	I	−0.16	1.33	Texas	8	−2.51	0.99
Maine	J	0.90	0.30	Utah	9	0.73	0.40
Maryland	K	−0.12	−0.34	Vermont	A	1.19	0.61
Massachusetts	L	−0.52	−0.46	Virginia	B	−0.18	−0.21
Michigan	M	−0.92	−0.50	Washington	C	−0.11	−0.37
Minnesota	N	−0.38	−0.28	West Virginia	D	0.63	0.65
Mississippi	O	0.68	0.83	Wisconsin	E	−0.32	−0.30
Missouri	P	−0.32	−0.11	Wyoming	F	1.22	0.42

approach. Since the distance measure used is based on locations in the attributes, it is possible to examine the correlation between the states' values on these attributes (income, etc.) and their positions on the two derived dimensions. Here, the ALSCAL program was used to regress each of the 11 original variables used in forming the distance measures against the two derived dimensions. The regression coefficients are shown in Table 17.5, and they (fortunately) generally confirm the names arrived at earlier.

BRAND CHOICE AND SWITCHING-BASED MAPS

There is nothing sacred about using judged similarities or derived distances as an input to MDS programs. One would expect more brand switching among similar brands, as they are closer substitutes. Hence by using brand-switching probabilities as similarity measures, a behavior-based map can be derived. (Since clearly some switching among different brands can be expected due to variety seeking, exactly how to interpret the map is unclear.) The results in the case of the soft drink study are shown in Figure 17.15 (Lehmann, 1972). The major (horizontal) axis appears to be diet–nondiet, and the

TABLE 17.5 Regressions of Original Variables versus the Two Derived Dimensions

| | Dimension | | |
Variable	1	2	R^2
Income	.14	−1.24	.61
Population	−.68	−.30	.92
Population change	.35	−.26	.17
Percent urban	−.33	−.54	.42
Tax	−.10	−.94	.46
Government expenditures	−.67	−.35	.94
College students	−.66	−.39	.94
Mineral production	−.42	.74	.34
Forest acreage	−.27	−.94	.35
Manufacturing output	−.61	−.33	.78
Farm output	−.55	.28	.43

cola versus lemon-lime dimension is somewhat muddled. This suggests (as in fact happened) that consumers would be more likely to give up flavor than to switch from a nondiet to a diet drink, or vice versa. It also indicates that preference dimensions may be different from the dimensions on which consumers make similarity judgments portrayed in Figure 17.11.

Scanner panel data have been used to generate market maps (e.g., Shugan, 1987). Panel data on brand usage have also been used to develop simultaneously market segments based on brand shares by person and market structure based on brand switching (Grover and Srinivasan, 1987), and to examine the impact of marketing variables such as promotion on the resulting market maps (Moore and Winer, 1987).

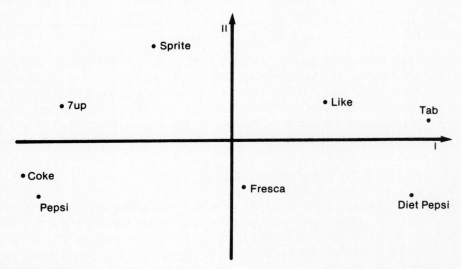

FIGURE 17.15
Soft Drinks Based on Brand Switching
Source: Donald R. Lehmann, "Judged Similarity and Brand-Switching Data as Similarity Measures" from *Journal of Marketing Research* 9 (August 1972): 333. Copyright © 1972 by the American Marketing Association. Reprinted with permission of the publishers.

MDS AND CLUSTER ANALYSIS

Both multidimensional scaling and cluster analysis "operate" on a similarity matrix and put similar objects together. The main difference is that MDS attempts to geometrically portray the objects in a space of two or more dimensions, while cluster analysis either simply indicates groups of similar objects or produces a tree representing the similarities. The best approach to use in a particular situation depends on how customers think about the alternatives (Johnson and Fornell, 1987). Nonetheless, the information obtainable is relatively similar.

In addition to being alternative ways to analyze similarity data, MDS and cluster analysis can often be used in conjunction with each other. For example, a researcher facing a large database (e.g., a sample of 800) may first want to cluster observations based on similarity judgments and then produce a separate MDS picture for each derived segment. Alternatively, a small (pilot) sample might be asked to generate similarity measures for a large number of brands. By clustering these brands, a sample can be drawn for use in a large-scale survey such that all the major types of brands are represented. A key point, therefore, is that MDS and cluster analysis (and any of the other multivariate procedures as well) can be viewed as alternatives for a particular task or as complementary components of a complete analysis plan.

USING MAPS

Attribute-based market maps can be used for a variety of purposes, such as new product idea generation, potential estimation, and advertising/promotional strategy selection. Consider the hypothetical example of Figure 17.16, where the numbers represent segments and the letters represent existing alternatives. Quick perusal of this graph suggests that alternative B is in excellent shape, having segment 1 representing 30 percent of the total market essentially to itself. In contrast, alternative A seems to appeal mainly to segment 6 with 10 percent of the market. To see how this picture could be used to stimulate the results of marketing decisions, consider the following two problems.

New Product Identification

Assume you needed to develop a new product for this market. Technical/production problems aside, two major alternatives appear to exist:

Target on segment 2 by making a product that is a "2" on attribute I and a "2.9" on attribute II. Since E, C, and D are all somewhat removed from segment 2, it appears there is a reasonable chance of capturing the bulk of this segment and, hence, close to 20 percent of the market. (Also, since the product lies between E and C, it is probably a feasible product to produce.)

Target on segment 1 by making a product that is "3" on attribute I and "4.5" on attribute II. The advantage is that this segment has 30 percent of the market. The disadvantage is that B already is there, and, if they are a strong competitor, you are going to be in a big war if you target here.

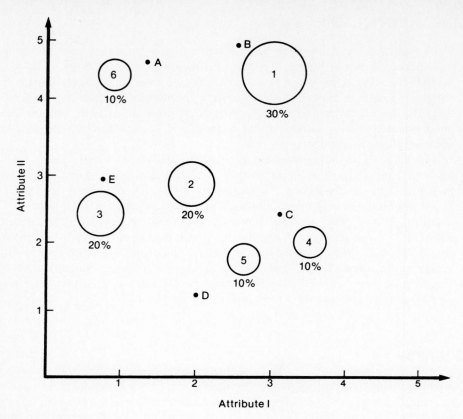

FIGURE 17.16
Hypothetical Joint Space Configuration

Now complicate the problem somewhat by assuming your company already makes C, D, and E. If we still go for segment 2, we will largely cannibalize sales of our own products. Hence segment 1 looks more appealing. However, the decision about which (if any) to produce depends heavily on likely competitors' actions and reactions. If we "attack" alternative B, the makers of alternative B may well attack us by going for segment 2. On the other hand, if we fail to attack, there is no guarantee that competitors will do likewise. What the map provides is a good focus for highlighting some implications of these strategic decisions. An example of a product developed in this fashion was Maxim coffee, which came from an R&D effort targeted to produce rich *and* convenient coffee (alas, Taster's Choice now dominates this market).

Repositioning

Assume you were put in charge of alternative D. After updating your résumé in anticipation of possible termination, you might consider trying to reposition the product. While many repositionings are theoretically possible, moving D up on attribute II to appeal to segment 2 seems most promising. This could be done by changing the actual product. Alternatively or additionally, advertising could stress that "product D is full of attribute II." If product D is an old brand, "new product D with attribute II added" might be introduced.

Limitations

The two previous examples suggest that attribute-based maps can serve as market simulators for the purpose of considering various product policy and promotional strategy decisions. In such use, however, it is important to recognize some of the major limitations of these maps:

> *Their reliability is not perfect.* To use such maps, it is important to have the basic dimensions constant over time. Yet changes in the market often make assumptions of constant maps over time untenable.
>
> *The dimensions may not be usable.* Often, dimensions appear which are either uninterpretable or so compound/abstract that it is unclear exactly what they are, much less how we give a product more of them (e.g., what gives a toothpaste more sex appeal?).
>
> *Many products are infeasible.* The general state of technology as well as company strengths and weaknesses often preclude many "obvious" strategies. (While a segment usually exists that wants a low-cost, high-quality product, producing one may prove an elusive goal.)
>
> *The rational model may be wrong.* Choice may not be determined by this mapping/trade-off type of decision making. Consequently, predictions of behavior based on this type of model can be quite deceptive.

Summary

This section has presented several methods for producing maps of alternatives. More detail on them is available (cf. Cooper, 1983; Dillon, Frederick, and Tangpanichdee, 1985; Green and Carmone [1970], Green and Rao [1972], and Green and Wind [1973]). While more elegant procedures exist for developing maps (e.g., correspondence analysis), for most applied users either MDS based on similarity data or derived distances or some simplification of direct ratings (e.g., factor analysis) will generally prove adequate.

The major uses of mapping models are twofold. First, they are very useful for generating hypotheses/ideas (which then should be further investigated). Even small samples (e.g., 15 office workers) occasionally produce interesting results. While MDS-based attribute models can be used to track markets over time (Moore and Lehmann, 1982), they are usually most appropriate as exploratory devices. Second, these maps are extremely useful communication devices. They often serve to get a room full of people to agree on a general plan of attack and this agreement, sometimes more than the plan, can lead to improved performance.

Geometric modeling portrays brands (and customers) graphically, based on either judged similarity data or direct ratings on attributes. In contrast, conjoint analysis deduces the values of various attribute levels based on ratings of products described in terms of combinations of levels on several attributes. Thus, geometric modeling is useful for discovering or portraying market structure, whereas conjoint analysis evaluates the desirability of various positions (brands) in a market.

For many frequently purchased products, however, it is unlikely that consumers actively process information about many brands on many attributes before making a choice. Rather, their behavior is likely to be relatively routinized. Hence, these models are useful for explaining preference formation and indicating likely long-run equilibrium positions but are not necessarily good models of repetitive decision making.

PROBLEMS

1. Assume you were brand manager for Lay's potato chips. Also assume people make choices based on multiattribute models. What data would you collect and how would you analyze them if you had
   a. A budget of $10,000 and two months?
   b. A budget of $100,000 and four months?
   c. A budget of $250,000 and eight months?

2. Assume you had the following distance data:

Objects	Object					
	1	2	3	4	5	6
1		4	6	5	6.5	3.5
2			4.5	6	9	8
3				3.5	7	8
4					4	6
5						4.5
6						

What is the underlying configuration? (Hint: Try graphing by hand.)

3. Your boss indicates an interest in conjoint analysis, which the boss says is "better than MDS." Outline a 15-minute talk you would give to explain the two techniques and their relative merits.

4. A series of subjects rated soft drinks on the following:
   1. Carbonation
   2. Calories
   3. Sweetness
   4. Thirst quenching
   5. Popularity with others

These ratings were on 1 to 6 scales, where 6 represented a rating of "very high" and 1 a rating of "very low." Subjects also rated importances of the attributes on a scale of 1 to 6, where 6 represents "very important." Given the following data for two individuals:

Respondent	Attribute	Importance	Brand								
			Coke	7-Up	Tab	Like	Pepsi	Diet Sprite	Pepsi	Fresca	Ideal
A	1	3	5	3	2	2	6	5	3	4	3
	2	2	3	5	2	4	6	2	6	5	3
	3	2	6	5	6	5	6	5	5	5	4
	4	1	3	6	5	5	1	4	5	3	6
	5	6	5	5	2	4	4	6	2	1	6
	Preference ranking		2	5	7	6	1	4	3	8	
B	1	3	5	4	2	2	4	4	3	3	3
	2	2	4	4	4	4	4	3	3	5	2
	3	2	3	4	5	4	3	4	5	3	4
	4	2	4	5	5	4	4	4	4	3	6
	5	3	5	5	2	5	3	4	3	3	4
	Preference ranking		6	3	8	4	2	1	7	5	

a. Using the attitude model

$$\sum_{1}^{5} (\text{Importance}) \cdot |\text{Brand rating} - \text{Ideal}|$$

calculate the predicted ranking of the eight brands and compare it with the actual ranking.

b. If you drop the ideal point and importances from the model, what are the results?

5. Professional launderers prefer different detergents for different types of clothing. The preferred level of "harshness" and "color fastness" and also the fraction of each type of business are as follows:

Clothing	Share of Total	Preferred Level	
		Harshness	Color Fastness
Heavy whites	50	1	5
Fine whites	10	5	5
Heavy colors	20	2	1
Fine colors	20	5	1

The four present brands have the following properties:

Brand	Harshness	Color Fastness
A	2	4
B	4	5
C	2	2
D	4	2

a. Estimate the shares of sales of each brand by assuming:

$$(1)\ \text{Distance to brand} = \sum |\text{Actual} - \text{Preferred level}|$$

$$(2)\ \text{Share}_j = \frac{(1\ /\ \text{Distance to } j)}{\displaystyle\sum_{i=1}^{4} (1\ /\ \text{Distance to } i)}$$

b. Estimate the share of sales that a new "general-purpose" detergent might achieve if it had a harshness level of 3 and a color-fastness level of 3.

c. What does your model assume? What does your model ignore? Can you think of a new model that you like better for addressing question (b)?

REFERENCES

BASS, FRANK M., EDGAR A. PESSEMIER, AND DONALD R. LEHMANN (1972) "An Experimental Study of Relationships Between Attitudes, Brand Preference, and Choice," *Behavioral Science*, 17, November, 532–41.

BECKWITH, NEIL E., AND DONALD R. LEHMANN (1975) "The Importance of Halo Effects in Multi-Attribute Models," *Journal of Marketing Research*, 12, August, 265–75.

CARROLL, J. DOUGLAS, AND JIH-JIE CHANG (1970) "Analysis of Individual Differences in Multidimensional Scaling Via an N-Way Generalization of 'Eckart-Young' Decomposition," *Psychometrika*, 35, January, 283–320.

COOPER, LEE G. (1983) "A Review of Multidimensional Scaling in Marketing Research," *Applied Psychological Measurement*, 7, Summer, 18–24.

DESARBO, WAYNE S., AND DONNA L. HOFFMAN (1987) "Constructing MDS Joint Spaces from Binary Choice Data: A Multidimensional Unfolding Threshold Model for Marketing Research," *Journal of Marketing Research*, 24, February, 40–54.

DILLON, WILLIAM R., DONALD G. FREDERICK, AND VANCHAI TANGPANICHDEE (1985) "Decision Issues in Building Perceptual Product Spaces with Multi-attribute Rating Data," *Journal of Consumer Research*, 12, June, 47–63.

GREEN, PAUL E., AND FRANK J. CARMONE (1970) *Multidimensional Scaling and Related Techniques in Marketing Analysis*, Boston: Allyn and Bacon.

GREEN, PAUL E., AND VITHALA R. RAO (1972) *Applied Multidimensional Scaling: A Comparison of Approaches and Algorithms*, New York: Holt, Rinehart and Winston.

GREEN, PAUL E., AND YORAM WIND (1973) *Multiattribute Decisions in Marketing, a Measurement Approach*, Hinsdale, Ill.: Dryden.

——— (1975) "New Way to Measure Consumers' Judgments," *Harvard Business Review*, 53, July–August, 107–17.

GROVER, RAJIV, AND V. SRINIVASAN (1987) "A Simultaneous Approach to Market Segmentation and Market Structuring," *Journal of Marketing Research*, 24, May, 139–53.

HAUSER, JOHN R., AND FRANK S. KOPPELMAN (1979) "Alternative Perceptual Mapping Techniques: Relative Accuracy and Usefulness," *Journal of Marketing Research*, 16, November, 495–506.

HOLBROOK, MORRIS B., WILLIAM L. MOORE, AND RUSSELL S. WINER (1982) "Constructing Joint Spaces from Pick-Any Data: A New Tool for Consumer Analysis," *Journal of Consumer Research*, 9, June, 99–105.

HUBER, JOEL, AND MORRIS B. HOLBROOK (1979) "Using Attribute Ratings for Product Positioning: Some Distinctions among Compositional Approaches," *Journal of Marketing Research*, 16, November, 507–16.

JOHNSON, MICHAEL D., AND CLAES FORNELL (1987) "The Nature and Methodological Implications of the Cognitive Representation of Products," *Journal of Consumer Research*, 14, September, 214–28.

KRUSKAL, J. B. (1964) "Multidimensional Scaling by Optimizing Goodness of Fit to a Nonmetric Hypothesis," *Psychometrika*, 29, March, 1–27.

——— (1964) "Nonmetric Multidimensional Scaling: A Numerical Method," *Psychometrika*, 29, June, 115–29.

LEHMANN, DONALD R. (1972) "Judged Similarity and Brand-Switching Data as Similarity Measures," *Journal of Marketing Research*, 9, August, 331–34.

MCINTYRE, SHELBY H., AND ADRIAN B. RYANS (1977) "Time and Accuracy Measures for Alternative Multidimensional Scaling Data Collection Methods: Some Additional Results," *Journal of Marketing Research*, 14, November, 607–10.

MCLAUCHLAN, BILL (1987) "How to Design a Perceptual Mapping Study," *Proceedings of the Sawtooth Software Conference on Perceptual Mapping, Conjoint Analysis, and Computer Interviewing*, 179–88.

MALHOTRA, NARESH K. (1987) "Validity and Structural Reliability of Multidimensional Scaling," *Journal of Marketing Research*, 24, May, 164–73.

MOORE, WILLIAM L., AND MORRIS B. HOLBROOK (1982) "On the Predictive Validity of Joint Space Models in Consumer Evaluations of New Concepts," *Journal of Consumer Research*, 9, September, 206–10.

MOORE, WILLIAM L., AND DONALD R. LEHMANN (1982) "Effects of Usage and Name on Perceptions of New Products," *Marketing Science*, 1, Fall, 351–70.

MOORE, WILLIAM L., AND RUSSELL S. WINER (1987) "A Panel-Data Based Method for Merging Joint Space and Market Response Function Estimation," *Marketing Science*, 6, Winter, 25–42.

NEIDELL, LESTER A. (1972) "Procedures for Obtaining Similarities Data," *Journal of Marketing Research*, 9, August, 335–37.

SHEPARD, ROGER N. (1962) "The Analysis of Proximities: Multidimensional Scaling with an Unknown Distance Function I," *Psychometrika*, 27, June, 125–39.

——— (1962) "The Analysis of Proximities: Multidimensional Scaling with an Unknown Distance Function II," *Psychometrika*, 27, September, 219–46.

SHUGAN, STEVEN M. (1987) "Estimating Brand Positioning Maps Using Supermarket Scanning Data," *Journal of Marketing Research*, 24, February, 1–18.

STEFFLER, VOLNEY (1968) "Market Structure Studies: New Products for Old Markets and New Markets (Foreign) for Old Products," in Frank M. Bass, Charles W. King, and Edgar A. Pessemier, eds., *Applications of the Sciences in Marketing Management*, New York: John Wiley and Sons, 251–68.

APPENDIX 17-A

SAS ALSCAL ON 50 STATES DATA

MDS: STATES DATA

ITERATION HISTORY FOR THE 2 DIMENSIONAL SOLUTION (IN SQUARED DISTANCES)
YOUNGS S-STRESS FORMULA 1 IS USED.

ITERATION	S-STRESS	IMPROVEMENT
1	0.40427	
2	0.20003	0.20423
3	0.18702	0.01302
4	0.18680	0.00022

ITERATIONS STOPPED BECAUSE
S-STRESS IMPROVEMENT LESS THAN 0.001000

STRESS AND SQUARED CORRELATION (RSQ) IN DISTANCES

RSQ VALUES ARE THE PROPORTION OF VARIANCE OF THE SCALED DATA (DISPARITIES) IN THE PARTITION
(ROW, MATRIX, OR ENTIRE DATA) WHICH IS ACCOUNTED FOR BY THEIR CORRESPONDING DISTANCES.

STRESS VALUES ARE KRUSKAL'S STRESS FORMULA 1.

STRESS = 0.233   RSQ = 0.925

MDS: STATES DATA

CONFIGURATION DERIVED IN 2 DIMENSIONS

STIMULUS COORDINATES

STIMULUS NUMBER	PLOT SYMBOL	DIMENSION 1	2
1	1	0.2194	0.4004
2	2	3.0832	-2.1087
3	3	0.7186	0.0264
4	4	0.7210	0.7048
5	5	-5.3162	-1.8998
6	6	0.1511	-0.2865
7	7	0.0628	-0.5075
8	8	0.7661	-0.1555
9	9	-0.3858	-0.4179
10	A	-0.1318	-0.1665
11	B	0.7642	-0.3043
12	C	1.1436	0.4483
13	D	-1.6750	-0.4567
14	E	-0.5154	-0.0954
15	F	-0.3804	0.6474
16	G	-0.0498	0.1781
17	H	0.1125	0.4773
18	I	-0.1559	1.3328
19	J	0.9011	0.3031
20	K	-0.1162	-0.3391
21	L	-0.5178	-0.4593
22	M	-0.9198	-0.5035
23	N	-0.3763	-0.2833
24	O	0.6755	0.8266
25	P	-0.3222	-0.1067
26	Q	0.8419	0.1302
27	R	0.2881	0.1603
28	S	1.1294	-0.2948
29	T	1.0279	0.4748
30	U	-0.6274	-0.4670
31	V	0.8944	0.5985
32	W	-3.3451	-1.7976
33	X	-0.2157	-0.0580
34	Y	0.8608	0.5515
35	Z	-1.1828	-0.1953
36	1	0.1498	0.4115
37	2	0.2951	-0.2752
38	3	-1.1489	-0.3743
39	4	0.5978	0.3199
40	5	0.4587	0.4741
41	6	0.8662	0.7380
42	7	0.0062	0.1609
43	8	-2.5099	0.9938
44	9	0.7307	0.4002
45	A	1.1883	0.6066
46	B	-0.1811	-0.2127
47	C	-0.1053	-0.3743
48	D	0.6278	0.6480
49	E	-0.3203	-0.2959
50	F	1.2173	0.4220

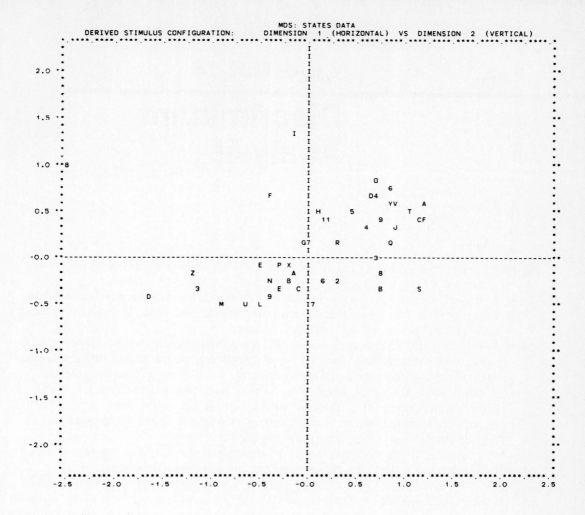

CHAPTER 18

Discriminant Analysis

A large number of problems entail predicting and describing membership in groups:

- A financial service company wants to understand which customers concentrate their assets in fixed investments, domestic stocks, and more speculative vehicles such as foreign stocks and currency futures.
- A furniture manufacturer is interested in the difference between customers who prefer different materials such as wood, plastic, or metal tables, different styles such as early American and Danish modern, or different colors or patterns.
- A bank needs to decide whether to issue a loan to a customer and is concerned with whether the customer will default or repay the loan.
- A soft drink manufacturer is interested in understanding the differences among regular drinkers of Coke, Pepsi, Dr Pepper, and Sprite.
- A consumer goods company wants to understand the major demographic and psychographic differences between heavy, medium, and light users.

All these problems share a common structure. The outcome (or dependent variable) is categorical (e.g., repay loan or not repay loan) and is a function of several factors or independent variables. For example, a bank may use a person's credit history, income, etc., to decide whether or not he or she should be approved for a loan.

This problem structure is very similar to regression, which also relates independent variables to a dependent variable. Therefore one may be tempted to use regression to approach these problems. However, while regression implicitly treats the dependent variable as continuous (or at least ordinally scaled), the dependent variables in many problems are categorical. At this point, the reader may be thinking, "this sounds like a technical distinction that probably doesn't matter." And in many cases, regression will produce "reasonable" results, especially when there are only two groups or outcomes. However, in some cases regression can lead to serious misinterpretation. For example, using demographics to predict preference among the three primary colors via regression is not meaningful. If a categorical scale of 1 = Blue, 2 = Red, 3 = Yellow is the dependent variable, "silly" regression coefficients can result (what would a positive coefficient mean?). Therefore, an alternative approach for assessing differences is clearly needed when there are three or more groups that are categorical in nature. For the sake of simplicity of exposition, we first discuss two-group discriminant analysis; then, we discuss the three-or-more-group case.

TWO-GROUP DISCRIMINANT ANALYSIS

Basic Concept

One technique for analyzing which characteristics "discriminate" (differentiate) members of the groups and their relative importance is imaginatively called *discriminant analysis*. Discriminant analysis has two major uses, prediction and understanding. For predictive purposes, discriminant analysis provides a simple method for determining which group a particular observation is more likely to be a member of. Rather than having to calculate the likelihood of a multivariate normal distribution (an unappealing task to most), one simply calculates an index and compares it to a cutoff value. For example, if a weighted combination of income, education, and years worked at the same job is above some value, a person may be likely to be a good credit risk and hence be given a loan.

The weights in the index indicate the impact of the variables (e.g., income) on group membership (e.g., good vs. bad credit risk). Exactly as in regression analysis, a big (in absolute value) weight indicates a variable has a large impact on (or at least is highly correlated with) group membership (e.g., creditworthiness). Also as in regression, the predictor variables should be either intervally scaled or dummy variables.

To understand how discriminant analysis works, consider a graph representing the incomes and ages of purchasers (P) and nonpurchasers (N) of a particular product (Figure 18.1). Purchasers of this product appear to be younger and richer than nonpurchasers. Hence if a 30-year-old drove up to my store in a Mercedes, he (assuming he hadn't stolen it) would be a good prospect for my product, whereas a 65-year-old pensioner would not be. In this case, both age and income discriminate between purchasers and nonpurchasers.

Now consider Figure 18.2. In this situation, height is apparently a perfect discriminator between purchasers and nonpurchasers, while liking of yogurt is essentially worthless as a discriminator.

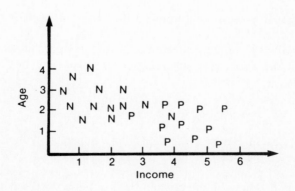

FIGURE 18.1
Purchasers (P) vs. Nonpurchasers (N) by Age and Income

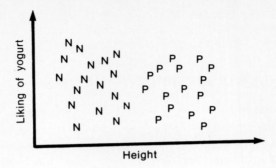

FIGURE 18.2
Purchasers (P) vs. Nonpurchasers
(N) by Height and Liking of
Yogurt

The process of plotting members of the two groups on axes to find out which variables discriminate has some severe limitations. First, it allows for considering only two independent variables at once. Second, it is tedious. And third, it does not give concise results that indicate quantitatively the effect of each of the characteristics on group membership. Therefore, a more formal approach is usually employed.

The Discriminant Function

An effective way to analyze which variables discriminate between members of two groups is to build an index that separates the two groups on the basis of their values on the measured characteristics. When the procedure called discriminant analysis is used, the index is called (again ingeniously) the discriminant function, and the characteristics become the independent variables:

$$f = w_1 x_1 + w_2 x_2 + \cdots + w_k x_k$$

where

$x_1, x_2, \ldots, x_k$ = the measured characteristics (variables);

f = the index (discriminant function);

w_i = the weight (discriminant coefficient) of the ith characteristic in discriminating between the two groups.

Discriminant analysis finds the set of weights that spreads the index values for the two groups as far apart as possible.

Returning to the example involving purchasers (group 2) and nonpurchasers (group 1) (see Figure 18.1), we see that the best index involving income and age might be as follows:

$$f = 3\,(\text{Income}) - 2\,(\text{Age})$$

We can represent this graphically, as in Figure 18.3. Consider the person with both age and income equal to 2. The value of the index for this person would be $3(2) - 2(2) = 2$. Similarly, the person with age of 1 and income of 5 would have an index of $3(5) - 2(1) = 13$. In fact, all the people in the sample can now be represented by a position on the new index

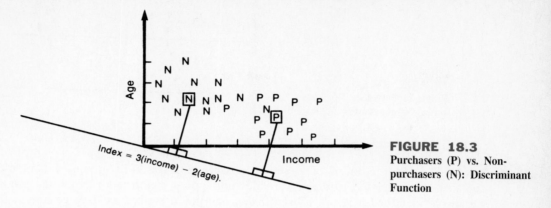

FIGURE 18.3
Purchasers (P) vs. Non-purchasers (N): Discriminant Function

(Figure 18.4). Thus, we can predict group membership based on a person's score on the discriminant function. If the score is closer to the mean of the purchasers, the person would be classified as a purchaser, and vice versa. This is equivalent to drawing a "cutoff" line through the space such that, as much as possible, the purchasers lie on one side of the line and the nonpurchasers on the other side. (For a more complete discussion of the weights and the use of discriminant analysis for classification, see Appendix 18-A.)

Relation to Regression Analysis   The basic approach of linear discriminant analysis is identical to that of linear regression analysis: using a weighted linear combination of independent variables to predict a dependent variable. The only difference is that the dependent variable in regression is a "real" variable (at least intervally scaled), whereas in discriminant analysis the dependent variable is group membership (and, hence, only nominally scaled). For two groups, however, it is easy to generate a dummy variable to represent group membership (i.e., code 1 for group 1 membership and 0 for group 2 membership). By using such a dummy variable as the dependent variable, a regression can be run. The resulting regression coefficients will be proportional to the weights that would have been obtained from discriminant analysis. Hence two-group discriminant analysis is essentially equivalent to regression analysis using a dummy dependent variable.

Using Discriminant Analysis: Basics

The purpose of discriminant analysis is to identify what variables are the best predictors of group membership. Since this usually requires a computer program, the key questions are what to input and what to look at in the output.

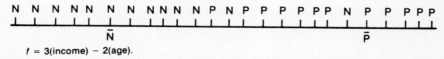

$f = 3(\text{income}) - 2(\text{age})$.

FIGURE 18.4
Positions on the Discriminant Function

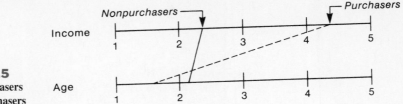

FIGURE 18.5
Profile of Purchasers versus Nonpurchasers

Input   The input consists of a set of observations for both groups. Each observation contains values for the predictor variables plus group membership. Note that group membership is identified a priori. (Discriminant analysis describes existing groups; it does not find groups.)

Output   Like most computer output, there is more information given than can be profitably used (see Appendix 18-B). This overload is the result of two causes: (*a*) to debug a program, a lot of intermediate calculations are output to make it easy to see if the program is working correctly; and (*b*) the desire to output enough so specialized uses can be made of the results. While much of this output has some purpose, the general user will find the information that follows sufficient in most applications.

Means of the Variables for the Two Groups   The profiles of the groups in terms of means on the variables serve two basic purposes. First, they are useful to check whether the data were input correctly (a mean of 5.4 on a variable scaled 1 to 5 indicates the input is "messed up"). More important, they give the first indication of which variables distinguish between members of the two groups. Large differences in means on a particular variable suggest that the variable is an important discriminator between the groups. If all the variables have approximately the same standard deviation and there is relatively little correlation among the independent variables, the size of the differences between the means will provide the same ranking of the importances of the variables in discriminating as the size of the discriminant coefficients.

To summarize the results, a profile chart is often very effective. Returning to our hypothetical example, we could plot the purchaser and nonpurchaser groups as in Figure 18.5. Such a plot is very useful in understanding how the two groups differ.

The Discriminant Coefficients (w_is)   The discriminant coefficients indicate the relative contribution of a unit on each of the independent variables to the discriminant function. A large discriminant coefficient means that a one-unit change in that particular variable produces a large change in the discriminant function, and vice versa. In short, discriminant coefficients are interpreted exactly the same way as regression coefficients.

Discriminant coefficients (like regression coefficients) are affected by the scale of the independent variable. To remove this scale effect, many researchers either standardize the variables before inputting or multiply each discriminant coefficient (w_i) by the standard deviation of the variable (s_i), which in effect standardizes them. The resulting coefficients indicate how much a change of one standard deviation in each of the independent variables would affect the discriminant function. Whenever the scales of the independent variables vary widely (causing large differences in the size of the standard deviations), the unstandardized discriminant coefficients and the standardized discriminant coefficients may give very different importance ratings to the variables.

Discriminant coefficients are not proportional to the simple t values testing differences in means between the two groups for the variables when there is multicollinearity among the independent variables. In multiple regression, an independent variable may have a high simple correlation with the dependent variable, but the regression coefficient may be small and/or insignificant if the independent variable is also highly correlated with other independent variables. In discriminant analysis, a variable may be significantly different between two groups, but the discriminant coefficient insignificant due to collinearity with other independent variables. In other words, collinearity among the independent variables makes interpreting discriminant coefficients difficult exactly the way it makes regression coefficients unreliable and hard to interpret.

Returning to the example in Figure 18.1, we see that income is measured on a larger scale than age. Assuming these scales produce standard deviations of income and age equal to 1 and 2, respectively, we can compute a set of coefficients proportional to the standardized discriminant coefficients by multiplying the "regular" discriminant coefficients by the appropriate standard deviations, thus obtaining +3 and −2. The resulting measure of importance is shown in Table 18.1. In this hypothetical case, the relative importance of the variables in discriminating depends on your definition of importance.

Goodness of Fit   Most programs generate a measure of goodness of fit analogous to R^2. The two most popular are (*a*) the canonical correlation and (*b*) Wilks Lambda.

The canonical correlation is the correlation resulting from a regression of the independent variables on a dummy dependent variable[1] (e.g., 1 = user, 0 = nonuser). Its squared value is the R^2 from this regression.

Wilks Lambda is the ratio of within-group to total variance. Hence, it is essentially $1 - R^2$.

The Hit-Miss Table   Most discriminant analysis programs produce a hit-miss table (also known as a *classification table* or *confusion matrix*), which indicates how successful the discriminant function would have been in classifying the original observations (i.e., those used to form the function) back into their respective groups. (Usually, these tables are

TABLE 18.1   Alternative Measures of the Importance of a Variable

Variable	Raw Difference in Mean	Standard Deviation	Unstandardized Discriminant Coefficient	Standardized Discriminant Coefficient
Income	2.0	2	1.5	3.0
Age	−.5	1	−2	−2.0

[1] For the multiple-group case, there are multiple dependent variables. That is, for five groups, four dummy dependent variables are included to represent four of the five categories/groups.

constructed under the assumption of equal prior probabilities of group membership.) Such a table might look like the following:

Actual Group	Predicted Group	
	1	2
1	21	12
2	56	111

The percent correctly classified is often used as a summary measure of the value of the independent variables in predicting group membership and is somewhat analogous to R^2 in regression. In this case, the number of correct predictions is $21 + 111 = 132$. Since there were 200 observations in all, $\dfrac{132}{200} = 66$ percent is a measure of how effective the independent variables were in predicting group membership.

Statistical Aspects of Interpretation

Differences in Means The differences in means between the groups for each variable can be tested by the "old-fashioned" t test or the equivalent one-way ANOVA F test:

$$\frac{\bar{x}_{1j} - \bar{x}_{2j}}{S_{1j-2j}} \text{ is } t_{\alpha, n_1 + n_2 - 2}$$

or

$$\frac{\left(\bar{x}_{1j} - \bar{x}_{2j}\right)^2}{S_{1j-2j}^2} \text{ is } F_{\alpha, 1, n_1 + n_2 - 2}$$

Such a test can be applied to each of the independent variables.[2]

Rather than test the variables separately, it is possible to test all the variables simultaneously. This test examines whether the means on all the variables (e.g., income, age) are the same for the two groups. This multivariate analysis of variance test produces a variety of equivalent test statistics, the most common of which are an F statistic and the Mahalanobis D^2 (which turns out to be approximately chi-square distributed). A "large" (significant) F or D^2 indicates the means of the two groups are different on the variables and, hence, that the variables are helpful in separating the groups. A small F or D^2 indicates that the independent variables are essentially worthless as predictors of group membership.

The Percent Correctly Classified By examining the hit-miss table, the number of correct classifications can be calculated. The percent correctly classified can be compared statistically against the following three main criteria.

---

[2]Since many computer programs do not automatically produce these tests (a definite oversight in our opinion), they may require some effort to perform. The difference in means on the jth variable $\bar{x}_{1j} - \bar{x}_{2j}$ is easily computed from the means of the variables. The standard deviation often is not directly available and must be obtained from the square root of the jth diagonal element in the pooled variance-covariance matrix.

Random The easiest standard to compare the percent correctly classified (p) with is random classification. In the two-group case, that means 50 percent. The one-tail test statistic is

$$z = \frac{p - 50}{\sqrt{(50)(50)}} \sqrt{n_1 + n_2}$$

where z is standard normally distributed. Hence, when z is big (greater than 2), the independent variables have made a significant contribution to prediction. Returning to our previous example, we can compare 66 percent with 50 percent as follows:

$$z = \frac{66 - 50}{\sqrt{(50)(50)}} \sqrt{200} = \frac{16}{50} \sqrt{200} = 4.5 > 2$$

Thus, we have done significantly better than random at the 95 percent level. If this test fails to be significant, all the others will also.

The Largest Group Criterion The toughest test is to compare the percent correctly classified with the percent that would be correctly classified by assuming everyone was a member of the largest group. This criterion becomes extremely hard to beat as one group becomes dominant. In the previous example, 167 = 83.5 percent of the people are in the largest group (nonpurchasers). Simply saying everyone is a nonpurchaser will give the fewest misclassifications, since 83.5 is greater than 66. This criterion is somewhat inappropriate in a practical sense, however, since we are much more concerned with finding purchasers than with avoiding contacting nonpurchasers. Beating the largest group criterion is sufficient to demonstrate the worth of the independent variables but is not necessary for the variables to be useful.

The "Fairest" Criterion In some sense, the fairest criterion is to assume that likelihood of correct classification depends on both the probability of group membership (P_i) and the fraction assigned to each group (f_i) (Mostellar and Bush, 1954). The criterion is:

$$C_{\text{fair}} = f_1(P_1) + f_2(P_2)$$

In the previous example, that would be:

$$C_{\text{fair}} = \frac{77}{200} \left(\frac{33}{200} \right) + \frac{123}{200} \left(\frac{167}{200} \right) = 58 \text{ percent}$$

Therefore, we would compare the 66 percent correctly classified with 58 percent.

The Bias Problem Using the same observations to examine the ability of the discriminant function to classify observations correctly as were used to create the discriminant function produces an upward bias in the percent correctly classified. The obvious way to remove the bias is to split the sample into an analysis sample, which is used to construct the discriminant function, and a *holdout sample*. The holdout sample is then classified into groups based on the discriminant function derived from the analysis sample, eliminating the bias. The problem with this approach is that for a large sample ($n > 300$), the bias is relatively small. For a small sample ($n < 50$), on the other hand, there are probably not enough observations to split the data into two groups. Consequently, the "split-half" approach is useful mainly for moderate sample sizes.

An extreme but effective way to remove the bias in classifying is to run $n_1 + n_2$ separate discriminant analyses. In each of these analyses, one observation is the holdout observation. Hence, we use the discriminant function based on the $n_1 + n_2 - 1$ observations to classify the holdout observation. By rotating the holdout observation, one can estimate the percent correctly classified. Fortunately, for most situations such an extreme remedy is unnecessary.

Application Issues

Where   Two-group discriminant analysis can be applied anywhere the criterion variable can be divided into two groups. This means situations including purchasers versus non-purchasers, buyers of brand A versus buyers of all other brands, good risks versus bad risks, and so forth, are candidates for two-group discriminant analysis.

In everyday life, one need only apply for a credit card or a loan to be subjected to the results of discriminant analysis. Your income, age, length of residence, and so forth are all considered (and appropriately weighted) in deciding whether to give you a loan. The weights are often rounded to even numbers so a clerk can easily calculate your "score." If your score is above a certain level, you get the credit card or loan. If not, you have literally been discriminated against.

How   Building a discriminant model is equivalent to building a regression model. All the caveats and suggestions about model building made in the regression chapter apply here as well. Two other issues often are raised by users of discriminant analysis. One question is whether the two groups must be of equal size. As long as the objective is to find the best discriminant function possible, given a sample has already been drawn, the best approach is to use all the data points available. In short, the groups do not have to be of equal size. In designing a sample, on the other hand, guaranteeing relatively equal sample sizes in the two groups for a fixed total sample size will somewhat improve the reliability of the results.

Another issue is what will happen when the two basic assumptions of normality and equal covariances in the two groups are violated. Violation of the basic assumptions makes statistical interpretation of the results very difficult. If the covariances in the two groups are sufficiently unequal, the optimal discriminant function becomes nonlinear. Nonetheless, for the purpose of finding interesting relations, discriminant analysis is remarkably robust. Therefore, such relaxations as using binary (dummy) variables as independent variables can be done in practice if not in theory.

Examples

Innovators versus Noninnovators   The first example concerns the difference between personalities of innovators and noninnovators in the purchase of a new home appliance (Robertson and Kennedy, 1968). In this study, 60 innovators were compared with 40 noninnovators on seven personality variables (Table 18.2). The two groups are profiled in Figure 18.6. The discriminant coefficients indicate that venturesomeness is the best discriminator (among the seven personality measures studied) and that interest range is

TABLE 18.2 Differences Between Innovators and Noninnovators

	Innovator Mean	Noninnovator Mean	Discriminant Coefficient
Venturesomeness	4.88	4.12	3.59
Social mobility	3.93	3.20	3.08
Privilegedness	3.68	3.25	2.04
Social integration	4.13	3.78	2.44
Status concern	2.00	1.73	.95
Interest range	5.27	5.00	.59
Cosmopolitanism	2.77	3.03	−2.86

Source: Thomas Robertson and James Kennedy, "Prediction of Consumer Innovators: Application of Multiple Discriminant Analysis." Adapted from *Journal of Marketing Research* 5 (February 1968): 66–67. Copyright © 1968 by the American Marketing Association. Reprinted with the permission of the publishers.

the worst. You may notice that the size of the discriminant coefficients produces a ranking different from what would be generated by looking at the differences in the means on the variables. The reasons for this are (*a*) unequal variances of the variables and/or (*b*) multicollinearity among the predictor variables.

U.S. versus U.K. Purchasing Agents   This example deals with industrial purchasing agents (Lehmann and O'Shaughnessy, 1974). To compare purchasing agents in the United Kingdom with those in the United States, the importances they attributed to 17 attributes for four product types were analyzed. One part of the analysis involved discriminant analy-

FIGURE 18.6
Profile of Innovators and Noninnovators

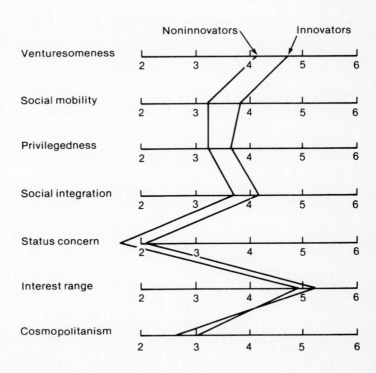

sis between U.S. and U.K. purchasing agents. Four two-group discriminant analyses were performed, one for each of the four product types. The resulting discriminant functions are shown in Table 18.3. Notice that here unstandardized discriminant coefficients are reported. Since the 17 attributes were all rated on the same scale and had approximately the same standard deviations, the standardized coefficients would be very similar to the unstandardized coefficients.

In interpreting these results, it is important to recognize that the function arbitrarily placed U.K. purchasing agents at the top of the scale. (This can be ascertained either by looking at the group means on the discriminant functions or by simply examining the group means on the separate variables and then deducing which way the function goes.) With this in mind, it is possible to interpret the results by looking for (relatively) big discriminant coefficients. In this example, any coefficient greater than 1 in absolute size was identified as "big" in interpreting the results.

U.K. purchasing agents place greater emphasis on reliability of delivery and maintenance for all four product types, on convenience in ordering for Type I and II products, and on sales service and financing for products that give rise to procedural (Type III) or political (Type IV) problems. U.S. purchasing agents, on the other hand, tend to stress reputation for Type I, III, and IV products, past experience for Type I and IV, training offered for Type II, III, and IV products, and price for Type I and II products. Hence, one might conclude that U.K. purchasing agents are more service oriented and U.S. agents somewhat more experience/reputation oriented. Interestingly, these results largely reinforce the results of simple t tests for differences in mean importance on the 17 attributes.

TABLE 18.3 Discriminant Functions: U.K. versus U.S. Purchasing Agents

	Product Type			
Attribute	I	II	III	IV
Reputation	−1.10	−.16	−.95	−1.02
Financing	−.01	.50	.85	1.64
Flexibility	−.19	.53	1.07	−1.73
Past experience	−1.16	−.11	−.27	−1.05
Technical service	.19	2.38	1.57	−.96
Confidence in salespersons	.81	.42	−.55	.48
Convenience in ordering	1.13	1.11	−.01	.18
Reliability data	−.58	−.67	−.24	.44
Price	−.81	−2.10	−.21	.27
Technical specifications	1.33	−.66	−.69	−.30
Ease of use	−.09	.18	.87	−1.17
Preference of user	−.45	−2.02	−.09	.88
Training offered	.15	−2.63	−.96	−1.16
Training required	−1.55	.39	−.45	−.12
Reliability of delivery	2.41	2.60	.64	1.36
Maintenance	.87	1.04	.42	1.50
Sales service	−.39	1.03	1.30	1.96

To get a measure of how well the 17 attributes predict group membership, there are two common approaches. The first is to test whether the independent variables taken as a whole differ significantly across the groups. Most programs calculate an F statistic to test this significance. In the current example, the test statistic used was a Mahalanobis D^2. This formidable sounding statistic is approximately chi-square (χ^2) distributed with (Number of groups − 1)(Number of variables) degrees of freedom. Here there were (2 − 1)(17) = 17 degrees of freedom. The Mahalanobis D^2s were 41.0, 50.8, 29.2, and 45.6, respectively, for the four product types. Since at the .05 significance level the cutoff for a significant chi-square with 17 degrees of freedom is 27.6, the independent variables contribute significantly (if not spectacularly) to predicting group membership. In other words, U.S. and U.K. purchasing agents attach significantly different importances to product attributes.

The other way to see how well the discriminant function performs is to use it to classify some observations and see how accurate its classifications are. Ideally, a fresh sample of observations should be classified. Since the purchasing agent project budget was exhausted, a fresh sample was not feasible. The next best approach is to use a holdout sample for classifications that was not used to compute the discriminant functions. Given the small sample size here (26 in one group, 19 in the other), this was not feasible. The least desirable approach is to see how well the discriminant function performs in classifying the observations used in constructing the functions. In spite of the inflated value this can give in terms of the percent correctly classified, the fact that most programs do this automatically makes this a common way to look at the results. In this case, the percents correctly reclassified were 84.4, 86.7, 77.8, and 84.4 percent, respectively, for the four product types. These are "pretty good" results and again support the notion that product attribute importances differ between U.S. and U.K. purchasing agents.

Fifty States Example   As a final example of two-group discriminant analysis, the 50 states in Table 9.1 were broken into two groups—15 in the South and the 35 others. The two groups were then compared, based on the other available variables (income, etc.). The first step in examining the results in Table 18.4 is to examine the means of the two groups. The big differences appear to be that in 1973 the South was lower in income and taxes and higher in mineral production. This is confirmed by the univariate F tests, which have 1 numerator and 48 denominator degrees of freedom. College enrollment differs on average, but apparently the within-group variation is so large that the difference is not statistically significant.

In examining the discriminant functions, we note that the most important discriminator is population. The reason this and not income, taxes, or mineral production is the best discriminator is multicollinearity among the variables. This emphasizes the point that the discriminant coefficients are not deducible from the means alone. It also suggests a more parsimonious model would probably predict group membership as well as this model.

Several other parts of the output are of some interest. The canonical correlation is a measure of the multiple correlation we would have obtained if we had run a regression with the dependent variable a dummy variable (e.g., 1 = South, 0 = other). Hence, $(.80)^2 = .64$ is the R^2, indicating a pretty good fit.

Wilks Lambda is the ratio of within-group to total variance. Therefore, it is essentially equal to $1 − R^2$, here $1 − .63 = .37$.

TABLE 18.4 Discriminant Analysis of Southern versus non-Southern States

Variable	Variable Means			Discriminant Function	
	South	Non-South	One-Way F	Unstandardized	Standardized
Average income	4.95	5.91	17.13	−0.43	−0.32
Population	4.45	4.19	0.05	0.92	4.15
Population change	1.37	1.19	0.30	−0.37	−0.39
Percent urban	57.00	58.37	0.03	0.02	0.33
Tax per capita	464.13	618.23	26.97	−0.01	−0.87
Government expenditures	286.13	281.54	0.00	0.00	0.75
College enrollment	165.20	192.45	0.14	−0.01	−2.03
Mineral production	2006.27	610.49	6.84	0.00	0.03
Forest acres	15.93	14.70	0.05	0.01	0.15
Manufacturing output	6.77	8.66	0.40	−0.27	−2.65
Farm receipts	1801.73	1943.37	0.06	−0.00	−0.40
Canonical correlation	.80				
Wilks lambda	.37				
Chi-square	42.71				
Degrees of freedom	11				

The chi-square value tests whether, overall, the variables help discriminate. Here, the 42.71 is compared with the chi-square table at 11 (the number of independent variables) degrees of freedom. Since the .001 level is 31.3, we have very strong evidence that the variables are significantly related to whether a state is in the South or not.

The classification matrix that results is, thus, not surprisingly fairly impressive:

Actual Group	Predicted Group	
	Non-South	South
Non-South	32	3
South	1	14

Consequently, 92 percent of the observations are correctly classified—much better than the random (50 percent) and largest group (70 percent) criteria. Obviously, this percent is somewhat overstated, since there are 11 predictor variables and only 15 southern states. A prudent researcher might, therefore, redo the analysis with fewer independent variables (e.g., population, college enrollment, and manufacturing output).

MULTIPLE-GROUP DISCRIMINANT ANALYSIS

The major approach to more-than-two-group discriminant analysis is to first attempt to find a single function that simultaneously spreads all groups apart as far as possible. Next, a second function (independent of the first) is found that best further explains differences in group membership, and so forth. For g groups, there will be $g - 1$ such functions. This can be viewed graphically as Figure 18.7. For the really curious reader, the functions are mathematically derived by canonical correlation (Appendix 18-D).

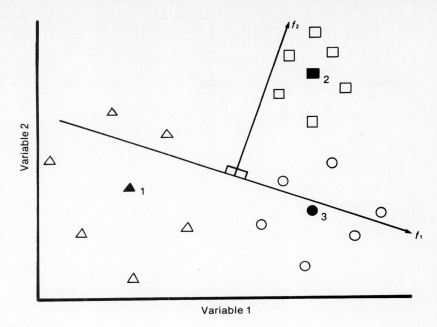

FIGURE 18.7
Simultaneous Approach to More Than Two-Group Discriminant Analysis

A Nutritional Example

Returning to the nutrition study, assume we are again interested in explaining weekly food consumption expenditures in terms of other characteristics. Since there were five response categories to the food expenditure question, we have five groups of respondents, ranging from those who spend less than $15 per week to those who spend more than $60 per week. (These data are really at least as well suited to regression—the alert reader will notice that food expenditure was the dependent variable in the regression example in the regression chapter—since food expenditure is at least ordinally and probably intervally scaled. This example is used, therefore, mainly for pedagogical purposes.)

The SPSS input and output appear in Appendix 18-B. The 853 respondents provided complete data in terms of education of both husband and wife, age, income, family size, how often they shopped, the number of alternatives considered, and information receptivity as well as food expenditures. Examination of the mean values shows "reasonable numbers" and relatively equal standard deviations. The group means are shown in Table 18.5. These means indicate that larger spenders tend to be more educated, be younger, have higher incomes and larger family sizes, and shop more extensively.

The significance of the differences among the five groups on a variable-by-variable basis is given by the F tests, which appear next in the output. The 106.0 for family size is the largest, with the 49.1 for income next biggest, indicating that these variables are the most important in separating the five groups. Interestingly, education, age, and how often they shop are all also significantly ($F > 4$) related to food expenditures. (Alas, our favorite variables—number of brands shopped and information sought—are not.)

TABLE 18.5 Variable Averages for Five Food Expenditure Level Groups

	Group				
	1 <$15	**2** $15–$29	**3** $30–$44	**4** $45–$59	**5** >$60
Education of wife	3.32	4.11	4.29	4.47	4.49
Education of husband	2.79	3.75	4.08	4.57	4.69
Age	4.09	3.46	3.06	2.50	2.72
Income	1.62	2.06	2.75	3.47	3.75
Family size	2.09	2.52	3.13	4.14	5.11
How often they shop	1.91	2.18	2.27	2.29	2.62
Number of brands shopped for	1.82	2.25	2.34	2.25	2.72
Information sought	1.91	1.91	1.81	1.84	1.87
Sample size	34	284	293	181	61

The program then (after giving some gratuitous information) proceeds to enter variables stepwise into a discriminant analysis in the following order:

1. Family size
2. Income
3. How often they shop
4. Age
5. Education of the wife
6. Number of brands shopped for

This order differs from what the size of simple Fs indicates, due to multicollinearity.

Next, the classification function coefficients are output (Table 18.6). These functions can be used for (*a*) classification and (*b*) finding the two-group discriminant function (unstandardized) between a particular pair of groups (see Appendix 18-B). Here, for example, the function that best discriminates between groups 1 and 2 is:

− .43	Education of wife
+ .20	Age
− .02	Income
− .25	Family size
− .73	How often they shop
− .17	Number of brands shopped for

while that between 2 and 3 is

+ .07	Education of wife
+ .05	Age
− .39	Income
− .44	Family size
− .27	How often they shop
− .01	Number of brands shopped for

TABLE 18.6 Classification Functions

	Group				
	1	**2**	**3**	**4**	**5**
Education of wife	2.92	3.35	3.28	3.21	3.22
Age	3.61	3.41	3.36	3.32	3.70
Income	.42	.44	.83	1.21	1.38
Family size	3.13	3.38	3.82	4.55	5.48
How often they shop	2.83	3.56	3.83	4.00	4.69
Number of brands shopped for	1.18	1.33	1.34	1.24	1.44
Constant	−19.61	−22.89	−25.23	−28.80	−37.02

It appears that the variable that best discriminates (at least it did in 1975) between those who spend under $15 and those who spend $15–$29 is how often they shopped, while what separates the $15–$29 from the $30–$44 spenders is income and family size.

The multiple discriminant functions are also output in both standardized and unstandardized forms. The first function is the most useful, the second next most useful, and so forth. The output indicated (by means of a chi-square test of Wilks lambda) that three functions are significant at the .01 level. The most important variables in the first function are family size, income, and how often they shop. The second function is related to age and family size. The results can be portrayed graphically as in Figure 18.8. Hence, these results largely reinforce the analysis of the means and simple *F* tests as well as the ANOVA and regression results of previous chapters.

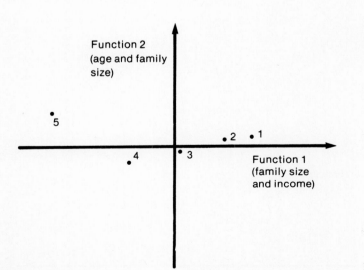

FIGURE 18.8
Group Means on First Two Discriminant Functions

PRODUCT MAPPING

Discriminant analysis also can be used to generate product maps. The basic input data are direct ratings of the alternatives on a set of prespecified attributes. Rather than plotting the results directly, however, multiple-group discriminant analysis (the canonical correlate type) is used to generate compound dimensions that explain the ratings. The trick is to generate input data by using the brands as groups. The brands thus appear as the groups in the output. The location of the brands on the attributes is given by the group centroids (means on the discriminant functions). The discriminant functions themselves are combinations of the original dimensions. These compound dimensions are relatively easy to name, since how closely related each of the original attributes is to each of the derived dimensions is part of the output. Since they depend totally on the prespecified attributes, however, discriminant analysis only simplifies the direct rating approach and does not deduce unknown dimensions.

TABLE 18.7 **Input Format for the Discriminant Analysis Approach for Deriving Attribute Models**

	Attribute Rating		
	1	2	8
	Flavor	Sweetness	...	Thirst Quenching

Group 1: Brand 1 (Coke)
  Subject
    1
    2
    .
    .
    .
    n
Group 2: Brand 2 (7-Up)
  Subject
    1
    2
    .
    .
    .
    n
    .
    .
    .
Group 8: Brand 8 (Fresca)
  Subject
    1
    2
    .
    .
    .
    n

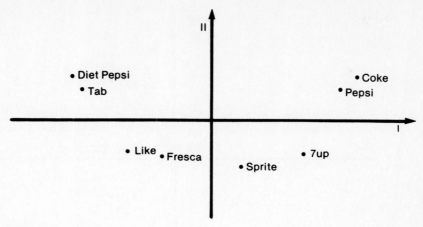

FIGURE 18.9
Basic Map

Some of the best examples of this approach appear in the work of Johnson (1971). One of his classic examples involved brands of beer. The two-dimensional solution consisted of a "premium–local" dimension and a "heavy" (Budweiser) versus "light" (Miller) dimension. Interestingly, in terms of some ingredients, Miller was heavier than Budweiser. The message here is that "there is naught but thinking makes it so." If you advertise with the Clydesdales, Ed McMahon, and a squat brown bottle you can convince people you're heavier than a "champagne of bottled beer" that is sold in a tall, clear bottle. Another classic example of Johnson's (1970) involved the 1968 pres-

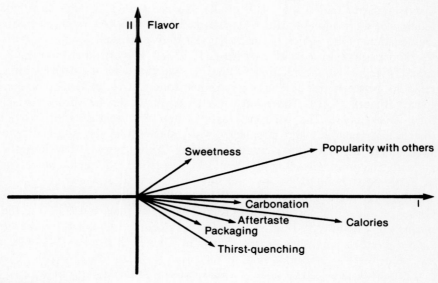

FIGURE 18.10
Relation of the Original Attributes to the Discriminant Function

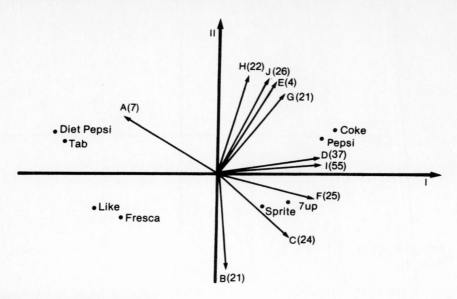

FIGURE 18.11 PREFMAP Results

idential campaign. The two-dimensional picture, which included both candidates and voter segments, provides an interesting vantage point for studying the strategies of the major candidates.

One example of the way discriminant analysis can be used to generate a map uses the by now infamous soft drink study again (Lehmann and Pessemier, 1973). The alternatives become the eight brands, and the eight attributes come from the questionnaire that was used (Table 18.7). The results can be viewed in three parts: the basic map, the relation of the original attributes to the derived dimensions, and (by means of PREFMAP) the location of 10 major segments in the derived space.

The basic map appears as Figure 18.9 and suggests that calories is the key dimension. To represent the relation of the original attributes to derived dimensions, the correlations between the attributes and dimensions can be used to plot the attributes in the space[3] (Figure 18.10). These attributes clearly indicate the vertical axis is flavor (lemon-lime versus cola). The horizontal axis is highly correlated with two attributes: calories (diet versus nondiet) and popularity with others. It is the appearance of the popularity with others attribute that is most surprising. This suggests that subjects may have been at least as concerned about the general acceptability of their choice (or its availability) as they were about its caloric content.

Subjects were grouped into 10 major segments, based on their frequency of purchase of the eight brands. The segments were then overlaid on the basic map by means of PREFMAP (Phase III). The segments (indicated by the letters) and their sizes (given in parentheses) are shown in Figure 18.11. For example, the biggest seg-

---

[3]This is done by using a vector to represent the original attributes. The length of the vector is proportional to the ability of the two derived dimensions to explain the original attributes. The correlation between the attribute and the discriminant function is used to determine the direction of the vector by using a form of $r = \cos(\text{angle})$.

ment (I) appears to prefer Coke and then Pepsi. These results clearly indicate that Coke and Pepsi will do well (they are the two biggest sellers) and that Like is left out in the cold.

SUMMARY

This chapter has discussed discriminant analysis, which complements previously discussed predictive procedures: tabular analysis, ANOVA, and regression. In subsequent chapters, we discuss a few others. However, predictive procedures have severely diminishing marginal utility. Running multiple predictive procedures on the same set of data is more likely to increase the computer bill than understanding. Also, very few people really understand these procedures. To really understand them requires a start-up cost in time and trial-and-error learning. Given time constraints and computer limitations, it is unrealistic to expect researchers to know all possible techniques well. It is effective, however, to understand one well (we vote for regression) and to know enough about the others (especially ANOVA and discriminant analysis) to know when their special properties make their use advantageous. Finally, don't be afraid to ask the "professional" a question; good ones can provide answers that are at least partially intelligible.

PROBLEMS

1. Assume I run a discriminant analysis on business school majors using aptitude scores as independent variables and get the following classification matrix:

	Predicted Group				
Actual Group	International Business	Marketing	Finance	Production	Others
International business	70	40	30	20	40
Marketing	50	90	30	10	20
Finance	20	20	80	60	20
Production	20	30	40	80	30
Others	20	20	40	20	100

   a. How well have I done (statistically)?

   b. What do the results indicate?

2. Explain the difference between discriminant analysis and classification.

3. In two-group discriminant analysis, could the *sign* of a discriminant coefficient and the *sign* of the difference between means on the variable differ? What would this mean?

4. Explain the difference between discriminant analysis and cluster analysis. Give an example of the type of marketing problems for which each is useful.

5. Your researcher wants to use a discriminant analysis to see if he or she can "predict the people who try a new brand" compared with those who do not try the new brand.

You know that the market share of the new brand is only 5 percent and observe that you can predict 95 percent of the population correctly by simply assuming each person did not try the new brand. Yet you are bothered by this assumption, because it suggests that the market share of the new brand should be zero. You do not think your researcher will be able to predict 95 percent correctly with his or her discriminant analysis model, and so you are reluctant to pay for such an investigation. Can anything possibly come out of the discriminant analysis research that might justify the cost of the investigation? What?

6. The following are the income (in $1,000) and age of a sample of 20 purchasers of an expensive automobile brand. A particular accessory was purchased by 12 of the sample but was not purchased by the other 8. The age and income of the sample were as follows:

Twelve Purchasers		Eight Nonpurchasers	
Age	Income ($000)	Age	Income ($000)
30	20	30	50
40	50	40	30
40	60	40	40
50	40	40	40
50	70	50	20
60	30	50	30
60	40	60	20
60	40	60	50
60	50		
60	60		
60	70		
70	20		

a. Graphically determine a linear discriminant function that will effectively predict the purchase of the accessory.

b. Determine the values of the discriminant function that correspond to nonpurchase, and the values that correspond to purchase of the accessory.

c. How well does the function discriminate?

7. Of what use are the following outputs of a discriminant analysis?

a. The Mahalanobis D^2 test statistic

b. The discriminant function in a two-group analysis

c. The first discriminant function in a three-group analysis

d. The second discriminant function in a three-group analysis

e. The hit-miss classification table for the estimation sample

f. The hit-miss classification table for a holdout sample

REFERENCES

BUCKLIN, RANDOLPH E., AND JAMES M. LATTIN (1991) "A Two-State Model of Purchase Incidence and Brand Choice," *Marketing Science*, 10, Winter, 24–39.

COOLEY, WILLIAM W., AND PAUL R. LOHNES (1971) *Multivariate Data Analysis*, New York: John Wiley and Sons.

DILLON, WILLIAM R. (1979) "The Performance of the Linear Discriminant Function in Nonoptimal Situations and the Estimation of Classification Error Rates: A Review of Recent Findings," *Journal of Marketing Research*, 16, August, 370–81.

GREEN, PAUL E., FRANK J. CARMONE, AND D. P. WACHSPRESS (1977) "On the Analysis of Qualitative Data in Marketing Research," *Journal of Marketing Research*, 14, February, 52–59.

HOLBROOK, MORRIS B., AND WILLIAM L. MOORE (1982) "Using Canonical Correlation to Construct Product Spaces for Objects with Known Feature Structures," *Journal of Marketing Research*, 19, February, 87–98.

HORA, STEPHEN C., AND JAMES B. WILCOX (1982) "Estimation of Error Rates in Several-Population Discriminant Analysis," *Journal of Marketing Research*, 19, February, 57–61.

JOHNSON, RICHARD M. (1970) "Political Segmentation," *Marketing Review*, 25, February, 20–24.

——— (1971) "Market Segmentation: A Strategic Management Tool," *Journal of Marketing Research*, 8, February, 13–18.

LEHMANN, DONALD R., AND JOHN O'SHAUGHNESSY (1974) "Difference in Attribute Importance for Different Industrial Products," *Journal of Marketing*, 38, April, 36–42.

LEHMANN, DONALD R., AND EDGAR A. PESSEMIER (1973) "Predicted Probability of Brand Choice Market Segments and Discriminant Attribute Configurations in Joint Space Market Analyses," Presented at Annual Meeting, Operations Research Society of America, Milwaukee, May.

MCLACHLAN, DOUGLAS L., AND JOHNY K. JOHANSSON (1981) "Market Segmentation with Multivariate AID," *Journal of Marketing*, 45, Winter, 74–84.

MORGAN, J. N., AND J. A. SONQUIST (1964) *The Determination of Interaction Effects*, Monograph No. 35. Ann Arbor: Survey Research Center, Institute for Social Research, University of Michigan.

MORRISON, DONALD G. (1969) "On the Interpretation of Discriminant Analysis," *Journal of Marketing Research*, 6, May, 156–63.

MOSTELLAR, FREDERICH, AND ROBERT R. BUSH (1954) "Selective Quantitative Techniques," in Gardner Lindzey, ed., *Handbook of Social Psychology*, vol. 1, Reading, Mass.: Addison-Wesley.

REYNOLDS, H. T. (1977) "Analysis of Nominal Data," Sage University Paper Series on Quantitative Applications in the Social Sciences, 07-007. Beverly Hills, Calif.: Sage.

ROBERTSON, THOMAS S., AND JAMES N. KENNEDY (1968) "Prediction of Consumer Innovators: Application of Multiple Discriminant Analysis," *Journal of Marketing Research*, 5, February, 64–69.

RYANS, ADRIAN B., AND CHARLES B. WEINBERG (1979) "Territory Sales Response," *Journal of Marketing Research*, 16, November, 453–65.

APPENDIX 18-A

TECHNICAL ASPECTS OF DISCRIMINANT ANALYSIS

THE DISCRIMINANT FUNCTION

The discriminant coefficients can be expressed as a matrix product as follows:

$$d = W^{-1}(\bar{x}_1 - \bar{x}_2) \tag{18A.1}$$

where

W = the pooled within-group covariance matrix
$\bar{x}_1$ = vector of means of the first group on all k variables
$\bar{x}_2$ = vector of means of the second group on all k variables

This formulation can be better understood by considering the special case where the predictor variables are perfectly independent of each other. In this case, the discriminant function becomes

$$d = \left[\frac{\bar{x}_{11} - \bar{x}_{21}}{s_1^2}\right] x_1 + \left[\frac{\bar{x}_{12} - \bar{x}_{22}}{s_2^2}\right] x_2 + \cdots + \left[\frac{\bar{x}_{1k} - \bar{x}_{2k}}{s_k^2}\right] x_k$$

Hence, the weight assigned a particular variable depends on (a) the difference in means between the two groups on that variable and (b) the variance of that variable. Practically, this means that variables on which the two groups differ significantly will be weighted heavily by the discriminant function. The relation between the difference in means between groups and standard deviation (variance) on a particular variable and the discriminant coefficient is summarized in Table 18A.1.

OPTIMAL CLASSIFICATION

The basic motivation of discriminant analysis is to determine which of a set of characteristics are most important as discriminators between members of the two groups. Discriminant analysis, therefore, is not primarily addressed to the objective of classifying an

TABLE 18A.1   The Effect of Difference in Mean and Variance on Discriminant Coefficients

Difference in Means	Variance	Discriminant Coefficient
Small	Small	Moderate
Small	Large	Close to Zero
Large	Small	Large
Large	Large	Moderate

individual into one of two groups based on the values the individual has on the predictor variables. The resulting discriminant function can, however, be used to optimally classify observations.

The basic approach in most classification procedures is to assign an individual to the group where the expected opportunity cost of misclassification is the smallest. This requires taking the following three pieces of information into account:

1. The cost of misclassifying a member of one group as a member of another:

    $C(1|2)$ = cost of classifying a person as a member of group 1 given he or she is really a member of group 2 (e.g., classifying a customer as a noncustomer);

    $C(2|1)$ = cost of classifying a person as a member of group 2 given the person is really a member of group 1.

2. The relative likelihoods that a person in the two groups would exhibit the values on the variables of the individual who is to be classified:

    $L(Z|1)$ = likelihood that a person in group 1 would exhibit a set of characteristics equal to Z;

    $L(Z|2)$ = likelihood that a person in group 2 would exhibit a set of characteristics equal to Z.

3. The overall (prior) probability that any individual will be a member of each of the two groups:

    $P(1)$ = probability that an individual is a member of group 1;
    $P(2)$ = probability that an individual is a member of group 2.

To classify a person as a member of group 1, the following inequality must hold:

$$\text{Expected cost of classifying as a 1} < \text{Expected cost of classifying as a 2} \qquad (18A.2)$$

or

$$[P(1)][C(2|1)][L(Z|1)] > [P(2)][C(1|2)][L(Z|2)]$$

This can be rewritten as:

$$\frac{[P(2)][C(1|2)]}{[P(1)][C(2|1)]} < \frac{L(Z|1)}{L(Z|2)}$$

For the case with equal priors and costs of misclassification, the formula reduces to classifying an observation as a member of group 1 if $L(Z|1) > L(Z|2)$.

To this point, nothing has depended on performing discriminant analysis. The likelihoods can be evaluated directly. Direct evaluation, however, is not very easy without a computer, given the messy formulas involved. Fortunately, the discriminant function can be used to get optimal classification if the following two assumptions are met:

1. The predictor variables are normally distributed.
2. The variances are equal in the two groups.

In this case, the linear discriminant function will provide optimal classification if the following rule is followed:

Let

$$K = \frac{[P(2)][C(1\,|\,2)]}{[P(1)][C(2\,|\,1)]} \qquad (18A.3)$$

$\bar{f}_1 \bar{f}_2$ = mean value of the groups on the discriminant function, which are calculated by multiplying the discriminant weights (w_is) times the means of the variables for each group:

$$\bar{f}_1 = w_1\bar{x}_{11} + w_2\bar{x}_{12} + \cdots + w_k\bar{x}_{1k} \qquad (18A.4)$$

$$\bar{f}_2 = w_1\bar{x}_{21} + w_2\bar{x}_{22} + \cdots + w_k\bar{x}_{2k}$$

n = total number of observations ($n_1 + n_2$);

$$f = w_1Z_1 + w_2Z_2 + \cdots + w_kZ_k \qquad (18A.5)$$

= value of the person to be classified on the discriminant function

Then (assuming $\bar{f}_1 < \bar{f}_2$) we would classify an observation as a member of group 1 if:

$$f < \frac{\bar{f}_1 + \bar{f}_2}{2} - \log_e k \qquad (18A.6)$$

For equal priors and costs of misclassifying, this reduces to:

$$f < \frac{\bar{f}_1 + \bar{f}_2}{2} \qquad (18A.7)$$

USING THE DISCRIMINANT FUNCTION FOR CLASSIFICATION

Recalling the earlier example involving nonpurchasers and purchasers measured in terms of age and income, we had:

$$f = 3(\text{Income}) - 2(\text{age})$$

If the group means on income and age were 2.5 and 2, respectively, for nonpurchasers, and the group means for purchasers were 4.5 and 1.5, the mean values for the two groups on the discriminant function are as follows:

$$\bar{f}_1 = 3(2.5) - 2(2) = 3.5$$

and

$$\bar{f}_2 = 3(4.5) - 2(1.5) = 10.5$$

Thus, the "cutoff" can be derived from formula (18A.7) as

$$\frac{\bar{f}_1 + \bar{f}_2}{2} = \frac{3.5 + 10.5}{2} = 7$$

Now assume we wished to classify a person as a member of group 1 or 2 based on the person's income of 3 and age of 2. In this case, $f = 3(3) - 2(2) = 5$. Since $5 < 7$, we would classify this person as a nonpurchaser.

APPENDIX 18-B

SAMPLE DISCRIMINANT ANALYSIS OUTPUT

```
STATISTICAL PACKAGE FOR THE SOCIAL SCIENCES SPSSH - VERSION 6.00          10/19/76     PAGE    1

          SPACE ALLOCATION FOR THIS RUN..

          TOTAL AMOUNT REQUESTED                        80000 BYTES


          DEFAULT TRANSPACE ALLOCATION                  10000 BYTES


               MAX NO OF TRANSFORMATIONS PERMITTED   100
               MAX NO OF RECODE VALUES               400
               MAX NC OF ARITHM.OR LOG.OPERATIONS    800

          RESULTING WORKSPACE ALLOCATION               70000 BYTES
               FILE NAME       LEHNUTRI
               VARIABLE LIST   EDUC1,EDUC2,AGE,INCOME,FAMSIZE,HOWOFTEN,EXPENSE,
                               BRAND,INFC
               INPUT MEDIUM    DISK
               N OF CASES      UNKNOWN
               INPUT FORMAT    FIXED(56X,2F1.0,17X,3F1.0/9X,F1.0,2X,F1.0,X,2F1.0////)


          ACCORDING TO YOUR INPUT FORMAT, VARIABLES ARE TO BE READ AS FOLLOWS

               VARIABLE   FORMAT   RECORD    COLUMNS

               EDUC1      F 1. 0      1       57-   57
               EDUC2      F 1. 0      1       58-   58
               AGE        F 1. 0      1       76-   76
               INCOME     F 1. 0      1       77-   77
               FAMSIZE    F 1. 0      1       78-   78
               HOWOFTEN   F 1. 0      2       10-   10
               EXPENSE    F 1. 0      2       13-   13
               BRAND      F 1. 0      2       15-   15
               INFC       F 1. 0      2       16-   16

THE INPUT FORMAT PROVIDES FOR   9 VARIABLES.   9 WILL BE READ
IT PROVIDES FOR  6 RECORDS ('CARDS') PER CASE. A MAXIMUM OF   78 'COLUMNS' ARE USED ON A RECORD.

               MISSING VALUES EDUC1 TO EXPENSE (0)
               READ INPUT DATA

AFTER READING   940 CASES FROM SUBFILE LEHNUTRI,  END OF FILE WAS ENCOUNTERED ON LOGICAL UNIT # 8



STATISTICAL PACKAGE FOR THE SOCIAL SCIENCES SPSSH - VERSION 6.00          10/19/76     PAGE    2
          DISCRIMINANT   GROUPS=EXPENSE(1,5)/VARIABLES=EDUC1 TO HOWOFTEN,BRAND,
                         INFO/METHOD=WILKS/
          OPTIONS        5,7,11,12,13,14
          STATISTICS     ALL
FIRST ANALYSIS LIST IS MISSING. ALL VARIABLES WILL BE  USED WITH INCLUSION LEVELS OF ONE.

***** WARNING *****     OPTIONS 13 THRU 19  AND STATISTICS 7, 8  ARE NOT YET IMPLEMENTED AND WILL BE IGNORED.

***** THIS DISCRIMINANT ANALYSIS REQUIRES   5624 BYTES OF WORKSPACE *****
```

STATISTICAL PACKAGE FOR THE SOCIAL SCIENCES SPSSH - VERSION 6.00   10/19/76   PAGE 3

FILE   LEHNUTRI (CREATION DATE = 10/19/76)

GROUP COUNTS

	GROUP 1	GROUP 2	GROUP 3	GROUP 4	GROUP 5	TOTAL
COUNT	34.0000	284.0000	293.0000	181.0000	61.0000	853.0000

MEANS

	GROUP 1	GROUP 2	GROUP 3	GROUP 4	GROUP 5	TOTAL
EDUC1	3.3235	4.1092	4.2901	4.4656	4.4918	4.2438
EDUC2	2.7941	3.7465	4.0751	4.5651	4.6885	4.0633
AGE	4.0882	3.4648	3.0648	2.4972	2.7213	3.0938
INCOME	1.6176	2.0634	2.7543	3.4696	3.7541	2.7022
FAMSIZE	2.0882	2.5211	3.1131	4.1181	5.1148	3.2427
HOWOFTEN	1.9118	2.1831	2.2730	2.2873	2.6230	2.2567
BRAND	1.8235	2.2465	2.3379	2.2541	2.7213	2.2966
INFO	1.9118	1.9120	1.8069	1.8358	1.8689	1.8581

STANDARD DEVIATIONS

	GROUP 1	GROUP 2	GROUP 3	GROUP 4	GROUP 5	TOTAL
EDUC1	1.3645	1.2854	1.1912	1.2044	1.1493	1.2500
EDUC2	1.6838	1.6769	1.5321	1.4499	1.4668	1.6202
AGE	1.5249	1.6156	1.4308	1.0586	0.8969	1.4634
INCOME	0.9539	1.3008	1.3451	1.2847	1.2471	1.4366
FAMSIZE	0.2879	0.8834	1.3083	1.2054	1.4503	1.3987
HOWOFTEN	0.6682	0.6685	0.6829	0.7034	0.7564	0.6977
BRAND	1.2666	1.3797	1.4165	1.4069	1.4724	1.4067
INFO	0.7535	0.7251	0.6807	0.6558	0.6449	0.6919

STATISTICAL PACKAGE FOR THE SOCIAL SCIENCES SPSSH - VERSION 6.00   10/19/76   PAGE 4

WILKS' LAMBDA (U-STATISTIC) AND UNIVARIATE F-RATIO WITH 4 AND 848 DEGREES OF FREEDOM

VARIABLE	WILKS' LAMBDA	F
EDUC1	0.9643	7.8525
EDUC2	0.9214	15.6173
AGE	0.9201	18.4185
INCOME	0.8119	49.1218
FAMSIZE	0.6667	106.0062
HOWOFTEN	0.9662	7.4155
BRAND	0.9880	2.5646
INFO	0.9958	0.8873

WITHIN GROUPS COVARIANCE MATRIX

	EDUC1	EDUC2	AGE	INCOME	FAMSIZE	HOWOFTEN	BRAND	INFO
EDUC1	1.5138							
EDUC2	1.1412	2.4565						
AGE	-0.4561	-0.8300	1.9765					
INCOME	0.6210	0.9189	-0.3880	1.6835				
FAMSIZE	0.0554	0.1346	-0.5932	0.1254	1.3103			
HOWOFTEN	-0.0036	-0.0498	0.2460	0.0426	-0.0979	0.4726		
BRAND	0.0959	0.2142	-0.3385	-0.0120	0.1527	-0.0106	1.9644	
INFO	-0.0890	-0.0988	0.0798	-0.0126	0.0043	0.0188	-0.1537	0.4789

WITHIN GROUPS CORRELATION MATRIX

	EDUC1	EDUC2	AGE	INCOME	FAMSIZE	HOWOFTEN	BRAND	INFO
EDUC1	1.0000							
EDUC2	0.5918	1.0000						
AGE	-0.2635	-0.3764	1.0000					
INCOME	0.3890	0.4519	-0.2125	1.0000				
FAMSIZE	0.0422	0.0750	-0.3683	0.0844	1.0000			
HOWOFTEN	-0.0042	-0.0462	0.2544	0.0478	-0.1244	1.0000		
BRAND	0.0556	0.0975	-0.1717	-0.0066	0.0952	-0.0110	1.0000	
INFO	-0.1046	-0.0910	0.0820	-0.0140	0.0055	0.0395	-0.1584	1.0000

STATISTICAL PACKAGE FOR THE SOCIAL SCIENCES SPSSH - VERSION 6.00   10/19/76   PAGE   5

TOTAL COVARIANCE MATRIX

	EDUC1	EDUC2	AGE	INCOME	FAMSIZE	HOWOFTEN	BRAND	INFO
EDUC1	1.5625							
EDUC2	1.2322	2.6251						
AGE	-0.5428	-0.5966	2.1414					
INCOME	0.7429	1.1668	-0.6340	2.0638				
FAMSIZE	0.2064	0.4482	-0.8878	0.2063	1.9563			
HOWOFTEN	0.0207	-0.0045	0.2063	0.1055	-0.0056	0.4868		
BRAND	0.1213	-0.2570	-0.3682	0.2450	0.2331	0.0083	1.9788	
INFO	-0.0945	-0.1084	0.0968	-0.0254	-0.0113	0.0165	-0.1551	0.4787

STATISTICAL PACKAGE FOR THE SOCIAL SCIENCES SPSSH - VERSION 6.00   10/19/76   PAGE   7

VARIABLE ENTERED ON STEP NUMBER 1..   FAMSIZE

		APPROXIMATE F	DEGREES OF FREEDOM		SIGNIFICANCE
WILKS' LAMBDA	0.66665	106.00616	4	848.00	0.000
RAO'S V	424.01978	CHANGE IN V 424.01978	4		0.0

F MATRIX - DEGREES OF FREEDOM: 1, 848

	GROUP 1	GROUP 2	GROUP 3	GROUP 4
GROUP 2	4.34259			
GROUP 3	25.38301	41.21944		
GROUP 4	91.79056	220.58722	86.24487	
GROUP 5	152.61307	257.78857	151.30698	22.61054

---- VARIABLES IN THE ANALYSIS ----

VARIABLE	ENTRY CRITERION	F TO REMOVE
FAMSIZE	106.00616	106.00616

---- VARIABLES NOT IN THE ANALYSIS ----

VARIABLE	TOLERANCE	F TO ENTER	ENTRY CRITERION
EDUC1	0.99822	5.11005	7.85746
EDUC2	0.99437	7.94118	15.61726
AGE	0.86432	4.42566	18.41850
INCOME	0.99287	26.45332	49.12177
HOWOFTEN	0.98452	10.83165	7.41548
BRAND	0.99094	1.48431	2.56460
INFO	0.99997	0.86361	0.88735

STATISTICAL PACKAGE FCR TFE SOCIAL SCIENCES SPSSH – VERSION 6.00   10/19/76   PAGE 12

VARIABLE ENTERED CN STEP NUMBER 6..   BRAND

		DEGREES OF FREEDOM		SIGNIFICANCE
WILKS' LAMBDA	C.55C66			
RAO'S V	65E.016E5			
APPROXIMATE F	22.8526	24	2942.09	0.000
CHANGE IN V	6.45825	4		0.167

F MATRIX – DEGREES CF FREECCM: 6,   843

	GROUP 1	GRCLP 2	GROUP 3	GRCLP 4
GROUP 2	4.25634			
GRCUP 3	11.24E04	13.42533		
GROUP 4	26.76587	55.89760	19.24C10	
GROUP 5	39.71443	6C.87253	34.04955	1C.43CC1

-------- VARIABLES IN THE ANALYSIS --------

VARIABLE	ENTRY CRITERION	F TO REMOVE
EDUC1	2.C6E56	2.02444
AGE	3.35772	2.956C4
INCCME	26.45332	21.00511
FAMSIZE	1C6.CC616	71.84845
HOMOFTEN	8.69083	7.48475
BRAND	1.55753	1.55752

-------- VARIABLES NOT IN THE ANALYSIS --------

VARIABLE	TOLFRANCE	F TO ENTER	ENTRY CRITERICN
EDUC2	0.54819	0.84227	0.89131
INFO	0.96163	0.84561	0.81323

F LEVEL INSUFFICIENT FCR FLRTHER COMPUTATICN

STATISTICAL PACKAGE FCR THE SOCIAL SCIENCES SPSSH - VERSION 6.00   10/19/76   PAGE 13

FILE   LEHNUTFI (CREATICN CATE = 10/19/76)

- - - - - - - - - - - - - - C I S C R I M I N A N T   A N A L Y S I S - - - - - - - - -

SUMMARY TABLE

STEP NUMBER	VARIABLE ENTEREC REMOVEC	F TC ENTER OR REMOVE	NUMBER INCLUDEC	WILKS' LAMBDA	SIG.	RAC'S V	CHANGE IN RAO'S V	SIG. OF CHANGE
1	FAMSIZE	106.00616	1	0.66665	0.000	424.01978	424.01978	0.0
2	INCOME	26.45332	2	0.59262	0.000	577.29126	153.27148	0.0
3	HOWOFTEN	8.69083	3	0.56923	0.000	628.94336	51.65210	0.000
4	AGE	3.39772	4	0.56022	0.000	642.81152	13.86816	0.008
5	EDUC1	2.08856	5	0.55473	0.000	651.55859	8.74707	0.068
6	BRAND	1.55753	6	0.55066	0.000	658.01685	6.45825	0.167

CLASSIFICATION FUNCTION COEFFICIENTS

	GROUP 1 GRCUP	2 GROUP	3 GRCLP	4 GPOLP	5
EDUC1	2.51570	2.35136	3.28176	3.27768	3.21836
AGE	3.60670	2.40733	3.26344	3.36958	3.69674
INCOME	0.41949	0.44196	0.62507	1.21068	1.37844
FAMSIZE	3.12635	3.38411	3.61591	4.55318	5.47836
HOWOFTEN	2.82546	2.56189	3.82536	3.55922	4.69368
BRAND	1.18224	1.32601	1.93864	1.23757	1.47319
CONSTANT	-19.61284	-22.88771	-25.23024	-28.75979	-37.01587

DISCRIMINANT FUNCTION	EIGENVALUE	RELATIVE PERCENTAGE	CANCNICAL CORRELATICN	FUNCTIONS (CERIVE)	WILKS' LAMBDA	CHI-SQUARE	DF	SIGNIFICANCE
				0	0.5507	505.055	24	0.0
1	0.72246	93.10	C.648	1	0.9495	44.769	15	0.000
2	C.02870	3.70	C.167	2	0.9757	20.820	8	0.008
3	0.02188	2.82	0.146	3	0.9971	2.499	3	0.475
4	C.0C296	0.38	0.054					

REMAINING COMPUTATIONS WILL BE BASED ON 4 CISCRIMINANT FUNCTION(S)

STATISTICAL PACKAGE FOR THE SOCIAL SCIENCES SPSSH - VERSION 6.00

10/19/76   PAGE 14

STANDARDIZED DISCRIMINANT FUNCTION COEFFICIENTS

	FUNC 1	FUNC 2	FUNC 3	FUNC 4
EDUC1	0.02931	0.01147	-0.70139	0.52128
AGE	-0.01743	0.80563	0.25404	-0.20102
INCOME	-0.41692	-0.42982	0.30218	-0.89749
FAMSIZE	-0.77391	-0.56026	0.25381	0.53745
HOWOFTEN	-0.20329	0.24330	-0.58126	-0.17733
BRAND	-0.01463	0.37179	-0.37260	-0.42580

UNSTANDARDIZED DISCRIMINANT FUNCTION COEFFICIENTS

	FUNC 1	FUNC 2	FUNC 3	FUNC 4
EDUC1	0.02345	0.00918	-0.56111	0.41702
AGE	-0.01191	0.55054	0.20093	-0.13737
INCOME	-0.29021	-0.29919	0.21035	-0.62473
FAMSIZE	-0.55331	-0.40056	0.21006	0.38425
HOWOFTEN	-0.29136	0.34870	-0.80440	-0.25415
BRAND	-0.01040	0.26430	-0.26487	-0.30270
CONSTANT	3.19721	-3.62650	2.93368	0.36612

CENTROIDS OF GROUPS IN REDUCED SPACE

	FUNC 1	FUNC 2	FUNC 3	FUNC 4
GROUP 1	1.02553	0.15579	0.64837	-0.05555
GROUP 2	0.59904	0.06620	-0.06331	0.04861
GROUP 3	0.04177	-0.05837	-0.06789	-0.06758
GROUP 4	-0.71423	-0.19783	0.06564	0.04565
GROUP 5	-1.44158	0.47234	-0.00654	-0.00484

STATISTICAL PACKAGE FOR THE SOCIAL SCIENCES SPSSH - VERSION 6.00   10/19/76   PAGE 17

PREDICTION RESULTS -

ACTUAL GROUP	NO. OF CASES	PREDICTED GROUP MEMBERSHIP				
		GP. 1	GP. 2	GP. 3	GP. 4	GP. 5
GROUP 1	34.	20. 58.8%	13. 38.2%	1. 2.9%	0. 0.0%	0. 0.0%
GROUP 2	284.	86. 30.3%	106. 37.3%	59. 20.8%	24. 8.5%	9. 3.2%
GROUP 3	293.	50. 17.1%	65. 22.2%	90. 30.7%	57. 19.5%	31. 10.6%
GROUP 4	181.	7. 3.9%	7. 3.9%	33. 18.2%	84. 46.4%	50. 77.6%
GROUP 5	61.	2. 3.3%	1. 1.6%	6. 9.8%	12. 19.7%	40. 65.6%

PERCENT OF "GROUPED" CASES CORRECTLY CLASSIFIED: 39.66%

APPENDIX 18-C

CLASSIFICATION FUNCTIONS AND DISCRIMINANT ANALYSIS

Discriminant analysis is closely related to classification. Optimal classification can be performed (assuming the variables are normally distributed) by computing the value of a classification function for each group. The bigger the value of a particular classification function, the more likely a person is a member of the group.

Assume for a moment I had three groups with the following classification functions:

Variable	CF_1	CF_2	CF_3
1	7	5	4
2	5	3	1
Constant	2	5	9

If I were to try to classify an observation with values 2 and 3 on the two variables into one of the three groups, I could directly use the multivariate normal distribution and a computer algorithm to find the likelihood that an observation with values 2 and 3 came from each of the three groups. A shortcut is available, however, by using the three classification functions:

$$\text{Value of } CF_1 = 7(2) + 5(3) + 2 = 31$$

$$\text{Value of } CF_2 = 5(2) + 3(3) + 5 = 24$$

$$\text{Value of } CF_3 = 4(2) + 1(3) + 9 = 20$$

Since the value of CF_1 is largest, it turns out that this particular observation is most likely to belong to the first group.

Classification functions are occasionally interpreted directly, with a big value attributed to a variable that is a major contributor to group membership. The classification functions can also be used to derive the two-group discriminant functions between pairs of groups. For g groups, there are $g(g - 1)/2$ two-group discriminant functions, one for each pair of groups. Mathematically, the discriminant functions turn out to be the differences between pairs of classification functions (e.g., $f_{12} = CF_1 - CF_2$).

Returning to our previous example, we would derive the two-group discriminant function between groups 1 and 3 (f_{13}) as follows:

$$f_{13} = (7 - 4)X_1 + (5 - 1)X_2 = 3X_1 + 4X_2$$

The constant is usually ignored. (It turns out, however, that the difference in the constant term produces the cutoff point for maximum likelihood classification. Hence, in this case, the cutoff point would be $2 - 9 = -7$. Alternatively, retaining the constant term makes the cutoff point equal to zero.)

APPENDIX 18-D

CANONICAL CORRELATION

Canonical correlation is the extension of regression to the case of multiple dependent variables. It produces sets of weights (regression coefficients) such that an index of the independent variables is "maximally correlated" with an index of the dependent variables:

$$a_1Z_1 + \ldots + a_kZ_k = b_1X_1 + \ldots + b_gX_g$$

Assuming the sets of variables are not perfectly redundant (collinear), the procedure will produce the minimum of k and g (usually g) canonical sets of weights.

Canonical correlation has been mainly used as a means of performing multiple-group discriminant analysis, although it has been used to generate perceptual maps by using dummy variable coding for group membership as the dependent variables (Holbrook and Moore, 1982). It also can be viewed as the special case of so-called structural equation or causal modeling where there are two constructs, as shown in the following:

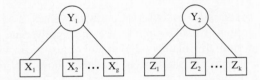

CHAPTER 19

Logit Models

In the last chapter, we discussed discriminant analysis and its use in discriminating or categorizing observations into distinct groups. Another procedure that predicts a categorical dependent variable is logit modeling. Discriminant analysis centers on the question, "Which group is the observation likely to belong to?" Common applications of logit models focus more on estimating "How likely is the observation to belong to each group?" Thus, while logit models fall somewhere between regression and discriminant analysis in application, both logit and discriminant analysis make quantitative predictions (à la regression) about categorical variables.

For example, suppose Chester, Inc. wanted to study how effective they are in reaching consumers over the age of 40. In response to this, they conducted a brand awareness study on a convenience sample of 100 consumers, which produced the data in Table 19.1.[1]

The variable AWARE is a 1 if the respondent was aware of the Chester brand, 0 if not. Most ages had AWARE values of both 0 and 1. Therefore, a manager at the firm reasoned that the best she could do was predict how likely a consumer of a given AGE was to be AWARE of the brand name. She had the idea of running a regression of the form AWARE = $B_0 + B_1 \times$ AGE.[2] However, a scatterplot of these data (Figure 19.1) looked different from those in other regressions she had run because of the binary (two-category) nature of the dependent variable, AWARE.

Some of the variability in AWARE can be removed by combining ages into groups. Table 19.2 contains the frequency of AWARE and not AWARE respondents for each age group as well as the mean of AWARE (i.e., the proportion of the age group aware of Chester). The proportion is essentially the probability that a person of that age is aware of the brand, Pr(AWARE). This table presents a clearer picture of the AGE-AWARE relationship than Figure 19.2.

---

[1] This is a disguised version of the coronary heart disease study presented by Hosmer and Lemeshow (1989), Chapter 1.

[2] As described in the last chapter, a regression with a 0–1 dependent variable is equivalent to a discriminant analysis.

TABLE 19.1 Age and Awareness of Chester Brand for 100 Respondents

ID	AGE	AWARE	ID	AGE	AWARE	ID	AGE	AWARE
1	20	0	35	38	0	68	51	0
2	23	0	36	39	0	69	52	0
3	24	0	37	39	1	70	52	1
4	25	0	38	40	0	71	53	1
5	25	1	39	40	1	72	53	1
6	26	0	40	41	0	73	54	1
7	26	0	41	41	0	74	55	0
8	28	0	42	42	0	75	55	1
9	28	0	43	42	0	76	55	1
10	29	0	44	42	0	77	56	1
11	30	0	45	42	1	78	56	1
12	30	0	46	43	0	79	56	1
13	30	0	47	43	0	80	57	0
14	30	0	48	43	1	81	57	0
15	30	0	49	44	0	82	57	1
16	30	1	50	44	0	83	57	1
17	32	0	51	44	1	84	57	1
18	32	0	52	44	1	85	57	1
19	33	0	53	45	0	86	58	0
20	33	0	54	45	1	87	58	1
21	34	0	55	46	0	88	58	1
22	34	0	56	46	1	89	59	1
23	34	1	57	47	0	90	59	1
24	34	0	58	47	0	91	60	0
25	34	0	59	47	1	92	60	1
26	35	0	60	48	0	93	61	1
27	35	0	61	48	1	94	62	1
28	36	0	62	48	1	95	62	1
29	36	1	63	49	0	96	63	1
30	36	0	64	49	0	97	64	0
31	37	0	65	49	1	98	64	1
32	37	1	66	50	0	99	65	1
33	37	0	67	50	1	100	69	1
34	38	0						

Source: Adapted from David W. Hosmer and Stanley Lemeshow, *Applied Logistic Regression*, page 3. Copyright © 1989 by John Wiley & Sons, Inc. Reprinted with the permission of the publishers.

The manager ran a regression of Pr(AWARE) against the age groups, each group represented by the midpoint of its age range. The resulting equation was

$$Pr(AWARE) = -0.468 + 0.020(AGE)$$

The R^2 was a healthy 0.960, and the t statistic for the AGE coefficient was over 12! In addition, the predicted values of Pr(AWARE) matched the actual values extremely well (Figure 19.3). This made her quite happy until she noticed that the equation predicted that

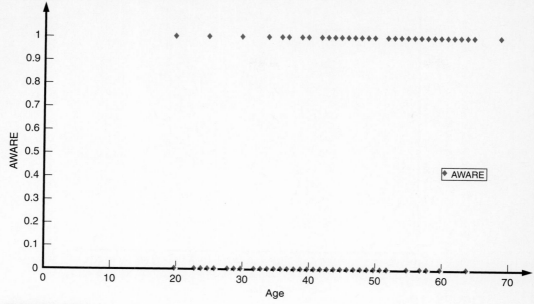

FIGURE 19.1

Plot of Aware by Age

Source: Adapted from David W. Hosmer and Stanley Lemeshow, *Applied Logistic Regression*, page 4. Copyright © 1989 by John Wiley & Sons, Inc. Reprinted with the permission of the publishers.

anyone who was less than 23 years old would have a negative probability of being AWARE and that anyone over 73 years old would have a probability greater than 1 of being AWARE. This disturbed her even though the sample included only one person under 23 and no one over 73. It suggested that this model could *not* be correct for extreme ages.

A colleague suggested that she just use the rule between 23 and 73 and set all predictions of Pr(AWARE) that are less than 0 (greater than 1) equal to 0 (1). While she conceded that this would in all likelihood be satisfactory in practice, she believed that there must be a less ad hoc way. She was right. Logit models and logistic regression provide the answer.

TABLE 19.2   **Frequency Table of Age Group by AWARE**

Age Group	Size of Group	# AWARE	# Not AWARE	Pr(AWARE)
20–29	10	1	9	0.10
30–34	15	2	13	0.13
35–39	12	3	9	0.25
40–44	15	5	10	0.33
45–49	13	6	7	0.46
50–54	8	5	3	0.63
55–59	17	13	4	0.76
60–69	10	8	2	0.80
Total	100	43	57	0.43

Source: Adapted from David W. Hosmer and Stanley Lemeshow, *Applied Logistic Regression*, page 4. Copyright © 1989 by John Wiley & Sons, Inc. Reprinted with the permission of the publishers.

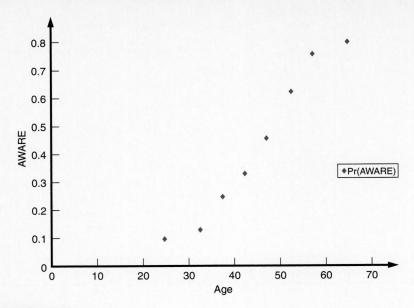

FIGURE 19.2
Plot of Mean of Aware in Each Age Group
Source: Adapted from David W. Hosmer and Stanley Lemeshow, *Applied Logistic Regression*, page 5.
Copyright © 1989 by John Wiley & Sons, Inc. Reprinted with the permission of the publishers.

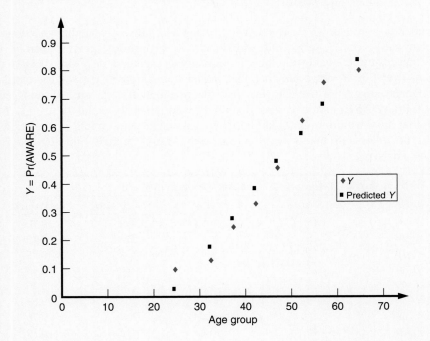

FIGURE 19.3
Probablility of Awareness by Age Group

In this chapter, we follow a pattern similar to that in the last (discriminant analysis) chapter. We begin with two-group logistic regression (a.k.a. *binary logit*) and then move to situations, such as brand choice, where the dependent variable has multiple categories (*multinomial and conditional logits*).

LOGISTIC REGRESSION

Basics

Logistic regression (a.k.a. binary logit) is very similar to ordinary least squares regression. The only real conceptual difference is that ordinary linear regression assumes that the outcome or dependent variable is continuous; logistic regression, on the other hand, assumes a dichotomous outcome (e.g., the consumer either buys or not; the respondent is either aware of the brand or not; etc.). The dependent variable can only take on the values 1 or 0.

Once the nature of the dependent variable is accounted for, the methods and philosophy of analysis are identical between linear and logistic regression, although the mathematical form of the two models differ. We begin with the simple regression model:

$$y = B_0 + B_1 X_1 + B_2 X_2 + \cdots + B_k X_k + \text{Error}$$

y has two possible values (1 and 0), each of which reflects an observation's membership in one of two categories.

The foundations of logistic regression rest on two modifications of the regression model. First, while we observe 0's and 1's in the outcome variable, what we really are interested in is not the actual observed outcome, but the probability of a certain outcome, $\Pr(y = 1)$. For example, the manager at Chester, Inc. was interested in the probability that any 45-year-old is aware of the Chester brand (i.e., the average of the variable AWARE for all 45-year-olds). If we substitute p (the probability that the observation takes on the value $y = 1$ for a given set of X's), we get

$$p = B_0 + B_1 X_1 + B_2 X_2 + \cdots + B_k X_k$$

This expression still can produce values for p outside the conventional range for probabilities (0 to 1). The second modification of the linear regression model solves that problem.

It turns out to be mathematically convenient to substitute the so-called logit transformation of p, $\ln\{p/(1 - p)\}$, for p. This is because $\ln\{p/(1 - p)\}$ can range between positive and negative infinity even if p is restricted between 0 and 1 (Figure 19.4). Therefore, the following logistic regression model is used:

$$\ln \frac{p}{1 - p} = B_0 + B_1 X_1 + B_2 X_2 + \cdots + B_k X_k$$

Solving for p, this is equivalent to

$$p = \frac{\exp\left(B_0 + B_1 X_1 + B_2 X_2 + \cdots + B_k X_k\right)}{1 + \exp\left(B_0 + B_1 X_1 + B_2 X_2 + \cdots + B_k X_k\right)}$$

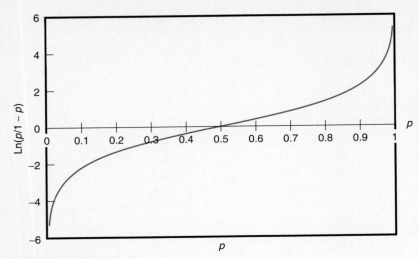

FIGURE 19.4
Plot of Logit Transformation

FIGURE 19.5
A Plot of Simple
Logistic Regression
$(B_0 = 0;\ B_1 = 1)$

$$P = \frac{1}{1 + \exp(-X)}$$

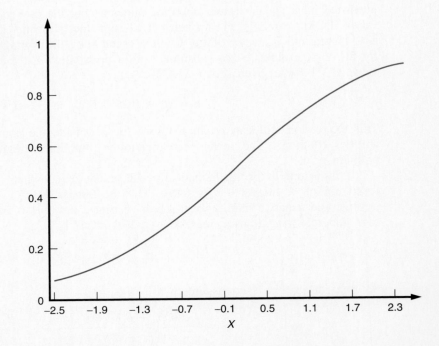

which is always between 0 and 1 (Figure 19.5). The graph of the logit model is somewhat S-shaped, and yields predictions that are never below 0 or above 1. Looking back at Figure 19.2, we see that this plot is somewhat S-shaped.

From this point, we can build a logistic regression model in the same way that we build an ordinary linear one. We can transform some of the Xs to be quadratic terms to allow for nonlinearities[3]; we could incorporate dummy variables to allow for nominally scaled predictors; and so forth.

Fitting the Logistic Regression Model

In linear regression, the model is fit by least squares; that is, the parameters are estimated to be those that minimize the sum of the squared errors of prediction. Errors in linear regression can take on any value. The statistical tests used with linear regression assume that the errors follow a normal distribution. In logistic regression, on the other hand, the error can only take on two values. If y is 1, the error is $1 - p$, and if y is 0, the error is p. Ideally then, we would like to choose estimates of the Bs so that the predicted values of p would be close to 1 when $y = 1$, and close to 0 when $y = 0$.

The method commonly used to fit the logistic regression model is the *method of maximum likelihood*, which turns out to be identical to least squares for linear regression, but not for logistic.[4] The complete details of this method are beyond the scope of this text. However, some intuition can be gained by noting that maximum likelihood estimation chooses the parameter values that maximize the probability of observing the existing data. We develop this idea a bit more in Appendix 19-A.

Table 19.3 presents the results from using a maximum likelihood logistic regression package on the data in Table 19.1. The resulting model is

$$\Pr(\text{AWARE}) = \frac{\exp(-5.31 + 0.111 \cdot \text{AGE})}{1 + \exp(-5.31 + 0.111 \cdot \text{AGE})}$$

and the logit transformation is

$$\ln \frac{p}{1 - p} = -5.31 + 0.111 \cdot \text{AGE}$$

TABLE 19.3 Results of Logistic Regression on Data from Table 19–1

Variable	Estimated Coefficient	Standard Error	Coeff/SE
Age	0.111	0.024	4.61
Constant	−5.310	1.134	−4.68

Source: Adapted from David W. Hosmer and Stanley Lemeshow, *Applied Logistic Regression*, page 1. Copyright © 1989 by John Wiley & Sons, Inc. Reprinted with the permission of the publishers.

---

[3] Although we may be less likely to want to do so since the model is already nonlinear with respect to p.
[4] Widespread availability of software still leads some marketing researchers to prefer least squares estimation for logit models even though it is not the statistically preferred approach (Flath and Leonard, 1979; Malhotra, 1984). There are only a few circumstances (e.g., Appendix 19-B) where this practice is reasonable.

The final two columns in Table 19.3 are analogous to the standard error and t statistics in linear regression and are discussed in the next section.

Testing the Significance of the Coefficients

The simplest, and most commonly used, approach to testing whether a variable affects the probability that $y = 1$, or equivalently, that the coefficient is (statistically) significantly different from zero, is the Wald test. The test is analogous to significance tests in linear regression. We reject the null hypothesis of H_0: $B = 0$ if the value of the ratio of the coefficient to its standard error is greater than a critical t value. The t value has the same number of degrees of freedom as the No. of observations – No. of parameters estimated. Usually, this is large enough (i.e., above 30) to use a critical Z cutoff rather than a t (i.e., reject the hypothesis of no impact of the variable at the .05 level if Coefficient/Standard error is not between -1.96 and $+1.96$). The Wald test would reject the hypothesis that AGE is not related to AWARE for the Chester, Inc. data (Coefficient/Standard error = 4.610). Despite the ease of this test, some statisticians prefer another test based on log-likelihoods (see Appendix 19-C).

Interpreting the Coefficients

In a linear regression, the coefficient is equal to the change in the expected value of the outcome variable per unit change in the corresponding independent variable. For example, suppose the regression equation was $y = B_0 + B_1 X + \text{Error}$. As X goes from X' to $X' + 1$, the predicted value of y increases B_1 units.

Unfortunately, there is no equally convenient interpretation of the coefficients in a logistic regression. The most intuitive interpretation relates to elasticities, the percent change in one variable that is associated with a percent change in another. The elasticity of the binary logit probability (p) with respect to independent variable X_j can be shown mathematically to be equal to

$$E_j^* = B_j X_j^* (1 - p^*)$$

where B_j is the coefficient of X_j in the model, X_j^* is a specific value of X_j, and $1 - p^*$ is computed from particular values of the independent variables.[5] As such, E_j^* is a function of not only the coefficient and variable in question, but also the independent variables and other coefficients as well (via p^*). In other words, E_j^* differs for different values of the independent variables (which is why it is denoted E_j^*).

Another interpretation is more in tune with linear regression. Following logic similar to that of linear regression, it is easy to see that an increase of one unit in an independent variable with a coefficient of B_1 in the logistic regression model increases $\ln[p/(1 - p)]$ by B_1 units. Since $p/(1 - p)$ is the *odds* of the event corresponding to $y = 1$ occurring, B_1 is the size of the increase in the "log odds" of the dependent-variable event per unit increase in the corresponding independent variable.

---

[5]See Guadagni and Little (1983).

Assessing Fit

In linear regression, R^2 provides a measure of fit of the model. Unfortunately, there is no such universally endorsed measure for logistic regression. Still, as in discriminant analysis, the proportion of correct predictions is widely used as a measure of fit. In this approach, we make "all or nothing" predictions by stating that the model's prediction is $y = 1$ if the predicted probability is greater than 0.5. If the predicted probability is less than 0.5, the prediction is $y = 0$. These predictions can then be compared with the actual observations as

$$\frac{\text{\# Correct predictions}}{\text{\# Observations}}$$

Most other fit measures are based on the log-likelihood as described in Appendix 19-B. The closer the log-likelihood gets to 0, the better the fit. Malhotra (1984) discusses these measures in a readable way.

Application: Telecommunications Adoption

In a study reported by Green, Carmone, and Wachspress (1977), AT&T was interested in relating the adoption of a new telecommunications service to three descriptor variables: respondent education, mobility, and income. Each of the three predictors was classified as a two-level variable and could therefore be coded with a single dummy each. The variables, levels, and coding are

1. Education
   a High school graduate or below (LOWEDUC = 1)
   b. Some college or above (LOWEDUC = 0)
2. Mobility
   a. No change in residence over past five years (NOCHG = 1)
   b. One or more moves (NOCHG = 0)
3. Income
   a. $12,500 or less (LOWINC = 1)
   b. More than $12,500 (LOWINC = 0)

The probability of adoption in the sample was 0.155. Casual inspection of Table 19.4 reveals that this probability varies considerably from cell to cell. A logistic regression was run using weighted least squares to uncover how this probability varied as a function of the descriptors. The resulting equation is

$$\ln \frac{p}{1-p} = -0.903 - 0.164 \cdot \text{LOWERDUC} - 0.986 \cdot \text{NOCHG} - 0.438 \cdot \text{LOWINC}$$

which suggests (as casual inspection of Table 19.4 would) that the likelihood of adoption increases for highly educated, mobile, high-income households and is particularly sensitive to mobility.

TABLE 19.4   Probability of Adoption of Telecommunications Service

Income	High School or Below		Some College or Above	
	Nonmobile	**Mobile**	**Nonmobile**	**Mobile**
≤ $12,500	0.071 (2,160)	0.199 (1,137)	0.069 (886)	0.214 (1,091)
> $12,500	0.108 (1,363)	0.254 (547)	0.149 (1,925)	0.270 (1,415)

Total sample estimated probability = 0.155
Numbers in parentheses are within-cell sample sizes on which proportions of adoption were based.
Source: Green, Carmone, and Wachspress (1977), p. 53.

Application: Database Marketing and Credit Cards

As an illustrative example of the use of logistic regression in database marketing, consider the credit card solicitation studied by Bult (1993) based on one firm's database in the Netherlands in the early 1990s. The database used contained information on demographic (age, family structure), socioeconomic, and psychographic characteristics (e.g., leisure interests, reading behavior) as well as product ownership for 1 million of the just over 6 million Dutch households. Credit card ownership was also included. A logistic regression to predict credit card ownership was run on a sample of 2,000 randomly selected households. The specific predictor variables in Table 19.5 emerged from prior analysis. All variables, except for RES, were significantly different from 0 at the .05 level; RES was significant at the .10 level.

For the model to be useful, it would have to predict current or impending ownership for households not in the database from which the binary logit was estimated. Such predictions can be made by inserting the data for each household into the logit formula in order to create an index; if the index value was above a certain cutoff, the prediction would be that the household would OWN. The model created for this example predicted correctly for 94.3 percent of the individuals in another randomly selected collection of 34,225 households.

The generalization of such an analysis to database marketing is straightforward. Imagine the firm mailing a credit card solicitation to 2,000 households randomly selected from its database of, say, 1,000,000 households. It would first estimate a model to predict response to the solicitation based on those households. It could then use that model to predict response for the remaining 998,000 households in the database and use those predictions to select its target customers efficiently. Alternatively, if the firm had mailed

TABLE 19.5   Logistic Regression Results

Variable	Desciption	Parameter	Standard Error	Z-Score
Intercept		−.906	.053	
CAR	Value of car owned	.040	.009	4.44
NRC	Reading newspaper	.195	.053	3.68
NHS	Covered by national health service	.230	.051	4.51
NW	Ownership of microwave	.173	.042	4.11
SKI	Interested in skiing	.153	.042	3.64
RES	Visiting restaurant	.065	.039	1.67
IF	Invested money in funds	.171	.04	3.48

to all 1,000,000 households, a model could be estimated on the complete data set and used to predict response for a future offering deemed similar to this one.

MULTINOMIAL LOGIT MODELS

Suppose the Chester, Inc. manager no longer wanted to study advertising awareness, but was now interested in brand choice. The binary logistic regression model could be used if the observation $y = 1$ was used to denote choice of the Chester brand and $y = 0$ was used to denote choice of *any other* brand. While this is a good start, some potentially useful insights may be obscured. In particular, there may well be a lot of information contained in *which* other brand is bought. The simple binary logit will not pick this up.

For example, suppose one of Chester's competitors frequently garners a great deal of share because it has a price much lower than that of Chester and the other competitors. If the manager at Chester ran the logit $\ln\{p_C/(1 - p_C)\} = B_0 + B_1 \times \text{PRICE}_C$, where the subscript C is used to denote the choice probability and price of the Chester brand, the impact of other competitors would not be evident. One could recode the price variable to represent a price relative to the "rest of the market" (i.e., Chester price − Average price or Chester price/Average price). This might help, but the full details of the market dynamics would still be obscured. Fortunately, logit can be extended to model the probabilities of observations that fall into one of several (more than two) categories, such as probability of brand choice.

Marketers care about modeling brand choice probabilities because they serve as surrogates for long-run market share. Considering this, we use the context of brand choice in much of this section. Of course, other choice problems can and have been studied using logit. Gensch and Recker (1979) studied (grocery) store choice; Punj and Staelin (1978) studied students' choices of business schools. Interestingly the alternatives in these categories have taken on the appearance of brands in recent years.

Multinomial Logit

Suppose we were interested in a three-brand market, with the brands denoted by 0, 1, and 2. The information that determines the ith individual's choice among them is captured in the K independent variables X_{i1}, X_{i2}, ..., X_{iK}. These variables could include attributes of the brands, the ith individual's perceptions of them, personal characteristics of the ith consumer, marketing variables of the brands, and so forth.

We can use the same framework as before if we select a "reference brand." We will arbitrarily choose brand 0. Then we form a series of binary logits, each presuming that the choice was between the reference brand and one other brand[6]:

$$\ln \frac{p_1}{p_0} = B_{10} + B_{11}X_1 + B_{12}X_2 + \cdots + B_{1k}X_k$$

and

$$\ln \frac{p_2}{p_0} = B_{20} + B_{21}X_1 + B_{22}X_2 + \cdots + B_{2k}X_k$$

---

[6]We can drop the subscript i if we keep in mind that the variables X_1, X_2, ..., X_K vary across individuals.

where p_j denotes the choice probability for brand j. Since the X's can vary across individuals, the p's can also. While the coefficients on the right-hand side of each binary logit can be different across equations, most marketing applications assume that they are not. With this, we write the expression

$$\ln \frac{p_j}{p_0} = B_0 + B_1 X_1 + B_2 X_2 + \cdots + B_k X_k, \text{ for } j = 1, 2$$

This does not mean that $\ln(p_1/p_0) = \ln(p_2/p_0)$. In the same way that the X variables vary across individuals, they vary across brands too (e.g., prices differ for different brands). So, although the equations for $\ln(p_1/p_0)$ and $\ln(p_2/p_0)$ look the same, the X's that go into them are different.

To simplify notation even further, we denote the right-hand side of each of the foregoing expressions as V_{ij}. The subscripts recognize that the right-hand sides can vary across individuals (i) and brands (j). V_{ij} can be interpreted as brand j's value (relative to the reference brand) for the ith individual.

It follows, then, as in the case of the binary logit, that

$$p_0 = \frac{1}{1 + \exp(V_{i1}) + \exp(V_{i2})}$$

$$p_1 = \frac{\exp(V_{i1})}{1 + \exp(V_{i1}) + \exp(V_{i2})}$$

$$p_2 = \frac{\exp(V_{i2})}{1 + \exp(V_{i1}) + \exp(V_{i2})}$$

These probabilities are each between 0 and 1 and collectively add up to 1, as should be the case in all logically consistent probability models.

A general expression for all probabilities here is

$$p_j = \frac{\exp(V_{ij})}{\exp(V_{i0}) + \exp(V_{i1}) + \exp(V_{i2})}$$

where the V function (or equivalently, its coefficients) is arbitrarily defined to be 0 for the reference brand. (This is necessary for technical reasons. Without such a designation, the model would not have a unique set of estimates.)

Clearly, this formulation can be extended to any number of alternatives, say J. We obtain

$$p_j = \frac{\exp(V_{ij})}{\exp(V_{i0}) + \exp(V_{i1}) + \cdots + \exp(V_{iJ})}$$

Higher values of V lead to higher choice probabilities. Therefore, variables that lead to increases in choice probabilities for an alternative (brand) have positive coefficients in the V function, and those that lead to decreases have negative coefficients. In particular, it can be shown that the elasticity of the choice probability p_j with respect to a specific variable X_k is equal to $B_k X_k (1 - p_j)$, as in the binary logit.[7]

Although the term *choice probability* implies an individual making a choice and the alternative (choice theory) development of the logit model in Appendix 19-D uses the context of an individual making a choice, logit models have rarely been applied to *individual* brand choice data. Rather, it is generally applied at a more aggregate (e.g., market, market segment) level with the B coefficients being constant within either the entire market or a set of segments. (Not only is it more managerially meaningful to analyze the impact certain X variables have in the aggregate, but this assumption also eases the data requirements for reliable estimation.)

This does not mean, however, that all consumers within a segment have the same choice probabilities, only that the independent variables have the same impact on choice. The choice probabilities differ because different individuals can have different Xs. While some X variables that govern brand choice, such as list price, do not vary across consumers, many do. If some of the variables are product attributes, the individuals may have different perceptions of them. Other variables may be personal characteristics (e.g., income, past purchases), and individuals certainly differ on these.

The expressions for p_j and V_{ij} are the bases for what are called the *multinomial* and *conditional* logit models. The distinction between these two stems from the independent variables used in them. Specifically, the conditional logit model includes independent variables that reflect characteristics of each specific choice occasion (e.g., existence of promotion). In practice, this distinction is meaningless; the same model applies; we introduce the terminology for cultural reasons.

Statistical Procedures

Almost everything discussed in the previous section on logistic regression carries over to the more general logit models. In particular:

1. Models are generally estimated by the method of maximum likelihood.
2. The statistical significance of the coefficients can be tested either by the Wald test or by comparing log-likelihoods.
3. Coefficients can be interpreted as the marginal increase in the "log odds" of the choice probability for a particular alternative (relative to the reference alternative) per unit increase in the corresponding independent variable. More commonly, though, elasticities are used to convey the sensitivities of choice probabilities to specific variables.
4. There is no agreed upon fit statistic, although most software packages contain something that resembles the R^2 of linear regression (Malhotra, 1984).

Application: Ground Caffeinated Coffee

This application was originally reported by Guadagni and Little (1983). Coffee provides an excellent illustration for us because price changes are relatively common. It also is

---

[7]See Guadagni and Little (1983, pp. 235–237) for details.

a frequently promoted category. The data that were analyzed in the model reported here came from scanner panel data collected on 100 randomly chosen households in Kansas City. This group made 1,037 purchases of the brands and sizes studied in the 32-week period between March 8 and October 17, 1979. Complete data were available for all but 16 purchases.

Previous studies of the coffee market showed that people were often brand and size loyal. Therefore, we evaluate brand-size combinations, designated as Small A, Large A, Small B, Large B, Small C, Large C, Small D, and Small E, as the choice alternatives.

Variables for the Value Function   There are two classes of variables: those unique to the alternative, and those common to all alternatives. All information endemic to a brand-size combination is contained in the set of dummy variables that take on the value 1 for one brand-size combination and 0 otherwise. Each alternative has its own dummy variable except the reference one, arbitrarily chosen to be Large A, and is denoted by the alternative's name (e.g., SMALLA, LARGEC). The coefficients of these variables are often interpreted as measures of brand image or equity.

The variables that are common to all alternatives, both in existence and (assumed) magnitude of effect, include regular price (REGPRI), whether or not the brand-size is on promotion (PROMO, another 0–1 dummy), the size of the promotional price cut (PROCUT), and whether the purchases made immediately prior and two occasions prior to the current one were of the current brand on promotion (PRIORPRO and PRIOR-PRO2, two more 0–1 dummies).

The Value function is thus

$$V_j(X) = B_0 + B_1 \cdot \text{PROMO} + B_2 \cdot \text{PROCUT} + B_3 \cdot \text{REGPRI} + B_4 \cdot \text{PRIORPRO}$$
$$+ B_5 \cdot \text{PRIORPRO2} + B_6 \cdot \text{SMALLA} + \cdots + B_{12} \cdot \text{SMALLE}$$

Results   Table 19.6 contains a summary of the output of this model. The coefficients were estimated by maximum likelihood and are significantly different from 0. It is difficult to compare magnitudes since the variables are measured in different units. One exception is the price variables, both of which are measured in dollars. It is interesting to note the approximate equality of the regular price and promotional price cut coefficients. This suggests that dollars are dollars. People respond to market price. A 25 cent increase in price lowers the V term by $(28.02)(.25)$ through the REGPRI term. However, if the price increase is followed by a 25 cent price promotion, the decrease in V is essentially balanced by a $(26.98)(.25)$ increase through the PROCUT term. Furthermore, there is also a boost that a brand gets with a promotion (indicated by a positive and significant PROMO coefficient), perhaps because it draws attention to the brand. So a brand may be better off listing at $2.00 and promoting to $1.75 than it is listing at $1.75.

The prior promotion variables are positive. This probably reflects loyalty more than it does the effect of any prior promotional purchase, as the above specification does not account for loyalty in any way. In fact, this suggests the model has left something out, and some term to account for household preferences should be included in the Value function. In general, when such models are applied to scanner data, a household loyalty variable is included, as in the SPSS example presented in Appendix 19-E.

TABLE 19.6 Coffee Study Logit Model

Variable	Coefficient	Coefficient/Std. Error
PROMO	1.40	11.5
PROCUT	26.98	8.0
REGPRI	−28.02	−7.8
PRIORPRO	0.62	4.5
PRIORPRO2	0.49	3.3
SMALLA	0.48	3.5
LARGEA	0	N/A
SMALLB	0.41	3.1
LARGEB	−0.35	−2.3
SMALLC	1.49	11.6
LARGEC	0.59	4.2
SMALLD	0.10	0.4
SMALLE	−1.88	−6.2
Log-likelihood ($N = 1021$): −1488		

Source: Peter M. Guadagni and John C. Little, "A Logit Model of Brand Choice Calibrated on Scanner Data" from *Marketing Science* 2 (Summer 1983), page 218. Copyright © 1983 by The Institute of Management Science (currently INFORMS). Reprinted with permission of INFORM, 2 Charles Street, Suite 300, Providence, RI 02904, USA.

The brand-size coefficients are substantively different. They represent unique product qualities. As suggested previously, brand managers attempting to build brand equity are trying to get high coefficients for their brand. Small C seems to have been the most successful[8], and Small E the least.

A Limitation

Logit models are often criticized because they are saddled with the seemingly undesirable "Irrelevance of Independent Alternatives" (IIA) property. To understand IIA, imagine that you live in a small town with two restaurants, one Chinese and one Italian. Suppose you like both equally. The food pleases you the same; you enjoy both atmospheres equally, and the quality of service at both is indistinguishable. Logically, your choice probabilities should be .5 for each restaurant. That is what the logit model would dictate too, since $V_{\text{Chinese}} = V_{\text{Italian}}$.

Now suppose that a second Italian restaurant, identical in every important way to the first, opened. Logically, it makes sense to argue that the choice probabilities would be .5 for the Chinese restaurant and .25 for each Italian restaurant. The new Italian restaurant would draw its share entirely from the old Italian restaurant. However, the logit model implies that all three restaurants would have 1/3 choice probability since $V_{\text{Chinese}} = V_{\text{old Italian}} = V_{\text{new Italian}}$, and it predicts that the new Italian restaurant would draw its share equally from the Chinese and the old Italian restaurants.

McFadden (1980, p. 516) argues that IIA is likely to be "unsuitable for marketing applications where the patterns of perceived similarities of brands have a significant influ-

---

[8]Large C also has a high coefficient, indicating that there is value to the brand name C.

ence on market shares." Some relatively simple tests for IIA have been designed by McFadden, Tye, and Train (1977). If a data set fails these tests and the researcher has reason to be concerned about IIA, he or she could resort to one of several alternative "logit-style" models that are not encumbered by this difficulty. Currim (1982) discusses and compares many of them.

One of these, the so-called *nested logit* model, partitions alternatives into subsets where the alternatives in any given subset are more similar to each other than they are to alternatives in the other subsets. The subset a consumer's choice comes from is decided via a logit model. The final choice is made from the chosen subset, also via a logit model. Thus the name *nested logit*. This model conceptualizes choice as a hierarchical process where (say) a consumer might first choose to dine on Chinese or Italian food and then, after this choice is made, select a specific restaurant. However, in spite of the limitations of the IIA property, the garden-variety logit model presented here dominates most marketing applications.

SUMMARY

Logit models, like discriminant analysis, focus on the relationship between group membership and a set of independent variables (predictors). The basic form of a logit model is

$$\frac{\exp(\text{Value of being in group } j)}{\exp(\text{Value of being in group } 1) + \cdots + \exp(\text{Value of being in group } J)}$$

where J is the number of groups. The value of being in group j is modeled as a linear function of the set of independent variables:

$$\text{Value of being in group } j = B_0 + B_1 X_1 + B_2 X_2 + \cdots + B_k X_k$$

where the Xs vary over individuals and groups, but the Bs generally do not.

Although estimating the parameters of a logit model requires maximum likelihood methods (Translation: You need statistical software; unlike regression, it is awfully hard—but not impossible—to do it in Excel), they have become increasingly popular for modeling brand/product choice in existing markets. In practice, developing a logit model follows the same logical steps used to build a regression model.

PROBLEMS

1. Discuss the relationship between regression, discrimination analysis, and logit models.

2. Of what use are the following outputs of a logit model?

   a. model coefficients

   b. *t*-statistics.

   c. log likelihoods

3. The following are the income (in $1000) and age of a sample of 20 purchasers of an expensive automobile brand. A particular accessory was purchased by 12 of the sample but was not purchased by 8 of the sample. The age and income of the sample were as follows:

Twelve Purchasers		Eight Nonpurchasers	
Age	Income ($000)	Age	Income ($000)
30	20	30	50
40	50	40	30
40	60	40	40
50	40	40	40
50	70	50	20
60	30	50	30
60	40	60	20
60	40	60	50
60	50		
60	60		
60	70		
70	20		

a. Graphically determine a logistic regression which will predict the purchase of the accessory.

b. Determine the coefficients of the logit model which predict purchase of the accessory.

c. How do the relative magnitudes of these coefficients compare to those for the discriminant function you computed for the same data in the problems in the last chapter?

4. ABB Electric used a multinomial logit model to study how firms made choices in the "medium power transformers" market. (*Source*: Dennis H. Gensch, Nicola Aversa, and Steven P. Moore [1990], "A Choice Modeling Market System that Enabled ABB Electric to Expand Its Market Share," *Interfaces*, 20 [January–February], 6–25.). A respondent from each firm in the sample rated each supplier on several attributes and indicated the supplier the firm had chosen most recently. The logit model coefficients are as follows:

Variables	Coefficient	t-value
Invoice price	3.45	1.45
Energy losses	7.45	3.29
Appearance	4.32	2.11
Availability of spare parts	2.45	0.99
Clarity of bid document	1.62	0.36
Knowledgable salesmen	2.78	1.12
Maintenance requirements	2.64	1.31
Warranty	8.22	4.05

a. How important is price in this model?

b. Can you suggest a more parsimonious model?

c. How might you assess the quality of the model?

d. How might you use the model to target potential customers? (Hint: Think in terms of relative choice probablities.)

5. Mathematically show that the multinominal logit model has the "independence from irrelevant alternatives property."

6. Your researcher shows you the Coffee Logit Model in Table 19.6. You want to use it to predict purchases of individual consumers but notice that the model would make identical predictions for everybody in the market regardless of past purchasing behavior. How might you modify the model to account for brand loyalty in particular?

REFERENCES

BULT, JAN ROELF (1993) "Semiparametric versus Parametric Classification Models: An Application to Direct Marketing," *Journal of Marketing Research*, 30, August, 380–90.

CURRIM, IMRAN S. (1981) "Understanding Segmentation Approaches for Better Prediction and Understanding from Consumer Mode Choice Models," *Journal of Marketing Research*, 18, August, 301–09.

——— (1982) "Predictive Testing of Consumer Choice Models Not Subject to the Independence of Irrelevant Alternatives," *Journal of Marketing Research*, 19, May, 208–22.

FLATH, DAVID, AND E. W. LEONARD (1979) "A Comparison of Two Logit Models in the Analysis of Qualitative Marketing Data," *Journal of Marketing Research*, 16, November, 533–38.

GENSCH, DENNIS H., AND WILFRED W. RECKER (1979) "The Multinomial, Multiattribute Logit Choice Model," *Journal of Marketing Research*, 14, February, 124–32.

GREEN, PAUL E., FRANK J. CARMONE, AND DAVID P. WACHSPRESS (1977) "On the Analysis of Qualitative Data in Marketing Research," *Journal of Marketing Research*, 14, February, 52–59.

GUADAGNI, PETER M., AND JOHN D. C. LITTLE (1983) "A Logit Model of Brand Choice Calibrated on Scanner Data," *Marketing Science*, 2, Summer, 203–38.

HAUCK, W. W., AND A. DONNER (1977) "Wald's Test as Applied to Hypotheses in Logit Analysis," *Journal of the American Statistical Association*, 72, December, 851–53.

HOSMER, DAVID W., AND STANLEY LEMESHOW (1989) *Applied Logistic Regression*, New York: Wiley.

JENNINGS, D. E. (1986) "Judging Inference Adequacy in Logistic Regression," *Journal of the American Statistical Association*, 81, July, 471–76.

MCFADDEN, DANIEL (1974) "Conditional Logit Analysis of Qualitative Choice Behavior," in P. Zarembka, ed., *Frontiers in Econometrics*, New York: Academic Press, 105–42.

——— (1980) "Econometric Models for Probabilistic Choice," *Journal of Business*, 53, 513–29.

MCFADDEN, DANIEL, WILLIAM B. TYE, AND KENNETH TRAIN (1977) "An Application of Diagnostic Tests for the Independent of Irrelevant Alternative Property of the Multinomial Logit Model," *Transportation Research Record*, 637, 39–46.

MALHOTRA, NARESH K. (1984) "The Use of Linear Logit Models in Marketing Research," Journal of Marketing Research, 21, February, 20–31.

MOOD, ALEXANDER M., FRANKLIN GRAYBILL, AND DUANE C. BOES (1974) *Introduction to the Theory of Statistics*, 3rd ed., New York: McGraw-Hill.

PUNJ, GIRISH N., AND RICHARD STAELIN (1978) "The Choice Process for Graduate Business Schools," *Journal of Marketing Research*, 15 November, 588–98.

RAO, C. R. (1973) *Linear Statistical Inference and Its Applications*, 2nd ed., New York: Wiley.

APPENDIX 19-A

MAXIMUM LIKELIHOOD ESTIMATION OF THE BINARY LOGIT MODEL

All observations that take on the value 1 occur with the binary logit probability of

$$p = \frac{\exp\left(B_0 + B_1X_1 + B_2X_2 + \cdots + B_kX_k\right)}{1 + \exp\left(B_0 + B_1X_1 + B_2X_2 + \cdots + B_kX_k\right)}$$

and all observations that take on the value 0 occur with the probability

$$1 - p = \frac{1}{1 + \exp\left(B_0 + B_1X_1 + B_2X_2 + \cdots + B_kX_k\right)}$$

If we take the appropriate probability function for each observation and insert the appropriate values of the Xs, we get the probability of that observation. Further, if we multiply them together,[9] we get the probability of observing the entire existing data set. The maximum likelihood estimates maximize this product.

For example, consider the data set that was given in Table 19.1. The probability that someone who is 45 years old is aware of the Chester brand, p_{45}, is

$$p_{45} = \frac{\exp\left(B_0 + B_1X_{45}\right)}{1 + \exp\left(B_0 + B_1X_{45}\right)}$$

The probability that a 45 year old is not aware is

$$1 - p_{45} = \frac{1}{1 + \exp\left(B_0 + B_1X_{45}\right)}$$

The data set has two 45-year-olds in it; one is aware (ID #54) and the other is not (ID #53). The probability of this occurring, sometimes called the *likelihood*, is $p_{45}(1 - p_{45})$, the product of the two above probabilities. Similarly, the probabilities of a 46-year-old being aware and not aware are

$$p_{46} = \frac{\exp\left(B_0 + B_1X_{46}\right)}{1 + \exp\left(B_0 + B_1X_{46}\right)}$$

and

$$1 - p_{46} = \frac{1}{1 + \exp\left(B_0 + B_1X_{46}\right)}$$

There are two 46-year-olds in the sample—one aware and the other unaware. The likelihood of this is $p_{46}(1 - p_{46})$, where p_{46} and $1 - p_{46}$ are as above.

---

[9]The multiplication assumes the observations are independent.

What the computer does when it performs maximum likelihood estimation is first compute the likelihood for each age and then multiply the likelihoods to get a joint likelihood, that is, the probability of observing all the observations in the data set. Next, the computer finds the values of the Bs that maximize this product (as opposed to minimizing the sum of squared prediction errors). In short, maximum likelihood estimation finds the values of the Bs that make it most likely that we would observe what we did indeed observe.

Finally, suppose that the impossible occurred and we had a model that "perfectly fit" the data. It predicts $y = 1$ has a probability 1 whenever it occurs and 0 when it does not. If this were to miraculously happen, the likelihood would be 1 (the product of all 1s). Of course, this would not happen for any real data. In those cases, the joint likelihood, being the product of probabilities, would be between 0 and 1. Computer outputs for logit models have a quantity called the log-likelihood. This is somewhat analogous to regression's R^2. In regression, a perfect model would have an R^2 of 1 and all real values will be between 0 and 1. A perfect logit model would have a likelihood of 1 or a log-likelihood of 0 (recall that the log of 1 is 0). So real-life logit models have log-likelihoods that are negative numbers (recall that the logs of numbers between 0 and 1 are negative). We use log-likelihoods rather than likelihoods because large samples such as those inherent in scanner data would produce likelihood numbers that are awfully hard to interpret (e.g., 0.00000000000000000000000000000000000000000000000024582946189).

APPENDIX 19-B

LEAST SQUARES ESTIMATION OF THE BINARY LOGIT MODEL

There are some cases in which least squares estimation can be used for the binary logit model. One case is when the independent variables are categories, that is, are nominally scaled! When the manager at Chester, Inc. combined the ages into groups, she formed a categorical variable. The increased viability of least squares is made evident by comparing Figures 19.1 and 19.2.

If the independent variables in the Chester example were SEX (male or female) and EDUCATION (high school or below, some college, college graduate, or some postgraduate school), one could form a 2×4 contingency table, the entries of which were the number of respondents qualifying for that cell and the proportion of those respondents who were aware of the Chester brand:

	HS or Below	*Some College*	*College Grad*	*Some Post Grad*
Male				
Female				

Unfortunately, the least squares procedure most appropriate for binary logit problems is not ordinary least squares (OLS). The logit transformation, $\text{Ln}[p/(1 - p)]$, introduces heteroscedasticity into the data. To fix this, the data must be differentially weighted by a procedure called weighted least squares (WLS). WLS estimation is also beyond the scope of this book. The interested reader is referred to Flath and Leonard (1979) , Green, Carmone, and Wachspress (1977), and Malhotra (1984).

APPENDIX 19-C

LIKELIHOOD METHOD OF TESTING THE SIGNIFICANCE OF COEFFICIENTS

As in linear regression, the significance of a variable's coefficient relates to the question of *whether a model with that variable describes the data better than a model without that variable.* Some statisticians (Hauck and Donner, 1977; Jennings, 1986) recommend another test based on this question. First, fit a model with the variable to be tested included, and then fit the same model without the variable. Does the first model fit significantly better than the second? If so, then the variable is significant. The models are compared using statistics called log-likelihoods that are part of any logistic regression package (e.g., Table 19.3). It turns out that $-2 \times$ (the difference in log-likelihoods) has a chi-squared distribution with one degree of freedom.[10] The variable will be significant if this statistic is greater than a critical chi-square value taken from an appropriate table. Some software packages not only give you the log-likelihoods, but perform these significance tests as well.

APPENDIX 19-D

CHOICE THEORY DEVELOPMENT OF THE LOGIT MODEL

We begin with a consumer i that must make a choice from among J alternatives denoted by $j = 1, 2, \ldots, J$. The standard economic assumption is that the consumer chooses the alternative that maximizes his or her utility. Furthermore, the utility the consumer has for alternative j, U_{ij}, is seen as the sum of two components,

$$U_{ij} = V_{ij} + e_{ij}$$

where V_{ij} is a fixed component of utility, which can be calculated from observable (independent) variables (i.e., the X's), and e_{ij} is a random component, which is assumed to be independent and identically distributed across alternatives j, choice occasions, and consumers i.

---

[10]Details of this chi-squared test can be found in Mood, Graybill, and Boes (1974).

V_{ij} is modeled in a manner similar to that in the chapter:

$$V_{ij} = B_0 + B_1 X_1 + B_2 X_2 + \cdots + B_k X_{ik}$$

The probability that alternative j is chosen is now

$\Pr(U_{ij} > U_{ik}$, for all k not equal to $j)$, or

$\Pr(V_{ij} + e_{ij} > V_{ik} + e_{ik}$, for all k not equal to $j)$, which is the same as

$\Pr(e_{ij} - e_{ik} > V_{ik} - V_{ij}$, for all k not equal to $j)$

McFadden (1974) shows that if the distribution of all the random error terms are I.I.D. type-II extreme value (a distribution readers are not likely to have encountered before), the choice probabilities are equal to

$$\frac{\exp(V_{ij})}{\exp(V_{i1}) + \cdots + \exp(V_{ik})}$$

If the errors are normally distributed, the result is called a "Probit" model, which cannot be written in a convenient form and is even less convenient to estimate than a logit model.

APPENDIX 19-E

SAMPLE SPSS OUTPUT FOR BINARY LOGIT MODEL

Figure 19E.1 presents selected portions of SPSS output for the estimation of a logit model on peanut butter brand choice. The data were collected through supermarket scanners by Nielsen from 300 households in Springfield, Mo., and Sioux Falls, S.D., in the late 1980s. Each observation is a peanut butter purchase. The data set centered on two brands, a nationally known premium brand (Brand C) and a second brand that served as a proxy for all local private labels (i.e., the private labels of all stores in both cities were treated as if they were the same brand). There were other national brands in the market, but we leave them out for illustrative purposes.

The data set has 988 purchases of the two brands. A purchase of Brand C (denoted as the variable "BRAND" in the output) was coded as BRAND = 1, and a private label purchase was coded as BRAND = 0. The data set also included the regular price for each brand, the size of any temporary discount (measured as a negative number), if any, and whether each brand was on display or included in the store's feature ad. Furthermore, the data set included a loyalty variable for each brand; this was intended to measure the degree to which a household exhibited loyalty for that brand. This variable is essentially a weighted average of past purchases. (See Guadagni and Little [1983] for a precise definition.)

Since we are interested in modeling brand choice, we form relative variables. For example, the relative regular price of Brand C, denoted RREGPRC in the output, is the difference between the regular price of Brand C and the regular price of the private label. Similar operations are performed to obtain relative loyalty, discount, feature, and display (RDLAMTC, RLOYALC, RFEATC, RDISPC). These variables were the predictors in the logit model. The first page of the output simply describes some of the details of the data (e.g., how many observations there are). The second page gives some details about the estimation. Rather than presenting the log-likelihood, it presents $-2 \times$ log-likelihood because that is used in significance testing (Appendix 19-C). The second page also includes a classification table, which enables us to calculate the number of correct predictions. The brand more likely to be chosen is the one predicted to be chosen. The proportion of correct predictions is 92.61 percent, and so the logit model seems to fit this data set quite well.

The third page presents a table that allows us to write the logit model:

PR (Brand C is chosen) =

$$\frac{\exp(1.94 + 5.19 \cdot \text{RLOYALC} - .66 \cdot \text{RREGPRIC} - 1.64 \cdot \text{RDLAMTC} + 1.15 \cdot \text{RFEATC} + 1.39 \cdot \text{RDISPC})}{1 + \exp(1.94 + 5.19 \cdot \text{RLOYALC} - .66 \cdot \text{RREGPRIC} - 1.64 \cdot \text{RDLAMTC} + 1.15 \cdot \text{RFEATC} + 1.39 \cdot \text{RDISPC})}$$

The first column lists the variables in the model, the second the coefficients, and the third the standard errors. The fourth column presents the result of the Wald test. The chapter presents the Wald test as the ratio of the coefficient to the standard error and uses a t test. SPSS presents the square of the ratio of the coefficient to the standard error and uses an F test (the square of a quantity that has a t distribution with k degrees of freedom follows an F distribution with 1 and k degrees of freedom, so the tests are equivalent). The sixth column presents the significance levels from the Wald test for each coefficient. The seventh presents R, Rao's (1973) statistic, something we will not discuss (because no one we know in marketing uses it).

The results of the model make sense. Loyalty has a positive impact on the purchase probability. So do features and displays. The price and deal variables have the expected signs. Higher prices lead to lower choice probabilities. The negative sign for RDLAMTC implies that higher deal values lead to higher choice probabilities. (Recall that discount appears in the data set as a negative number.) Furthermore, the magnitude of the deal coefficient is much higher than the regular price coefficient. This implies that a manager would be better off (i.e., have a higher choice probability) if he were to raise his price 1 cent and offer a 1 cent deal. The net effect on the exponent in the logit model would be $-0.6622(1) - 1.6406(-1)$, or about plus 1!

19 Feb 97 SPSS for MS WINDOWS Release 6.1

        Total number of cases: 988 (Unweighted)
        Number of selected cases: 988
        Number of unselected cases: 0

        Number of selected cases: 988
        Number rejected because of missing data: 0
        Number of cases included in the analysis: 988

Dependent Variable Encoding:

Original   Internal
Value   Value
     .00   0
    1.00   1

---

19 Feb 97 SPSS for MS WINDOWS Release 6.1

Dependent Variable..   BRAND

Beginning Block Number 0. Initial Log Likelihood Function

-2 Log Likelihood   1275.853

* Constant is included in the model.

Estimation terminated at iteration number 7 because
Log Likelihood decreased by less than .01 percent.

 -2 Log Likelihood   341.726

Classification Table for BRAND
                        Predicted
                        .00   1.00   Percent Correct
                         0   1
Observed
    .00   0   305   38   88.92%

   1.00   1   35   610   94.57%

                        Overall 92.61%

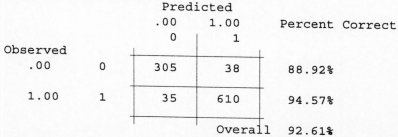

FIGURE 19E.1
Sample SPSS Output for Binary Logit Model

19 Feb 97 SPSS for MS WINDOWS Release 6.1

Page 3

------------------ Variables in the Equation ------------------

Variable	B	S.E.	Wald	df	Sig	R¹	Exp(B)
RLOYALC	5.1861	.4410	138.2762	1	.0000	.3268	178.7719
RREGPRC	-.6622	.1466	20.4060	1	.0000	-.1201	.5157
RDLAMTC	-1.6406	.1648	99.1033	1	.0000	-.2759	.1939
RFEATC	1.1515	.5183	4.9360	1	.0263	.0480	3.1629
RDISPC	1.3901	.3869	12.9114	1	.0003	.0925	4.0152
Constant	1.4943	.2850	27.4855	1	.0000		

CHAPTER 20

Additional Data Analytic Techniques

This final chapter on data analytic methods discusses a potpourri of techniques that have emerged in the marketing research industry in the last decade. While previously discussed (and often simpler) methods can be used in their place, these procedures have advantages for several situations. The particular methods we present are correspondence analysis, log-linear models, a variety of nonparametric regression techniques, latent class analysis, and structural equation modeling.

CORRESPONDENCE ANALYSIS

Correspondence analysis is a recently popularized technique that produces maps from nominally scaled or categorical data. Its popularity stems from limitations of two techniques previously discussed in this book. First, perceptual maps built from factor analyses require that the raw data be intervally scaled. They have difficulty with nominally scaled variables such as color or brand preference. Second, the relationships among nominally scaled data are usually analyzed via visual inspection of cross-tabs. If statistics is used at all, it tends to be in the form of a chi-square test of independence. Chi-square tests only reveal whether there is evidence of any relationship between two sets of variables; they unfortunately do not reveal the nature of that relationship. Correspondence analysis presents a picture of that relationship. The variables may be product descriptors, usage occasions, users, or all at the same time.

The input for correspondence analysis is a two-dimensional contingency table with R rows reflecting different levels of one categorical variable and C columns reflecting those of another. The variables may be product descriptors, usage occasions, users, and so forth. The assumption of categorical data is not limiting, since most intervally scaled data can be meaningfully broken out into categories (e.g., age: 20–29, 30–39, 40–49, etc.). The r, c-th cell of such a table records the number of observations in the data set that simultaneously have the rth level of the first variable and the cth level of the second.

The primary way contingency tables arise is through the cross-tabulation of two categorical variables. There are others, however. For example, a common consumer task has respondents list all the attributes that apply to a given product. Alternatively, they can be given a list of attributes and asked to pick the two (or three, or K, or an unspecified number) that best describe the product. In either case, a contingency table can be constructed with the number of times a product was described by each attribute as entries. Such a data collection produced the contingency table about snack foods studied by Rogus and Berry (1986), which is given in Table 20.1. A sample of 750 users of snack foods were each asked to rate three randomly chosen foods by placing a check mark next to any characteristic they felt described the food "extremely well."

Correspondence analysis assigns numerical values or scores to the rows and columns of the contingency table that maximize the relationship between selected row and column variables. All variables (attributes, adjectives, etc.) and products can be plotted in the same geometric space to reveal the structure of the data. In that sense, correspondence analysis belongs more to the family of techniques for "exploratory data analysis" (Tukey, 1977) than it does to formal statistical methodology. The particular details are beyond the scope of this book, but Figure 20.1 presents an example based on the data in Table 20.1.

The triangles in Figure 20.1 represent snack foods, and the points represent the characteristics. Foods on the left of the map (e.g., chips, crackers, and nuts) are similar: they are all "dry," "salty," and "crispy." Foods on the right (e.g., pies, ice cream, and cookies) are all "sweet," "flavorful," and "soft." Although some of the brands are confidential, we can say the those products near the top tend to have chocolate and are all available in vending machines. In general, the characteristics listed near a given food seem to make sense.

This correspondence analysis focused on products by characteristics data. Other analyses are possible for other variables in contingency tables. For example, Rogus and Berry (1986) also present products by occasions (What snack foods are appropriate for what occasions?) and products by users (Who is most likely to use which snack food?). The ability to position products with respect to any type of data (e.g., attitudes, usage occasions, customers) probably accounts for the emerging popularity of correspondence analysis.

Correspondence analysis maps invite comparisons to factor analysis maps and multidimensional scaling of similarity data. There are some (perhaps subtle) differences. MDS and correspondence analysis employ the related concepts of similarity between products. In correspondence analysis, similarity is defined in terms of sharing the same levels of some categorical variables. With respect to factor analysis, two distinctions emerge. First, the variables in correspondence analysis are categorical, while those in factor analysis are generally intervally scaled. Second, correspondence analysis plots both variables and products in the same map directly. In particular, just as products are related if they share the same levels of categorical variables, variable levels are related if they appear in the same products.

LOG-LINEAR MODELS

Log-linear models provide another way to analyze contingency tables. Unlike correspondence analysis, the contingency tables in log-linear models can be of more than two dimensions. Also unlike correspondence analysis, log-linear models present a statistical analysis as opposed to a visual map. As such, log-linear models extend chi-square tests of independence in simple cross-tabs.

TABLE 20.1   Frequency Counts for Snack Food Descriptors

Base: Rated (Snack)	Type of Chips	Nuts	Type of Crackers	Home-made Pies	Individual fruit Pies	Crisp Cookies	Home-made Cookies	Soft Cookies	Type of Candy	Bulk Ice Cream	Portable Ice Cream	Fresh Fruit	Toast/ Muffins
Good with dips	60%	8%	67%	6%	4%	11%	5%	8%	6%	8%	18%	12%	42%
Salty	60	64	48	5	3	3	2	5	3	a	6	a	1
Crispy	76	32	80	11	10	79	34	17	17	5	10	35	28
Dry	65	63	62	4	4	44	20	19	12	a	5	2	38
No sugar	18	41	42	9	1	2	7	10	9	1	3	38	36
Not bad for teeth	28	65	64	16	14	15	14	19	11	29	20	16	45
Has grain	21	4	26	12	5	12	25	18	4	1	10		31
High fiber	11	28	17	3	5	5	20	20	3	4	9	37	32
Good right out of bag	80	81	83	14	61	82	28	64	66	36	47	38	21
Easy to handle	62	52	56	28	40	57	60	61	43	34	40	58	54
All natural	18	70	25	50	11	8	28	22	8	32	24	85	40
Easy to fix	66	68	61	28	67	63	46	55	45	67	51	69	60
In vending machines	58	28	43	14	44	37	17	32	48	19	50	30	3
Made by well-known company	41	28	43	14	45	37	17	38	32	42	24	8	28
Wholesome	19	54	31	44	23	20	37	30	3	52	42	79	46
Lots of vitamins	7	54	11	24	12	6	25	22	8	16	16	62	30
Quality ingredients	24	44	43	62	31	18	61	41	13	53	35	48	37
Easy to chew	37	42	51	70	36	13	75	72	13	48	63	49	41
Good with milk	17	21	55	82	70	72	81	81	10	28	31	27	63
Good with coffee	8	14	39	55	52	59	67	64	13	19	34	16	55
Has chocolate	2	5	7	2	11	53	58	47	12	63	68	14	4
Sticky/gooey	a	1	10	27	35	3	15	11	22	25	26	6	5
Lots of flavors	19	17	20	66	64	51	46	40	82	77	63	44	19
Sweet	4	2	3	71	66	59	64	63	66	69	60	47	6
Soft/chewey	2	5	12	45	55	11	55	78	20	34	40	27	28
Homemade	2	3	7	81	14	30	64	46	16	23	17	10	40
Fruity	1	2	3	64	87	12	23	30	34	35	18	72	8

a Less than .5%.

Source: Carol A. Rogus and Elisabeth M. Berry, "Correspondence Analysis: The Picture That's Worth a Thousand Numbers" from *Marketing Review* 41, no. 7 (1986). Copyright © 1986 by the American Marketing Association. Reprinted with the permission of the publishers.

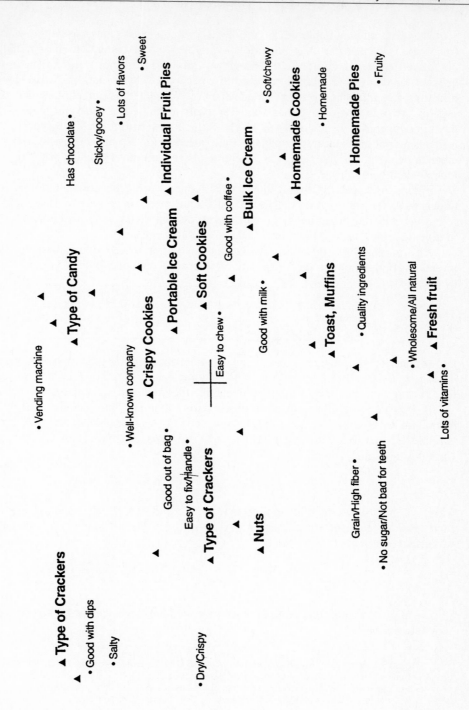

FIGURE 20.1

Correspondence Analysis Map of Snack Foods

Source: Carol A. Rogus and Elisabeth M. Berry, "Correspondence Analysis: The Picture That's Worth a Thousand Numbers" from *Marketing Review* 41, no. 7 (1986). Copyright © 1986 by the American Marketing Association. Reprinted with the permission of the publishers.

The contingency table in Figure 20.2 presents a 2 (marital status—variable a) $\times$ 3 (income—variable b) $\times$ 3 (occupation—variable c) $\times$ 2 (intend to buy radial tires or do not intend to buy—variable d) contingency table of a sample of 252 males between the ages of 18 and 64 collected for a study performed by a national marketer of automobile tires (DeSarbo and Hildebrand, 1980). We present the four-dimensional table as three separate two-dimensional tables (one for each level of the third variable) with each cell having two entries (one for each level of the fourth variable). This type of table is typical of marketing research analyses that attempt to explain differences between a discrete dependent variable, such as intention, based on several categorical or "categorized" independent variables.

Figure 20.2 tells us that 14 of the 252 men were blue collar, not married, and earn under \$10,000 (the $c_2 b_1 a_1$ cell). Six of them intended to buy replacement radial tires ($c_2 b_1 a_1 d_1$). On the other hand, of the 31 respondents who were white collar, married, and middle income, 18 of them intended to buy the tires.

Any of the three descriptor variables can be summarized in a simple cross-tab with intention. For example, the cross-tab of intention and occupation is

	c_1	c_2	c_3
Intend to Buy	60	54	32
Do Not Intend to Buy	52	44	10

Unfortunately, simple chi-square tests of independence of this cross-tab (as well as the analogous ones for marital status and income) do not give a complete picture of the relationship among intention, marital status, income, and occupation.

If N_{ijkl} denotes the number of observations that fall into the ith category of variable a, the jth category of variable b, the kth category of variable c, and the lth category of variable d, the following main-effects ANOVA-type expression is appropriate if all the variables are independent:

$$\log N_{ijkl} = B_0 + B_i^a + B_j^b + B_k^c + B_l^t$$

where B_0 is a constant that applies to all N_{ijkl}, and B_i^a, B_j^b, B_k^c, and B_l^d are constants for each level of each of the variables.[1] As usual, the B's all satisfy the typical analysis of variance constraints:

$$\sum_i B_i^a = \sum_j B_j^b = \sum_k B_k^c = \sum_l B_l^d$$

To allow for possible violations of independence, we can add two-, three-, and four-way interactions:

---

[1] To see where this expression comes from, suppose that we have two variables a and b instead of all four. The ith level of a and jth level of b are denoted by a_i and b_j. If a and b are independent, the probability that a randomly chosen observation has the values a_i and b_j (i.e., falls into the contingency table cell $a_i b_j$) is $\Pr(a_i) \times \Pr(b_j)$. These probabilities are equal to the number of respondents in each category divided by the total sample size, N. Using the notation N_{ij}, N_{i+}, and N_{+j} for the number of observations in $a_i b_j$, a_i, and b_j, we can write $N_{ij}/N = (N_{i+}/N) \times (N_{+j}/N)$. Taking logarithms leaves us with $\log(N_{ij}/N) = \log(N_{i+}/N) + \log(N_{+j}/N)$, or $\log N_{ij} = \log N_{i+} + \log N_{+j} - \log N$. So $B_0 = -\log N$, $B_i^a = \log N_{i+}$, and $B_j^b = \log N_{+j}$.

VARIABLE a: MARITAL STATUS
              a_1 = Other
              a_2 = Married

VARIABLE b: INCOME
              b_1 = Below 10K
              b_2 = 10K–20K
              b_3 = Over 20K

VARIABLE c: OCCUPATION
              c_1 = White collar
              c_2 = Blue collar
              c_3 = Other

VARIABLE d: INTENTION
              d_1 = Intends to buy
              d_2 = Does not intend to buy

c_1		
	a_1	a_2
b_1	$d_1 = 6$; $d_2 = 8$	$d_1 = 4$; $d_2 = 3$
b_2	$d_1 = 6$; $d_2 = 6$	$d_1 = 18$; $d_2 = 13$
b_3	$d_1 = 6$; $d_2 = 1$	$d_1 = 20$; $d_2 = 21$
c_2		
	a_1	a_2
b_1	$d_1 = 6$; $d_2 = 8$	$d_1 = 4$; $d_2 = 6$
b_2	$d_1 = 12$; $d_2 = 9$	$d_1 = 23$; $d_2 = 15$
b_3	$d_1 = 7$; $d_2 = 3$	$d_1 = 2$; $d_2 = 3$
c_3		
	a_1	a_2
b_1	$d_1 = 7$; $d_2 = 0$	$d_1 = 2$; $d_2 = 1$
b_2	$d_1 = 7$; $d_2 = 4$	$d_1 = 5$; $d_2 = 2$
b_3	$d_1 = 11$; $d_2 = 2$	$d_1 = 0$; $d_2 = 1$

Source: DeSarbo and Hildebrand (1980), p.41.

FIGURE 20.2
A Four-Way Contingency Table
Source: Wayne S. DeSarbo and David K. Hilderbrand, "A Marketer's Guide to Log-Linear Models for Qualitative Data Analysis" from *Journal of Marketing* 44 (Summer 1980): 41. Copyright © 1980 by the American Marketing Association. Reprinted with the permission of the publishers.

$$\log N_{ijkl} = B_0 + B_i^a + B_j^b + B_k^c + B_l^d + B_{ij}^{ab} + B_{ik}^{ac} + B_{il}^{ad} + B_{jk}^{bc} + B_{jl}^{bd} + B_{kl}^{cd}$$
$$+ B_{ijk}^{abc} + B_{ikl}^{acd} + B_{jkl}^{bcd} + B_{ijkl}^{abcd}$$

This complete model is called a *saturated model*. The *B*'s in the saturated model also obey the usual constraints,

$$\sum_i B_{ij}^{ab} = \sum_j B_{ij}^{ab} = \cdots = \sum_k B_{ijkl}^{abcd} = \sum_l B_{ijkl}^{abcd} = 0$$

The independence of all four variables can be assessed by testing the hypotheses that all interactions in a saturated model are equal to zero. If the saturated model is superior to the main-effects one, there is some association among the variables. By examining which interaction terms are significant, one can determine the source of the association. In addition, the parameter estimates allow for predictions of cell counts. Perhaps most important, however, is the ability to form a predictive model of the response variable, intention in this case. Green, Carmone, and Wachspress (1977) present a log-linear model–based approach for doing this. Appendix 20-A presents some SPSS output for the log-linear modeling of Figure 20.2.

NONPARAMETRIC REGRESSION

In some instances, the relations between predictors and a dependent variable are quite complex. Linear regression can be adapted to account for nonlinearities and interactions among the predictors. Sometimes, however, these nonlinearities and interactions are either too complex for linear regression or are completely unknown to the analyst.

Classes of methods falling under the umbrella of nonparametric regression can handle these problems. Nonparametric regression is so named because there is no underlying parametric statistical model such as $Y = a + b_1X_1 + b_2X_2 + \ldots + b_kX_k + e$ that needs to be specified. These methods are essentially computer search algorithms that build a prediction rule between a set of predictors and a dependent variable or variables. They all tend to involve tree or network diagrams that track the flow from the input to the prediction rule to the output. We will discuss two major classes of nonparametric regression: segmentation trees and neural networks.

Segmentation Trees

Segmentation trees divide observations (e.g., consumers) into mutually exclusive and exhaustive subgroups (segments) that differ with respect to levels of predictor variables that have the strongest relationship with a dependent variable (e.g., purchase behavior). For example, men may buy the largest quantities of a given product (with no differences among age groups); women under 40 buy the least; and women over 40 buy a moderate amount.

The general approach to segmentation trees begins by finding the predictor variable that divides the sample so that the difference among the new subsamples with respect to a dependent variable is the greatest. At the next stage, each subgroup is then further divided into smaller subgroups via the same approach: the remaining predictor variables are examined to find the one that divides the subgroup into further subgroups (sub-sub-groups) so that the difference among them on the same dependent variable is as large as possible. The predictor variable used in the second division generally will not be the same for each subgroup produced at the first division. This process continues until either no predictor variables are left, none produce statistically significant differences (for the dependent variable) within the new subgroups, or the subgroups are too small to divide further. The end product is usually shown graphically in a treelike structure. The final subgroups are often taken to be market segments.

Because they deal with subgroups, segmentation trees can handle more complex inter-actions than is common with regression. For example, suppose the dependent variable is "intend to buy," and the first subdivision is gender (male vs. female). Males are further divided by income (high vs. low) and females are further divided by employment (work-ing vs. not). This implies an interaction of sex and income, and sex and employment, of a nature difficult to extract from regression.

However, tree models (like most stepwise procedures) are susceptible to the influ-ence of a few unusual observations. Furthermore, they lack the statistical precision of regression models. In fact, tree models are not really models at all; they are somewhat ad hoc procedures designed to find the best combination of subgroups for a given sam-ple of data.

The first segmentation tree method popularized in the marketing literature, Automat-ic Interaction Detection (AID) (Morgan and Sonquist, 1963), assumed that the dependent variable was intervally scaled (e.g., purchase quantity). AID examines all possible two-way splits of each subgroup for each variable and selects the split that produces the most significant t statistic for the difference in means of the dependent variable between the two subgroups. However, AID cannot handle important categorical dependent vari-ables like buyer vs. nonbuyer, and has been replaced in practice by methods that empha-size categorical dependent variables. These can handle all types of variables, since we can always convert intervally scaled variables to nominal ones simply by dividing the range of the variable into categories.

We examine two of these segmentation tree analytic methods, CART and CHAID. The difference between them (and others in the literature) lies in the methods of divid-ing samples into segments, the number of subcategories allowed at each division, and the method of final tree formation.

CART In CART (Classification and Regression Trees), each observation is a collection of nominal and/or intervally scaled predictor variables with a known dependent-variable category assignment. The objective is to predict the dependent variable. This is essen-tially the structure of discriminant and logit analysis. CART's advantage over these approaches is its ability to handle complex interactions and to uncover these interactions through the data analysis rather than specify them a priori. Its disadvantage, since it is based on stepwise sample splits and not precise values, is potentially unstable results.

Initially, the tree contains all N observations. The algorithm performs a search across all binary splits on the data to determine the optimal split s_{opt}. Optimality is determined by one of two very technical criteria (Gini and twoing) that we won't bore you with here.[2] The important things to note are that (a) all splits are binary, and (b) they are performed with respect to maximizing the differences between groups on a dependent variable.

For ordered variables (intervally scaled or ordered categories), splits occur at a boundary (e.g., income $\geq$ \$40,000 vs. income $<$ \$40,000). For categorical variables, all possible splits of the levels into two parts are examined (e.g., for three cities there are three possible splits: say, New York and Los Angeles versus Hong Kong; New York and Hong Kong versus Los Angeles; and New York versus Los Angeles and Hong Kong).

Splitting continues until a large "terminal" tree is formed. Often, there will be too few observations in each terminal branch to be practical. (Would you want to deal with a market that has 146 segments, each with about 3 consumers, from a random sample of 500?). In these cases, the large tree is then pruned backward (i.e., some of the splits are removed) in a way that keeps the percentage of the sample misclassified on the dependent variable small. The terminal branches of the pruned tree are taken as the final segments. A detailed discussion of pruning is given in Brieman et al. (1984).

Examples help clarify these principles. Morwitz and Schmittlein (1992) performed CART analyses on the PC and automobile categories. Their objective was to predict purchase given the demographic and product usage variables listed in Table 20.2. They computed separate CART models for respondents who intended to buy and those that did not. The dependent variable was purchase, yes or no. The four models (intenders and nonintenders for each of the two categories) are in presented in Figure 20.3. For example, the root of the intending households' tree for PCs reflects the 1,765 observations, 13.65 percent of which bought. The root has two branches defined by different sets of occupa-

TABLE 20.2 Predictor Variables Used in CART Analyses

Automobile Data	Personal Computer Data
Size of household	Size of household
Annual household income	Annual household income
Age of head of household	Age of head of household
Household composition	Household composition
Marital status	Marital status
Household stage of life	Household stage of life
Type of residence	Type of residence
Home ownership	Home ownership
Employment of head of household	Employment of head of household
Race	Race
Occupation of head of household	Presence of children
Number of cars owned	Socioeconomic status
Year of car to be replaced	Region
	Use of PC at work or school

Source: Vicki G. Morwitz and David C. Schmittlein, "Using Segmentation to Improve Sales Forecasts Based on Purchase Intent: Which 'Intenders' Actually Buy?" from *Journal of Marketing Research* 29 (November 1992): 397, 398. Copyright © 1992 by the American Marketing Association. Reprinted with the permission of the publishers.

---

[2]Brieman et al. (1984) define and discuss these criteria.

Personal Computers

1. *Intenders*

1,765 Households

Occupation
Student
Professional
Mgr./Own
Sales
Farm
Laborers

Occupation
Clerical
Craftsman
Operative
Military
Service
Retired
Unknown

647 Households
9.27% Buy

Region
New England
Mid Atlantic
E N Central
South Atlantic
Mountain
Pacific

Region
N W Central
E S Central
W S Central

872 Households
18.23% Buy

246 Households
8.94% Buy

2. *Nonintenders*

Use of PC
At Work,
School,
or both

Use of PC
Neither at Work
nor at School

2,652 Households
7.88% Buy

7,699 Households
1.40% Buy

Automobiles

1. *Intenders*

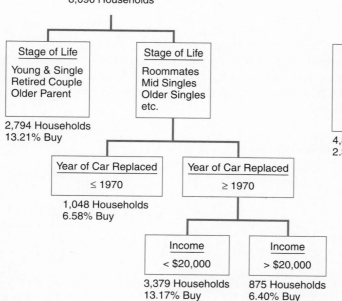

8,096 Households

Stage of Life
Young & Single
Retired Couple
Older Parent

Stage of Life
Roommates
Mid Singles
Older Singles
etc.

2,794 Households
13.21% Buy

Year of Car Replaced
≤ 1970

Year of Car Replaced
≥ 1970

1,048 Households
6.58% Buy

Income
< $20,000

Income
> $20,000

3,379 Households
13.17% Buy

875 Households
6.40% Buy

2. *Nonintenders*

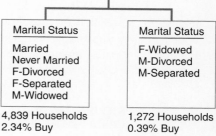

Marital Status
Married
Never Married
F-Divorced
F-Separated
M-Widowed

Marital Status
F-Widowed
M-Divorced
M-Separated

4,839 Households
2.34% Buy

1,272 Households
0.39% Buy

FIGURE 20.3
CART Analysis of PC and Authomobile Data
Source: Vicki G. Morwitz and David C. Schmittlein, "Using Segmentation to Improve Sales Forecasts Based on Purchase Intent: Which 'Intenders' Actually Buy?" from *Journal of Marketing Research* 29 (November 1992): 397, 398. Copyright © 1992 by the American Marketing Association. Reprinted with the permission of the publishers.

tions, the best predictor of whether or not an intender bought. The right branch indicates that 9.27 percent of the 647 observations in that branch bought. The left-hand branch is divided again, by region. Segment 1 were the most likely to buy of all the CART-derived PC segments (18.23% bought). In the automobile market, the intending segment characterized by the stage of life split (young and single, retired couple, or older parent as opposed to roommates, midlife singles, or older singles) was the most likely to buy.

CHAID The underlying principles behind CHAID (CHi-square Automatic Interaction Detection) are very similar to those behind CART. The differences are

1. The predictor variables must all be categorical.
2. The splitting is not constrained to be binary.
3. The splitting is based on a chi-square test, not a Gini or twoing measure.
4. No variable is included unless there is a statistically significant association between the dependent variable and the predictor.
5. There is no pruning of the final tree.

Given our ability to categorize intervally scaled variables, the categorical restriction is not severe. That variables can be split into more than two parts adds flexibility. The chi-square criterion may make users more comfortable because of their familiarity with the analysis of cross-tabs.

A simple tree is found in Figure 20.4, a CHAID analysis of the DeSarbo and Hildebrand (1980) data presented earlier in the chapter (Figure 20.2). The diagram indicates that 57.94 percent of the sample intended to buy the tires. The lone significant (based on the chi-square test) predictor entered in the CHAID analysis was occupation: 54.29 percent of the white- and blue-collar workers intended to buy, whereas 76.19 percent of the "others" did. Chi-square tests establish that "Occup." is the only variable that can be shown to be not independent of "Intend."

A more complex data set involves a direct marketing promotion used to enlist magazine subscribers.[3] Households sent a promotion were categorized as responders or nonresponders depending on whether they returned the form sent with the promotion. Predictor variables included age of head of household, household income, occupational status of the head of household ("Occupation"), whether the household has a bankcard,

FIGURE 20.4
CHAID Analysis of Desarbo-Hilderbrand (1980) Data

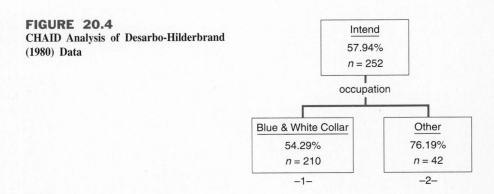

---

[3]This data set and its analysis are described in Magidson (1993).

whether children reside in the household, the sex of the head of the household ("Gender"), and the number of people in the household ("Hhsize"). The CHAID tree from this analysis is presented in Figure 20.5. Each node on the CHAID tree represents a population subgroup. The three rows of information in each node describe the subgroup. The data in each node indicate the number of cases in that subgroup and the percentage of cases in that subgroup that responded to the promotion.

For example, the initial node represents the entire sample, 81,040 observations, 1.15 percent of which responded to the promotion. The initial node has four *descendants*, formed by the categories of Hhsize, the best predictor of whether or not a household responded to the promotion. The node second from the left in this row represents the two- and three-person households. Of the 16,132 of these, 1.52 percent responded. The descendants of this node refine the prediction. The variable Occupation (white or blue color) is the best remaining predictor of which of these would respond. Similarly, the sex of the head of household is the best remaining predictor of which households of unknown size (denoted "?") would respond.

The lack of pruning is seen as a major disadvantage of CHAID by some. Once a split is built into the tree, it stays. On the other hand, CART reviews a tree once built and prunes it so that it might be more useful. One major advantage of CHAID, in addition to allowing splits to be more than binary, is that it is part of SPSS (Magidson, 1993).

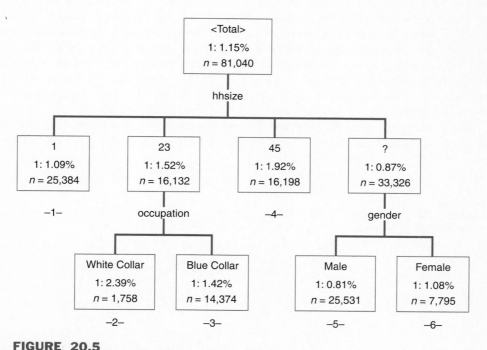

FIGURE 20.5
CHAID Analysis of Magazine Promotion
Source: Jay Magidson, *SPSS for Windows: CHAID, Release 6.0*, page 4. Reprinted with the permission of SPSS Inc.

Neural Networks

Neural networks are used for building predictive models in situations where the analyst has little knowledge about the form of the relationship between the independent and dependent variables. As such, they are particularly useful for pattern recognition tasks. For example, firms active in database marketing often have a huge amount of information on each of many potential customers or prospects (e.g., demographics, past purchases, media habits). Such a firm might want to know what products each customer in its database are likely to be in the market for. Another firm with sales subject to fluctuations in patterns of economic conditions, investment decisions, and the allocation of marketing resources might want to forecast sales. Previous chapters in this book have presented tools that could be used for these purposes (e.g., linear regression, logistic regression, discriminant analysis). However, these techniques assume very specific mathematical forms (often linear) in the pattern relating independent and dependent variables. When the patterns are too complex to be captured by these forms, neural networks provide a viable alternative.

Neural networks draw their inspiration from research on the workings of the human brain. The brain is a large, highly connected network of simple computing elements called "neurons." Each neuron accepts electrical signals from several others in a prior layer of the network, transforms them, and sends the output to several others in a subsequent layer. Neural networks are built as a collection of artificial neurons as in Figure 20.6. The top layer of the network represents the independent variables in the analysis, the input into the neural network, and the bottom level represents the dependent variables, the output of the network. There may be one or more (usually one in practice) intermediate layers, called *hidden layers*. Each node in the network operates as a neuron in the human brain. This metaphor is fully explored by Hinton (1992) in a detailed but layman (if not Lehmann) accessible discussion. For our purposes, Figure 20.7 will suffice.

Each artificial neuron performs a simple calculation. In Figure 20.7, i_k and o_k are used to denote the input to and output from unit ("neuron") k. The output is a

FIGURE 20.6
A Common Neural Network

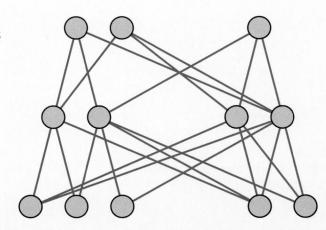

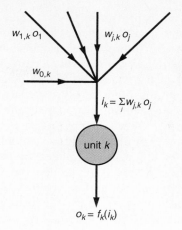

FIGURE 20.7
Neural Network Computation at a Single Unit
Source: Hal S. Stern, "Neural Networks in Applied Statistics" from *Technometrics* 38 (August 1996): 206. Copyright © 1996 by American Statistical Association and the American Society for Quality Control. Reprinted with the permission of American Statistical Association.

function (transformation), $f_k(i_k)$, of the input; this function is often called an *activation function*. Common forms of $f_k(i_k)$ include

$$\text{Linear or identity: } f_k(i_k) = i_k$$

$$\text{Logistic: } f_k(i_k) = \left(1 + \exp(-i_k)\right)^{-1}$$

$$\text{Threshold: } f_k(i_k) = 0, \text{ if } i_k < 0; \ 1, \text{ otherwise}$$

The neurons in the network are connected in the sense that the output from one unit serves as part of the input to others that follow it in the network. Each "connection" has a weight associated with it. The weight reflects the influence that the output of one unit has on the input of another. If the weight of the j, k connection is w_{jk} (where j precedes k in the network), the input to unit k is modeled as $i_k = w_{0k} + \Sigma \ w_{jk}o_j$, where the sum is taken over all units in the layer immediately preceding the one that unit k resides in. The connection weights w_{jk} are conceptually similar to regression coefficients, and w_{0k}, called a *bias*, is similar to a regression intercept.

Hidden layers play a role similar to that of factors in factor analysis.[4] They transform and combine the input variables into forms more useful for further analysis. Suppose there is one hidden layer. That layer transforms the independent variables, which after transformation are then analyzed with respect to a dependent variable. This is exactly what happens when we do a regression on factor scores as discussed in Appendix 16-A.

There is great flexibility in constructing the hidden layers of a neural network. However, the first and last layers are determined by the independent and dependent variables. When there are multiple dependent variables (e.g., the database marketing firm alluded to earlier wanting to predict need for each of several products), there would be multiple output units at the last layer. If there is only one dependent variable (e.g., as in a sales forecast), only one output unit would be present.

The value of neural networks stems from the fact that by varying the number of hidden layers, the nodes in each layer, the activation functions, the connection weights,

---

[4]Later in the chapter we will see yet another similar concept, structural equation modeling.

and the biases, we can approximate any functional relationship to any desired degree of accuracy. That is why neural networks are useful when either the analyst has very little knowledge about the form of the relationship between the independent and dependent variables or the relationship is very complex.

Most models (with the exception of cluster and correspondence analyses) discussed in earlier chapters in this book involve statistical estimation of an underlying model. Segmentation trees are heuristically derived in an ad hoc way. In contrast, neural networks are "trained." There is no prespecified mathematical model relating input and output. Training algorithms improve initial estimates of connection weights by calculating the errors the network makes in prediction on a "training sample." The weights are then changed so as to reduce the error. This process continues until the network achieves minimal prediction errors with respect to the training sample. The most popular approach appears to be the back-propagation algorithm of Rummelhart, Hinton, and Williams (1986). Its popularity stems from its ease of implementation. Hinton (1992) describes this algorithm in an intuitive way.

Interestingly, many of the data analytic approaches discussed in this book can be modeled as neural networks. Discriminant analysis is depicted in Figure 20.8 as a single neuron (i.e., the outputs do not input to another layer). The activation function is the threshold function, and the connection weights are the discriminant coefficients. If we substitute the identity function for the threshold function, we have the familiar multiple regression model. Stern (1996) develops the model for a time series regression.

Keep in mind that lack of an underlying statistical model places an extremely heavy burden on the data in the training sample. Without a model, they almost exclusively determine the final prediction mechanism. To ensure that the mechanism is not an artifact of the specific data employed, some split-sample validation is recommended; that is, train the model on a subset of the data and see how well the derived mechanism predicts the rest of the data.

Kumar, Rao, and Soni (1995) performed an empirical comparison between neural networks and logistic regression on supermarket buyers' decisions about adding new products. On one hand, neural networks tended to provide somewhat superior predictions (to the data used to estimate and train the models as well as to a holdout sample). The reason is that hidden layers in networks are able to extract complex features of input data. On the other hand, Kumar and his colleagues argue that neural networks are not intuitive, may often be difficult to interpret, and require special software.

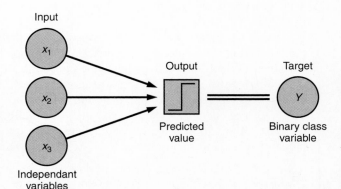

FIGURE 20.8
Discriminant Analysis as a Neural Network
Source: Warren S. Sarle (1995), "Neural Networks and Statistical Models" from *Proceedings of the Nineteenth Annual SAS, Users Group International Conference* (Cary, North Carolina: SAS Institute, 1994). Copyright © 1995 by SAS Institute Inc. Reprinted with the permission of the publisher.

STRUCTURAL EQUATION MODELING

A number of researchers have become interested in so-called structural equation modeling (e.g., the entire November 1982 issue of the *Journal of Marketing Research* was devoted to this topic). These approaches blend two basic procedures:

1. Simultaneous equation regression
2. Factor analysis

Essentially, structural equation models use multiple measures to improve reliability and simultaneous equation models to estimate "causal" impact. Consider the following simple example:

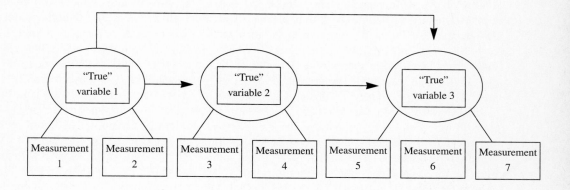

A simple approach to this situation is to first form indexes of the variables based on the measures and then run regressions on the indexes. The index formation can be done via factor analysis or by simply averaging the measures (assuming their scales are comparable):

$$\text{Index 1} = (\text{Measure 1} + \text{Measure 2}) / 2$$
$$\text{Index 2} = (\text{Measure 3} + \text{Measure 4}) / 2$$
$$\text{Index 3} = (\text{Measure 5} + \text{Measure 6} + \text{Measure 7}) / 3$$

The following regressions are then run:

$$\text{Index 2} = B_{02} + B_{12}(\text{Index 1})$$
$$\text{Index 3} = B_{03} + B_{13}(\text{Index 1}) + B_{23}(\text{Index 2})$$

Since the indexes are based on multiple measures, they are generally more reliable than a single measure. In many situations, however, the measures themselves may be correlated. For example, if measures 2 and 5 are both measured on six-point scales, response style would tend to increase the correlation between the variables. To take into account such relations, as well as to more efficiently (in a statistical sense) estimate the parameters, some relatively elaborate procedures have been developed.

The essence of these procedures is that the true variables (constructs) are unobserved. Therefore, the "game" is to estimate both the relations of the measures to the constructs and the causal relations among the constructs simultaneously.

Two different approaches to estimating the parameters of these models exist.[5] The first is that of Jöreskog and Sörbom (1982) and Bagozzi (1980), known as LISREL, which is now available as part of the SPSS package. The second is known as PLS (partial least squares), and derives from Wold (1979) and Fornell and Larcker (1981). Both have considerable promise.

LATENT CLASS MODELS

Latent class models share conceptual elements with both cluster and factor analysis. Like cluster analysis (and segmentation trees, for that matter), latent class models try to uncover the structure of segments within a data set. Unlike cluster analysis, though, it does not do so based on a set of variables that characterize each consumer. Instead, it tries to discern the segments that when combined produce observed aggregate market behavior. In that sense, latent class methods are similar to factor analysis (and structural equation models) in that an essential component of what is being studied is unobservable. In factor analysis, it is the factors; in latent class models, it is the segments or "latent classes."

To explain latent class methods, it is useful to consider how an aggregate market would look if we knew the segments, their relative sizes, and their behavior. Here, we focus on segments with different brand preferences. Assume two segments exist. In segment 1, customers buy brand A with probability .9 and brand B (the only other brand) with probability .1. In segment 2, the probabilities are .2 for brand A and .8 for brand B. Further, assume segment 1 accounts for 60 percent of sales and segment 2 for 40 percent.

The aggregate market share for brand A therefore is

$$= (0.6)(0.9) + (0.4)(0.2)$$
$$= 62\%$$

and the market share for brand B is 38 percent.

Furthermore, if purchase occasions are independent, the brand switching probability from A to B =

(Relative size of segment 1) • (Probability of buying A in segment 1) • (Probability of buying B in segment 1) + (Relative size of segment 2) • (Probability of buying A in segment 2) • (Probability of buying B in segment 2) = (.6)(90%)(10%) + (.4)(20%)(80%)
$$= 5.4\% + 6.4\% = 11.8\%$$

The same calculation can be shown to hold for the switching probability from brand B to A.

---

[5]They differ conceptually in the assumption they make about whether the measures are *caused* by the true variables (LISREL) or combine to form them (PLS). LISREL relies on a maximum likelihood estimation procedure, whereas PLS does least squares estimation. The major advantage of these procedures is that they focus attention on both measurement issues and the structural/causal relations. At present, their use is largely restricted to academics.

Similarly, the probability of repeat buying brand A

$$= (.6)(90\%)(90\%) + (.4)(20\%)(20\%) = 48.6\% + 1.6\% = 50.2\%$$

and the probability of repeat buying B

$$= (.6)(10\%)(10\%) + (.4)(80\%)(80\%) = .6\% + 25.6\% = 26.2\%$$

Hence, the aggregate (market) brand switching matrix would be

	A	B
A	50.2 / 62 = 81.0%	11.8 / 62 = 19.0%
B	11.8 / 38 = 31.1%	26.2 / 38 = 68.9%

Latent class analysis attempts to work this process in reverse. That is, it begins with the aggregate switching and share data and tries to deduce the underlying segments and their brand loyalties (Grover and Srinivasan, 1987). For two brands and two segments, this means estimating one purchase probability parameter for each segment[6] plus one more for the relative segment sizes. The total is three parameters. There are also three "independent" bits of data, one for market share and one for each brand's repeat rates. Hence, in this case, the results can be obtained algebraically (three equations in three unknowns). More segments would produce more parameters than number of data bits and, consequently, an unestimable model.

In the more general case of r brands and g segments, there are $(r - 1)g + g - 1 = rg - 1$ parameters to estimate and $r(r - 1) + r - 1 = (r + 1)(r - 1) = r^2 - 1$ pieces of information. Hence, one can only get estimates when $rg - 1$ is less than or equal to $r^2 - 1$, or when the number of segments is less than or equal to the number of brands.

SUMMARY

This chapter presented several methods that have evolved over recent years in response to specific situations. The techniques discussed include

Correspondence analysis—a technique for producing market maps from contingency tables

Log-linear models—models that investigate the structure of multidimensional contingency tables or cross-tabs

Nonparametric regression—a class of techniques for predicting a dependent variable from a set of predictors when the mathematical form of the relationship cannot be assumed to be linear or made linear

Segmentation trees—computer algorithms such as CART and CHAID, which divide a sample of observations into groups that allow the prediction of a

---

[6]When one purchase probability is estimated, the other follows automatically since they must add up to 1.

dependent variable from the combination of predictor variables that define each group

Neural networks—computer algorithms that mimic the human brain in building predictive models that are very nonlinear, complex, and involve the interaction of several variables

Structural equation models—models that use multiple measures to improve the reliability of construct measures

Latent class models—models that try to uncover unobservable segments (i.e., "latent classes"), the behavior of which when combined produce aggregate market statistics

While sometimes useful, these various methods are not general substitutes for such standard procedures as simple data description and regression analysis. Further, they rely on quality input data. Put bluntly, in most situations assuring quality data is more important than knowledge and use of complex techniques.

REFERENCES

BAGOZZI, RICHARD P. (1980) *Causal Models in Marketing*, New York: Wiley.

BRIEMAN, LEO, JEROME H. FRIEDMAN, RICHARD A. OLSHEN, AND CHARLES J. STONE (1984) *Classification and Regression Trees*, Belmont, Calif.: Wadsworth.

DESARBO, WAYNE S., AND DAVID K. HILDEBRAND (1980) "A Marketer's Guide to Log-Linear Models for Qualitative Data Analysis," *Journal of Marketing*, 44, Summer, 40–51.

FORNELL, CLAES, AND DAVID F. LARCKER (1981) "Two Structural Equation Models: LISREL and PLS Applied to Consumer Exit Voice Theory," *Journal of Marketing Research*, 18, February, 440-52.

GREEN, PAUL E., FRANK J. CARMONE, AND DAVID P. WACHSPRESS (1977) "On the Analysis of Qualitative Data in Marketing Research," *Journal of Marketing Research*, 14, February, 52–59.

GROVER, RAJIV, AND V. SRINIVASAN (1987) "A Simultaneous Approach to Market Segmentation and Market Structuring," *Journal of Marketing Research*, 24, May, 139–53.

HINTON, GEOFFREY E. (1992) "How Neural Networks Learn from Experience," *Scientific American*, 267, September, 144–51.

HOFFMAN, DONNA L., JAN DE LEEUW, AND RAMESH V. ARJUNJI (1995) "Multiple Correspondence Analysis," in Richard P. Bagozzi, ed., *Advanced Methods in Marketing Research*, Cambridge, Mass.: Blackwell, 260–94.

JÖRESKOG, KARL G., AND DAG SÖRBOM (1982) "Recent Developments in Structural Equation Modeling," *Journal of Marketing Research*, 19, November, 404–16.

KUMAR, AKHIL, VITHALA R. RAO, AND HARSH SONI (1995) "An Empirical Comparison of Neural Network and Logistic Regression Models," *Marketing Letters*, 6, October, 251–64.

MAGIDSON, JAY (1993) *SPSS for Windows: CHAID, Release 6.0*, Chicago: SPSS, Inc.

MORGAN, JAMES N., AND JOHN SONQUIST (1963) "Problems in the Analysis of Survey Data and a Proposal," *Journal of the American Statistical Association*, 58, 415–34.

MORWITZ, VICKI G., AND DAVID C. SCHMITTLEIN (1992) "Using Segmentation to Improve Sales Forecasts Based on Purchase Intent: Which "Intenders" Actually Buy?" *Journal of Marketing Research*, 29, November, 391–405.

ROGUS, CAROL A., AND ELISABETH M. BERRY (1986) "Correspondence Analysis: The Picture That's Worth a Thousand Numbers," *Marketing Review*, 41, (7).

RUMMELHART, DAVID E., GEOFFREY E. HINTON, AND RONALD J. WILLIAMS (1986) "Learning Internal Representations by Error Propagation," in *Parallel Distributed Processing: Exploration in the Microstructure of Cognition*, vol. 1, Cambridge, Mass.: MIT Press, 318–62.

SARLE, WARREN S. (1995) "Neural Networks and Statistical Models," SAS Technical Paper 320, Cary, N.C.: SAS Institute.

STERN, HAL S. (1996) "Neural Networks in Applied Statistics," *Technometrics*, 38, August, 205–14.

TUKEY, JOHN W. (1977) *Exploratory Data Analysis*, Reading, Mass.: Addison-Wesley.

WHITE, H. (1992) *Artificial Neural Networks: Approximation and Learning Theory*, Oxford, U.K.: Blackwell.

WOLD, HERMAN A. (1979) "Estimation and Evaluation of Models Where Theoretical Knowledge Is Scarce: An Example of Partial Least Squares," in J. Ramsey and J. Kmenta, eds., *Evaluation of Econometric Models*, New York: Academic Press.

APPENDIX 20-A
SAMPLE SPSS OUTPUT FOR LOG-LINEAR MODELS

Figure 20A.1 presents part of the SPSS output for the saturated log-linear model of the full data in Figure 20.2. The tests of *K*-way (and higher-order) effects suggest that the four-way interaction is not significantly different from zero. However, interactions at all other levels are. Therefore, the variables in the contingency table are not independent. The tests of partial associations identify the main effects and interactions that are significantly different from zero. At a .05 level, the significant effects are

Three-way interactions: income–marital status–occupation
Two-way interactions: income–marital status
                        income–occupation
                        marital status–occupation

and all main effects. Interestingly, unless we relax the .05 significance level, intention is not present in the list of significant interactions. Thus, it might be difficult to predict intention from the other three descriptors.

02 Feb 97 SPSS for MS WINDOWS Release 6.1   Page 1

* * * * * *   H I E R A R C H I C A L   L O G   L I N E A R   * * * * * *

DATA   Information

    252 unweighted cases accepted.
      0 cases rejected because of out-of-range factor values.
      0 cases rejected because of missing data.
    252 weighted cases will be used in the analysis.

FACTOR Information

    Factor Level Label
    INCOME   3
    INTEND   2
    MARITAL   2
    OCCUP   3

FIGURE 20A.1
SPSS Output for Linear Analysis of Tire Intentions Data

```
02 Feb 97 SPSS for MS WINDOWS Release 6.1                          Page 4

* * * * * *  H I E R A R C H I C A L   L O G   L I N E A R  * * * * * * * * *

Tests that K-way and higher order effects are zero.

   K   DF   L.R. Chisq   Prob   Pearson Chisq   Prob   Iteration

   4    4      2.980     .5611       2.586       .6294      4
   3   16     34.053     .0053      29.822       .0189      4
   2   29    108.596     .0000     103.533       .0000      2
   1   35    176.445     .0000     183.429       .0000      0

   - - - - - - - - - - - - - - - - - - - - - - - - - - - - - - - - - - - - -

Tests that K-way effects are zero.

   K   DF   L.R. Chisq   Prob   Pearson Chisq   Prob   Iteration

   1    6     67.849     .0000      79.895       .0000      0
   2   13     74.543     .0000      73.711       .0000      0
   3   12     31.072     .0019      27.236       .0071      0
   4    4      2.980     .5611       2.586       .6294      0


>Note # 13865
>DF used for these tests have NOT been adjusted for structural or sampling
>zeros. Tests using these DF may be conservative.
```

FIGURE 20A.1
SPSS Output for Linear Analysis of Tire Intentions Data

(continued)

```
02 Feb 97 SPSS for MS WINDOWS Release 6.1                    Page 5

* * * * * *   H I E R A R C H I C A L   L O G   L I N E A R   * * * * * *

Tests of PARTIAL associations.

Effect Name              DF   Partial Chisq   Prob    Iter

INCOME*INTEND*MARITAL     2       3.490       .1746    4
INCOME*INTEND*OCCUP       4       4.267       .3710    3
INCOME*MARITAL*OCCUP      4      21.923       .0002    4
INTEND*MARITAL*OCCUP      2        .352       .8386    5
INCOME*INTEND             2       1.233       .5397    4
INCOME*MARITAL            2      12.272       .0022    3
INTEND*MARITAL            1        .561       .4538    4
INCOME*OCCUP              4      27.872       .0000    4
INTEND*OCCUP             2       5.726       .0571    4
MARITAL*OCCUP            2      23.677       .0000    3
INCOME                   2      20.442       .0000    2
INTEND                   1       6.376       .0116    2
MARITAL                  1       4.601       .0319    2
OCCUP                    2      36.430       .0000    2
```

FIGURE 20A.1
SPSS Output for Linear Analysis of Tire Intentions Data
(continued)

CHAPTER 21

Summary

This book has focused on methods for market research. While a substantial portion of the book is devoted to data collection, given the widespread availability of data the key problem is often to interpret and synthesize rather than collect information. Therefore, we conclude by focusing on three topics: (1) which of the more complex analytical procedures apply to various types of data; (2) which combination of procedures is most useful for addressing a number of common problems; and (3) how the results of past studies can be assembled to develop a knowledge base for use in decision making.

WHICH PROCEDURE IS APPROPRIATE?

Why Use Multivariate Procedures?

There are many reasons why the use of multivariate procedures has become increasingly widespread in marketing research:

1. Multivariate procedures can assess complex interrelationships among variables more efficiently than simpler procedures such as cross-tabs. This is especially important when a key variable (e.g., sales) is assumed to depend on several other variables simultaneously.
2. Given the large data sets available, multivariate procedures are useful for simplifying them. This simplification often leads to the development of a model that captures much of the information contained in the full data set in a more parsimonious way (e.g., a data set containing a key variable, such as sales, and 107 possible influences on sales can often be reduced to a model that has sales related to 5 to 10 variables).
3. Multivariate procedures often uncover relations that simpler procedures such as two-way cross-tabs overlook. Conversely, multivariate procedures sometimes indicate that apparently important correlations or cross-tabs are illusory.
4. Multivariate procedures are easy and relatively cheap to use given computer

programs. (This has led to considerable misuse as well as use.) Also, more researchers and managers have at least been exposed to such methods.

5. Some people attribute to users of multivariate procedures special technical competence (which may or may not be true) as well as greater general competence in making decisions (rarely true). This leads some researchers to use multivariate procedures to increase their perceived credibility.

There are, then, at least five reasons for the increased use of multivariate procedures. While the fourth (increased availability) may be the most important reason, the first three reasons (advantages vis-à-vis simpler procedures) are good enough to outweigh the fifth (false scientification), so that multivariate procedures are a net positive addition to the researcher's toolkit.

A Typology

There are innumerable ways to distinguish between types of analyses. Two of the best known appear in Sheth (1971) and Kinnear and Taylor (1971). Most such typologies place considerable importance on the form of the data in terms of its scale properties (nominal, ordinal, interval, or ratio). While the type of data available has an important role to play in determining which technique to use, the more crucial issue is to match the technique to its general purpose (to discover a relation, to predict, etc.). Therefore, this typology focuses on the purpose of the researcher. As such, it is related to the type of studies (exploratory, descriptive, causal).

The typology discussed here assumes that analysis ranges from simple perusal of the data to careful model testing and refinement. For the sake of simplicity, most analytical methods can be classified into four categories: descriptive, relationship portrayal, structure derivation, and effect assessment.

Descriptive   Descriptive procedures make no assumptions about the data; they merely describe data. The major example of this type is tabulation, which simply reports the percentage of the time each answer was recorded. Other examples include medians and percentiles (if the data are ordinal) and means (if the data are intervally scaled). Most of the univariate procedures used in exploratory studies fit this category. Descriptive measures are quite useful and should be the first step before any "fancy" analysis is conducted.

Relationship Portrayal   These procedures examine variables (usually one pair at a time) to see if they are related. No prior notion about the nature of the relationship is required. The major example of this type of analysis is cross-tabs. If the general nature of the relationship is known, more "powerful" procedures such as Spearman's rank correlation coefficient (if the relationship is ordinal) or the product-moment correlation (if the relationship is linear) become useful. Such procedures are often used in descriptive studies, especially to uncover which variables are related to two or three key variables.

Structure Derivation   These procedures assume that data are generated according to some underlying but unknown structure; they attempt to deduce the structure from the data and, hence, to simplify it. For example, cluster analysis assumes that the observations came from groups and attempts to rediscover the groups. Factor analysis is a special case of cluster analysis that attempts to group either variables (based on the correlations between variables across people) or people (based on the correlation of people in terms of their values on the variables across variables). Multidimensional scaling assumes that similarity or preference data were generated by a geometric model of the stimuli and tries to deduce this underlying geometric model.

Effect Assessment These procedures assume that there is a particular kind of relationship in the data. They assume that one variable (called the *dependent* or *criterion variable*) depends on a number of other variables (called *independent* or *predictor* variables) in a particular mathematical way. They then proceed to assess/estimate the strength of the dependence of the criterion variable on the predictor variables. The appropriate method of this type to use depends on the scale type of the independent and dependent variables. Examples of this type of analysis include ANOVA, regression analysis, and discriminant analysis. The advantage of these techniques is that when the researcher correctly identifies (*a*) the critical variables and (*b*) the way they relate to each other, these techniques produce more information than simpler techniques. Their disadvantage is that, if the researcher incorrectly identifies the variables or the form of the relationship, the results may be misleading.

A summary of the major types of analytical procedures appears in Table 21.1. Generally, all the techniques in a given category are substitutes for each other and complements to the techniques in the other categories. Put differently, an analysis plan that includes tabulations, factor analysis, and regression may be reasonable, while one that attempts to study the relationship of sales to a collection of other variables by means of ANOVA, CHAID, regression analysis, and discriminant analysis is relatively inefficient.

Summary On balance, multivariate procedures provide a useful competitive advantage for the researcher who knows how to use them. Three caveats are in order. First, proper use of them requires a reasonable amount of understanding and experience. Second, because many of the techniques are related, there is a diminishing marginal utility of multivariate techniques. Put differently, there is no reason to try every conceivable analytical procedure on a given study—pick the most appropriate one or two. Finally, communication of the results often causes considerable problems. The "uninitiated" may respond with either unabashed (and unjustified) approval or open distrust (often arising from insecurity). To make the results genuinely useful, every attempt should be made to convert them to a simple form so that the implications can be seen and understood by nontechnicians.

A final point is that it is not necessary to have a deep understanding of the intricacies of all the procedures. Regression analysis has been in the past and will be for the foreseeable future the most widely used "fancy" marketing research technique. In fact, its versatility allows a researcher who understands it, plus the basic analytical procedures, to handle almost any situation. The moral of this is, if you have to pick one of these techniques to learn, pick regression. It is also true that understanding regression makes learning other multivariate procedures much easier.

TABLE 21.1 Typology of Analytical Procedures

General Category	Specific Type	Data Scale
Descriptive	Tabulations	Categorical (nominal)
	Medians, percentiles	Ordinal
	Mean	Interval
Relationship portrayal	Cross-tabulation	Categorical
	Log-linear	
	Correspondence analysis	
	Rank correlation	Ordinal
	Product-moment correlation	Interval
Structure derivation	Cluster analysis	Different procedures for each type
	Factor analysis	Interval
	Multidimensional scaling	Ordinal
Effect assessment	ANOVA	Dependent-interval
		Independent-categorical
	CHAID	Dependent-categorical
		Independent-categorical
	Regression analysis	Dependent-interval
		Independent-interval
	Discriminant analysis	Dependent-categorical
	Logit	Independent-interval

TYPICAL RESEARCH APPROACHES TO COMMON MARKETING PROBLEMS

The purpose of research and all the techniques discussed previously is to help managers make better decisions. In this section, we briefly discuss some of the common marketing problems faced by managers and then indicate which multivariate techniques may be appropriate to address them. A summary of the problems and approaches used is given in Table 21.2. More extensive discussions appear in books such as Lehmann and Winer (1997).

Uncovering Customers' Needs

Most marketing issues require understanding customer needs. As a starting point, this may involve focus groups and other qualitative research methods to give us some idea of consumers' decision processes and the attributes they use in their decisions. For example, if a company wants to start a new Internet service, a focus group of target customers may tell us why people use such a service (e.g., entertainment, information), what factors affect their choice of a particular service (e.g., price, speed of access, quality of content), who makes the decision, and so on. Typically, this process generates a long list of potential factors that consumers consider when they select an online service. To narrow down this list to a few distinct "factors," we can use factor analysis. It is also possible to obtain similarity ratings of different competing products (e.g., online service, TV, newspaper) from the consumers and use multidimensional scaling (MDS) to uncover the underlying attributes that go into their decision processes.

TABLE 21.2 Common Information Needs and Research Approaches

Typical Problems	Common Approaches
Uncovering customer needs	MDS of similarity data
	Factor analysis of attribute importances or brand ratings
Segmenting markets	Cluster analysis of potential customers based on customer characteristics (general or specific market responsiveness)
	Factor analysis of attitudinal data (e.g., attribute importances or brand ratings)
Profiling customers/product users	Regression of usage vs. customer (e.g., demographic) and market (e.g., prices) characteristics
	CART
	CHAID
	Neural nets
Predicting group/segment membership	Discriminant analysis
	Logit
	Regression analysis (if only two groups)
Portraying competitive structure	MDS
	Factor analysis
	Cluster analysis
	Discriminant analysis
Assessing marketing mix effectiveness	Conjoint analysis
	Regression of sales on market characteristics
	Multinomial logit of brand choice
Evaluating new concepts	Conjoint analysis
Forecasting	Regression of sales vs. time or customer and market characteristics

Segmenting Markets

A second task for our manager could be to uncover market segments. Clearly, customers are different in their needs, and it is imperative to understand these differences. A typical approach for segmentation is cluster analysis. This analysis could be done on customers' attitudes, needs, market responses, etc. For example, we can ask customers to rate different attributes in terms of their importance and then cluster customers with similar importance ratings into groups. Alternatively, we could use the part-worths from conjoint analysis (which tell us the utility or value placed by each consumer on various attributes at different levels) as an input to cluster analysis. The results of this analysis will reveal the number of segments with different needs (benefits rated highly) and their relative sizes.

Profiling Users

In many cases, we may wish to identify segments and users based on their usage behavior. For example, our online company manager may want to find what factors distinguish the different usage rates of online service customers. Unlike the cluster analysis approach, here we have a criterion variable (usage rate) that defines segments, and our goal is to describe them. This problem can be addressed by regression, CART, or CHAID. All three techniques attempt to find the relationship between consumer/market characteristics (e.g., consumer demographics) and usage. CART and CHAID provide tree-like structure (e.g., find the difference in usage between those younger than 25 years whose average monthly usage of online service is 60 hours and those older than 25 whose average monthly usage is 20 hours), which many managers find intuitive and easy to interpret. Note that if we wish to use many variables (e.g., age, education, income) to "split" the population into segments, then CART and CHAID require a large sample size. Some companies, such as those in the financial services industry and many direct marketers, have large databases of their customers and their transactions and, therefore, find these techniques especially appealing.

Predicting Group/Segment Membership

While the previous approaches "uncover" segments, many applications require predicting membership of consumers in predefined segments or categories. For example, a bank may wish to categorize consumers into two groups—those who should be given a loan versus those who should not be. Here, the segments or groups are clear and predefined. The task is to develop a prediction rule that will allow the bank manager to use information about a new applicant (e.g., income, credit history) and assign him or her into one of the two categories. Discriminant analysis and logit models are appropriate techniques for such applications.

Portraying Competitive Structure

In addition to understanding customers, a company must understand the competitive structure of the marketplace. A better understanding of the competitive landscape will enable the company to address such strategic questions as:

> "What should be the positioning of our product with respect to competing brands?"
>
> "If we introduce a new product, where are we likely to draw share from and how much will the new product cannibalize our existing products?"

Several techniques help managers address these issues by constructing perceptual maps using consumers' perceptions or choice data. To construct these maps, factor analysis and discriminant analysis use consumers' perception ratings of various brands or brand switching, MDS uses consumers' perceptions of similarity among brands or brand switching, and correspondence analysis uses frequency data (e.g., frequency of product purchase).

Assessing Marketing Mix Effectiveness

Having understood the customers and competition, and after choosing the appropriate segments and positioning, it is essential for a marketing manager to allocate marketing resources appropriately. Typical queries at this stage include

> "What should be the price of my product (should I lower the price)?"
>
> "Is my advertising effective (should I cut the advertising budget)?"

"How effective are my promotions (is it better to allocate more resources to promotions than to advertising)?"

While these are complex questions and require detailed and sometimes sophisticated analyses, some simple techniques can provide useful guidelines. For example, a manager can use the historical sales and marketing mix (price, advertising, promotion, etc.) data from different geographical areas and time periods to run a regression and assess the impact of various marketing instruments. Alternatively, the manager can use data from consumer panels (e.g., scanner data) that have a record of the brands a particular household bought, the price paid, whether or not a coupon was used, and so on, in a logit model to understand the relative impact of various marketing actions. In the case of a new product, the manager can create hypothetical product profiles and conduct a conjoint analysis to assess the relative impact of, say, price changes on market share. Once we know the market's reaction to changes in our actions, we can use this and cost information to guide us in resource allocation.

Evaluating New Concepts

Another typical problem is to decide what type of product or service to offer to consumers, what should be its value proposition, and what acceptance or share can be expected from the marketplace for each of these offerings. Conjoint analysis is an obvious way to address these issues. For example, we could first find the attributes that consumers consider important. Then we would decide on the different levels of each attribute that we wish to consider based on technical possibilities and the competitive situation (e.g., the company may wish to assess demand for its service at three different price levels). Next we would create a set of profiles based on experimental design considerations. Consumer ratings or rankings of these profiles become input to conjoint analysis, and the results tell us the relative importance of various attributes to different customers. We can also conduct simulations to assess the expected market share from each potential offering. Using the share results in combination with cost and margin information, we can estimate the profit potential of different new product options.

Forecasting

Sales forecasting is another, and perhaps the paramount, issue faced by managers. It is important to recognize that sales depend on many environmental factors as well as decisions made by the company and its competitors. Once we understand all the factors that drive the sales of our product or service, we can run a regression with sales as the dependent variable and these factors (e.g., price, inflation) as independent variables. This regression equation then allows us to forecast sales, assuming we know what the values of the independent variables are going to be in the future. There is always uncertainty about the latter (e.g., we do not know for sure what the price of a competitive brand will be). Therefore, it is advisable to conduct sensitivity analysis and estimate a range of sales forecasts under different scenarios (e.g., optimistic, best estimate/guess, pessimistic) rather than to rely on a single estimate.

Summary

Obviously, a wide variety of problems exist. Here we have tried to highlight some of the most common and suggest which methods are likely to be most useful. However, this text and the summary (Table 21.2) are simply guides; analytical strategies must be tailored to the knowledge level and "comfort zones" of users as well as to the problem/task and specifics (e.g., scale) of the data.

CUMULATING KNOWLEDGE FROM PAST STUDIES: META-ANALYSIS

One of the most fruitful avenues for analysis is exploring what can be learned from past studies. For example, an advertising agency that has studied the impact of increasing advertising 237 times can learn more from synthesizing the information in the 237 studies than from running the 238th. The process of combining information from past studies is known as empirical generalization and/or meta-analysis (that is, the analysis of past analyses). The basic premise is that we can learn from other (past) situations. In essence, then, meta-analysis is quantitative benchmarking.

Conduct

Quantitative meta-analysis requires four basic steps:

1. First, you need to identify some quantifiable variable worth studying. Examples include survey response rates, the response of the market to elements of the marketing mix (e.g., price, coupon promotions, advertising spending measured as a percent change or elasticity), or sales patterns (e.g., diffusion rates).

2. Next, you must collect studies (from published/secondary sources and/or company records) that provide measures of the variable of interest (e.g., advertising elasticity) as well as information on situational and methodological characteristics that potentially affect the variable of interest (e.g., the product/service involved, area where the study was conducted, measurement method). These characteristics generally fall into two broad categories: (*a*) situation (including both the product itself and the circumstances—e.g., region, level of competition—describing where the study was done) and (*b*) methodology (including both issues of measurement and modeling/estimation). In essence, meta-analysis examines whether the overall average (e.g., impact of advertising on sales) is a good descriptor of all the possible conditions described by these characteristics (e.g., when the impact is measured with linear regression models of durable goods in Asia) or, if not, how much results differ across conditions.

3. Third, a database is formed with each measure of the variable of interest and the (other) characteristics (e.g., product class) forming a single observation. Note that a single past study may contain multiple observations on the variable of interest. The focus here is on the variable of interest (e.g., advertising elasticity), and so a study that reports, say, 10 elasticities provides 10 observations to the meta-analysis. Table 21.3 presents a small-scale example of how such a data set might look with one situational and one methodological variable.

4. Finally, you need to analyze the data. This is typically done in two stages:
   a. First, the mean and variance are computed and/or the variable displayed

graphically. This gives a quick summary/overview of the variable (e.g., the average price elasticity is −0.2, or the average response rate is 3 percent).

b. Second, a systematic analysis of the impact the situational and methodological characteristics have is often produced. Since the characteristics are often quite collinear and there are fewer observations than the number of combinations, simple contingency analysis such as conditional averages (e.g., the response rate in December is 6%, in March 2%) can be misleading. Thorough analysis requires more sophisticated analyses (e.g., dummy variable regression to estimate the impact of the characteristics on the variable of interest, such as advertising elasticity).

Returning to the simple example of Table 21.3, we see a mean of .09 and a range from .01 to .38. Quick inspection of the first eight observations suggests new products have higher elasticities (consistent with actual results of Eastlack and Rao (1989), Batra et al. (1995), and Lodish et al. (1995)) of .24, .22, and .38 (average = .28) vs. .02, .01, .03, .01, and .06 (average = .03), whereas the measurement method makes little difference. Simple inspection is less useful when there are many observations and the characteristics of the studies are confounded/correlated (which in practice they typically are). Therefore, it is common to run a standard dummy variable regression to estimate the impact of the characteristics:

$$\text{Advertising elasticity} = B_0 + B_1(\text{If new product}) + B_2(\text{If scanner data used})$$

The results would be a large B_1 (close to $[(.24 + .22 + .38)/3] - [(.02 + .01 + .03 + .01 + .06)/5]$, but not necessarily equal due to collinearity) and a B_2 close to 0. (The interested reader, a.k.a. one without a life, can verify this.) In practice, dealing with confounding among characteristics (collinearity) is the second most difficult aspect of applying meta-analysis. (The first is the tedious task of digging through studies to set up the data set in the first place.)

TABLE 21.3 Data for Hypothetical Meta-analysis

Meta-analysis Observation	Variable of Interest Advertising Elasticity	Situational Variable Product Category		Methodological Variable Type of Data	
		Mature	New	Experiment	Scanner
1	.02	1	0	0	1
2	.01	1	0	0	1
3	.03	1	0	0	1
4	.24	0	1	0	1
5	.22	0	1	1	0
6	.01	1	0	1	0
7	.38	0	1	1	0
8	.06	1	0	0	1
. . .					

Use

Meta-analysis has two primary uses. The first is to provide a base (benchmark) value. For example, the impact of a 100 percent increase in customer access lines might produce on average a 4 percent sales increase, with a range of 1–12 percent. In assessing the likely return to a proposed doubling of lines, one would hope that a 4 percent sales increase would generate enough incremental margin to cover the costs. Certainly if even a 12 percent increase would not break even, you would wonder if the proposal was a good idea (in essence asking the question, "what makes your product, or in this case lines, so special?").

The other use of meta-analysis is to aid in prediction. For example, it is difficult to project a product's sales over the life cycle early in the cycle based on sales data alone (i.e., if you only have two years' data, you can't even estimate a nonlinear model of sales). On the other hand, by combining the early data with the general pattern found for other new products, an early forecast becomes more feasible and accurate (Sultan, Farley, and Lehmann (1990)).

Most companies currently do not utilize such formal procedures to gain insight from their own and others' data. However, under increasing competitive and budget pressure and a growing realization of the critical role knowledge plays in determining competitiveness, movement in this direction is beginning, likely to increase, and potentially very beneficial. Put bluntly, you can often learn more from examining the drawers/shelves full of past studies of related products than you can from conducting the $(n + 1)$st study, and do so at a lower cost.

CONCLUSION

This book has attempted to describe research as it is and should be conducted. In the future, changes are inevitable. For example, the following all are likely to have an impact:

1. Technology, in particular the Internet as both data collection method and market
2. Politics, in particular concerns over privacy and who owns customer record data
3. Competition, which seems to be more intense and more global every year

These trends will demand increased customer and competitor knowledge (a.k.a. market orientation). They will also increase pressure for measuring the impacts of action on shareholder value or at least its close predecessors (sales, share, brand equity) rather than more traditional measures of the impact of marketing (e.g., awareness, attitude). Further, a movement toward automated decision making, where routine decisions are handled by algorithm/decision support systems rather than a manager, seems inevitable. Most important, the world seems to require continuous updating of both customer knowledge and the tools to acquire it. We live in interesting times. Keep learning and good luck.

REFERENCES

Assmus, Gert, John U. Farley, and Donald R. Lehmann (1984) "How Advertising Affects Sales: Meta-Analysis of Econometric Results," *Journal of Marketing Research*, 21, February, 65–74.

Batra, Rajeev, Donald R. Lehmann, Joanne Burke, and Jae Pae (1995) "When Does Advertising Have an Impact? A Study of Tracking Data," *Journal of Advertising Research*, 35, September–October, 19–32.

Eastlack, Joseph O., Jr., and Ambar G. Rao (1989) "Advertising Experiments at Campbell Soup Company," *Marketing Science*, 8, Winter, 57–71.

Farley, John U., and Donald R. Lehmann (1986) *Meta-Analysis in Marketing: Generalization of Response Models*, Lexington, Mass.: Lexington Books.

Farley, John U., Donald R. Lehmann, and Alan Sawyer (1995) "Empirical Marketing Generalization Using Meta-Analysis," *Marketing Science*, 14, September, G36–G46.

Kinnear, Thomas C., and James R. Taylor (1971) "Multivariate Methods in Marketing Research: A Further Attempt at Classification," *Journal of Marketing*, 35, October, 56–58.

Lehmann, Donald R., and Russell S. Winer (1997) *Product Management*, 2nd ed., Burr Ridge, Ill.: Richard D. Irwin.

Lodish, Leonard M., Magid Abraham, Stuart Kalmenson, Jeane Livelstoerger, Beth Lubetkin, Bruce Richardson, and Mary Ellen Stevens (1995) "How TV Advertising Works: A Meta-Analysis of 395 Real World Split Cable TV Advertising Experiments," *Journal of Marketing Research*, 32, May, 125–39.

Sheth, Jagdish N. (1971) "The Multivariate Revolution in Marketing Research," *Journal of Marketing*, 34, January, 13–19.

Sultan, Fareena, John U. Farley, and Donald R. Lehmann (1990) "A Meta-Analysis of Applications of Diffusion Models," *Journal of Marketing Research*, 27, February, 70–77.

Tellis, Gerard J. (1988) "The Price Elasticities of Selective Demand: A Meta-Analysis of Econometric Models of Sales," *Journal of Marketing Research*, 25, November, 331–42.

Appendices

APPENDIX A: RANDOM NUMBERS

56970	10799	52098	04184	54967	72938	50834	23777	08392
83125	85077	60490	44369	66130	72936	69848	59973	08144
55503	21383	02464	26141	68779	66388	75242	82690	74099
47019	06683	33203	29603	54553	25971	69573	83854	24715
84828	61152	79526	29554	84580	37859	28504	61980	34997
08021	31331	79227	05748	51276	57143	31926	00915	45821
36458	28285	30424	98420	72925	40729	22337	48293	86847
05752	96065	36847	87729	81679	59126	59437	33225	31280
26768	02513	58454	56958	20575	76746	40878	06846	32828
42613	72456	43030	58085	06766	60227	96414	32671	45587
95457	12176	65482	25596	02678	54592	63607	82096	21913
95276	67524	63564	95958	39750	64379	46059	51666	10433
66954	53574	64776	92345	95110	59448	77249	54044	67942
17457	44151	14113	02462	02798	54977	48340	66738	60184
03704	23322	83214	59337	01695	60666	97410	55064	17427
21538	16997	33210	60337	27976	70661	08250	69509	60264
57178	16730	08310	70348	11317	71623	55510	64750	87759
31048	40058	94953	55866	96283	40620	52087	80817	74533
69799	83300	16498	80733	96422	58078	99643	39847	96884
90595	65017	59231	17772	67831	33317	00520	90401	41700
33570	34761	08039	78784	09977	29398	93896	78227	90110
15340	82760	57477	13898	48431	72936	78160	87240	52710
64079	07733	36512	56186	99098	48850	72527	08486	10951
63491	84886	67118	62063	74958	20946	28147	39338	32109
92003	76568	41034	28260	79708	00770	88643	21188	01850
52360	46658	66511	04172	73085	11795	52594	13287	82531
74622	12142	68355	65635	21828	39539	18988	53609	04001
04157	50070	61343	64315	70836	82857	35335	87900	36194
86003	60070	66241	32836	27573	11479	94114	81641	00496
41208	80187	20351	09630	84668	42486	71303	19512	50277
06433	80674	24520	18222	10610	05794	37515	48619	62866
39298	47829	72648	37414	75755	04717	29899	78817	03509
89884	59651	67533	68123	17730	95862	08034	19473	63971
61512	32155	51906	61662	64430	16688	37275	51262	11569
99653	47635	12506	88535	36553	23757	34209	55803	96275
95913	11085	13772	76638	48423	25018	99041	77529	81360
55804	44004	13122	44115	01601	50541	00147	77685	58788
35334	82410	91601	40617	72876	33967	73830	15405	96554
57729	88646	76487	11622	96297	24160	09903	14047	22917
86648	89317	63677	70119	94739	25875	38829	68377	43918
30574	06039	07967	32422	76791	30725	53711	93385	13421
81307	13114	83580	79974	45929	85113	72268	09858	52104
02410	96385	79067	54939	21410	86980	91772	93307	34116
18969	87444	52233	62319	08598	09066	95288	04794	01534
87863	80514	66860	62297	80198	19347	73234	86265	49096
08397	10538	15438	62311	72844	60203	46412	65943	79232
28520	45247	58729	10854	99058	18260	38765	90038	94209
44285	09452	15867	70418	57012	72122	36634	97283	95943
86299	22510	33571	23309	57040	29285	67870	21913	72958
84842	05748	90894	61658	15001	94005	36308	41161	37341

APPENDIX B: STANDARD NORMAL DISTRIBUTION

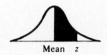

Mean z

z	.00	.01	.02	.03	.04	.05	.06	.07	.08	.09
0.0	.0000	.0040	.0080	.0120	.0160	.0199	.0239	.0279	.0319	.0359
0.1	.0398	.0438	.0478	.0517	.0557	.0596	.0636	.0675	.0714	.0753
0.2	.0793	.0832	.0871	.0910	.0948	.0987	.1026	.1064	.1103	.1141
0.3	.1179	.1217	.1255	.1293	.1331	.1368	.1406	.1443	.1480	.1517
0.4	.1554	.1591	.1628	.1664	.1700	.1736	.1772	.1808	.1844	.1879
0.5	.1915	.1950	.1985	.2019	.2054	.2088	.2123	.2157	.2190	.2224
0.6	.2257	.2291	.2324	.2357	.2389	.2422	.2454	.2486	.2518	.2549
0.7	.2580	.2612	.2642	.2673	.2704	.2734	.2764	.2794	.2823	.2852
0.8	.2881	.2910	.2939	.2967	.2995	.3023	.3051	.3078	.3106	.3133
0.9	.3159	.3186	.3212	.3238	.3264	.3289	.3315	.3340	.3365	.3389
1.0	.3413	.3438	.3461	.3485	.3508	.3531	.3554	.3577	.3599	.3621
1.1	.3643	.3665	.3686	.3708	.3729	.3749	.3770	.3790	.3810	.3830
1.2	.3849	.3869	.3888	.3907	.3925	.3944	.3962	.3980	.3997	.4015
1.3	.4032	.4049	.4066	.4082	.4099	.4115	.4131	.4147	.4162	.4177
1.4	.4192	.4207	.4222	.4236	.4251	.4265	.4279	.4292	.4306	.4319
1.5	.4332	.4345	.4357	.4370	.4382	.4394	.4406	.4418	.4429	.4441
1.6	.4452	.4463	.4474	.4484	.4495	.4505	.4515	.4525	.4535	.4545
1.7	.4554	.4564	.4573	.4582	.4591	.4599	.4608	.4616	.4625	.4633
1.8	.4641	.4649	.4656	.4664	.4671	.4678	.4686	.4693	.4699	.4706
1.9	.4713	.4719	.4726	.4732	.4738	.4744	.4750	.4756	.4761	.4767
2.0	.4772	.4778	.4783	.4788	.4793	.4798	.4803	.4808	.4812	.4817
2.1	.4821	.4826	.4830	.4834	.4838	.4842	.4846	.4850	.4854	.4857
2.2	.4861	.4864	.4868	.4871	.4875	.4878	.4881	.4884	.4887	.4890
2.3	.4893	.4896	.4898	.4901	.4904	.4906	.4909	.4911	.4913	.4916
2.4	.4918	.4920	.4922	.4925	.4927	.4929	.4931	.4932	.4934	.4936
2.5	.4938	.4940	.4941	.4943	.4945	.4946	.4948	.4949	.4951	.4952
2.6	.4953	.4955	.4956	.4957	.4959	.4960	.4961	.4962	.4963	.4964
2.7	.4965	.4966	.4967	.4968	.4969	.4970	.4971	.4972	.4973	.4974
2.8	.4974	.4975	.4976	.4977	.4977	.4978	.4979	.4979	.4980	.4981
2.9	.4981	.4982	.4982	.4983	.4984	.4984	.4985	.4985	.4986	.4986
3.0	.49865	.4987	.4987	.4988	.4988	.4989	.4989	.4989	.4990	.4990
4.0	.4999683									

Source: *Fundamental Statistics for Business and Economics*, 4th ed. by John Neter, William Wasserman, and G. A. Whitmore, Copyright © 1973 by Allyn and Bacon, Inc. Reprinted with permission.

APPENDIX C: THE *t* DISTRIBUTION

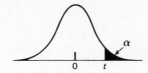

d.f. \ α	.10	.05	.025	.01	.005
1	3.078	6.314	12.706	31.821	63.657
2	1.886	2.920	4.303	6.965	9.925
3	1.638	2.353	3.182	4.541	5.841
4	1.533	2.132	2.776	3.747	4.604
5	1.476	2.015	2.571	3.365	4.032
6	1.440	1.943	2.447	3.143	3.707
7	1.415	1.895	2.365	2.998	3.499
8	1.397	1.860	2.306	2.896	3.355
9	1.383	1.833	2.262	2.821	3.250
10	1.372	1.812	2.228	2.764	3.169
11	1.363	1.796	2.201	2.718	3.106
12	1.356	1.782	2.179	2.681	3.055
13	1.350	1.771	2.160	2.650	3.012
14	1.345	1.761	2.145	2.624	2.977
15	1.341	1.753	2.131	2.602	2.947
16	1.337	1.746	2.120	2.583	2.921
17	1.333	1.740	2.110	2.567	2.898
18	1.330	1.734	2.101	2.552	2.878
19	1.328	1.729	2.093	2.539	2.861
20	1.325	1.725	2.086	2.528	2.845
21	1.323	1.721	2.080	2.518	2.831
22	1.321	1.717	2.074	2.508	2.819
23	1.319	1.714	2.069	2.500	2.807
24	1.318	1.711	2.064	2.492	2.797
25	1.316	1.708	2.060	2.485	2.787
26	1.315	1.706	2.056	2.479	2.779
27	1.314	1.703	2.052	2.473	2.771
28	1.313	1.701	2.048	2.467	2.763
29	1.311	1.699	2.045	2.462	2.756
30	1.310	1.697	2.042	2.457	2.750
40	1.303	1.684	2.021	2.423	2.704
60	1.296	1.671	2.000	2.390	2.660
120	1.289	1.658	1.980	2.358	2.617
∞	1.282	1.645	1.960	2.326	2.576

Source: Hoel, *Elementary Statistics*, 3rd ed. New York: John Wiley & Sons, 1971 c.

APPENDIX D: THE x^2 DISTRIBUTION

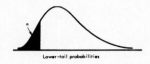

Lower-tail probabilities

df \ α	.001	.005	.010	.025	.050	.100
1	.000	.000	.000	.001	.004	.016
2	.002	.010	.020	.051	.103	.211
3	.024	.072	.115	.216	.352	.584
4	.091	.207	.297	.484	.711	1.06
5	.210	.412	.554	.831	1.15	1.61
6	.381	.676	.872	1.24	1.64	2.20
7	.598	.989	1.24	1.69	2.17	2.83
8	.857	1.34	1.65	2.18	2.73	3.49
9	1.15	1.73	2.09	2.70	3.33	4.17
10	1.48	2.16	2.56	3.25	3.94	4.87
11	1.83	2.60	3.05	3.82	4.57	5.58
12	2.21	3.07	3.57	4.40	5.23	6.30
13	2.62	3.57	4.11	5.01	5.89	7.04
14	3.04	4.07	4.66	5.63	6.57	7.79
15	3.48	4.60	5.23	6.26	7.26	8.55
16	3.94	5.14	5.81	6.91	7.96	9.31
17	4.42	5.70	6.41	7.56	8.67	10.1
18	4.90	6.26	7.01	8.23	9.39	10.9
19	5.41	6.84	7.63	8.91	10.1	11.7
20	5.92	7.43	8.26	9.59	10.9	12.4
21	6.45	8.03	8.90	10.3	11.6	13.2
22	6.98	8.64	9.54	11.0	12.3	14.0
23	7.53	9.26	10.2	11.7	13.1	14.8
24	8.08	9.89	10.9	12.4	13.8	15.7
25	8.65	10.5	11.5	13.1	14.6	16.5
26	9.22	11.2	12.2	13.8	15.4	17.3
27	9.80	11.8	12.9	14.6	16.2	18.1
28	10.4	12.5	13.6	15.3	16.9	18.9
29	11.0	13.1	14.3	16.0	17.7	19.8
30	11.6	13.8	15.0	16.8	18.5	20.6
35	14.7	17.2	18.5	20.6	22.5	24.8
40	17.9	20.7	22.2	24.4	26.5	29.1
45	21.3	24.3	25.9	28.4	30.6	33.4
50	24.7	28.0	29.7	32.4	34.8	37.7
55	28.2	31.7	33.6	36.4	39.0	42.1
60	31.7	35.5	37.5	40.5	43.2	46.5
65	35.4	39.4	41.4	44.6	47.4	50.9
70	39.0	43.3	45.4	48.8	51.7	55.3
75	42.8	47.2	49.5	52.9	56.1	59.8
80	46.5	51.2	53.5	57.2	60.4	64.3
85	50.3	55.2	57.6	61.4	64.7	68.8
90	54.2	59.2	61.8	65.6	69.1	73.3
95	58.0	63.2	65.9	69.9	73.5	77.8
100	61.9	67.3	70.1	74.2	77.9	82.4

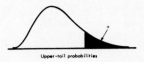

Upper-tail probabilities

df \ α	.100	.050	.025	.010	.005	.001
1	2.71	3.84	5.02	6.63	7.88	10.8
2	4.61	5.99	7.38	9.21	10.6	13.8
3	6.25	7.81	9.35	11.3	12.8	16.3
4	7.78	9.49	11.1	13.3	14.9	18.5
5	9.24	11.1	12.8	15.1	16.7	20.5
6	10.6	12.6	14.4	16.8	18.5	22.5
7	12.0	14.1	16.0	18.5	20.3	24.3
8	13.4	15.5	17.5	20.1	22.0	26.1
9	14.7	16.9	19.0	21.7	23.6	27.9
10	16.0	18.3	20.5	23.2	25.2	29.6
11	17.3	19.7	21.9	24.7	26.8	31.3
12	18.5	21.0	23.3	26.2	28.3	32.9
13	19.8	22.4	24.7	27.7	29.8	34.5
14	21.1	23.7	26.1	29.1	31.3	36.1
15	22.3	25.0	27.5	30.6	32.8	37.7
16	23.5	26.3	28.8	32.0	34.3	39.3
17	24.8	27.6	30.2	33.4	35.7	40.8
18	26.0	28.9	31.5	34.8	37.2	42.3
19	27.2	30.1	32.9	36.2	38.6	43.8
20	28.4	31.4	34.2	37.6	40.0	45.3
21	29.6	32.7	35.5	38.9	41.4	46.8
22	30.8	33.9	36.8	40.3	42.8	48.3
23	32.0	35.2	38.1	41.6	44.2	49.7
24	33.2	36.4	39.4	43.0	45.6	51.2
25	34.4	37.7	40.6	44.3	46.9	52.6
26	35.6	38.9	41.9	45.6	48.3	54.1
27	36.7	40.1	43.2	47.0	49.6	55.5
28	37.9	41.3	44.5	48.3	51.0	56.9
29	39.1	42.6	45.7	49.6	52.3	58.3
30	40.3	43.8	47.0	50.9	53.7	59.7
35	46.1	49.8	53.2	57.3	60.3	66.6
40	51.8	55.8	59.3	63.7	66.8	73.4
45	57.5	61.7	65.4	70.0	73.2	80.1
50	63.2	67.5	71.4	76.2	79.5	86.7
55	68.8	73.3	77.4	82.3	85.7	93.2
60	74.4	79.1	83.3	88.4	92.0	99.6
65	80.0	84.8	89.2	94.4	98.1	106.0
70	85.5	90.5	95.0	100.4	104.2	112.3
75	91.1	96.2	100.8	106.4	110.3	118.6
80	96.6	101.9	106.6	112.3	116.3	124.8
85	102.1	107.5	112.4	118.2	122.3	131.0
90	107.6	113.1	118.1	124.1	128.3	137.2
95	113.0	118.8	123.9	130.0	134.2	143.3
100	118.5	124.3	129.6	135.8	140.2	149.4

APPENDIX E: CRITICAL VALUES OF THE F DISTRIBUTION

Appendix E: Five Percent Level of Significance

Degrees of freedom for denominator	\	Degrees of freedom for numerator																		
		1	2	3	.4	5	6	7	8	9	10	12	15	20	24	30	40	60	120	8
1		161	200	216	225	230	234	237	239	241	242	244	246	248	249	250	251	252	253	254
2		18.5	19.0	19.2	19.2	19.3	19.3	19.4	19.4	19.4	19.4	19.4	19.4	19.4	19.5	19.5	19.5	19.5	19.5	19.5
3		10.1	9.55	9.28	9.12	9.01	8.94	8.89	8.85	8.81	8.79	8.74	8.70	8.66	8.64	8.62	8.59	8.57	8.55	8.53
4		7.71	6.94	6.59	6.39	6.26	6.16	6.09	6.04	6.00	5.96	5.91	5.86	5.80	5.77	5.75	5.72	5.69	5.66	5.63
5		6.61	5.79	5.41	5.19	5.05	4.95	4.88	4.82	4.77	4.74	4.68	4.62	4.56	4.53	4.50	4.46	4.43	4.40	4.37
6		5.99	5.14	4.76	4.53	4.39	4.28	4.21	4.15	4.10	4.06	4.00	3.94	3.87	3.84	3.81	3.77	3.74	3.70	3.67
7		5.59	4.74	4.35	4.12	3.97	3.87	3.79	3.73	3.68	3.64	3.57	3.51	3.44	3.41	3.38	3.34	3.30	3.27	3.23
8		5.32	4.46	4.07	3.84	3.69	3.58	3.50	3.44	3.39	3.35	3.28	3.22	3.15	3.12	3.08	3.04	3.01	2.97	2.93
9		5.12	4.26	3.86	3.63	3.48	3.37	3.29	3.23	3.18	3.14	3.07	3.01	2.94	2.90	2.86	2.83	2.79	2.75	2.71
10		4.96	4.10	3.71	3.48	3.33	3.22	3.14	3.07	3.02	2.98	2.91	2.85	2.77	2.74	2.70	2.66	2.62	2.58	2.54
11		4.84	3.98	3.59	3.36	3.20	3.09	3.01	2.95	2.90	2.85	2.79	2.72	2.65	2.61	2.57	2.53	2.49	2.45	2.40
12		4.75	3.89	3.49	3.26	3.11	3.00	2.91	2.85	2.80	2.75	2.69	2.62	2.54	2.51	2.47	2.43	2.38	2.34	2.30
13		4.67	3.81	3.41	3.18	3.03	2.92	2.83	2.77	2.71	2.67	2.60	2.53	2.46	2.42	2.38	2.34	2.30	2.25	2.21
14		4.60	3.74	3.34	3.11	2.96	2.85	2.76	2.70	2.65	2.60	2.53	2.46	2.39	2.35	2.31	2.27	2.22	2.18	2.13
15		4.54	3.68	3.29	3.06	2.90	2.79	2.71	2.64	2.59	2.54	2.48	2.40	2.33	2.29	2.25	2.20	2.16	2.11	2.07
16		4.49	3.63	3.24	3.01	2.85	2.74	2.66	2.59	2.54	2.49	2.42	2.35	2.28	2.24	2.19	2.15	2.11	2.06	2.01
17		4.45	3.59	3.20	2.96	2.81	2.70	2.61	2.55	2.49	2.45	2.38	2.31	2.23	2.19	2.15	2.10	2.06	2.01	1.96
18		4.41	3.55	3.16	2.93	2.77	2.66	2.58	2.51	2.46	2.41	2.34	2.27	2.19	2.15	2.11	2.06	2.02	1.97	1.92
19		4.38	3.52	3.13	2.90	2.74	2.63	2.54	2.48	2.42	2.38	2.31	2.23	2.16	2.11	2.07	2.03	1.98	1.93	1.88
20		4.35	3.49	3.10	2.87	2.71	2.60	2.51	2.45	2.39	2.35	2.28	2.20	2.12	2.08	2.04	1.99	1.95	1.90	1.84
21		4.32	3.47	3.07	2.84	2.68	2.57	2.49	2.42	2.37	2.32	2.25	2.18	2.10	2.05	2.01	1.96	1.92	1.87	1.81
22		4.30	3.44	3.05	2.82	2.66	2.55	2.46	2.40	2.34	2.30	2.23	2.15	2.07	2.03	1.98	1.94	1.89	1.84	1.78
23		4.28	3.42	3.03	2.80	2.64	2.53	2.44	2.37	2.32	2.27	2.20	2.13	2.05	2.01	1.96	1.91	1.86	1.81	1.76
24		4.26	3.40	3.01	2.78	2.62	2.51	2.42	2.36	2.30	2.25	2.18	2.11	2.03	1.98	1.94	1.89	1.84	1.79	1.73
25		4.24	3.39	2.99	2.76	2.60	2.49	2.40	2.34	2.28	2.24	2.16	2.09	2.01	1.96	1.92	1.87	1.82	1.77	1.71
30		4.17	3.32	2.92	2.69	2.53	2.42	2.33	2.27	2.21	2.16	2.09	2.01	1.93	1.89	1.84	1.79	1.74	1.68	1.62
40		4.08	3.23	2.84	2.61	2.45	2.34	2.25	2.18	2.12	2.08	2.00	1.92	1.84	1.79	1.74	1.69	1.64	1.58	1.51
60		4.00	3.15	2.76	2.53	2.37	2.25	2.17	2.10	2.04	1.99	1.92	1.84	1.75	1.70	1.65	1.59	1.53	1.47	1.39
120		3.92	3.07	2.68	2.45	2.29	2.18	2.09	2.02	1.96	1.91	1.83	1.75	1.66	1.61	1.55	1.50	1.43	1.35	1.25
8		3.84	3.00	2.60	2.37	2.21	2.10	2.01	1.94	1.88	1.83	1.75	1.67	1.57	1.52	1.46	1.39	1.32	1.22	1.00

Appendix E: One Percent Level of Significance

Degrees of freedom for numerator

Degrees of freedom for denominator	1	2	3	4	5	6	7	8	9	10	12	15	20	24	30	40	60	120	∞
1	4,052	5,000	5,403	5,625	5,764	5,859	5,928	5,982	6,023	6,056	6,106	6,157	6,209	6,235	6,261	6,287	6,313	6,339	6,366
2	98.5	99.0	99.2	99.2	99.3	99.3	99.4	99.4	99.4	99.4	99.4	99.4	99.4	99.5	99.5	99.5	99.5	99.5	99.5
3	34.1	30.8	29.5	28.7	28.2	27.9	27.7	27.5	27.3	27.2	27.1	26.9	26.7	26.6	26.5	26.4	26.3	26.2	26.1
4	21.2	18.0	16.7	16.0	15.5	15.2	15.0	14.8	14.7	14.5	14.4	14.2	14.0	13.9	13.8	13.7	13.7	13.6	13.5
5	16.3	13.3	12.1	11.4	11.0	10.7	10.5	10.3	10.2	10.1	9.89	9.72	9.55	9.47	9.38	9.29	9.20	9.11	9.02
6	13.7	10.9	9.78	9.15	8.75	8.47	8.26	8.10	7.98	7.87	7.72	7.56	7.40	7.31	7.23	7.14	7.06	6.97	6.88
7	12.2	9.55	8.45	7.85	7.46	7.19	6.99	6.84	6.72	6.62	6.47	6.31	6.16	6.07	5.99	5.91	5.82	5.74	5.65
8	11.3	8.65	7.59	7.01	6.63	6.37	6.18	6.03	5.91	5.81	5.67	5.52	5.36	5.28	5.20	5.12	5.03	4.95	4.86
9	10.6	8.02	6.99	6.42	6.06	5.80	5.61	5.47	5.35	5.26	5.11	4.96	4.81	4.73	4.65	4.57	4.48	4.40	4.31
10	10.0	7.56	6.55	5.99	5.64	5.39	5.20	5.06	4.94	4.85	4.71	4.56	4.41	4.33	4.25	4.17	4.08	4.00	3.91
11	9.65	7.21	6.22	5.67	5.32	5.07	4.89	4.74	4.63	4.54	4.46	4.25	4.10	4.02	3.94	3.86	3.78	3.69	3.60
12	9.33	6.93	5.95	5.41	5.06	4.82	4.64	4.50	4.39	4.30	4.16	4.01	3.86	3.78	3.70	3.62	3.54	3.45	3.36
13	9.07	6.70	5.74	5.21	4.86	4.62	4.44	4.30	4.19	4.10	3.96	3.82	3.66	3.59	3.51	3.43	3.34	3.25	3.17
14	8.86	6.51	5.56	5.04	4.70	4.46	4.28	4.14	4.03	3.94	3.80	3.66	3.51	3.43	3.35	3.27	3.18	3.09	3.00
15	8.68	6.36	5.42	4.89	4.56	4.32	4.14	4.00	3.89	3.80	3.67	3.52	3.37	3.29	3.21	3.13	3.05	2.96	2.87
16	8.53	6.23	5.29	4.77	4.44	4.20	4.03	3.89	3.78	3.69	3.55	3.41	3.26	3.18	3.10	3.02	2.93	2.84	2.75
17	8.40	6.11	5.19	4.67	4.34	4.10	3.93	3.79	3.68	3.59	3.46	3.31	3.16	3.08	3.00	2.92	2.83	2.75	2.65
18	8.29	6.01	5.09	4.58	4.25	4.01	3.84	3.71	3.60	3.51	3.37	3.23	3.08	3.00	2.92	2.84	2.75	2.66	2.57
19	8.19	5.93	5.01	4.50	4.17	3.94	3.77	3.63	3.52	3.43	3.30	3.15	3.00	2.92	2.84	2.76	2.67	2.58	2.49
20	8.10	5.85	4.94	4.43	4.10	3.87	3.70	3.56	3.46	3.37	3.23	3.09	2.94	2.86	2.78	2.69	2.61	2.52	2.42
21	8.02	5.78	4.87	4.37	4.04	3.81	3.64	3.51	3.40	3.31	3.17	3.03	2.88	2.80	2.72	2.64	2.55	2.46	2.36
22	7.95	5.72	4.82	4.31	3.99	3.76	3.59	3.45	3.35	3.26	3.12	2.98	2.83	2.75	2.67	2.58	2.50	2.40	2.31
23	7.88	5.66	4.76	4.26	3.94	3.71	3.54	3.41	3.30	3.21	3.07	2.93	2.78	2.70	2.62	2.54	2.45	2.35	2.26
24	7.82	5.61	4.72	4.22	3.90	3.67	3.50	3.36	3.26	3.17	3.03	2.89	2.74	2.66	2.58	2.49	2.40	2.31	2.21
25	7.77	5.57	4.68	4.18	3.86	3.63	3.46	3.32	3.22	3.13	2.99	2.85	2.70	2.62	2.53	2.45	2.36	2.27	2.17
30	7.56	5.39	4.51	4.02	3.70	3.47	3.30	3.17	3.07	2.98	2.84	2.70	2.55	2.47	2.39	2.30	2.21	2.11	2.01
40	7.31	5.18	4.31	3.83	3.51	3.29	3.12	2.99	2.89	2.80	2.66	2.52	2.37	2.29	2.20	2.11	2.02	1.92	1.80
60	7.08	4.98	4.13	3.65	3.34	3.12	2.95	2.82	2.72	2.63	2.50	2.35	2.20	2.12	2.03	1.94	1.84	1.73	1.60
120	6.85	4.79	3.95	3.48	3.17	2.96	2.79	2.66	2.56	2.47	2.34	2.19	2.03	1.95	1.86	1.76	1.66	1.53	1.38
∞	6.63	4.61	3.78	3.32	3.02	2.80	2.64	2.51	2.41	2.32	2.18	2.04	1.88	1.79	1.70	1.59	1.47	1.32	1.00

Subject Index

Author

Index

Aaker, D. A., 177
Aaker, J. L., 177
Abraham, M. *See* Lodish,
    L. M.
Acito, F., 24
Ackerman, L. J., 251
Ackoff, R. L., 314
Addleman, S., 158, 546, 547
Ahtola, O. T., 259
Akaah, I. P., 546
Albaum, G., 241
Alpert, M. I., 173
Anderson, E. W., 177
Anderson, J. C., 255
Anderson, T. W., Jr., 586
Arabie, P. J., 574, 581, 585
Arbitron, Inc., 116
Armstrong, J. S., 21
Arnold, S. J., 135
Arnould, E. J., 136
Assmus, G., 28
Association for Consumer
    Research, 498
Aversa, N., 707

Bagozzi, R. P., 260, 261, 281,
    732
Balasubramanian, S. K., 191
Barach, J. A., 172
Bass, F. M., 162, 176, 499,
    638

Bateson, J. E. G., 192
Batra, R., 177, 259, 747
Bauer, R. A., 172
Baumgartner, H., 260, 261
Bazerman, M. H., 35, 42, 43
Bearden, W. O., 261
Beatty, S. E., 174, 175
Bechtel, G. G., 248
Beckwith, N. E., 185, 642
Belk, R. W., 135, 176
Bellenger, D. N., 131. *See
    also* Parameswaran, R.
Belsley, D., 483
Bender, S. D. F. G., 307
Berenson, C., 309
Bernhardt, K. L., 131
Berry, E. M., 717, 718, 719
Berry, L. L., 177, 261
Best, R., 241
Bettman, J. R., 185
Bickart, B. A., 259
Birdwell, A. E., 172
Bither, S. W., 173
Bitner, M. J., 186
Blair, E., 186, 188
Blankenship, A. B., 203
Bloom, P. N., 75, 76
Bock, H. H., 574
Bolton, R. N., 181
Bonoma, T. V., 90
Booms, B. H., 186

Boulding, W. R. S., 177
Boyd, H. W., Jr., 94
Bradburn, K., 259
Bradburn, N. M, 203, 269.
    See also Blair, E.
Bretton-Clark, 585
Brieman, L., 724
Brinberg, D., 251
Brown, R. V., 384, 385
Bruce, G. D., 172
Brucks, M., 136
Bruneau, C. *See*
    Chakravarti, D.
Bruner, G. C. II, 261
Bruno, A., 173
Bryson, M. C., 315
Buchanan, B., 187
Buckley, M. R., 275
Bult, J. R., 700
Burke, J. *See* Batra, R.
Burke, R. R., 149
Burnett, M. S., 136
Burton, S., 186
Bush, A. J., 305
Bush, R. R., 663
Buzzell, R. D., 384, 385

Calder, B. J., 90
Cameron, T. A., 247
Campbell, D. T., 255. *See
    also* Webb, E. J.